# THE LETTERS
# OF SIR WALTER RALEGH

EDITED BY
AGNES LATHAM
AND
JOYCE YOUINGS

UNIVERSITY
*of*
EXETER
PRESS

First published in 1999 by
University of Exeter Press
Reed Hall, Streatham Drive
Exeter EX4 4QR
UK
*www.ex.ac.uk/uep/*

© Joyce Youings 1999

**British Library Cataloguing in Publication Data**

A catalogue record of this book
is available from the British Library

ISBN 0 85989 527 0

Typeset in Stempel Garamond
by Colin Bakké Typesetting, Exeter

Printed and bound in Great Britain
by Short Run Press Limited, Exeter

FLORIDA STATE
UNIVERSITY LIBRARIES

OCT 25 1999

TALLAHASSEE, FLORIDA

# THE LETTERS OF SIR WALTER RALEGH

*Frontispiece.* Sir Walter Ralegh, attributed to the monogrammist H (?Hubbard), NPG 7. Largely repainted, except for the face. (Courtesy of the National Portrait Gallery, London)

# CONTENTS

List of the Letters . . . . . . . . . . . . . vii
List of Plates . . . . . . . . . . . . . . xv
List of Abbreviations . . . . . . . . . . . . xvi

FOREWORD by Emeritus Professor David Quinn, FBA . . . xix

PREFACE . . . . . . . . . . . . . . . . xxi

INTRODUCTION
   The Collection . . . . . . . . . . . . . xxv
   Previous Publication of the Letters . . . . . . . . xxx
   A Brief Biography: Sir Walter Ralegh 1554–1618 . . . . xxxiv
   The Recipients of the Letters . . . . . . . . . xxxvii
   The Subject Matter of the Letters
      Ireland and Virginia . . . . . . . . . . . xxxviii
      Ships, Privateering and the Sea Wars . . . . . . . xl
      The Queen and the Court . . . . . . . . . xlii
      Patronage . . . . . . . . . . . . . xliv
      The Sherborne Estate . . . . . . . . . . xlvi
      The Westcountryman . . . . . . . . . . xlviii
      Guiana . . . . . . . . . . . . . . li
      The Man behind the Pen . . . . . . . . . liv
   The Writing of the Letters
      Spelling and Style . . . . . . . . . . . lvii
      Ralegh's Clerks and Carriers . . . . . . . . lviii

Editorial Conventions . . . . . . . . . . . . . . lx
Acknowledgements . . . . . . . . . . . . . . lxi

## THE LETTERS . . . . . . . . . . . . . . . 1

## APPENDICES
1. Letter 31a. To Master [James] Gold from the Court, 10 October [1589] . . . . . . . . . . . . 379
2. Sir Walter Ralegh's Will, 8–10 July 1597 . . . . . 381
3. Agnes M.C. Latham: Bibliography . . . . . . 388

## INDEX . . . . . . . . . . . . . . . . 389

# LIST OF THE LETTERS

1. To Lord Burghley from Cork, 22 February 1581 . . . . . . . 1
2. To Sir Francis Walsingham from Cork, 23 February 1581 . . . . . 3
3. To Sir Francis Walsingham from Cork, 25 February 1581 . . . . . 5
4. To Lord Grey from Cork, 1 May 1581 . . . . . . . . 8
5. To the Earl of Leicester from Lismore, 26 August 1581 . . . . . 10
6. To Sir Humphrey Gilbert from Richmond, [15] March 1583 . . . . 12
7. To Thomas Egerton from the Court, 10 April 1583 . . . . . 13
8. To Lord Burghley from Greenwich, [10] May 1583 . . . . . 14
9. To Edward Seymour from the Court, 20 March [c.1584/c.1597] . . . 15
10. To Dr David Lewis, c.11 April 1584 . . . . . . . . 16
11. To Dr Valentine Dale from the Court, c.1584/5 . . . . . . 18
12. To Dr Richard Howland and others from the Court, 9 July 1584 . . . 20
13. To Master Richard Duke from the Court, 26 July 1584 . . . . . 24
14. To Sir Edward Stradling from the Court, 26 September 1584 . . . . 25
15. To Robert Norgate from the Court, 10 February 1585 . . . . . 26
16. To Robert Norgate and Others from the Court, 20 February 1585 . . . 28
17. To the Privy Council (with Sir Thomas Heneage), 7 May 1585 . . . 29
18. To John Sotherton from the Court, 9 May 1585 . . . . . . 31
19. To John Sotherton from the Court, 1 January 1586 . . . . . 31
20. To the Earl of Leicester from the Court, 29 March 1586 . . . . 32
21. To Sir William More, [?early 1586] . . . . . . . . 34
22. To Sir John Gilbert from the Court, 25 May 1586 . . . . . . 35
23. To the Earl of Leicester from Windsor, 8 October [1586] . . . . 36
24. To Sir Walter Mildmay from the Court, 25 November 1586 . . . . 37
25. To Dr Roger Hovenden from the Court, 15 August 1587 . . . . 38
26. To Lord Burghley from Exeter, 21 December 1587 . . . . . . 39

27. To Sir John Gilbert from the Court, 27 February 1588 . . . . . . 42
28. To Sir Thomas Egerton, 8 March 1588 . . . . . . . . . 43
29. To the Privy Council, [July/August 1588] . . . . . . . 44
30. To [Sir John Gilbert] from the Court, 13 September 1588 . . . . . 45
31. To Lord Burghley, [before 8 May 1589] . . . . . . . . 47
32. To Sir William Fitzwilliam from London, 12 November 1589 . . . . 49
33. To Sir George Carew [from London], 28 December 1589 . . . . . 50
34. To Sir Francis Walsingham, January 1590 . . . . . . . . 52
35. To the Subdean and Chapter of Wells Cathedral, [?] September 1590 . . . 54
36. To Sir Robert Cecil from Durham House, 13 October [?1591] . . . . 55
37. To Lord Burghley from Durham House, 16 October [1591] . . . . . 57
38. To Sir John Gilbert from the Court, 30 December 1591 . . . . . 59
39. To Sir John Gilbert, 10 February 1592 . . . . . . . . 60
40. To Sir John Gilbert from the Court, 3 March [1592] . . . . . . 61
41. To Sir Robert Cecil from Chatham, 10 March [1592] . . . . . . 62
42. To Sir John Gilbert from Portland, Dorset, 31 March [1592] . . . . 64
43. To Sir John Gilbert from Falmouth, 24 April 1592 . . . . . . 65
44. To Lord Burghley from Durham House, 8 June 1592 . . . . . . 66
45. To Sir Robert Cecil, [late July 1592] . . . . . . . . 68
46. To Sir Robert Cecil [from Durham House], [c.26 July 1592] . . . . 70
47. To Sir Robert Cecil [from Durham House], [c.30] July 1592 . . . . 71
48. To Charles Lord Howard [from Durham House, late July 1592] . . . 72
49. To Lord Burghley and Charles Lord Howard [from the Tower], 27 August 1592 . . . . . . . . . . . . . 74
50. To Charles Lord Howard with Sir John Hawkins [from the Tower], 27 August 1592 . . . . . . . . . . . . . 76
51. To Lord Burghley from the Tower, [13] September 1592 . . . . . 78
52. To Lord Burghley from London, 16 September 1592 . . . . . . 80
53. To Lord Burghley and Charles Lord Howard from Hartley Row, 17 September 1592 . . . . . . . . . . . . . 82
54. [To Lord Burghley] from Dartmouth, [?21] September 1592 . . . . 84
55. To Lord Burghley, Charles Lord Howard and Lord Buckhurst from Durham House, 13 December 1592 . . . . . . . . 85
56. [To Lord Burghley, ?late January 1593] . . . . . . . . 87
57. To the Justices of the Peace of Devon from Durham House 15 February 1593 . . . . . . . . . . . . . 88
58. To the Queen [23 February 1593] . . . . . . . . . 90

## LIST OF THE LETTERS

| | |
|---|---|
| 59. To the Countess of Shrewsbury from Mile End, 8 March [?1593] | 92 |
| 60. To Sir Robert Cecil from Sherborne, 10 May 1593 | 93 |
| 61. To Lord Burghley from Durham House, 15 June 1593 | 96 |
| 62. To Sir Robert Cecil from Sherborne Castle, 15 August 1593 | 97 |
| 63. To Sir Robert Cecil from Gillingham Forest, 27 August 1593 | 99 |
| 64. To Sir Robert Cecil from Weymouth, 8 October 1593 | 100 |
| 65. To Sir Robert Cecil from Sherborne Castle, 25 February 1594 | 101 |
| 66. To Sir Robert Cecil from Sherborne Castle, 25 February 1594 | 102 |
| 67. To Sir Robert Cecil from Sherborne Castle, 3 March 1594 | 104 |
| 68. To Sir Robert Cecil from Dorchester, 4 March 1594 | 105 |
| 69. To Sir Robert Cecil from Sherborne, 14 April 1594 | 106 |
| 70. To Master Pytt from Sherborne Castle, 28 April 1594 | 107 |
| 71. To Sir Thomas Egerton from Sherborne Castle, 2 May 1594 | 108 |
| 72. To Edward Knoyle from Sherborne Castle, 28 May [1594] | 110 |
| 73. To Lord Burghley from Sherborne, 15 June 1594 | 111 |
| 74. To Sir Robert Cecil from Sherborne, 15 June 1594 | 112 |
| 75. To Charles Lord Howard from Sherborne, 20 June 1594 | 113 |
| 76. To Sir Robert Cecil from Sherborne, 9 July 1594 | 115 |
| 77. To Michael Hickes from Sherborne, 9 July [1594] | 116 |
| 78. To Michael Hickes from Sherborne, 12 July [1594] | 117 |
| 79. To Sir Robert Cecil from Sherborne, 20 July 1594 | 118 |
| 80. To Sir Robert Cecil [from Durham House], 20 September 1594 | 119 |
| 81. To Sir Robert Cecil from Alresford, Hants, [7/14] December 1594 | 120 |
| 82. To Sir Robert Cecil from Sherborne, 21 December 1594 | 121 |
| 83. To Sir Robert Cecil from Sherborne, 26 December 1594 | 122 |
| 84. To Sir Robert Cecil from Sherborne, 1 January 1595 | 123 |
| 85. To Sir Robert Cecil [?from Sherborne, ?late January 1595] | 124 |
| 86. To Sir Robert Cecil from Sherborne, 10 November 1595 | 125 |
| 87. To Sir Robert Cecil from Sherborne, [12] November 1595 | 126 |
| 88. To the Privy Council from Sherborne, 25 November 1595 | 128 |
| 89. To Sir Robert Cecil from Sherborne, [26] November 1595 | 132 |
| 90. To Charles Lord Howard from Sherborne, 30 November 1595 | 134 |
| 91. To Sir Robert Cecil from Weymouth, 18 January 1596 | 135 |
| 92. To Sir Robert Cecil, 3 May 1596 | 136 |
| 93. To Sir Robert Cecil from Blackwall, 3 May 1596 | 138 |
| 94. To Sir Robert Cecil from Mile End, 3 May 1596 | 139 |

95. To Sir Robert Cecil [? from Mile End], 3 May 1596 . . . . . 140
96. To Sir Robert Cecil from Northfleet, 4 May 1596 . . . . 140
97. To Sir Robert Cecil from Queenborough, 6 May 1596 . . . . . 142
98. To Sir Robert Cecil from Dover, [c.13] May 1596 . . . . . 143
99. To Sir Robert Cecil from Plymouth, 26 May 1596 . . . . . 143
100. To Sir Robert Cecil from Plymouth, 29 May 1596 . . . . . 144
101. To Arthur [Gorges] from Cadiz, 21 June 1596 . . . . . 145
102. To Sir Robert Cecil from aboard ship off Cadiz, 7 July [1596] . . 151
103. To [Sir Robert Cecil] from Plymouth, 6 August [1596] . . . . 153
104. To Sir Robert Cecil, 24 January 1597 . . . . . . . 154
105. To John Rashleigh of Fowey, 14 April 1597 . . . . . . 156
106. To Lord Burghley and Charles Lord Howard from Chelsea, 24 April 1597 . . . . . . . . . . . 157
107. To Sir Robert Cecil from Weymouth, 6 July 1597 . . . . . 158
108. To Sir Robert Cecil from Plymouth, 18 July 1597 . . . . . 160
109. To Sir Robert Cecil from Plymouth, 20 July 1597 . . . . . 163
110. To Sir Robert Cecil from Plymouth, 26 July 1597 . . . . . 165
111. To [the Privy Council from Plymouth, end of July 1597] . . . 166
112. To Sir Robert Cecil from Terceira, 8 September 1597 . . . . 168
113. To the Earl of Essex, with Lords Thomas Howard and Charles Mountjoy, from Plymouth, 29 October 1597 . . . . . . . . 170
114. To Sir Robert Cecil from Plymouth, 30 October 1597 . . . . 172
115. To Lord Burghley from Durham House, 16 January 1598 . . . 175
116. To Sir William More and others from the Court, 20 May 1598 . . 176
117. To [Sir Thomas Norris] from the Court, 15 June 1598 . . . . 177
118. To Sir Robert Cecil, 26 October 1598 . . . . . . . 178
119. To [Sir Robert Cecil] from the Channel, 25 August [1599] . . . 179
120. To Sir Thomas Fane with Thomas Lord Howard from the Downs, 27 August, 1599 . . . . . . . . . . . 182
121. To Sir Robert Cecil [from Sherborne], 2 February [1600] . . . 183
122. To Sir Robert Cecil, [February 1600] . . . . . . . 185
123. To Sir Robert Cecil [from Durham House, February/March 1600] . . 185
124. To Sir Robert Cecil from Durham House, 15 March 1600 . . . 187
125. To Sir Robert Cecil [from Sherborne], 27 March 1600 . . . . 188
126. To Lord Cobham [from Sherborne], 6 April [1600] . . . . . 189
127. To Sir Robert Cecil from Sherborne, 21 April 1600 . . . . . 190
128. To Lord Cobham from Bath, 29 April [1600] . . . . . . 191

LIST OF THE LETTERS xi

129. To Sir John Gilbert II, 26 May [1600] . . . . . . . 192
130. To Thomas Reynell, Christopher and Robert Hamlyn and to John Swete, from Sherborne, 1 September 1600 . . . . . . . . . . 194
131. To Lord Cobham from Sherborne, 14 October [1600] . . . . . 195
132. To Sir Robert Cecil from Sherborne, 15 October 1600 . . . . . 196
133. To Lord Buckhurst and Sir Robert Cecil from Radford, 4 November 1600 . . . . . . . . . . . 198
134. To Sir Robert Cecil from Sherborne, 13 November [1600] . . . . 200
135. To Sir Robert Cecil from Sherborne, 15 November 1600 . . . . 201
136. To Sir Robert Cecil [?from London, after 17 January 1601] . . . . 202
137. To Sir Edward Coke from Durham House, [between 20 February and 13 August 1601] . . . . . . . . . . . 203
138. To Sir John Gilbert II [?from London], 14 July [1601] . . . . . 204
139. To Sir Robert Cecil from Sherborne, 13 August [1601] . . . . . 205
140. To Lord Cobham from Sherborne, 13 August 1601 . . . . . 207
141. To Lord Cobham from Sherborne, [27 August 1601] . . . . . 209
142. To Sir Robert Cecil from London, 7 September 1601 . . . . . 210
143. To Lord Cobham from Basing, [12 September 1601] . . . . . 212
144. To Sir Robert Cecil from Sherborne, 19 September 1601 . . . . 213
145. To Sir Robert Cecil from Sherborne, 25 September 1601 . . . . 214
146. To the Jurats of Jersey from Sherborne, 25 September 1601 . . . . 216
147. To Sir Robert Cecil from Weymouth, 26 September 1601 . . . . 217
148. To Sir Robert Cecil from Sherborne, 27 September 1601 . . . . 219
149. To Sir Robert Cecil, [c.10] October 1601 . . . . . . 220
150. To Sir Robert Cecil from Sherborne, 13 and 14 October 1601 . . . 222
151. To Sir John Gilbert II [from the Court], 31 October [1601] . . . . 223
152. To Sir John Gilbert II from the Court, 11 November [1601] . . . . 224
153. To Sir John Gilbert II [from London, late November 1601] . . . . 226
154. To the Bailiff and Justices of Jersey from the Court, 15 December 1601 . 227
155. To Sir Robert Cecil [?from Sherborne, ?late 1601] . . . . . 228
156. To the Western Assize Judges from the Court, 3 March [1602] . . . 229
157. To Sir John Gilbert II, [late April 1602] . . . . . . 232
158. To Sir Robert Cecil [from the Court, late June] 1602 . . . . . 235
159. To Sir Robert Cecil (and Lord Cobham) from Jersey, 20 July 1602 . . 237
160. To Lord Cobham from Weymouth, 12 August [1602] . . . . . 238
161. To Sir Robert Cecil from Weymouth, 21 August 1602 . . . . . 240
162. To Sir Robert Cecil from Bath, 15 September 1602 . . . . . 242

163. To [Sir Robert Cecil, before 25 March 1603] . . . . . . . . 244
164. To Sir Thomas Egerton, Sir John Popham and Sir Edward Coke, [on or before 9] June 1603 . . . . . . . . . . . . . 245
165. To Lady Ralegh [from the Tower, on or shortly before 27 July 1603] . 247
166. To the Earls of Nottingham, Suffolk and Devonshire and Lord Cecil [from the Tower, shortly after 13 August 1603] . . . . . . . 251
167. To Lord Cecil [from the Tower, before 10 November 1603] . . . . 254
168. To King James [from the Tower, before 10 November 1603] . . . 256
169. To Lord Cobham from Bagshot, [c.11/12 November 1603] . . . 257
170. To King James I [from Winchester, shortly after 17 November 1603] . 258
171. To the Earls of Suffolk and Devonshire, Lord Cecil, Henry Lord Howard and Henry Lord Wotton [from Winchester, 27/28 November 1603] . . 260
172. To Lady Ralegh [from Winchester, 4–8 December 1603] . . . . . 263
173. To the Lords Commissioners for the Trial [from Winchester, 9 December 1603] . . . . . . . . . . . . . . . . 266
174. To Lord Cecil [from Winchester, on or shortly after 10 December 1603] . 268
175. To the King [from Winchester, 11–15 December 1603 . . . . . 269
176. To Lord Cecil [from the Tower, late December 1603–early January 1604] . 270
177. To the Lords Buckhurst and Cecil and Sir George Hume [from the Tower, soon after 14 February 1604] . . . . . . . . . . . . 273
178. To the Privy Council [from the Tower, after 14 February 1604] . . 276
179. To Lord Cecil [from the Tower, 16/17] June 1604 . . . . . . 278
180. To Lord Cecil [from the Tower, shortly after 16 June] 1604 . . . 279
181. To King James [from the Tower, shortly after 16 June 1604] . . . 280
182. To Lord Cecil from the Tower, [between 25 March and 3 August] 1604 . 281
183. To Lord Cecil from the Tower, [before 3 August] 1604 . . . . . 283
184. To Lord Cranborne [from the Tower, late] 1604 . . . . . . . 284
185. To Lord Cranborne [from the Tower, winter 1604–5] . . . . . 286
186. To Sir Michael Hickes from the Tower, 10 November 1604 . . . 288
187. To Lord Cranborne [from the Tower, late December] 1604 . . . 289
188. To Levinus Munck [from the Tower, c.April 1605] . . . . . . 290
189. To the Earl of Salisbury from the Tower, [shortly before 16 July] 1605 . 291
190. To the Earl of Salisbury [from the Tower, before November] 1605 . . 293
191. To the Privy Council [from the Tower], 9 November 1605 . . . 295
192. To the Earl of Salisbury [from the Tower, c.July] 1607 . . . . . 297
193. To Viscount Haddington [from the Tower, c.July 1607] . . . . 299
194. To Henry Prince of Wales [from the Tower, c.November 1607] . . 301

## LIST OF THE LETTERS

195. To [?Sir Henry Hobart from the Tower, mid-1608] . . . . . . 304
196. To [?Lord Salisbury from the Tower, ?1608] . . . . . . . 306
197. To Sir Robert Carr from the Tower, 2 January 1609 . . . . 307
198. To John Shelbury, 3 January 1609 . . . . . . . . . 310
199. To the Earl of Salisbury [from the Tower, c.29 July 1609] . . 310
200. To [the Earl of Salisbury from the Tower], December 1609 . . 313
201. To Queen Anne [from the Tower, ?late 1609/early 1610] . . . 316
202. To Walter Ralegh Junior [from the Tower, ?c.1610] . . . . 317
203. To Sir Robert Cotton [from the Tower, ?c.1610] . . . . . 319
204. To Sir Edward Phelips [from the Tower] 19 June [1611] . . . 320
205. To the Earl of Salisbury [from the Tower, 1611] . . . . . 322
206. To [the Earl of Salisbury] and the Privy Council from the Tower, [before July] 1611 . . . . . . . . . . . . . 325
207. To Queen Anne [from the Tower, after 11 July 1611] . . . . 327
208. To King James [from the Tower, after July 1611] . . . . . 330
209. To Sir Walter Cope [from the Tower], 5 October [1611] . . . 331
210. To Sir Ralph Winwood [from the Tower], July 1615 . . . . 333
211. To Sir Ralph Winwood from the Tower, [early 1616] . . . . 335
212. To Sir George Villiers [from the Tower], 17 March [1616] . . 337
213. To Master Peter Van Lore, 1 July 1616 . . . . . . . . 338
214. To Sir William St John from Lee, Essex, 19 March [1617] . . 339
215. To Monsieur de Bisseaux from Plymouth, 14 May [1617] . . 340
216. To Sir Richard Boyle from Rostellan, co. Cork, 28 June 1617 . 342
216a. To Sir Richard Boyle [from Rostellan, ?early/mid August 1617] . 343
217. To Lady Ralegh from Cayenne, 14 November 1617 . . . . 344
218. To Sir Ralph Winwood from St Christophers, 21 March 1618 . 347
219. To Lady Ralegh from St Christophers, 22 March 1618 . . . 353
220. To Lord Carew from Plymouth, [c.11] June 1618 . . . . . 356
221. To King James [from Plymouth], 16 June 1618 . . . . . . 362
222. To [Lord Carew, late July/early August 1618] . . . . . . 364
223. To the Marquess of Buckingham from the Tower, 12 August 1618 . 368
224. To Lady Ralegh from the Tower, 18 September 1618 . . . . 370
225. To Lady Ralegh from the Tower, 4 October 1618 . . . . . 371
226. To King James from the Tower, 4 October 1618 . . . . . 373
227. To King James from the Tower, [?between 24 and 28 October 1618] . . 375
228. To [?Queen Anne from the Tower, ?late October 1618] . . . 376

Permission to publish the texts, and in certain cases photographs, of manuscripts in their custody has been given by:

The Marquess of Salisbury for 87 letters in the Cecil Papers; the Marquess of Bath for Letters 50, 51, 52, 53, 77, 78, 186, 195 and 212; the Marquess of Tavistock and the Trustees of the Bedford Estate for Letter 200; His Grace the Duke of Devonshire and the Trustees of the Chatsworth Settlement for Letters 117 and 216; the Earl of Leicester and the Trustees of the Holkham Estate for Letter 137; the Trustees of the Knole Estates for Letters 156 and 221; Major Hyne of Baldock, Herts, for Letter 154; Major J.R. More-Molyneux and the Surrey History Service for Letter 116; the Controller of Her Majesty's Stationery Office in respect of Crown copyright material in the Public Record Office, including Plates 6, 7, 8 and 12; the British Library for 20 items in the Department of Manuscripts, and Plate 5; the National Library of Wales, Aberystwyth, for Letter 214; the Keeper of Western Manuscripts, the Bodleian Library, Oxford, for Letters 23, 222 and 223; the Warden and Fellows of All Souls College, Oxford for Letters 25 and 165; the Syndics of Cambridge University Library for Letters 12, 15 and 16 (in the Cambridge University Archives); the Trustees of Lambeth Palace Library for Letters 32 and 33; the Dean and Chapter of Wells for Letter 75; the Masters of the Bench of the Inner Temple for Letter 197; Dr Williams's Trust for Letter 227; the Guildhall Library, London, for Plate 4; the Society of Antiquaries of London for Plate 9; the Harry Ransom Humanities Research Center at the University of Texas at Austin for Letters 6, 30, 42, 151 and 153; the Director of the Huntington Library, California, for Letters 7, 38, 164 and 169; the Folger Shakespeare Library, Washington DC, for Letters 21, 101, 163 and 213; the Office of Special Collections, the New York Public Library, for Letters 31, 130 and 157; the Librarian, the Pierpont Morgan Library, New York, for Letters 43, 152 and 209; the Historical Society of Pennsylvania, Philadelphia, for Letter 39; the Rare Book Department, the Free Library of Philadelphia, for Letter 138; the Maine Historical Society, Portland, for Letter 40; the Houghton Library, Harvard University, Cambridge, Mass., for Letter 146; the University of North Carolina at Chapel Hill for Plate 2; Basle University, Switzerland, for Letter 70; the Keeper of Archives in the Castle of Simancas, Spain, for Letter 215; the heads of the Archives Services of Bradford, Yorkshire, for Letters 194, 211 and 217; of Cornwall for Letter 105; of Devon for Letters 9, 13 and 57; of Dorset for Letter 72; of East Sussex for Letter 120 and of Somerset for Letters 204 and 218. Letters 27 and 59, whose present whereabouts are unknown, are printed from photographs in their auction catalogues by courtesy of Messrs Christies and Sothebys of London respectively. Every effort has been made to trace the present owner of Letter 28, but without success, and the owner of Letters 205, 206, 208 and 210, while allowing them to be printed, wishes to remain anonymous. Finally Mr John Wingfield Digby, the present owner of Sherborne Castle, has given permission for the printing (Appendix 2) of Ralegh's Will.

# LIST OF PLATES

*Frontispiece:* Portrait of Sir Walter Ralegh 1588: National Portrait Gallery

| | | |
|---|---|---|
| Plate 1. | Ralegh to Dr Valentine Dale, c.1584/5 | 19 |
| Plate 2. | Wine Licence, 4 December 1583 | 22 |
| Plate 3. | Ralegh to Sir Francis Walsingham, January 1590 | 53 |
| Plate 4. | Durham House, from John Norden 1593 | 56 |
| Plate 5. | Sherborne Castle c.1592 | 109 |
| Plate 6. | Ralegh to Sir Robert Cecil, 6 July 1597 | 159 |
| Plate 7. | Ralegh to Lord Cobham, 13 August 1601 | 208 |
| Plate 8a. | Ralegh to Sir Robert Cecil, 15 September 1602 | 243 |
| 8b. | ditto, flyleaf | 243 |
| Plate 9. | The Bloody Tower, from Hayward and Gascoyne, 1597 | 271 |
| Plate 10. | Ralegh to John Shelbury, 3 January 1609 | 311 |
| Plate 11. | Ralegh and others to the Earl of Salisbury, December 1609 | 315 |
| Plate 12. | Ralegh to Queen Anne, [after 11 July 1611] | 328 |

# LIST OF ABBREVIATIONS

| | |
|---|---|
| Addit. | Additional Manuscripts |
| Andrews 1964 | K.R. Andrews, *Elizabethan Privateering*, Cambridge, 1964 |
| Andrews 1984 | K.R. Andrews, *Trade, Plunder and Settlement*, Cambridge, 1984 |
| APC | *Acts of the Privy Council 1577–1625*, ed. J.R. Dasent, 46 vols, 1890–1964 |
| Bagwell | R. Bagwell, *Ireland under the Tudors*, 3 vols, 1885–90, reprinted 1962 |
| Birch 1751 | *Works of Sir Walter Ralegh*, 2 vols, ed. T. Birch, 1751 |
| Bodleian | Bodleian Library, Oxford |
| BL | British Library, Department of Manuscripts |
| *Cabala* | *Cabala ... mysteries of state etc. ... 1654*, repr. 1663, 1691 |
| Cayley 1806 | Arthur Cayley, *Life of Sir Walter Ralegh Knt*, 2 vols, 1806 |
| CCM | *Calendar of Carew Manuscripts in the Lambeth Palace Library 1515–1624*, 6 vols, ed. J.S. Brewer and W. Bullen, 1867–73 |
| Collins 1746 | Arthur Collins (ed.), *Letters ... written and collected by Sir Henry Sidney ...*, 2 vols, 1746 |
| Cotton | Cotton Manuscripts |
| CSPD | *Calendar of State Papers Domestic, Edward VI, Mary, Elizabeth and James I*, 12 vols, ed. R. Lemon and Mrs Everett Green, 1856–72 |
| CSPI | *Calendar of State Papers relating to Ireland, Henry VIII, Edward VI, Mary and Elizabeth*, 11 vols, ed. H.C. Hamilton, E.G. Atkinson and R.P. Mahaffy, 1860–1912 |
| DAT | *Devonshire Association, Reports and Transactions* |
| de Ricci | *Census of Medieval and Renaissance Manuscripts in the United States and Canada*, 3 vols, New York, 1935–40 |

## LIST OF ABBREVIATIONS

| | |
|---|---|
| D'Ewes 1682 | Simonds D'Ewes, *Journals of all the Parliaments during the reign of Queen Elizabeth*, ed. P. Bowes, 1682 |
| DNB | *Dictionary of National Biography*, 63 vols, 1885–1900 |
| Edwards | Edward Edwards, *Life of Sir Walter Ralegh*, 2 vols, 1868 |
| EHR | *English Historical Review* |
| Folger | Folger Shakespeare Library, Washington DC |
| Fynes Moryson 1907 | Fynes Moryson, *Itinerary*, 1917, reprinted Glasgow 1907 |
| Greg 1932 | W.W. Greg, *English Literary Autographs 1550–1650*, Oxford, 1932 |
| Grosart | A.W. Grosart, *Lismore Papers*, Series 1 and 2, 10 vols, 1886–9 |
| Harl. | Harleian Manuscripts |
| Harlow, *Last Voyage*, 1932 | V.T. Harlow (ed.), *Sir Walter Ralegh's Last Voyage*, 1932 |
| Hasler | P.W. Hasler (ed.), *The House of Commons 1558–1603*, 3 vols, 1981 |
| Hatfield CP | Hatfield House, Herts, Cecil Papers |
| HCA | High Court of Admiralty |
| HMC Bath | Historical Manuscripts Commission, *Calendar of the MSS of the Marquess of Bath at Longleat*, 5 vols, 1904–80 |
| HMC Foljambe | Historical Manuscripts Commission, 15th Report, Appendix V, 1897 |
| HMC Rutland | Historical Manuscripts Commission, 12th Report, Appendices IV and V, 1888, 1889 |
| HMC Salisbury | Historical Manuscripts Commission, *Salisbury (Cecil) MSS*, vols II–XXI, 1888–1970 |
| Huntington | Huntington Library, San Marino, California |
| Hutchins 1861–70 | J. Hutchins, *History and Antiquities of the County of Dorset*, 1774, revised edn, 4 vols, 1861–70, reprinted 1973 |
| Jackson 1940 | W. Jackson, *Carl H. Pforzheimer Library*, New York, 3 vols, 1940 |
| Lansd. | Lansdowne Manuscripts |
| Lefranc 1968 | Pierre Lefranc, *Sir Walter Ralegh Écrivain*, Quebec and Paris, 1968 |
| Longleat | Longleat, Warminster, Wilts. |
| McClure 1939 | N.E. McClure (ed.), *Letters of John Chamberlain*, 2 vols, Philadelphia, 1939 |
| *Maxims* 1642 | ?Sir Walter Ralegh, *The Prince or Maxims of State*, 1642 |
| Monson | M. Oppenheim (ed.), *Naval Tracts of Sir William Monson*, 5 vols, Navy Records Society, 22, 23, 43, 45, 47, 1902–14 |

| | |
|---|---|
| Murdin 1759 | Murdin, William (ed.), *Collection of State Papers ... left by William Cecil, Lord Burghley*, vol. 2, 1759 |
| Oldys 1736 | W. Oldys, 'Life of Ralegh', in 11th edn of Ralegh's *History of the World*, 1736, reprinted in *Works* 1829 |
| Pierpont Morgan | Pierpont Morgan Library, New York |
| Pope Hennessy | Sir John Pope Hennessy, *Sir Walter Raleigh in Ireland*, 1883 |
| PRO | Public Record Office, Kew, Surrey |
| Purchas | S. Purchas (ed.), *Hakluytus Posthumus or Purchas his Pilgrimes*, 20 vols, Glasgow, 1906 |
| Quinn 1962 | D.B. Quinn, *Raleigh and the British Empire*, 1947, revised edn 1962 |
| Quinn, *Gilbert* 1940 | D.B. Quinn (ed.), *Voyages and Colonising Enterprises of Sir Humphrey Gilbert*, 2 vols, Hakluyt Society, Series 2, LXXXIII, 1940 |
| Quinn, *Roanoke* 1955 | D.B. Quinn (ed.), *Roanoke Voyages 1584–90*, 2 vols, Hakluyt Society, Series 2, CIV–V, 1955 |
| Ransom Center | Harry Ransom Humanities Research Center, University of Texas at Austin |
| *Remains* | *Remains of Sir Walter Raleigh*, 1657, 1661, 1664, 1669, 1675, 1681, 1702, 1726 |
| *Skeptick* 1651 | *Sir Walter Raleigh's Skeptick*, 1651 |
| Sloane | Sloane Manuscripts |
| SP9 | State Papers Miscellaneous |
| SP12 | State Papers Domestic, t. Elizabeth |
| SP14 | State Papers Domestic, t. James I |
| SP15 | State Papers Domestic, *Addenda* |
| SP46 | State Papers Supplementary |
| SP63 | State Papers Ireland |
| Stebbing, 1899 | William Stebbing, *Sir Walter Ralegh*, Oxford, 1891, reprinted Oxford, 1899, New York, 1972 |
| Strype, *Annals* | J. Strype, *Annals of the Reformation ...* 4 vols, 1709–31, and Oxford, 1824 |
| Tytler 1833 | P.F. Tytler, *Life of Sir Walter Raleigh*, Edinburgh, 1833 |
| Vivian, *Cornwall* | J.L. Vivian, *Visitations of Cornwall*, Exeter, 1887 |
| Vivian, *Devon* | J.L. Vivian, *Visitations of the County of Devon*, Exeter, 1895 |
| *Works* 1829 | *Works of Sir Walter Ralegh*, 8 vols, Oxford, 1829, reprinted in facsimile, New York, 1965 |

# FOREWORD

by Emeritus Professor David Quinn, FBA

Sir Walter Ralegh's private archive has perished, though he left a substantial body of personal papers in his scattered correspondence. This has hitherto been accessible in print only in a mid-Victorian edition and has been badly in need of enlargement, with authoritative texts and apparatus, an undertaking which was for long the preoccupation of the late Agnes Latham, the distinguished editor of Ralegh's poetry. Although greatly assisted in her searches by Professor Pierre Lefranc, with advancing years she found it impossible to complete her task to the standard which she had set for herself and wisely entrusted the presentation of her texts for publication to Joyce Youings. The letters have been re-checked and some further additions made, including a number of newly-discovered contemporary manuscript copies. Agnes Latham's very extensive historical annotation has been both refined and updated and a substantial Introduction provided. The consequent edition is one of admirable academic scope which will, I am sure, remain standard for many years. It is my privilege to commend it to its users.

Liverpool, May 1998                                       David B. Quinn

# PREFACE

THE NAME of Agnes Latham is known and respected by literary historians all over the world as that of the compiler of the standard edition of the poetry of Sir Walter Ralegh, first published in 1929 and reprinted in a revised edition in 1951.[1] Throughout the 1930s Ralegh's writings continued to absorb her and she began her search for his letters, with a view to publishing a much-needed revision and expansion of the second volume, containing the texts of the letters, of Edward Edwards's *Life of Sir Walter Ralegh*, published as long ago as 1868.[2] It was a mammoth task, facilitated in its early stages by a two-year research fellowship at Westfield College in the University of London but thereafter requiring great determination to continue without the stimulus of a university teaching post. As early as 1930 she published a letter in *The Times Literary Supplement* seeking help in locating certain specified Ralegh letters and before 1932 she had been able to supply Professor Vincent Harlow with source material for his work on the second Guiana voyage. Shortly after this she made a useful contribution to Seymour de Ricci's guide to historical manuscripts in North America.[3] In 1939 she published a paper in

---

1. A complete list of Agnes Latham's published work will be found in Appendix 3.
2. Edward Edwards (ed.), *The Life of Sir Walter Ralegh*, 2 vols, 1868. He himself looked forward (vol. II, p. lxxxi) to publishing a revised edition, but there was never even a reprint. Vol. I contains a biography.
3. *TLS*, 1930, p. 554; V.T. Harlow, *Ralegh's Last Voyage*, 1932, pp. 114 and 145 and S. de Ricci and W.J.Wilson, *Census of Medieval and Renaissance Manuscripts in America and Canada*, 3 vols, New York, 1935–40. It was at de Ricci's insistence that Agnes Latham subsequently wrote a letter to *The Times Literary Supplement* reporting her discovery in the Public Record Office (SP9) of an unlisted collection of transcripts of Ralegh letters to the Gilberts: *TLS* 4 February 1939, p. 74 and correspondence with de Ricci among her papers. By then most of her earlier queries had been answered.

which, after much careful reasoning, she courageously declared her confidence in the authenticity of Ralegh's farewell letter to his wife of July 1603, of which only a copy survives (Letter 165), and this in spite of its reference to an apparently unknown daughter. Thirty years later, with the discovery in Sherborne of a will made by Ralegh in 1597,[4] she was to be triumphantly vindicated.

After the war, by then Lecturer, and from 1958 Reader, in English Literature at Bedford College, London, she redoubled her work on the letters and published further papers. She also continued her searches far beyond London. It was in 1947 that her request for access to the muniment room at Lismore Castle, co. Cork, one-time haunt of the young Ralegh, brought from the Duke of Devonshire a charming and helpful response, including the offer of some salmon-fishing on the Blackwater which he promised her would be more thrilling than the discovery of a hitherto unknown document![5]

Not long before her retirement in 1971 she was invited by Professor Pierre Lefranc of Laval University in Quebec, Canada, an established Ralegh scholar,[6] to join a research team based at Laval and financed by the Canada Council, which was to prepare an edition of all the identified writings of Sir Walter Ralegh, published and unpublished, literary and archival, under his general direction. Agnes Latham's assignment covered Ralegh's letters. The association was a great encouragement to her, the project's resources enabling her to add substantially to her own material, in particular as a result of the world-wide searching of libraries and record repositories carried out by one of Pierre Lefranc's research assistants, John Roberts, who also served as Secretary of the enterprise. Through the project, too, she made many useful contacts with the international fraternity of Ralegh scholars, including Professor Ernest Strathmann of California[7] and Professor George Story of Memorial University, Newfoundland, and renewed an association dating back to the late 1930s with Professor David Quinn, still happily the leading authority on Sir Walter Ralegh and his

---

4. See Appendix 2.
5. Letter in Agnes Latham's papers. Whether she went to Ireland is uncertain: the letters she was seeking (117 and 216) are now at Chatsworth in Derbyshire.
6. Pierre Lefranc, *Ralegh Écrivain, l'œuvre et les idees*, Quebec and Paris 1968.
7. Ernest Strathmann, *Sir Walter Ralegh: a study in Elizabethan Skepticism*, New York and Oxford, 1951.

world,⁸ and his late wife, Alison. On several occasions the editors met and conferred in London and at least once in Liverpool.

The publication of the 'Complete Works' was a splendid idea. It was also a very ambitious enterprise, including as it did Ralegh's own *History of the World*, which was one of the responsibilities assumed by Professor Lefranc, and it met with problems which, within a very short time, brought it virtually to a standstill. By 1975 the Canadian-based project had collapsed, the Director having moved elsewhere, leaving his associate editors entirely free to complete and publish their assignments independently.

Now living once more in her native Yorkshire, Agnes Latham, with occasional visits to the library of the University of York and several extended journeys to the British Library in London,⁹ continued her work for a while but found it increasingly difficult, with advancing years, to complete her edition of Ralegh's letters for publication, although by then nearly all those which she and her former collaborators had identified had been transcribed, partially edited and very extensively annotated. Her particular concern had been the collating of the vast number of contemporary transcripts, especially those of which the original letters have not survived; this enabled her to spring once more into action in the later 1970s to make an invaluable contribution to the section on Ralegh in the *Index of English Literary Manuscripts*, then being compiled at the University of Leeds by Dr Peter Beal, with whom she carried on a characteristically lively correspondence.¹⁰ But there was a danger that over fifty years' work on the complete edition of the Letters would be wasted. It was in 1990 that one of her former research students, Miss Marion Glasscoe of the School of English at the University of Exeter, alerted an Exeter colleague, a Tudor specialist with a particular interest in maritime history and in the editing of historical texts—and, as it happens, like Ralegh a Devonian.¹¹ A visit to the small flat in Pickering led to an undertaking, with the enthusiastic support of Professor David Quinn, to complete the work for publication and to the

---

8. See, in particular, *Roanoke Voyages 1584–90*, 2 vols, Hakluyt Society, Series 2, 104–5, 1955 and *Set Fair for Roanoke*, Chapel Hill and London, 1985.
9. Her meticulously-filed application slips show that she paid her last visit in 1985.
10. P. Beal (compiler), *Index of English Literary Manuscripts*, 2 vols, London and New York, 1980. My thanks are due to Dr Beal for providing copies of Agnes Latham's letters to him between 1975 and 1979.
11. Joyce Youings, *Sixteenth-Century England*, 1984, 'Ralegh's Country and the Sea', *Proceedings of the British Academy*, LXXV, 1989 and co-editor and contributor, *New Maritime History of Devon*, 2 vols, 1991–2.

transportation, in blizzard conditions in a small car, of the whole of Agnes Latham's working papers on Ralegh's letters to Thorverton, near Exeter in Devon, not far as the crow flies from Ralegh's place of birth in the parish of East Budleigh.[12]

Agnes Latham was delighted with this outcome and, although eager to hand over full responsibility, followed with interest the progress towards publication. She was most patient with Ralegh's competitors for his new editor's time, work only being resumed in earnest towards the end of 1994. Sadly she did not live to see her life's work in print. Agnes Mary Christabel Latham died on 13 January 1996, within a few weeks of her ninety-first birthday,[13] not, however, before giving her blessing to the offering of Ralegh's Letters to the University of Exeter Press for publication.

Joyce Youings

---

12. Included in the load were eight original letters of Lady Ralegh and a number of other early seventeenth-century manuscript books, containing contemporary transcripts of Ralegh's letters, all of which, as agreed with Agnes Latham, have since her death been placed permanently in the Department of Manuscripts at the British Library, with the exception of a volume once part of the Bacon-Frank collection which has rejoined the series in the Bodleian Library, Oxford.

13. See the obituaries in *The Times*, 8 February 1996, and the *Independent*, 14 February 1966.

# INTRODUCTION

## THE COLLECTION

In order to keep the length of the new edition within reasonable bounds the term 'letter' has been rigorously defined so as to include only communications written or composed by Ralegh, signed by him personally and addressed to particular, i.e. named, recipients. This has led to the exclusion of several letters included by Edwards in his *Life of Sir Walter Ralegh*, published in 1868, which were composed by others and to which Ralegh was only a signatory. Exceptions have been made in the case of two letters (31 and 200) which, though strictly legal documents, were cast in letter form. The surviving letters of Lady Ralegh and the remaining manuscripts included by Edwards which are not in letter form have not been included. Nevertheless, so many new letters have been discovered in the last 130 years that while Edwards's admissible tally was 159 this edition runs to 228 individual items, including 32 not hitherto published *in extenso*, of which 17 are virtually unknown. New finds in the state papers in the Public Record Office and the British Library have been few, with fewer still among the Cecil Papers at Hatfield, a tribute to Edwards's thoroughness. The main additions to his tally, a few of them already in print, have been in the English county record offices and in a number of American libraries.

Today's editors of historical documents, that is, records created in the course of business or administration, public or private, as opposed to literary texts whose subsequent revision may well be crucial to their interpretation, will always prefer to derive their texts as far as possible from the original manuscripts. It was not always so. For nearly a quarter of his texts Edwards relied upon copies, either texts already in print or contemporary or later manuscript transcripts. Of these, all but ten of the original letters have since been traced, including three of the four he derived from the often incomplete and faulty texts printed by John Strype, the eighteenth-century antiquary. In this new and much expanded edition over five-sixths have been taken from the original manuscripts and most of the remainder from what may be regarded as very reliable copies.

Indeed, this new collection would be very much the poorer were it not for the fact, peculiar to Ralegh among the great historical figures of his day, that in addition to the surviving original letters actually despatched by him there exists an incredible number of early manuscript transcripts, that is more or less exact copies, incredible not so much for the total number of individual letters copied as for the number of copies made of the more popular letters, especially those written during the two most critical years of his life, 1603 and 1618. The original letter (172) written to his wife from Winchester early in December 1603 has not survived, but no less than 74 manuscript copies have been identified, some of them of a shorter recasting which Agnes Latham believed to have been made by Ralegh himself. She selected for this collection a transcript made for Sir Robert Cotton (1571–1631) of the longer, and earlier, version as showing more the writer's state of mind,[1] although she regarded the edited version, the one he no doubt intended for circulation, as the finer work of art. Letter 197, begging Sir Robert Carr in January 1609 to refuse the King's gift of Ralegh's former estate at Sherborne, of which the original is also missing, is extant in at least 45 copies. There is little variation but the copy in the library of the Inner Temple is unique in preserving both the address and the date. These transcripts, embracing only a small fraction of Ralegh's surviving letters, are to be found scattered among the manuscript collections of England, with a few in North America.[2] Some were made on Ralegh's own instructions (e.g. see Letters 218 and 219) so that the news they contained could be circulated more widely or, in the case of the letter to Carr, not with any hope of saving his estate but rather to make public his wrongs. On occasion Ralegh would have copies made for others to read. In his letters to Sir Ralph Winwood (210 and 211) in 1615 and 1616, he mentions that he is enclosing for information copies of his letters to the Earl of Salisbury and to King James. No written copy will ever be facsimile, but the ultimate in transcripts must be the translations into Spanish, made either from the originals or from contemporary copies, of Ralegh's letters to his friend

---

1. See below, footnote 25.
2. A list of all manuscript collections containing these transcripts, but without particulars of the individual letters, was contributed by Agnes Latham to Beal, *Index*, ii, pp. 374–5.

Sir George Carew (Letter 220) and to King James (Letter 226) in 1618. Sent to the King of Spain by his ambassador in England, they are now in the Spanish archives and are here printed as re-translations into modern English. But most of those extant were undoubtedly made, at their own behest, for private collectors, for every possible reason, including curiosity, 'last' letters being particularly valued. Those made some time after the originals were written, many as late as the eighteenth century, were usually entered into bound volumes along with transcripts of the letters of other public figures.

A great deal can be done by careful collation of multiple texts to establish lineage and hence to select the transcript most likely to be the nearest to a missing original. Certain collections, and even certain scribes, win the experienced editor's confidence and Agnes Latham regarded the inclusion of addresses and superscriptions as a good guide to authenticity.[3] A small collection of transcripts now in Bradford, Yorkshire, which she knew about but never actually saw, is so stained with gall (applied by some previous owner in the hope of improving legibility) that the four Ralegh items are now readable only with the help of numerous other copies, but in one case (Letter 194) it has been given priority by the present editor because it alone contains copies of both subscription and signature and in another (Letter 211) because, unlike other copies, it is dated. Additional confidence derives from the fact that another transcript in the Bradford collection is very nearly identical with the original letter (221) to King James which survives a hundred miles away and which has, of course, taken priority. Near-contemporary transcripts are not only indispensable in the absence of the original letters, but are also extremely useful in cases where the originals themselves (e.g. Letter 157) have been very badly damaged. Unfortunately, even those in English are only too likely to have been 'edited' by over-zealous copyists, especially with regard to spelling, each, it would appear, having his own idea as to how Ralegh spelled his name. Finally, attention must be drawn to a group of four letters (205, 206, 208 and 210) the texts of which have been taken from what is described as a 'common-place' book. All date from the years when Ralegh was planning his second voyage to Guiana, with which all are concerned, but although clearly transcripts, each, as the list of contents tells us, is 'entituled' by Ralegh in his own hand, which lends them peculiar authenticity. Unfortunately this particular

---

3. Agnes Latham's very extensive notes on the transcripts will be deposited, for the use of accredited scholars, in Exeter University Library.

collection is now back in private hands although when Agnes Latham transcribed the Ralegh items they were in a Cambridge museum.[4]

There has been no advance on Edwards in that no letter has been found dating from earlier than 1581, by which time Ralegh was in his late twenties, but thereafter they are spread, though unevenly, up to the end of his life in 1618. From the following table it will be seen that the last decade of the reign of Queen Elizabeth has by far the greatest coverage. Five years, 1582, 1606 and 1612–14, are totally unrepresented, the first when Ralegh was making his first real infiltration into the Court circle and the rest when he was settling down to life in the Tower without any prospect of release. No exact comparison of chronology with Edwards's collection can be made owing to the extensive corrections made in this new edition in the dating of the undated letters, mostly from internal evidence. Wherever appropriate, readers have been alerted to possible forgeries, but these are remarkably few.

*Number of Extant Letters of Sir Walter Ralegh.*

| Years | No. | Years | No. |
| --- | --- | --- | --- |
| 1581–1585 | 18 | 1601–1605 | 56 |
| 1586–1590 | 17 | 1606–1610 | 12 |
| 1591–1595 | 55 | 1611–1615 | 7 |
| 1596–1600 | 45 | 1616–1618 | 18 |

The present edition follows that of Edwards in that a very considerable part of the collection draws upon the survival of no less than 87 of Ralegh's letters among the Cecil Papers at Hatfield and of 43 in the State Papers, Domestic, Foreign and Irish, in the Public Record Office, together with 19 in the British Library, 5 in the Bodleian Library at Oxford and 2 in the Cambridge University Archives. Several have come to light since Edwards's time in the muniment rooms of three other great English country houses,

---

4. It is ironic that the volume containing these four transcripts can be traced through the salerooms *before* it reached Cambridge but not after it left there. Edwards (vol. II, p. 337) identified it, probably correctly, with a volume once in the possession of Sir Joseph Jekyll, Master of the Rolls, which was sold at auction in London in 1739, the four Guiana letters then being described as being wholly in Ralegh's hand, which Edwards rightly doubted. It next appeared as Lot 207 in Sotheby's sale of the Bright collection on 8 June 1844, and finally as Lot 248, from the collection of Harry L. Bradfer-Lawrence FSA, at Christie's in 1954 where it was purchased by Quaritch for the Fitzwilliam Museum. Of these four letters Edwards printed only Letter 206 which he took from a far less reliable transcript.

Longleat, Holkham and Chatsworth. Six county record offices, particularly those of Devon and Somerset, have produced new finds and, last but not least, Ralegh's letters have found their way to a number of American libraries, notably the Huntington in California and the Folger in Washington, but also some less likely institutions such as the New York Public Library, after changing hands several times in the auction houses of London and New York. Apart from the translations already mentioned, only one (Letter 70) has been found as yet in European archives but, even so, the letters here published are located in over 30 separate locations on either side of the Atlantic.

The migration of many of Ralegh's surviving letters is almost a tale in itself. Many of those sent to the Cecils, father and son, moved no further than the distance between Burghley House in the Strand and the new mansion at Hatfield, those which remained with the state papers only from the Tower of London to the Rolls House in Chancery Lane, though even as this is being written the latter are in the course of being transported to the new Public Record Office at Kew in Surrey. It is the smaller collections which have faced the greater hazards. For example, 13 letters which Ralegh wrote to members of the Gilbert family, his half-brothers Sir John and Sir Humphrey, and the former's son, also Sir John, were in the mid-eighteenth century in the possession of a descendant, one Major Pomeroy Gilbert of the 72nd Foot, stationed c.1750 at Plymouth. Subsequently the collection passed through many hands, including those of the editor of the *Edinburgh Review*, eventually to be split up, via the auction rooms, between no less than six American libraries, including three in New York, from one of which, the Pforzheimer, five of the letters have moved quite recently to what must surely be their final resting-place, the Harry Ransom Humanities Research Center in the University of Texas at Austin. The present location of one of the Gilbert letters (28) is no longer known, although it passed through a London saleroom as recently as 1975 and is reported to be in private hands in Venezuela.[5] Inevitably some of the letters, especially those that have changed hands several times, and even some which are in the national repositories, have in the course of time suffered wear and tear, not to speak of wanton damage. Letter 213, one of the few in the collection addressed to anyone in Europe and now in Washington, has lost its important subscription and signature, presumably to a collector of autographs,

---

5. Beal, *Index*, ii, p. 374.

since it was copied and published by William Oldys in the early eighteenth century. At least one (Letter 103) has suffered fire damage. But we must be grateful for the care which has been bestowed upon most of them by their curators. Agnes Latham liked to relate how, on her early visits to Hatfield in the 1930s, the Librarian, when he needed to fetch a new log for the fire, insisted on taking with him the manuscript on which she was working. Her story of his further insistence, no doubt kindly meant, that she accompany him home to a leisurely lunch, will find a sympathetic echo in the memories of all who recall the heroic days of record searching.

No such collection will ever be complete, even to the extent of including all surviving manuscripts. There is ample evidence in the surviving texts that Ralegh wrote and sent many letters that have almost certainly not survived. It is to be hoped, however, that in the course of time more will come to light. Indeed, there are those who believe that one day the fabric of Ralegh's new castle at Sherborne in Dorset will release its secrets, for it is a fact that Sir Walter's own papers, which must once have been considerable, have never been found. Such treasure trove, of course, would produce only draft outgoing letters, of which, one suspects, Ralegh wrote a great many, some of which he probably never despatched. Compared with the situation in Edwards's day finding aids now proliferate. What benefits will accrue from the Internet only time will tell. It may assist scholars to obtain particulars, even instant photocopies, of their sources less laboriously, but it is to be feared that twenty-first century discoveries of archival goldmines may well prove as elusive as Ralegh's own El Dorado.

# PREVIOUS PUBLICATION OF THE LETTERS

In addition to the apparent demand for transcripts the interest in acquiring copies of Ralegh's letters was seized upon, though much more slowly, by the printed book trade. The first to be printed was its author's own revision of Letter 172 which he wrote to his wife early in December 1603 in expectation of imminent execution. That it appeared in 1644 (in a small pamphlet 'printed in London for R.H.') under the title *To day a man, To morrow none: or Sir Walter Rawleighes Farewell to his Lady the night before he was beheaded* [sic] ... can only be attributed to artistic licence. It was followed in 1648 by the inclusion of the texts, both of this letter and of that which Ralegh wrote to King James in November 1603 (Letter 170) begging for his life (the original of which survives at Hatfield), in Sir John Overbury's *Arraignment and Conviction of Sir Walter Ralegh*, an account of the trial of 1603, which reproduces them very faithfully. Two other letters (194 and 222) followed in 1650, printed in *Judicious and Select Essayes and Observations ...*, a collection largely of Ralegh's naval writings, along with the 'Apologie' for Guiana. A work once attributed to Ralegh but now regarded as spurious, *The Prince, or Maxims of State*, printed in 1651 with many subsequent editions, contained the texts of eight, and later of eleven, letters and in the same year the publication of *Sceptick, or Speculations ...*, another work no longer universally attributed to Ralegh,[6] added a few more, as also did *Cabala: Mysteries of State in letters of the great ministers of K. James and K. Charles* in 1654. In 1660 there appeared *A Collection of Letters made by Sir Tobie Mathews* [sic] which included two attributed to Ralegh and printed here (Letters 196 and 228) for which this is the only textual source. Edwards was dismissive[7] but there seems to be no *a priori* reason to doubt their authenticity.

For the next hundred years the printing of Ralegh's prose works continued to be sustained by public interest, his *Remains*, which succeeded the *Maxims* in 1657, going into no less than eight editions, each with its small complement of his letters 'to divers persons of quality'. These, however, tended to be the same ones, so that by 1751 there were still only about a dozen in print, some of them carelessly copied, most to some extent edited and all of them reproduced in current spelling.

In 1736 William Oldys published the first substantial biography, prefixed to the eleventh edition of Ralegh's *History of the World*, with the now traditional appendix of letters. In 1751 the *Works of Sir Walter Ralegh* in two volumes contained a new biography by Thomas Birch who had obtained access to more of the original letters and added marginally to the number available in print. Both of these biographies, together with twenty-four of Ralegh's letters, were included in the greatly expanded edition of the *Works* published in eight volumes by Oxford University Press in 1829.[8] Meanwhile, in 1759 a small selection of the Ralegh letters at Hatfield was newly transcribed and printed, fairly accurately, though in modern spelling,

---

6. ibid., p. 368.
7. Edwards II, pp. lxiv–lxv.
8. Vol. 8 contains the letters. A facsimile edition was published in New York in 1965.

by William Murdin.⁹ In 1805 Arthur Cayley, in his *Life of Sir Walter Ralegh*, the first really scholarly biography, added his own selection, 17 in all, scattered throughout the two volumes. Not long after this the notorious forger of Elizabethan literary manuscripts, John Payne Collier, was reporting, mostly in the respectable pages of *Archaeologia*, his discoveries of new Ralegh letters, all of them genuine though Collier was inclined to claim as originals texts which were only near-contemporary or later copies.¹⁰ In the 1860s, during the first real flush of Victorian historical scholarship based on documentary sources, while Edwards was burrowing away in England, S.R. Gardiner made an exploratory search of the archives of Spain,¹¹ an initiative which has not, to this day, been adequately followed up. Scholars were now to be well served by the publication, beginning in 1856, of the *Calendars of State Papers Domestic*, which, however, had only reached the year 1594 by the time Edwards went to press in 1868, which explains his description of many of the late-Elizabethan letters as being among 'unarranged papers'. The Jacobean volumes were already in print but those for Ireland only as far as the year 1585, which explains why Edwards missed Letters 34, 73, 74 and 76 which are here for the first time published *in extenso*. The earlier calendars were fairly complete in content but still no real substitute for complete texts, though many eminent historians have regarded them as such. Some of the most interesting recent discoveries (e.g. Letters 18, 19 and 129) have been from PRO, SP9 and 46, classes which still lack printed calendars and the latter even a detailed manuscript list.¹²

From 1888, however, there began to appear the Historical Manuscripts Commission's publication of the Cecil Papers at Hatfield House. The early volumes reproduced almost verbatim texts, though in modern spelling, but later retreated to abstracts with cross-references, where appropriate, to Edward Edwards, indicating how thorough had been his search there: he missed only a handful of the Ralegh letters. There was, however, a limit to his peregrinations and it fell to the Commission's inspectors to report finds of new Ralegh letters in the other great country-house collections, notably

---

9. William Murdin and Samuel Haynes, *Collection of State Papers ... left by William Cecil, Lord Burghley*, 2 vols., 1740, 1759. Volume II, edited by Murdin alone, contains the Ralegh letters, including the texts of two (Letters 41 and 45) which are now missing from the collection at Hatfield.
10. *Archaeologia* 34 (1852), pp. 149–59, 160–70; 35 (1853), pp. 213–22; *Notes and Queries*, series 3, 5 (1864), pp. 7–8, 108–9 and 207–8.
11. 'The Case against Sir Walter Raleigh', *Fortnightly Review*, new series 1, 1867.
12. A.M.C. Latham, 'Ralegh's Letters', *The Times Literary Supplement*, 4 February 1939.

that of the Marquess of Bath at Longleat in Wiltshire,[13] and, at least until the Second World War, many of these were printed in full, though often in modern spelling. Increasingly in the 1920s they appeared in the form of brief abstracts, as too was the case with the printed calendars of state papers as their custodians strove to keep up with the demand for more finding aids from scholars able and anxious to read the originals.

When Agnes Latham began her search for Ralegh's letters in the early 1930s the chief interest was by specialists in New World Discovery, beginning with V.T. Harlow's work on Ralegh's expeditions to Guiana.[14] Only in 1966 did the literary historian, Pierre Lefranc, begin to publish his findings with the printing of the texts of two hitherto unknown Ralegh letters (101 and 169) of which he found transcripts in the Huntington Library, California,[15] to be followed in 1968 by *Sir Walter Ralegh, Écrivain*, published in Canada and still, regrettably, without an English translation. Not the least useful of its contents was a list (pp. 579–82) of 64 Ralegh letters then known to him which are not in Edwards, each of which, incidentally, is included in this volume. The Second World War having cut short Agnes Latham's publication of her work on Ralegh's letters which had begun so promisingly (Letter 165) in 1939, she began again in 1951 on an all-too-brief series of Ralegh papers which appeared largely in literary journals.[16] Her last paper, published in 1971, told of the discovery among the estate documents at Sherborne of the will Ralegh made in 1597. As she printed only extracts from this very illuminating manuscript the opportunity has been taken of including the full text as one of the appendices to this volume.

Meanwhile, for over a century countless biographers have reprinted extracts, and even whole texts (such as those in Sir John Pope Hennessy's *Raleigh in Ireland*, 1883) copied verbatim, and not always with due acknowledgement, from Edward Edwards's massive work. This is not the place for a new biography, badly as one is needed. Indeed, for a really comprehensive 'life' it is still necessary to go back to William Stebbing's *Sir Walter Ralegh*, first published in 1891 but, unfortunately for a work which is soundly based on the sources available at the time, entirely lacking

---

13. *HMC Bath*, II, 1907.
14. V.T. Harlow (ed.), *English Colonising Expeditions to the West Indies and Guiana*, 1925 and *Voyages of Great Pioneers*, Oxford, 1929, both including Ralegh's two expeditions to Guiana, followed by *Discoverie of ... Guiana*, 1928 and *Ralegh's Last Voyage*, 1932.
15. 'Ralegh in 1596 and 1603: Three unprinted letters in the Huntington Library', *Huntington Library Quarterly*, xxix, 4, 1966, pp. 337–345.
16. See Appendix 3.

in footnotes.[17] Most of the innumerable biographies which followed in the twentieth century have been lightweight in original scholarship, virtually the only exception being the all too brief but authoritative *Raleigh and the British Empire* by David Beers Quinn. This was first published in 1947 and revised in 1962, but does, however, remain true to its title and, in any case, must be read today in conjunction with the author's subsequent published work on Ralegh's enterprises in Ireland and the Americas.[18] One of the most readable of the post-war and more popular biographies is Robert Lacey's *Sir Walter Ralegh*, published in 1973, but the most original recent work, apart from that of Quinn, has been much more specialized, such as E.A. Strathmann's *Sir Walter Ralegh: a study in Elizabethan Skepticism* (New York and London 1951) and S.J. Greenblatt's *Sir Walter Ralegh: the Renaissance Man and his roles* (New Haven, 1973). Indispensable as companion pieces to any full-scale historical study of Ralegh are the late A.L. Rowse's *Ralegh and the Throckmortons* (1962) and John W. Shirley's *Thomas Harriot* (Oxford, 1983), the latter a highly technical study of the great mathematician which also contains a lot of new material on his employer. For the rest, readers are referred to *Sir Walter Ralegh: an Annotated Bibliography* (Chapel Hill, North Carolina, 1987), an invaluable work of reference compiled by Christopher M. Armitage, its contents, including full details of Ralegh's own published works, running to nearly two thousand items. Also useful, though primarily concerned with Ralegh's literary output, is 'Recent Studies in Ralegh', *English Literary Renaissance* 15, 1985, pp. 225–44, by J.L. Mills.

## A BRIEF BIOGRAPHY

All that can be provided here, merely to identify the pattern and progress of Ralegh's career, is a brief though not entirely factual biography written by Agnes Latham some years ago, one of several she supplied for various encyclopaedias.

---

17. In a reprint of 1899 Stebbing added fourteen pages of 'Authorities' but these still do not make it very easy for the reader to identify his sources.
18. In particular, *The Elizabethans and the Irish*, New York 1966; 'The Munster Plantation: Problems and Opportunities', *Journal of the Cork Historical and Archaeological Society* 71, 1966, pp. 19–40; with A.M. Quinn and Susan Hillier (eds), the five-volume *New American World*, 1979, which contains the texts of several of Ralegh's letters and the quadricentennial *Set Fair for Roanoke*, Raleigh, North Carolina and London, 1985, in which he deals in minute detail with Ralegh's attempts to settle English people in his 'Virginia'.

## Sir Walter Ralegh 1554–1618

The Raleghs were an old Devonshire family, of some standing in the county. Walter, born in 1554,[19] was the youngest of three brothers and his half-brothers were the Gilberts, Humphrey, John and Adrian. His cousins were innumerable. But comparatively speaking he was a nobody, a young gentleman who had come down from Oxford without a degree and who still spoke with a strong provincial accent. The young Walter was handsome and well-built, with soft dark hair and eyes, and a delicate complexion. He might have bent his mind to marrying money, settling down near his boyhood home in east Devon and becoming, in the fullness of time, a justice of the peace. Instead he chose the hazards and uncertain rewards of soldiering, first in the French wars and then in Ireland. In the latter, besides his sword, he used his tongue and pen, giving lucid and energetic advice on the whole Irish question, thereby coming to the notice of his superiors and finally of the Queen, who found something in him—was it the clear brain? or the driving power?—that was extremely attractive. From her he received a knighthood, office, income and lands, and became for a time the ruling favourite and the close friend of Robert Cecil, Lord Treasurer Burghley's second son.

Although he himself rarely at this time left the Court, during the later 1580s he was one of the country's leading promoters of maritime ventures, especially those directed against the power of the Spanish empire. From 1584, with a royal grant of almost incredible proportions, if only he could exercise it, on the eastern seaboard of North America, he was the inspiration, promoter and the chief financial backer of the first attempt to settle English people in the New World. At the same time, and with rather more success, he was one of the leaders of English settlement in Ireland.

When he was nearly forty he married.[20] His wife was Elizabeth Throckmorton, a maid of honour at Court, and in gaining her he lost the Queen who felt his secret affiliation as a deadly wound. His position, even without this *faux pas*, was in any case precarious, since the young Earl of Essex had for some time been his rival for the Queen's favour, with all

---

19. A.M.C. Latham, 'A Birth-date for Sir Walter Ralegh', *Etudes Anglaises*, 3, 1956, pp. 243–5, arguing very convincingly for 1554, which is now generally accepted as correct.
20. Cf. P. Lefranc, 'La Date du Mariage de Sir Walter Ralegh: un document inédit', *Etudes Anglaises*, 3, 1956, pp. 193–211, arguing a much earlier date which has not won general acceptance.

the splendour of his lineage and the strong following which Ralegh lacked. Imprisoned in the Tower of London when the news of his marriage reached the Queen, Ralegh bought his release with the forfeiture of the enormous profits of his most successful privateering venture. It took him the best part of ten years to regain his good standing with the ageing Queen.

In 1595 he crossed the Atlantic for the first time as leader of an expedition to Guiana in South America, received the homage of the native rulers and listened avidly to their tales of El Dorado and of the gold and silver his agents had failed to find in Virginia. With minimal interest at Court and, in spite of the defeat of the Spanish Armada, a worsening international situation nearer home, Ralegh's services as a naval commander were now given a new, if limited, rein. In 1596 he acted as rear-admiral to the Earl of Essex on the expedition to Cadiz and in 1597 he was with Essex again on the Islands Voyage, in the course of which their rivalry escalated. Partly as a result of Essex's rising against the Queen in 1602, Ralegh once again basked in royal favour.

But the future now lay not with the ageing Queen but with James VI of Scotland who allowed himself to be convinced, before ever he arrived in England, that Ralegh was one of his most dangerous and determined adversaries. Plots were soon discovered: to put Lady Arabella Stuart on the throne, and to make peace with Spain. One of the leaders was Lord Cobham, an erstwhile friend, who, in an effort to clear himself, incriminated Ralegh, whose desperate declarations of a lifelong hatred of Spain carried little weight with a king who had now decided to have peace. Ralegh was convicted, saved from the scaffold at the last moment and committed to life imprisonment in the Tower.

For the next decade or so Ralegh's main energies were devoted to saving his estate at Sherborne in Dorset for his son, or at least sufficient income to maintain his wife and growing family, and not least himself, in some degree of comfort. It was the most broken and despairing period of his life, not made more bearable by deteriorating health. He finally lost Sherborne in 1609. But he had some resources which could not be taken from him and bestowed on James's favourites. His mind's treasure was inexhaustible, his arrogant intellect as keen as when he had told Queen Elizabeth what to do with Irish rebels. He began to write a history of the world, showing how kings have always paid in the end for their crimes and innocent blood never cried to heaven unanswered. He read voraciously, kept in close touch with the outside world and at the same time contrived to occupy himself with science and metallurgy. This last preoccupation was not unconnected with his brooding over a scheme whereby England could exploit the gold and silver-bearing mountains of Guiana without necessarily offending Spain.

He was at last released in 1617, a not-too-fit man of 63, to search, at his own expense, for his El Dorado, knowing, as indeed did King James I, that in the eyes of Spain he was an intruder. When he came home, storm-beaten, fever-stricken and empty-handed, having buried his eldest surviving son, he was naturally disowned by his sovereign. When he realized that this time there was no hope he composed himself to die with dignity. He was executed on 29 October 1618.

## THE RECIPIENTS OF THE LETTERS

As by far the greater number of Ralegh's surviving letters are to be found among the state papers, including those at Hatfield, it is inevitable that most of them are addressed to the principal officers of state, and hence to the Cecils, father and son, 18 to Lord Burghley and no less than 91 to Sir Robert, the later Viscount Cranborne and finally Earl of Salisbury. Next come King James and Lord Cobham, each with eight, and no one else with an appreciable number unless those to Ralegh's Gilbert half-brothers and nephew are taken together, one to Sir Humphrey, eight to Sir John senior and six to his young namesake. Of what must surely have been a large number written to his most loyal friend, and distant cousin, Sir George Carew, only three have survived. Neither the Earl of Bath, Devon's Lord Lieutenant, nor Sir Richard Grenville, to whom Ralegh must frequently have written, left behind any papers. They or their descendants were either careless or discreet where their correspondence was concerned. Nor has a single letter from Ralegh to Thomas Harriot been found among the large collection of papers left by the great mathematician, partly no doubt because they were able to communicate verbally in the fastness of Durham House, and occasionally at Sherborne. The greatest loss is of the many letters Ralegh almost certainly wrote to the Queen, only one of which has survived. We must be grateful indeed to those who copied for posterity six of those he wrote to his wife.

But one cannot complain about the variety of the recipients of Ralegh's letters, these being extant to such diverse subjects of the Crown as Dr Roger Hovenden, Warden of All Souls, and Sir Robert Cotton; Sir Richard Boyle and Robert Carr; the Earl of Essex and Sir Michael Hickes; the Lord

Admiral, Charles Lord Howard, and John Rashleigh of Fowey; not forgetting Bess of Hardwick as well as Bess Ralegh. By no means the least interesting challenge of the collection is the need to distinguish the private from the official communication; the occasions when Ralegh was just being himself from those when he was acting a part; to decide to what extent, if any, his style of writing reflected the identity of those to whom he addressed himself; and, perhaps most difficult of all, to imagine the impact of his letters on those to whom they were addressed.

# THE SUBJECT MATTER OF THE LETTERS

What follows is not a comprehensive analysis but an indication of what the reader may expect to find. Those letters which have not hitherto been published *in extenso* are indicated by an asterisk. References to other source material will usually be found in the endnotes.

## *Ireland and Virginia*

The first five of Ralegh's letters to survive are those despatched by the young army captain from Munster in 1581. Only one is in his hand, not surprisingly that written to the Earl of Leicester in August complaining of the ineffectiveness of the Lord Deputy to whom, three months earlier, he had communicated his dissatisfaction with his commanding officer, Lord Ormond. Three were in the hand of a very competent clerk, to whose identity we have a clue in the chronicle of John Hooker of Exeter, who adds to Ralegh's own story of his escape from being ambushed by the Seneschal of Imokilly (Letter 2) the fact that among his small company was his 'man, Jenkin', who was carrying some £200 in cash. Already, in these early letters, there is evidence of Ralegh's interest in staking a claim to the land of the Irish rebels, but the story of his acquisition in 1587 of the largest seignory of all finds no place in his letters, which only show the extent to which his duties in England, and his own concern to be near the Queen, delayed his return. He was over there, however, for several months in the late summer of 1589, seeing to his 'prize' (Letter 33) and meeting, in his new role as landlord, a somewhat mixed reception, not least from the new Lord Deputy.

But it was an encounter of a different kind which called forth later that year a letter from Ralegh addressed to one Master James Gold of Cork. With regret, especially on account of its interesting revelations about the identity of the mother of Ralegh's illegitimate daughter, it has not been included in the main sequence of letters but, in view of what must be grave suspicions about its authenticity, it has been printed, numbered Letter 31A, in Appendix 1, to which readers' attention is drawn for further details. There follow three letters, two of them not hitherto published *in extenso*, in which Ralegh propounds his solutions to the troublesome state of Ireland, including urging on the Lord Deputy (Letter 32*) the recruitment to the latter's Council of his Devonshire 'cousin', Sir George Carew, and, a frequent theme later on, the winning over of certain potentially loyal Irishmen to be carefully detached from what he clearly regarded (Letter 34*) as the incurably rebellious majority. In 1592, when he had troubles enough in England, he was conscious that his 'disgraces' (Letters 45 and 47) were also undermining his position as an Irish landlord, and his burgeoning feud with Lord Deputy Sir William Fitzwilliam led to many complaints to Sir Robert Cecil, now the most powerful member of the Queen's Privy Council. But his air of self-righteousness never deserted him. In May 1593 (Letter 60), from his 'fortress fold' in Sherborne, he chided not only her advisers but the Queen herself, for not listening to an expert on Ireland: 'the Trojan Southsayer [sic] cast his spear agaynst the wodden horse but [was] not beleved.'

Meanwhile, other letters testify to his efforts, even as an absentee landlord, to make his estate pay, especially (Letters 61 and 63) his great timber resources along the Blackwater river for which there was a foreign market in the form of wine-barrel staves. A series of letters, including several hitherto unpublished (73*, 74*, 76* and 77), show Ralegh continuing, even as new risings threatened, to support his Irish protégés, especially his former 'page', Charles MacCarthy, like the others a former rebel. He also sought, not without success (Letters 92 and 117), to influence clerical appointments. By the later 1590s, however, his chief concern, expressed or implied in many of his letters, was the danger of Ireland being used as a backdoor to England by the forces of the King of Spain, and we see him, usually from his vantage point in Dorset, doing his best to keep Cecil informed. These culminated in his reports of the Spanish landing at Kinsale in October 1601 (Letters 147–50). However, underlying all his missives to Cecil is the barely disguised effort to improve his standing with the Queen. In May 1593 (Letter 60) he even sympathized with her about the cost of controlling Ireland, and for a passing moment wondered whether it was all worthwhile.

Indeed, after his disposal of his Irish estate to Sir Richard Boyle in 1603 and during his long imprisonment in the Tower, Ireland and its affairs, at least on the evidence of his letters, ceased to concern him. Once only, on his way to Guiana in June 1617, did he again make landfall there. Lying storm-bound in Cork harbour he wrote to Boyle (Letter 216) asking for the loan of some horses so that he could go hawking, adding that he would either 'prosper' or 'perish', there being 'no other way'. He was thinking of Guiana but he might as well have been contemplating his involvement with Ireland.

It is disappointing to have to report that, whereas nearly forty of Ralegh's extant letters are concerned partly or wholly with Ireland, only two have been found, either by Edward Edwards or by more recent scholars, relating to his colonizing enterprises in North America, and both date from after 1600 when the main thrust had evaporated. The letter (161) of 1602 to Sir Robert Cecil is therefore all the more valuable, though its real importance lies in its indication that Ralegh was, even then, still hoping to contact his lost 'people' in Virginia, though endeavouring at least to cover his costs by trading and, as a corollary, by defending his rights under the charter of 1584. Letter 201 to Queen Anne, ostensibly seeking her support for a voyage to 'Virginia', was transparently a plea for release from the Tower, his trans-Atlantic ambitions by now, i.e. 1609–10, being directed towards the goldfields of Guiana.

## Ships, Privateering and the Sea Wars

Nearly half of the letters in this collection are concerned, wholly or partly, with the sea, including the naval expeditions to Cadiz in 1596 and to the Azores the following year, in both of which Ralegh played a leading role. But very few of Ralegh's surviving letters were written aboard ship for the very good reason that the sea was not his element. Until he went to Guiana in 1595 he had not left European and, indeed, barely English Channel waters. When in command of a naval squadron at the siege of Cadiz, although claiming (Letter 101) considerable seamanship, he really longed for the moment when he would acccompany his soldiers ashore. On their return, while the now elderly Lord Admiral, Charles Howard, remained aboard ship from Plymouth to the Thames, his 43-year-old junior, pleading a sore leg, preferred (Letter 103) to take to the notoriously bad west-

INTRODUCTION                                                                xli

country roads. He frequently complained (Letters 110 and 119) of not being able to sleep aboard ship and was altogether an unwilling seafarer. In a fragment of one of the very last of his surviving letters (Letter 227*), he begs King James to consider whether, merely to have gained his liberty, he would have left

> this steady Tower [*for*] a rolling ship, to change the diet of soft bread and fresh meat for hard biscuit and salt beef, to drink unsavoury water instead of wine and beer and to disorder an aged, worn and weak body with watching, travail and the distempered heat of the Indies, besides a world of other harms and hazards.

But as an organizer of maritime ventures (Letters 38*, 48–50 and 54), particularly those with the chance of prizes, he can have had few if any contemporary superiors, having in particular a facility with figures (Letters 37*, 51 and 56) probably unrivalled outside the merchant communities and concerning whose sedentary maritime adventuring he could on occasion (Letter 56) be withering in his comments. Only weeks before his death he was instructing his wife from the Tower (Letter 225) regarding the winding up of the accounts of himself and his fellow adventurers in the recent Guiana voyage. He knew exactly how to use his local contacts, especially his relations, to obtain at short notice (Letters 38* and 39*) supplies of dried Newfoundland fish and Devonshire cider, the westcountry seaman's staple diet. He was also something of an expert on the problem of recruiting and retaining ships' companies (Letters 40 and 42), even to the extent, in 1596 (Letter 96), of personally searching for absconders among the hiding-places of the Thames estuary. Unlike the 'mercenary men' (Letter 54) employed by his fellow adventurers for shares in the profits, his own crews served for wages, which he did his best to pay (Letters 41, 48 and 52). Besides being good psychology it tells of a man confident of his success and determined to maximize his own share of the proceeds.

As to what those proceeds actually were, the letters are understandably uninformative. Only in his resigned acceptance (Letter 51) of the almost total surrender to the Crown of his profit from the capture in 1592 of the great Portuguese carrack, the *Madre de Dios*, does he produce some detailed accountancy (Letter 56), but even with the considerable additional documentation elsewhere in the state papers it is unlikely that the full story of that astonishing episode will ever be told. It is clear, however, from his advice to his somewhat wayward nephew, the second Sir John Gilbert, in

1600 (Letter 129*) that he wrote as one experienced in keeping just within the letter of the law of the High Court of Admiralty of which he himself was an officer. Indeed, one searches in vain in the letters for any mention of his duties from 1585 as Vice-Admiral of both Devon and Cornwall or, in contrast to his touchiness over the Duchy of Cornwall seal in 1604 (Letter 179), evidence of any regret at surrendering his seals as Vice-Admiral.

Although there is little in the letters about Ralegh's ownership of seagoing vessels, one letter in particular leaves no doubt about his considerable knowledge of their construction, and indeed, contrasting oddly with his dislike of the sea, of their handling. This is the letter of advice he wrote from the Tower in or about 1607 (Letter 194) to his friend the young Prince Henry on how to design a ship for the times. Probably less professional, though he certainly regarded himself as more than competent to give advice thereon, especially on the way to the siege of Cadiz in 1596 (Letters 101 and 102), was Ralegh's knowledge of naval strategy, though he probably had every right to pit his wits in this respect against those of his fellow, or just slightly senior, commanding officer, the Earl of Essex. What he did understand (Letter 60), as an experienced soldier as much as a sailor, was the value of good 'intelligence', both of the enemy's strength and of his whereabouts. Ralegh was particularly well placed during his residence at Sherborne between 1592 and 1603, to act as a clearing-house (Letters 36, 75, etc.) for reports on enemy shipping brought in to the channel ports of Devon and to Weymouth in Dorset by those all-seeing but often unseen small trading vessels and 'fishermen' in which the South West abounded.

## The Queen and the Court

Ralegh's letter to the Earl of Leicester from Munster in August 1581 (Letter 5) must have been one of the first of his many declarations of loyalty to those mightier than himself, combined with expressions of thanks for reciprocal services, real or imagined. It hardly squared with his already well-developed self-confidence but it helped to oil the wheels which for the next ten years carried him into the confidence of the Queen, if not entirely that of her ministers. The unctuous expressions of mutual trust which characterized all Ralegh's letters to those in positions of power and influence flowed lightly off his pen, but his eyes, like those of most of his social equals, were fixed upwards, not just towards Westminster and the Court but towards the actual physical presence of the Queen and her immediate successor.

# INTRODUCTION xliii

Between 1582 and 1592 he moved fairly steadily in the direction he desired so passionately, and his letters go far to plot his progress. By March 1583 (Letter 6) he was addressing himself to Sir Humphrey Gilbert in the manner of the Queen's personal secretary and in May (Letter 8) was writing to Lord Burghley as though he was more in her confidence than was her Lord Treasurer. Time and again he wrote (e.g. Letter 33) of his 'nearness' to Her Majesty, and that it was a literally physical propinquity is borne out by his acute sense of separation when in late July 1592, after news of his marriage had reached her, he watched, from his vantage point in Durham House (Letter 46), his 'nymph' leave on one of her progresses. The 'disgrace' so soon to befall him seems almost inevitable from the moment, five months earlier, when (Letter 41) he clearly, and very stupidly, lied about his marital commitment to the man who was to be his greatest single enemy. From then until the end of the Queen's reign his life was one long struggle to climb back into her confidence. Almost every letter he wrote during this period reflects his anxiety and, as the change of dynasty approached, his realization of his failure. To the Lord Admiral in 1595 he expressed (Letter 90) his willingness to 'purchase Her Majesty's favour with what labour or perill [*what*]soever'. He tried (Letter 138*) to put a good face on his disappointments and even to pretend (Letters 142–3) to enjoy acting as hospitality officer to the Queen's foreign visitors. He was, of course, still Captain of the Queen's Guard, but it was political office, at the heart of things, that he craved. His term as the Queen's representative in Jersey (Letters 126, 131–2, 146, 154 and 159–60), for all that it gave him scope for pursuing his interest in military fortification, was little consolation. To Sir Robert Cecil in 1602 (Letter 158) he wrote of the 'difficulty and torment' he experienced to 'obtain the smallest favour', this in connection with his monopoly (Plate 2) of the right to license retailers of wine, granted him by the Queen in his heyday ten years before. There is a great deal in the letters on this subject, including Ralegh's extraordinarily naïve attempts in the 1580s to challenge the entrenched authorities of the University of Cambridge (Letters 12 and 15–16). Among the most interesting new finds is Ralegh's request in 1589 to Lord Burghley (Letter 31*, now in New York and carrying the elder statesman's conditional, signed agreement) to be allowed to assemble his licensed vintners for their annual review. Ralegh no doubt took the Lord Treasurer's guarded response as a slight, but it was to be expected of one always suspicious of assemblies in whatever guise. It was a devastating loss at the beginning of the new reign (Letters 172 and 186–7) not only to be deprived of his wine patent but also of the collection of the arrears which, in the manner of the times, he regarded as a useful nest-egg to fall back on when other sources failed.

## Patronage

A high proportion of Ralegh's letters were written on behalf of suitors, i.e. persons whom he felt under some obligation to support. The system, seen at its height in Elizabeth's reign, operated both ways, the writer, explicitly or implicitly, promising to those he addressed his own future services, often expressed simply as 'friendship' or even 'love'. So, when volunteering a service, such as 'intelligence' of enemy shipping movements, he would claim the recipient's ongoing goodwill as a kind of accumulating investment. At his most optimistic Ralegh would include the services of his own dependants, as in August 1618 (Letter 223) when he promised, of all people the king's favourite, the Marquess of Buckingham, the support of one hundred gentlemen, all of them his kinsmen, in return for his good offices. The system was not dependent on the offer of material inducements and, indeed, these are mentioned but rarely (Letters 77, 78 and 119).

Ralegh's clients, that is those for whom he sought favours, included, very much first and foremost, his blood relations (Letters 32*, 62, 84, 127, 152 and many more), no matter, it would seem (e.g. Letters 11* and 14), how remote that relationship might be. Then there were the members of his extended family, former household servants such as Charles MacCarthy (Letters 76, 77, 83 and 94), casual acquaintances such as the Italian fencing master (Letter 21*), a Devonshire gentleman whom he had known as a law student (Letter 24*), an old friend the celebrated navigator John Davis (Letter 67*), and even total strangers (Letter 35*) who had been commended to him. One particularly interesting and hitherto unpublished letter to the magistrates of Surrey (Letter 116*) was on behalf of one of Ralegh's 'band' as Captain of the Queen's Guard, whom he maintained should not have been prosecuted without his leave. There was, of course, nothing inherently stable about the system. As Ralegh had come to realize by the end of 1595 (Letter 85), only his own personal standing could ensure his continuing credibility as an advocate.

Like all who sought to climb up in the world, or, as was his own particular need, to climb back from degradation, Ralegh needed friends in high places. The letters show his chosen path, first (Letters 2–3 and 34*) to the ageing Sir Francis Walsingham, and soon after (Letters 5 and 20) to the Earl of Leicester. For a while in the 1590s, while he struggled to re-establish himself, acting the part of the gracious host (Letter 110), he cultivated the favour of the Earl of Essex, though thereby clearly set on pleasing the Queen. Indeed, he can be seen (Letters 102 and 109) as virtually presuming to patronize Essex by flattery as they made their separate ways back from Cadiz to Court, each intent on making his own tale good in the Queen's eyes. Not altogether surprisingly, when Essex's sun was setting Ralegh was unforgiving in his condemnation (Letter 123). This was the occasion for an interesting comment on the political instability of dynasties.

Of an entirely different character was his altogether more personal liaison with Henry Brooke, from 1597 the 11th Lord Cobham, with whom he became almost infatuated, calling him in 1601 (Letter 143) his to command 'before all the world'. It was, in fact, in this same letter that for a short spell he showed some recognition of his friend's vulnerability, striving to persuade Cobham not to distance himself from the Queen. In almost the last of his surviving letters to Cobham, written from Bagshot on or about 11 November 1603 when both were on their way to be tried at Winchester on a charge of treason, Ralegh writes (Letter 169) with all the old familiarity. They are in the same boat and perhaps they can help each other. If Cobham will withdraw his accusations against him, i.e. that he knew of the 'Spanish imaginations', all will be well. For a short while Cobham did his bidding. It is true that Ralegh made no reciprocal promises, but although before he even left London he admitted to his wife (Letter 165) that he was charged 'by the word of an unworthy man', he wrote, possibly for public consumption, rather in sorrow than in anger and continued to exhibit (Letter 173) extraordinarily charitable feelings towards his former friend. As to his own guilt, the evidence of the letters is that at worst Ralegh denied all knowledge of anything likely to be incriminating, and his only admission, and this in a confidential letter to Cobham (Letter 169), was of having been 'offered' the Spanish money. On this account he was surely guilty only of 'misprision' of treason.[21]

Ralegh expressed to his wife (Letter 165) even greater dismay at having been deserted by another whom he had thought to be his friend, Sir Robert Cecil. Their surviving correspondence—or at least Ralegh's side of it—dates from before the latter's 'disgrace', and it was to the young Privy Councillor, nearly ten years his junior that (Letter 41) he categorically

---

21. Cf. Mark Nicholls, 'Sir Walter Ralegh's Treason: a Prosecution Document', *EHR*, CX, 438, 1995, pp. 902–24, which presents new material on the government's case against Ralegh and Cobham, especially concerning the nature of their alliance, but fails to show that Ralegh did more than *contemplate* treason.

denied the fact of his marriage, assuring Cecil that if the rumours were true he would have been the first to hear. The original letter has disappeared, perhaps removed by a later 'friend', since the mid-eighteenth century. It was clearly to someone he regarded as a friend that he poured out his misery (Letter 46) when in due course he was physically separated from the Queen. His subsequent rough treatment by Cecil at Dartmouth (Letter 54) did nothing to interrupt the continuous flow of letters, asking for favours and remitting news, in tones which became ever more obsequious and, especially in moments of despair, more and more endearing. Even allowing for the high proportion of the letters which derive from the Cecil Papers, Sir Robert, as the Queen's reign drew to its close, seems to have become Ralegh's lifeline. Rarely, in fact, during the last five years of her reign does he mention the Queen. She was not 'remembered' in his will in 1597 (Appendix 2), and indeed the only beneficiary outside his immediate household, and then only as a residuary, was his 'friend', Robert Cecil. In the last of his surviving letters to the now Earl of Salisbury in 1611 (Letter 206) he professed to believe that his friend had promised him what above all else he desired, a free pardon under the Great Seal. But by then (Letter 207, Plate 12), he thought he had an even more influential patron, no less a person than James's Queen, Anne of Denmark, together, of course, with her relations.

## The Sherborne Estate

Ralegh's status as an English landowner has never been accurately delineated, but it is clear, even from his letters, that apart from a brief period between 1599 and 1603 when he enjoyed undisputed ownership as well as occupation of the estate at Sherborne in Dorset, it was always precarious.

In spite of his many connections, by blood and by marriage, with the landowning establishment both of the West Country and further afield, as the youngest son of Walter Ralegh senior (ob. 1581), an impecunious gentleman turned privateering shipowner, he enjoyed no landed inheritance. When his grant of the wine patent in 1583 necessitated a residential description for insertion on the vintners' licences, he styled himself (Plate 2) 'of Colyton Raleigh in the county of Devon', a parish in which he had acquired by purchase (Letter 13) a small farm, almost certainly the only land he owned in England then or for some time to come. Hence his residential style in his will of 1597 (Appendix 2).

His knighthood early in the following year and even his election as knight of the shire in the parliament of 1584, were not, presumably in view of his position in the Queen's service, contingent on his ownership of land, nor, apparently, was his appointment in 1585 as Lord Lieutenant of Cornwall. Indeed, his lack of endowment by the Queen in this latter year is in stark contrast to that showered by her father, King Henry VIII, in 1539 on John Lord Russell, later the 1st Earl of Bedford. It was, in fact, the second earl's death without an adult male heir in 1585 which had, as it were, catapulted Ralegh into westcountry affairs, but Queen Elizabeth was more careful than her father to avoid creating local landed dynasties.

It was just prior to his marriage in 1592 that Ralegh obtained possession of the estate at Sherborne. The timing, though in the circumstances very convenient for him and his bride, was of no particular significance, merely the culmination of long negotiations between the Queen and the estate's former owner, the Bishop of Salisbury. And even then Ralegh was only leaseholder of the property from the Crown. Not until 1599 did he at last become the owner, though liable for a substantial annual rent-charge payable to the Bishop, by whom, he later complained (Letter 119), he was worse treated than if he were a Turk.

The only other serious irritation, at least as far as life at Sherborne was concerned, was the presence of 'those rogues the Meeres' (Letter 141). John Meere junior was an example of that type very common in early-modern provincial society, the local man-of-affairs, trained in the law, whose personal—in this case inherited—standing was put in jeopardy by the replacement of absentee clerical landlords by a resident master who brought to the job his own tried and trusted servants. There is much in the letters about their relations, including Ralegh's eventual conviction that Meere was an accomplished and active forger (Letters 145 and 156 and Plate 10), and even the steward's inclusion in the will of 1597 (Appendix 2) may well have been intended as a bribe to secure his loyalty.

Only four years after obtaining the freehold of the Sherborne estate, almost coinciding with, though as it turned out not primarily as the result of, his attainder, Ralegh's tenure of the estate became the subject of a legal wrangle which lasted for some six years and forms the subject-matter of some dozen of his letters during the early period of his incarceration in the Tower of London. The retention of Sherborne by his heirs might so easily have been secured and it is difficult not to ascribe the main responsibility for its ultimate loss to the efforts of Ralegh himself to obtain his liberty, combined, at the last minute, with what appear (Letter 196) to have been the machinations not of King James but of the now Earl of Salisbury. The letters do not tell the whole story but only Ralegh's reaction to events as they unfolded. For the legal background, which is really quite simple, the chief source is the collection of title deeds still at Sherborne which have still not been fully explored by local historians. The gist of their story is that in 1599, like so many other landowners with sons under age, in order to avoid the possibility of his property falling into the clutches of the Court of Wards and also, no doubt, in view of the uncertainties of the times and in particular of his own future, Ralegh conveyed the estate to trustees. This should have safeguarded his family's possession in 1603, but for 'want of a word' (Letter 197), i.e. a small omission in the legal verbiage, the blame for which Ralegh placed on his eminent legal adviser (and fellow-Devonian), Sir John Doddridge, the 1599 transfer was eventually declared by the Crown's legal officers to be invalid, effectively making the property forfeit to the King. But Lady Ralegh and her small son Walter, plus, from 1605, baby Carew, were permitted to continue in residence while alternative arrangements were made. Indeed, *pace* Sir Walter (Letters 185 and 197) the King seems not to have been unkindly disposed towards them. Not only was the estate put in the hands of a new body of trustees, all of whom were friends and relations of the Raleghs, but Lady Ralegh was granted a lump sum from which to draw income which would, to some extent, compensate for her husband's other losses of revenue, including the wine licences. It is true that until a final settlement was reached Lady Ralegh was in some distress, but her pleas, far from encouraging Sir Walter to accept what was offered with good grace, only drove him to suggest (Letter 190) that, given a good title, he might hand the estate over to Salisbury. Although, even after the King had decided to give Sherborne to his favourite, Robert Carr, some compensation for the Raleghs was provided, Sir Walter himself would still not give up hope of being able to shame the young man by a grovelling letter (197) which was hardly worthy of him, even bearing in mind their relative circumstances. The final settlement of 1609–10 is beautifully encapsulated in a hitherto unpublished manuscript now at Woburn Abbey (Letter 200\* and Plate 11), with its impressive array of signatures. It was not ungenerous and Ralegh could go to Guiana, and ultimately to his death, knowing that Bess and young Carew would not be penniless.

## The Westcountryman

County lord lieutenancies, the new offices which dated only from the reign of Edward VI, had so far only been bestowed on members of the peerage, and for Devon the tradition was followed in 1585 by the appointment of William Bourchier, 4th Earl of Bath. His unfitness for the office, both by inclination and experience, was recognized by the insertion in his terms of appointment, totally without precedent, that he should lean on his deputies, who fortunately included a number of very able knights, especially Ralegh's half-brother, Sir John Gilbert. Equally unprecedented, however, was the appointment of Ralegh, a commoner, as Lord Lieutenant of Cornwall. Together with his appointments as Vice-Admiral of both Devon and Cornwall and as Chief Steward of the Duchy of Cornwall and Lord Warden of the Stannaries in the two counties, the virtually landless knight held sway in the West Country entirely at the Queen's pleasure. His power base, if indeed he had one, lay not in his tenantry, not even in his very extensive westcountry 'cousinage', but as the Queen's deputy. It says something for him that as long as she lived he was never replaced.

As the arrival off the south-west coast and the landing of a Spanish army became a very real possibility, it was Ralegh's military experience that was called into play. In December 1587 it was by virtue of a special commission rather than *ex officio* that he was sent to the South West to investigate and report on the area's state of readiness. Pulling no punches he reported (Letter 26) on what he found, taking obvious pleasure in exposing the shortcomings, as he saw them, of many of the leading knights and gentlemen, though sparing the Earl, Gilbert and, as well he might, Sir Richard Grenville, who was to bear the brunt of refurbishing the defences of Cornwall (Letter 29). The citizens of Exeter, who until 1581 had included his own father, were singled out as unco-operative. He was, however, sympathetic to what he saw as the South West's unstable economy, a concern which found an echo in many of his later letters.

In the next decade, although he rarely crossed the Dorset border, he developed a very keen understanding of the land-defence potentialities of the south-western peninsula and their relation to the region's economy, and especially its manpower. His response to yet another inquiry by the Lords of the Privy Council in November 1595 (when his mind was really on Guiana and its gold mines) demonstrates (Letter 88) an intimate knowledge of local topography and hence of the practical problems likely to arise in moving men and horses across the county boundaries.

He also enjoyed, in so far as he chose to exploit it, a very special relationship, judicial as well as military, with that extraordinarily diverse body of residents of Devon and Cornwall, the tinners. An anonymous contemporary critic of Ralegh's virtual monopoly of royal power in the South

West wrote dismissively of his ability, especially considering his landless state, to control 'so rough and mutinous a multitude, whose number we judge to be a 10,000 or 12,000 [of] the most strong able men of Yngland'.[22] In fact, those who, as 'tinners' in Devon and Cornwall, claimed to be subject to no other superior (the Queen, of course, excepted) included not only the workmen and all owners as well as occupiers of tin-mines, but all who directly or indirectly derived their living from the extraction and sale of tin. It was a formidable army which only the Lord Warden could muster, the envy, no doubt, of many a large landowner who could only number his tenants or his militia men in hundreds. Oddly enough, the subject of mustering the miners only crops up in the letters in connection with the needs of Elizabeth's armies overseas, including Ireland, for 'pioneers' (Letters 20, 29, 79 and 149). Indeed, he seems in general to have had little faith in the westcountry yeomanry and peasantry as soldiers, his company in Ireland in the early 1580s (Letter 1) having clearly been raised in London. For that matter, he clearly found the government of the tinners, especially those of Cornwall (Letter 131), a somewhat tiresome diversion and for the most part seems to have left them, with the help of his deputies, to solve most of their own problems. A letter discovered in a New York library (Letter 130*) shows him interfering with a heavy hand in a dispute concerning a Devon mine. He enjoyed a fight, of course, and in 1600 (Letter 135) gladly took up the case of a gentleman tinner, William Crymes, against the corporation of Plymouth which had the backing of Sir Francis Drake's brother and heir. There may have been an old personal score to settle and he appears to have won his case. Another letter (66*) which concerned his battling on behalf of tinners found him supporting men of some substance, and when in 1594 he defended the tinners' right to be summoned only in the stannary courts, he was in effect defending his own, or the Queen's, prerogative. One case where he certainly claimed to be on the side of the working tinners and those owners working their mines themselves surfaces in a letter of 1600 (Letter 133) concerning the pre-emption of tin. It serves to alert us to the fact that, contrary to general belief, based on words attributed to Ralegh himself in the great Commons debate of 1601, he did not have a personal patent of monopoly in the pre-emption of tin but was acting in this connection simply as the Queen's deputy. But on at least one occasion (Letter 66) he waited for the involvement of the Lords of

---

22. PRO, SP15/29/126: no signature, dated 7 July [1586], endorsed by Lord Burghley.

the Privy Council before picking up the matter himself, thereby risking censure which at the time he could ill afford.

There were probably some financial or other gains to be made out of the exercise of patronage by way of Duchy offices and after 1603 Ralegh certainly regarded 'the stannary' (Letter 178) as among his lost sources of income. Beyond this, the letters are uninformative. He clearly set great store by his office which was, of course, quite prestigious, and when deprived of it by James I he stood very firmly on his dignity (Letters 179–80) in refusing, from the Tower, to hand over the Duchy seal to anyone other than the King or his Principal Secretary.

## Guiana

No less than 44 of the surviving Ralegh letters are concerned entirely or incidentally with his two voyages to that part of South America centred on the lower Orinoco river-basin known as Guiana. Of these only ten deal with the first voyage in 1595, that of his so-called 'Discovery' of its potential, and there are no letters extant for this year actually written overseas. Indeed, the earliest letter to mention this first expedition is a short note to Cecil in September 1594 (Letter 80) in which he is at pains to conceal his real destination. His concern two months later (Letter 81) with, it must be said, some justification, at the number of his own countrymen 'going for the [West] Indies' helps to put his 'enterprise' into perspective. At this stage he had a reasonable chance of success. He spent Christmas at Sherborne, 'waiting for a wind' to bring his ships from the Thames and to carry him to what he dramatically called his 'destiny' (Letters 83–4), and he sailed, almost certainly from Plymouth, on 6 February. For what followed we are dependent on other sources, including his own journal. We next hear from him at first hand, at least as far as his letters are concerned, the following November when, back home in Dorset, he seeks (Letter 86), somewhat petulantly, to hear from Cecil what they make of his voyage at Court, 'whether it pass for a history or a fable', a reference to rumours then circulating that he had been no further than Cornwall! But the real importance of this letter, and that which followed a day or so later (Letter 87), is his claim, which he steadfastly maintained to the end of his life (Letter 217), that he had won the friendship of the native rulers, and the fears he expressed of what other, less scrupulous, adventurers would do which would spoil the alliance. He does not, at this stage, mention the Spaniards, although he went on to claim his right to be allowed to 'conquer' the country for the Queen. With its references to Harriot's map of Guiana and to the gold, diamonds, and pearls he had brought back with him and which he was having assayed, Letter 87 is a key text, one which although at Hatfield and included by Edwards, is not among those printed by Harlow.

It seems, from a letter to Cecil from Sherborne at the end of November 1595 (Letter 89), that Ralegh was impatient to return to Guiana the following summer, but, after begging the Lord Admiral a few days later (Letter 90) for 'a resolution for our enterprise of Guiana', as far, at any rate, as his surviving letters are a guide, he then put the matter right out of his mind. What the effect was on his enthusiasm of the news that spring of the death in the Indies of both Hawkins and Drake, we can only guess. Ralegh himself was only too aware (Letter 87) that because of his continuing 'disgrace' men might fear to adventure with him.

Be that as it may, no more is heard of Guiana until he had spent four years in the Tower and then, in July 1607, apparently totally relaxed, he sent a carefully composed letter (192) to the Earl of Salisbury. It deserves careful reading, including his admission—a shrewd move—that the idea that he was primarily interested in obtaining his liberty 'might rightly fall into the cogitation of a wise man'. So anxious was he to return to Guiana that, and it must have cost him dearly, he offered (Letters 192–3) to sail not in command but as a 'private man'. He had great confidence in the Queen's support, and indeed, in 1609/10 he addressed himself (Letter 201) directly to Her Majesty, repeating an earlier offer of his service 'in Virginia', and even of his wife's life if he fail in his duty. All such promises ring a little hollow, however, when read along with the extraordinarily naïve guarantee with which he concluded Letter 192, that he would 'break no peace'.

There then follow a series of letters, written at long intervals, largely to the Earl of Salisbury and after 1615 to Sir Ralph Winwood, refining his plans, reiterating his promises, rebuffing criticism and always regretting opportunities lost, even (Letter 210) playing on the King's susceptibilities regarding Parliament. For the first time in the letters, apart from a brief mention in 1603 (Letter 165), we hear (Letters 205 and 206) of Lawrence Keymis. He had been Ralegh's second-in-command in 1595 and, as his master freely admitted, without his topographical knowledge the expedition would be pointless. In both these two letters to Salisbury, Ralegh declared that he had been promised in the long run his liberty and in the meantime his free pardon under the Great Seal, which, incidentally, he was confident was to be kept for him, not, as has always been believed, by the King but,

# INTRODUCTION

if the new transcript of the letter is to be accorded precedence, by his friend the Queen. In one last desperate attempt (Letter 208) to approach the King through his consort, Ralegh returns yet again to the charge that all he wants is his liberty. Would anyone but a 'slavish marriner' prefer a long sea voyage to imprisonment in the Tower! He even goes on (Letter 210) to castigate the refusal of his offer as irresponsible—a charge hardly likely to counteract the influence of the Spanish ambassador—and, even nearer the bone, to accuse the King (Letter 211) of taking false counsel.

By 1616, if not before, the Guiana voyage was clearly inextricably mixed up with domestic as well as international politics. But then, quite suddenly and for reasons upon which there will always be debate, Ralegh was allowed to leave the Tower. He chose (Letter 212) to thank the future Marquess of Buckingham before devoting himself to preparing for the voyage, the preparations including (Letters 213 and 215) the seeking of support in kind from abroad. What followed the fleet's departure, unlike what happened in 1595, is laid bare in great detail in Ralegh's five letters (216–219) from overseas, the first from no further than the coast of Ireland. The work of determining who was to blame for the two principal disasters, the English assault on the Spanish town of San Thomé and the failure to reach the goldmine, must take account of other source material as it emerges, including that in the archives of Spain. But the trail must commence with Ralegh's own accounts, in particular his confidential letters of March 1618 from St Christophers in the West Indies to his friend Sir Ralph Winwood (Letter 218*, an undamaged, hitherto unpublished copy) and to Lady Ralegh (Letter 219). Unaware as yet of the charges which would be laid against him, he had no reason to speak anything but the truth as he knew it. For the fight at San Thomé in which he lost his own son he blamed those in London who had betrayed his plans to the Spanish authorities but he was clearly also very bitter about Lawrence Keymis's failure to reach the mine. In the circumstances this was a fair assumption of responsibility by the overall commander of the expedition. It may not have been the whole truth. Indeed, the substitution in this collection of the original letter to King James (221*) which we now know was written by Ralegh at Plymouth on 16 June, and not on 24 September as the transcripts had led historians to suppose, throws an altogether new light on its contents. It was clearly not dashed off in a hurry and can only have been the result of much cogitation and the receipt of much 'intelligence' from London, at least since his arrival at Kinsale at the end of May. It shows, too, that the *Destiny* reached Plymouth at least five days earlier than previously reported.

## The Man behind the Pen

Interest in Ralegh as a writer has concentrated on his poetry and, to a lesser extent, on his treatises and hardly at all on his letters, and yet this collection, most of it long available in print, contains some of the finest prose which has come down to us from the Elizabethan and early Stuart period. Helped along with a modicum of punctuation, in particular full stops, each of his letters is a joy to read. Almost invariably Ralegh wrote with an economy of words which is the hallmark of style and even when under pressure, including (e.g. Letter 165) deep melancholy, he could produce balanced cadences and inversions which lift his prose way above the practicalities of his current situation. Equally impressive, and of course intended to impress, were his reverberating classical Latinisms (e.g. Letters 189 and 190). But, particularly towards the end of his life, he showed himself equally if not more at home (Letters 139 and 171) with the Book of Common Prayer and the Bible, the latter in both the Latin and English versions. These were for real: even when in the depths of despair he could, by recalling the words of the prophet Job (Letter 165), regain some of that fortitude and magnanimity which won him, at his trials and particularly after his death, so much popular adulation.

Except during periods of deepest despair his mind was always fully occupied and with a range of pursuits which almost passes belief. Above all else, his new-found leisure in the Tower, where his bibliographical *desiderata* (Letter 203) were astonishing, was put to good use. His knowledge of geology, though probably largely dependent on those he could persuade to work for him (Letters 87 and 89), was impressive, and in contrast, even before he can have had much time for study, his grasp of the Common Law (e.g. Letters 190 and 199) was remarkable in one who had in his youth spent only a few terms as a law student. Indeed, in defending his estate he showed a degree of legal cunning which he can only have inherited from his Devon ancestors.

Although born in the country and eager to obtain at least a country 'seat' (Letter 13) Ralegh was, for the greater part of his active life, a city dweller, almost a Londoner. From about 1584 most of his letters were written from the upper storey of Durham House on the Strand river-front, cheek by jowl with the town mansions of Elizabeth's ministers whose ranks he yearned to join but, equally, if not more importantly, within sight of, and a short row to, the Queen's Palace of Whitehall (Plate 4). Although his occupation was always tenuous he was maintaining a very substantial household in Durham House at the time of his summary eviction early in 1603 (Letter 164). By comparison, his establishment at Sherborne must have been minimal. Sherborne, in fact, was his family's home only from 1592 until 1603, with only fitful residence by Lady Ralegh and her sons thereafter, and total eviction, lock, stock and barrel, by 1609 at the very latest. It was during the decade 1593–1603, the period of his greatest activity at sea, that Ralegh built the nucleus of a new mansion, not on the site of the decayed episcopal castle, which it may at an early stage have been intended to resemble (Plate 5),[23] but a short distance away in the midst of an open park such as he might well have contrived at Hayes in East Budleigh had he secured his youthful heart's desire (Letter 13). Only one letter (70*) survives concerning these building operations, an order for limestone from Portland, of which, in 1594, he needed 'great store'. There are none from the brief period of his governorship concerning the building of Elizabeth Castle on the island of Jersey, except one expressing admiration of the skills of the military architect, Paul Ivey, who was with him at Sherborne in October 1600 (Letter 132). But it was in this letter that Ralegh expressed a liking for the much older Mont Orgueil and a resolve to save it from demolition, for which posterity, not least Jersey's present administration, must surely be grateful.

By 1609 (Letter 199) he was, at least momentarily, happy to be rid of his 'fortress fold' (Letter 60) in Dorset, and indeed, in the company of his friends he seems to have been more at home in Bath (Letters 126 and 128). However, there are several glimpses in the letters of domestic life at Sherborne where the Raleghs kept a good table, at any rate when they were expecting company (Letter 141). Although Sir Walter did not always keep his wife fully informed about his affairs, even those which closely affected her (Letter 81), the marriage was, without doubt, a happy one, Ralegh being obviously genuinely relaxed in his wife's company (Letters 128 and 139–40) and valuing her presence with him in the Tower, not least for its

---

23. This Elizabethan pictorial map (Plate 5) of the town of Sherborne, Dorset, and its surrounding area (BL, Addit. 52522) has been confidently dated 1569–78 on the assumption that it was drawn for the bishop of Salisbury: P.D.A. Harvey, 'An Elizabethan Map of the manors of North Dorset', *British Museum Quarterly*, 29, 1964–5, pp. 82–4 and Katherine Barker, 'An Elizabethan Map of North-West Dorset', in Katherine Barker and Roger Kain (eds), *Maps and Map History in South-West England*, 1991, pp. 28–53. There is, however, the distinct possibility, one might even suggest the probability, that it was drawn for Ralegh in about 1592–3, when he was still intending to restore the old castle. However that may be, this splendid map depicts the estate at Sherborne very much as Ralegh knew it.

effect on his domestic economy (Letter 209). Only once, in 1605 (Letter 189), do we see him apparently driven to distraction when, as he told Salisbury, she arrived at the Tower with young Walter at her heels and baby Carew in her arms, 'crying and bewailing' her situation, but his dramatic outburst was possibly a pretence intended to move the Earl, as it were man to man, for some relief from his incarceration. But, genuine as was his affection, he was also a realist. Of the two highly emotional letters (165 and 172) which Ralegh wrote to his wife in 1603, one before and one after his trial, the first, while clearly a 'cry for help' not intended for her eyes alone, contains passages expressive of deeply-held philosophies concerning the bonds of matrimony. As in Letter 219 in which, many years later and from the other side of the Atlantic, he sought to comfort her on the death of their elder son, he took a very practical, and almost insensitive, view of their parting, not even mentioning the possibility of a reunion and echoing, in fact, sentiments expressed many years before (Letter 104) in his letter of condolence to Sir Robert Cecil on the death of his wife. In the first letter he not only urges Bess to remarry, but to do so for material ends, 'to avoid poverty' for herself and young Walter, rather than 'to please sense', as he presumably assumes she had done in marrying him. The second letter, written when he must have felt nearer to death than at any time before he mounted the scaffold, and without, at the time, a wider readership in mind, finds him more positive about their continuing relationship, both with each other and with their son, and also with God, to whom he refers at this time with more than his usual conventional piety. Indeed, neither here nor elsewhere in the letters do we meet up with the atheist leanings with which he has been credited, largely on the basis of some of his literary works and one small and probably exaggerated episode in Dorset. Rather, as behoved a good Christian facing imminent death, all the 'last letters' to his wife show him much preoccupied with the winding up of his affairs. Not for the first or last time (cf. Letters 11, 45, 158 and 214) did he exhibit an anxiety to settle his debts, especially to 'poor men', not simply, it must be admitted, as an act of charity but in order to maintain the personal credit he so much desired.

These are some of the subjects illuminated by this collection: many others lie waiting to be identified. Inevitably readers will look for those that particularly interest them, but it is to be hoped that, although they are far from being a random selection, Sir Walter Ralegh's surviving letters will be read

INTRODUCTION                                                          lvii

as a whole and, as presented here, in chronological order, providing as they do, and better than exists for any of his contemporaries, a kaleidoscopic view of the life of a remarkable man.

## THE WRITING OF THE LETTERS

### *Spelling and Style*

Of the 190 original letters which have survived, 134 (70 per cent) are entirely in Ralegh's own hand, the rest being written by various clerks but signed by him, almost invariably following a subscription in his own hand declaring his everlasting friendship or loyalty. There was often appended a postscript, again usually in his own hand. In the 1580s and 1590s Ralegh employed clerks to write about half his surviving letters but from his second imprisonment in the Tower in 1603 until the end of his life he wrote very nearly all of them himself. Only one draft survives (Letter 170), that of a letter to King James in November 1603, the fair copy being at Hatfield. They are nearly identical, except for the handwriting.

Basically Ralegh wrote two hands. Like most gentlemen of his generation he had no doubt been taught—tradition has it by the vicar of East Budleigh—the set, i.e. formal, 'secretary' hand, not unlike that of his clerks (e.g. Letter 11, Plate 1). But the postscript to this same letter shows that by the age of 30 the young courtier could also write the more fashionable italic script which, although not necessarily quicker to write, was easier to read, even when written in great haste. But to the end of his life his usual hand was 'mixed', that is basically 'secretary' but including certain italic letters, and even when the italic character of his hand was most pronounced (Letter 200, Plate 11), or indeed almost pure, as in the letter to Queen Anne (Letter 207, Plate 12), certain features of English 'secretary' letter forms were present, notably c, reverted e and a sinuous h with the second vertical stroke prolonged below the line. By contrast (Letter 140, Plate 7), Lady Ralegh wrote, probably as she had been taught, a purely italic hand. At its best (Letters 34, 107 and 162, Plates 3, 6 and 8) Ralegh's usual 'mixed' hand, if not especially stylish, was tidy, controlled and fairly easily readable: at its worst, but this was rare, it became an almost undecipherable scrawl. His use of capital letters, however, was erratic to say the least and his punctuation practically non-existent, an oblique stroke (virgule) normally making do for a full point (stop), except when a sentence ended at the end of a line when it was dispensed with altogether. He very rarely crossed anything out, but it must be borne in mind that virtually all his surviving letters are originals or transcripts of the fair copies which were actually sent and received.

Doubts which occasionally arise as to whether a letter was written by Ralegh can usually be resolved by the presence, or absence, of certain peculiarities of spelling, especially his unmistakable 'yow' for 'you', 'mich' for 'much' and 'frinde' for 'friend', eccentricities which, though not entirely peculiar to him,[24] were rarely copied by his clerks. There was also his habit of writing 'on' for 'one' and, very common in his subscriptions, 'humble' which he would no doubt have pronounced 'humbly'. On the whole, however, and unlike his wife (Letter 140), Ralegh spelled in conformity with contemporary norms, only occasionally coming up with such oddities as 'phello' (Letter 45 and also Appendix 1) and 'octores' for 'authorise' (Letter 52 and elsewhere), which may echo contemporary pronunciation. Only very occasionally, usually when writing under some pressure, does he resort to his legendary westcountry dialect, so that one cherishes such a rare example as 'manghangled' (Letter 48). Misspellings such as 'sarsephraze' for 'sassafras' (Letter 161) probably reflect contemporary pronunciation.

Much has been made of the seemingly endless ways of spelling his surname, and indeed, as the endorsements by the recipients of his letters show, he appeared under many guises, but not as far as his own signature was concerned. Until 1584, the year before he was knighted, and except in his wine licences (Plate 2), he was always 'W Rauley', without a point. Only once (Letter 11, c.1584–5), as far as the extant letters go, did he experiment with 'Raleigh' and thereafter, to the end of his life, his signature was invariably 'Ralegh', with his initial usually elided to make one word, i.e., 'WRalegh'. Was this, perhaps, the nearest he ever got to a peerage?

## Ralegh's Clerks and Carriers

The rest of the letters were written by professional clerks. Even as a young soldier in Ireland Ralegh had at least one in his entourage, but he frequently wrote himself, even at the height of his fortunes, and he seems to have had no regular clerical help while confined in the Tower of London between 1603 and 1617.

---

24. An instance of the spelling 'yow' for 'you' occurs in a letter of the Earl of Bath at Longleat: see *HMC Bath* II, p. 54.

No attempt has been made to distinguish or to identify these clerks, all of whom wrote very much alike in the elegant 'secretary' hand which they had been taught (Letter 11, Plate 1). No doubt much could be done by a specialist, but a detailed palaeographical survey is beyond the scope of this edition.[25] Nor does there seem to be any clear indication of when they acted as 'audio' scribes and when merely as fair copiers. There is some evidence of mis-hearing or mis-reading but on the whole they wrote sense and were probably more reliable than Ralegh's posthumous transcribers, any deliberate editing by them being liable to discovery.

As the vast majority of Ralegh's extant letters, and probably most of those which have not survived, were addressed to persons at Court or in its vicinity, carriage was not a problem except when he was out of London. Between Ireland and the capital there seems always to have been much coming and going and even when on the other side of the Atlantic, Ralegh could usually find a passing ship. Cross-channel shipping was considerable and when he was on naval service there were the Crown's own messengers or 'pursuivants'. Sending letters from Sherborne and further west would probably have been more difficult had not such a large proportion concerned suitors who could be relied upon to deliver promptly. There is, however, ample evidence on the letters that by 1595 (Letter 89), if not before, Ralegh was making use of the system of royal 'posts' which by then was well established from Plymouth to London, via Staines, including, between Crewkerne in Somerset and Shaftesbury in Dorset, facilities for the despatching of private letters in the little town of Sherborne.[26] The covers enclosing the packets, where they have survived, and in some cases the flyleaves of individual letters, carry the postmasters' receipts and these (e.g. Letters 147 and 159) indicate that letters from Sherborne regularly reached London in little over 24 hours, and sometimes even less. Apparently letters out of London took rather longer, as in August 1601 (Letter 139) Ralegh complained to Cecil that the Queen's Principal Secretary's letter had taken two days to reach him, adding that he himself could do the journey in half a day less. Nor was he confident that in a time of crisis

---

25. The anonymous and appropriately nicknamed 'Feathery Scribe', whose enormous output in the 1620s and 1630s has recently been identified (Peter Beal, *In Praise of Scribes: Manuscripts and their Makers in Seventeenth-Century England*, Oxford 1998, Chapter 3 and Appendix II), was a copyist rather than a clerk. Only Letter 172 has been printed from his copy.
26. See M. Brayshay, 'Royal post-horse routes in England and Wales: the evolution of the network in the later-sixteenth and early-seventeenth century', *Journal of Historical Geography*, 17, 4, 1991, pp. 373–89.

things would improve. Further west towards Plymouth the pace was decidedly slower, partly, no doubt, due to the notoriously bad state of the highways. However, Ralegh's letter from Terceira in 1597 (Letter 112), which took nearly a month to reach the little Devon port of Lyme Regis in an English merchant ship, was promptly sent on its way by the Mayor to the regular staging post at Crewkerne, where it arrived within 24 hours of landing. It was when writing to Cecil from Bath in September 1602 (Letter 162, Plate 8b), enclosing naval intelligence brought to him from Jersey by the owner of a small fishing or merchant vessel, that Ralegh underlined for the carrier the urgency of 'Her Majesties especiall service' by adding a small sketch of a gallows.

# EDITORIAL CONVENTIONS

All Agnes Latham's original transcriptions, with only a few exceptions due to their being in overseas repositories, were made from the actual manuscripts. Fortunately, largely with the help of the Canadian funding, she was later able to obtain good photocopies and this has enabled her associate editor to proceed with the checking and finalizing of the text with minimal recourse to the original manuscripts.

By and large, the editors have followed the conventions now generally used in the publication of early-modern English historical manuscripts. Capitalization and the use of the letters 'i' and 'j' (except where used as the terminal figure in sums of money), 'u' and 'v' and 'c' and 't' have been brought into line with current usage in order to make for easier reading and comprehension. To the same end, the punctuation, or lack of it, of the original texts has been modernized, any editorial doubts in these respects being noted, and likewise in the silent extension of scribal abbreviations. Words ending in 'ton' or 'con', with superscript abbreviation marks, have been printed as 'tion'. The letter 'y' has been printed as 'th' when used for such words as 'the' and 'that'. Otherwise the original spelling has been reproduced exactly. Wherever words appear to be missing or are now illegible or the sense was thought to be unclear, words or phrases have been added to the text, in all cases in italics and enclosed in square brackets. Words crossed out by the writer, unless thought to be of some significance, have been ignored, but all interlineations and marginal insertions in a different hand from that of the original scribe have been indicated. To assist readers all archaic or technical words and phrases have been elucidated, either in endnotes or, where this could be done economically, italicized and enclosed in square brackets in the body of the text. All words and phrases in Latin, including quotations from classical texts, have been italicized, but ships' names have not, except in the Introduction and in endnotes, the preceding 'the', however, being given a capital 'T'. Dates are printed as they appear in the manuscripts, but elsewhere, including the headings, they follow a calendar year commencing on 1 January.

The letters are printed, as far as dates can be established, in chronological order. Headings in larger type are followed by the present location, call-mark and calendaring or listing of the manuscript or other source supplying all or most of the text, the writer and the hand, and a note, where appropriate, of the physical condition of the manuscript. There then follow similar details of the principal early transcripts, if any, and finally the main printed versions.

All persons and places named in the text have, where necessary, been identified, either in square brackets or in endnotes, but annotation other than textual has been kept as short as possible, with the minimum of interpretation, intended only to enable readers to understand the text. Most has been selected from the very extensive annotation provided by Agnes Latham, and only where appropriate has it been extended by her associate editor to take account of recent publications or her own research. The main object has been to provide reliable texts of the letters, for the use both of future biographers and of specialists writing on any of the multiplicity of topics touched upon, and, it is hoped, for the enjoyment of non-specialist readers.

## ACKNOWLEDGEMENTS

Our first, and most important, debt is to the owners and custodians of the original manuscripts, both for permitting access and the making of photocopies and for permission to publish. Their names are listed above, p. xiv. Agnes Latham felt particularly indebted to the archivists and librarians who, in the days when few private papers had been deposited in local record offices, opened their doors to her, mentioning especially the Revd Stanhope-Lovell, one-time librarian at Hatfield House and one of his successors, Miss Clare Talbot, to whom the writer would add the name of the present librarian and archivist, Mr Robin Harcourt Williams, who has responded so helpfully to her queries. Agnes Latham remembered with gratitude the University of Oxford and Westfield College London who made it possible for her to begin work on Ralegh's letters. Although she herself had long since searched virtually all the public and private collections in Great Britain, she was also very mindful of her enormous debt to Pierre Lefranc and his research team at Quebec, especially John Roberts, for extending her horizons, and to the Canada Council whose funding made their searches possible. For assistance with the Spanish texts she was indebted to Dr John Allan Jones, of the department of Spanish in the University of Hull and to the late Mrs Norma Jacob (née Sherlock) of Somerville College, Oxford, and there will have been many others unknown to the present writer who helped and encouraged her along the way. After her death her nephew, Dr Nathaniel Booth, was most helpful in providing access to her remaining books and papers.

In my turn I would like, first and foremost, to thank Professor David Quinn, but for whose encouragement and advice at a particularly crucial stage I would probably not have undertaken what has been a formidable but very enjoyable task, and who has kindly contributed a Foreword. Almost the only other person to have known both Agnes Latham and myself is Peter Beal, who, at different times has put his specialist knowledge of Elizabethan and early Stuart scribes at our disposal. Besides these, many friends and former colleagues at Exeter have contributed their time and expertise. Whatever our destination, be it North Yorkshire or the Outer Banks of North Carolina, Marjorie Bird has been unfailing in her provision of companionship and logistical 'backup'. Marion Glasscoe not only effected the first introduction but has been a continual source of practical help, not least in preparing for inclusion as Appendix 3 a full list of the published work of her friend and former tutor. Besides bringing that to the notice of today's younger scholars it will also alert them to the need to look beyond their own specialist journals. Richard Hitchcock and Keith Cameron gave me invaluable assistance with the translating of the Spanish and French letters. Although Agnes Latham's own transcripts were made with great care, she would have been the first to insist on a final checking and to have welcomed the generous offer of my friend and former colleague, Audrey Erskine, lately archivist to the Dean and Chapter of Exeter Cathedral, to read the whole of the edited texts against the photocopies. Besides ensuring thereby that this new edition of Ralegh's letters is as near to what he wrote as a practised eye can determine, she and her husband, R.A. Erskine (who, as Deputy Registrar, was the architect of Exeter University publications), undertook the formidable task of reading the proofs. It also gives me great pleasure to express my appreciation not only of the professional skills of Simon Baker, Publisher at the University of Exeter Press and his staff, in particular Genevieve Davey, Anna Henderson and Rosemary Rooke, but also of their unfailing kindness and consideration which have made my visits to Reed Hall such a pleasure. I am fortunate, too, to have had the services of Colin Morgan, who tidied up my Introduction and annotation to such good effect, of Colin Bakké who converted my computer disks so efficiently into camera-ready copy, and of Delphine Jones and her colleagues in the University's Graphics Unit, who designed the book jacket.

Finally, on behalf of Agnes Latham and myself, and of the University of Exeter, I acknowledge with thanks grants towards pre-publication and publication costs, respectively, from the British Academy and from the Scouloudi Foundation in association with the Institute of Historical Research.

Thorverton, Exeter, 1 September 1998                    Joyce Youings

# THE LETTERS

1. TO LORD BURGHLEY FROM CORK,
   22 FEBRUARY 1581

   PRO, SP63/80/73, *CSPI 1574–85*, p. 288. Written by a clerk, with signature in Ralegh's hand.

   Edwards II, pp. 7–8; Pope Hennessy 1883, pp. 151–3, from Edwards.

ARMY PAY AT SEA

[*addressed*] To the right honorable and my very good lord the Lord Burgheley,[1] Lord Highe Thresourer of England

[*endorsed*] 22 February 1580, Master Rawley to my lord from Corke. For payment of his and his bandes [= *companies*] entertaynement during there aboade at the [*Isle of*] Wight

Maye yt please your honor to understand that uppon the receavinge of my footebande of one hondrethe men when I departed from London towardes this land there was then delivered into my handes (besides one hundred powndes in imprest which is defalted [= *deducted*] uppon my enterteynment heere)[2] so mutche mony as amownted to six dayes wages for myself, my leuetenante, officers and soldiers at accustomed rates, viz iiij*s per diem* for my selfe, ij*s per diem* for my leuetenante, xiiij*d* le peece for iiij officers and viij*d* a peece for every soldier.[3] After thexpiration of which six dayes (by order from your honor and the rest of my lords of Her Majesties Pryvy Counsell) wee entered into the Isle of Wighte where wee contynued xv dayes, and then beinge imbarked in Her Majesties shippes, yt was xvii dayes more before wee arryved heere, durings all which tyme of xxxii dayes in the whole wee receaved only vittells after the rate of vj*d* sterlinge *per diem* for eache one, so that duringe those xxxii dayes there growethe due to every of my company ij *d* sterlinge *per diem* as a remaynder of theire wages at viij *d* sterlinge per diem. And also to my selfe, my leutennante and officers our whole enterteynment for the lyke tyme at the rates abovesaid. So yt is my good and honorable lorde that at the importunate suyte and exclamation of my company I have bin enforced to paye and satisfy every of them of that remaynder. And seekinge to have the same to be allowed mee agayne heere I am therefore referred to your honors order and the residue of my lords of Her Majesties Privy Councell in England, beinge answered by Her Highnes offycers heere that wee are neyther to be entered into paye nor no other manner of waye [sic] to be allowed heere, but from the day of our arryvall in this land.[4] In consideration whereof I am a moste humble sutor to your honor and the residue of my said lordes for allowaunce of that mony as hathe bin heretofore by your lordships good meanes in the like case allowed to Sir William Morgan,[5] and that the same maye be payd to the gentleman which shall deliver this letter to your honor, whom I have desired to attend your lordship for that purpose and who shall present unto you as well a perfect accompte thereof as also a suffycient certifycate or testemony of the tyme of our contynuaunce in the Wighte and of the daye of our arryvall heere. I moste humbly desier your honor to farther this my request as spedey as you conveniently maye because I have appointed the mony to be imployed in England abowte the providinge of sutche wantes as bothe my self and company doe greatly stand in neede of.[6]

Thus I commyt your lordship to God, my poore self remayninge alwayes at your honors service and commaundement.

    Corke this 22 of February 1580
        Your lordships most humble to commaunde
           W Rauley

1. William Cecil, Lord Burghley (1520–98), the Queen's Principal Secretary and from 1572 Lord Treasurer.
2. In July 1580, 300 men were ordered to be levied in London for service in Ireland against the Earl of Desmond (see Letter 2, note 9), Ralegh and Edward Denny to have charge of 100 each and 100 'to go with the ships'. The Lord Treasurer was instructed to advance Ralegh £100: *APC* XII, pp. 96–7. In fact, it had already been paid on 22 June: PRO, E351/230/f.206.
3. This was to correspond to the allowances separately made to the 100 seamen, 'for avoyding of contention emonge the officers': *APC* XII, pp. 117–18.
4. Once in Ireland the companies were the responsibility of the authorities in Dublin.
5. Morgan had gone to Ireland in October 1579 as Constable of Dungarvan Castle with 100 soldiers, and, on 6 October 1580, the Lord Treasurer was instructed to pay him £100 out of

the £149 18s. 10d. which he claimed to have spent on the journey: *DNB* and *APC* XI, p. 280 and XII, p. 223.
6. On 24 April 1581, the Lord Treasurer was authorized to pay Ralegh and Captain Edward Denny, who had sailed to Dublin, £43 14s. 8d. each for the wages of themselves and their companies for 32 days: *APC* XIII, pp. 12–13.

2. TO SIR FRANCIS WALSINGHAM FROM CORK, 23 FEBRUARY 1581

PRO, SP63/80/74, *CSPI 1574–85*, p. 288. Written by a clerk, with signature in Ralegh's hand.

Edwards II, pp. 9–10, with errors; Pope Hennessy 1883, pp. 154–6, from Edwards.

## SOLDIERING IN MUNSTER

[*addressed*]   To the honorable Sir Francis Wallsingam,[1] knighte, Principal Secritory to Her Highnes geve thes
[*endorsed*]   23 February 1580, from Master Walter Rawley

I receved of late a letter from your honor wherin I finde your honors dispo[si]tion and oppinion more favorable then I can any way deserve.[2] Notwithstandinge I hope your honor shall finde that my forwardnes to advance Her Majestes service shall not be lest [*sic*] according to my smale strenght. Wheras of late a cumpany of yonge cumpanions linket together in rebellion, who, because they can no longer covertly assiste the proclaymed traytors[3] do at lenght manifeste their good mindes to Her Hightness [*sic*] and the Inglyshe nation: as Davy Barrey,[4] sonn and heir to Lorde Barrey now in the Castle of Develin [*Dublin*], Morrice Roche, eldest sonn to the Lorde Roche, Finnin Macartey,[5] Patrik Conndon,[6] and divers others,[7] my Lorde Generall [*Ormond*][8] is now cum hither who wee hope, ether by force or pollecy, will sufficiently hampre them. Thes ar farr of greater strenght then the Earl of Desmond and Johne.[9]

In my returne from Develin I made a hard escape from the Seneshall.[10] He sett on me in Barres Countre (wher he is allwayes fostered)[11] with xiiij horsmen and threscore footmen. I was three horsmen and foure shot[12] on horsbake t[w]o Irishe footmen. I coveted to recover a litle old castle[13] and in that retire [= *retreat*] I lost[14] three men and three horses. The manner of myne own behavior I leve to the report of others,[15] but the escape was strong [sic] to all men. The castle was a longe mile of from the place wher he first sett on us. Ther is great need of a supply in Munstre for the bandes ar all miche decayed;[16] the bandes of Tanner and Barnishe[17] were so ordered in the cashiringe [= *dismissing*] that no man was the better, for the officers had the furniture [= *equipment*] and the soldiers ran away. Beside the men ar suche poore and misserable cretures as ther captaynes dare not lead them to serve. If your honors beheld them when they arrive here you would think them far unfitt to fight for Her Majesties crown. And, like your honor, ther is no fitt place to lande them that their captaynes may receve them furnished but Corke, from whence they may most conveniently be delivered over. This [sic] besechinge you to continew your favorable oppinion of mee I humble take my leve, restinge allways most ready to do yow all honor and service.

From Corke the xxiij of February 1581.

  Your honors most humble to cummande

    W Rauley

1. Sir Francis Walsingham (c.1532–1590), Privy Councillor, Principal Secretary since 1573 and master of 'intelligence'.
2. Ralegh's feats of arms since his arrival in Ireland in 1580, including responsibility for one wholesale massacre and a major role in a second, were described in vivid terms, almost certainly by his Exeter friend and mentor, John Hooker, in the 'Chronicle of Ireland' published in R. Holinshed, *Chronicles*, etc., 1587, pp. 1–71. See also Bagwell III, pp. 74–7 and Quinn 1962, pp. 33–4.
3. These included Viscount Roche, who submitted to Lord Justice Pelham in May 1580 (*CCM 1575–88*, p. 257) and James FitzRichard Barry, Viscount Barrymore, now in Dublin Castle and who died there in April 1581: *CSPI 1574–85*, pp. 249 and 304.
4. David Fitzjames Barry (1556–1617), son of the above, was proclaimed a rebel in May 1581 and submitted in July: *CCM 1575–88*, pp. 267–8.
5. Finnin, usually known as Florence, MacCarthy, heir to MacCarthy Reagh, lord of Carbery. See also below, Letters 4, 68 and 149.
6. Patrick Condon was at this juncture a supporter of Desmond (Bagwell III, p. 94) but see below, Letters 73 and 74.
7. Donnell More MacCarthy, natural son of Donnell Macarthy More, Earl of Clancare, Callough MacTeige, brother of Sir Cormac MacTeige MacCarthy of Blarney Castle and Philip O'Sullivan had combined with David Barry and Maurice Roche to become 'Robin Hoods', according to a letter of 23 February from Sir Warham St Leger, Provost Marshall of Munster (see below, Letter 5, note 3) to Burghley: *CSPI 1574–85*, p. 287.
8. Thomas Butler, 10th Earl of Ormond (1532–1614), Lord General of the Province of Munster.
9. Gerald FitzGerald, 16th Earl of Desmond, who joined the rebellion after the death in 1579 of James FitzMaurice FitzGerald, the Catholic enthusiast who inaugurated it. Desmond had been proclaimed traitor on 1 November 1579 and was to be killed on 11 November 1583: *DNB* and Bagwell III, pp. 23–5, 31.
10. John FitzEdmund FitzGerald, Seneschal of Imokilly (between Cork Harbour and Youghal at the mouth of the Blackwater), became on the death of FitzGerald the real head of the rebellion: *DNB* and Bagwell, pp. 34, 55–6.

11. Barry's lands were Barry's Court, Inchinibackye; Castell-Lions; Botevante and Lescarroll in Orerye; Timologe, Ratheharry and Lislie in Ybawne: *CCM 1589–1600*, p. 513.
12. Cf. Edwards II, p. 9, which has 'and soune set …'.
13. Ralegh was probably attacked at Midleton or Ballinacurra and took refuge at Ballivodig: Bagwell III, p. 85.
14. Cf. Edwards II, p. 10, which has 'in that resun I left …'.
15. The incident modestly alluded to is recounted at length by the author of the 'Chronicle of Ireland' (op. cit. p. 173) who allots the Seneschal six horsemen 'and certeine kerne'. He says that Ralegh crossed the ford alone and went back to rescue his servant, Henry Moile, whose horse had foundered.
16. On 13 January 1581, Sir Henry Wallop, Under-Treasurer of Ireland, told Burghley in a letter from Dublin that there was 'great deficiency in the bands [= *companies*] because the new come men die so fast'. The Lord Deputy (see below, Letter 3, note 3) had hanged several for runnning away: *CSPI 1574–85*, p. 280.
17. Captains Roger Tanner and Arthur Barnes were each appointed to take 100 soldiers over from Bristol in October 1580: *APC* XII, p. 217.

---

## 3. TO SIR FRANCIS WALSINGHAM FROM CORK, 25 FEBRUARY 1581

PRO, SP63/80/82; *CSPI 1574–85*, p. 289. Written by a clerk, with signature in Ralegh's hand.

Edwards II, pp. 11–13; Pope Hennessy, pp. 157–61, from Edwards; Norman Lloyd Williams, *Sir Walter Raleigh*, 1962, pp. 33–5, from Edwards, spelling modernized.

### THE LORD GENERAL OF MUNSTER

[*addressed*] To the honorable Sir Francis Walsingham Knighte, Principall Secritory to Her Highnes

[*endorsed*] 25 May 1580 [*in another hand*] From Master Walter Rawleighe

The day after the writinge of my letter to your honor by Leuetenant Rigges[1] news came[2] that Davy Barrey had broken and burnt all his castles and entred publikly into the action of rebellion. It plesed my Lorde Deputy[3] att my beinge at Develin (forseinge wherunto this trator was bent) to bestow on mee the kepinge of on of his castles called Barre Court and the Iland adjoyninge therunto,[4] which hows he gave mee in charge to keap to Her Majesties use, beinge a great strenght to the countre and a safty for all passingers betwen Corke and Youghall, notwithstandinge becaus my Lord Generall [*Ormond*] was presently to cum up and Barrey redy to go out (having befor undre grond broken the fondations of the rest of his castles) I made stay to take this Barrey Court as well for that my Lord Generall should not alledge that I crost hyme in any service or did anythinge within his goverment without his privity, as also because it should not be sayd that ther takinge therof was the hasteninge of Barries rebellion. But when my Lord [*Deputy*] came and Barrey had burnt all the rest the Lord Generall, ether meninge to kepe it for hyme self, as I think all is to litle for hyme, or els unwilling any Inglishman should have any thing, stayd the taking therof so longe, meninge to put a gard of his own in it, as it is, withe the rest, defaced and spoled. I pray God Her Majesty do not finde that, what with the defence of his own countrie assalted on all sides, what with the beringe and forberinge of his kindred, as all thes traytors of this new rebellion ar his own cussen germayns, what by reason of the incomperable hatred betwen hyme [*Barry*] and the Garantines,[5] who will rather dy a thowsand deathes, entre into a million of mischiefes and seek soccor of all nations, rather then they will ever be subdued by a Butler,[6] that aftre Her Majesty hathe spent a hundred thousand pound more she shall at last be driven by to dere experience to send an Inglyshe presedent [*of Munster*] to follow thes mallicious traytors with fier and sword, nether respectinge the aliance nor the nation.

Would God your honor and Her Majesty, as well as my poore self, understoode how pitifully the service here goethe forward. Considering that this man [*Ormond*], havinge now byn Lord Generall of Munstre now about too yeares, their ar at this instant a thowsand traytors more then ther were the first day. Would God the service of Sir Humfry Gilbert[7] might be rightly lokt into, who, with the third part of the garrison now in Irland, ended a rebellion not miche inferior to this in to monethes, or would God his own behavior were such in peace[8] as it did not make his good service forgotten and hold hyme from the preferm[*ent*] he is worthy of. I take God to wittnes I speake it not for affection but to discharge my duty to Her Majesty, for I never hard nor rede of any man more fered then he is amonge the Irishe nation. And I do assuredly know that the best about the Earle of Desmond, ye[*a*] and all the unbridled traytors of thes partes, would cum in[*to*] hyme and yeld them selves to the Queens mercy were it but known that he were cum amonge them. The end shall prove this to be trew.

And for myne own part, God is my judge, it grevethe mee to receve Her Majestys pay (although God knowes it be but a poor entreteynment) to see her so miche abused, and I will rather begg then live here to indure it. I would most willingly geve over my charge—and did offre it to the Lord

Generall, God is my judge—if I could, and serve Her Majesty privatly with a dussen or ten horse duringe the wares. I beseich your honor to take my bold writing in good part, protesting befor hyme that knowethe the thoughtes of all hartes that I writ nothing but [am] moved therunto for the love I bere to Her Highnes and for the furtherance of her service. And further I humble crave at your honors handes that yow will reserve my letters to your self, and if your honor will promise mee so miche and geve me leve I will from tyme to tyme advertise your honor trewly of this estat, myself being on that your honor shall allways finde most ready to venture my life to do yow all honor and service during my lyfe. I beseiche your honor that I may by your means injoy the keping of this Barrey Court and they [sic] Iland, or that it will pleas your honor but to writ to my Lorde Deputy that he will confirm it unto mee, whom I find most willing to do mee any good, being my honorable good lord.[9]

This humble I take my leve, reposing myself and my estat uppon your honors favor.

From Corke the xxv of February, your honors most humble ever to cummand

    W Rauley

1. Gregory Rigges (not Biggs as in Edwards), a sea-captain, appears frequently in the state papers in connection with Ireland.
2. Already reported in a letter dated 20 February from St Leger: *CSPI 1574–85*, p. 287.
3. Arthur, 11th Lord Grey of Wilton, had been appointed Lord Deputy of Ireland in June 1580.
4. Barry's Court Castle, now a ruin, lies south of the village of Carrigtohill. The Great Island is in Cork harbour. See below, note 9.
5. The Geraldines, led by the Earl of Desmond.
6. Ormond preferred not to see the country ravaged and his kinsfolk slain, a point of view with which the Queen had a certain sympathy in view of the cost of sending English troops to Ireland. By and large the English establishment in Ireland, including St Leger, shared Ralegh's lack of confidence in his superior: Bagwell III, pp. 105–12.
7. Ralegh's half-brother, who had been appointed Colonel of Munster in October 1569, had fought with great savagery and been knighted for his services by the then Lord Deputy, Sir Philip Sidney: *CSPI 1509–73*, p. 425. He was now (1581) absorbed in planning an Atlantic voyage. Ten years his senior, Gilbert had not only encouraged Ralegh in his military career but introduced him to the Court.
8. In a recent dispute in Chancery between Gilbert and William Hawkins of Plymouth, Ralegh had been only lukewarm in his support of his half-brother: PRO, C24/150.
9. According to the 'Chronicle of Ireland', loc. cit., pp. 172–3, after Ralegh had received a 'commission' from the Lord Deputy to take possession of the island, due to the dilatoriness of Ormond, Barry had managed to install his mother. See also *CSPI 1574–85*, pp. 344–5. In August 1583, following his submission and pardon, Barry obtained official restitution: C. Smith, *Ancient and present state of Cork*, Dublin 1750, reprinted Cork 1893–4, p. 144. Ralegh's disappointment at failing to secure what would have been a valuable personal base in Munster must have been acute at the time: see also below, Letter 4.

4. **TO LORD GREY FROM CORK, 1 MAY 1581**

PRO, SP63/83/16(i), *CSPI 1574-85*, p. 304, a contemporary transcript, with writer's name in cypher, enclosed with a letter dated 14 May 1581¹ from Grey to Walsingham.

Edwards II, pp. 14-16; Pope Hennessy 1883, pp. 162-6, from Edwards.

## HOME TRUTHS FROM MUNSTER

[no address]
[endorsed]   2 May 1581: Copie of a letter to the Deputy from Corke

Fering that it shoulde seme strainge unto your Lordshipe the litle service don in thes partes, I presume to wryte unto your honor in myne owne excuse lest your Lordshipe should growe in ill opinion of us that ar and have byne continually in the presenc of the general [*Ormond*] to be directed. The bandes of Sir George Bowser,² Edward Bartley,³ Captayne [*John*] Dowdall⁴ and of my self have bine ever since the seconde weeke of Lent remayninge in Corke and both the great woode of Conolothe, Harlo, Clenlis and all the countye of Lymbricke and the counties betwene the Dingle and Kilkeny left without any companies ether to defend it self or anoy the enemy. Since which tyme wee have made to jurneys, theone towardes Kilkenny to give convoye to my Lord and attend his returne and the other into Conolothe, by which jurnes, the one being in horible wether and the other utterly botles [= *to no purpose*], being don without draught [= *plan*] or espiall, and besyde inforst to walke such unreasonable march as, wher wee dispatched a churrell [= *common soldier*] of the traytors, wee lamede, lost or left behynde unservicable a soldier ye [?*or*] two of our owne. The poor bandes have curste the change they made in leving to follow your honor, as they have tould the Lord Generall many tymes. And this fyrst of May wee ar going a nother posting convoy towardes Kilkeny, but to culler [= *disguise*] the matter wee shall march some two dayes out of our way to seeke wee know not whome. The store of Corke, exept it be a smale quantitie of wheat and butter, is all spent within the walles, and now it wilbe aleged that wee cannot serve for want of victles or els because the bandes ar not supplied, allthowgh wee were nevere less then fore hundred stronge and yet both of Sir Georg Bowcers and Capteyne Bartles left at Kilmallock and Asketon.

We have spent thes two monethes of the spring in parles with Davey Barrey, Barrey Rowe, the Countes of Desmonde and Finnin Macartey,⁵ and wee thinke it willbe two moneth more er he [*Ormond*] be resolved whether thes ought to be followed or no, and yet ther is no day passeth without some trayterous villonies by the Barres committed. The Countes of Desmonde is retourned and brought so many followers with her hither to carrye provision with her as the Earle for his parte shall be the better able to keepe the feild all this summer; and at her going away none of her trayne ether sercht or lokt over. Barrey Rowe is protected, the Lady Barrey having gathered her goodes into Corke and fering that by the atteyndure of her husband those wilbe found for the queene.[6] Her young sonne, that five dayes before sett on the garrisons of Youghall, is brought in to serve that turne to carye the goodes into Osyllevantes [*O'Sullivan's*] countrey[7] or els wher for the more saftie, and besides this man shall keep some store of cattell and such impotent people as cannot follow Davey Barrey in the feild, with many othe[r] profits ether for the Queen or for the knaves. I thinke your honor hard of the losse of the warde [= *garrison*] of Asketon [*Castle*].[8] Okenif and his sonn wer both slayne by Jhon of Desmonde, gentelmen of Macdonoths countrey and very good subjectes.[9]

Barres Courte and the Iland, which your honor willed me to keepe,[10] theon hath since bin many tymes defaced and theother spoylde and preyed. From this Iland the traytors can never wante nether wine nor salte, iron or any other necessary provision, or if neede bee advertisment from Spayne or els wher, being common for any man to lande on. Notwithstanding it is left naked and the castle broken that stood in the entrance therof for defence. I have, by great perswation of the commissioners, gott leve to edifie the same and leve a ward therin, and if it shall please your honor to thinke mee woorthie the keeping and custodie therof, I will at myne owne coast [*sic*] buyld it up agayne and defende it for Her Majestie. I would the rather bee an humble and ernest suter to your honor for it in that I heire the Lord Generall purposeth, when I have taken the toyle in making it defencible and bin at the charg, to turne me over for my charges to the Queene and dispose of the Iland to some other.[11] I hope your honor will stand my good lord therin.

If it please your honor to give commission ther may bee an other hundreth soldiors leyd [= *quartered*] uppon the cuntre heire aboute.[12] I hope it willbe a[13] most honorable matter for your Lordshipe, most acceptable to Her Majestie and profitable for the countre, and the ryght meane to banish all idle and frutles galliglas and kyrne,[14] the ministers of all mischeife.

This most humblie beseeching your honor not to condemne any of us that are willing to deserve your Lordshipps good favour, I humble take my leve from Corke the fyrst of May.
        Copie [............][15]

1. Lord Grey wrote asking to be discharged from office since he could no longer with conscience implement the Queen's conciliatory policy and included Ralegh's letter to support an appeal for reinforcements. 'Yow maye a lyttle geather by Capt. Rawley's letter that oothers heere thynk no impossibilitie in it': PRO, SP63/83/16, *CSPI 1574–85*, p. 304.
2. Sir George Bourchier, Colonel of Munster, was the third son of the 3rd Earl of Bath (ob. 1561), of Tawstock in north Devon. He drew his soldiers from both the north and east parts of Devon: ibid., p. 422.
3. Captain Barkeley had arrived at Waterford on 9 November 1580 with no less than 700 men. His chief recruiting area was Somerset: ibid., pp. 269 and 423.
4. Another professional soldier, whose family had longstanding Irish roots, with considerable experience in the Queen's service, including being for a time muster-master to the Devon militia. See also below, Letter 45.
5. See Letter 2, note 5.
6. Marginal insertion, probably by Grey, 'viz Barrie Roe' but should have been inserted after 'sonne'.
7. Bear Haven and Bantry. The clerk first wrote 'Urselevantes'.
8. 'hard ... Asketon' underlined. Marginal insertion: 'xi of them were distressed that fondly aventured owte to far for sum cowes'.
9. Not identified. The Macdonoghs held Dowalla, the modern Duhallow.
10. See above, Letter 3, especially note 9.
11. But see ibid.
12. A further insertion reads 'this is in the beeginyng of that platt which by Master [*Geoffrey*] Fen[*ton*] [*secretary to the Lord Deputy*] I have advertized of, for the fynding of a certayne garrison gratis to her Majestie'. For Ralegh's plan for Ireland see PRO, SP63/96/30–31, printed in part in Pope Hennessy 1883, pp. 227–32.
13. 'I ... a' underlined.
14. Irish soldiers, the 'galliglass' being tall, strong, men, who carried battle-axes and the 'kerne' the lightly-armed foot-soldiers.
15. In cypher.

---

## 5. TO THE EARL OF LEICESTER FROM LISMORE, 26 AUGUST 1581

BL, Harl. 6993, f. 5. In Ralegh's pure 'secretary' hand.

Cayley 1806, I, pp. 39–40, spelling modernized; Edwards II, pp. 17–18; Greg 1932, plate LXXV, with partial transcript.

### IN SEARCH OF A PATRON

[*addressed*]   To the righte honorable lorde my very good lord the Erle of Leycester,[1] of Her Majestes moste honorable Pryvy Counsell
[*endorsed*]   26° August 1581   W. Rawley
[*headed in left-hand top margin*]   Book of Hand. 26 August 1581 Raughly

I may not forgett continually to put your honor in mind of my affection unto your lordshipe, havinge to the world bothe professed and protested the same. Your honor havinge no use of suche poore followers hathe utterly forgotten mee. Notwithstandinge if your lordshipe shall please to thinke mee yours, and I am, I wilbe found as redy, and dare do as miche in your service as any man you may cummande, and do nether so miche dispaire of my self but that I may be someway able to performe as miche. I have spent some tyme here under the Deputy [*Grey*] in suche poore place and charge as were it not for that I knew hyme to be on of yours I would disdeyn it as miche as to keap sheepe.[2] I will not troble your honor with the bussnes of this loste lande for that Sir Warram Sentleger[3] can best of any man deliver unto your lordshipe the good, the badd, the mischeiffes, the meanes to amend and all in all of this common welthe, or rather common woo.[4] He hopeth to finde your honor his assured good lorde, and your honor may most assuredly cummande hyme. He is lovingly inclyned towardes your honor and your lordshipe shall win by your favor towardes hyme, a wise, faythfull and valient gentleman whos worde and deade your honor shall ever find to be on[e].

Thus, having no other matter but only I desire the continuance of your honors favor, I humble take my leve.

From the camp at Leishmore[5] in Irland, August the 26,
 Your honors faithfull and obedient
  W Rauley

[*postscript*] I am bold being bond by very conscience to commend unto your honors consideration the pitifull estate of John Fittes Edmondes of Cloyne,[6] a gentleman and the only man untucht and proved tru to the Queen bothe in this and the last rebellion. Sir Warram can declare his servise, what he is and what he deservethe.[7]

---

1. Robert Dudley, Earl of Leicester (*c.*1532–88), Privy Councillor, Master of the Horse.
2. Ralegh had been appointed one of the three commissioners for Munster: Bagwell III, p. 84. For another reference to the keeping of sheep, see below, Letter 126.
3. Son of a previous Lord Deputy of Ireland, Sir Warham (*c.*1525–97) had been nominated by Sir Henry Sidney, Lord Deputy, to the post of President of Munster, but, having personally quarrelled with Ormond, in October 1579 he had been made Knight Marshal instead: *DNB*. They were Kentishmen, only distantly related to the St Legers of Annery near Bideford in north Devon.
4. From George Gascoigne's *The Steele Glas*.
5. Lismore, co. Waterford, in the Blackwater valley north-east of Cork.
6. John FitzEdmund FitzGerald, to be distinguished from his namesake, the Seneschal of Imokilly. In May 1582 the Queen granted him an annuity of 200 marks, partly out of escheated land: *CSPI 1574–85*, p. 368.
7. See ibid., pp. 283 and 300.

## 6. TO SIR HUMPHREY GILBERT FROM RICHMOND, [15]¹ MARCH 1583

Ransom Center, Pforzheimer 106, Jackson 1940, III, pp. 852–3, *in extenso* with facsimile. In Ralegh's 'mixed' hand.

BL, Add. 4231, f. 85 and PRO, SP9/55/12(i), eighteenth-century transcripts, the former made for Thomas Birch.

Cayley 1806, I, pp. 47–8, from BL, spelling modernized; Tytler 1833, I, f. 116; Edwards II, p. 19, from BL, dated 17 March; Quinn, *Gilbert*, 1940, ii, p. 348, from BL and PRO; N Lloyd Williams, op. cit., p. 53, from Edwards, spelling modernized.

### WITH A JEWEL FROM THE QUEEN

[*addressed*]   To my brother Sir Humphrey Gilbert knight²
[*endorsed*]   Reseived the 18th of Marche 1582

Brother, I have sent yow a token from Her Majesty, an ancor guyded by a Lady as yow see,³ and farther Her Highness willed mee to send yow worde that she wished as great good hap and safty to your ship⁴ as if her sealf were ther in parson, desiring yow to have care of your sealf as of that which she tendereth, and therefore for her sace [*sic*] yow must provide for hit accordingly. Farther she cummandeth that yow leve your picture with mee.⁵ For the rest I leve till our meetinge or to the report of this berer, who would needs be the messengre of this good newses [*sic*].

So I commit yow to the will and protection of God, who send us such life or death as he shall pleas or hath appoyncted.⁶

Richmond this Fryday morninge
    Your trew brother
        W Rauley⁷

---

1. 18 March 1583 (see endorsement) was a Monday, so Friday was 15 March.
2. See above, Letter 3, note 7.
3. Described by Maurice Browne, a close friend of Gilbert, in a letter of April/May 1583 to John Thynne as 'a very excellent Jewell ... an anckor of gold set with 29 diamondes with the portracture of a Queene ... On the back side of the ankor is written ... *Tuemur sub sacra ancora* ... and herewith receyved a letter of very greate favore': Longleat, Thynne Papers, V, ff. 252–253v., printed in David B. Quinn and Neil M. Cheshire, *Newfoundland of Stephen Parmenius*, Toronto 1973, p. 205.
4. Gilbert sailed in June 1583 with a fleet of five ships on a colonizing expedition to North America. His largest vessel was Ralegh's own *Bark Ralegh*, c.200 tons, equipped by her owner at great cost, only to turn back two days out: Quinn, *Gilbert* 1940, I, pp. 83–4.
5. Revd John Prince reported having seen at Compton, Devon, Gilbert's former home, a portrait

of Sir Humphrey wearing on his breast 'the Golden Anchor, with the pearl at peak', given him by Queen Elizabeth: *Worthies of Devon*, 1701, reprinted Exeter 1810, p. 419. No such portrait survives today.
6. Gilbert perished at sea on his way home.
7. See below, Letter 9, note 9.

---

## 7. TO THOMAS EGERTON FROM THE COURT, 10 APRIL 1583

Huntington, EL. 1317. Written by a clerk, with signature and subscription in Ralegh's hand.

J.P. Collier (ed.), *Egerton Papers*, Camden Society, Old Series 12, 1840, p. 94; Edwards II, 20, from Collier.

### ALL SOULS LEASES

[*addressed*] To my worshipfull freinde Master Eggerton esquier,[1] Solycytor [*General*] to Her Highnes

[*endorsed*] Master Rawley's letter for Hattens [*sic*][2] maner

Master Solycyter: Yt hathe pleased Her Majestie to bestowe the leases of Scotney and Newlande,[3] lately graunted unto her from Alsolne [*All Souls*] Colledge in Oxon, uppon me, or any other that I shall agree withall.[4] And for that of late I have barganed with William Touse and Clemente Stupney[5] for the lease of Scotney, I ame to requeste yow that the assignement maye passe by your good helpe from Her Majestie to them, they payenge all fees and chardges therto belonginge.[6] And soe with hartie thankes for many other courtesyes, I byd yow farewell from the Court the xth of Aprille 1583.

    Your very lovinge frinde to cummande
    W Rauley

1. *c*.1540–1617, Solicitor-General from 1581, the later Lord Chancellor.
2. A clerical error, perhaps confused with Sir Christopher Hatton's estate at Bletchingley in Surrey.
3. The manor of Scotney alias Bletching Court in the parish of Lydd in Kent and Newlands Farm in Romney Marsh.
4. Ralegh had obtained a letter from the Queen to All Souls as recently as 14 March 1583, acting on 'the information and lewd setting on of William Langherne, late Fellow of All Souls [*and*] then servant to Sir Walter Raleigh knight, highly favoured of Her Majesty ... which suit Langherne and one Arthur Gorges [*a kinsman of Ralegh, see below, Letter 101*] did follow at the college' in the Warden's absence: C.R.L. Fletcher, 'All Souls College versus Lady Jane Stafford, 1587' in *Collectanea* I, Oxford Historical Society, 1885, Appdx. p. 231.

5. William Towse came from Essex and Stepney was a jurate of Lydd in Kent.
6. The assignment of Scotney was effected on 13 May 1583, but the lease of Newland seems to have remained with the Queen. In 1587 when Ralegh was seeking a further lease from the college he was reminded of 'those two our best leases demised to Hir Highnes in your worship's behalf, to our great hindrance': Fletcher, op. cit., p. 214. See also below, Letter 25.

---

## 8. To Lord Burghley from Greenwich, [10]¹ May 1583

BL, Lansd. 39, f. 130a. In Ralegh's neatest hand, his signature underlined with an elaborate flourish. Right-hand lower edge damaged.

J. Strype, *Annals* 1731, IV, suppl., p. 17; Edwards II, pp. 21–2; Greg 1932, plate LXXIV, with full transcript.

### THE EARL OF OXFORD

[*addressed*] To the right honorable my very good lord the Lord Tresorer of Inglande

[*endorsed in Burghley's hand*] xij Maij 1583 [*Sunday*] Master Walter Rauley con[*cerning*] the Erle of Oxon [*Outer leaf shows the mark, a tick, of Michael Hicks, Burghley's secretary, an anchor, and a third mark, not identified.*]

The eveninge aftre the recept of your lordship[*s*] letter I spake with Her Majesty, and ministringe sum occasion touchinge the Earle of Oxford² I told Her Majesty how grevously your lordship receved her late discumfortable awnswere. Her Majesty, as your lordship had writen (I know not by whom lately and strangly perswaded), purposed to have new repetition [= *to reopen the case*] between the Lords Haward [*sic*], Arundle and others, and the Earle, and said it was a matter not so slightly to be passed over.³ I awnswered that beinge asured Her Majesty would never permit any thing to be proceuted to the Earles dangre, if any such possibilly [*sic*] were, and therfore it were to small purpose, aftre so longe absence and so many disgraces, to call his honor and name agayn in question, wherby he might apeare the less fitt ether for her favor or presence. In conclusion Her Majesty confessed that she ment it only therby to geve the Earle warninge, and that, as it semed to mee, beinge acquaynted with his offences, her grace might seme the more [*word omitted*] in remittinge the revenge or punishment of the same. I delivered her your lordships lettre, and what I sayd farther, how honorable and profitable it weare for [*Her*] Majesty to have regard of your lordship[s] health and quiett, I referr to the wittnes of God and good report of Her Highness.

And the more to witness how desirous I am of your lordships favor and good opinion [of me *deleted*], I am content for your sake to lay the serpent before the fier, as mich as in mee lieth, that [*he*] havinge recovered strenght my sealf may be most in dangre of his poyson and sting. For awnswere Her Majesty would geve mee no oth[er] but that she would satisfy your lordship, of whom she ever had and wou[ld] ever have speciall care and regard.[4]

Thus beinge unfenedly willinge to deserv[e] your lordships good favor I humble take my leve. Grenwich this present Friday.

    Your lordships most willing to be cummanded,
       · W Rauley

1. The Friday before 12 May.
2. Edward de Vere, 17th Earl of Oxford (1550–1604), hereditary Great Chamberlain, who was married to Lord Burghley's elder daughter: *DNB*, sub Vere.
3. Having earlier been high in the Queen's favour, in December 1580 Oxford had confessed to having joined with Lord Henry Howard (see below, Letter 165, note 11), Charles Arundel and Francis Southwell, not only in a secret profession of Catholicism but also in a conspiracy against the regime. Their subsequent falling out among themselves (Oxford was a wild and quarrelsome young man) had put an end to the matter. In 1582 the Earl had been placed under house arrest for an affray with Thomas Knevett of the Privy Chamber, and his father-in-law had asked Sir Christopher Hatton and Ralegh to intercede for him with the Queen, although Oxford was known to be jealous of Ralegh's rapid rise to royal favour: B.M. Ward, *The Seventeenth Earl of Oxford*, 1928, chapter 5 and Conyers Read, *Lord Burghley and Queen Elizabeth*, 1960, pp. 274–6.
4. On 2 June 1583, the Earl of Rutland learned that 'after some bitter words and speeches in the end all sins ar forgiven and he [*Oxford*] may repayre to the Court at his plesure. Master Ralley whas a great mean herin', which was not to the liking of Hatton: *HMC Rutland* I, p. 150.

---

9.   To Edward Seymour from the Court, 20 March [*c.*1584/*c.*1597][1]

    Devon Record Office, 1392M/L1599/41, transcribed by Alison M. Quinn, but not previously printed. In Ralegh's hand, written in great haste.

## PROPERTY DEALING

[*addressed*]   To my very loving cussen Master Edwarde Semore[2]

Cusen Semore: I have now agreed with Master Lowman[3] for the leas. I thank yow for youre kinde dealinge therin and I wilbe reddy to requite it to my uttermost poure. And yet a mallicious knave dwellinge in Sherburne, on Stocker,[4] hathe made offer of purpose to make me pay the deerer knowing how mich I affected the place.[5] Butt how soever it be I will acknowledge that Sir W[illiam] Courtney[6] hathe dealt very kyndly with me therin.

For Sandrige[7] I will returne yow aunswere very shortly and in the mean tyme for your sake I will promis that Master Yarde[8] shalle have the refusall therof and that better cheape then any elce.

And yeven so wishing yow right welle, I rest your very assured loving frind and kynsman,

W Ralegh[9]

Court the 20th of March

1. No year is given but it was in 1584 that Ralegh began to look for land in the West Country: see below, Letter 13. For evidence that it was not earlier see below, note 9, but see also below, Letter 165, note 30, which points, but without any certainty, to c.1597, as does the reference to Ralegh's familiarity with a resident of Sherborne.
2. 'Master Edward' (1563–1613), of Berry Pomeroy near Totnes, was the grandson of the Protector Somerset. His wife was Elizabeth, daughter of Ralegh's uncle, Sir Arthur Champernon: Vivian, *Devon*, pp. 702–3 and Hasler III, pp. 369–70. He was not created a baronet until 1611.
3. Probably John Lowman, gentleman (ob. 1585), of the parish of Whitstone near Exeter, who was assessed for tax on his landed property there in 1581: Vivian, *Devon*, p. 533, and T.L. Stoate, *Devon Taxes 1581–1660*, Bristol 1988, p. 94. His son and heir was Philip (1561–1617).
4. A John Stocker was Sheriff of Dorset in 1601/2: PRO, *Lists and Indexes*, IX, 1898, p. 39.
5. Possibly a property in Colaton Raleigh where both the Courtenays (see note 6) and the Seymours owned land, as indeed did Ralegh himself: see below, Letter 13, note 7.
6. Of Powderham on the Exe estuary and now the senior line. Sir William (1553–1630) owned extensive landed property across south Devon. He was Sheriff of Devon in 1579/80: PRO, *Lists and Indexes* IX, p. 36.
7. Sandridge, in the parish of Stoke Gabriel on the River Dart, which was part of the ancient Pomeroy lordship now held by the Seymours. For Ralegh's later interest in the property see below, Letter 165, note 30.
8. Possibly George Yarde esq., of Churston Ferrers in south Devon, son and heir of Edward (ob. 1583) but more likely Francis Yarde, gentleman, of Clyst Honiton in east Devon, both being taxed on their land in 1581: Vivian, *Devon*, p. 830 and Stoate, op. cit., pp. 64, 74.
9. Until 1583 Ralegh usually signed his name 'Rauley'. From 1584 he always spelled it 'Ralegh', which helps to date this letter.

---

## 10. TO DR DAVID LEWIS, c.11 APRIL 1584

PRO, HCA 14/22/100. In Ralegh's hand.

C. L'Estrange Ewen, *Times Literary Supplement*, 4 March 1939, p. 136 and *The Golden Challice*, privately printed, Paignton 1939; Quinn, *Gilbert* 1940, II, p. 428 and *New American World*, 1979, IV, p. 112.[1]

## GILBERT'S SHIP

[*addressed*]   To the righte wor[*shipful*] my very good frend Master Doctor Lewis[2]
[*no endorsement*]

Master Lewis ther is a matter between my brother Sir John Gilberd[3] and a Skottisman[4] about a shipp which he [*Gilbert*] now possesseth. First she was taken by a piratt,[5] delivered to the Queens use, praysd [= *valued*] and sold, befor Sir John had her. Aftre ward she was leaft att Newfoundland, [*whome* crossed out] from whence he was att great charge to bringe her home. Then she arived in Cornwall wher she spent her mastes. Besids he hath new built her, so that I thinke he should be very extremly [= *hardly*] dealt withall to have the ship taken from hyme without recumpence, having first bought her by good ordre and, havinnge lost a great ship goinge to Newfoundland, he hath sent her thither with another small barke to save sum part of his charges.

Sir, I pray lett hym have your lawfull favor and yow shall cummand mee in a greatre matter.

       Your very asured frinde,
          W Ralegh[6]

---

1. Annexed to the letter are recognizances from Walsingham to Lewis dated 11 April 1584, printed by Quinn, *Gilbert* 1940, II, p. 429–31.
2. Formerly Judge, now Joint Commissioner, of the High Court of Admiralty, he died on 27 April 1584: *DNB*.
3. Ralegh's elder half-brother (c.1536–96), a pillar of local government, Sheriff in 1573–4, Vice-Admiral of Devon and a deputy-lieutenant, but no seaman: J. Roberts, 'Sir John Gilbert', *DAT* XCI, 1959, pp. 92–106.
4. Presumably her rightful owner: see below, note 5.
5. In fact, John Callice or Callis, a well-known pirate, had taken the *Swallow* of Leith in April 1577 and renamed her the *Golden Challice*. In early June 1583, Sir Humphrey Gilbert (see above, Letter 3, note 7) took her from Callice in the English Channel and included her, without legal formalities, as the *Swallow*, in the fleet he was assembling to sail to Newfoundland. For further details see Quinn, *Gilbert* 1940, I, pp. 83–9. Such claim as he had on her rested on Sir John's inheritance of his childless brother's estate, but ownership was now being sought by one Richard Boyse, who claimed that Sir Humphrey had made over the *Swallow* to him in Newfoundland: Quinn, *Gilbert* 1940. II, pp. 429–30. Ralegh must have known how weak was Sir John Gilbert's case, especially in view of the interest of yet another party, the Crown. The final outcome is not known.
6. See above, Letter 9, note 9.

## 11. To Dr Valentine Dale from the Court, c.1584/5[1]

PRO, SP15/30/125; *CSPD Addenda 1580–1625*, p. 260, Plate 1. Not previously printed *in extenso*. Written by a clerk in a particularly fine hand, with postcript and signature in Ralegh's almost pure italic hand.

### A HELPING HAND

[*addressed*] To my very lovinge freinde Master Doctor Dale[2] of the [*Court of*] Requestes

These be to praye your favor according to justice. That whereas one William Toiker of the citie of Exon [*Exeter*][3] and Barnard Drake esquires[4] have exhibityd a byll to Here Majestie in here most honorable Courte of Requeste[5] against Hugh Wilson of the said citie of Exon,[6] to whom the said Toiker was bounde by obligation to assure and convaye one tenemente in Exon by heme sold to the said Hugh Wilson. By means thereof the said Toiker, beinge not able to performe the same, the said Wilson hath not onlie receavid xx*li* and the profytes of the same which [?*while*] it remayneth in his possession, worthe x*li* above the money he paid for the same, but also prosecuteth (contrary to reason and conscience) against the said Barnard Drake a bande [= *bond*] of a C markes [= £66 6s. 8d.] wherein he stode bounde for the apparance of the said William Toiker in Here Majesties Courte of Common Pleas. But sithence the said William Toiker is dessessed and his wyfe, my poore kindswoman,[7] with many poore children ar, without your helpe, like to be utterlie undonne. The remedye whereof I desire you to be carefull for at my requeste and I will geve you thankes in my poor kindswomans behalf. And in the meane time I comende me to you and you to Gode. From the Courte the [*blank*].

[*subscription crossed out*]

Master Dale I pray favor this cause in what yow may for my sake and I wilbe redy to requot [*sic*] yow in any thinge I may.
  Your very asured frinde
  W. Raleigh[8]

---

1. See notes 2, 3 and 4.
2. Dale was a Master in the Court of Requests from 1576 and died in 1589: Hasler II, pp. 5–6.

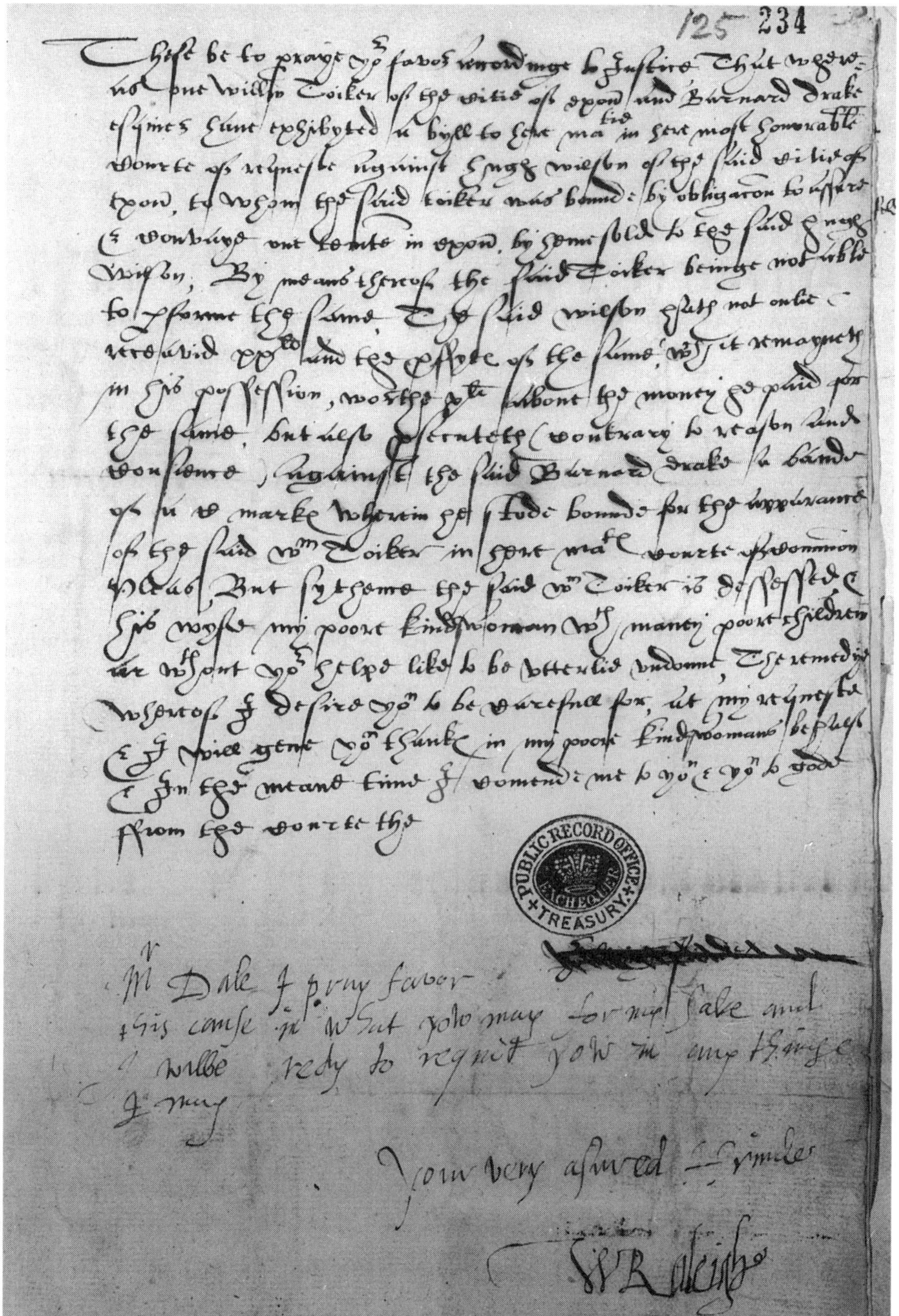

Plate 1. Letter 11: Sir Walter Ralegh to Dr Valentine Dale, c.1584/5.
(PRO, SP15/30/125)

3. One of the sons of Robert Tucker, Mayor of Exeter in 1543–4, William Tucker became a freeman of the city in 1553: M.M. Rowe and A.M. Jackson (eds), *Exeter Freemen 1266–1967*, Exeter 1973, p. 79. According to the evidence presented to the Court of Requests (see note 4) William Tucker died in or after February 1583.
4. Of Ash in Musbury, east Devon, he was a nephew of Joan Drake, first wife of Walter Ralegh senior and hence the writer's step-cousin. Knighted in 1586, he was an energetic and professional oceanic adventurer, hardly an eligible suitor in the Court of Requests, but widow Tucker may have had problems.
5. See PRO, Requests, Proceedings, 58/60.
6. Described as a merchant, having been apprenticed to Robert Hunt, when he was admitted to the freedom of the city in 1562–3: Rowe and Jackson, op. cit., p. 85.
7. Tucker married a Cornish gentlewoman, Honor Erissey, whose mother was Christian Grenville, sister of Sir Richard: Vivian, *Cornwall*, Exeter 1887, pp. 155, 191. Her relationship with Ralegh has not been established. One of the reputedly poor Tucker children, another William, was to become one of the Queen's chaplains and Dean of Lichfield: John Prince, *Worthies of Devon*, 1810 edn, p. 735.
8. See above, Letters 9 and 10. This is the only extant signature (except for those printed on Ralegh's wine licences: see below, Letter 12) to include the letter 'i', which was, and still is, a regular constituent of 'Raleigh' place-names in the South West.

---

## 12. TO DR RICHARD HOWLAND AND OTHERS FROM THE COURT, 9 JULY 1584

Cambridge University Library, University Archives, Lett.9, B20(a). Written by the clerk who wrote Letter 11, with subscription and signature in Ralegh's hand.

Transcript in University Archives, Baker MS 29, Mm.1.40, p. 342.

C.H. Cooper, *Annals of Cambridge*, II, 1843, pp. 399–400, from Baker; Edwards II, pp. 24–5, from Baker, and pp. lxxxi–lxxxiii, revised.

## WINE LICENCES

[*addressed*] To the Worshipfull my Loving Frendes Master Doctor Howland,[1] Vice-Chauncellor of the Unyversitie of Cambridge and others the Maisters of the same

[*endorsed*] Master Raleghes letter concerning Keymer[2]

I comend me to you: Beinge lothe to greyve or discontent you, whome I love and am willinge any waies I maye to pleasure, I have thoughte good to informe you of a late hard part and riotouse demeanor done by some of your unyversytie which I can as yet but take in contempte of Her Majesties graunt to me,³ not dealinge further therby then lawfullie (as I am informed) I maye doe. Yf otherwise the conference offered by my deputeis to one Baxster and others, your late dealers in that cause for the spedie and quyett dissidinge the matter by your learned councell and myne, shold have bene accepted.⁴ The abuse done was sutche as yf I shall not understand of some reformation or correction to be done to the malefactors wherby this barer John Keymer, Her Majesties subjecte lawfullie lycenced by me to sell wynes in your towne, doe quyetlie enjoye the same untill by lawe (that governethe us all) it be otherwyse determyned, I will devyse some other course for reformation herein.

This barers haste awaye (to comforte his poore wife who by violence offered was in case by sondrye soundes and passions [sic] likelie to have died) was suche as tyme served me not to move my verye good lord the Lord Treasurer [Burghley] for his honors letter in reformation hereof which I dowted not to have had, but I do rest asured that yorselves will take suche directe and lawfull corse herein as neyther my selfe nor you, nor anye other that will comaund us, shall have occasion further herein to be trobled, which I hartelie wyshe, not desiringe so fullie and lawfullie to extend Her Majesties graunt in your towne as maye further greve your vynteners, the onlie styrrers herein, respectinge more their gayne then quyett governement. I crave your spedie answere in wrightinge by this barer, for that the unlawfull and riotous partes must not rest unpunyshed.

And so I bidd you all hartelie farwell, from my lodging at the Cort this ixth of Julie 1584.⁵

    Your very asured loving frinde,
        W Ralegh

1. Richard Howland, Vice-Chancellor 1577–8 and 1583–4: J. Venn, *Alumni Cantabrigiensis*, 1921, pt i, vol. 2, p. 419.
2. John Keymer, the bearer of this letter, a vintner of Cambridge who had been licensed by Ralegh to retail wine in accordance with the latter's royal grant of 4 May 1583 of the sole right to license vintners throughout the kingdom: T.N. Brushfield, *DAT* XII, 1909, pp. 182–3.
3. There had been an attempt to take down Keymer's sign which he had resisted with considerable violence: Cooper, *Annals*, p. 405. In June 1584, Howland and the heads of colleges had written to both Burghley and the Earl of Leicester, Chancellor and High Steward, respectively, of the University, requesting them to persuade Ralegh to withdraw his licence to Keymer: BL, Lansd. xli, arts 51 and 52.
4. Ralegh himself, in reply to a letter from the Vice-Chancellor, had suggested that the matter be referred to his counsel and a representative of the University. John Baxter, bedell, had been licensed by the University to sell wines in 1563/4: J. Venn, *Grace Book Delta*, p. 181.
5. See below, Letter 15.

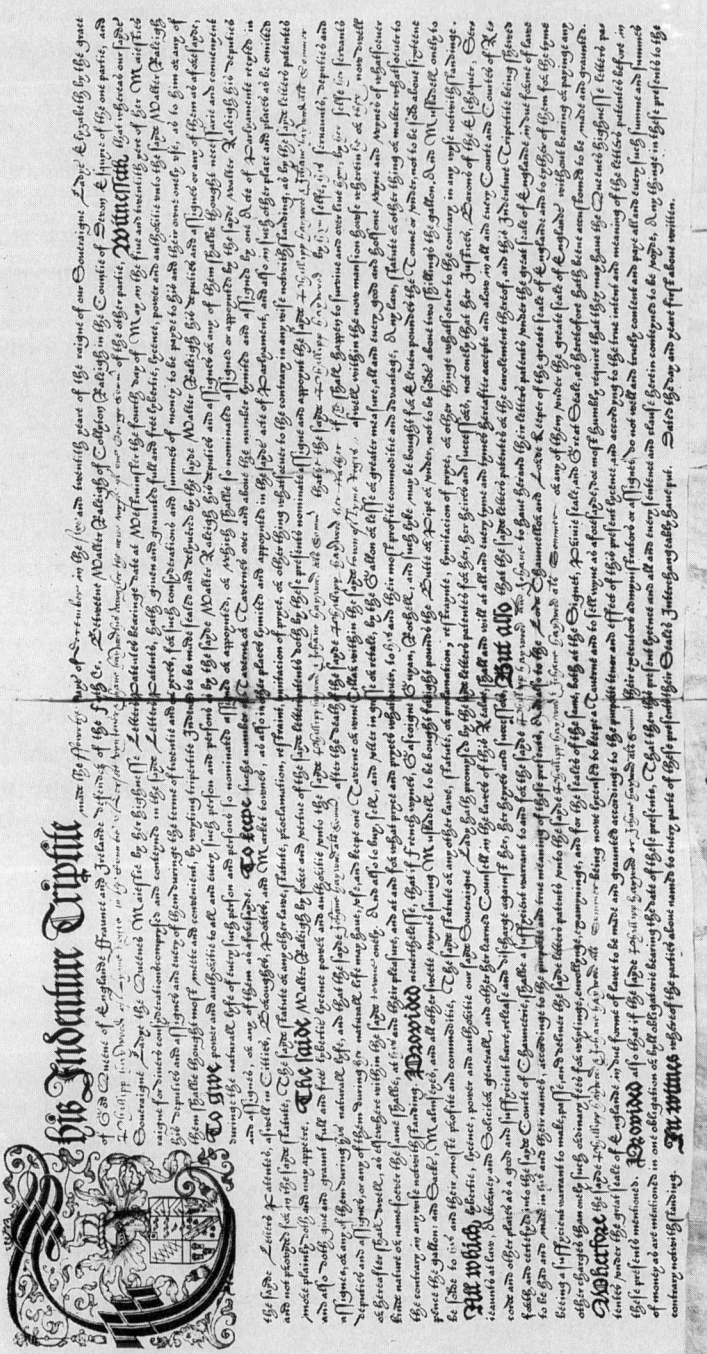

Plate 2. Licence to sell Wines: Walter Raleigh esquire to Phillip Haywood of Lyme Regis and his daughter, Joan Somer, 4 December 1583. Printed on vellum, with hand-written insertions and signed with a stamp. Considerably reduced. (Courtesy of the Raleigh Collection, University of North Carolina at Chapel Hill, N.C.)

THIS INDENTURE TRIPARTITE made the fourth day of December [1583] ... betweene Walter Raleigh of Collyton Raleigh in the countie of Devon, esquire, of the one part and Phillipp Haywood of Lyme Regis in the countie of Dorsett vyntener and Johane Haywood his daughter, the nowe wyfe of one George Somer, of the other part, WITNESSETH THAT WHEREAS ... the Quenes Majestie ... by letters patentes bearing date at Westminster [4 May 1583] ... hath given and graunted full and free libertie, lycence, power and authoritie unto the sayde Walter Raleigh, his deputies and assignes and every of them, duringe the terme of twentie and one yeres, for such considerations and summes of money to be payde to his and their only use, as to him or any of them shalbe thought most meete and convenient ... TO GIVE power and authoritie to all and every such person and persons as by the sayde Walter Raleigh [etc.] ... shalbe thought necessarie and convenient duringe the naturell lyfe of every such person and persons ... TO KEEPE suche number of Taverne or Tavernes over and above the number lymeted and assigned by one Acte of Parlyamene [7 Edward VI, c.5] recyted in the sayde letters patentes, aswell in Cities, Boroughes, Portes and Market Townes, as also in other places lymited and appoynted in the sayde act of parlyament and also in such other place and places as be omitted and not provyded for in the sayd statute ... THE SAIDE Walter Raleigh, by force and vertue of the sayd letters patentes, doth by these presents nominate, assigne and appoynt the sayde Phillipp Haywood and Johanne Haywood alias Somer ... [to] have, use and keepe one Taverne or wine Cellar within the sayde town of Lyme Regis aswell within the now mansion wherein he or they now dwell or hereafter shall dwell as elsewhere in the sayde towne onely. And also to buy, sell and utter in grosse or retcle by the Gallon or greater measure all and every good and holsom wyne and wynes of whatsoever kinde, nature or name soever the same shalbe, at his and theire pleasure and at and for what pryce and pryces whatsoever to his and their most profite, commoditie and advantage, any law, statute or other thing or matter whatsoever in any wise notwithstanding. PROVIDED nevertheless that if French wynes, Gascoigne, Guyan, Rochell and suchlike may be bought for Eleven poundes the tonne or under, not to be solde above sixteene pence the gallon, and Sacke, Malmseyes and other sweete wynes, saving Muskadell, to be bought for eight poundes the Butte or Pipe or under, not to be solde above two shillings the gallon. And Maskadell onely to be solde to his and their moste profite and commoditie ... IN WITNESS whereof the parties above named to every parte of these presentes their Seales interchangeable have put. Dated the day and yeare first above written.

[stamp] W. Raleigh

[signed] by me Phyllyp Haywood

*Transcript of Plate 2.*

## 13. TO MASTER RICHARD DUKE FROM THE COURT, 26 JULY 1584

Devon Record Office, 2850Z/Z3. In Ralegh's hand.

Transcripts in Bodleian, Ballard xi, f. 2 and Aubrey vi, f. 75.[1]

John Aubrey, *Lives of Eminent Men*, ed. P. Bliss and J. Walker, 1813, II, pp. 520–21; Edwards II, p. 26, from Aubrey, parts omitted; T.N. Brushfield, 'The Birthplace of Sir Walter Ralegh', *DAT*, XXI, 1889, pp. 319–20;[2] Joyce Youings, *Ralegh's Country*, Raleigh, N.C., 1986, pp. 5–6, with facsimile.

### REQUEST TO PURCHASE HIS BIRTHPLACE

[*no address*]
[*endorsed in a later hand*] Sir W[alter] Rawleyes letter

Master Duke:[3] I wrate to Master Prideux[4] to move yow for the purchase of Hayes, a farme sumtyme in my fathers possession.[5] I will most willingly geve yow what so ever in your conscience yow shall deeme it worthe, and if yow shall att any tyme have occasion to use mee yow shall find mee a thanckfull frind to yow and youres. I have dealt with Master Sprinte[6] for suche things as he hathe att Colliton[7] and ther aboute and he hathe promised mee to depart with [= *transfer*] the moety of Otertowne[8] unto yow in consideration of Hayes accordinge to the valew, and yow shall not find mee an ill neighbere unto yow here after. I am resolved, if I cannot intreat yow, to build att [Otterton *crossed out*] Colliton, but for the naturall disposition I have to that place [*Hayes*], beinge borne in that howse, I had rather seat my sealf ther then any wher els.[9]

This leving the matter att large to Master Sprint I take my leve, resting redy to countervaile [= *match*] all your courteses to the uttermost of my power. Court the xxvi of July 1584.

    Your very willing frinde in all I shalbe able,
        W Ralegh

---

1. Carries a note by Aubrey that he thinks he sent the original letter to Anthony Wood. Early in the present century it was in the Royal Albert Memorial Museum at Exeter.
2. Prints the three previous versions and his own.
3. Richard Duke of Otterton, Devon (ob. 1607), son of John, younger brother and heir of Richard (ob. 1572), Clerk of the Court of Augmentations t. Henry VIII and purchaser of much former monastic property in east Devon: Vivian, *Devon*, p. 311, Joyce Youings (ed.), *Devon Monastic Lands*, Devon and Cornwall Record Society, New Series I, 1955, pp. 7, 29, 31–2 and 78.
4. Probably Edmund Prideaux esquire of Netherton in Farway parish in east Devon, like Ralegh he had been at the Inner Temple and was now a practising lawyer: Vivian, *Devon*, p. 621.

5. The manor of Hayes in the east Devon parish of East Budleigh had come to the Dukes, who earlier in the century were Exeter merchants, by marriage with an heiress. The home farm had been leased to Walter Ralegh senior and his first wife, Joan, who died about 1530, and in 1551 the tenancy had been renewed for a term of 80 years or their lives to Walter senior and his second son, John: DRO, Rolle MSS, 96M/Box 32/bundle 10.
6. Gregory Sprente of Templecombe, Somerset, son-in-law of Richard Duke senior. His wife, Christianne, née Duke, was the widow of George Brooke younger son of the 9th Lord Cobham: Vivian, *Devon*, p. 311 and Hasler III, p. 428.
7. Colaton Raleigh in east Devon, where Ralegh's father (Walter senior, ob. 1581) had owned a small ancestral estate: PRO, Chancery, Inquisitions post-mortem, 194, 2. Ralegh himself had acquired an even smaller property in the parish called Hawkerland which had formerly belonged to Dunkeswell Abbey: Youings, op. cit., p. 118 and R. Polwhele, *History of Devonshire*, 1797, p. 224. It was his only freehold property at this time and he described himself, for example in his wine licences, as 'of Colaton Raleigh' (see above, Letter 12, note 2 and Plate 2.) though there is no evidence that he ever resided in the parish or pursued his intention of building a house there. According to Sir William Pole (*Collections towards a history of Devon*, 1791, pp. 162–3) he sold the property in 1589, but he was still reputed to be the owner of 'the manor of Colaton Raleigh' in 1609: Hutchins, *Dorset* IV, pp. 216–17.
8. It is not known how Sprente had acquired half of the former Syon Abbey manor of Otterton, the whole of which had been granted by Henry VIII in 1540 to Richard Duke senior: Youings, op. cit., p. 7. Was it perhaps Christianne's dowry?
9. He did not succeed in his ambitions. His father's lease of 1551 substantiates Ralegh's claim to have been born in the house later known as Hayes Barton, but it was never owned by the Raleghs. In the mid-1560s, when Walter junior was still in his early teens, his parents had moved into Exeter where the then Sir Walter's widowed mother, the redoubtable former Lady Katherine Gilbert, née Champernon, died in 1594: A.J. Howard and T.L. Stoate (eds), *The Devon Muster Roll for 1569*, 1977, p. 246 and T.N. Brushfield, *DAT* XXVIII, 1896, pp. 272. John Ralegh died in 1588: DRO, Wolborough Parish Register. The present house at Hayes dates almost entirely from the early seventeenth century and bears little resemblance to the modest farmhouse which Ralegh coveted and would, no doubt, have enlarged or rebuilt if Master Duke had been prepared to sell.

---

14. TO SIR EDWARD STRADLING FROM THE COURT, 26 SEPTEMBER 1584

BL, Add. 28852, f. 63 v., a contemporary transcript in a letter-book.

J.M. Traherne (ed.), *Stradling Correspondence*, 1840, pp. 22–3.

## A WELSH MARRIAGE

[*addressed*]   To the R[ight] Worshipful Sir Edward Stradlinge knighte[1]

Sir Edward: Her Majestye hath nowe thrise caused letters to be written unto you that you suffer not my kinsewoman[2] to be bought and sold in Wales without Her Majesties pryvetye and the consent or advise of my Lord Chamberlayne (Hunsdon) and my selfe, her father's cosen germayns, consideringe that she hath not anie nirer kyn nor better. Her father and my selfe came of twoe systers, Sir Philipp Champernowne[s] daughters.[3] I doubte not but, all other perswasion sett aparte, you will satisfie Her Highnes and withall do us that curtesie as to acquaint us with her matchinge, yf you desire anie matche for her of youre owne kynn.[4] Yf you acqaynt us withall you shall fynde us ready to yeilde to anie reason. I hope, Sir, you will deale heerein most advisedlie and heerin you shall ever fynde us redye to requite you in all thinges to our power.[5]

And soe with my verie hartye comendations I end. In haste from the Courte, the xxvith of September 1584.

Youre moste willinge frend,

W Ralegh

1. Of St Donat's, Glamorgan, ob. 1609: Traherne, op. cit., pp. x–xii.
2. Barbara Gamage, aged 22, granddaughter and heiress of Robert Gamage of Coity, Glamorgan, whose son, also Robert, had died on 8 September 1584.
3. Barbara's mother was Joan, sister of Ralegh's mother, Katherine, née Champernon. Gamage was Joan's second husband.
4. One of Barbara's great aunts, Catherine Gamage, had been the first wife of Sir Thomas Stradling and it was his son, Sir Edward, her uncle by marriage, who was the recipient of this letter. On 20 September 1584, Sir Francis Walsingham had written to Stradling ordering him to bring the young heiress to Court where she would be in the custody of the Lord Chamberlain, Henry Carey, Lord Hunsdon, the mother of whose son-in-law (Charles Howard) was a sister of Sir Robert Gamage: Traherne, pp. 27–8.
5. However, Walsingham wrote again the next day, in a milder tone, saying that he had heard confidentially that Barbara was to marry Robert Sidney, younger brother of Sir Philip, which match the Queen would 'noe waye miselike thereof', and that 'the Lord Chamberlaine, Master Rawley and the rest of the younge gentlewoman's kynsfolkes doe greatly desyre yt'. Barbara was married to Robert Sidney on 23 September, two hours before Walsingham's second letter arrived: Traherne, op. cit., pp. 19, 27–30. In fact, as Burghley pointed out in a letter of 24 September, Barbara was of age and could marry whom she wished (BL, Lansd. 102, f. 213), so Ralegh's reference to her being 'bought and solde', as if she was a ward, was quite uncalled for.

## 15. To Robert Norgate from the Court, 10 February 1585

Cambridge University Library, University Archives, Lett.9, B20(b), Written by a clerk, with subscription and signature in Ralegh's hand.

Transcript in University Archives, Baker MS 29, Mm.1.40, p. 341.

C.H. Cooper, *Annals of Cambridge*, II, 1843, p. 404, from Baker; Edwards II, pp. 27–8 and, corrected from Baker, pp. lxxxiii–lxxxiv.

# WINE LICENCES

[*addressed*]  To my lovinge frend Master Vycechaunceller[1] and the reste of the Maysters of the Unyversytie of Cambridge

[*endorsed*]  for Keymer   x° February 1584   Sir Walter Ralegh[2] to the vice chancelor and heds of the howses in Cambrige   Keymer

Master Vyce Chauncellor: beinge (by information) perswaded that your selfe, with the grave and well disposed of your universitie, were so greved with the unseamelye owtrages latelie comytted by the yonge and unbridled heddes of the same, in contempte of the Quenes Majesties prerogatyve and graunt unto me and to my discredytt. As suffycyent order by you had ben taken for this bearers[3] quyett, which caused me to reste from requyringe reformation therin at my verye good Lord Threasurers [*Burghley's*] handes, who (by me) as yet understandeth not of those ryottes.[4] And I did forbare, contrarye to the advyse of my learned councell, in procedinge to enquyer by lawe of the same ryottes of good will I beare to your universitie. And [I] ment so to deale with you for the other foure tavernes,[5] as sholde have suffycyentlie contented you. But my to favorable dealinge with you hathe geven suche encorage as this daie, I am informed, you have warned this barer to appeare before you, whose willes therin I have willed hym to performe.[6] And I am further informed you mynd to disturbe hym ageyne from usinge his honeste and lawfull trade of wynesellinge, aucthorysed therunto by the Quenes Majesties graunt under the Great Seale of Ingland. And althoughe I knowe you not, yet your place sholde tell me that your prosedinges wilbe with hym juste and laufull, which onlye I desyer of you. So yow shall pleasure your selves and contynewe my redynes to do you anye good I maye. I hope uppon your answere I shall fynd thes informations to growe rather uppon jelosey then juste matter.

So I leave you to God, from the Cort at Somersett Howse this xth of February 1584

    Your very willing frind,
      W Ralegh

1. Robert Norgate, Master of Corpus Christi, 1573–87, Vice-Chancellor 1584–5: J. Venn, *Alumni Cantabrigiensis*, pt I, iii, 1924, p. 263.
2. Ralegh was knighted in January 1585.
3. John Keymer, whom Ralegh had licensed to sell wine in Cambridge without consulting the University authorities: see above, Letter 12.
4. The 'riots' of 1584: see above, Letter 12.
5. Those kept by John Baxter, Philip Scarlet, John Cutbard and Thomas Ventris, though the last of these had lost his licence in 1581: J. Venn, *Grace Book Delta*, pp. 181, 240, 248, 345.

6. In fact, on 19 February 1585, Keymer was jailed for resisting the writ. He was released on 2 December 1586 with a prohibition against selling wine in Cambridge: Cooper, *Annals*, V, p. 6.

---

## 16. To Robert Norgate and Others from the Court, 20 February 1585

Cambridge University Library, University Archives, Lett.9, B20(c). In Ralegh's hand, in great haste.

Transcript in University Archives, Baker MS 29, Mm.1.40, pp. 342–3.

C.H. Cooper, *Annals of Cambridge*, 1843, p. 405, from Baker; Edwards II, pp. 28–9 and, corrected from Baker, p. lxxxiv; N. Lloyd Williams, op. cit., 1962, p. 64, from Edwards, spelling modernized and with minor errors.

### WINE LICENCES

[*addressed*]  To the Vycechauncellor and the reste of the maysters of the Unyversytie of Cambridge

[*endorsed*]  Sir W. Raleighes letter xx° February 1584, the originall  Sir Walter Raighles letter concerninge the sellinge of wine in anno 1584

I cannot a litle marvaile att your peremtory and proud mannner of delinge. I was content to use all manner of curtesy towards yow in respect of my Lord Tresorer, my honorable good lorde, but I parceve that my reasonable or rather to submis[*sive*] deling hath bread in yow a proceding unsufferable. Yow have cummitted a poor man to the prison[1] having don nothing but warranted by the Great Seal of Ingland, your sealvs supposing a priveledge by charter.[2] I do not know that any man, or any men or society, would take so mich uppon them before triall made. But as I reverence the place of whence yow ar the governors so I will not willingly take any wrong or disgrace from yow. And I am asured my Lord Tresorer, who may command mee mich, wilbe indifferent in this case, for the matter so mich concerneth the validety of my patent elswher as well as in your uneversety as I will try the uttermost of my right as well for this one, which I was content to be satisfied withall, as for all the other foure.[3]

And so having thought yow would have vouchsafed an awnswere of my last letters I end.[4] Court this xxth of Febriary 1584,

       Your frind as yow shall geve cause,
          W Ralegh

1. See above, Letter 15, note 6.
2. Probably a reference to the Statute of 7 Edward VI, c.5 (1552–3) 'to avoyde the greate price and excesse of Wynes' which recognized the privileges of the two universities.
3. Ralegh had licensed four other Cambridge vintners: see above, Letter 15, note 5.
4. The Vice-Chancellor replied on 28 February following, reproving Ralegh as a gentleman, a scholar and a courtier for his discourteous language: Cooper, *Annals*, II, 406 and also W. Oldys in *Works* 1829, p. 62. On 26 July 1585 Burghley supplied a statement by Christopher Wraye and Edmund Anderson, Chief Justices of the Queen's Bench, declaring the privileges of the University to be lawful: T.N. Brushfield, 'Ralegh Miscellanea', *DAT* XLI, 1909, p. 209. Ralegh had met more than his match, but a year later, according to a letter from the Vice-Chancellor to Burghley, he was behind Keymer and other University vintners in a case in the Exchequer against overcharging: Cooper, *Annals*, p. 421.

---

## 17. TO THE PRIVY COUNCIL (WITH SIR THOMAS HENEAGE), 7 MAY 1585

PRO, SP12/178/78, *CSPD 1581–90*, p. 243. Written by a clerk, in a formal set hand, with signatures of Heneage and Ralegh.

Edwards II, pp. 30–31.

## A CAPTIVE IN BARBARY

[*addressed*] To the righte honorable and oure verie good lordes the Lordes of Hir Majestes most honorable Pryvie Counsell
[*endorsed*]  i. May 1585 d.7. From Sir Thomas Henneag¹ and Sir Walter Ralegh.
 ii. What they have donn in the matter between Morgan Powell² and Jones³ abowt the money paid for the redeminge of a captive in Barbary⁴

It maie please your good lordships: Accordinge to your Lordships pleasures dyrected unto us from your honorable lordships and others of Hir Majestes most honorable Pryvie Counsell upon a complainte exhibited by this bearer Morgan Powell, we called before us the parties to whome the cause doth apperteyne. And upon twyce hearinge therof and what was produced by the learned councell of both sides, and also themselves, we conceyve the matter to stande even as it is sett downe in a paper hereinclosed.⁵ And we fynde the hardenes of the case to consist in this: that the iiij$^{xx}$v$li$ sent by this compl[ainant] unto John Owen[6] accordinge to the direction of the Lord Maior[7] to be payde to William Symcotes[8] for the captyves ransom was, by the procurement of the said Lord Maior, attached in the name of Johnes in the handes of the said Owen as the goodes of one Jon Symcottes deceased,[9] for that the said Johnes as it appearith was then indebted to the Lord Maior, by which devise the said iiij$^{xx}$v$li$ so sent by this compl[ainant] for the captyves ransom is comm to the handes of the said Lord Maior for the answeringe of the said Johnes his debt. Wherby (as we take it) this compl[ainant] is muche wronged. In trothe it hath directlie been approved before us that the captyve was redeemed by William Symcottes goodes and that the byls of exchange thereupon made by the captyve in Barbary were to the use of the said William Symcottes. And therfore it seemith strange unto us and ageinst all equitie that this compl[ainants] money shold (to any other purpose[)] be deteyned. We also fynde that the saide William Simcotes hath recovered against the said captyve in Hir Majestes Courte of Common [Pleas][10] at Westminster his whole somme of iiij$^{xx}$v$li$ for the ransom and x$li$ for damages besides, so that both the captyve and this compl[ainant] are lykely to be twice charged for the satisfaction of one debt, unlest your lordships take order to the contrary. We had ordered and ended the matter to the satisfaction of all parties and to the hinderance only of William Symcotes (but with his consent) save that the Lord Maior refused it and referred himself and the cawse to your lordships consideration, to whom we humblie commende us.

    Your lordships humble at comaundment,

      T: Heneage     W Ralegh

1. Of the Queen's Privy Chamber, the later Vice-Chamberlain: *DNB*.
2. Presumably a Welshman.
3. Almost certainly the Nicholas Jones of Weymouth who was a well-known privateer and also captain of Portland Castle under Ralegh: Andrews 1964, pp. 142–3 and *APC XXIII*, p. 68.
4. Thomas Powell, William's brother, and Peter Williams had been taken captive in Barbary in 1581, but the former only was redeemed: see note 5. At this time there was a brisk trade with 'Barbary', i.e. the coast of North Africa, especially Morocco, where sugar and gum were traded for English (and Welsh) cloth and firearms: T.S. Willan, *Studies in Elizabethan Foreign Trade*, Manchester 1959, chapter IV.
5. A statement, signed by Heneage and Ralegh, of the complicated financial details of the case, from which notes 6–8 have been derived. For the full text see Edwards II, pp. 31–2.
6. Of London, linen draper.
7. Alderman Pulison.
8. Not identified.
9. Brother of William.
10. Manuscript torn.

18. TO JOHN SOTHERTON FROM THE COURT,
    9 MAY 1585

    PRO, SP46/33/f.268a. Written by a clerk, with subscription and signature in Ralegh's hand. Not previously printed.

## A COURTEOUS REQUEST

[*addressed*] To his very lovinge freind Master Sowtherton, one of Her Majesties Barrons of Thexchequeur these [*to*] be delivered
[*no endorsement*]

After my hartye comendatiouns etc, havinge occasion to use your freindshippe in a matter that dothe concerne Her Majesty and myselfe, wherin some examination must be had,[1] I have sent unto you by this my servaunt[2] certaine interrogatories and doe by these fewe earnestlye entreate that you would take the paines therupon to examyne suche persons as may or shalbe produced on the parte and behalfe of Her Heighnes. And what you doe therin in favoure shalbe accepted of me in most thankful manner to move requitall on my parte in a greater matter.

Thus ceasinge I committe you to God, from the Courte the ix$^{th}$ of Maye 1585.

  Your very asured lovinge frinde,
    W Ralegh

1. Presumably connected with Ralegh's lease of the Alnage of Woollen Cloth in Yorkshire: see below, Letter 19.
2. Dalyson [?Dallison]: see Letter 19.

---

19. TO JOHN SOTHERTON FROM THE COURT,
    1 JANUARY 1586

    PRO, SP46/34/f.1. Written by a clerk, with subscription and signature in Ralegh's hand. Not previously published.

## CLOTH DUES IN YORKSHIRE

[*addressed*] To his very lovinge freind Master Sowtherton, one of Her Majesties Barrons of Thexchequer d[?*elive*]r these
[*endorsed*] 1 January 1585/6

After my heartye commendatiouns, havinge occasion to use your freindshippe as heartofore in a matter that dothe concerne Her Majestie and myselfe touchinge the Alneage[1] of Yorkeshier, wherin some further examination must be had, I have sent unto you by Dalyson my man certaine interrogatoryes[2] that therupon you would att my entreatye proceede to the examynation of such persons as may or shalbe produced for Her Heighnes. For your great paines alreadye taken I yeilde you due thankes and shall thinke my selfe so much the more beholden yf that I maye entreate your further trouble herein.

And so I leave you, from the Courte the first of Januarye 1585

Your asured frinde to requit you in all I can,

W Ralegh

1. The alnage, also known as the 'ulnage', was the ancient levy payable, with some exemptions, to the Crown or its assigns on all woollen cloths put up for sale. It was by now regularly farmed, and presumably Ralegh, the date of whose grant is unknown (H. Heaton, *Yorkshire Woollen and Worsted Industries*, Oxford 1965 edn, p. 178), was hoping to lean on the Exchequer to establish his claims on certain clothiers. What profit he made is nowhere revealed, but the fact that he never included it in his lost 'estate' in and after about 1603 may be significant.
2. Missing.

---

### 20. TO THE EARL OF LEICESTER FROM THE COURT, 29 MARCH 1586

BL, Harl. 6994, f. 2. In Ralegh's hand.

Cayley 1806, I, pp. 84–5, in modern spelling; *Works* 1829, XIII, pp. 654–5, from Cayley; Tytler 1839; Edwards II, pp. 33–4; G.F. Warner, *Facsimiles of Royal ... Autographs ... in the British Museum*, 3rd Series, 1898, no. 6; Lloyd Williams, op. cit., 1962, p. 72, from Edwards, spelling modernized.

## IN SEARCH OF A FRIEND?

[*addressed*] To the right honorable my singuler good lord the earle of Lester, Governour of the Low Countres for Her Majesty
[*endorsed*] 29 Martii Sir W. Rawlegh

My very good Lorde: Yow wrate unto me in your laste letters for pioners to be sent over,[1] wher uppon I moved Her Majestye and found her very willing in so mich as order was geven for a cummission, but since the matter is stayd, I know not for what cause.[2] Also according as your lordshipe desired I spake for on Jukes for the office of the Back Howse

[= *Bakehouse*], and the matter well liked.³ In ought elce your lordshipe shall finde me most asured to my poure [= *power*] to performe all offices of love, honor and service towards yow.

But I have byn of late very pestilent reported in this place to be rather a drawer bake then a fartherer of the action wher yow govern.⁴ Your lordshipe doth well understand my affection [= *feelings*] towards Spayn and how I have consumed the best part of my fortune hating the tirranus sprosperety [*sic*] of that estate⁵ and it were now strange and monnsterous that I should becum an enemy to my countrey and conscience. But all that I have desired att your lordships hands is that yow will evermore deal directly with mee in all matters of suspect dubleness, and so ever esteme mee as yow shall find my deserving good or bad.

In the mean tyme I humble beseich yow lett no poeticall scrib⁶ worke your lordshipe by ony device to doubt that I am a hollo or could sarvant to the action, or a mean wellwiller and follower of your own.

And yeven so I humble take my leve, wishing yow all honor and prosperety. From the Courte the xxix of March 1586.
    Your lordships to do yow service,
      W Ralegh

The Queen is in very good tearms with yow and, thank be to God, well pacified and yow ar agayne her sweet Robyn.

1. On 3 February 1586, Leicester informed Burghley that he had asked Ralegh for one thousand 'pioneers', i.e. sappers, of whom one hundred should be miners, and that he had written to Ralegh asking him to find them 'out of his jurisdiction in Cornwall and Devon': J. Bruce (ed.), *Correspondence of the earl of Leicester from the Low Countries*, Camden Society, XXVII, 1844, p. 86. Ralegh alone was empowered, as Lord Warden of the Stannaries, to enlist the tin-miners.
2. As always, the root cause was financial: J. Neale, 'Elizabeth and the Netherlands 1586–7', *EHR*, XLV, 1930, pp. 373–96. A warrant was issued to Ralegh in April to find one hundred tinners for the Low Countries (Murdin 1759, p. 784) and on 11 May the Council ordered him to have them embarked: *APC* XIV, p. 102). However, on 31 May Leicester was still reporting that Ralegh had written to say that one hundred miners were 'ready to come': Bruce, op. cit., p. 285.
3. Leicester had asked Ralegh to recommend one Edward Jukes, a yeoman 'garritor', i.e. watchman, as Sergeant of the Bakehouse. He later gave way to a nominee of Nicholas Gorges, but Jukes obtained the post: *CSPD Foreign* XXI, pt ii, p. 28, BL, Lansd. 69, f. 154v. and *CSPD Addenda 1580–1625*, p. 526.
4. On 1 April 1586, Walsingham informed Leicester that the Queen had called on him to deny that Ralegh had been 'an yll inst[*rument*] towardes her agaynst' Leicester: Bruce, op. cit., p. 207. Was Ralegh hinting that he did not support the Queen's misliking of Leicester's acceptance of the title of Governor?
5. A reference, no doubt, to the Virginia voyages of 1584/5.
6. Probably a code-name for Walsingham, implying that he had a persuasive tongue.

21. TO SIR WILLIAM MORE,
    [?EARLY 1586]¹

Folger, L.b.37, from the More-Molyneux papers formerly at Loseley Hall, Surrey, *HMC 7th Report*, Appendix I (Molyneux), p. 665, incomplete. Written by a clerk, with subscription and signature in Ralegh's hand. Not previously published in full.

## FOR AN ITALIAN FENCING MASTER

[*addressed*]   To my very lovinge frende Sir William More, knight²
[*endorsed*]   Signor Rocco built houses on Master More's ground
                                                            Blackfriers

Sir: My hartie comendations remembred, understandinge by the bearer hereof, Signior [*sic*] Rocco,³ that he hathe bestowed all his wealthe in buyldinge certayne howses upon your ground⁴ without your consent and therby is endetted unto dyvers and sondrye persons in the somme of two hundrethe poundes, by reason wherof he hathe byn constrayned [? *in prison*] by the space of one halfe yere heretofore, aswell as at this present is to kepe his house as prysoner, to his utter undoinge. And farther understandinge the matter hathe byn labored by certayne honeste gentilmen⁵ to desire you to graunte him some reasonable tyme to countervayle his charges, at whoes entreatye of your owne free will you graunted him seven yeres more to the smale number whiche he hathe alreadye. These are in his behalfe to desire yow, the rather at my requeste, to consider his poore estate, to bestowe fower or fyve yeres more to those seven yeres already graunted, and in so doenge you shall not onlye requeste the lyke at my handes but I take it shall do God good service, being not desirous to be enryched withe the utter undoenge of a pore stranger. And he therby shalbe releeved and accordynge to his trewe and honest meanynge [= *intention*] discharge those creditors to whome he is endetted by reasone of the same.

   Thus muche beinge boulde to troble you for that I have a verye good opinion of the poore gentilman, whose honeste behaviour and singuler good qualities deservethe great comendation. [*about 10 words crossed out*] ... I comytt yow to Thalmightye.
           Your very lovinge frinde,
                 W Ralegh

1. See below, note 5.
2. (1520–1600) of Loseley Hall, Surrey, Sheriff in 1579–80.
3. Rocco Bonetti, a fashionable Italian fencing master whose success in teaching the new style of

duelling, with rapier and dagger, made him unpopular with his English competitors. He died c.1590. G. Silver, *Paradoxes of Defence*, 1599, pp. 64–72.

4. Sir William More owned property in the liberty of Blackfriars, a part of London much favoured for fencing and dancing, tennis and, of course, theatres. More had apparently promised Bonetti a longer lease but changed his mind when the Italian ran into debt for his buildings.

5. Lord Peregrine Willoughby and Sir John North between July 1584 and January 1586. More had extended Bonetti's lease of the old Butler's Lodging by ten years in March 1585. Other correspondence on the subject in the Loseley papers (A.J. Kempe (ed.), *Loseley Manuscripts*, 1835, *passim*) comes to an end in January 1586. As Ralegh refers to a 7-year extension already having been made, a date for his letter after that is surely indicated, possibly though unlikely, as late as 1589/90.

---

## 22. TO SIR JOHN GILBERT FROM THE COURT, 25 MAY 1586

BL, Sloane 1519, f. 139; PRO, SP9/55/12, an eighteenth-century transcript of a missing original. In Ralegh's worst hand, presumably in great haste.

Edwards II, pp. 34–5; Greg 1932, plate LXXV, with full transcript.

## VICTUALLING A SHIP

[*addressed*]   To my loving brother Sir John Gilbert knight
[*endorsed by Gilbert*]   Sir Walter Rylly [*sic*][1] For the cownte [*sic*] of the Admyralty and for provysyons for hys shyppes
   25 May 1586 for the acownte off the Admyralty and for the provyssyon for his barkes

Good brother: Lett the bread which was left of my cussen Chydles[2] proportion be in redines, for my barks[3] ar cumming about for hit and the sider [= *cider*] which I wrat to yow for.[4] My Lord Admiralls Judg[5] calleth out for accompt[6] and says I shall forfet my office.[7] If any s[*hip*]s[8] will go to Newfonland in consort [= *convoy*] to [?*take*] Spanierds wee will sett out sume from hence and go together.[9] I pray inquire of the hoers [? = *huers, lookouts for pilchards*].
   From the Curt the 25 of May, your most asured loving brother,
      W Ralegh

1. Spelling peculiar to Gilbert: see also Letters 39, 42 and 43.
2. John Chudleigh, gentleman (1565–89), of Ashton, Devon, Gilbert's brother-in-law. Still barely 22 years old, he was an ambitious, if somewhat foolhardy seafarer, who nevertheless found

time in 1586 to sit with Sir Walter Ralegh in Parliament as knight of the shire for Devon. He died in 1589/90 while on a voyage of circumnavigation: Hasler I, p. 608 and Andrews 1964, pp. 67–9.
3. In June 1586, Ralegh sent out from Plymouth two privateers, the *Serpent* and the *Mary Sparke*, under the command of Captain Jacob Whiddon: R.C. Anderson (ed.), *Book of Examinations*, Southampton Record Society xxvi, 1926, p. xxxi.
4. No such letter has survived.
5. Dr Julius Caesar, appointed 1584.
6. Gilbert had seized wine from a French ship to supply Ralegh's privateers, but although it was decreed by the High Court of Admiralty to be no lawful prize, Ralegh refused to pay for it. The Council ordered payment or restitution but he claimed right of reprisal for one of his ships seized in Brittany: *CSP Foreign* XX, pp. 584 and 698, XXI, pt i, pp. 33, 65 and Quinn, *Roanoke* 1955, I, pp. 474–5.
7. Presumably his Vice-Admiralty of Devon and Cornwall. His wardenship of the Stannaries can hardly have been affected and he did not become Captain of the Queen's Guard until early in 1587.
8. The manuscript is torn.
9. In June 1585, Ralegh had contributed his ship, the *Job*, to a fleet led by his cousin Bernard Drake and his brother Carew Ralegh, which had taken several Spanish ships off Newfoundland. Gilbert and Drake were appointed to distribute the profits and were said to have appropriated the greater part for themselves. Ralegh seems, nevertheless, to have been eager to be involved in any further such enterprises, the first overt English acts in the war with Spain: *CSPD 1581–90*, pp. 246, 273, *APC* XVII, pp. 283–4 and 412.

## 23. TO THE EARL OF LEICESTER FROM WINDSOR, 8 OCTOBER [1586][1]

Bodleian, Tanner 79, f. 117. In Ralegh's hand.[2]
Edwards II, p. 35, dated 1587, with facsimile as frontispiece.

### FOR SIR FRANCIS DRAKE

*[no address or subscription]*[3]

My very good lord: With mich ado I procured Her Majesties leve for Sir Francis to visitt your excelency *[in the Netherlands]*, which I would most willingly have donn my sealf wear it possible, but wher soever I remayn none shall be more redy to serve your excelency then my sealf. Sir Francis is in good hope to return for the Indies if it may be brought to pass.[4] I doubt not but all shalbe recumpenced.[5] I hope your excelency will assist what yow may. Hyme sealf can deliver best the estate of all things here.

And so with my humble dewty I kiss your hande.[6]
   From Windsor this 8 of October, your excelences to serve yow,
     W Ralegh

1. See note 3.
2. In a very hasty scrawl such as Ralegh rarely used when writing to a social superior.
3. There is a near-contemporary note added in the bottom left-hand corner of the manuscript giving the year as 1587, which Edwards accepted, although internal evidence points clearly to 1586: see below, note 4.
4. Drake had returned on 27/28 July from a voyage to the Indies, bringing with him most of Ralegh's Virginian colonists: D.B. Quinn, *Set Fair for Roanoke*, North Carolina 1985, pp. 138–9.
5. Possibly a reference to Drake's recent voyage which had so far brought little joy to the investors: M.F. Keeler (ed.), *Sir Francis Drake's West Indian Voyage 1585–6*, Hakluyt Society, series 2, 148, 1981, p. 41.
6. It would no doubt have suited Ralegh to have had a continuing English naval presence off the North American coast.

---

## 24. To Sir Walter Mildmay from the Court, 25 November 1586

PRO, SP46/34/f.107. Written by a clerk, with subscription and signature in Ralegh's hand. Not previously published.

### ON BEHALF OF A DEVONSHIRE GENTLEMAN

[*addressed*] To the ryghte honorable Sir Walter Mildmaie knighte,[1] Chawncellor of Her Majesties Courte of Eschequer
[*no endorsements*]

Maie it please your honor, these ar to desire your favour in the behalfe of the bearer heerof, Master George Evelegh: that wheras his father, latelie deceased, was Collector for the Subsedie of the East Division in the cowntie of Devon, his whole charge amowntinge to ix$^c$*li* [= £900],[2] parte wherof was collected in his fathers lyfe and the greatest parte remaininge yet in the petie collectors and others handes, neverthelesse, as I am geven to understande, the younge gentleman[3] sithence his fathers deathe hathe paide into Her Majesties Exchequer this terme fowre hundred*li*. And for that the residew of the saide monie cannot so speedelie bee collected and browghte in, as the partie desirethe, my request unto your honor is that he maie finde suche favour that suddenlie he maie not bee proceeded against by proces [*of law*] but that reasonable time maie bee geven to collecte and make accompte for the same, and I shalbe heerafter reddie to deserve your honors goodnes to him in this behalfe extended.

Thus most humblie I take my leave, Cowrte this xxv of November 1586.

Your honors to do yow service,

W Ralegh

1. (c.1523–89) of Apethorpe, Northants, Chancellor of the Exchequer since 1559: Hasler III, pp. 53–6.
2. In 1581, the last occasion before the date of this letter when a parliamentary subsidy was levied, one John Eveleigh esq. was named as High Collector for the hundreds of Axminster, Colyton and seven others, his total liability being £560 1s. 4d.: T.L. Stoate, *Devon Taxes 1581–1660*, Bristol 1988, p. 1. He was far from poor, his personal liability as the second richest inhabitant of Ottery St Mary was based on a notional income from land of £20: ibid., p. 77.
3. George was his eldest surviving son (Vivian, *Devon*, p. 336) and he and Ralegh had been contemporaries at the Inner Temple: H.A.C. Sturgess, *Register of Admissions at the Inner Temple*, 1949, sub 1574–5.

---

## 25. To Dr Roger Hovenden from the Court, 15 August 1587

All Souls College, Oxford, Appeals and Injunctions IV, 76. Written by a clerk, with subscription and signature in Ralegh's hand.

C.R.L. Fletcher (ed.), *Collectanea* I, Oxford Historical Society, V, 1885, pp. 202–3.

## COLLEGE LEASE

[*addressed*]  To the worshipful my very good frind Master Doctor Hovenden, Warden of Alle Soulne College, gyve this
[*endorsed*]  Sir W Raughlies letter

Master Hovenden: Whereas yt pleased Her Majestie to wryte her gracious letters to your colleadge in the behalfe of my lady Stafforde[1] for a lease of your woods in Mydd[*lesex*] which you goe aboute to denye [*her*], alleaginge a few vayne reasons for your excuse, which beinge by Her Majestie comytted to the examynation of my Lord Treasorer [*Burghley*] are founde by his judgment to be very fryvelous and of no suffyciency to ground your undutiful refusall of Her Highnes request. Her Majestie, advertised thereof, greately disdayned to wryte twyse to subjects of your qualytie for a matter so reasonable and therfore willed my lord to admonych you that you shold presently [= *at once*] performe the contents of her former letters, or awnswere to the contrary here in your owne person.

I thought good therfore to advise you to have dew regard of your duty herein, for howsoever the company escape, the burden of this contempt wyll light uppon you. And I and other of my lad[*y's*] frends and kindsfolks that are neare about Her Majestie must prosecute yt to the uttermost of oure powers. Yeat because I have bene in som sorte beholdinge unto you, and ever redy to doe you good, I wold wyshe you shold doe that willingly which (beinge so reasonable a motion) you wilbe inforsed to yeald unto, and assure yourself that I and other of my lad[y's] frends will bothe excuse you for that ys don and be alwaies willinge to further your preferment in anny thinge we may, in such sorte that you shall have cause to thinke this benefyt well bestowed.[2]

And so with my hartie comendations I byd you farewell. Court the xvth Auguste anno 1587

    Your very willing frind,
      W Ralegh

1. Lady Jane Stafford was probaby the daughter of Sir Edward Gorges of Wraxall in Somerset and aunt of Ralegh's cousin and friend, Sir Arthur Gorges: see below, Letter 101. Sir Robert Stafford was her second husband and she died in 1591: R. Gorges, *The Story of a Family*, Boston, 1944. Other possible identifications lack the connection with Ralegh.
2. On 20 August, Hovenden replied that the lease would be 'altogether prejudiciall' to the college and asked Ralegh to take into consideration the leases it had already made to the Queen: Fletcher, op. cit., p. 214. See also above, Letter 7. Lady Stafford's powerful friends seem subsequently to have lost interest in her case: Fletcher, ibid., *passim*.

---

## 26. To Lord Burghley from Exeter, 21 December 1587

PRO, SP12/206/40, *CSPD 1581–90*, p. 445. In Ralegh's hand except for the address.
J.P. Collier, *Notes and Queries*, 3rd Series, V, 1864, p. 207; Edwards II, pp. 36–7.

### SOUTH WEST DEFENCES

[*addressed*] To the righte honorable my singuler good lord the Lord Highe Tresourer of Ingland d[*elivere*]d
[*endorsed in Burghley's hand*] 21 December 1587 Sir Walter Ralegh, lev[*ying*] of 2000 foot, 200 hor[*se*], in Devon and Cornwall

My singuler good lord: Accordinge to your lordships and the rest of my lords [*of the Council*] directions[1] I have attended the Earle of Bath[2] and conferred with the Deputes of Devon and the cittey of Exon[3] for the drawinge together of 2000 foote and 200 horse, and I finde great differences in oppinion amonge them. Sume are of oppinion that this burden wilbe grevous unto the countrey, standinge att this tyme voyde of all traficque,[4] the subside not beinge yet gathered[5] and the past musters having byn very chargable. Sir John Gilbert, Sir Richard Granvile[6] and the Earle hym self, being more zelous both in religion and Her Majesties service, who have allways founde a reddy disposition in their devisions[7] and willingnes to beare whatsoever shalbe though[t] meet for Her Majesties service by the people, ar of oppinion that the matter and service wilbe very fesible. It is most asured that the carefull usage of the action by the Deputes in their severall devisions will easely induce the inferior sort to whatsoever shalbe though[t] necessary for Her Majesties saufty and their own defence, but sume other of the cummission of Devon[8] (in my conscience before the Lorde[)], beinge both infected in religion and vehemently malcontent, who by how mich they more the ar [= *the more they are*] temperat by so mich the more [*they are*] dangerous, are secreatly great hinderence of all actions tendinge to the good of Her Majesty or [*the*] saufty of the present state. Thes men make doubt that your honors instructions alone ar not [sic] sufficient and saufe warrant for their discharge and that if any refuse to contribute the[y] see not by what they should be inforsed, with a thowsand dillitory cavelations.

For myne own oppinion, under your lordships correction, if it might notwithstandinge stande withe Her Majesties likinge to beare theon [= *the one*] half of the charge, beinge great, it would be very consonant to all good pollecy, and the countrey, as I judge, will willingly defray the rest, which onles ther wear ministers of other disposion[9] will not be so saufly and easely brought to effect.[10] I have sent your lordshipe an estemate of the whole,[11] with which I humble pray your lordship to acquaynt Her Majesty, and not otherwise to impart my letter because I am bold to write my simple oppinion playnly unto your lordshipe, the same beinge as the Lord doth judge, without respect or parttiality, havinge vowed my travaile and life to Her Majesties service only and forever.[12]

I have writen to the Deputes of Cornwale[13] and am reddy to repaire thither with all dillegence to performe the rest of Her Majesties cummanded [sic] geven mee in charge by your lordships.

And yeven so, humble cummending my service unto your Lordshipe favorable construction, I take my leve from Exon this xxi of December.

Your lordships to do yow all honor and service,

The cittisens of Ex[e]ter as yet refuse to beare such part as was thought meet by the leuetenants of Devon and the rest.[14]

W Ralegh

---

1. On 7 December 1587, the Council resolved to write to Ralegh, as Lord Warden, instructing him to hold musters 'proportionable, chosen out of the trained men of Devon and Cornwall, and to be placed in forme of a campe ... against anie suddaine invasion', and see to the repair

of deficiencies in the defence of the south-western counties; but on 13 December it decided to put on hold its order for 2,000 foot and 200 horse: *APC* XV, pp. 297, 302. On 15 December, however, it was reported that 'Sir Walter Rawley is gon westward': J.W. Stoye, 'An early letter from John Chamberlain', *EHR* LXII, 1947, p. 528.

2. William Bourchier, 3rd Earl of Bath (1557–1623), had succeeded the late Earl of Bedford as Lord Lieutenant of Devon in September 1585 but, being young and with little military experience, was told to be guided by his Deputies: *APC* XIV, p. 239–40 and *HMC Foljambe*, p. 19.
3. These were, for the county of Devon, Ralegh himself, Sir William Courtenay of Powderham, Sir Robert Dennis, Sir John Gilbert, Hugh Fortescue esquire and George Cary esquire of Cockington: *HMC Foljambe*, p. 25. The city of Exeter, a county of itself since 1537, was represented in 1587–8 by the Mayor (John Periam), the Recorder (a distinguished lawyer), two former mayors (Nicholas Martyn and Thomas Brewerton) and one Richard Prowse, gentleman, a formidable team.
4. An exaggeration, but all the Devon ports, north and south, were suffering to some extent from the open conflict with Spain which had begun in 1585, and, as the Mayor of Barnstaple pleaded early in 1588, were not yet enjoying the profits of legalized piracy: PRO, SP12/209/77, *CSPD 1581–90*, p. 474.
5. See above, Letter 24. The assessment of the parliamentary subsidy of 1587 survives for Exeter only: Stoate, *Devon Taxes 1581–1660*, p. ix.
6. Sir Richard Grenville (1542–91) had earlier in the year been sent to survey the coastal fortifications of the South West and the readiness of the local militia: *HMC Foljambe*, pp. 20 and 22.
7. Devon was divided for judicial as well as military purposes into three parts, North, East and South.
8. The Commission of the Peace for Elizabethan Devon numbered about 30 active individuals, excluding *ex officio* members, and that for Cornwall about 20: *Calendar of Patent Rolls 1569–72*, pp. 222–3.
9. Presumably a further warning about the gentlemen of the South West, among whom Ralegh had few friends other than his family circle.
10. There were no county funds, and without help from Westminster the whole cost had to be borne by the parishes, which, in effect, meant local landowners and the more substantial yeomen farmers and clothiers.
11. Filed with this letter in the State Papers is a detailed costing of pay and supplies for an army, including officers, of 2,000 foot and 200 horse to be provided by Devon, Cornwall, the city of Exeter and the tinners, but it is undated and there is no evidence to connect it with Ralegh's letter of December 1587. It is printed in full in Edwards II, p. 39.
12. Ralegh's letter had reached Westminster by 24 December, for on that day the Council resolved to inform the Earl of Bath that the Queen was 'lothe to laye any further burthen' on the county and that he should 'forbeare to assemble the saide forces in any great number'. Again he was urged 'to use the advyse of Sir Walter Rawleighe [sic]': *APC* XV, pp. 307–8. But well into 1588, with the risk of invasion becoming ever more serious, a Committee of Defence, of which Ralegh was a member, was still pressing for the Crown to pay half the cost of training the south-western militia: PRO, SP12/209/49.
13. In 1587 these were Sir Francis Godolphin, Sir William Mohun, Peter Edgcombe esquire, Richard Carew esquire of Antony, and Sir Richard Grenville: *HMC Foljambe*, p. 26. Ralegh himself had been Lord Lieutenant of Cornwall since 1585 and his authority in the two south-western counties had been immensely increased by his appointment to the late Earl of Bedford's post as Lord Warden of the Stannaries, but he had his critics: PRO, SP15/29/126, *CSPD Addenda 1580–1625*, pp. 181–2.
14. Ralegh's cloth and wine patents won him no friends in civic circles, as he had already discovered in 1586 when seeking contributions towards his Virginia ventures: Quinn, *Roanoke 1955*, I, p. 471.

27. **TO SIR JOHN GILBERT FROM THE COURT, 27 FEBRUARY 1588**

Present location unknown. From facsimile in sale catalogue, Messrs Christies, London, 2 April 1975, photocopy, BL, RP 1213. In Ralegh's hand.

PRO, SP9/55(ii), an eighteenth-century transcript.

Quinn, *Roanoke* 1955, II, pp. 559–60, from SP9; Lloyd Williams, op. cit., 1962, p. 85, from Quinn, with omissions, spelling modernized.

## RESTRAINT OF SHIPPING

[*addressed*] To the righte worshipful my very loving brother, Sir John Gilbert knighte

[*endorsed*] To John Gilberte

Sir: Hereing of late that ther is lyttle regarde tak[en of][1] the generall restraint made heretofore by the lords of the [*Privy*] Counsell of shipping and mariners,[2] but that every man providethe to goe for Newfoundland[3] and other places at ther pleasures as though the restraynte wer forgotten, or not to be respected, I thoughte good therfore to put you [*in*] mynde to have speciall care that none passe withoute speciall order from the lords of the Counsell, praying you to write to the costomers and serchers[4] and other officers that they suffer none to goe into any forrayn partes withoute speciall lycence unles they receave other dyrections from the Counsell, that Her Majestie maye not be unfurnished of shipping and mariners upon any occasion that maye happen. Whereof I doubt not but you will have suche care as to a matter of suche importance apertayneth.

And so with my very hartye comendations I byd you farewell.

From the Courte the 27 of February 1587.

    Your loving brother
      W Ralegh

Such as I acquaynted yow withall to whom I have geven leve yow may lett them steale away.[5]

[*at foot of page*] Ther is no newse att all wo[r]th the writinge. With a thowsand commendations to your sealff and my sister[6] I commit yow to God. I have written agayne to Master [*sic*] Drake[7] touching the Danskers.[8] I will take order to shorten his octorety.[9]

---

1. From the transcript, the original manuscript being obscured by staining.
2. On 9 October 1587, all ships and mariners throughout the kingdom were 'stayed' from going to sea: *APC* XV, p. 254.

3. Devon ships and seamen, especially those of Dartmouth, near Gilbert's home, had been going to Newfoundland to fish since the 1540s: Todd Gray in M. Duffy *et al.* (eds), *New Maritime History of Devon*, I, 1992, p. 142.
4. Port customs officers, to be found principally at Exeter, Dartmouth and Plymouth, and at Barnstaple in north Devon.
5. Probably included two small Bideford ships which, on 22 April 1588, were the only ones permitted to sail to Virginia with supplies for Ralegh's colonists: Quinn, *Roanoke* 1955, II, pp. 554-5 and 559-62 and *Set Fair for Roanoke*, 1985, pp. 301-3.
6. Probably Ann, née Aucher, Sir Humphrey Gilbert's widow: see below, Letter 30, note 5.
7. One might query whether this is Sir Francis but for note 8 below.
8. Ships from the Baltic port of Dantzig. On 9 February 1588, Dr Julius Caesar, Judge of the High Court of Admiralty, complained to Burghley that Sir Francis Drake would not allow certain German and Dutch merchants to sail from Plymouth to La Rochelle, in spite of their having Burghley's permission: BL, Lansd. 157, f. 380.
9. On 1 April 1588, the Council reprimanded Gilbert for permitting certain ships 'of great burden and fytt for service', which had been 'stayed' by Drake, to go to sea, and in general for showing 'little regard' for the authority of the Queen's Admiral: *APC* XVI, pp. 17-18.

---

28. TO SIR THOMAS EGERTON,[1]
    8 MARCH 1588

    Present location unknown, said by Collier (below) to be among the Ellesmere MSS at Manchester House.[2] From facsimile in unidentified sale catalogue in possession of the editors. Written by a clerk, with postscript and signature in Ralegh's hand.

    J.P. Collier, *Archaeologia* XXXV, 1853, p. 369, accurate; Edwards II, p. 40, from Collier.

## RENEWAL OF WINE PATENT

*[No address or endorsement]*

Sir: Whereas the Quenes Majestie hath heretofore given unto me by her letters patentes aucthoritie to graunte licenses for the sellinge of wynes by retayle,[3] Her Highnes pleasure is to revoke and make voyde the same and by new letters patentes to regraunte unto me the aucthoritie and benefytt thereof for a farther terme of yeres.[4] Wherefore I pray you hartely to peruse the drafte which this bearer, my servant, shall bring unto you and sett your hande thereunto, redie for Her Highnes to signe, and I wilbe redie to requyte your courtesie. So, hopinge your carefull dealing for me accordinge to my requeste, I bid you hartely farewell. This 8th of March 1587.

      Your lovinge frende,
         W Ralegh

Sir: [*Her*] Majesty her sealf cummaunded mee to acquaynt yow with the booke [= *text*] and therfore yow shall not need to doubt, for you may take knowledg of her pleasure by thes my letters, beseechinge yow to frinde me so much to make expedition herein, and yow shall cummaunde mee in what I may stand yow in steede.⁵

1. Solicitor-General. No address but identity of recipient clear from his reply: see below, note 5.
2. It is not with the Ellesmere MSS in the Huntington Library, California and all efforts to trace its present whereabouts have drawn a blank.
3. See above, Letter 12, note 2.
4. Ralegh claimed that he had been cheated by his agent, one Richard Browne, and hoped that a new grant would be more satisfactory.
5. Egerton also looked at a draft of Ralegh's proposed new agreement with Browne and found it 'intricatelie penned and with so great disadvantage for your [*Ralegh's*] part that I doubte the course which you are directed will hardlie satisfie your expectation': Collier, op. cit., pp. 369–70 and Edwards II, pp. 40–41. See also T.N. Brushfield, 'Ralegh Miscellanea, part II', *DAT* XLI, 1909, pp. 181–99. The new grant was made on 9 August 1588: PRO, Patent Roll 30 Elizabeth, pt vi. For the sequel, see below, Letter 31.

---

## 29. TO THE PRIVY COUNCIL, [JULY/AUGUST 1588]¹

PRO, SP12/211/90, *CSPD 1581–90*, p. 496, dated June 1588. Written by a clerk, with subscription and signature in Ralegh's hand.

J.P. Collier, *Notes and Queries*, 3rd series, V, 1864, p. 207. Not in Edwards.

### CORNISH MILITIA FOR LONDON

[*Headed*]   Order for the puttinge in a reddines of 2000 footmen accordinge to your honors directions
[*no address*]
[*endorsed*]   Order for the 2000 men in Cornewal

2000 men under captayns to repaire to the Court or elswher att my lords [*of the Council's*] directions:

| | |
|---|---|
| Sir R[*ichard*] Grenvill with his band of | 300 |
| Richard Carew [*of Anthony*] with his | 300 |
| Sir John Arrundell [*of Trerice*] with his | 200 |
| Master [*William*] Bevill [*of Talland*] with his | 200 |
| The Provost Marshall² John Wrey [*of Sourton, Devon*] | 200 |

| | |
|---|---|
| Thomas Lower [*of Lewannick*] with his | 200 |
| Tristram A[r]scote [*of Tetcott, Devon*] with | 200 |
| John [*Jonathan*] Trela[w]ny [*of Menheniot*] with his | 200 |
| John Reskener [*of Helston*] with his | 200 |

Wee have apoynted 4 waynes [= *carts*] to each hundred and vitles for fourteen dayes and wee accompt to mount the one half on hacknes for expedition. Wee provede tooles for 200 pioners as well for own incampinge as to serve Her Majesty in her camp reall [= *royal*]. Also wee have ordayned a cornett [= *troop*] of horsmen to be in areddines if your honors shall cummand the same, to be added to the 2000 footmen. And if I shall not be cummanded down [*to Cornwall*] my sealf[3] I have thought good to direct Sir Richard Grenvill to have the conduction of this regiment to bringe them to the campe, wher after your honors may otherwise dispose of the charge as it shall best like your wisdomes.

    Your honors humble att cummand,

        W Ralegh

---

1. On 27 June 1588, when the Spanish fleet was preparing to sail, the Council informed the lords lieutenants that part of their forces would be required to go to London to help defend the Queen. On 28 July, by which time the Armada was approaching the Lizard, they had orders to send up their contingents by 4 August, but by 7 August the crisis was over and the orders were countermanded: *HMC Foljambe*, p. 45. See also below, note 3.
2. Officer in charge of discipline.
3. Although Ralegh was not necessarily in Cornwall at the time he despatched this report, this evidence of his preoccupation with military matters casts doubt on Camden's story that he joined Howard's fleet at sea on or about 23 July. In any case, he had a prior responsibility as Captain of the Queen's Guard and he was certainly back at Court by 2 August when he was sent to the south coast to 'confer' with Lord Admiral Howard: *APC* XVI, p. 212. Grenville was perfectly capable of looking after Cornwall: A.L. Rowse, *Sir Richard Grenville*, 1937, p. 261.

---

## 30. To [Sir John Gilbert] from the Court, 13 September 1588

Ransom Center, Pforzheimer 107, Jackson 1940, pp. 853–4, *in extenso*. Written by a clerk, with subscription, signature and postscript in Ralegh's hand. In poor condition, illegible words supplied from PRO transcript.

PRO, SP9/55/9iii, *CSPD Addenda 1580–1610*, p. 260, an eighteenth-century transcript.

Tytler 1833, I, f. 231.

## SPANISH ARMADA WINE

*[no address or endorsement]*

Sir: With muche adoe wee have gotten order for you to sell the wyne and so to satisfye yourself.[1] Yf this had not byn broughte to passe you mighte perhapps have looked for your monye a good while. Ther is allso order sent you to send up xvi [tonnes *crossed out*] buttes of the wyne to be devided among the lords and others of the Consell. When yt comithe I praye you take suche a course that I maye have a letter directed to me to have the presenting of yt to my Lord Admirall [*Howard*] for by that meanes I maye happ gett a butt for myself.[2] Of the rest of the wynes appoynted to be sold I pray you take xx$^{tie}$ [tonnes *crossed out*] buttes into your seller preysed [= *valued*] at as reasonable rate as you can. And Sir Richard Greynvill as he goyth home[3] shall com by you and paye ready monye for yt. I must allso praye you to sett a syde xxv toonnes of the ieron hooped e[*mpty*] caske for me, preysed in suche reasonable sort as you maye for I shall have great use of them. And yf my lord of Comberland[4] or any other make meanes to have them you may answer that they are [*preysed*] and solde, or that Her Majestie hathe gyven them to me, but in any case lett them be kept for me.

And so with my moste hartie comendations to your sealf and my good Ladye[5] I byd you farewell.[6]

Courte the xiij$^{th}$ of September 1588,
    Your most loving brother,
        W Ralegh

I pray you cummend mee to [*m*]y sister[7] many tymes.

---

1. This was the wine, thought to have been some 130–40 barrels in all, which was on board the *Nuestra Senora del Rosario*, when on the night of 21/22 July 1588 she became separated from the rest of the Spanish Armada and, on the instructions of Sir Francis Drake, was brought into Torbay by the joint action of the *Margaret and John* and the *Roebuck*, both owned by Ralegh. Subsequently she was moved into the Dart estuary in the custody of Sir John Gilbert, whose residence was upstream of the town of Dartmouth, and George Cary esquire, of Cockington behind Torbay, both of whom had a legitimate claim to reimbursement for the expenses they had incurred in handling the ship and feeding her crew until alternative arrangements could be made for the seamen's accommodation. Needless to say, many barrels had already left the ship before the order to sell reached Dartmouth. For a full account of the whole affair, including the dispersal of the ship's contents, see Paula Martin, *Spanish Armada Prisoners*, Exeter 1988, chapter 2, *passim*.
2. Ralegh had no claim to the *Nuestra* as a prize, her capture as an act of war delivering the ship and her contents into the hands of the Queen.

3. To Stowe, his house in the north Cornwall parish of Kilkampton, Dartmouth being not as far out of his way there as it might seem.
4. George Clifford, 3rd Earl of Cumberland, the privateer.
5. As Ralegh mentions her separately from his sister[-in-law], Elizabeth Gilbert, 'my Lady' was probably Ann, née Aucher, widow of Sir Humphrey, to whom both Ralegh and Sir John Gilbert were very attached.
6. Whether any of Ralegh's requests were complied with is not on record, but Gilbert and Cary very soon fell out, Cary self-righteously complaining to the Council about Gilbert's liberality and, as late as October, writing in despair at not being able to render an account: Martin, op. cit., p. 33. In any case, 'all the best wines [were] gone'. On 9 September the Council ordered Gilbert to make good the value of the wines he had disposed of 'without sufficient warrant' and hand over the proceeds to Sir Thomas Dennis and Master Cary, and there were further remonstrances on 30 December (APC XVI, pp. 293 and 378–9), but with little hope of success.
7. See above, note 5.

---

## 31. TO LORD BURGHLEY, [BEFORE 8 MAY 1589][1]

New York Public Library, Gilbert Holland Montague Collection 1307. Written by a clerk, with signature in Ralegh's hand and additions, with signatures, by Sir John Popham and Burghley. Not previously printed.

## THE WINE LICENCES

[addressed]    To the right honorable the Lord High Tresorer of England

Humbly sheweth unto your honor your suppl[icant] Sir Walter Raleigh [sic] knight, that whereas the Quenes Majestie by her letteres patentes under the great seale of England dated in Auguste laste[2] hathe geven auctorytie unto your said suppl[icant] to graunt lycences for the sale of wynes by retail, and hath lykewise, emongst other things in the said letteres patentes, geven power and auctorytie to your said suppl[icant] and to his deputie and deputies to vew and examyn all lycences hertofor graunted, aswell by Sir Edward Horsey[3] as by hym your said suppl[icant], his deputies or assignes, which cannot be don without greate charge to your said suppl[icant] but by comission to the Shereffe and other officeres of every shere to cause the vintneres of every shere to appeare in one certen place of the same, and whereas, Right Honorable, divers complaintes have been made out of diveres sheres unto your said suppl[icant] that his assignes hath let more licences in sundry townes then by the statute of vijth Edwardi sexti,[4] or by Her Highnes graunt unto your said suppl[icant], they

ought to doe, and hath comitted diveres and sundry faltes and misdemeaneres to the greate abuse of Her Highnes statute lawes and graunte and to the greate disceipt and hindrance of her lovinge subjectes. And for asmuch as your said suppl[icant] ys determyned by all meanes that he may to see a spedie reformation of the said abuses, and hath appointed his sufficient deputies, Randell Knevet, gentleman, Peter Wilcox and Richard Okham, gentleman, to travell throughout all the realme to that ende, and to take further order for the ease of the subjectes, which they cannot possibly doe nor sufficiently prosecute because one of your suppl[icants] assignies heretofore deputed to deale in the matteres of wynes[5] dothe detaine all lycences, bookes, bondes and other wrytinges concerning the office without Her Highnes speciall comission out of the Exchequer. May it therfore please your honour, considering the premyses and how necessary yt ys for ease of the vintneres, and for abuses to appeare more manifest, to graunte Her Highnes comission accordinge to the articles hereunto annexed,[6] which commision beinge raytorned with the abuses into thexchequer, Her Highnes shall have remedy to punych the offender for doinge contrary to the statute and abusinge of her graunt and the poor subjectes shall also have remedy of abuses don unto theym and shall have good cause to pray for your honores prosperous estate longe to continew.
  W Ralegh

I thynke so as [= *provided*] the parties whom it concernythe be not dreven to travell to farre from their dwellinges it may be permytted, which may be holpen [= *helped*] by syttinge in sundry [?*places*].
  J Popham[7]

W Burghley Master Fanshaw[8] make a comission as is required with a direction to ye shyrrifes that they call no persons to any place above twelve myles from his dwellynge howse.[9]

1. See below, note 9.
2. Ralegh's first patent (1583) had been revoked at his request on 4 May 1588 and a new one granted on 9 August 1588: see above, Letter 28, note 4.
3. Ralegh's predecessor as patentee.
4. See Letter 16, note 2.
5. Richard Browne: see Letter 28 and below, note 9.
6. No longer attached to the petition.
7. Sir John Popham, later Lord Chief Justice, who was to preside over Ralegh's trial in 1603.
8. Thomas Fanshaw, Queen's Remembrancer, an officer of the Exchequer.
9. On 8 May 1589, the Council ordered Browne to deliver to Ralegh or his 'councell learned', 'true copies in wrytinge of all the bookes and notes concerninge the matter in variaunce': *APC* XVII, p. 167.

## 32. TO SIR WILLIAM FITZWILLIAM[1] FROM LONDON, 12 NOVEMBER 1589

Lambeth Palace Library, MS 618, f. 27r., a contemporary copy, *CCM 1589–1600*, p. 14, abstract, otherwise not previously printed. The spelling suggests that the original was written by a clerk.

### ON BEHALF OF SIR GEORGE CAREW[2]

[*marginal heading*] Sir W[alter] Ralegh's letter to my Lord Deputye the 12th of November 1589 A request for his letters unto the Councell [*of Ireland*] in Sir G[eorge's] behalf to the lyke effect as his Lordship wrote unto him as touching his sufficiencye to be one of the Councell

When as I was with your Lordship I forgatt (after the desier to see you) even my chiefest sute, which was to intreat your lordship to wryte your letter in the behalf of my cossen Sir George Carewe, to suche effecte as it pleased your lordship to wryte unto me, recommendinge his sufficiencye, longe service[3] and experience, as also the weaknes of his office,[4] to be of Her Majesties Councell. Itt is verye trewe that I shewed your lordships letter unto Her Majestie who toke the same as rightlye wrytten and well commended, and I assure your lordship she wylled me (that the matter might have the better inducement) to intreat your lordship to write asmytche ether to herself or [*the*] Councell, which also she wylled Master Dellves[5] by worde of mouthe to delyver. Wherefore I praye your lordship to performe the same, assuringe your lordship that the gentleman ys one that undyssymulatly honoreth you and commendeth your honour for sundry vertues. And for my owne parte, as I have many tymes boldened my selff to trouble you with many letters and requestes, so I assure your lordship that you cannot by any favour so muche bynde me (no, were it for anye good for my owne particular) as your lordship shall by favoringe and grasinge my said kynseman, and in leu [= *return*] thereof all the power and credytt and service and all that anye frende maye performe shalbe perfected, to do your lordship honour and service everye where and at all tymes. From London.

    Your lordships assured lovinge kynesman to commaunde
    W R
    deliv. per G C[6]

---

1. Lord Deputy of Ireland, 1571–5 and 1588–96.
2. Carew (1555–1629), a very junior member of the east Devon branch of this very prolific West Country family, had been a soldier in Ireland on and off since 1574. Like Ralegh he had sailed

with Sir Humphrey Gilbert in 1578 and returned to Ireland, where he was knighted the following year, at about the same time as his elder brother, Sir Peter, was killed by the rebels: Hasler I, pp. 539–40. He and Ralegh were together in Ireland in the summer of 1589 and returned to London early in November: see Appendix I. His blood relationship with Ralegh was somewhat distant, Carew's aunt, Catherine, being Ralegh's maternal grandmother: Vivian, *Devon*, pp. 135 and 162–3.

3. When approached on his behalf by Sir Thomas Heneage in May 1589, the Queen had said that Carew, then aged 34, was 'young yet': *CCM 1589–1600*, p. 5.
4. Carew was Master of the Ordnance in Ireland from February 1588 until August 1592 when he became Lieutenant General of the Ordnance in England: Hasler, op. cit.
5. George Delves, Fitzwilliam's brother-in-law, a frequent conductor of troops to Ireland and carrier of letters: *CCM 1589–1600, passim*.
6. Fitzwilliam wrote to Heneage, Burghley and Ralegh on his behalf on 20 February 1590, describing Carew as 'virtuously given and of a judgement beyond his years' and he was appointed to the Irish Council in the following August: ibid., pp. 20, 41.

---

## 33. TO SIR GEORGE CAREW [FROM LONDON], 28 DECEMBER 1589

Lambeth Palace Library, MS 605, f. 140, *CCM 1589–1600*, p. 15. Damaged at right-hand edge. In Ralegh's hand.

Edwards II, pp. 41–3; Pope Hennessy 1883, pp. 120–22, from Edwards; Lloyd Williams, op. cit., 1962, p. 97, part only, from Edwards, spelling modernized.

### TALES FROM IRELAND

[*addressed*] To my lovinge cussen Sir George Carew, Master of the Ordinance in Irland.

[*headed by or for Carew*] Ralegh 1589. A private letter from Sir Walter Raleighe to Sir G.C. 27 [*sic*] December 1589

[*endorsed by or for Carew*] From Syr Walter Ralegh the 28th of December 1589

Cussen George: For my retrait from the Court it was upon good cause, to take order for my prize.¹ If in Irlande they thincke that I am not worth the respectinge they shall mich deceve them sealves. I am in place to be beleved not inferior to any man to plesure or displesure [*word erased*] the greatest. And my oppinion is so receved and beleved as I can anger the best of them. And therfore if the Deputy² be not as reddy to steed [= *support*] mee as I have bynn to defend hyme, be it att is [= *as it*] may. When Sir William Fitts Williams shalbe in Ingland I take my sealf farr his better, by the honorable offices I hold,[3] as also by that nireness to Her Majestye which still I injoy, and never more. I am willinge to continew towards hyme all frindly offices and I doubt not of the like frome hyme, as well towards mee as my frinds.[4] This mich I desire he should understand, and for my part ther shalbe nothinge wantinge that becumeth a frinde, nether can I but hold my sealf most kindly dealt withall by hy[m] heretherto [= *hitherto*], of which I desire the continuance, [I] hav[ing] deserved all his curteses in the hiest degree.

For the sut[e] of Lesmore I will shortly send over order from the Queen for a dismis of their cavelations.[5] And so I pray deale as the matter may be respeted [= *delayed*] for a tyme, and cumm[end] mee to Master Sollicitor[6] with many thanks for his frindly delinge therin: and I assure yow on myne honor I have deservde it att his hands in places wher it may most steed hyme. For Hardinge[7] I will send unto yow mony by exchange with [*all*] possible spead, as well to pay hyme (if he suffer the recoverye) as all others. And till then I pray if my builders[8] want, supply them.

I look for yow here this springe, and if possible I may I will returne with yow. The Queen thinks that George Carew longes to see her, and therfore see her.[9] Farewell noble George my chosen frinde and kinsman, from whom nor tyme nor fortun nor adversety shall sever mee.

    the xxviii of December
        W Ralegh

---

1. There was no reason for Ralegh to lie to Carew. Was he called to Plymouth to deal with the *Angel Gabriel*, alias the *Jobe* of Hamburg, which one of his privateers had brought in on the grounds that she was carrying Spanish goods? He was having to defend himself against charges laid in the High Court of Admiralty: BL, Lansd. 144, ff. 57–60, printed in Edwards II, pp. 415–17. On the other hand, he may have been using the word 'prize' as a euphemism for his Irish seignory: see below, Appendix 1.
2. Sir William Fitzwilliam, who was apparently no longer Ralegh's ally.
3. He had been appointed Captain of the Queen's Guard in 1587.
4. Ralegh was clearly using Carew as an intermediary.
5. Lismore Castle, formerly the residence of the Bishop of Waterford and Lismore, was held on lease by Ralegh from a tenant of the Bishop. There were other claimants: see Quinn, 1962, p. 147.
6. Roger Wilbraham, Solicitor-General for Ireland since 1585.
7. Probably a seaman of Youghal, of which Ralegh had recently been elected 'Mayor': S. Hayman, *Handbook for Youghal* (1858), p. 23.
8. Possibly his English 'settlers' in Ireland (see below, Letter 45) but more likely referring to those engaged in the rebuilding of Lismore Castle where Ralegh hoped to reside.
9. This was no doubt Carew's cue to write fulsomely to the Queen, on 10 February 1590, that he was seeking leave from the Lord Deputy to visit home in order to see her. He was in England from May to October: *CCM 1589–1600*, pp. 18, 36, 50, 61.

## 34. TO SIR FRANCIS WALSINGHAM, JANUARY 1590

PRO, SP63/150/30, *CSPI 1588–92*, p. 103, no. 30, Plate 3. Otherwise not previously printed. In Ralegh's hand.

### ON BEHALF OF TEIG ONORSI

[*addressed*] To the right honorable Sir Francis Wallsingnam, knight, Principall Secretory to Her Majestye

[*endorsed*] Januarie 1589. From Sir Walter Rawleigh in favour of Teig McNursey[1] to have letters to the Lord Deputie to accept of his surrender according to his petition in that behalf

Sir: I humble beseich yow to procure a letter for this poore gentleman, Teig a Nursey, for his surrender.[2] And if my Lord Deputy [*Fitzwilliam*] finde that any other of his kindre[d] make clayme as well as hyme sealf, that yet his lordship will favor hyme in the sute in respect of his good services dun and his abillety to do, being on very sufficient and hath many able men that follow hyme. And I assure your honor that the contenting of this man wilbe to great purpose, for no man is better followed of thos dangarous men of the west parts [*of Ireland*] than hyme sealf.[3]

And this with rem[em]brance of my humble deuty I take leve this present Twesday,

    Your honors ever to be cummanded
        W Ralegh

---

1. Teig Onorsi (alias Teig MacDermot MacCarthy) was the younger brother of one Cormac Donn (alias Cormac MacDermot MacCarthy) who had murdered his cousin, one Cormac MacFinin, who, contrary to Irish custom, had taken possession of MacCarthy lands in county Cork. In 1576 Cormac Donn was hanged by the English for his crime, but Teig had been recognized by his compatriots as the rightful heir: *CSPI 1586–8*, p. 463, no. 66.
2. In 1587 Teig had accompanied Ralegh to England to surrender the lands and have them regranted in order to bar the claim of young Finin MacCormac, son of Cormac MacFinin, only to be told that they had been forfeit to the Queen on the hanging of Cormac Donn, a recognition that by Irish law he had been in lawful possession.
3. In June 1590, 'in consideration of the favourable report made of him to Her Majesty by Sir Walter Raleigh', the Queen leased the land to Teig at a low rent: *APC* XIX, pp. 53–4, *Cal. Chancery Rolls of Ireland 1576–1602*, II, p. 202.

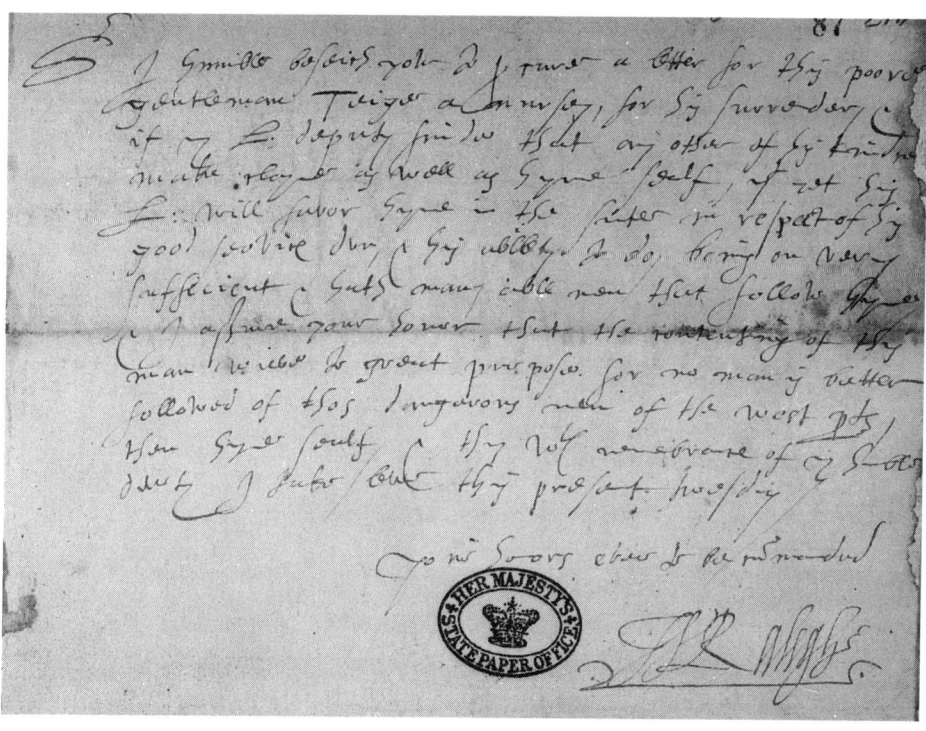

*Plate 3.* Letter 34: Sir Walter Ralegh to Sir Francis Walsingham, January 1590.
(PRO, SP63/150/30)

## 35. TO THE SUBDEAN AND CHAPTER OF WELLS CATHEDRAL, [?] SEPTEMBER 1590

Wells Cathedral Library, Dean and Chapter Archives, Series II/948. Written by a clerk, with subscription and signature in Ralegh's hand. In poor condition at right-hand edge. Not hitherto printed.

### FOR WILLIAM TAWSWELL, VICAR CHORAL OF WELLS

[*addressed*]   To the right worshipfull my very loving frinds Master James Bisse, subdean,[1] and the chapter of Wells d[*eliver*]
[*no endorsement*]

After my verye hartie comendations, wheras I am credibly in[*formed*] that the berar hereof, Willyam Tawswell, having se[*rved*] his yeare of proof in your churche as a singin[g *man*], and being then to be admitted as a vicar, [*was*] withoute any cause aleaged agaynst him [?*rejected*], to his utter undoing, having a wife a[*nd*] childeren and no other meanes to maynetey[*ne*] him self and them. I was earnestly sue[?*d*] unto to procure Her Majesties lettre in his beh[*alf*], but hoping, the cause being so reasonabl[*e*], that I might intreat your favour for his admittaunce, I have omitted all other meane[s] which I wold willingly have used for h[*im*], being so earnestly intreated by such of his frindes as I wold gladly pleasure,[2] and [*I do*] moste hartely intreat you the rathe[*r*] for my sake to have compassion upon h[*is*] distressed case and to admit him in to the roome [= *office*] that he hath served for. If he hav[*e*] offended any of you he hathe promised with all humblenes to submitt him. Which I hope will be as great a recompence as any of you will requyr at a mans hand of his fortune. So, praying you to do this charitable dede at my request[3] I rest ready to do you or any of you what pleasure I may, and byd you hartely farewell this [*blank*] of September 1590.

       Your very loving frind,
        W Ralegh

1. Formerly of Magdalen College, Oxford, Tawswell had been subdean of Wells since 1585. Ralegh had earlier tried to obtain leases of parts of the episcopal estates but without success: P.M. Hembry, *The Bishops of Bath and Wells 1540–1640*, 1967, pp. 148–9.
2. Who these 'friends' were is not known.
3. Tawswell was admitted a 'perpetual vicar' on 9 July 1593. In 1600 and 1601 he was in trouble with his superiors, accused first of incontinence and then of being out at night playing at tables: *HMC Dean and Chapter of Wells Cathedral*, II, 327, 341–2.

## 36. To Sir Robert Cecil from Durham House, 13 October [?1591][1]

Hatfield, CP56/17, *HMC Salisbury* XIII, p. 453. In Ralegh's hand.
Edwards II, pp. 179–80, dated 1597.

### SPANISH NAVAL PREPARATIONS

[*addressed*]   To my honorable frinde Sir Robert Cicill knight[2]
[*endorsed by or for Cecil*]   13 October 1597 [*sic*] Syr Walter Ralegh to me

Sir: This bearer[3] will go presently into Spayne and vew all the portes, by whome yow shalbe ascertianed [*sic*] of all the kings preparations,[4] what is becume of this late fleet that was att the Ilands,[5] whe[the]r thos with the rest be held in reddines or discharged. I will undertake for the honesty of the man. Hee hath the kings pass wherby hee may saufly look into all the ports. Hee only desirs to carry for the countenance of the matter a small buck[et] of wheat or rye. Yow canot devise a fitter waye to discover all his pretences: therfore I pray cummend it and dispatch it with hast.
   From Derhum hows this xiii of October,
      Your asured frinde to do yow service,
         W Ralegh

If I had bynn well I would have wayted on yow my sealf.

---

1. There is an error in the endorsement, which must have been made some years later during a similar panic about Spain. The year cannot have been 1597 when Ralegh was away on the Islands voyage, from which he returned on or about 20 October: Wernham, *Return of the Armadas*, pp. 182–3. There is confirmation of the year suggested in the form of the address, which was to his 'friend', a formula later dispensed with by his clerks and only used by Ralegh himself when writing in his own hand: e.g. Letter 69. Also, he was at Durham House in October 1591: see Letter 37.
2. (1563–1612), younger son of William, Lord Burghley, knighted in May, Privy Councillor from August 1591.
3. Not identified.
4. Cf. *HMC Salisbury* IV, p. 158 for instructions given on 8 November 1591 to one Austen Halfacre, who was to gather naval intelligence in Spain.
5. Presumably he means the Spanish fleet which had given battle to the English fleet led by Howard, in which Sir Richard Grenville had lost his life in September. Ralegh was to have sailed as Howard's rear-admiral but the Queen forbade it: A.L. Rowse, *Sir Richard Grenville*, 1937, pp. 192–3. One of Ralegh's own ships was with Howard, and he victualled others.

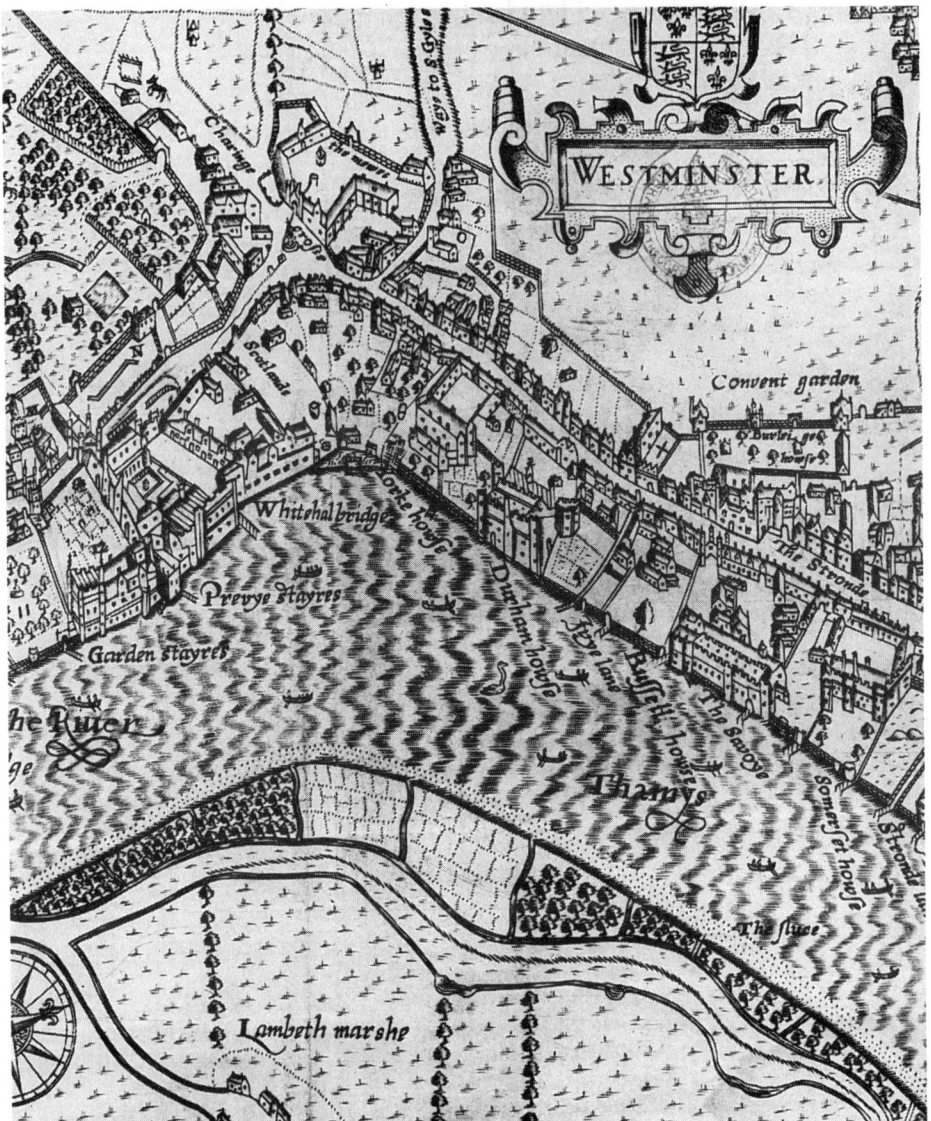

*Plate 4.* Durham House (right of centre), The Strand, from the 'Plan of Westminster' in John Norden's *Speculum Britanniae*, 1593. (Courtesy of the Guildhall Museum, London)

### 37. TO LORD BURGHLEY FROM DURHAM HOUSE, 16 OCTOBER [1591][1]

BL, Lansd. 69, f. 60.[2] F. 60v. in Ralegh's hand, written in great haste. F. 60r. not hitherto printed *in extenso*.

Edwards II, pp. 43–4, f. 60r. summarized only; part facsimile in Greg, 1932, plate LXXIV(b).

CONCERNING MASTER WATTS'S PRIZES

[*no address*]
[*endorsed in Burghley's hand*]   A note and vallew of any shippes taken by Wattes[3] and his company

[*f. 60v.*]
May it pleas your lordship: Uppon Her Majesties motion for the understandinge of the valew of thes late prises brought in by Master Watts shipps,[4] wee have conferred together and sett downe the trew valew of all, what parts go out and what remayns amonge twelve of us[5] [I do faythfully sett downe *crossed out*], all which amownteth not to the increas of on for on, which is a small returne.[6] Wee might have gotten more to have sent them afishinge, I ashure your lordshipp. What soever is taken fifty of the hundred goes cleare away from the adventurers [= *investors*] to the mariners, the Lord Admirall and to the Queene.[7] The rest, being but fourteen thowsand pounde or ther about, is a small matter amonge twelve adventurers, and of which fourteen the setting out [= *equipping*] cost us very nire eyghthowsande. This is the very trewth I asure your lordship before the livinge God as nire as wee can sett down or gett knowledge of, of which, if ought should be taken, ther would never our men of warr put out, and so all our shipps may rote, our mariners run awaye and Her Majesty lose the best part of her custome, and besydes the sume not worth the looking after.

This humble praying your lordships favorable consent in our rightfull cause, I humble take my leve, from Derhum Howse this xvi of October.

      Your lordships humble to do yow service,
        W Ralegh

[*f. 60r., marginal notes by Burghley*]
[*left-hand margin*]   To be devyded
Goodes brought to London by the shipps of John Wattes merchaunt and others in company

First in bullion and cutchinella [= *cochineal or red dye*] by
    estimation                                                    6900 *li*
Item: brought to London of ginger, hides, and sugares which
    was taken out of ij prices [= *prizes*]                       4000 *li*
Item: ij prices arrived in Bristowe laden with hides, sugar
    and ginger                                                    4000 *li*

[*margin*]   Dartmouth
Item: one prize in Dartmouth with 48 chestes of cutchenell
    and 4800 hides                                                4000 *li*

[*margin*]   Dar[t]mouth
Item: in bullion in The John being at Dartmouth, 750 pounde
    weight at Ls per pounde                                       1900 *li*
Item: in rialles of plate [*Spanish silver coins*] in the same shipp    1200 *li*

[*margin*]   Falmouth
Item: in The Harry and John being in Falmouth in bullion
    700 weight at Ls the pounde                                   1750 *li*
Item: in rialles of plate in The Harry and John 900 *li*          0900 *li*
    more amongst all the shipp shared by the marrineres
    and company in parte of ther thirdes                          6000 *li*
                                            Sum 31150 *li*
Wherout is to be deducted for the third of the
    marrineres partes                                            10383 *li*
For my Lord [*Admiral*] his tenthes                               3015 *li*
For the Queen's custom                                            1600 *li*
In charges for bringinge the goodes about                         1200 *li*
                                            Sum 16198 *li*
Rest unto the owneres and victuellares to be devided
    emongest twelve                                              14952 *li*

[*margin*]   Sir Walter Raleghe 16.7.b.

---

1. The text omits the year but it was in the summer of 1591 that John Watts's ships (see note 3) took the prizes listed on f. 60r. Ralegh had no great maritime project of his own in 1591.
2. The folio has been bound with the letter on the dorse.
3. John Watts (c.1550–1616), a London merchant who was to be Lord Mayor in 1606–7, has been rated as 'perhaps the greatest privateering promoter of his time': Andrews 1964, p. 104. In 1591 he had five ships at sea from April to September, setting sail in consort with ships of Lord Thomas Howard (in partnership with the Queen) and Sir George Carey, but they parted company before Watts's ships took rich prizes between Havana and Cape St Anthony: BL, Lansd. 67, f. 172v.

4. All were owned in whole or in part by Watts: BL, Lansd. 67, ff. 141 and 159.
5. The nature and extent of Ralegh's stake in the voyage is not known, but besides his clear intimation in the letter there is a list of eleven adventurers, largely in Burghley's hand (BL, Lansd. 67, f. 141), headed by Ralegh. His letter suggests that there were in fact twelve investors. For Watts's involvement with Ralegh in 1590 in attempts to supply the Roanoke colony, Watts entering into a bond of no less than £5,000 to see the job done, see D.B. Quinn, *Set Fair for Roanoke*, Chapel Hill and London 1985, pp. 316–17. There may have been some commitment by Watts to succour Ralegh's colony in 1591, but if so nothing happened.
6. Andrews (loc. cit.) calculates the profit at over 200 per cent, pointing out that Ralegh ignored the fact that 'part of the initial capital outlay (i.e. the ships) returned with scarcely diminished value'.
7. The profits of an Elizabethan privateering voyage, after the deduction of the Queen's customs and the 'tenths' due to the Lord Admiral, were supposed to be divided equally between the owners of the ships, those who victualled them and the ships' companies: BL, Lansd. 73, f. 38.

---

## 38. To Sir John Gilbert from the Court, 30 December 1591

Huntington, HM 21227. In Ralegh's hand, in great haste. Parts barely legible except with help of transcript. Not previously printed.

PRO, SP9/55/12(iv), an eighteenth-century transcript.

### CIDER FOR VICTUALLING

[*addressed*]   To my brother [Adrian *crossed out*] Sir John Gilbert, knight.
[*endorsed*]   My brother for 50 tonnes off [*ci*]der   30 December 1591. Syr Walter for 50 tones of syder, 10000 [*Newfound*]lande fyshe

Brother: The Queene cummanded mee to write yow thancks for your care in her service,[1] and so shee also cummanded my Lord [*Admiral*] to do. Here is no newse worthe the writinge, but all things stand in the same state as of olde. I pray lett Salter[2] provide mee fifty toones of [sider in good *interlined*] caske and hoped with iron hopes and rackte [= *decanted*], [or your selfe yf yow please to provide yt *interlined*]. The mony shalbe payde here, to be returned [by *crossed out*] to Master Smithe of Exceter.[3] I pray, good brother, lett it be carfully dun. This also I would have, ten thowsand of dry Newfoundland fishe provided and sent to Plymothe.

This with my most affectionate comendations I cummit yow to God.
From the Court this xxx of December,
  Your ever as my owne,
    W Ralegh

I pray remember mee to my sister.[4]

1. As Vice-Admiral of Devon, Gilbert had been concerned with victualling men enlisted for Brittany and in getting Ralegh's fleet to sea: *CSPD 1591–94*, p. 66 and see below, Letter 40, note 1.
2. See Letter 39.
3. In Letter 40 Ralegh refers to 'my servant Richard Smith', but this is more likely to have been George Smith of Exeter, merchant, Mayor in 1586–7.
4. Ralegh's sister-in-law, Lady Elizabeth Gilbert, née Chudleigh: see above, Letter 30.

---

## 39. TO SIR JOHN GILBERT, 10 FEBRUARY 1592

Historical Society of Pennsylvania, Gratz Autograph Collection, 12/15. In Ralegh's hand, except for the address. Not previously printed.

PRO, SP9/55/12vi, an eighteenth-century transcript.

### CIDER FOR VICTUALLING

[*addressed by a clerk*]   To my verie lovinge brother, Sir John Gilbart theise
[*endorsed by Gilbert*]   10th Febriary 1591. Syr Walter Rylley for the provysyon to be imbarked for [? *Torbaye and Falmothe*]

Brother: I pray lett thriscore toons of sider [*be*] made reddy and brought to Dartmouthe, and a bark provided to bringe it into the Tore bay to us, wher I will take it in if weather serve. If not that the bark may go with us to Falmouthe for I dare not tarry att Plymothe.[1] Our provisions I would have reddy by the fine [= *end*] of this moneth of Febriarye, the rest of the mony I would have imployed to furnishe John Fleor[2] whom I pray healpe what yow cann.

I have dealt with the Queen who hath geven me her honor to defend yow and esteeme yow in my absence that yow shall not need to doubt [= *fear*] your enemis.[3] This is all for the present. I pray be carefull to stay the shippinge, especially about Dartmouth and Exmothe.[4]

Farewell in hast this xth of Febriary,
    Your most asured loving brother,
        W Ralegh

I have stayd Salter[5] here this longe.

1. Was this something to do with Drake's current fall from favour at Westminster?
2. John Floyer was one of Ralegh's sea-captains: see below, Letter 49.

3. Gilbert had a feud with his neighbour, George Cary of Cockington, especially about musters: *APC* XIX, pp. 211–13, XXIII, pp. 173–6, *HMC Salisbury* IV, pp. 171, 228–9, 458–9 and *CSPD 1591–4*, pp. 266, 274. See also above, Letter 30.
4. Presumably to enable Ralegh to take up mariners.
5. Not identified.

---

## 40. TO SIR JOHN GILBERT FROM THE COURT, 3 MARCH [1592]¹

Maine Historical Society, Portland, John S. Fogg Autograph Collection, vol. 14. In the hand of a clerk, with subscription and signature in Ralegh's hand.

PRO, SP9/55/12v, an eighteenth-century transcript.

Edwards II, pp. 105–6, dated 1594, from a transcript made for the then owner, the editor of the *Edinburgh Review*.

## IMPRESSMENT OF SAILORS AND MARINERS IN DEVON AND CORNWALL

[*addressed*] To my verie lovinge brother, Sir John Gilbart knight, theise [*endorsed by Gilbert*]² ... [*four lines illegible*] 20 of Marche

Brother: Wher by my last letteres directed unto yow concerninge the levienge of sailores and marriners I gave direction that they should be readie against the xvteneth of this moneth at Dartmouth, which I am now, thorowe manie urgentt occacions, constrained to deferr, herebie prainge yow to have speciall care that they be levied from places least infected [*by plague*]³ and to be readie at [Dartmouth the twentith *underlined*]⁴ daie of this present moneth to take shippinge. I have sent money by Luskombe⁵ for the conduct [= *payment to sailors*]. I praie supplie anie thinge necessarie that is wantinge. I will see yt aunswered at my cominge about. I have likewise sent by him proclamations⁶ to be proclamed with yow and sent unto my servaunt Richard Smith into Cornwall, or to Sir William Bevill⁷ to be delivered unto Smith with all spede ([*even*] if I be at charge of sending a foteman of purpose). And hereof I desire yow to have care first that good and sufficient menn be ymprested and ther names taken and then that yow cause the proclamation to be published, and not before, for that the best sort will absent themselves not having received ther prest [= *conduct money*] before, and to write the like direction unto Smith and appoint him to be likewise readie at Falmouth⁸ at the same daie with the Cornishe menn.

And so commendinge me unto yow I comytt yow to God. Court this thirde.⁹

    Your lovinge brother,
    W Ralegh

Post scr[*ipt*]: I praie lett Luscomb have the levienge of the menn in Devon, or, if they be alreadie ymprest, if he know menn of better sufficiency to ympress them a new and leave out some of the worser sort for them alreadie ymprest.

    Sir John Gilbart

1. The letter is clearly connected with Ralegh's intended expedition to the West Indies, serious planning of which began early in the New Year, 1592, with a scheduled departure date of February: Monson I, p. 283. He must also have had his wife's condition very much on his mind: she was already at her brother's house awaiting her confinement: A.L. Rowse, *Ralegh and the Throckmortons*, 1962, p. 160. Their son was born on 29 March.
2. See below, Letter 42.
3. South Devon had been badly hit in 1589–91: P. Slack, *The Impact of Plague in Tudor and Stuart England*, 1985, p. 90.
4. Left-hand margin, probably by Gilbert: 'Dartmouthe the 20 off Marche'.
5. For a Hugh Luscombe, described in 1588 as Gilbert's servant, see *APC* XVI, p. 378, but it was a very common name in south Devon.
6. On 2 March 1592, a royal proclamation was issued ordering all mariners impressed for service with Ralegh, who is described as 'fully ready', to proceed at once to their appointed ships on pain of death: P.L. Hughes and J.F. Larkin, *Tudor Royal Proclamations*, II, p. 106.
7. A Cornish magistrate: see above, Letter 29.
8. Left-hand margin, probably by Gilbert: 'Fawmowthe the 24'.
9. In fact, Ralegh and his fleet did not leave, from Falmouth, until 6 May: Rowse, op. cit., p. 161.

---

## 41. TO SIR ROBERT CECIL FROM CHATHAM, 10 MARCH [1592]¹

Murdin, 1759, pp. 663–4, from the original then at Hatfield House but subsequently lost. Probably, from the nature of contents and the spelling, in Ralegh's hand.

*Works*, 1829, VIII, pp. 658–9, from Murdin; Edwards II, pp. 44–6, from Murdin.

## PREPARATIONS FOR A NAVAL EXPEDITION AND RALEGH'S MARRIAGE

[*no address or endorsement included*]

Sir, I receved your letters this present day at Chattame concerninge the wages of the mariners and others. For myne own part I am very willing to enter bond, as yow perswaded mee, so as the Privy Seale be first sent for my enjoying the third,[2] but I pray consider that I have layd all that I am worth and must do, err I depart on this voyage.[3] If it fall not out well I can but loose all, and if nothinge be remayning wherewith should[4] I pay the wages.[5] Besides, Her Majestie told mee herseoalf that shee was contented to paye her part,[6] and my Lord Admiral his,[7] and I should but discharge for myne own shipps.[8] And farther, I have promised Her Majestie that if I can perswade the [*ships*'] cumpanies to follow Sir Marten Furbresher [*Frobisher*],[9] I will without fail returne and bringe them but into the sea but sume fifty or thriscore leagues, for which purpose my Lord Admirall hath lent me The Disdayne, which to do Her Majestie many tymes, with great grace, bedd [= *bade*] me remember,[10] and sent me the same message by Will Killegrewe,[11] which, God willinge, if I can perswade the cumpanies, I meane to performe, though I dare not be acknown [= *admit*] therof to any creature.

But, Sir, for mee then to be bounde for so great a sume uppon the hope of another man's fortune, I will be loth, and besids, if I were able, I see no privy seale for my thirds.

I mean not to cume away, as they say I will,[12] for feare of a marriage and I knowe not what.[13] If any such thing weare I would have imparted it unto your sealf before any man livinge. And therefore I pray believe it not, and I beseich yow to suppress what you can any such mallicious report. For I protest before God ther is none on the face of the yearth that I would be fastned unto.[14]

And so in hast I take my leve of your honour. From Chattame the 10th of March.

   Yours ever to be cummanded,
    W Ralegh

---

1. The letter's contents clearly indicate the year.
2. To the men for their wages, although he had no letters of Privy Seal from the Queen promising payment of his share of the profit as the owner of some of the ships: see below, Letters 51 and 52.
3. It is not known exactly how much Ralegh personally contributed by way of cash.
4. Edwards has 'shall'.
5. Murdin has inserted a question mark, but Ralegh never uses them.
6. Her ships were the *Garland*, 700 tons, and the *Foresight*, 400: BL. Add. 6177.
7. For the *Lion's Whelp*, 120 tons, see ibid.
8. The *Roebuck*, 350 tons, and the *Galleon Ralegh*, 250.
9. The now-elderly Yorkshire navigator, best known for his attempts in the 1570s to discover a north-west passage.
10. The Queen had first given, and then withdrawn, her permission to Ralegh to lead the expedition, leaving him no option but to hand over in the long term to Sir Martin Frobisher and

Sir John Burgh. But Ralegh obtained the Queen's agreement that he should sail with the fleet when it left England and would return home from the Azores: BL, Ashmole 830, f. 83.
11. A Cornishman, Groom of the Privy Chamber, Vice-Warden of the Stannaries.
12. Murdin has '... cume away, as they say, I will for feare of ...'.
13. Ralegh had, in fact, already married Elizabeth Throckmorton, a Lady of the Queen's Bedchamber, but the Queen was still in ignorance of what many in high places already knew. Cf. Pierre Lefranc, 'La Date du Marriage de Sir Walter Ralegh', *Etudes Anglais*, IX, 1956, pp. 192–211 and A.L. Rowse, *Ralegh and the Throckmortons*, p. 160. If Ralegh meant 'for fear of a [*forced*] marriage' it was an ingenious prevarication, but it seems more likely that he meant fear of the Queen's reception of the news. On either interpretation the phrase was designed to mislead.
14. Rather than admit that Ralegh was lying, Edwards (vol. I, pp. 137–8 and vol. II, p. 146) suggested that he meant to write 'would *rather* be fastned unto' but current opinion is less charitably inclined. In any case the statement is meaningless for he was already married.

---

## 42. To Sir John Gilbert from Portland, Dorset, 31 March [1592]¹

Ransom Center, Pforzheimer 109, Jackson 1940, p. 856, *in extenso* with gaps and minor errors, dated 1 May. In Ralegh's hand.
PRO, SP9/55/12/no.7, an eighteenth-century transcript with some gaps, dated 31 March.
Tytler 1833, I, f. 169.

### PROVISIONS FOR THE FLEET

[*addressed*]   To my loving brother Sir John Gilbert knight
[*endorsed by Gilbert*]   Syr Walter Rylly² for the dyspach of the cyder, fish, etc.

Wee ryde all a cross att Portland reddy to take the first winde, or if the weather continew faire wee will tyde it up³ to the bay.⁴ If yow had geven order to the cunstables of the country to lay [= *search*] the villages yow might have taken thos mariners agayne that ranne away, for wee shalbe undun if wee miss them. I [?*hope*] to be with yow as soun as this bearer. I pray that yow order our fishe be imbarked in all possible hast to cum out into the bay to us, for wee dare not putt in with our great shipps. When I cum I will defray all charges. Therefore good brother gett all abord reddy for us. Wee hoped to have gotten some long pikes⁵ here att Portland but they be Spanish short pickes [*sic*]. Therfore if yow can procure us one hundred or more for reddy money they [?*ma*]y be supplyed agayne from

London. Good brother [?*make*] us not stay longe in the bay, but lett all [?*be*] imbarked agaynst wee cum.

This in hast I bidd yow farewell from Portland this [*last of March*]
>    Yours
>        W Ralegh

1. The date on the original manuscript is now illegible. The year is clearly 1592, and the date read by the eighteenth-century transcriber is likely to be accurate, the manuscript almost certainly being more legible then than it is now.
2. See above, Letter 22.
3. Nautical term for navigating a ship by taking advantage of the tide and anchoring when the tide turns.
4. Torbay, near Gilbert's home at Compton in the parish of Marldon. He was apparently using this as his principal residence rather than his 'poor' ancestral home at Greenway on the River Dart: *HMC Salisbury*, IV, p. 459.
5. For the soldiers who would form part of the ships' companies. On 13 September, Frobisher wrote to Burghley from Dartmouth saying that he had 'some hundred soldiers that belonged to Sir Walter Rawley': BL, Lansd. 70, f. 92.

---

## 43. TO SIR JOHN GILBERT FROM FALMOUTH, 24 APRIL 1592

Pierpont Morgan, REIII.EI-1.44. In Ralegh's hand. Not hitherto printed.
PRO, SP9/55/12viii, an eighteenth-century transcript.

### ACKNOWLEDGMENT OF DEBT

[*addressed*]   To my very loving brother Sir John Gilbert knight
[*endorsed*]   24 Apryel 1592   Sir Watter Rylly from Fawmowthe etc.

Good brother: I thank yow for your many charges. If wee live wee hope to repay all agayne, if not wee shall reccon in the kingdome of Heaven. I have written to satisfy old Souhcot[1] as yow see. I pray hasten away The Adrien,[2] and so in all haste I cummit yow to God. From Falmouth this xxiiii of Aprill.[3]
>    Your ever and ever,
>        W Ralegh

I pray cumend me to my sister.[4]

1. Probably Thomas Southcot (1525–1600), of Shillingford, Clerk of the Peace for Devon. He may have been an investor.
2. A pinnace, probably that owned by Ralegh's half-brother, Adrian Gilbert: *HMC Salisbury* IV, p. 234.
3. The fleet sailed on 6 May from Falmouth bound for the Indies, but by 18 May Ralegh, by prior agreement with the Queen, was back in Plymouth (Rowse, *Ralegh and the Throckmortons*, p. 161) leaving Frobisher in charge of a fleet which was to wait for the Spanish carracks as they neared home: *HMC Salisbury* IV, p. 200.
4. Elizabeth, Lady Gilbert.

---

## 44. To Lord Burghley from Durham House, 8 June 1592

PRO, SP12/242/48, *CSPD 1591–4*, pp. 232–3. In Ralegh's hand.
Edwards II, pp. 46–8.

### COURTESY, OR PILLAGE, AT SEA

[no address]¹
[endorsed]   8 Junii 1592. The awnsweare of Sir Walter Raleigh to the letter of the merchantes of Middleborough [*Middleburg in Zealand*]

My very good lord: I have seen the letter of the deputes of Midelburgh to which I am bold in this manner to awnswere.

About the thirteen day of Maye, as I remember, early in the morninge about fortye leaugs of[f] the Cape Finister wee discried a fleet of thirteen shipps, the admirall [= *flagship*] cariinge a redd flage and the viceadmirall a white, which wee veryley thougt to have bynn the fleet of Saint Mallos,² whereof wee had harde and was upon returninge. Thes shipps, notwithstandinge they might well know us to be Inglishmen and might easely perceve Her Majesties shipp³ to be admirall, bare [= *stood further off*] from us all the[y] could and keipt out their flages in great bravery till The [Row Bucke *underlined*], reachinge the admirall, shote att hyme and made hyme strike [= *salute by lowering flags*]. Which dun all strake and bare with mee but foure who, contrary to their bonds and promises to follow theire admirall, packt on all the sayle the[y] could and left their own admirall and us, being att hand with them, and knew us as well as our sealvs. After whom three of our smaler shipps⁴ followed.

I asked the admirall and the rest why the rest rane away, knowing Her Majesties shipp to be ther. Hee told mee he knew not what the Flemings suspected of them sealvs or whos goods they caried. Thos seven, after I had taken out Davis⁵ from them and to other passengers which I sent your lordship, I dismissed and suffred not the valew of a farthinge to be taken from any of them. The rest, as it is confessed, first forsooke ther admirall, ranne from Her Majesties shipp and fought it out afterward as longe as shee [sic] could agaynst thos three Inglish shipps, beinge apoynted so well as they weare by their own confession, notwithstandinge hee had seen his own admirall strike, which in my oppinion douth make it very playne that the [first written they] monye belonged to thos of Anwerpe [Antwerp], who dayly fraight shipps of Zeland for the trade of Spayne to abuse Her Majestye.

Besids, if Maunsfeld⁶ had not had good reason for that hee did hee would not have caried the shipp back towards his admirall, thriscore and fyve leauges, but would have turnde her of[f] and gonn aweye, ether into Irland⁷ or [first written and] Wales. Besids it is in their letter confessed that Mansfeld did urge sume of the cumpany to confess it was belonginge to thos of Anwarpe, so as it apereth it was confessed to be so.

In my oppinion the Flemings canot say less for them sealvs than they do, and if they can recover xx thousand pound for⁸ the askinge I cannot blame them. I protest before the levinge God I am of oppinion that nether Mansfeld or any of the rest durst any more robe any Fleminge or other (beinge charged and instructed as they weare) then they durst hange them sealvs. Besids the masters of bothe the shipps be very honest and [?religious *crossed out*] sufficient men, and of good wealth, especially the on.⁹

From Derum Howse this 8 of June,
    Your honors humble att cummandment,
        W Ralegh

---

1. Edwards (loc. cit.) thought this letter was addressed to Howard, the Lord Admiral, but it is endorsed by Burghley's clerk. Both would have seen it. The incident here referred to had occurred early in May near Finisterre, but this letter confirms the evidence of the Throckmorton diary that Ralegh was back in London, still a free man, by early June.
2. St Malo in Brittany. In fact, the fleet encountered by Ralegh on 14 May had come from San Lucar, Cadiz. The admiral was a Norwegian, the vice-admiral a Frenchman and the rest Flemings who later said they had mistaken the English ships for Frenchmen or Biscayans because they were flying white flags: see below, note 9.
3. The *Garland* or the *Foresight*: see above, Letter 41, note 6.
4. The *Lion's Whelp*, 120 tons; the *Susan Bonaventure*, 300 tons, and the *Margaret and John*, 300 tons.
5. Nevil Davis, an Englishman who had escaped from the Spaniards and was on board the French vice-admiral: *HMC Salisbury* IV, p. 200.
6. Robert Mansfield alias Mansell (1573–1656), of Margam in Glamorgan, Captain of the *Lion's Whelp*, which belonged to the Lord Admiral. He boarded a Dutch vessel and was alleged to

have taken away 115 bags of money and some cochineal and indigo, declaring that it belonged to merchants of Antwerp trading with Spain.
7. Edwards has 'gonn away otherside ...'.
8. From here to the end, including Ralegh's signature, written vertically in the left-hand margin.
9. The case against the Englishmen was heard in the High Court of Admiralty in the autumn of 1592. Mansell was made to reimburse those he had robbed: PRO, HCA, Examinations XXX; HCA III/61, IV/4 and Acts XXII.

---

## 45.   To Sir Robert Cecil, [late July 1592][1]

Murdin 1759, p. 658, from a manuscript at Hatfield now lost. The spelling suggests that the letter was in Ralegh's hand.

Edwards II, pp. 48–50, from Murdin; Pope Hennessy 1883, pp. 173–5, from Edwards.

### IRISH SETBACKS

[*addressed*]   To my honorable frinde Sir R Cicill knight, of Her Majesty's most honorable Privy Councell
[*no endorsement recorded*]

Sir: I wrat unto your father how I am dealt withall by the Deputye,[2] to whom my disgraces[3] have bynn highly cummended. Hee supposed a debt of four hundred pounds to the Queen for rent[4] and sent order to the Shiriff to take away all the cattell my tenants had and sell them the next day unless the money weare payd the same day. All Munster hath scarce so mich mony in it, and the debt was indeed but fifty marks [= £33 6s. 8d.], which was payde, and it was the first and only rent that hath yet bynn payd by any undertaker.[5] But the Shirife did as he was commanded and tooke away five hundred milch kine from the poor people. Sume had but two, and sume three, to releve their poore wives and children, and in a strange country newly sett downe to builde and plant. Hee hath forcible thrust mee out of possession of a castell, because it is in law between mee and his cousin Winckfeld[6] and will not here my atornes speake. He hath admitted a ward,[7] and geven it to his man, of a castell which is the Queens[8] and hath bynn by mee new built and planted with Inglishe this five years, and to profitt his man with a wardshipp looseth Her Majesties inheritance and would plant the cussen of a rebell in the place of Inglishe men, the castell standinge[9] in the most dangerous place of all Munster.

Besids ther is a band of soldiers which a base phello O'Dodall[10] hath in Yoholl [*Youghall*] which duth cost the Queen twelve hundred pound a yeare and hath not ten good men in it. But our poorest people muster and serve hyme for threepence a day and the rest of his soldiers do nothing but spoyle the country and drive away our best tenants. If the Queen be over rich it may be mayntayned; but I will, att three days warninge, rayse her a better bande, and arme it better tenfold, and better men, whensoever shee shall need it. And in the mean tyme it may ether be imployed in the North or discharged, for ther is in Munster besids a band of horse and another of foot, which is more than needeth. In this, if yow pleas to move it, yow may save Her Majestye so mich in her coffers.[11]

For the rest I will send my man to attend yow, although I care not ether for life or lands, but it will be no small weakninge to the Queen in thos parts, and no small comfort to the ill-affected Irishe, to have the Inglishe inhabitants driven out of the countrey which are yet stronge enough to master the rest without her charge.[12]

    Yours to do yow service,
    W Ralegh

1. As dated by both Murdin and Edwards, who may have seen an endorsement. See also notes 3 and 11.
2. Sir William Fitzwilliam: see Letters 32 and 47.
3. It was not until late July that news of Ralegh's matrimonial affairs was broken to the Queen. On 18 July she granted land in Cork on his recommendation: *Calendar of Irish Chancery Rolls 1576–1602*, p. 202.
4. The rent payable by Ralegh for his Irish lordships had been set at 50 marks (£33 13s. 4d.) per annum for 1591–4 and thereafter at 100. Part had, in fact, been paid: *CCM 1589–1600*, p. 61, *CSPI 1592–6*, p. 57 and Quinn 1962, p. 149
5. = one who had been granted Irish seignories by the Crown.
6. Richard Wingfield, whose mother, Christian, was Fitzwilliam's sister. He had recently been successful in establishing a prior claim to the manor of Ardmore and other property of which, on 15 January 1591, Ralegh had been granted a 101-year lease by the Bishop of Lismore and Waterford, Thomas Wethered: Grosart, Series i, VI, pp. 43 and 242 and M.E. Wingfield, *Family of Wingfield*, 1894, p. 38. See below, note 12.
7. A military governor.
8. Not identified.
9. Edwards has 'stanetinge'.
10. John Dowdall, a professional soldier (see above, Letter 4) who was to be knighted in 1593. He garrisoned Youghall in 1588, and possibly at other times. Ralegh's ill-humour is reflected in his use of the native Irish prefix to Dowdall's name.
11. In December 1592 it was recommended that Dowdall's band be dispensed with, a saving to the Queen put at £1417 8s. 4d. per annum, but no action seems to have been taken: Grosart, op. cit., p. 301, *CCM 1589–1600*, p. 128 and *CSPI 1592–6*, p. 50.
12. To compound Ralegh's loss, Wingfield transferred his claim to Ardmore to John Dowdall who succeeded in ejecting Ralegh in January 1593 and who was still in possession at the time of the inquiry into Ralegh's Irish estates in 1614: Grosart, Series i, V, pp. 43, 42 and Wingfield, op. cit., p. 38.

46. TO SIR ROBERT CECIL [FROM DURHAM HOUSE],[1] [c.26 JULY 1592][2]

Hatfield, CP21/58, *HMC Salisbury* IV, p. 220. In Ralegh's hand.
Murdin, 1759, p. 657; *Works* 1829, II, pp. 685–6; Edwards II, pp. 51–2, from Murdin.

## HOUSE ARREST

[*addressed*] To my honorable frind Sir Robard Cicill knight, of Her Majestyes most honorable Privy Councell
[*endorsed*] Julie 1592
[*in a different hand*] Sir Walter Rawleighe to my master

Sir: I pray be a mean [= *intercessor*] to Her Majestye for the signing of the bills for the gards coates,[3] which ar to be made now for the prograce [and which the cleark of the cheeck[4] hath importunde mee to write for *interlined*]. My hart was never broken till this day that I here the Queen goes away so farr of[f] whom I have followed so many yeares with so great love and desire, in so many jurneys, and am now left behinde her and in a darke prison [all alone *interlined*].[5] While shee was yet nire att hand, that I might here of her once in to or three dayes my sorrows weare the less, but yeven now my hart is cast into the deapth of all misery. I that was wount to behold her ridinge like Alexander, huntinge like Diana, walkinge like Venus, the gentle winde blowinge her faire heare about her pure cheekes like a nimpth [*sic*], sumtyme sitting in that shade like a [nimp *crossed out*] goddes, sumtyme singinge like an angell, sumtyme playinge like Orpheus. Behold the sorrow of this worlde, once amiss hath bereved mee of all. Oh love[6] that only shineth in misfortune, what is becum of thy asurance. All wounds have skares [= *scars*] but that of fantasye, all affections their relentinge but that of wooman kinde. Who is the judge of frindship but adversetye, or when is grace wittnesed but in offences. Ther weare no devinitey but by reason of cumpassion, for revenges ar brutishe and mortall.[7] All thos tymes past, the loves, the sythes [= *sighs*], the sorrowes, the desires, can they not way doune one fraile misfortune. Cannot one drope of gall be hidden in so great heapes of sweetness.[8] I may then conclude *spes et fortuna valete*: shee is gonn in whom I trusted, and of mee hath not on thought of mercy nor any respect of that that was. Do with mee now therfore what yow list. I am more wery of life then they are desirus I should perishe, which if it had bynn for her, as it is by her, I had bynn to happelye borne.[9]

    Yours not worthy any name or title,
        W R

1. Ralegh had been under house arrest in Durham House, in the charge of his cousin, Sir George Carew, since early June. His study window commanded extensive views of the Thames: O.L. Dick (ed.), *Aubrey's Brief Lives*, 1962, p. 317. He did not go to the Tower until 7 August: Rowse, op. cit., p. 162.
2. See below, notes 5 and 9.
3. Appointed to succeed Sir Christopher Hatton as Captain of the Queen's Guard in 1587, Ralegh had only assumed full responsibility on Hatton's death in 1591.
4. Edward Wingate, Keeper of the Roll of the Queen's Servants: *CSPD 1591–4*, p. 549.
5. The Queen moved from Greenwich to Nonsuch in Surrey between 25 and 27 July: Nichols, *Progresses of Queen Elizabeth*, 1823, III, pp. 38, 124.
6. Murdin read this as 'glory'.
7. See above, note 1.
8. His grant of Sherborne was formally confirmed on 27 June: BL, Lansd. 163, p. 190a.
9. Ralegh's frenzy at this time is borne out by the account given to Robert Cecil of his behaviour at Durham House on 26 July when he was said to have caught sight of the royal barges assembled at Blackfriars. Struggling with Carew he swore 'that he wolde disguyse hymselfe and gett into [*sic*] a pare of oares to ease hys mynde butt with a syght of the Quene, or els, he protest[ed], his harte wolde breake ...': Bodleian, Ashmole 1729, f. 177, printed in H.E. Sandison, 'Arthur Gorges: Spencer's Alcyon and Ralegh's friend', *Modern Language Association*, 43, 1928, pp. xxvi–xxvii.

---

47. TO SIR ROBERT CECIL [FROM DURHAM HOUSE], [c.30][1] JULY 1592

Hatfield, CP21/59, *HMC Salisbury* IV, p. 221. In Ralegh's hand.

Murdin 1759, pp. 658–9; *Works*, 1829, VIII, pp. 657–8, from Murdin; Edwards II, pp. 50–51, also from Murdin.

## REBELLION IN CONNAUGHT

[*addressed*] To my very lovinge frinde Sir Robard Cicill knight, of Her Majestyes most honorable Privey Councell

[*endorsed*] Julie 1592   Sir Walter Rawleighe to my master

Sir: I pray send me the newse of Irlande. I here that ther ar three thowsand of the Burgks[2] in arms and younge Odonell and the soonns of Shane Oneale.[3] I wrate in a letter of [*to*] Master Killegrews[4] ten dayes past a prophesye of this rebellion which, when the Queen redd, she made a scorne att my conceate, but yow shall finde it but a shoure of a farther tempest.[5] If yow pleas to send mee worde of what yow here. I will be laught att agayne in my oppinion towchinge the same and be bolde to write yow my [oppinion *crossed out*] farther suspicion. Your cussen the dotinge deputye[6] hath dispeopled mee, of which I have written to your father alreddye. It is a signe how my disgraces have past the seas and have bynn highly cummended to that wise governoure who hath used mee accordinglye. So I leve to troble yow att this tyme, being becum like a fishe cast onn dry lande, gaspinge for breath, with lame leggs[7] and lamer [*lunges crossed out*] loonges.

  Your for the litle while I shall desere to do yow service,
   W Ralegh

1. See above, Letter 46, note 1.
2. Ulick Burke and his followers in county Mayo were reported, in June 1592, to number no more than 240 men, and by September to have all surrendered: *CSPI*, IV, pp. 523–4, 578–9.
3. Hugh Roe O'Donnell (?1571–1602) and the two sons of Shane O'Neill, Earl of Tyrone, had escaped from Dublin Castle on Christmas Eve 1591: D. Murphy (ed.), O'Clery, *Life of O'Donnell*, Dublin 1893, p. 19.
4. See Letter 41, note 11.
5. Although O'Donnell submitted to the Lord Deputy on 2 August 1592, the rebellion which Ralegh foresaw smouldered on for the next five years and flared up in 1598.
6. Cecil's mother, Mildred, was the daughter of Lord Deputy Fitzwilliam's father's half-sister, Ann Cooke.
7. His friend Arthur Gorges (see below, Letter 101), describing the struggle between Ralegh and Carew at Durham House on 26 July (Letter 46, note 9), adds 'al lameness was forgotten', which suggests that Ralegh affected at this time of acute emotional shock what Gorges, at any rate, recognized as a psychosomatic affliction.

---

48.  TO CHARLES LORD HOWARD
   [FROM DURHAM HOUSE,
   LATE JULY 1592][1]

   PRO, SP12/242/131, *CSPD 1591–4*, p. 265, dated ?August 1592. In Ralegh's hand. Edwards II, pp. 52–4, dated ?August.

## THE FRUSTRATIONS OF CAPTIVITY

[*addressed*] To the right honorable the Lorde High Admirall of Ingland
[*endorsed*] Admiralty

My very good lorde: I have sent to Sir John Hawkings[2] to have his oppinion as towchinge The Great Susan,[3] and both hee and my sealf do verely thinke that in removing the vitles att this tyme of the yeare, the drink turnde on the leese [= *dregs*], all wilbe spoyled. So as I see noway but to leve the shippe and sell the remayne of the provisions, for I know noboddye but my sealf (if I had byne att libertye) that would undertake to sett her out, and a good strenght is tharby wantinge, especially wher a [*sic*] farr more ayde is required.

It is hard to lessen that that was, but it is more profitable to punishe my great treasons then that I should ether strenghthen [*sic*] the flet or do many other thinges that lye in the diches.

Here ar besides all the mariners that came in the prize and the soldiers. They run up and down exclayminge for paye. I dare not speake with them that I might cumpare their names with my booke to know when they entreat [= *entered*][4] into pay and what hath byn imprested, and so that order may be directly taken for their discharge. For now both thos of good and ill decsart ar mixt without respect, theon unpunished theother unpayde. I beseich your lordship, if it be thought fitt, that order be gaven to Sir Georg [*Carew*][5] that they may cum unto mee to stay all farther exclamation.[6]

I was yesterdey advertesed from a man of myne cumminge from the coast of Britayne [*Brittany*] that ther ar twentye shipps of warr for the Leauge[7] that lye between Silley and Ushent to take up our Newlandmen[8] and to watch for any prises that shalbe sent home. If any of the shipps in the Narrow Seas[9] weare sent for a tyme, or sume other course taken, it weare most necessarye, or elce wee shall lose all and be a scorne to all nations. But wee ar so mich busied with the affaires of other nations (of whose manghangled[10] trobles ther will never be end) that we forgett our own affaires, our profitt and our honor. Hee is of a mean consait [= *imagination*] that lookes not into the purpose of this peace[11] which may as well be turnde over, *finesse contra finesse*, to our most advantage, but in the meanwhile the few mean actions of our own ar utterly neglected.[12]

To conclud I must humble thanck your lordshipp for your most honorable care of mee in this unfortunate accident.[13] But I see ther is a determination to disgrace mee and ruin mee, and therfore I beseich your lordship not to offend Her Majestye any farther by sewing [= *suing*] for mee. I am now resolved of the matter. I only desire that I may be stayd no one howre from all the extremetye that ether lawe or presedent can avowe, and if that be too letle would God it weare withall concluded, that I might feed the lions as I go by[14] to save labor. For the torment of my mind cannot be greater, and for the boddye, would others did respect themsealvs as miche as I valew hit att litle. [*vertically in left-hand margin*] And so with my humble dewtye and thancks which I cannot express I leve your lordship to God.

    Your lordships poore kinsman[15] to do yow service for ever,
      [W Ralegh]

1. Possibly very early August, but before the 7th when he went to the Tower: see below, note 14.
2. Treasurer and Comptroller of the Navy Board since 1577 and 1589 respectively.
3. 350 tons, belonging to Paul Bayning, Warden of the Grocers Company of London, she had been part of Ralegh's fleet but had been sent home with a prize, the *Sante Clara*, a Biscayan ship taken off the Spanish coast: Monson I, p. 281, note 1.
4. Compare Letter 1, line 24.
5. See above, Letter 46, note 1.
6. On 13 August the Council ordered Ralegh to pay the *Great Susan*'s crew, if necessary from a sale of goods, and later that the profits on the prize goods be used to pay the *Foresight*'s crew for the Queen: *APC* XXIII, pp. 117–18, 204.
7. The Catholic League in France.
8. English ships, especially from Dartmouth, going to Newfoundland to fish.
9. The eastern end of the English Channel.
10. = mixed in a wild and confused manner, a West Country term.
11. Peace between religious adversaries in France was much talked about at this time: *CSPD 1591–4*, p. 251.
12. On 21 August, Burghley noted that the band in the Low Countries numbered 2,400, that in Brittany 1,200 and in Normandy 4,000: *CSPD 1591–4*, p. 254.
13. His marriage and, in particular, the Queen's displeasure.
14. Indicating that when he wrote this letter he had not yet been sent to the Tower.
15. Possibly through Howard's mother, a Gamage of Coity: see Letter 14.

---

## 49. TO LORD BURGHLEY AND CHARLES LORD HOWARD [FROM THE TOWER], 27 AUGUST 1592

BL, Lansd. 115, f. 173, enclosed with a letter from Howard to Burghley, ibid., f. 261, dated 28 August. Written by a clerk in a particularly fine set hand, with place-names in italic script, subscribed and signed by Ralegh.

Edwards II, pp. 56–8.

## A TRIO OF UNHOLY BOTTOMS

[*addressed*] To the right honorable my verie good lords the Lord Th[resur]er and Lord Admirall of England
[*no endorsement*]

My verie good lords: I have receaved a lettre from your lordships concerning the taking of a shipp of Bayon[ne] laden with fish by Captain John Floire, whereunto your lordships require my aunsweare.¹ I acquainted the Judg of Thadmiraltie [*Sir Julius Caesar*] and Captain Floire with the complaint and do finde that in the Bay of Portugal² John Floire, meeting with this shipp of Bayon[ne], which a little before was taken going into Spaine with victuell without licence by a man of warr of Diep[pe] (as was said), though Captain Floire judged him rather to be of Newhaven,[3] was earnestly entreated to succor and rescue them from the captain and others which were putt abord from the man of warr. Captain Floire, perceaving that they were the Fr[ench] kings frends and like to be spoiled by the Leaguers, caused the supposed captain of Diep[pe] and the master of the shipp of Bayon[ne] to come abord his shipp, where one accused thother, thone for carying victuel to thenemy, thother for landing the greatest parte of his men in Spaine. Hereuppon the master, standing uppon his integritie and innocencie, promised Captain Floire great recompence to rescue him and to bring his shipp and lading safelie into some port of England, affirming that in France he shold be oppressed by the Liguer and find no justice in recovery of them againe.

During which time there arose a great tempest so violent Captain Floire could neither return the Fr[ench] captain and master to the shipp from whence they came nor receave his own men out of the shipp of Bayon[ne]. This storm severed the shipps and the Fr[ench] ship was by Captain Floires men (which did swim abord her) caried to Uphil in Severne[4] with intent to have made spoile of her.[5] Which Captain Floire understanding [he] was forced to putt into Plymmouth and to victuel his ship for a moneth longer, all which time he followed the Fr[ench] shipp and took her againe. Within 2 or 3 daies after came commission from you my Lord Admiral to take the ship and fish from Captain Floire, which he accordinglie obeyed and delivered the same to your lordships officer with a very small diminution.

What became afterwards of the ship and goods Captain Floire protesteth he is ignorant. Neither was he inquisytive because he held himselfe discharged of anie farther account uppon receipt of your lordships commission. Onelie he hath heard that by the negligence of such as had charge thereof the ship was lyke to perish in harbour, and the fish being removed and landed did begin noisomelie to smell. And so it seemeth some losse was susteined after John Floire was commaunded to leave her, himselfe making no benefytt by the ship or her lading, although they made him great promises of recompence before he rescued them.[6] Besides he lost the benefitt of his voyage to the Indies, victuelled his ship twise and is almost undone in seeking their safetie, never receaving [a] penny for his travel [= *trouble*], charges and losse of time.

Thus I make bold to dilate unto your lordships the particularities at large, because Captain Floire is reputed and known to be my man and the

ship mine[7] wherein he was going to the Indies, yet do I write nothing partyallie but what shalbe confirmed by the testimonies of honest persons.
And so do humblie take my leave the 27th of August 1592.[8]

    Your lordships humble att cummandmente,
        W Ralegh

Lord Thr[easurer]
Lord Admiral

1. A complaint had been lodged with the Privy Council on or before 6 June and passed to Ralegh: *CSPD 1591–4*, pp. 230–31 and *APC* XXIII, p. 57. John Floyer's family held land near Exeter and he, or a namesake, had sailed with Ralegh in 1578: Quinn, *Gilbert* 1940, I, p. 212.
2. The sea off the coast of Portugal between Oporto and the headland of Cintea.
3. Le Havre, a Catholic League port. Ralegh is suggesting that the unnamed vessel was pretending to be from a Protestant port, thus justifying Floyer's intervention.
4. At the mouth of the River Axe south of Bristol.
5. The Bayonne vessel was said to have been a flyboat, that is a small boat used for supplies, laden with 108,000 dry fish, 4,000 green fish and 14 hogsheads of train oil, worth 6,000 crowns, and to belong to Pierre de Hody, a merchant of Bayonne: *CSPD 1591–4*, p. 231. Hody charged certain 'rich merchants' of Bristol with pocketing the proceeds of the sale of his goods.
6. However, several Englishmen, including Carew Ralegh, had found easy targets in Bayonne merchantmen: ibid.
7. In his initial complaint, Hody had described Floyer's ship as one victualled by merchants of Bristol (ibid.), and while Ralegh would have been taking a great risk in lying to the Privy Council, it seems odd that members of Floyer's crew should take their captive up the Bristol Channel. However, Andrews 1964, p. 261, lists a Bristol vessel, name unknown, captain John Flegon (*sic*), as having in 1591 seized a cargo of French fish, the promoters being certain merchants of Bristol and Sir Walter Ralegh.
8. In Howard's rather brisk note to Burghley enclosing Ralegh's letter, the Lord Admiral stated that he had instructed the Vice-Admiral of Somerset to deliver the ship and part of her cargo to the Frenchman, but in October Hody was still claiming £1,000 and Ralegh was again ordered by the Privy Council to answer for his ship lest the French take reprisals on English merchantmen: BL, Lansd. 115, f. 261, Edwards II, p. 55 and *APC* XXIII, p. 221.

---

## 50. TO CHARLES LORD HOWARD WITH SIR JOHN HAWKINS [FROM THE TOWER], 27 AUGUST 1592

Longleat, Wilts, Portland Papers I, f. 147, *HMC Bath*, II, p. 38, *in extenso*. Written by a clerk, with postscript and signature in Ralegh's hand and also signed by Hawkins.

Strype, *Annals* 1751, IV, pp. 177–82, with errors; W. Oldys, *Life of Ralegh*, 1736, pp. 154–5 and *Works*, 1829, from the original then in BL.

## CONVOY FOR THE GREAT CARRACK

[*addressed*]   To the right honorable our verie good Lorde the Lord High Admirall of England

[*endorsed*]   Sir Walter Rawlighe and Sir John Hawkins to the Lord High Admiral 27 Auguste 1592

2v 7ᵇ [*sic*] Sent to me [*Michael Hicks*] by the Lord Admyral  Desiring 3 ships to guard the great Indian ship Sir John Burgh was bringing into Plimouth [*sic*]

Oure verie good Lord: We have conferred together about the East Indian shippe[1] to be brought to Plymmoth by Sir John Burgh,[2] and in our opinions she can be no lesse worth then five hundreth thowsand pounde, being a shippe of so great burthen and laden with so rich commodyties[3] as appeareth she is. Wherefore we have considered that the Spanish men of warre lying upon the coast of Britaigne [*Brittany*], hearing of so great a prize taken from the King [*of Spain*] or the merchantes of that cuntrie, and envying that such a benefytt should grow to us, to their hindrance and dishonour, will endevour by all possible meanes, being distaunt but a daies or nights sayling, either to recover the shipp againe or to burne her and all her lading,[4] rather then it shalbe deteined here, seing that the places of defence where the shipp may remaine is not able to resist their power.[5] In our opinions, therefore, we thinke fitt, and do praie your lordship, that the three shippes of Her Majesty which are appointed to keep the Narrow Seas[6] may, by your lordships lettre and direction, be appointed to goe westward and there to guard the Indyan shipp for a time, untill The Gardland [*Garland*][7] and some of the same fleete be returned, whose arrivall can not be anie long time expected,[8] or untill some other order maie be taken for the unlading or keeping of her otherwise, which we praie your lordship may be done with some expedition.

And so do humblie take our leaves this 27th of August 1592.
    Your lordships humble att cummandmente
        W Ralegh
        John Hawkyns

[*left-hand margin, near-contemporary hand, unidentified*]
Called The Mother of God, 165 foot in length, 7 decks high and manned with 600 men. This huge carrack was met with about the Azores where Sir Walter Raleigh appoyted some ships to wait for the Spanish East Indian ships.

[*postscript ditto*]
But when she was brough[t] home the booty was but about 150000 *li*, the commanders, seamen and soldiers having purloined and embezzelled the rest. For the retrieving of which the Q[ueen] issued out a proclamation and appointed commissioners to examine al that were concerned, or suspected, upon their oaths. And some of them ventured to foreswear themselves rather then part with their spoil.

1. She was the *Madre de Dios*, 1,600 tons, an East Indiaman, captured off the Azores on 3 August, but only now, three weeks later, had the news reached London.
2. (1562–1594), a younger son of William, 4th Lord Burgh of Gainsborough, and admiral aboard the *Roebuck*, one of Ralegh's aborted West Indian fleet. Both Ralegh and Hawkins had vested interests in the fleet's prizes, but there were other ships involved in the taking of the *Madre de Dios*. For the fullest accounts yet published, see C.L. Kingsford, 'The taking of the Madre de Dios 1592', in *The Naval Miscellany*, vol. II, Navy Records Society, XL, 1912, Andrews 1964, *passim* and R.B. Wernham, *After the Armada*, Oxford 1984, pp. 446–8.
3. The estimate proved to be somewhat optimistic but she was, nevertheless, the greatest prize ever taken by Englishmen, her cargo consisting of jewels, spices, drugs, perfume, silks, cottons, carpets, dye stuffs, ivory, porcelain, coconuts, hides and tropical woods, but above all of pepper.
4. Burgh had failed to take the first carrack that he encountered off the Azores, the *Santa Cruz*, because her crew contrived to beach and burn her.
5. Meaning not clear.
6. These were the *Rainbow*, the *Vantage* and the *Answere*: APC XXIII, p. 206.
7. 660 tons, one of the Queen's ships.
8. Burgh brought the Great Carrack into Dartmouth on 8 September: Stebbing 1899, p. 97.

---

## 51. To Lord Burghley from the Tower, [13][1] September 1592

Longleat, Wilts, Portland Papers I, f. 149, *HMC Bath* II, pp. 38–9, *in extenso*. In Ralegh's hand. Right-hand edge now very much damaged, lost words supplied from *HMC Bath*.

Strype, *Annals*, 1731, IV, p. 129, with errors and omissions; Edwards II, pp. 67–8, from Strype, 1824 edit., repeating errors and omissions.

## NEGOTIATIONS FROM THE TOWER

[*addressed*] To the right honorable my singular good Lord the Lord Tresorer of Inglande, etc.

[*endorsed*] [*September 1592*] Sir Walter Raleighe to my lord

May it pleas your lordship: Sir George Carew[2] hath dealt with mee to know in parti[cular] how Her Majestye might be profited by the carecke[3] accordinge to the offer I ma[de].[4] My promis was not to buy my bondage but my libertye and the hope of Her Majesties favor. For setting downe of the accompts [= *liabilities*] I cannot for I have receved none, and I [*am*] to take reckininge of twentye severall persons, sume that made my provisions in the west countrey, others that imprested men in all the maritime sheires, the vitle[r]s, coopers, smiths for iron hoopes, brewers, bakers, shipp carpenters, [*armo*]rers and divers others that provided aparell, canvas, wullen clothe, etc.[5] Before I [*harde*] of the takinge of the carecke I thought it not worth the labor and, my seal[*fe*] beinge the greatest adventurer, I was contented rather to smother my [*loss*] then labor to publeshe [= *make known*] a hopeless overthron estate.

In breif this mich may [*it*] pleas your lordship to know: that of five thowsand toons of shippinge[6] Her Majesty hath but aleven hundred, of eyghteen thowsande pounde in mony Her Majestie hath but fifteen hundred pounde, for the other fifteen hundred was imployed [*on*] her too shipps, as by Sir John Hawkings accompt will apeare. To conclude, Her Majesties adventure will cume but to the tenth part, which of too hundred thowsand pounde (such I thinck is the valew of the carecke)[7] Her Majesties p[*art*] wilbe but twentye thowsand pounde, and I know Her Majestye will not take the rights of her subjects from them contrary to her hand and seale, consider[*ing*] that for her service sake and the rather for your lordships perswation they wea[*re*] contented to adventure, and this is not the last tyme that Her Majestye shall need their contribution. If Her Majestye had sett out the jurney [*at*] her own charge it would have cost her fortye thowsande pounde, and [?*now*][8] it stoode her but fifteen hundred pounde, besids her too shipps. In steed of this twentye thowsande pounde if [= *as*] I had made it a hundred thowsande [*and*] donn injury to none but my sealf I hope it may be thought that it procee[*ded*] from a faithfull minde and a true desire to serve her.

Fore score thowsande pounde is more then ever any man presented Her Majestye as yet. If God have sent it for my ransome I hope Her Majestye of her abundant goodness will accept it. If I speake with the least [= *the minimum*] a greater sume wilbe more thancks worthye. If my imprisonment or my life might do Her Majestye more good I protest before God I would never desire ether libertye or farther respett of breathinge, and if Her Majestye cannot beat me from [her *crossed out*] my affection I hope her sweet nature will thinck it no conquest to afflict me. What her will shalbe I shall as willingly obaye.

And so I humble take my leve of your lordship from this unsavory dongeon this [*blank*][9] of September.

        Your lordships most redy to do yow ser[*vice*],
          W Ralegh

1. On 11 September, Hawkins informed Burghley that Ralegh was willing to discuss terms for his release, and as the Court was in Gloucestershire from 9 to 12 September, Carew can hardly have received instructions to visit Ralegh before the 13th. On the 14th the Queen, then at Sherborne, signed the order for Ralegh's conditional release: BL, Lansd. 70, f. 88.
2. See above, Letter 46, note 1.
3. The *Madre de Dios*, see Letter 50, note 1.
4. See above, note 1 and Letters 48 and 49.
5. 'For settinge downe ... wullen clothe etc.' omitted by Edwards.
6. Cf. Edwards who has 1,800 and 1,200, ameriding Strype who reproduced the figures correctly.
7. Allowing for some 1,210 tons for Cumberland's fleet.
8. *HMC Bath* II, p. 39 has 'as [now?]' but 'and [now?]' is more certainly the correct reading.
9. Ralegh left the Tower with his keeper, Sir Michael Blount, on Friday 15 September: Stebbing 1899, p. 97.

---

## 52. To Lord Burghley from London,[1] 16 September 1592

Longleat, Wilts, Portland Papers I, f. 151, *HMC Bath* II, pp. 39-40, *in extenso*. In Ralegh's hand.

Strype, *Annals*, 1731, IV, p. 182, in note form; Edwards II, p. 69, from Strype, with omissions.

## DARTMOUTH AHOY

[*addressed*] To the right honorable my singuler good lorde the Lorde Tresorer of Inglande

[*endorsed*] 16 September 1592 Sir Walter Raleigh to my lord

[*No salutation*] By your lordships great favor I have obteyned libertye to ride downe.[2] I hope it shalbe profitable for Her Majestye and a quietness and satisfaction to the rest. I here that the rest of your shipps[3] ar arived ther also and present payment must be made that they run not in farther charge. The Lions Whelpe of my Lord Admiralls is cum to the Ile of Wight with too prises. I have dispach away a messenger to see them ordered accordingly.

The way to profitt Her Majestye muste be in this wise: first to take a fift part for her custome,[4] secondlye a tenth part or more for her particular adventure,[5] and next and cheefest I will put the therd part of all into her handes for the mariners, which I did undertake to paye and of right belongeth unto my sealf.[6] Which will amount to the on half of the careke [*the Madre de Dios*], for althoughe Her Majestye was offended with Sir

Robard Cicill for not taking bounde of mee for the payment of the wages, yet, my lord, I did binde my sealf to all the shipps cumpanies to paye them, which indeed I did not confess to Sir Robarde while I was prisoner.[7]

That this part may cum unto Her Majestye as of her own dew and not by mee I will avowe that I undertooke it as in the Queens right, who had promised mee to save me harmless [= *give me legal immunity*], hopinge of Her Majesties goodness otherwise, for I protest before the levinge God both my three years pension of the customhowse which was six thowsand pounde,[8] and all I have besids is in this jurney.

Now your lordship must remember that the earle of Cumberland can be in no privat consort [= *convoy*] with thes three shipps[9] but hee must cum in with all our fleet, for all ours weare in consort in sight and out of sight, and the agrement of any part cannot breake the rest, otherwise hee would clayme the on half.

I pray your lordship to send mee order for sume 2000*li* to pay the shipps here wher the most part are, and to pay them for the Queene. I have payd allredd[y] about 1200*li* here in Lundun and all the wages will not amount [to] six thowsand for which the [crews'] thirds I doubt not but wilbe worth thriscore thowsande. I here of great outrage still cummitted[10] ther [*Dartmouth*] and therfore it is tyme I weare gonn. I beseich your lordship to beare with my hast for this tyme.

Ther wants a cummission there to Billingsly and Barns[11] to examine all persons that cum to Lundun and that have convoyed goods, and to arest it [*sic*]. Also your lordships letter to octores [= *authorize*] us att Dartmouth to fraight shipps to bring about the goods: it is as good cheap from thence as from Porsmouth [*sic*] and in Dartmouth will be found warlike shipps enough to do it, att Porsmouth none. Besids it weare a desperat adventure to bring her [= *Madre de Dios*] about.[12] I beseich your lordship to take order for thes with sume speade for the charge will groe dayly and winter weather cumes on.

This xvi of September 1592.

  Your lordships evermore to serve yow,
    W Ralegh

1. See above, Letter 51, note 9.
2. To Dartmouth where the *Madre de Dios* lay. After visiting Ralegh in the Tower, Sir John Hawkins had written to Burghley on 11 September that he saw no-one 'of so reddy a disposytion to lay the grownd howe Her Majesties porcyon may be increasyd as he ys and can best brynge it abowt': BL, Lansd. 70, f. 88.
3. Ralegh was only too ready to credit Burghley with the enrolment of investors from the city of London.

4. The normal custom payable on all prize goods.
5. Largely ships.
6. See above, Letter 50.
7. He had not anticipated being in a position to do so: see Letter 51.
8. Presumably his income from his sole right to license the export of remnants and overlength cloths.
9. There is no evidence that Cumberland contemplated making such a claim, but Ralegh counted upon there being no honour among privateering entrepreneurs.
10. From here to the end vertically in left-hand margin.
11. Alderman Henry Billingsley, haberdasher, who was to be Lord Mayor of London in 1596, and Sir George Barnes, also a haberdasher, knighted in 1587 at the end of his Lord Mayoralty: A.B. Beaven, *Aldermen of the city of London*, II, 1913, p. 208.
12. The Privy Council thought that if she were brought to Chatham she could be sold, but were happy that she be sold in Dartmouth if a buyer were to come forward offering the right price: *APC* X, p. 269. In fact, she remained at Dartmouth, 'being so huge and unweldie a ship as shee was never remooved out of that harbour, but there laid her bones' (Purchas, XVI, p. 17), to which one is tempted to add, 'or what was left of them' after the local shipwrights had had their pickings. Ralegh appears to have washed his hands of her.

---

## 53. To Lord Burghley and Charles Lord Howard from Hartley Row,[1] 17[2] September 1592

Longleat, Wilts, Portland Papers I, f. 153, *HMC Bath*, II, pp. 40–41, incomplete. In Ralegh's hand.

Strype, *Annals*, 1731, p. 178, modern spelling, with slips; Edwards II, pp. 70–71, from Strype.

### EN ROUTE FOR THE WEST COUNTRY

[*addressed*]   To the ryght honorable my syngular good lords the Lord Treasurer and Lord Admyrall of Englande   With speade

[*endorsed*]   17 September 1592   Sir Walter Raleigh to the Lord Tresurer and Lord Admirall

[*in another hand*]   Desiring a Commission to examine persons on oath

My humble dewtye remembred: If it pleas your lordships to send us by this bearer a cummission to examine uppon oath as well mariners as townsmen, and all strangers of other places, what hath bynn bought or solde, I doubt not but wee shall finde out many things of importance, for the earle of Cumberlands shipps who had the cheefest pillage[3] arived at Plymouth, made port sale of diamonds, rubies, muske, ambergreece and all other commodetes, and not on of the cummissioners[4] ever moved or sent thither but only sacked my shippe, which only attended the careke, yeven to the very keilson.⁵ The earls shippes, The Dayntye, The Dragon, The Foresight and the rest ran from her in to severall ports and have solde all;⁶ only my poore men and shippe was stript for her good attendance, and if shee had forsaken the careke as thes rest did shee had bynn cast awaye.⁷

Also if it pleas your lordship to send a cummission to Alderman Marten⁸ and others to make inquiry in Lundune what goldsmiths or jewellers ar gon down [*to Devon*] and that att ther retorne the[*y*] may be examined uppon oath what stonn or perrele [= *pearl*] they have bought, I doubt not but many thinges wilbe discovered. If I meet any of them cumming upp, [*even*] if it be uppon the wildest heath, in all the way I mean to stripp them as naked as ever the[*y*] weare borne, for it is infinite [= *beyond doubt*] that Her Majestye hath bynn robbed and that of the most rare things.⁹

Wheras I wrate to your lordship for 2000 *li*,¹⁰ if wee lode the same shipps with the goods we shall not need to pay but part, and the rest att Lundun, so as I thinck one thowsand will serve.

This in hast I humble take my leve, from Hartelbery¹¹ this Sunday morninge.

   Your lordships humble att cummandment,
    W Ralegh

If it pleas your lordships to se[*n*]d cummission to my sealf, Sir John Gilbert, Sir Francis Drake, Master Killegrew, Master Christopher Harris and Master Payden [*Payton*], the Customer and Tristram Gorge,¹² because other[*s*] dwell uppon Saltashe river and shalbe able amonge their tenants to find out many things.

---

1. 'Hartelbery' (or 'Hartlebury' as in *HMC Bath*) can only be Hartley Row in the parish of Hartley Witney between Basingstoke and Bagshot, a regular staging post on the road to the South West. Sir Arthur Throckmorton stayed at the 'George' there in 1595: Rowse, op. cit., p. 195.
2. The letter is undated but Ralegh had been released from the Tower on 15 September (see above, Letter 51, note 9) and 17 September was a Sunday. On 16 September, Sir Robert Cecil had been appointed to oversee the unloading of the carrack and on the 19th he wrote from Exeter remarking that he had outridden the Queen's captive and would reach Dartmouth before him: *CSPD 1591–4*, pp. 272–3. Cecil reached Sir John Gilbert's house, Greenway, on the River Dart, late on the 19th, and Ralegh reached Dartmouth on the 20th: BL, Lansd. 70, p. 98 and Addit. 6177, pp. 154–5.
3. Technically spoil taken on deck by boarders, but a right very loosely interpreted.
4. On 28 August, Sir John Gilbert and Mr Christopher Harris of Radford near Plymouth had been appointed commissioners for the carrack to act on Ralegh's behalf, and Sir Francis Drake for the Queen: BL, Lansd. 70, p. 64, but by 6 September the Privy Council had joined Drake with William Killigrew, esquire (see above Letter 41, note 11), and a John Bland,

5. Keelson = internal timber under the floor of a ship, in this context 'to the very bottom'.
6. On 9 September, Burgh wrote from Dartmouth concerning great abuses at Plymouth. Drake's very success was causing local 'envy' of conditions in Saltash: BL, Lansd. 70, f. 76.
7. By no means all of Ralegh's fleet returned to Dartmouth.
8. Sir Richard Martin, a former Lord Mayor, Master of the Mint since 1581 and Prime Warden of the Goldsmiths Company 1592–3: Beaven, *Aldermen of London*, II, pp. 40, 174.
9. This is confirmed by Cecil's letter of 19 September: see above, note 2.
10. Above, Letter 52.
11. Ralegh was writing in great haste: see above, note 1.
12. Neither Thomas Payton nor Tristram Gorges seem to have been particularly active, and indeed Drake's personal involvement is nowhere on record.

---

## 54. [TO LORD BURGHLEY][1] FROM DARTMOUTH, [?21][2] SEPTEMBER 1592

From Strype, *Annals*, 1731, IV, pp. 126–7, from a lost original, spelling and punctuation modernized, it appears to be a complete transcript. Probably in Ralegh's hand.

Edwards II, pp. 71–2, from Strype, 1824 edition.

## UNLADING THE CARRACK

[*headed by Strype*]   Sir Walter Raleigh to the Lord Treasurer concerning the robbbing of the great Spanish carrack, upon Sir Robert Cecil's coming down to examine the matter, September 21 1592

The particularities of all done your lordship shall receive from Sir Robert Cecil. If the like diligence had been used at Plymouth where the earl [*of Cumberland*]'s ships arrived,[3] at Portsmouth where The Foresight arrived, [*and*] at Harwich where The Dainty arrived, as hath been [*done*] here, their value of the carrack would then have resembled itself in some sort. But if the earl were presented of voluntary gift with so many thousands of pearls and diamonds, and these only from such of his men as were abiding in the carrack, what is to be thought of the rest remaining. His own ships I leave to your lordship's discretion, and what was unpresented [= *not recorded*] was of some acccount if it had been recovered, for mercenary men[4] are not so affectionate or religious but that they can, with safe conscience, lick their own fingers.

What will be done hereafter I know not, but I dare give the Queen ten thowsand pounds sterling for that which is gained by Sir Robert Cecil's coming down, which I protest before the living God I speak of truth, without all affection or partiality (for God is my judge) he hath more rifled my ship [*the Roebuck*] than all the rest, and yet she only [= *alone*] stayed by the carack, lost most men, [*was*] most of all spoiled and only remaineth here under commandment. The rest are gone, every one his way. And truly, my lord, Cross⁵ was most to blame, and dealt lewdly to leave the carack, and afterwards to steal from Sir Martin [*Frobisher*].⁶ I have always served him to my power, but his mad behaviour is too insolent in this action.

Thus with remembrance of my duty I humbly take my leave and remain most ready to do your lordship all honour and service.
    W Ralegh

1. The single addressee can only have been Burghley. His name may have been on the original letter which Strype copied.
2. Strype gives the date as 21 September, which he may have taken from the original letter, but the reference to all but Ralegh's own ship having left Dartmouth would appear to put it later.
3. See above, Letter 53.
4. Ralegh's crews served for the certainty of wages rather than 'shares'.
5. Robert Cross, Captain of the *Foresight*.
6. See above, Letter 41, note 9.

---

## 55. To Lord Burghley, Charles Lord Howard and Lord Buckhurst from Durham House, 13 December 1592

PRO, SP12/243/89, *CSPD 1591–4*, p. 294. Written by a clerk, with subscription and signature in Ralegh's hand.
Edwards II, pp. 75–6.

### THE *UGGERA SALVANIA*

[*addressed*] To the right honorable my verie good lords the Lord Th[reasu]rer, Lord Admirall and Lord Buckhurst¹
[*no endorsement*]

My verie good lords: I understand by Master Middleton² of your lordships proceedinge in the cause between Corsina³ and us, and although it be prejudiciall unto us, yet in reguard your lordships have so prescribed I am contented to submit my selfe therinto. And do humblie pray your lordships that theis enclosed articles[4] may (if you shalbe so pleased) be performed by such as particulerlie are nominated therein by your lordships order. Thereby Corsina is to have the benefytt of making sale of the goods which are valued at 12000*li* and the use of the money which wilbe worth unto him 3000*li*.

In my opinion if your lordships will allow thereof it were more fytt that the goods might remaine as presentlie they do, in sequestration, untill your lordships finall resolution shalbe known therein, because the venting and dispercing thereof will extenuate [= *underrate*] the price of the caracke [*the Madre de Dios*] goods when they shalbe sold, being all of one nature and kinde.[5] Or that they may be delivered to Her Majesties use at suche rate as they are prized. And so all parties uppon determination of the varyance to receave their due portion allotted unto them. If this course shall be deemed requisite both parties will travell [= *work*] for a speedie end and Her Highnesse wilbe benefited therebie above 3000*li*: otherwise they will seeke by protraction of time to delaie an absolute triall and composition for some of theire private lucre.[6]

Thus humblie praying your lordships direction herein by this bearer, my servaunt, I take my leave, from Dirrham House the xiii[th] of December 1592.

    Your lordshipps humble att commandmente,
       W Ralegh

[*bottom left-hand margin*] Lord Thr[*easur*]er
                          Lord Admiral
                          Lord Buckhurst

1. Special commissioners appointed to adjudicate concerning a Spanish vessel, the *Uggera Salvania*, captured in 1590 by Captain John Davis and others and brought into Plymouth as lawful prize. Its cargo, chiefly pepper, was declared by one Filippo Corsini to be the property of Italians, having been taken out of a Venetian ship: *APC* XX, pp. 77–8, 295, XXI, pp. 39–40. John Davis (c.1555–1605) was the Devon-born navigator whom Ralegh will have known as a boy on the River Dart.
2. Thomas Myddelton, the great London merchant and privateer: Andrews 1964, pp. 113–18.
3. Filippo Corsini, a native of Florence, who was one of the most important of London's alien merchants, agent of the Duke of Tuscany and with European-wide commercial connections.
4. See the six pages (PRO, SP12/243/89, articles i and ii) summarized in *CSPD 1591–4*, pp. 294–6, but note that Ralegh makes no mention of whether or not he has agreed to stand surety for Davis.
5. Eventually the prize pepper was sold.
6. The case had already been before the High Court of Admiralty and had regularly occupied the Privy Council. The Admiralty Judge, Dr Julius Caesar, did his best to be fair to the powerful opposing parties but in April 1593 Corsini complained that he was still being 'led about in a ring without end': Andrews 1964, p. 25.

## 56. [TO LORD BURGHLEY, ?LATE JANUARY 1593][1]

BL, Lansd. 70, f. 217. Written by a clerk and lacking signature.
Strype, *Annals*, 1731, IV, p. 128, with minor errors; Edwards II, pp. 76–8, from BL.

## THE DIVISION OF THE SPOILS

[*endorsed*]   Sir Walter Raleighes cawse [= *case*] for the carick

| | |
|---|---|
| The accompt of our whole charge amounteth to | 34000 *li*. |
| Her Majesty hath given order that we shall receve | 36000 *li*. |
| So as there is given us of profyt | 2000 *li*. |

The city of London is to have 6000 *li* profytt by Her Majesties order. Then are they to have Her Majesties allowance of 2000 *li* uppon all and 4000 *li* profitt aswel out of our principall. By that meanes we are to lose 4000 *li* of mony disbursed.

To help which we have 3000 *li* of the Queens, and then we lose but 1000 *li*. But of that 3000 *li* of the Queens, 1200 *li* was bestowed on her own ships to make them perfect.

Then there remaineth 1800 *li* towards the losse of 4000 *li*, so the losse wilbe 2200 *li*.

In respect hereof we have the remaines and our ships againe, but we are not allowed for our ships in this accompt as they were worth in adventure but onelie according to the losse which we sustein by them, and therefore that remain is nothing to us for wee take our shipps in part of payment.

The Erle of Cumberland is allowed also 36000 *li* and his accompt came but to 19000 *li*, so as he hath 17000 *li* profytt, who adventured for himselfe, and we that served the Queen and assisted her service have not our own again. Besides I gave my ships sayles and cables to furnish the caraque and bring her home, or els she had perished. My ship first boarded her and onely [= *alone*] staid with her and brought her into harborough or els she had also perished uppon Silley [*the Isles of Scilly*]. I was not present and therefore had no extraordinary profyt.[2] I was the cause that all this came to the Queen and that the King of Spaine spent 300,000 *li* the last yere. And I lost in the last yere in the voiage of my lord Thomas Howard[3] 1600 *li*, besids the interest of 11000 *li* which I have paid ever since this voiage began.

And farther my ship and [*that of*] Sir John Hawkins,[4] that were takers with The Foresight of the Q[*uee*]ns, have no other allowance then those that were absent, and whereas the city onely disbursed 6000*li*, and have 12000*li* againe, the same being taken out of the halles of London[5] amonge a multitude, I that adventured all my estate lose of my principall and they have double. I tooke all the care and paines, caried the ships from here to Falmouth and from thence to the north cape of Spaine, and they only sate still and did but disberse 6000*li* out of the common store, for which double is given to them and lesse then mine own to me, and to the Earle of Cumberland 17000*li* profytt, who adventured for himselfe, and I for the Queen.

1. To whom else, other than the Queen, could Ralegh have addressed his appeal? With regards to the date, it could have been his response to a final settlement dated 24 January 1593 (BL, Lansd. 73, ff. 38–40) but there are discrepancies in the figures. That he came out badly from the 1592 adventure is beyond doubt, but the importance of his appeal lies not so much in the accuracy of his figures as in his reasoning.
2. i.e. opportunity for private looting.
3. To the Azores in 1591. Ralegh had victualled the *Revenge*.
4. The *Dainty*. Ralegh's was, of course, the *Roebuck*.
5. The headquarters of the city gilds.

---

## 57. To the Justices of the Peace of Devon from Durham House, 15 February 1593

Devon Record Office, QS 1/i, Quarter Sessions Order Book 1592–1600, p. 45, a contemporary copy. The spelling of certain words suggests that the original letter was in Ralegh's hand.

A.H.A. Hamilton, *Quarter Sessions from Queen Elizabeth to Queen Anne*, 1878, pp. 350–51, in modern spelling.

## PRIVILEGES OF THE DEVON TINNERS

[*marginal heading*]   A lettre from Sir Walter Raleighe [*sic*]
[*addressed*]   To my very lovinge frinds the Justices of Peace in the countie of Devon

After my verie heartie commendations: Complainte hath bene made unto me by Peter Burges, Richard Lanxford, William Stockman and Anthony Sleman, tynners within the countie of Devon[1] and connstables[2] of hundreds and severall parishes there that they have bene summoned to appere before Master Serjeante Glanvyle[3] and, refusinge to contribute towardes the reparaton of a pryvate bridge (induced thereunto for the maintenaunce of the charter and customes of the Stannaries), were compelled to enter into recognizaunce for their appearaunce at the laste sessions holden in Devon, and do yet stand bound for aunsweringe their refusall therein at your next sessions, contrary to there said charter and Her Majesties late lettres.[4] Forasmuch as the said bridge was in former tyme accustomed to be repayred by the boroughe of Okehampton at the chargs of thinhabitants and for that tynners are not usuallie constrayned to yeld to any taxations and ymposytions for repayringe of bridges out of there owne hundredes and parishes, beinge continually charged with expences bestowed upon the ruines of there owne, and not holpen with anye contribution from other hundreds, I have thought good to signifye unto yow that in myne opinion they ought to be forborne in any of theis courses, and doe therfore pray youe to discharge them of there recognizaunces for further aunsweringe this cause and to desist from demaundinge any rate or taxe which is overburthensome to poore men in regard of there daily travell [= *labour*] and disbursements employed about the mynes.

If yow doe persist in the contrary I shalbe urged [= *compelled*] to have the cause heard before the lordes of Her Majesties Privy Councell and then, if hitt shall appeare that they ought to contribute, I will by my authorititye [*sic*][5] cause them to yeld to anie reasonable charge that shalbe thought indifferent.

And soe I commit yow to God, from Dirham House the 15th of February 1592.

      Your lovinge frynde,
          W Raleighe

I will my selffe geve order that the tynners shall contribute unto the bridge if uppon examination I find cause to urge them therunto, but not by anye forren aucthoritie.[6]

---

1. Peter Burges, gentleman, Richard Lanxford, gentleman, and Anthony Sleeman were 'jurats', i.e. representatives, of the stannary court of Tavistock; and William Stockman, gentleman, was a jurat of the court of Plympton in the Great Court or Parliament of the Stannaries of Devon held in October 1600, over which Ralegh presided as Lord Warden: H.P.R. Finberg, 'An unrecorded Stannary Parliament', *DAT*, LXXXII, 1950, p. 297.
2. The officers responsible for collecting local rates.
3. Sir John Glanville, Sergeant-at-Law, Judge of the Devon Assizes.
4. The most recent charter was that of Henry VII in 1508, but on 28 June 1589, presumably in response to an earlier complaint, the Queen had written to the 'Justices of Assizes' in Devon

and Cornwall reaffirming the tinners' right not to be 'taxed, charged or rated with any ymposition, charge or service' except by their Warden: G.R. Lewis, *The Stannaries*, 1908, p. 41 and DRO, QS1 (Quarter Sessions Order Book 1592–1600), p. 134. See also BL, Addit. 24746, f. 92.
5. Ralegh had been appointed to the office of Lord Warden of the Stannaries in 1585.
6. The response of the JPs is not on record but three years later a further letter from Ralegh, the text of which does not survive, apparently complaining about an infringement of his jurisdiction as Warden of the Stannaries, resulted in a spirited reply by the JPs that he has been misinformed by certain persons intent on making mischief: Hamilton, op. cit., pp. 351–2.

---

## 58. TO THE QUEEN, [23 FEBRUARY 1593]¹

Hatfield, CP83/35, *HMC Salisbury* XI, p. 538, dated 1601, listed only. In Ralegh's almost pure italic hand, with unusual signature in far bottom right-hand corner.

BL, Add. 4160, f. 77, copy made for Birch.

Cayley, 1806, I, pp. 142–4, from BL, spelling modernized; *Works*, 1829, VIII, pp. 661–2, from Cayley; Edwards II, pp. 259–60, from the original but dated 1602 and P. Lefranc, 'Un inédit de Ralegh sur la succession', *Etudes Anglaises*, XIII, 1960, pp. 42–3, from the original, dated 23 February 1593.

## ON THE SUCCESSION TO THE THRONE

[*addressed*]   For the Queens most excelent Majestye²
[*endorsed, probably in Sir Robert Cecil's hand*]   Sir Walter Ralegh

I presumed to present your Majestye with a paper contayninge the dangers which might groe by the Spanish faction in Skotlande:³ how it pleased your Majestye to accept therof I know not. I have since harde that divers ill-disposed [?*persons*] have a purpose to speake of succession.⁴ If the same be supprest I am gladd of it, yet fearinge the worst I sett downe sume reasons to prove the motive meerly vayne, dangerus and unnescesarye, and because I durst not my sealf speake in any matter without warrant,⁵ I have sent your Majestye thos arguments which may perchance put others in minde of sumewhat not impertinent [= *irrelevant*], and who, beinge graced by your Majesties favor, may, if need require, use them amonge others more worthy. Without glory I speake it, that I durst ether by writinge or speach satisfye the worlde in that poynct and in every part of their foolish consaytes, which for shortnes of tyme⁶ I could not so amply insert, this beinge after onn houres warninge but onn houres worke.⁷ I humble beseich your Majestye not to acquaynt any withall unles ccasion be offred to use them.

Your Majestye may perchance speake hereof to thos seeminge my great frinds, but I finde poore effects of that or any other supposed ametye, for your Majesty havinge left mee I am left all alone in the worlde⁸ and am sorry that ever I was att all. What I have dunn is out of zeale and love and not by any incoragement, for I am only forgotten in all rights and in all affaires and myne enemis have their wills and desires over mee.

Ther ar many other things concerninge your Majesties present service which mee thincke ar not as the[y] ought [to be] remembred and the tymes pass away unmesured of which more profett might be taken. But I feare I have allreddy presumed too mich, which love stronger then reason hath incoraged, for my errors ar eternal,⁹ and thos of other mortall,¹⁰ and my labors thanckless—I mean unacceptable, for thancks belongeth not to vassalls. If your Majestye pardun it it is more then to great a rewarde.

And so most humble imbracinge and admiringe the memory of thos celestiall bewtes (which with the people is denied mee to renew) I pray God your Majestie may be eternall in joyes and happines.

     Your Majesties most humble slave,
     WR

---

1. P. Lefranc, op. cit., pp. 38–42. Cf. Edwards II, p. 259, who dated the letter 1602, accepting a later endorsement on Ralegh's enclosure (see below, note 7) which Lefranc (p. 42, note 9) suggests may refer to its later removal from Cecil's files when the subject arose again.
2. There is no evidence that the letter was ever read by the Queen.
3. The paper has never been identified. On 26 February, Robert Cecil spoke in the House of Commons of the hostile designs of the King of Spain and of the possibilities of Spain's use of Ireland as a bridge, a subject of considerable interest to Ralegh: Simonds D'Ewes, *Journals of the Parliaments in Elizabeth's reign*, ed. P. Bowes, 1682, pp. 559–60.
4. On the afternoon of 23 February 1593, Peter Wentworth was interrogated concerning his intention of speaking the next day in Parliament on the forbidden subject of the succession, and was immediately sent to the Tower: J.E. Neale, *Elizabeth I and her Parliaments 1584–1603*, 1957, pp. 257–60.
5. Having represented the county of Devon in the Parliaments of 1584 and 1586, in 1593 Ralegh had to be content with the small borough of Michell in Cornwall. Even so, he was not prevented from contributing to debates. In fact his parliamentary activity now increased dramatically, always in the the government's interest, no doubt as part of his effort to regain the Queen's favour. He not only spoke quite frequently but in a spirited manner, quite unlike the mood of his letter to the Queen: Hasler III, pp. 274–5.
6. Ralegh seems, however, to have been remarkably well-informed.
7. His enclosed memorandum, which was hardly fit for public discussion, is also with the Cecil Papers, *HMC Salisbury* XIV, (*Addenda*), p. 244. See also Lefranc, op. cit., pp. 43 and 46.

8. Cf. Letter 46. In 1593 he was still forbidden the Court, a ban not lifted until 1597.
9. See below, Letter 60.
10. Bitter that he, unlike others whose crimes were no greater than his, will never be forgiven, he introduces at this point what Lefranc (op. cit., p. 41) calls 'quelques gouttes d'acide' into what is otherwise a largely ingratiating letter.

---

## 59. To the Countess of Shrewsbury from Mile End, 8 March [?1593][1]

From facsimile in Sotheby's *Catalogue*, 14 August 1942, Lot 15, dated 1596, facsimile, with flyleaf bearing Ralegh's seal (not illustrated). Previously in Bacon–Frank papers at Campsall Hall, Yorks, *HMC*, 6th Report, p. 456, *in extenso*. Resold Park-Bernet, New York, June 1974, Lot 483. Present location unknown. In Ralegh's neatest hand.

### APOLOGIZING FOR NEGLECT

[*addressed*][2]  To the Countess of Shrewsbury[3]

Right excelent ladye: If I had not hoped longe or this to have bynn restored to that poure [= *power*] of fortune as I might therby rather have shewed good effects of my desire to honor and serve yow then have [*con*]sorted with thos that only make payment with cerremony and protestations, I had not so longe foresloed [= *delayed*] your ladeshipps attendance, or left mysealf for so many dayes under the judgment of ingratetudes for the disposition which I have ever norished to performe, sumewhat the better to valew my sealfe in your favorable oppinion, being as yet left poureless, ether thorugh myne own ill desteny or the strenght of counterworkinge, hath also withhelde mee from thos whom I have most honored, and perswaded mee rather to acc[*om*]panye myne own disgrace then agayne and evermore to present butt the withered leves of an unprosperus and blasted fortune. Other fault or forgettfullness I hummble beseech yow to excuse, and that yow wilbe pleased to beleve that as your virtue and excelent spirritt have bynn the adamants [= *strengths*] which have drawn mee to honor and reverence the same, so did I never admire any of thos the more whom the tyme had bewtefied and declared for happye, or ever preferred that polletike care of sealf estate as in respect therof to relinquish any dewtye or indevor that might witness my uttermost thanckfullness and zealous afffection, esteeming the contrary only to proceed from a cowardly forgettfullness of foreproved fryndlines and forgonn honorable regardes.

But havinge now, right honorable ladye, so longe deferred the performance of my dewtye, lookinge eache day after other to have founde mean therby to have made the better offer of my service, I am driven first to intreat your favorable consaite [= *esteem*] by these messengers, being ever as reddye to be disposed and as farr cummanded as any in whom yow have most interest or greatest pour over.

    Your ladeshippes to be cummanded,
        W Ralegh

Mile End[4] this 8th of Marche

1. This is the only possible year, shortly after his 'disgrace': in March 1594 he was in Sherborne (Letters 66–9) and by March 1595 he was on his way to Guiana. He was in London in March 1593, Parliament being in session from 19 February to 10 April: *Handbook of British Chronology*, 1986 edn, p. 574.
2. From *HMC*, 6th Report, p. 456.
3. Elizabeth (Bess), née Hardwick, c.1520–1608, widow of George Talbot, 6th Earl of Shrewsbury, said to have been a friend of both Ralegh and his wife.
4. Ralegh went to Mile End when he needed to be in close touch with London's shipping. His brother-in-law, Sir Arthur Throckmorton, had a house there, where Lady Ralegh's first child was born in 1592: A.L. Rowse, *Ralegh and the Throckmortons*, p. 160.

---

## 60. TO SIR ROBERT CECIL FROM SHERBORNE, 10 MAY 1593

Hatfield, CP22/93, *HMC Salisbury* IV, pp. 310–11. In Ralegh's hand.

Murdin II, pp. 664–5; *Works* 1829, VIII, pp. 659–61, from Murdin; Edwards II, pp. 78–80; Pope Hennessy, 1883, pp. 178–81.

### IRISH AFFAIRS

[*addressed*] To the right honorable Sir Robert Cicill knight, of Her Majesties most honorable Privy Councell

[*endorsed*] 10 Maii 1593    Sir Walter Rawley to my master

Sir: I am very sorry for Master Wilkenson[1] and the rest that I here ar lost in the river of Burdeus [*Bordeaux*],[2] but for my part I was resolved of the succes before hand and so mich I tolde Willkensonn before his departure.

    Of this Irishe combination[3] Her Majestye shall fynde it remembred to her sealf not longe time since, but the Trojen Southsayer cast his spear agaynst the wodden horse but [*was*] not beleved.[4] I did also presume to speake sumewhat how to prevent this purpose and I thinck it not over hard to be yet donn. And if I had by any chance bynn acquaynted with the Lord Burghs instructions[5] I would have putt yow in mynde to have woonne the Earle of Argile[6] rather then all the rest of Skotland, for by hyme this fier must be only mayntayned in Ulstell [*Ulster*]. But for mee to speake of theon or the other I knowe my labors are prejudicate [= *prejudged*] and I cannot hereafter deserve ether thancks or acceptance. Less then that number of men apoynted, I tacke it, will serve the turne if the garrisons be placed aright to impeache the assembles and sume smale pineses ordered to ly between Cantirr [*Kintyre*] and Odonells countrey [*Tyrconnell*], but herein the order and the tyme hath most poure. Therbe also others in Irland that lye in waite not suspected, which I most feare, and others, most able and fitt to make them neglected and discoraged, which smale matters would have hartned to great purpose as the tyme will better wittness. I had bynn able my sealf to have raysed to or three bands of Inglishe, well armed, till I was driven to relinquishe and recale my people[7] of which the loss shall not be alone to mee, howsoever I am tumbled down the hill by every practize.

Wee ar so busyed and dandled [= *toyed with*] in thes French warrs,[8] which ar endless, as wee forgett the defens next the hart. Her Majesty hath good cause to remember that a million hath been spent in Irland not many yeares since. A better kingdome might have bynn purchased att a less prize and that same defended with as many pence if good order had bynn taken, but the question now may be whether for so great expence the estate be not less asured then ever. If Her Majestye conseder it aright shee shall fynde it no small dishonor to be vexed with so beggarly a nation, that have neather armes nor fortification, but that acursed kingdome hath alwayes bynn but as a trafique for which Her Majestye hath payde both fraight and custome and others receved the marchandize, and other then such shall it never bee.

The kinge of Spayne seeketh not Irlande for Irlande but havinge raysed up troops of beggers in our backs shalbe able to inforce us to cast our eyes over our shoulders while thos before us strike us on the braynes. Wee have also knowne the levell [= *purpose*] of his subversion, but destiney is stronger than councell and good advise, ether neglected or weakly executed, hath tought our enemis to arme thos parts which before lay bare to the sworde. Prevention is the doughter of intelligence [= *information*], which cannot be borne without a mother, and the good wooman hath so many patrons as the on referreth her cherishinge to anothers trust, and in the mean while shee liveth baren and frutless.

Sir these poore countres [*the South West*] yeild no newse. I here of a frigott that taketh up fishermen for pilatts in the west. I am my sealff here att Sherburne in my fortrus folde.⁹ Wher ever I be and while I am yow shall cummande mee. I thinck I shall need your farder favor for the little parke, for law and conscience is not sufficient in thes dayes to upholde mee. Every foole knoweth that hatred ar the cinders of affection and therfore to make mee a sacrifize shalbe thanksworthye. Sir I pray remember my dewty to my Lord Admirall and to yor father if it pleas yow.

From Sherburne this x^te of May,

    Yours most asured to do yow service,

        W Ralegh

I am the worse for the Bath¹⁰ and not the better.

---

1. Probably Edward Wilkinson of Tower Hill, a ship's captain with Mediterranean and West Indian experience: K.R. Andrews, *Privateering Voyages*, pp. 51–3. In November 1592 he was in charge of English merchants trading in and out of Bordeaux: *APC* XXIII, p. 293.
2. There seems to be no other record of this mishap.
3. Hugh O'Donnell, Lord of Tyrconnell, and Hugh O'Neill, Earl of Tyrone, combined forces in April 1593: *CSPI 1592–6*, pp. 94–5.
4. Cf. Letter 58 in which Ralegh refers to his warning 'paper' to the Queen concerning the danger of the 'Spanish faction in Scotland'.
5. Thomas Lord Burgh was sent to Scotland on a diplomatic mission early in 1593: *CSP Scotland 1593–5*, pp. 64–7.
6. Archibald Campbell, 7th Earl of Argyll, whose kinswoman Finola had married, as her third husband, Hugh O'Donnell. Ralegh's fears of a Scottish–Irish alliance proved to be well-founded. In 1594 there were reported to be 3,000 Scots in Tyrconnell: *CCM 1589–1600*, pp. 94–5.
7. See above, Letter 45.
8. A campaign was being fought in Brittany against Spain under Sir John Norris with miserably inadequate resources, both of men and supplies: J.S. Nolan, *Sir John Norreys*, Exeter, 1997, chapter XIII. Various considerations, not least the conversion of Henry IV of France to Catholicism the following July, encouraged even the hawks in Elizabeth's Council to think of peace. Ralegh, of course, knew his Queen's own preferences well enough to play on them for his own purposes. But as recently as 3 March 1593 he had spoken in Parliament in defence of a subsidy bill which he had linked with the necessity of attacking the Spanish forces in Brittany: D'Ewes *Journals*, 1682, p. 484.
9. All previous editors have read this as 'fortuns folde', but 'fortress', which Mrs Audrey Erskine regards as an equally acceptable reading, better describes the old Castle at Sherborne where Ralegh and his family had taken up temporary residence pending their move into the new 'Lodge': see below, Letter 70, note 1. The royal grant of Sherborne had preceded Ralegh's fall from grace. In January 1592 the Queen had obtained from the Bishop of Salisbury a 99-year lease, subject to an annual rent of £200 16s. 1d., of the Bishop's extensive estate in and near the Dorset market town. A few days later she had transferred her interest to Ralegh (W.B. Wildman, *Short History of Sherborne*, 1930 edn, p. 139) and he probably installed his wife and child down there in the autumn of 1592, immediately after his release from the Tower and his exertions at Dartmouth: see above, Letter 54. This, however, is the

first of his surviving letters to have been written there. It was far from being the rural paradise which some of his biographers have imagined, the medieval castle providing few of the material comforts and other advantages which Ralegh himself continued to enjoy in that part of Durham House on the Thames waterfront in Westminster, a short distance from the Court, which he had occupied, at the Queen's pleasure, since the early 1580s.

10. The newly fashionable spa possibly had other than strictly medical attractions for Ralegh. The Queen had been there in 1574 and Lord Burghley would be in June 1593: Phyllis Hembry, *The English Spa 1560–1815*, 1990, pp. 28–9.

---

## 61. TO LORD BURGHLEY FROM DURHAM HOUSE, 15 JUNE 1593

Hatfield, CP22/100, *HMC Salisbury* IV, p. 332, with omissions. Written by a clerk, with subscription, signature and postscript in Ralegh's hand.
Edwards II, pp. 81–2.

### FOR THE FREE EXPORT OF IRISH TIMBER

[*addressed*]   To the right honnorable my very good lord the Lord High Thr[*eas*]urer of England
[*endorsed*]   15 Junii 1593   Sir Walter Rauley to my lord

My honorable good lord: By reason of your lordships letters and the rest of the lords of Her Majesties Privie Councell written to the Lord Deputie[1] and Councell of Ireland for a restraint of transportaton of pipe-staves[2] out of that realme to the [*Canary*] Islands[3] we have a great quantitie of barrell and hogshead bords alreadie cutt and made which, for want of venting and expending, will rott uppon the ground if we maie not receave some order for their utteraunce [= *sale*]. Besides we must be forced to draw home a great number of able men from thence which are appointed to serve Her Majestie with their weapons uppon anie occasion, which will prove to be a great weakening of the province of Munster.[4] Wherefore if it please your lordship for the keeping and enterteyning [= *supporting*] of theis men in worke, which otherwise cannot live there, and for venting of this commoditie which must needs perish if longer staie be made of them there, to write to the Lord Deputie and Councell that according to your lordships meaning signified in your former lettres we maie be licensed to transport from thence into England such barrell and hogshead bords as we have made and maie be spared out of our own woods, the rather because those of the west cuntrie here have great want of this caske.⁵ [and *crossed out*] We will putt in such bands [= *boards*] to Her Majesties use before th'officers of the ports where they are to be laden as are required in your lordships said lettres for th'assured transporting thereof into England and to no other place.

And so I most humblie take my leave, from Dirrham House the xvth of June 1593,

    Your lordships for ever to be cummanded,
       W Ralegh

[*in Ralegh's hand*] For the bringinge of caske into Irland⁶ I hope wee shall rather deserve thankes then that wee shall need to make any great sutes for it, yet so mich it hath plesed the Deputye to mallice my particuler as I know without your lordshipps healpe geven so mich will hardly be afforded. I do humble desire your lordship to favor mee so mich as to writ your lordships own letters unto hyme that I may receve justice att his hands, and acknowledging my sealf only bound and susteyned by your lordships goodnes, I wishe your lordship eternall health, and humble take my leve.⁷

1. Sir William Fitzwilliam, no friend to Ralegh: see above, Letters 45, 47.
2. Wooden boards for making barrels.
3. In 1589, Ralegh and three partners had obtained a 14-year patent from the Queen to export barrel-staves, i.e. pipe-staves (*CSPI 1592–6*, p. 83 and *HMC Salisbury* IV, p. 464), but in January 1593 Fitzwilliam secured a restraint on the grounds that they were carrying on an illegal trade with Spain: *APC* XXIV, pp. 6–7 and below, Letter 63.
4. Ralegh was reported to be employing 200 men, mostly English settlers: *Edwards* II, pp. 418–19 and *HMC Salisbury* IV, p. 464.
5. See also postscript.
6. i.e. the introduction of the industry.
7. On 28 June, in response to a petition from Ralegh and his partners, the Council released the export of Irish timber, but strictly for use in England: *APC* XXIV, pp. 335–7. None was to be felled on the lands of Patrick Condon, he being outlawed and his property forfeit to the Queen.

## 62. To Sir Robert Cecil from Sherborne Castle, 15 August 1593

Hatfield, CP23/31, *HMC Salisbury* IV, p. 356, with omissions. Written by a clerk, with subscription and signature in Ralegh's hand.

*Edwards* II, pp. 83–4.

## FOR RICHARD KELLY OF DARTMOUTH

[*addressed*]   To the right honorable Sir Robert Cecill knight, one of Her Majesties most honorable Privie Councell

[*endorsed*]   Sir Walter Rawley to my master

Sir: I am earnestlie entreated by my brother Sir John Gilbert to write unto you in the behalfe of Master Kelley, a marchant of Dartmouth, his very honest freind. And because his and my perswasion may the better prevaile in his behalfe I have sent you as well his [*Gilbert's*] lettre to testefie the honest behavior of the gentleman[1] as [*also*] my servant Hancocke[2] to certifie the truth according to my brothers mot[i]on.

The matter importeth the deliverie of a lettre sent from Kellies factor sent by Nicholas Fitzharbert written to Thomas Fitzharbert. The lettre uppon the deliverie to Master Fizharbert was openlie read and nothing found therein ether offensive to the estate [*sic*] or to any particuler person, as your honnor, if you please, maie at large understand.[3] Sir John Gilbert wilbe bound for him in a thowsand pounds and I will undertake for his honest cariage and demeanure. And because you shalbe the better perswaded of his integritie and good affection to the Queen's Majestie and the opinion conceaved of him by his neighbors, I have sent you my brothers lettre[4] to testifie the same. I beeseech your honnor therefore not to suffer anie wrongfull informations [= *charges*] to prevaile against him and to give order for his dispatch[5] assoone as your honnor shall thinke convenient, that I may by this bearer understand [= *learn*] some newes.

And so I committ your honnor to the tuition [= *care*] of th'almightie,

From Sherborn Castle the xvth of August 1593,[6]

    Ever to do yow honor and service,

        W Ralegh

I have sent Hancocke chiefelie to understand some newes and to see yow and to certifie me the rest att his return.

---

1. If, as is probable, Kelly was a younger son of John Kelly, esq., of Kelly near Tavistock, he was a brother of Elizabeth Kelly who was later to marry Rawleigh Gilbert (b. 1580), son of Sir Humphrey and heir of Sir John: Vivian, *Devon*, p. 406. Assuming that the couple were already betrothed, this may explain Ralegh's frantic anxiety to exculpate the young man.
2. Edward Hancock of Combe Martin in north Devon, Ralegh's secretary.
3. On 24 July 1593, the Privy Council had decreed that a letter be sent to Sir John Gilbert ordering him to send up one Robert [*sic*] Kelly to face a charge of carrying letters for Nicholas Fitzherbert, 'a person most lewdlie affected and a pencioner of the kinge of Spaine': *APC*

XXIV, p. 418. Fitzherbert had been attainted for recusancy in 1580 and had fled to Rome. Thomas Fitzherbert, a priest, was his cousin and was presumably still living somewhere in England.
4. Missing.
5. Gilbert had apparently carried out his orders.
6. On 31 August 1594, Gilbert Smith, an Exeter merchant, testified before the Privy Council that when in Italy on business he had fallen sick in Rome and been visited by Nicholas Fitzherbert asking for news of England. He had agreed to deliver two letters to Richard Kelly, one addressed to Fitzherbert's brother and one to a near kinsman: *HMC Salisbury*, IV, p. 598. Smith said he had heard nothing spoken against the Queen, only that there was an evil religion maintained in England, and that he had no knowledge of what Kelly did with the letters. Smith seems to have been pardoned. What Kelly said in his own defence is not on record but Ralegh's efforts seem to have borne fruit.

---

## 63. To Sir Robert Cecil from Gillingham Forest, 27 August 1593

Hatfield, CP23/41, *HMC Salisbury* IV, p. 363. Written by a clerk, with subscription, signature and postscript in Ralegh's hand.
Edwards II, pp. 84–5.

## THE EXPORT OF IRISH PIPE-STAVES

[*addressed*]  To the right honorable Sir Robert Cecil knight, one of Her Majesties most honorable Privie Councell
[*endorsed*]  27 August 1593  Sir Walter Rawley to my master

Sir: You know our long suite to the lords of Her Majesties Privie Councell for the continuance of transportaton of pipestaves out of Ireland to the [*Canary*] Islandes according to Her Majesties graunt by her lettres patents under the Great Seale.¹ Master Pine² as I understand is now at Court to sollicite your honnor and the rest, in our behalfe, for a dissoluton of the restraint procured by the Lord Deputies lettres uppon his suppositon of some enormities and surmised inconveniences which therby will never ensue. I beeseech your honnor to fauvor our proceedings therein and to assist us as much as you maie for the obteyning of our suite. And if you please to acquaint my Lord Admiral [*Charles Howard*] with my poore request I doubt not but his lordship will farther so honest a motion. If their lordships wold be pleased thoroughlie to consider the state of the cause and have patience to peruse the contents of our demaund (which Master Pine will shew your honnor in all points according to the truth)³ they wold assuredlie allow of our trade to the Islands and conceave better of those which undertake the same.

And so I humblie take my leave, from Gillingham Forrest⁴ the 27th of August 1593,

    Your honors humble att cummandment,
        W Ralegh

Sir, the Indien falcon⁵ is sike of the buck worme and therfore if yow wilbe so bountefull to geve another falcon I will provide yow a winter gelding.

1. See Letter 61.
2. Henry Pyne, Constable of Mogeely Castle, one of Ralegh's partners in the grant of 1589 (see Letter 61), who has presumably persuaded Ralegh, contrary to his letter of 15 June, to insist on their right to export the timber anywhere, incuding the dominions of the King of Spain.
3. Hatfield, CP24/68, probably the original document.
4. In Dorset, of which the Queen had appointed Ralegh to the office of Ranger in July 1584.
5. The *falco sacer* and the *falco lanarius* were imported in large numbers from North Africa and Asia: E.B. Michell, *The Art and Practice of Hawking*, 1900, reprinted 1970, pp. 23–4.

---

## 64. To Sir Robert Cecil from Weymouth, 8 October 1593

Hatfield, CP23/77, *HMC Salisbury* IV, p. 384. Written by a clerk, with subscription, signature and postscript in Ralegh's hand.
Edwards II, pp. 85–6.

### FOR JOHN WOLRIDGE ABOUT A WARDSHIP

[*addressed*] To the right honorable Sir Robert Cecill knight, one of Her Majesties most honorable privie Councell
[*endorsed*] 8 October 1593 Sir Walter Rawley to my master

Sir: This gentleman Master John Wollridge¹ hath been written unto by my Lord Thresurer² about the deliverie of a ward, his wives sonne. If he shall have need of your honnors fauvor therein, which he is able himselfe lawfullie to aunswere, except he be overborn by his adverse partie, I praie you in reguard of the honestie of the gentleman and of the desire he hath to deale indifferentlie [= *without prejudice*] and uprightlie, to assiste him so farre that he maie receave no hard measure.

And so I humblie take my leave, from Weymouth the 8th of October 1593

    Your honors to do yow service,
      W Ralegh

Sir: I have written to my Lord Admirall the newse of Rimonde³ att large, from whom I pray yow to be acquaynted.

This bearer Wulredge, being sent for by my lord your father, was here stayde sumewhat longer to examyne a cause of the Admiralty, so as I beseich yow to excuse hyme.

1. John Wolridge of Winfrith Newburgh, near Wareham in Dorset, a local Admiralty official.
2. Burghley was Master of the Court of Wards.
3. George Raymond of Chichester, naval adventurer, who was lost on a voyage to the East Indies in 1593: Andrews 1964, *passim*.

---

## 65. To Sir Robert Cecil from Sherborne Castle, 25 February 1594

Hatfield, CP22/49, *HMC Salisbury* IV, p. 483. In Ralegh's hand, except for the address. Edwards II, pp. 86–7.

### A FRENCH PRIZE

[*addressed, by a clerk*] To the right honorable Sir Robert Cecill knight, one of Her Majesties most honnorable Privy Councell
[*endorsed*] 25 February 1593    Sir Walter Rauleigh to my master    In favour of Captain Harry Thynne

Sir: This gentleman Harry Thynne,¹ without sending for, is cum up to awnswere the cumplaynt of the French men for [*which*] my brother [*Carew*] was lately caled before yow.² He was an adventurer in that jurney and lost all. For the fishe prize hee did nothing but by cummission and hath accompted for the same. I beseich yow to favor hyme this mich that

hee be not charged with more then he receved and hee maye have tyme till the next terme to bring in the accompt which now resteth in other mens hands and in the meane tyme no hard dealing be offred hyme.³ I shall think my sealf mich bound unto yow for any favor yow shall afford hyme, and so being allwayes yowr servant to be cumanded I humble take my leve.
    W Ralegh

From Sherburne Castell this 25 of February

1. Son of Sir John Thynne of Longleat, Wilts.
2. Thynne had been Captain of the *Galleon Dudley*, alias the *Galleon Ralegh*, which, together with another privateering ship, the *Elizabeth Bonaventure* (Captain Robert Cross), both owned by Carew Ralegh, had in September 1591 taken the *Holy Ghost* of St Jean de Luz in France, laden with fish and oil, which they had brought into Milford Haven. It would seem that with the consent of the Lord Admiral and the Lord Treasurer they had sold her perishable cargo but, contrary to instructions from the High Court of Admiralty, instead of restoring the ship to her French owners, they had allowed her to founder and rot, with the result that English merchants trading at St Jean were threatened with reprisals: *CSPD 1591–4*, pp. 248–51, *APC* XXII, pp. 66, 496–7 and BL, Lansd. 148, ff. 102, 243.
3. As late as January 1597 the King of France wrote personally to the Queen complaining of 'la foule et multitude des plaintes et clameurs de nos subjets depredes en mer par les votres, ausquels toute justice a este en effect desniee' (*HMC Salisbury* VII, p. 16), but no more is heard of this particular case.

---

## 66. To Sir Robert Cecil from Sherborne Castle, 25 February 1594

PRO, SP12/247/89, *CSPD 1591–4*, p. 441. Otherwise not previously published. Written by a clerk, with subscription and signature in Ralegh's hand.

### DISPUTED TIN-MINE

[*addressed*] To the right honorable Sir Robert Cecill knight, one of Her Majesties most honorable Privy Councell
[*endorsed*] 25 February 1593   Sir Walter Rauley to my master   Concerning the controv[ersy] for the Tynneworke

Sir: The Lords of the Councel have written their lettres to the deputie lieutenauntes of Cornwall to see certen orders sett down formerly by Sir

John Fortescue[1] and me with th'advise of some of the Judges to be observed according to our directions concerning the right of [sic] a tynworke in Cornwall called St Margaret[2] which hath longe depended [= *hung*] in variance between [Peter] Bevill, [Peter] Courtney and others[3] of th'one parte and Sergeant [*John*] Glanvile[4], Master Arundell and others of th'other parte.[5] And now I understand that the said Bevil, Courtney and his confederates have lingred here in the cuntry untill they understood that I was returned from London and are now hastely repayred to the Court to renew their ancient complaintes and importunities and to take th'advantage of my absence, thinking to prevaile in their shameless requestes when there are none to contradict them or to shew their contemptes and misdemeanures.

I beseech you lett me rely upon your honorable care herein that if any complaint be by them made against me or Master Sergeant Glanvile and his pretences, any further proceedings there may be staied untill the next terme, at which time we will attend yow to satisfie yow in any thing that shalbe now brought in question against me or them [*Glanville etc.*] and that yow wilbe pleased to commaund them to sett down their requestes in writing that we maie uppon receipt of copies thereof aunswere our procedinges with indifferency and equity.[6]

And so I humblie take my leave, from Sherborn Castle the 25th of February 1593.

    Your honors to do yow service,

        W Ralegh

---

1. Chancellor of the Court of Exchequer, the department which administered the Duchy of Cornwall's finances.
2. In the stannary of Blackmore near St Austell.
3. The 'others' included John Connock and a William Samuel: see below, note 5.
4. Assize Judge for Cornwall 1592–1603.
5. The matter had been in dispute for some time. Ralegh had apparently failed to resolve it and it had already been before the Privy Council on several occasions. As long ago as October 1591, following alleged violence against Connock at the mine, the Council had ordered Courtney and his associates to appear before it and on 25 December [*sic*] 1592 had put the matter back in Ralegh's hands: *APC* XXII, pp. 11–12 and XXIII, pp. 380–81. In March 1593 Courtney and Bevill had complained that when, after some delay, they had received from Ralegh a copy of the order agreed upon it did not tally with their own draft: *APC* XXIV, pp. 119–20, 228–9 and 245. At the Council's suggestion, and by then presumably conscious that he was being accused of partiality, Ralegh had then sought the assistance of the Lord Chief Justice of the Court of Common Pleas (Sir John Woolley) and the Chancellor of the Exchequer, both of whom had sat with him at Durham House in May 1593: *APC* XXIV, pp. 266–7.
6. In 1594 the Privy Council finally upheld Ralegh's judgment against Courtney and for Arundell: G. Harrison, *Report on the Stannaries*, 1835, p. 136.

## 67. To Sir Robert Cecil from Sherborne Castle, 3 March 1594

PRO, SP12/248/4, *CSPD 1591–4*, p. 452. Not otherwise previously printed. Written by a clerk, with subscription and signature in Ralegh's hand.

## FOR JOHN DAVIS

[*addressed*] To the right honorable Sir Robert Cecill knight, one of Her Majestes most honorable Privy Counsell

[*endorsed*] 3 March 1593 Sir Walter Rauleigh to my master In favour of John Davis

Sir: This gent[*leman*], Captain Davies,[1] is come unto yow with the poursuivant.[2] He was comming before, uppon advertisement [= *advice*] from me, but being intercepted by the messenger is brought by him. He is accused of some notorious villany but, the matter being examined by some of the best gent[*lemen*] in Devon is found to be frivolous, and nothing, as I understand, can be proved against him concerning that objection. His accuser is a dissolute and fugitive person, he reguargeth [= *regardeth*] not his vowes, he hath nothing to loose, he hath coined money and, as I thinke, shalbe hainged here in this countrey at this Assises. I praie your honnor to favvour him [*Davis*] herein and suffer him to departe assoone as you may lest some other matters maie be laid to his charge which concern him and others, being no cause of estates [= *public concern*] but depending between subject and subject as yow know, and fitt to be tried by course of law and not by aucthority.[3]

And so I humblie take my leave, from Sherborn Castle the 3ᵈ of March 1593.

    Your honors humble [*at*] cummandment
      W Ralegh

Sir: this Milburn[4] that accused John Daves begatt Daves wife[5] with child in his absence and, being brought in question for quoyninge of monye, wherof the greatest proofe resteth on John Daves, this Milburne vaunted that hee would device matter agaynst John Daves to lay hyme up, by meane wherof John Daves might neather follow the matter of quoyninge nor other revendge agaynst hyme for his wife.

1. See above, Letter 55, note 1. Davis had returned in June 1593 from his disastrous voyage to the Strait of Magellan with Thomas Cavendish, in the course of which he became the first European to sight the Falkland Islands, since when he had been compiling his *Seaman's Secrets* which he published from his home in the parish of Stoke Gabriel on the River Dart in August 1594: C.R. Markham, *Sir John Davis*, 1889.
2. A royal messenger with power of arrest.
3. The Privy Council's jurisdiction was an extension of the royal prerogative.
4. Not identified.
5. She was Faith, thought to have been a daughter of Sir John Fulford, a former Sheriff of Devon (Markham, op. cit.), but although Fulford had many children, she is not named in the family pedigree: Vivian, *Devon*, p. 379.

---

## 68. TO SIR ROBERT CECIL FROM DORCHESTER, 4 MARCH 1594

Hatfield, CP22/52, *HMC Salisbury* IV, pp. 486–7. Written by a clerk, with subscription and signature in Ralegh's hand.

Edwards II, pp. 89–90.

## FOR LORD BARRY

[*addressed*]   To the right honorable Sir Robert Cecill, knight, one of Her Majesties most honorable Privy Councell

[*endorsed*]   4 March 1593   Sir Walter Rauleighe to my master   Lord Barry

Sir: This honorable gent[*leman*] the Lord Barry,[1] one that is well affected to Her Majesty and her estate, is an humble suitor to Her Majesty and hath entreated my lettre to your honnor that such fine or benefitt as Florence McCarty[2] hath by graunt obteined from Her Majesty by reason of his [*Barry's*] former offence in Ireland,[3] which is well knowen to your honnor, may be again revoked and remitted. And if my opinion herein maybe reguarded I thinke that his pardon, which Her Highnes graunted him, hath wrought his true affection and his entire disposition to honnor and serve Her Majesty with such unfeined obedience as can be required, and therfore not fitt to be discountenanced by Florence McCarty, being a man reconciled to the Pope, daungerous to the present state, beloved of such as seke the ruine of the realme, his native cuntrie and not worthie to be releived by Her Majesties goodnes. He may for a time dissemble and, in revealing his poverty by occasion of his imprisonment in the Tower, protest that obedience which he ought to performe, but he is not to be trusted. His alliance and freinds in Ireland are great and manie and he wanteth nothing but mony to execute his practises whereunto the Pope hath animated him.

    This noble gentleman hath to my knowledg a long time lived civilly and conformable to all Her Majesties directions and commandmentes and hath not deserved theis troubles and discontentmentes. I praie you so much to favour him by yourself, or by the meane of my honorable good lord your father, that he maie be discharged of this demaund and I will reckon it amongst the rest of your favours.

    And so I humblie take my leave, from th'assises at Dorchester the 4th of March 1593.

        Your honors humble att cummandment,

          W Ralegh

1. David, son and heir of James, Viscount Barrymore (ob. 1581): see above, Letters 2–4.
2. Florence (Finnin) MacCarthy (see above, Letters 2 and 4) had spent much of his life in the Tower of London, but he had nevertheless contrived in 1589 secretly to marry Ellen, heiress of Donnell MacCarthy More, whom the Queen had made Earl of Clancare: Bagwell III, p. 200. The prospect of the union of two Munster lordships was viewed with as much suspicion in Ireland as in England.
3. In August 1593 the Queen had granted MacCarthy £500 to repay his debts, the money to be recovered from Lord Barry who still owed her £500 for his pardon in 1582: D. MacCarthy, *Life and Letters of Florence MacCarthy Reagh*, 1867, Cal. Chancery Rolls Ireland, p. 252 and *CSPI 1592–6*, pp. 139, 199. He was also allowed to return to Ireland, but failed to extract the cash from Lord Barry: Bagwell III, pp. 240–41.

---

## 69. To Sir Robert Cecil from Sherborne, 14 April 1594

Hatfield, CP26/25, *HMC Salisbury* IV, pp. 510–11. In Ralegh's hand. Edwards II, p. 91.

### TAKING OF A CATHOLIC PRIEST

[*addressed*] To the right honorable my very good frinde Sir Robert Cecell [*endorsed*] 14 April 1594    Sir Walter Rauleighe to my master    John Moone a Jesuit[1] taken in the La[*dy*] Sturtons house

Sir: This night the 13th of Aprill wee have taken a notabell Jesuite in the Lady Sturtons howse, wife to old Sir John Arrundell,[2] with his copes and bulles. Ther hath byn keipt in this howse, as I have formerly informed yow, above thirtye recusantts.[3] Sir Georg Trencher, Sir Raufe Horsey and my sealf ar now ryding to take his examination which by the next yow shall receave att large. Sir Georg and Sir Raufe have used great dillegence in the fynding of this notable knave.[4]

Being in hast I do for the present humble take my leve from Shorburne this 14th of Aprill.

     Yours ever to do yow service,
        W Ralegh

He cales hyme sealf John Moone but hee is an Irishman and a notable stout villayne and I thinke can say miche.[5]

1. Better known as John Cornelius, he is said not to have been admitted to the Society of Jesus until after his capture: A.L. Rowse, *Tudor Cornwall*, 1941, p. 365, who writes at some length (pp. 358, 363–6) on his notable career, drawing on a near-contemporary biography.
2. Lady Stourton, daughter of Edward Stanley, 3rd Earl of Derby, married, as her second husband, Sir John Arundell of Lanherne in Cornwall, after whose death in 1591 she returned to the house in Chideock in Dorset of her first husband, Charles Lord Stourton: *APC* XXXII, pp. 28–9. Cornelius, born in Bodmin of Irish parents and a protégé of Sir John, had preached before the Pope before returning from Rome in 1583 to become Arundell's chaplain. He too moved to Dorset in or soon after 1591.
3. At first the Queen treated Lady Stourton and her household leniently, but the passage, in 1593, of two further parliamentary Acts of Uniformity was all that certain of the lay magistracy needed for them to target recusant priests.
4. Sir George Trenchard (c.1548–1630) of Wolveton near Charminster, MP for Dorset in 1584, and Sir Ralph Horsey (ob. 1612), who sat for the county in 1586 (Hasler III, p. 526 and II, p. 141), in 1586 had complained that 'the papists live at ease and have their conventicles in despite of the justices, do what they can': *CSPD 1586–8*, p. 361.
5. According to his biographer, Lady Arundell's daughter, Cornelius was taken to Trenchard's house where Ralegh spent the night disputing with his contemporary and 'offered to do all he could in London for his liberation'. However, it was also reported that at Cornelius's execution at Dorchester Ralegh prevented his prisoner from addressing the crowd for fear that, impressive speaker that he was, he might cause a breach of the peace: Rowse, loc. cit.

---

70.   To Master Pytt from Sherborne Castle, 28 April 1594

Basle University Library, Autographen-Sammlung Geigy-Hagenbach no. 299. Written by a clerk, with subscription and signature in Ralegh's hand. Not previously printed.

## PORTLAND STONE

[*addressed*]   To my very lovinge frend Master Pytt, one of the Tellers of the Exchequer and Surveyor of Her Majesties landes in Dorset at his office at Westminster gyve these

Master Pytt: My hope ys that you wilbe myndfull to dispatche my lease [= *contract*] for lymestone etc in Portland for I have present occassion to use great store.[1] What you doe for me in these businesses I wilbe ready to requite you in what I maye, prayeng you to take care of the present dispatch therof as my trust ys in you. And so I end in haste.
   Sherborne Castell thys 28th of Aprill 1594
      Your very loving frinde,
         W Ralegh

1. No doubt for the mansion he was building on the site of the old 'Lodge' to replace the medieval castle in which Walter and Bess were in temporary residence: see above, Letter 60. By March 1595, Lady Ralegh was writing from 'Sherborn Loge': Edwards II, pp. 398–9.

---

## 71. TO SIR THOMAS EGERTON FROM SHERBORNE CASTLE, 2 MAY 1594

BL, Harl. 6996, f. 132. Written by a clerk with subscription and signature in Ralegh's hand. Works 1829, pp. 662–3, Edwards II, pp. 92–3.

## TINNERS' PRIVILEGES

[*addressed*]   To the right honorable my very good lord the Lord Keeper of the Great Seale of England
[*endorsed*]   Sir Walter Rawley   For perjury in the Stannerye sued yn the Star Chamber

My verie good lord: There hath been a subpena graunted out of the Starre Chamber for th'appearaunce of one Thomas Whitford and William Dobb[1] before your lordship and the rest of Her Majesties most honorable Privie Councell for verefying their knowledg in a Stannary Court of witnesses in

*Plate 5.* Sherborne Castle and Park, from a pictorial map of part of the county of Dorset *c.*1592 (see Introduction, p. lv, note 23). BL, Addit. 52520)

an action uppon the case between one Denshire and Stevens. The triall and penaltie of the offence (if anie shalbe proved) is to be censured [*sentenced*] in Her Majestes absolute jurisdiction of the Stannery and Her Majesty hath been pleased of late uppon complaint by me made unto her to signifie to my honorable good lord the Lord Th[*reasu*]rer that the Stannary aucthoritie shall consist and continue according to the auncient custome and prerogative and not to be contradicted by private censure, and that all abuses uppon my information shalbe presentlie reformed.² I thinke your lordship is not thoroughlie acquainted herewith because a Stannary cause is suffred to be prosecuted in that court and therefore I am bold to putt you in mind thereof and to praie yow to dismiss the same out of the Starre Chamber to be tried in the Stanuries where it is determinable.

And so I humblie take my leave from my Castle at Sherborn the second of May 1594.

>Your lordshipps most humble att cummandment,
>  W Ralegh

1. None of the persons involved in the case has been identified.
2. See above, Letter 57.

---

## 72. To Edward Knoyle from Sherborne Castle, 28 May [1594][1]

Dorset Record Office, Dorchester, D/SHA:C2. In Ralegh's hand.

*Western Gazette*, 12 April 1940; *Somerset and Dorset Notes and Queries*, XXIII, CCv., June 1940, p. 180; J. Fowler, *Medieval Sherborne*, 1951, p. 381, all from a copy in the weekbook of the Master of the Almshouses of St John at Sherborne[2] which is in bad condition.

### FOR ELINOR DYER, A POOR WOMAN

[*addressed*]  To my very loving frend Master Edward Knoyll

1593/4

Master Knoyll: This poor woman Ellner Dyer hath bene d[*ivers*] times with me and Ser Raff Horsye[3] to complain aga[*inst*] the Masters [*sic*] of the allmeshouses off Sherburn [*of*] the wrongfull detaininge off a tennament[4] fro[m] her at such time as she was a very chilld when she had no frend to help her. And foras much as the wrong she receveth semeth to be aparent, as myself and Ser Raff [Ho]rsy ar enformed, and I think you canot denye, I pray you be a meane to the rest of that company that this poor soull may now at last be restored to her right and not dryven farther to complain against them in a mater so injustly begon and prosecuted by them that ar, or sholld be, protectors and not opresers off poor pepll. Wher off I hope you and the rest will have due consederatyon with owt geveng presedent off so great an ill.⁵

From my Castell this 28th off May,
    Your loving frind,
        W Ralegh

I have apointed Meer⁶ now att your court to deale for the exchange of the quilletes [= *small plots of land*] at the Castell.⁷

---

1. Since the matter was settled in July 1594 (see below, note 5) it seems likely that the letter was written earlier that year. See also note 2.
2. A medieval foundation, the almshouse had accommodation for 20 brethren, each serving in turn as Master for a year. Edward Knoyll was Master in 1593–4: J. Fowler, op. cit., p. 381.
3. See above, Letter 69, note 4.
4. This has been identified as part of the Old Church House in Half Moon Street in Sherborne: J. Fowler, op. cit., p. 321, note 1.
5. The property was restored to Elinor on 15 July 1594 and in the following year, 'at the instance of' Sir Ralph Horsey and under the heading of expenses for the poor, she was paid 20s.: Fowler, op. cit., p. 382, notes 1 and 2.
6. John Meere, Ralegh's bailiff: see Letter 141.
7. Connection with the main text unclear.

---

## 73. To Lord Burghley from Sherborne, 15 June 1594

PRO, SP63/175/6, *CSPI 1592–6*, p. 253. Not otherwise previously printed. Written by a clerk with subscription and signature in Ralegh's hand.

### FOR PATRICK CONDON, IRISH LANDOWNER

[*addressed*] To the right honorable my singuler good lord the Lord High Th[reasu]rer of England
[*endorsed*] 15 Junii 1594     Sir Walter Raleigh to my lord     By Patrick Condon

My verie honorable good lord: This gentleman, Master Condon,[1] hath been formerlie an humble suitor to your lordship and the rest of Her Majestes most honorable Privie Councell for possession of his lands in Ireland which your lordship was pleased he should enjoy and was by your honorable direction restored to the quiet possession thereof. Which he quietlie held until Master Hide, an undertaker, by another contrarie information dispossessed him.[2] He is now come out of Ireland to crave your lordships favvour that Hide maie not prevaile against his right in the lands which he can prove to appertein unto him, and I am bold to beeseech your lordship to consider of his petition. He is my neighbour in Ireland, his lands are adjoyning to mine and I know the gentleman to be well able and willing to serve Her Majesty. And therefore I humblie praie your good lordship that he maie be restored to his lands which by proofes may appeare to appertain unto him.[3]

And so I humblie take my leave, from Sherborn the 15th of June 1594.

Your honors ever to be cummanded,

W Ralegh

1. For Condon's past record see above, Letters 2 and 3, and also *APC* XXVII, pp. 148–9 (22 May 1597). He had eventually submitted to the Earl of of Ormond with the promise of his life and lands: ibid., XXI, pp. 339–41.
2. Arthur Hyde, second son of Willliam Hyde of Hyde in Berkshire, High Sheriff of Cork. For confirmation that he had taken possession of Condon's land (on the Blackwater), pretending that it was part of the property of supporters of the Desmond rebellion, and had refused to relinquish it, see ibid., XXII, p. 469. The land had profitable timber.
3. Ralegh had not always supported Condon (see above, Letters 2 and 3) and indeed the latter claimed, in 1594, that Ralegh had secured the 'countermandment' of one of his letters of restoration: *HMC Salisbury* V, p. 68. In 1597, in another effort to reinstate Condon, the Privy Council arranged for Hyde to receive partial compensation elsewhere, but not until 1610 did Condon's son, David, recover his inheritance: *APC* XXVII, pp. 148–9 and *CSPI 1608–10*, pp. 582–3. See also below, Letter 74.

---

## 74. To Sir Robert Cecil from Sherborne, 15 June 1594

PRO, SP63/175/7, *CSPI 1592–6*, p. 253. Otherwise not hitherto printed. Written by a clerk, with subscription, signature and postscript in Ralegh's hand.

## FOR PATRICK CONDON

[*addressed*] To the right honorable Sir Robert Cecill, knight, one of Her Majestes most honorable Privie Councell [endorsed] 15 June 1594 Sir Walter Raleigh to my master in favour of Master Condon

Your honnor maie be pleased to understand that this gentleman Master Condon is an humble suitor to your honnor and the lords of Her Majesties Privie Councell that he maie be restored to the possession of his lands in Ireland whereof he is dispossessed by one Hide, an undertaker.¹ Their lordships heretofore by their directions gave order for Master Condons possession, he quietlie enjoyed his lands untill Hide by a wrong information prevailed against him. I am bold to crave your honors fauvour in his behalfe. I have knowen him a long time, his lands are adjoyning to mine in Ireland as neighbours. I know him to be as well able to serve Her Majestie as any man in that parte, and therefore I humblie praie your honorable favour towards him that he maie be restored to his lands which by his proofes will appeare to belong unto him.
   And so I humblie take my leave from Sherborn the 15th of June 1594.
      Your honors to do yow service,
        W Ralegh

Sir: I humble beseich yow to favor this poore gentleman in all yow cann and I shall thinck my sealff mich bond unto yow for hyme.

1. See notes to Letter 73.

---

75. TO CHARLES LORD HOWARD FROM SHERBORNE, 20 JUNE 1594

   Hatfield, CP27/8, *HMC Salisbury* IV, pp. 551–2. In Ralegh's hand.
   Edwards II, pp 93–5.

NEWS FROM ACROSS THE CHANNEL

[addressed] To the right honorable my singuler good lord the Lorde Admirall of Inglande in hast
[endorsed] 21 Junii 1594 Sir Walter Rauleighe to my master¹

My honorable good lord: Your lordshippe may perceve by the intelligence sent by my brother [*Sir John Gilbert*] bothe of the strenght of the Spanishe fleet as also of their reddiness to sett sayle. The master hyme sealf which was taken out of [= *near*] Dartmouth is returned. The intelligence your lordship had before was from too of his men which weare sett free, but this master, called Makerell,² is a man of good judgment and very honest. If your lordship consider too things especially in this intelligence: first that some surprize is purposed by the hast, for the carpenters and all other about the fleete worke the saboth day. Next the hugeness of the shipps which must neads cary many soldiers or elce lesser vessells weare far fitter for the coast of Bryton [*Brittany*]. Ther are also many shipps taken of ours, sume of good burden, but all of good wealth as may apeare by the report sent the lords.³

How the Spanierds have proceeded about Brest⁴ your lordship may also understand by this report: first (havinge receved no impeachment [= *resistance*]) they have finished the fortification att Old Croydun [*Crozon*] which your lordship well knowes is within the port of Brest, and, the better to cummand the haven, they have also built a stronge peere att the very entrance. Now, if it pleas your lordship to pardun mee, I pray remember that their wilbe no entrance for the Queens fleet what weather so ever happen, for Blewett [*Blavet*] and Brest and Bel Ile [*off the Quiberon peninsula*] att [*sic*] ar theirs. The Spanishe shipps ar huge, wherof eyght ar between 800 and 1000 toones, 10 shipps more of good burden, divers galles and full filde with soldiers. I hope also that your lordship will remember it is the Queens honor and sawfty to assaile and not defende,⁵ and for ought I here your lordships fleet wilbe far to weake.

I hope your lordship will take my remembrance in good part, and if your lordship will vouchsawfe to move Her Majesty for mee to attend yow privatly in her service I hope I shall stand your lordship in the place of a poore marriner or soldier. I have no other desire but to serve Her Majestye and, seinge I desire nor place nor honor nor rewarde, I hope it wilbe easely graunted, if I be not condemned to the grave and no libertye nor hope left, that eyther tyme or the geving of my life may recover or be a sacrify[c]e for my offences. I hope your lordship wille not forgett my desire or that I am evermore,

        Your most assured pore kynseman to serve yow,
          W Ralegh

Sherburne the 21 of June

1. Indicating that Howard passed the letter on to Sir Robert Cecil.
2. Not identified.
3. On 23 May, six English merchant ships leaving Bayonne were taken by Pedro de Cubiaur: *HMC Salisbury*, IV, p. 540.
4. In 1593 a Spanish fleet had brought reinforcements to Port Louis, i.e. Bluett. The Spaniards had set about commanding the entrance to Brest, and very recently Burghley had been informed of a Spanish fleet preparing to sail for Brittany: *HMC Salisbury* IV, pp. 540, 550. For more details of preparations to send to Brittany an English force led by the Earl of Essex see R.B. Wernham, *After the Armada*, chapter XXIII.
5. Cf. above, Letter 60.

---

## 76. To Sir Robert Cecil from Sherborne, 9 July 1594

PRO, SP63/175/22, *CSPI 1592–6*, p. 257. Otherwise not hitherto printed. In Ralegh's hand except for the address.

### FOR CHARLES MACCARTHY

[*addressed*] To the right honorable Sir Robert Cecill knight, one of Her Majesties most honorable Privie Councell

[*endorsed*] 9 Julij 1594 Sir Walter Rauleighe to my master In favour of Charles McCartey

Sir: I will be bold to forbeare the awnswere of your too letters of the 17 of June and the 2th of July till my next writinge. Att this tyme my request and humble sute is unto yowr honor in the behalfe of this bearer my servant Charells Mac Cartye.[1] I have writen to my lorde your father and to my Lord Admirall in his behalfe. Hyme sealf will be bold to acquaynt yow with his desire which is very reasonable, conscionable and lawfull.[2] His adversary [*Cormac MacDermot*] is possessed of the land to which hee hath good right and by means of the profitts of the lands fyndeth [= *supports*] many frinds. I humble beseiche yow to favor hyme for my sake, havinge also the greatest right. My sealf would have bynn a suter in person for hyme if sume other advertisment [= *report*] receved of late had not for a while stayde mee, but I hope it will pleas your honor to respect hyme for my sake.

And for it, and the rest of your many honorable favors, I shall ever be reddy to [*do*] yow all honor and service.
   W Ralegh

Sherburne the 9th of July

1. Charles Carty, alias Cormac MacCormac MacCarthy, lately Ralegh's servant or page. See also below, Letters 77, 83 and 94.
2. The dispute was over a will. In March 1592, at which time MacCarthy was at sea with his master, the Privy Council had overruled the Lord Deputy and confirmed MacCarthy's right to the castle of Blarney but delayed a decision on the lordship of Muskerry, north-west of Cork. With Ralegh's disgrace in 1592 the situation changed: *APC* XXII, pp. 320–22, 579–80.

---

## 77.  To Michael Hickes from Sherborne, 9 July [1594][1]

Longleat, Wilts, Portland Papers, 1, f. 173, *HMC Bath* II, p. 42. In Ralegh's hand.

### PRESENT OF A PEARL

[*addressed*]  To my verie loving freind Master Michael Hext,[2] secretary to the Lord High Treasurer of England

[*endorsed*]  Sir W Raleigh

I confess I am your debter for a perrell, but the more yow frinde this bearer[3] the bigger the perrell wilbe founde; it shall grow as your good favor growes to my sarvent. And besids the perrell I wilbe farther thanckfull unto yow for hyme. His sute is honest and yow ar a man of conscience. I know you love justice for it sealf but to be carfull and earnest therin is often proceeding from mediation of frinds, of which number I hope yow esteeme mee.

 And so wishing yow a good rich and lustye wife[4] I cummit yow [*to*] God and rest your poore frind to do yow service.
  Sherburne the 9th of July,
   W Ralegh

1. This cannot be later than 1594 (see note 4) and that year Ralegh wrote from Sherborne, sending care of a bearer, on 9 July. Cf. 1593 for which letters survive written only in May and August.
2. Michael Hickes (1543–1612) was Burghley's patronage secretary and also a close friend of Sir Robert Cecil.

3. If the letter has been correctly dated the bearer was Charles Carty (see Letter 76) whose case it seems to fit.
4. Hickes married a rich widow in December 1594: A.G.R. Smith, *Servant of the Cecils: The Life of Sir Michael Hickes*, 1977, p. 102.

---

## 78. TO MICHAEL HICKES FROM SHERBORNE, 12 JULY [1594]¹

Longleat, Portland Papers 1/81, *HMC Third Report (Bath)*, p. 195. In Ralegh's hand.

A. Collins, *Baronettage of England*, 1720, pp. 56–7, spelling and punctuation modernized, from a faithful, unprinted transcript by Strype, according to Oldys, 1736, in *Works* 1829, I, p. 141, note 13; Edwards II, pp. 382–3, from Collins.

### CAPTAIN SPRING AND THE GOOD ANGEL

[*addressed*]   To my very loving frinde Master Michell Hext, secritory to the right honorable the Lord Tresorer of Inglande

[*endorsed, probably much later*]   Sir W Raleighe   Cap[tain] Spring   The Good Angel at Master Hextes elbow

Worthy Master Michell: I am most earnestly to entreat yow for this gentleman, Cap[tain] Springe,² that, partly for love and partly for honest consideration, yow will farther hyme with my Lord Tresorer for a debt of 300 *li* which Her Majestie douth owe hyme. It hath bynn longe dew and hee hath good warrant for it.³ Besids hee hath served Her Majestye very longe and hath receved many wounds in her service. Thes reasons delevered by a man of your utterance, and havinge the good angell⁴ att your elbow to instruct yow, I doubt not but it will take good and spedye effect. And in the conclusion I never wrate unto yow for any man or in any matter wherin yow shall more bynde mee unto yow then for this bearer.

And so not doubtinge of your asured frindliness I leve yow to God and remayne your most asured loving frind,

       W Ralegh

Alwayes remember yow must deale conscionable for my sake and I will requit it. From Sherburne the 12th of July

1. This cannot be during July 1595, 1596 or 1597, during all of which Ralegh was at sea, nor July 1598 by which time Burghley was too ill to be troubled with such minor business: Conyers Read, *Lord Burghley and Queen Elizabeth*, 1960, p. 545. Ralegh was probably in Sherborne in

July 1593 and 1594 (Letters 61, 62 and 77) and it seems more likely that it should follow Letter 77, being addressed to the same person and surviving in the same collection.
2. Probably Edward Spring who, through Ralegh's influence, had been freed from prison and pardoned for having supplied the rebel Earl of Desmond with provisions: Grosart, Series II, vol. I, pp. 272–3.
3. In April 1591 an Edward Spring had been recommended by Sir John Norris for service in France, and in June of that year a Captain Spring took 150 Somerset men from Weymouth to Brittany: *CSPD 1591–4*, p. 25 and *APC* XXI, p. 192.
4. A delicate way of offering a bribe, probably stemming from the coin known as the angel or noble, worth 6s. 8d. Cf. the 'large perrell' of Letter 77.

---

79. TO SIR ROBERT CECIL FROM SHERBORNE, 20 JULY 1594

Hatfield, CP27/46, *HMC Salisbury* IV, p. 566. In Ralegh's hand.
Edwards II, pp. 95–6.

## SPANISH BASES IN BRITTANY

[*addressed*]   To the right honorable Sir Robert Cecill knight, one of Her Majesties most honorable Privie Councell
[*endorsed*]   20 Julii 1594   Sir Walter Rauleighe to my master

Sir: It seemeth that the late advertisment [= *report*] of the Spanishe preparations[1] is now confirmed and this last weeke ther weare three great Spanishe men of warr that gave chace to an Inglishe shipp and her too prizes and drave them yeven to the very mouth of Dartmouth. It is likely that all our Newfoun[d]land men wilbe taken up by them if they be not speedely driven from the coast, for in the begininge of August our Newland fleet ar expected, which ar above a hundred sayle. If thos should be lost it would be the greatest blow that ever was geven to Ingland.

I beseich yow to remember my leve to go privately with my Lord Admirall.[2] I may perchance do Her Majestye sume service. I am now preparinge thos 50 myners for which I had direction,[3] but if Her Majesties letter had left it att large as well for Devon as Cornwale, Devon may better spare men then Cornwale, but I am now tyed by the letter to Cornwale which hath fewer men[4] and is nirer the enemye. I pray, Sir, vouchsaufe mee a lyne or too how things go on and who goes for Britayne.

Thus ever more bound to honor and serve yow and take leve.
W Ralegh

Sherburne the 20th of July

1. See Letter 75. Note that Ralegh's spelling is becoming slightly less eccentric, but he still uses the single letter e as a last syllable, for example in 'Britayne'.
2. Preparations to dislodge the Spaniards from Brittany were already under way in July 1594 but it was not until the following November that a combined land and sea force, led by Sir John Norris and Sir Martin Frobisher, made a successful attack on Brest: R.B. Wernham, *After the Armada*, pp. 532–54. While the participation of the Earl of Essex was blocked by the Queen herself, there is no evidence that Ralegh's offer of his services was ever considered.
3. The Queen's letter to Ralegh of 16 July asked that 50 'pioneers' be at Plymouth by 5 August. The number was later increased to 100: *CSPD 1591–4*, p. 528, *HMC Salisbury* IV, p. 563.
4. The population of Elizabethan Devon was at least twice that of Cornwall and the proportion of active miners probably about the same: Joyce Youings, *Ralegh's Country*, 1986, p. 11.

---

## 80. To Sir Robert Cecil [from Durham House],[1] 20 September 1594

Hatfield, CP28/40, *HMC Salisbury* IV, p. 609, dated 10 September. In Ralegh's hand, in great haste.

Edwards II, p. 100.

### PREPARING FOR GUIANA

[*addressed*]  To the right honorable Sir Robert Cicill knight, of Her Majesties [m]ost honorable Privy Councell

[*endorsed*]  20 September 1594  Sir Walter Raleigh to my master

Sir: Although Eatons[2] shipp be gonn yet the letter will do no harme for I may be frynded of hyme in sume thinge I want. Your own I have returned and I can say no more but what good shall happen in Ingland or in India[3] or elcewher, so God favor mee as I take it and confess it to be of your most honorable frindshipps towards mee and how mich for such respect I may be bound yow know and which I will acknowledg and performe to the end of my life.

With my humble dewtye to my Mistris[4] I leve and I am ever your servant,

    W Ralegh

I had a post this morning from Sherburne. The plauge is in the town very hote.[5] My Bess is on way sent, hir sonne[6] another way, and I am in great troble ther withe.

1. His usual residence in London where he was early in September: E. Lodge, *Illustrations of British History*, 1791, new edn 1838, III, p. 67.
2. Thomas Heaton, Mayor (1594), shipowner, customer and privateer of Southampton. He sent three ships to the West Indies in 1595: *HMC Salisbury* IV, p. 563 and Andrews 1964, p. 145.

3. He was being careful to conceal his destination (Guiana) from prying eyes.
4. Elizabeth, Lady Cecil, daughter of Lord Cobham.
5. Both school and church records confirm this: J. Fowler, *Medieval Sherborne*, Dorchester 1951, p. 382.
6. Their eldest surviving son, Walter, had been baptized at Lillington near Sherborne on 1 November 1593: Lillington parish register. It is possible that when this letter was written the baby was being wet-nursed by a woman of the town.

---

## 81. To Sir Robert Cecil from Alresford, Hants, [7/14][1] December 1594

Hatfield, CP29/61, *HMC Salisbury* V, p. 52. In Ralegh's hand.
Edwards II, pp. 104–5.

### WIDOW SMITH, THE SHERBORNE TITLE AND WEST INDIAN VOYAGES

[*addressed*] To the right honorable Sir Robert Cicill knight, of Her Majesties most honorable Privy Councell
[*endorsed*] December 1594   Sir Walter Raleighe to my master

Sir: You must esteeme mee for your yevell spirritt that haunts yow thus with so many tedius bussneses. I could not dispach with that debt of Symsons[2] for the widoe Smithe.[3] Shee hath a soonn[4] that waytes on the Keper [*of the Great Seal*],[5] and her doughter maried Master Wilkes[6] so as it wilbe the harder to clere. Yet seing I am butt a suretye for Spilman,[7] and never borrowed penny of her, it hath the more reasons. If it be not stayde all that I have wilbe taken upon the execusion in my absence, and if shee will not geve longer day [*to pay*] I thinke the next way wilbe that the shirrif of Dorsett be cummanded to execute no write [*sic*] uppon mee in that countrey, for although they can do no good by reason all the intrest [= *equity*] is in my soonn, yet the discreditt wilbe great if I be driven to shew that conve[*y*]ance.[8] And besyds by that means my wife will know that shee cann have no intrest in my livinge, and so exclayme [= *complain*]. On this all my estate dependeth and the Queen, having refused all other graces, I hope will save me yet from the ruin of others.

I leve it and my sealf to your honorable constant care [of my *crossed out*] on whom I only depend and love above all, and it is all I cann saye.

Your constantlye and sinserely to be cummanded,
W Ralegh

It is more then tyme that ther be a restraynt of all shippinge bound out to the warrs, for ther ar multetudes going for the Indies.[9] If any men be taken (as sume every yeare ar) the Queens purpose wilbe frustrate, and if Eatons[10] shipps go, who will attempt the chefest places of my enterprize. I shalbe undun and I know they wilbe beaten and do no good.

From Alsford this Saterday after I left yow, with a hart half broken.

1. Cf. Letter 82, which follows, written on Saturday 21 December.
2. Probably Egis Simpson, a London goldsmith.
3. Probably Joan, widow of Ambrose Smith, a London mercer, for whom Ralegh seems to have stood surety.
4. Possibly Henry Smith, who in 1586 was described as 'Her Majesties servant ... lodging at his mothers at the Gilt Keye in Cheapsyde': R.C. Anderson, *Letters of the Fifteenth and Sixteenth Centuries*, Southampton Record Society, 1921, p. 98.
5. Sir John Puckering, Lord Keeper of the Great Seal, 1592–6.
6. Thomas Wilkes, a Clerk of the Privy Council from 1576, MP for Southampton 1589 and 1593. He was frequently employed in diplomatic missions abroad and had been knighted by Henry of Navarre in 1592: Hasler III, pp. 619–21.
7. See below, Letter 190, note 3.
8. In 1609, Ralegh was to claim that in the year 1598 he had conveyed his lease of the Sherborne estate to his son Walter, 'without power of revocation', subject to a payment of £200 a year to Lady Ralegh after his, Sir Walter's, death: Wildman, *Short History*, pp. 139–40. He subsequently mislaid the indenture, perhaps deliberately, and, as this letter indicates, his memory regarding the date of the conveyance was at fault. His 'interest' in the estate was, of course, still only that of a tenant of the Bishop of Salisbury: see above, Letter 60, note 9.
9. Between 1589 and 1595 'we know of 77 voyages' from Europe to the West Indies: Andrews 1984, p. 283.
10. See above, Letter 80, note 2.

---

## 82. TO SIR ROBERT CECIL FROM SHERBORNE, 21 DECEMBER 1594

Hatfield, CP29/44, *HMC Salisbury* V, 42–3. In Ralegh's hand.
Edwards II, p. 102.

### THE MISSING LETTER AND THE WIDOW SMITH

[*addressed*]   To the right honorable Sir Robert Cecill knight, of Her Majesties most honorable Privey Councell
[*endorsed*]   21 December 1594   Sir Walter Raleighe to my master

Sir: My carelessness in loosinge the coppy of the letter I cannot excuse butt it concernd no boddy butt my sealf and therfore the less matter. But how it came to the earles[1] hand I beseich yow lerne by sume means, that I may butt know wher it weare lost or otherwise imbeseled.

What yow have vouchsawfed for the staye of my sutes in law, especially for the widdo Smith[2] I humble pray yow to lett mee know, for I stay butt for the winde to bringe about the shipp.[3] I shalbe wiser on day, and I shall withall, I hope, do yow sume service after so many of thes troblesume affaires.

    Till then and ever I shalbe your debter and [m]ost yours of all livinge.
           W Ralegh

Sherburne the 21 of December

1. The missing letter has not been identified. Nor is it known which earl Ralegh suspected. It was probably Essex, but there were others, such as Cumberland, who were no doubt inquisitive about his current maritime project.
2. See above, Letter 81.
3. He was awaiting the arrival of his ships from the Thames with some anxiety, the passage down the Channel often being more hazardous than the crossing of the Atlantic.

## 83. To Sir Robert Cecil from Sherborne, 26 December 1594

Hatfield, CP29/53, *HMC Salisbury* V, p. 49. In Ralegh's hand.
Edwards II, p. 103.

### FOR CHARLES MACCARTHY

[*addressed*] To the right honorable Sir Robert Cecill knight, of Her Majesties most honorable Priveye Councell

[*endorsed*] 26 December 1594 Sir Walter Raleighe to my master in favour of Charles that was sometyme his page

Sir: I am importuned so by this bearer[1] as I cannot refuse hyme to write unto yow. His desire is to retayne towards [= *serve*] yow. What your disposition hath byn in these things I know well, butt hee will not be other wise awnswered att my hands. I would be gladd he would sew [= *sue*] to serve the earle of Essex, to which I have persuaded [= *advised*] hyme.[2]

I hope to here how yow do, and for my self this wynde breakes my hart. That [*which*] should cary mee hence now stayes mee heere and holds my shipps in the river of Temes. As soune as God send them hither I will not lose on houre of tyme.
        Ever more yours to do yow service,
           W Ralegh

Sherburne the 26 of December

1. See above, Letter 76.
2. Was Ralegh anxious to be rid of a man for whom he no longer had any use and who was becoming somewhat of a nuisance?

---

## 84. TO SIR ROBERT CECIL FROM SHERBORNE, 1 JANUARY 1595

Hatfield, CP24/76, *HMC Salisbury* V, p. 77. In Ralegh's hand.
Edwards II, pp. 106–7.

### FOR WILLIAM STRODE

[*addressed*]  To the right honorable Sir Robert Cecill knight, of Her Majesties [*m*]ost honorable Privey Councell
[*endorsed*]  Primo January 1594  Sir Walter Raleighe to my master

Sir: This gentleman, my especiall frinde and kynsman,[1] hath sume controversye with the towne of Plymouth, and hath desired mee to recummende unto your honor his just and reasonable desire, and therin no farther to be favored then it shall apeare lawfull.[2] If it shall therfore pleas your honor to be his honorable favorer herein I shall acknowledge it as dun to my sealf and shalbe very proude if it pleas yow to make hyme know (that as I am yours in all love and service) so hee may fynde that yow pleas for my sake, in this his great right, to aforde hyme sume testimony therof.

And yeven so only gasing [= *gazing*] for a wynde to carye mee to my destiney, I humble take my leave. From Sherburne this first of January.
    Your honors to do yow service,
      W Ralegh

---

1. William Strode of Newnham in Plympton, near Plymouth. The relationship could, no doubt, be established but it was not close: Vivian, *Devon*, pp. 718–19.
2. Strode owned land on Plymouth waterfront, including a plot called Lambhay, overlooking the harbour on which he wanted to erect buildings. The town raised objections on account of military and naval security and appears to have had a good case. On 19 January 1595, the Privy Council appointed a commission of inquiry, including Sir Francis Drake and Sir John Gilbert, which persuaded Strode simply to amend his plans, a solution with which, on 2 April, the Council pronounced itself satisfied. Drake claimed the credit for persuading Strode to climb down. How far Ralegh's intervention affected the outcome is impossible to say: its significance is that Strode should think his support worth having: R.N. Worth (ed.), *Plymouth Municipal Records*, 1893, pp. 214, 58, 136, 197–8 and *CSPD 1595–7*, pp. 76, 81.

## 85. To Sir Robert Cecil [?from Sherborne, ?late January 1595][1]

Hatfield, CP58/52, *HMC Salisbury* VI, pp. 327–8, dated July 1597. In Ralegh's hand.
Edwards II, p. 101, dated ?September 1594.

## STILL BECALMED

[*addressed*]   To the right honorable Sir Robard Cecill knight, of Her Majesties most honorable Privey Councell
[*endorsed*]   Sir Walter Rawley

I am sorry to be now [= *still*] so nire that my letters may cum to your hands, but this unfortunate yeare is such as thos that weare reddy and att seas too moneths before us ar beaten bake agayne and distressed.[2] This longe staye hath made mee a poore man, the yeare farr spent and what shalbe cum of us God knowes. The boddy is wasted with toyle, the purse with charge and all things worne. Only the minde is indifferent to good fortune or adversety.

There is no newse from hence worth the writtinge. If I were more fortunate I should be the more worth the cummandinge.[3] As I ame yow may dispose of mee. And thus for the present I leve yow to all good fortune, and my sealf *quo me fortuna retrudet*.[4]

    Yours ever to do yow service,
      W Ralegh

I pray be gracious to my frends in my absence, [but *written over* and] not to [kinde *crossed out*] credulous, and farther that yow wilbe pleased if any of my officers be suters unto yow in my behalf that yow will vouchsafe your favor towards them. I pray excuse mee to my lord your father, having nothinge worth his reeding to write of.

---

1. This must be before July 1596 when Cecil became Principal Secretary, so Ralegh's imminent departure must be on his first voyage to Guiana, and the degree of his despair must put it after Letters 82–4. Late January seems most likely as he finally sailed, almost certainly from Plymouth, on 6 February 1595: V.T. Harlow (ed.), *Discoverie of Guiana*, 1932, p. 11. The reference to a 'yeare farr spent' may be thought to indicate a slightly earlier date, but Ralegh's year ended on 25 March.
2. Drake and Hawkins did not depart from Plymouth until 28 August 1595.
3. A sentence pregnant with meaning.
4. A *cri de cœur* which was surely answered by the arrival of his ships.

## 86. TO SIR ROBERT CECIL FROM SHERBORNE, 10 NOVEMBER 1595[1]

Hatfield, CP36/4, *HMC Salisbury* V, pp. 444–5. In Ralegh's hand.
Edwards II, pp. 107–8.

## MARITIME MATTERS

[*addressed*]   To the right honorable Sir Robert Cicill knight, of Her Majesties most honorable Privey Councell
[*endorsed*]   10 November 1595   Sir Walter Ralegh to my master

Sir: From this desolate place I have litle matter, from my sealf less hope, and therefore I thinke the shorter the discource the better wellcum.

I receved from Lyme [*Regis*], a port town in this shire, by a smale bark lately arived, that ther ar lately many French shipps imbarged in Spayne, and of good burden and very serviceable, notwithstanding that the same went by pasport and asurance from Spayne, and all the marriners likewise imprested, and that ther ar a fleet ether gone or goinge of sixtye saile, as the[*y*] saye, for Irlande.[2] It seemeth asuredly that the preparations ar great and do dayly increase. If your honors conceve therof aright or looke into the nirest mischeif wee shall do the better, butt I feare, by your favors, ther is somewhat more in the enemis intent then is supposed. Wee that have mich ado to gett bread to eat have the less to care for, unless mich lost labor and love awake us, that ar also thanckless bus[*ied*] in things ether beyound our capasetes or cares.

What becumes of Guiana I miche desire to here, whether it pass for a history or a fable.[3] I here Master Dudley[4] and others ar sendinge thither. If it be so, farewell all good from thence, for although my sealf like a cockscome [= *fool*] did rather preferr the future in respect of others, and rather sought to wine [= *win*] the kings to Her Majesties service[5] then to sack them, I know what others will do when thos kings shall cum simpely [= *innocently*] into their hands. If it may pleas yow to acquaynt my Lord Admirall therwith, lett it then succeed as it will.

If my Lord [*Admiral*] will have a fyne pinnes [= *pinnace*] sent to the coast of Spayne to vew what is dunn I thinke for a matter of 40 or 50 *li* I can gett on that shall do service.

Sir, for conclusi[*on*] I will only say this mich, take good head least yow be not to slow. Expedition in a litle is better then mich to late. Butt your ministers of dispach ar not plentefull, neather is it every mans occupation.

God send yow all honor and health. I will wish yow both and be reddy ever to do yow service.
   W Ralegh

From Sherburne the 10th of November[6]

1. Ralegh had returned to Plymouth from Guiana early in September: *HMC Salisbury* V, p. 396.
2. The Earl of Tyrone was in open rebellion and the Lord Deputy had been warned of Spanish preparations on 29 October 1595: *APC* XXV, pp. 37–8. In fact, it was not until October 1596, by which time the Irish rebels had made a temporary peace, that Spain sent a fleet to Ireland. It was destroyed in a storm: *APC* XXIII, pp. 37–8.
3. Ralegh's account of his voyage was received with scepticism. It was even rumoured that he had not gone further than Cornwall: Harlow, *Discoverie*, pp. 4 and 9.
4. Robert Dudley, an illegitimate son of the Earl of Leicester. He had explored the Orinoco in February 1595, and then awaited Ralegh who arrived some six or eight weeks later.
5. Ralegh based the English claim to Guiana on treaties said to have been voluntarily entered into by native chiefs. See also Letter 87.
6. Two days later Sir John Hawkins died off Puerto Rico.

---

## 87.  To Sir Robert Cecil from Sherborne, [12][1] November 1595

Hatfield, CP36/9, *HMC Salisbury* V, pp. 457–8. In Ralegh's hand.
Edwards II, pp. 109–11.

### IN PRAISE OF GUIANA

[*addressed*]   To the right honorable Sir Robert Cycill knight, of Her Majesties most honorable Privy Councell
[*endorsed*]   13 November 1595   Sir Walter Ralegh to my master

Sir: Yow may perceve by this relation [= *description*][2] that it is no dreame which I have reported of Guiana, and if on image[3] have bynn brought from thence wayinge 47 kintalls [= *quintalls or hundredweights*] which cannot be so litle worth as 100 thowsand pounde, I know that in Manoa[4] ther ar store of thos. If the relation sent to the Spanishe kinge[5] had bynn also taken yow should therin have founde matter of great admiration. Butt howsoever this action be respected, I know that the like was never offred to any Christien prince. I know it wilbe presently followed both by the Spanishe and French, and if it be foreslowed [= *delayed*] by us I conclude that wee ar curst of God. In the mean tyme I humble beseich yow to move Her Majesty that none be suffred to foyle the enterprize and that thos kings of the borders which ar by my labor, perrill and charge woonn to Her

Majesties love and obedience be not by other pilferers lost agayne. I hope I shalbe thought worthy to direct thos actions that I have att myne own charge labored in and to govern that countrey which I have discovered[6] and hope to conquer for the Queen without her cost. I am sendinge away a barke to the countrey to cumfort and asure the people that they dispaire not nor yeild to any composition with other nations.[7]

I know the plott [= *map*] is by this tyme finished which yf yow pleas to cummand from Heriott[8] that Her Majestye may see it. If it be thought of less importance then it deserveth Her Majestye will shortly bewayle her negligence therin, and the enemy by the addition of so mich wealth weare us out of all. Sir, I pray esteeme it as the afaire requireth if yow love the Queens honor, profitt and sawftye. If I be thought unworthy to be imployed, or that because of my disgrace all men feare to adventure with me, if it may not be otherwise I wishe sume other of better sufficiency and grace might undertake it, that the Queen loose not that which shee shall never fynde agayne.

Yow fynd that ther ar besids gold both diamounds and peorell [= *pearl*] and I brought with mee, taken up amonge the sands, a stone which beinge cutt is very rare. I pray do mee the favor to cummand Peter van Lore[9] to deliver yow thos too which I gave hyme to prove, which hee made litle accompt of butt I will have them cutt by Pepler[10] who is skilfull and dwells here with A[drian] Gilbert.[11] I have sent yow on that was cutt here which I think is amatist and hath a strang blushe of carnation. Butt I asure my sealf that ther ar not more diamounds in the Est Indies then are to be founde in Guiana, which yow see also verefied by the relation of the Spanishe letters.

I have another cutt of another sort and if it be no diamound yet it is exceeding any diamound in bewtye, butt I am not in hast to lett it go out of my fingers. Butt thee stonns beare wittness of better, and ther is enough for all the world if wee have the grace. Butt we must cast so many doubts and this dolt [= *dullard*] and that gull [= *simpleton*][12] must be satisfied or elce all is nothing. If the Spaniards had bynn so blockishe and slouthfull wee had not feared now their poure, who by their gold from thence vex and indanger all the estates of Europe. Wee must not looke to mayntyne warr uppon the revenus of Ingland: if wee be once driven to the defensive, farr well my part, butt as God will so it shalbe who governs the harts of kings.

    I rest your asured to be cummanded, poor or rich,
      W Ralegh

[*left-hand margin*] Sherburn this Wensday morning an houre after the recept of your letter, the 13 of November.

1. 12 November was a Wednesday in 1595.
2. According to his own statement (Harlow, *Discoverie*, 1932, p. 77), the 'relation' which Ralegh sent to the Privy Council was a package of extracts from Spanish manuscripts which he had acquired in November 1595 from Captain George Popham who had come by them on his way to the Indies the previous year. Ralegh printed them in translation as an Appendix to his *Discoverie* (ibid., pp. 79–85). What are probably the originals, dated 7 November 1593, survive (PRO, SP12/246/5 (*CSPD 1591–4*, pp. 383–5) although there is some variation in the spelling of personal and place names.
3. The legendary image of the Indian idol: Harlow, ibid., p. 84.
4. The capital of Eldorado, known to Ralegh only by report.
5. The fuller version (above, note 2) of which Ralegh had only extracts. A transcript of the originals (now in the Archivo General de Indias at Simancas) is in BL, Add. 36316, ff. 30 et seq.
6. An echo of his ambitions for a seignory over his 'lost colony' of Virginia ten years previously. He had not, in fact, financed the voyage to Guiana entirely out of his own pocket, Cecil himself, for one, having contributed: Andrews 1984, p. 290.
7. Ralegh sent out Laurence Keymis (see below, Letter 165, note 31) in January 1596.
8. Thomas Harriot (1560–1621), the highly gifted 'mathematical practitioner' and cartographer, who had been among those sent by Ralegh to Virginia in 1585: for his relationship with Ralegh see John W. Shirley, *Thomas Harriot, a Biography*, Oxford 1983, *passim*. The 'plott' referred to is almost certainly that now in the British Library (Add. 17940A, reproduced as a frontispiece in Harlow, *Discoverie*, 1932) which has place-names thought to be in Ralegh's hand: J. Lorimer (ed.), *English and Irish settlement on the river Amazon 1540–1646*, Hakluyt Society, Series II, CLXXVI1, 1989, p. 12, but see also R.A. Skelton, 'Ralegh as a geographer', *Virginia Magazine of History and Biography*, LXXII, 1963, pp. 140–41, who suggested that that map was one produced by Harriot after Keymis's expedition of 1596.
9. A London jeweller: see below, Letter 213.
10. Not identified.
11. Ralegh's elder half-brother whom he employed as his agent at Sherborne.
12. Shakespeare, *Othello*, v, ii, 163: 'Oh gull, oh dolt, as ignorant as durt'.

---

## 88. To the Privy Council from Sherborne, 25 November 1595

Hatfield, CP36/26, *HMC Salisbury* V, pp. 466–9, enclosed with Letter 89. In the hand of a clerk, place-names in italic, with address, subscription and signature in Ralegh's hand.

Edwards II, pp. 112–17.

## THE LAND DEFENCES OF THE SOUTH WEST

[*addressed*] To the right honorable the lords and others of Her Majesties most honorable Privy Councell

[*endorsed*] 25 November 1595 Sir Walter Raleghe to [my master *crossed out*] the lords

My dewtie most humblie remembred: In the letters which I receaved from your honors bearing date the xvth of this November yt hath pleased yow to order that mutuall succour be gyven from the counties of Devon and Cornwall to each other by renforsing of each with 4000 men upon notice gyven from me to the erle of Bath[1] for the succour of Cornewall and the like from his lordship to me for Devon.[2] Yt is trewe that before this tyme wee had not anie warrante to send out of the counties under our charge any releeffe to the neighbour places invaded, for remedy whereof your lordships have gravelye ordered this course of seconding each other. Notwithstanding bycause I holde my selfe bounde in duetie to speak my knowledge of th'estate of Cornwall, wherewith it hath pleased Her Majestie to put me in trust, a charge both for the greatnes and grace farr beyonde any worth or deserte of myne,[3] I doe presume to put your honors in minde that according to my meane judgement yt were more fitt to supplie Devon out of Somersett then from Cornewall, hoping that your honors will receave my reasons for the same as in discharge of my duetie and not that I dare to offer them in any other sorte, being bound to obay and not to advice.

Yf there shall any disent [= *invasion*] be made by the enymye in either countye by the waie of surprise, and that the enymy doe but burne or sacke and depart, then can nether be releeved as aforsaied bycause ther wilbe noe tyme gyven to unite the forces of the same sheere where such attempt shalbe offered, much lesse for the drawing in of any mumbers from a farr, and for any such enterprize where their is noe purpose [*by the invaders*] to holde and possesse the places gotten, each shire with 4000 men shalbe able either to repell or resiste the same. But if the enymy dispose himselfe to fortyfye any parte in Cornewall, or to strengthen any neck of lande of advantaige and thereby begyne to dryve us to a defensive warr,[4] then there is noe country adjoyneth to Cornewall but Devon from whence any spedye supplie maie be had to impeach [= *prevent*] the begining of such a purpose. And if ought be attempted in Devon, of which Plymouth ys most to be feared, having in one indraught [= *inlet*] two goodly harboroughes, as Catt Water and Aishe [*Saltash*] Water,[5] then yt is also very likely that the enymye will either assure Cornewall or seek utterly to wast yt bycause it ys next his suplies, both from Spayne and Brittaine, and hath divers portes and good rodes [= *anchorages*] to receave a fleete.

Furthermore maye it please your lordships to consider that Cornewall is stretched owt all in lenght, and hath little bredth, the west partes whereof ar little lesse than 80 myles from Plymouth, and betwen the one and the other the great river of Tamar which is not fordable in any place within 12 myles of Plymouth,[6] and for 4000 men to march over at Newbridge above Calstock, which is the neerest passage, the yournye [*sic*] of one part of the succour wilbe of one 100 myles and more as they come to the towne of Plymouth, considering the coasting of the river on both sides.[7] And for other passaige there are but two ferries, the one at Stonehouse, the other at Aishe and those smale boates of no recept [= *capacity*] and by which nether carriage, horse, victuall, munition nor ought else fitt to folow an army can be conveyed but in a very longe time. Besides if therbe an intente for Plymouth yt is to be feared that the enymy will bring gallies[8] with them, aswell to assure there landing as to comaund the river of Tamar, and then all passages shalbe taken awaie but at Newebridge aforesaid, and yet the same maie be also easelie broken yf the gallies once possesse the saied river. And yf the enemy shoulde lande towarde the east of Plymouth, as at Saltcombe [*Salcombe*], Slapton, Dartmouth or Torbay, which I doe nowe thinke is likely, then shold also parte of the succours of Cornewall martche above one hundreth and 20 myles or 140 mile to the place attempted. Moreover may it please yow to consider that if 4000 men sholde at any time be drawen out of Cornewall, and the same knowen to the enymy, as it wilbe at the instant, I assure your honors that 300 soldiers either sent out of Brittaine (which maie be done in two tydes) or retorned in a gallye or two from Plymouth, wilbe strenght sufficient to indainger and distroy the whole shire, at least all the westren partes which ought most to be defended in respecte of the good harboroughes therein. For there is noe parte of Inglande so dangerouslie seated [= *settled*],[9] soe thynnly mande [= *manned*], so littell defensed and soe easilie invaded, having the sea on both sides (which noe other countye of Inglonde hath) and is withall so narrow that yf an enymy possesse any of two or three sraightes [= *necks*] neither can those of the west repair eastward nor those of the est westward, for betwyn Mounts Baye and the sea entring within St Tees [*St Ives*] it is but 3 miles and a halfe from sea to sea, without [= *beyond*] which their lyeth a good parte of the lande to the west in forme of a peninsula. Betwen Trewro, which standethe on the first sounde [= *stretch of sheltered water*] of the river of Falmouth, and St Piran [*Perranporth*] is but fyve miles over land passable, and the same also easilie garded, which is as much of Cornewall as the enemy should need, for within soe muche as lieth to the west of the two forthrightes [= *straight courses*][10] are the best portes and are very sufficient to receave the greatest fleet that ever swam. And [*this*] conteyneth 27 myles of lenght, very gardable, which in my simple juidgement is everie waie more to be sought for by the enymy then Plymouth, at least yf the same weare so well understode by them, which is not unlikely, for the enymy taking Plymouth and not possessing Cornewall there is then a whole country to the west of them and between them and their supplies. But possessing this part they ynyoye as good yf not a better porte then Plymouth and there is then noe lande betwen them and Britaine or Spaine. And if they have any purpose to make warr with us at home, and shalbe able to dryve us to a defensyve, then ys [ther *in margin in a different hand*] noe comparyson betwen the one and theother, for which I could yeilde your honors many reasons but that I feare I am over tedyouse in these. The countrye eastward ys also but narrowe, there being but 8 miles between the river of Padstowe and the bay of Trewardreth [*Tywardreth*]. Againe, Cornewall hath not anie one company of horse, either lance, lightehorse, petronell or pistall.[11]

Notwithstanding, if it shall please your honors to thinke it fitt, there maie be order given that all those companies which border the river of Tamar or Saltashe be reddy to releeve Plymouth upon any sudden [*descent*], bycause they maie be soone past over, if there were provision of better passage. But as yet there are but two ferries neere Plymouth, the one at Stonehouse, the other at Aishe as aforesaied, and two or three gallies will interrupte all transportation bycause there is not any place strengthened to gard or assure anie passage over the saied river neerer then Newebridge, which is 12 miles above within the lande.

Contrariewise Somerset lieth to Devon in great bredthe and is a cuntrye strongly formed, whereas the other is stretched all in lenght. Somersetshiere is not devyded from Devon by any river which is not fordable at all tymes and in all places so as both horse, foote, carryadge, victuall and whatsoever maie come in hast from thence to the succour of Devon. Cornewall hath Tamier [*sic*] noe waie passable neere Plymouth. Somersett is seated from daunger, having Devon towardes the south and on Severne side yt hath noe port capeable of any shippes of bourden,[12] and the indraughte is long and danngerous. All the north coast of Devon and Cornewall lyeing betwen the waters of Somerset, which are Dunster, Minniett [*Minehead*] and Bridgewater, into which smale barques cannot aryve without precise observation of the tyde. Cornewall is but an arme of lande which stretcheth itselfe even to the bosome of the enemye and hath the best portes of Ingland on the south and better then any in Somerset on the north, and also betwen them and harme. Somerset ys verie riche and full of horse, aswell for cariadge as service, many welthie gentlemen and aboundeth in victuall. Cornewall hath noe horse of service, the cuntrie poore, fewe gentlemen and those of meane livinge, and by reason that their riches consisteth in tynn workes there is little corne and lesse of all thinges else.[13] For these respectes I hope that your honors will have favorable regarde towardes us, being notwithstanding redye to performe whatsoever it shall please Her Majestie to determine or your lordships to comaunde.

And even soe craving pardon for my presumption herein I humblie take my leave from Sherborne this 25 of November 1595.

    Your honors in all to be cummanded,
        W Ralegh

---

1. William Bourchier, 3rd Earl of Bath, Lord Lieutenant of Devon, lived at Tawstock near Barnstaple in north Devon and rarely travelled far from home: John Roberts, 'The Armada Lord Lieutenant', *DAT*, 102, 1970, pp. 71–85 and 103, 1971, pp. 103–22. His part in the defeat of the Armada was minimal.
2. Bath was to expect reinforcements in an emergency to the number of 13,000 men, including 2,000 from Wiltshire: APC XXV, pp. 64–8. See also ibid., pp. 69–72.
3. Ralegh was, in fact, one of the very few commoners appointed by Queen Elizabeth to a lieutenancy and that in spite of his owning very little land in Cornwall: G. Scott Thompson, *Lords Lieutenants in the Sixteenth Century*, 1923, p. 61, note and *passim*.
4. There had recently been several such 'descents' in Cornwall by small Spanish squadrons, but no serious attempts to establish defensive positions: A.L. Rowse, *Tudor Cornwall*, 1941, pp. 400–407.
5. At the mouths of the Rivers Plym and Tamar respectively, the latter also known as the Hamoaze.
6. Forming for most of its course the boundary between the two counties.
7. Both the main stream and its creeks follow the most tortuous courses.
8. Galliasses, barge-like vessels impelled by sails or oars.
9. i.e. with so few resident gentlemen.
10. Cf. Shakespeare, *The Tempest*, III, iii, 3, 'through forth rights and meanders'. Edwards read this as 'indraughtes', and for the revised reading printed here the editors are indebted to Mrs Audrey Erskine.
11. Horseman carrying light firearms.
12. The accuracy of Ralegh's observation is confirmed by the national survey of shipping made in 1582–3 where Bridgwater, the only coastal port in Somerset, is credited with no vessels over 60 tons: PRO, SP12/156/45, p. 90v.
13. Cf. Richard Carew, *Survey of Cornwall*, 1603, ed. F.E. Halliday, 1953, p. 101, who drew attention to an increase in husbandry of late.

---

## 89. To Sir Robert Cecil from Sherborne, [26][1] November 1595

Hatfield, CP36/44, *HMC Salisbury* V, pp. 472–3. In Ralegh's hand.
Edwards II, pp. 117–18.

## DISINTEREST IN GUIANA

[*addressed*]   To the right honorable Sir Robert Cecill knight, of Her Majesties most honorable Privey Councell
   Hast post hast   W Ralegh[2]
   [*Shaftesbury, 26 November, 1 pm; Salisbury 5 pm; Andover 8 pm; Basingstoke 11 pm; Hartford Bridge, 27 November, 1 am, and Staines 8 am.*]
[*endorsed*]   November 1595   Sir Walter Ralegh to my master

Sir: I beseich yow lett us know whether wee shalbe travelers or tinkers, conquerors or crounes [= *imbeciles*], for if the winter pass without making provision ther can be no vitling in the summer. And if it be now forslowed [= *delayed*] farewell Guiana forever. Then must I determyne to begg or run away, honor and gold and all good forever hopeless. I do not here how yow like the white stonn.[3] I have sent for more of each: as soune as they cume yow shall have them.

I have written this letter [88] to the Lords [*of the Privy Council*] in awnswere of that which I receved about mutuall supplies between Devon and Cornwale, a matter soun written butt not possible to performe. Somersett may best releve Devon, for if it be apoynted to Dorsett it is more and [*than*] need, for Dorsett hath never a haven capable of any great shipp,[4] without which ther is no feare of any disent [= *invasion*].

I beseich yow lett us here sumewhat as soun as yow cann. And so with my most humble dewtye to my Mistris,[5] I care not mich for yowr idle honor.
   W R

Sir, I have sent the letter unsealed. Hancocke[6] hath a seal of myne when yow have perused it. I humble pray yow that your footman may deliver thes too letters at Derum [*Durham*] Howse.

1. See note 2.
2. Interspersed with postmasters' endorsements.
3. Probably quartz, with traces of gold, then being assayed in London: Harlow, *Discoverie*, 1932, pp. 7–8.
4. The shipping survey of 1582–3 (above, Letter 88, note 12), f. 77d in fact credits Poole with six and Weymouth with three vessels over 100 tons.
5. Elizabeth (née Brooke), Lady Cecil.
6. Edward Hancock, Ralegh's secretary (see Letter 62, note 2). Presumably Ralegh's intention was that Cecil should read Letter 88 before forwarding it to Durham House where Hancock would seal it and deliver it to the Clerk to the Privy Council.

## 90. To Charles Lord Howard from Sherborne, 30 November 1595

Hatfield, CP36/42, *HMC Salisbury* V, p. 477. In Ralegh's hand.
Edwards II, 120–21.

### WARNING OF A SPANISH FLEET

[*addressed*] To the right honorable my singuler good lorde the Lorde Admirall of Inglande
[*endorsed*] Ultimo November 1595 Sir Walter Raleghe to the Lord Admirall A pynnasse to be sent after Sir Francis Drake

My very good lord: I thincke your lordship hath understoode by Watts[1] that came lately out of Spayne that ther wilbe a fleet sent after Sir Francis Drake and Sir John Hawkinges.[2] The man was curius [= *careful not*] to confess any particuler to mee butt I did ever gess it to be so. I thincke your lordshipp should do very honorable to cause a coople of smale carvells [= *small, fast vessels*] or pineses to be dispatcht with all hast with advise to them. The charge wilbe small to the Queen and it may save all her shipps[3] and people in that action, for as sure as God lives if the Spanishe fleet arive while the soldiers ar over lande bothe the ships att ancor and those att Panama wilbe both lost, and they may yet be warned in tyme sufficient. I dare take on mee to direct them to fynde them out by a sure and speedy course, butt your lordshipp can do it better your sealf and therfore ther needs nothing butt the resolution which God grawnt may be effected according to the greatness of the necessetye.[4]

If any fleet go for Ilande [*Ireland*][5] and that your lordshipp go not, I beseich your lordship to inable mee to the service, who would purchace Her Majestyes favor with what labor or perrill soever.

If your lordship send to Sir Francis it would be best dun from hence, I mean from Weemouth [*Weymouth*] or Plymouth, for a messenger may be with them from hence er they can cum about from London hither.

I would also humble pray your lordship to gett a resolution for our enterprize of Guiana, for if provision of vitle be not made in the winter it cannot be dun for this yeare. Her Majestye shall by foreslowing [= *delaying*] it lose the greatest asurance of good that ever was offred to any Christien prince and your lordship douth fynde that it is the surest way to devert all attempts from home.

This levinge thes afaires to your lordships honorable care and my sealf to your service I humble take my leve and will ever be [to] your lordship as your sarvant.

Sherburne the last of November      W Ralegh

1. Not positively identified but a George Watts, mariner, of Ratcliffe on the Thames, gave evidence in October 1594 in the High Court of Admiralty concerning a case of privateering in the Indies: K.R. Andrews (ed.), *English Privateering Voyages*, 1959, pp. 302–4.
2. They had sailed for the West Indies on 28 August knowing that the King of Spain was already fitting out a fleet to intercept them, and this was confirmed by Robert Sydney in a letter from Flushing on 27 November: *HMC Salisbury* V, p. 474. Hawkins had died on 12 November but the news had not yet reached England.
3. On 5 March 1596, Cecil informed Sir Horatio Pallavicino that 'certen pynasses' had been sent out to warn Drake on 20 December: K.R. Andrews, *Last Voyage of Drake and Hawkins*, Hakluyt Society, Series II, CXLII, 1972, pp. 739–40.
4. Drake and Hawkins's fleet contained no less than six of the Queen's ships: Andrews, ibid.
5. See above, Letter 86, for recent rumours of a Spanish fleet preparing to invade Ireland. The Queen had tried, but without success, to persuade Drake and Hawkins to divert their Indies expedition to the defence of Ireland, in lieu of whom her preference was for Sir Henry Palmer: *CSPD 1595–7*, pp. 88–9 and *APC* XXV, pp. 37–8.

---

91.    TO SIR ROBERT CECIL FROM WEYMOUTH, 18 JANUARY 1596

      Hatfield, CP30/1, *HMC Salisbury* VI, p. 18. In Ralegh's hand.

## A CASE OF MANSLAUGHTER

[*addressed*]    To the right honorable Sir Robert Cecill knight, of Her Majesties most honorable Prive[y] Councell
[*endorsed*]    18 January 1595    Sir Walter Raleghe to my master

May it please your honor to understande that since the writinge of my last letter[1] wherin I acquaynted your honor of Master Stautons [Staytons *overwritten*] mischance,[2] I have since lerned and do very well know by examination that Fitt James[3] strake the sayd gentleman and offred hyme [?*un*]indurable wronge before the fraye. And further it is very asured that Master Stauton had no weapon about hyme when hee was asalted by Fitt James, who also was known to be a very quarelsume yong man, and on the contrary Master Stauton ever known and reputed for very honest, civill and of modest caredge towards all menn. I hovie [sic] bynn moved by divers of the better sort to make knowne unto your honor the innosencye of the gentleman and to be farther a suter unto yow in his behalf, that it might pleas yow to favor hyme. The gentleman hyme sealf will ever be reddy to do yow service, and I shall take your favor towards hyme as bestowed on my sealf.

And so resting ever asured to be disposed and cummanded by yow, I humble take leve from Weemouth this xviii of January.

   Ever as your sarvent in all love and affectionn,
    W Ralegh

1. Missing.
2. On 25 January the Sheriff of Somerset informed Sir Robert Cecil that he had taken an inventory of the goods of one Master Thomas Stoughton pending the result of a coroner's inquest regarding 'the manslaughter or murder he standeth charged with': *HMC Salisbury* VI, p. 29.
3. There were Fitzjameses in both Dorset (see below, Letter 119, note 5) and Somerset, but the deceased was probably one of the family living at Redlynch in Somerset which was well known for its recusancy: Collinson, *Somerset*, 1731, I, pp. 225–6. On the other hand, one wonders how Ralegh came to be involved in a Somerset matter, except by special commission.

---

## 92. TO SIR ROBERT CECIL, 3 MAY 1596

> Hatfield, CP40/52, *HMC Salisbury* VI, pp. 166–7. Written by a clerk, but not the usual one, with subscription, annotation and signature in Ralegh's hand.
> Edwards II, pp. 125–6.

### BISHOPRIC OF LISMORE AND WATERFORD

[*addressed*] To the right honorable Sir Robert Cecill knight, Councellor in Her Heighnes Prevye Councelles
[*endorsed*] 3 Maii 1596 Sir Walter Raleighe to my master in favour of the Bushop of Lesemore in Waterford

Thes maye be to seignyfye unto your honor that the Archebishopp of Cashell,[1] a man whome I thincke my Lord Treasour [sic] hathe lytell cause to favor, hathe of late delte verye badlye with me, contrarye to all faythe and promysse, touchinge diverse of my Irishe leases and landes. Whoes discortysies I wold gladlye mete [= *repay*] withall, and doe fynde noe better meanes in releffe of my self, fartheraunce of relygyon and comfort of all myne Inglyshe tenantes and frends, then in preferrynge some other of better sorte to the bishoppricke of Lesmore and Waterforde, whereof the Archebishop hathe but (a comendam)[2] and hathe besydes twoe or three other bishoprickes.[3] My desire is that you wilbe pleased to be a meane to preferr unto the same bishopricke of Lesmore and Waterford my very good frend Master Hughe Broughton,[4] a man well knowen to my lord His Grace of Caunterburye,[5] my Lord Treasour and all the lerned doctors and scollers of Englande, and a man unto whome I wishe moche good, beschinge you to have some conference with my cosen Goringe[6] aboughte the same, wherein the said Master Brouton is able to doe moche good and be a greate comforte to all our Inglishe nation there aboughtes, and encrease of relygyon. And the gentellman hym self wilbe verye thanckefull unto you for anye favor shewed unto hym, whome I leave to your good rememberance,[7] and your self to God.

This third of Maye 1596,

    Your honor to do yow service,

        W Ralegh

*[left-hand margin]*   To Sir Robert Cycill

---

1. Miles Magrath (?1523–1622), a former Franciscan friar, contrived both to resist anti-government forces and to give warning of his coming: W.D. Killen, *Ecclesiastical History of Ireland*, 1875, I, pp. 411–16, who says that an extremely plausible tongue kept him in the Queen's favour. Having previously granted Ralegh most of the temporalities of the see of Lismore, in August 1592, after the latter's disgrace, Magrath recovered most of the property with the assistance of the Lord Deputy, Fitzwilliam: H. Cotton, *Fasti Ecclesiae Hibernicae*, Dublin 1847–8: Munster, p. 9; *Cal. Close and Patent Rolls Ireland 1576–1602*, p. 244. See also *CSPI 1565–1654, Addenda*, pp. 622–3.
2. In temporary charge, until an incumbent be installed. There seems to be no reason for the brackets.
3. In 1604 he held the sees of Cashel, Waterford, Lismore and Emly, besides no less than 77 other livings: *CSPI 1603–6*, p. 143.
4. A Cambridge man and a puritan noted for his Hebrew scholarship, Broughton had been living in Ireland.
5. John Whitgift.
6. Relationship not established. In June 1596 George Goring was supported both by Ralegh and the Privy Council in his efforts, with one Herbert Pelham, to erect dwellings and ironworks in Munster to which some of Ralegh's other tenants objected: *APC* XXV, pp. 453–4. Goring was a friend of Sir Robert Cecil: *HMC Salisbury* VII, p. 192.
7. Ralegh's suit, like others made on Broughton's behalf, was unsuccessful and in 1597 his protégé went to Germany: *DNB*.

## 93. TO SIR ROBERT CECIL FROM BLACKWALL, 3 MAY 1596

Hatfield, CP40/55, *HMC Salisbury* VI, p. 168–9. In Ralegh's hand.
Edwards II, pp. 122–3.

## SHIPS FOR CADIZ

[*addressed*] To the right honorable Sir Robert Cecyll knight, of Her Majesties most honorable Privy Councell
[*endorsed*] 3 Maii 1596 Sir Walter Raleighe to my master

Sir: May it pleas yow to vouchsaufe to send for Master Burrough[1] the Controler of the Admeraltye and to geve charge unto hyme to repaire to Bralkwale [*sic*] and to Ratcleife[2] to cummand awaye thos flibotts [= *store ships*] and other shipps that remayne,[3] who [*Borough*] cann best informe yow of the possebilletye of thes things. I am not able to leve to row up and down every tyde from Grav[s]end to Londun and hee that lies here att Rackleif can easely judge when [?*where*] they rest and how the rest of the shipps may sale downe. I am cum up agayne as farr as Blake Wale and would attend yow if I knew how or where [?*when*]. The names of thos men that refuse to serve Her Majestye I have delivered to [*William*] Pope, Marshall of the Admiraltye: the rest shall also be sent hyme. The names of the shipps remayning I will send to Master Burrough whom I humble pray yow to speake withall.

And so being more greved then ever I was in any thing of this world for this rough weather I humble take my leve. From Blake Wale reddy to go down agyne this tyde.

       Your honors to do yow service,
       W Ralegh

The 3d of Maye

---

1. For William Borough (1536–99), a Devonian and author of the *Discourse on the Variation of the Compass* (1581), see Joyce Youings in M. Duffy *et al.* (eds), *New Maritime History of Devon*, I, 1992, pp. 32–4.
2. Blackwall and Ratcliff on the Thames estuary.
3. Ralegh's squadron, apparently unable because of weather conditions to set sail out of the Thames, was eagerly awaited by Howard and Essex who, with the rest of the fleet, were already in Plymouth.

## 94. TO SIR ROBERT CECIL FROM MILE END, 3 MAY 1596

Hatfield, CP40/50, *HMC Salisbury* VI, p. 166. Written by a clerk, with subscription and signature in Ralegh's hand.
Edwards II, p. 127.

### FOR CHARLES MACCARTHY

[*addressed*] To the right honorable Sir Robert Cecill knight, one of Her Majesties most honorable Privie Counsell
[*endorsed*] 3 Maii 1596 Sir Walter Raleighe to my master in favour of Charles Cartey[1]

Sir; This bearer my ancient [= *former*] servaunt, Charles Cartie, is an humble suitor to your honnor for the renewing and confirming of a lettre formerlie written by your honnor and the rest of the lords of Her Majesties Privy Councell to the Lord Deputie and Lord Chauncellor of Ireland[2] for the passing of certein concealed lands there graunted by Her Highnes to Patrick Grante, for which Charles hath agreed and compounded, for that he and his father have been possessed of the said lands a long tyme.[3] Your honnors lettres have not been obeyed and therefore he humblie desireth other lettres of lyke tenor to comaund performance thereof. He will show your honnor a lettre conceaved [= *drafted*] in writing which, if yow shall please to allow of as a reasonable request, he will ever remaine most bound for your honorable favor, without which he is like to be undone for that this is his chiefest living. And so I humblie take my leave, from Myle End[4] the 3d of May 1596.

    Your honors to do yow service,
        W Ralegh

1. Charles MacCarthy: see above, Letter 76.
2. In June 1596 the Privy Council expressed its disapproval of such 'bringing men's inheritance in dowbte and question after so longe tyme and quiet possession', but a few days later they called for an examination of any reasonable grounds upon which Charles could base a claim: *APC* XXV, pp. 491–2, 505–6.
3. The lordship of Muskerrry and the manor of Blarney: see above, Letter 76.
4. Probably at the house of his brother-in-law, Arthur Throckmorton, which was conveniently near Ratcliff where his ships were anchored.

95.   TO SIR ROBERT CECIL, [? FROM MILE END],
      3 MAY 1596

   Hatfield, CP40/51, *HMC Salisbury* VI, p. 166. In Ralegh's hand.
   Edwards II, p. 128.

## DEBT TO WIDOW SMITH

[*addressed*]   To the right honorable Sir Robert Cecill knight, of Her Majesties most honorable Privy Councell

[*endorsed*]   3 Maii 1596   Sir Walter Raleigh to my master

Sir: Beinge ever bolde to charge yow with many of my trobles and burdens I do still presume on your favor that yow wilbe pleased to be bounde for mee for the 500*li* which I stande in danger [= *debt*] to the Widdow Smithe for.[1] And because the conveyance [= *meaning*] of the statute[2] is intricatt and that I hope this very terme to cumpound for [= *settle*] it and to discharge yow, I beseich yow to accept of my counter bonde for your reasurance, in which I will not faile. I must hope that if other then sawftye accumpany my fortune in this enterprize that yow wilbe pleased to favor thos of myne that remayne who must only depend on yow as I have dun, so as of all other I shall take good order to free yow from any particuler charge or inconvenience.

   Thus hoping to take leve on yow er I depart I rest ever yours to be cummanded,
      W Ralegh

1. See above, Letters 81 and 82.
2. The Statute Staple for taking recognizances of debt.

---

96.   TO SIR ROBERT CECIL FROM NORTHFLEET,
      4 MAY 1596

   Hatfield, CP40/60, *HMC Salisbury* VI, p. 169. In Ralegh's hand.
   Edwards II, p. 128.

## CLEAR OF THE THAMES

[*addressed*]   To the right honorable Sir Robert Cecyll knight, of Her Majesties most honorable Privy Councell

[*endorsed*]   4 Maii 1596   Sir Walter Raleigh to my master

Sir: The shipps that remayne above [= *behind*] ar six. The great vlebote [= *flyboat*] of Bas[ ]nes[1] is on, riding att Blake Wale [= *Blackwall*]. Another great flebote of Londun caled The George another. The Jacobe of Agarslote[2] a third, The Jusua of Horne[3] a fourth, and sume too other. [*William*] Pope, the Marshall of the Admiraltye, can informe Master Burres [*William Borough*][4] for Pope prest [= *commandeered*] all the shipps. Hee can also informe yow how litle Her Majesties octoretye is respected, for as fast as wee press men on day they run away another and say the[y] will not serve.

[*I*] beseich yow Sir to vouchsauf to send for [*Robert*] Pope of Saynt Katerens[5] who hath taken great payns alreddy and tell hyme that I have recummended his service, and hee will do more then any.

Here ar att Grav[es]end and between this and Lee[6] sume 22 saile. Thos above that ar of great draught of water cannot tide it down[7] for the[y] must take the high water and dare not move after an houre ebb untill they be past Barking Shelf,[8] and now the wind is so stronge as it is impossible to turne down or to warpe[9] downe or to too[w]e downe. I cannot writ to our generalle [*Essex*] att this tyme for the pursevant [= *messenger*] found me in a countrie villag a mile from Grav[es]end hunting after runaway marriners and drugging [*sic*] in the mire from ale howse to ale howse, and [*I*] could gett no paper butt that the pursevant had this peece.

Sir, by the living God ther is nor king nor queen nor generall nor any elce can take more care then I do to be gonn, butt I humble prey yow butt to speake with Master Burroes and lett hym be sent for afterward before my Lord Chamberleyne[10] that they may here hyme speake wh[eth]er any man can gett down with this wind or no, which will satisfie them of me.

If this strong wind last I will steal to Blakewale to speak with yow and to kiss your hands.

    W R

From Norfleet[11] this Twesday

---

1. Not identified, but presumably a European port. Edwards reads it as 'Brasenes'.
2. In Ralegh's squadron: J.S. Corbett (ed.), *Naval Miscellany* I, Navy Record Society XX, 1902, pp. 48–9.
3. Hoorne, a port on the Zuider Zee. The *George* and the *Joshua* were intended to be part of Howard's squadron.
4. See Letter 93, note 1.
5. A London merchant who was Deputy Sergeant of the Admiralty: *APC* XXVII, pp. 50 and 62. St Katherine's parish was on the river, east of the Tower of London.
6. Leigh, a small port in Essex near Canvey Island.

7. 'tiding down' or 'over' = working with the tides against a contrary wind.
8. Barking Creek below Woolwich.
9. 'warping' = hauling with the help of a rope fixed to something on shore.
10. Henry Carey, Lord Hunsdon, presumably one of Ralegh's discreditors.
11. In Kent, a mile and a half west of Gravesend.

---

## 97. TO SIR ROBERT CECIL FROM QUEENBOROUGH, 6 MAY 1596

Hatfield, CP40/63, *HMC Salisbury* VI, p. 170. In Ralegh's hand.
Edwards II, pp. 130–31.

### FOR A FRIEND AND KINSMAN[1]

[*addressed*]   To the right honorable Sir Robert Cecyll knight, of Her Majesties most honorable Privey Councell
[*endorsed*]   6 Maii 1596   Sir Walter Raleighe to my master

Sir: This gentleman, my frinde and kynsman, hath intreated mee to be a suter unto yow in his behalfe that it would pleas yow to move Her Majestye after so many years disgrace to cumfort hyme with on gratius worde. I do not know how hee may be wronged unto Her Majestie butt I fynd no man more reddy and disposed, of his qualletye, to do her service, neather more willing to spend all he hath therin. I know his charge was great in the last discovery with me,[2] and ther is none now of his sort that douth so chargable prepare hyme sealf. I must leve me and all myne to your honorable favor and wee will all honor yow and serve yow.
                    W Ralegh

From Quinburrow[3] this 6th of Maye.

1. Unnamed, but internal evidence points to George Gifford who had served as Ralegh's vice-admiral on the *Lion's Whelp* on the Guiana voyage and went on the Cadiz expedition as his rear-admiral on the *Quittance*. His mother was Elizabeth, née Throckmorton, wife of John Gifford of Weston-under-Edge, Gloucestershire, and Lady Ralegh's aunt. In August 1597 he begged Cecil to deliver a petition to the Queen seeking her pardon, possibly for suspected recusancy: Harlow, *Discoverie* 1932, p. 34; *Naval Miscellany*, I, Navy Record Society XX, p. 49; [T.R. Nash], *Collections for a History of Worcestershire*, 1781–99, I, p. 452 and *HMC Salisbury* VII, p. 374.
2. The Guiana expedition of 1595.
3. Queenborough, a port on the Isle of Sheppey, 2 miles SSW of Sheerness.

## 98. TO SIR ROBERT CECIL FROM DOVER, [c.13][1] MAY 1596

Hatfield, CP173/73, *HMC Salisbury* VI, p. 175. In Ralegh's hand.
Edwards II, pp. 381–2.

### LOSS OF CABLES AND ANCHORS

[*addressed*]   To the right honorable Sir Robert Cecill knight, of Her Majesties most honorable Privy Councell in hast
[*endorsed*]   13 [*sic*] Maii 1596   Sir Walter Raleigh to my master from Dover

Since I sent my letter to your honor from Dover,[2] before I departed the rode [= *anchorage*] ther came up unto mee sume seven or eyght saile of the fleet who, being all like to perris[*h*] on Wensday after midnight, they weare driven to lett slipp all their cables and ancors. I humble beseich your honor to cause a letter to be written to the Maior of Dover to send a boat of the towne to save the sayd cables and ancors. Having all boyes uppon them they weare left on the northe[*a*]st part of Goodden [*Goodwin*] Sands in five or six fathoms.[3]

Thus I humble take my leve from Dover on howre after my former letter.

    Yours ever to do yow service,
     W Ralegh

1. Wednesday was the 12th of May.
2. Missing.
3. Cecil communicated accordingly on 14 May with the Lieutenant of Dover Castle, who replied on the 15th that he had the matter in hand and would send the lost tackle to Plymouth by sea: *HMC Salisbury* VI, p. 182.

---

## 99. TO SIR ROBERT CECIL FROM PLYMOUTH, 26 MAY 1596

Hatfield, CP41/14, *HMC Salisbury* VI, pp. 196–7. Written by a clerk, with address, subscription, signature and postscript in Ralegh's hand.
Edwards II, p. 131–2.

### FOR WILLIAM HILLIARD

[*addressed*]   To the right honorable Sir Robert Cecyll knight, of Her Majesties most honorable Privy Councell

[*endorsed*]  26 Maii 1596  Sir Walter Raleighe to my master in favour of Master Hilliard
[*probably in Cecil's hand*]  readde

Sir: I have written to Doctor Caesar[1] in the behalfe of Master William Hilliard,[2] a master of Arts and very learned, to move Her Majestie for her lettres to the Dean and Chapter of Exceter for his admittance to the next place that shalbe void of a prebend and canon there. I beeseech your honor to further him in his suite for the obteyning thereof. He will in dutifull service acknowledg your honorable favour and I shalbe bound for his sake to remember it to my power.

    And so I humbly take my leave. From Plymouth the 26th of May 1596.

      Your honors to do yow service,
        W Ralegh

Sir: I beseiche yow for my sake, because it standeth miche on my creditt, to favor the sute and I shall evermore acknowledge it in the highest digre.
      WR

1. Dr Julius Caesar (1538–1626), Judge of the Court of Admiralty, Judge and Master of Requests: *DNB*.
2. William Hilliard, MA, of Hart Hall, Oxford, chaplain to the Queen. An Exonian by birth and probably related to Nicholas Hilliard who painted the famous miniature of Ralegh in 1588, he had been vicar of Bickleigh in Devon and rector of Dunchideock and Charleton. He was appointed to an Exeter canonry later this year.

---

### 100. TO SIR ROBERT CECIL FROM PLYMOUTH, 29 MAY 1596

Hatfield, CP41/25, *HMC Salisbury*, VI, p. 200, abstract only. Written by a clerk, with subscription and signature in Ralegh's hand.
Edwards II, pp. 132–3.

### FOR JOHN RANDOLL

[*addressed*]  To the right honorable Sir Robert Cecyll knight, one of Her Highnes most honorable Privy Councell
[*endorsed*]  29 May 1596  Sir Walter Ralegh to my master in favour of Master Randoll

Sir: I am entreated by Master John Randoll [*of Weymouth*],[1] deputie vice-admirall of Dorsetshire, to desire your honorable fauvour towards him if, by reason of his office or other occasions, he shalbe urged by suites to sollicite your honnor. I beseech your honnor in regard of the honestie of the gentleman, and for the good opinion that is hereaboutes generallie conceaved of him, to favour him in such sort as the equitie of his causes shall require and himselfe deserve.²

And so I humblie take my leave, from Plymmouth the 29th of May 1596.
    Your honors to do yow service,
        W Ralegh

1. Randoll was Bailiff of Weymouth and deputy to Sir Carew Ralegh, Vice-Admiral of Dorset: *APC* XXV, p. 275.
2. Randoll was no doubt anticipating his summons before the Privy Council two months later to answer a charge of deserting his post. He excused himself on the grounds that he had been in London about a commission of oyer and terminer, and the charge was dismissed: *APC* XXVI, pp. 55–6.

---

## 101. TO ARTHUR [GORGES]¹ FROM CADIZ, 21 JUNE 1596

Folger, V.b.214, ff. 106v.–109 and Huntington, HM102, ff. 10v.–12, formerly Phillips MS 10665, de Ricci 1935, pp. 49–50, almost identical near-contemporary transcripts of the missing original.² Folger, V.b.214 is probably nearer the original in its spelling, HM102 following more modern forms but including short passages not in the Folger transcript. The original was almost certainly in Ralegh's hand.

P. Lefranc, 'Ralegh in 1596 and 1603: Three unprinted letters in the Huntington Library', *HLQ*, XXIX, 1966, pp. 340–44, from HM102.

### THE ACTION AT CADIZ

[*marginal heading*]   Sir Walter Rauglie, his letter concerning Calze³ Voyage 21 June⁴ 1596 Eliz. 38

Noble cosin: Though it be long since you haerd from us, yet we will send you good newes at the last.⁵

When we arrived at the entrance of Calze, myself being in the reargard of the fleete,⁶ the rest came all to anchor without the port. When I was arrived I found the Earle [*of Essex*] imbarquing the armie to take land and to attempt the towne at the west end. The winde was very strong, the billows much raysed and the place of dissent [= *landing*] a lee shore, so as ther could have beene no hope but of losse only. The reason hereof was that, in my absence, it was agreed on that the towne should first to [*be*] attempted to the end that the fortes of the same might beat uppon the Spanish fleete, upon the gallies and gallions, although two dayes before we had resolved, the wind falling out fayre, first to sett upon the navie. But when I beheld a toward [= *impending*] and an universall perrill, the Queenes honor and that of our nation under saile and readie to runne headlong against the rocks, I went first aborde the Earl [*in the Due Repulse*] and afterward to the Admirall [*Howard, in the Ark Royal*]. I declared unto him [*Essex*], in the presence of all his collonels and captaynes, that he was rather [?*either*] very exceeding desperat or wanted much of that judgement which I hoped heretofore to have found in him, and that if he respected neyther himself neyther yet so manie gallant gentlemen as were readie without anie enemie to be overwhelmed, yet he ought to remember the great cost Her Majestie had sett uppon this affaire. This orasion so well pleased the universall as they all protested they were bound to me for their lives and would evermore acknowledge the same. The Lord Generall [*Essex*] hard since [= *made sense*] of the perswation and, having ever pleased to take my foolish advise before any els, seemed much content with my bold reason and told me that my Lord Admiralls care of the shipes[7] was the cause, and that for his owne part he desired rather to attempt the shipes and enter the port, praying me (and withall perswaded of my power with the Admirall) that I would draw hime to yeld therunto, for which he would ever acknowledge himself my great debtor. Now as I plainly withstood thearle, so did I as plainly deliver unto the other what shame, danger and losse would follow, first in particular to himself, secondly to our armie and nation, if we entred not, the enemie taking hart to see us ride without as [*though*] possessed with feare. But I prevailed with my Lord Admirall and returned to the side of the earles ship, calling to him *intremus* [*entramus*], who, casting his hatte into the sea, prepared himself to weigh anchor.

Now the day was so farre spent, and it was so long ere the boates could returne againe from the Generalls sterne to their owne shipes, as when thearle came by me under sayle I desired him to anchor againe in the mouth of the harbor, some half a league nearer then before, and to give him reason of my desire I went aborde him in my shallope [= *ship's boat*]. I told him that it would be sunnesett [*bef*]or half the fleet would weigh anchor and that it was no evening worke.[8] I put him in mind that it was not determined in what order we should fight, nor who should lead, who for second, nor the manner of fighting, eyther by boarding or otherwise. Wheruppon he came to anchor, and so did all the rest, it being an howre within night ere all came in. Now you must think that we wanted not those that made constructions [= *interpretations*] of my retarding, and because they hoped on other mens care they gave the Italian shrugge⁹ at the stay. In the night I wrote a letter to my Lord Admirall, and to my Lord Generall, wherin I sett downe my opinion for the manner of the fight, and withall besought them that I might be imployd therin, [*it*] being unfitt the greatest shipes of all [*should*], being resolved to tast [*test*] the dispositions of the forwardest gallantes, and also, as I hope, with good reason mixte. The same being graunted I sent to warne the shipes assigned to follow me all night. The shipes of Her Majestie were The Wastspight [*the Warspite, Ralegh's flagship*],¹⁰ The Mariarose, The Foresight, The Lyon and The Rainebow, with The Rowbuck and eleven of the shipes of London with some others, of all which the Lord Thomas [*Howard, in the Merhonour*], finding himself agreeved to be left out, pressed the Generall to have the charge, or at least to be joyned, with whom I would not contend [= *argue*], meaning notwithstanding to lead the daunce. Now my Lord Thomas was appointed to goe into The Nonparella¹¹ because The Honor was unfitt to be adventured, which he willingly accepted.

At the very opening of day I wayed anchor and bare in crying *Vive la Reigna d'Angleterre*. I gat the start and lead before all a good distance which, when it was perceived, the whole navie folowed, as well those appointed as the rest. As soon as the gr[e]at Saint Phillip¹² one of the admirals under saile, and many other prepared to follow, she let slipp her anchor and sett sayle till she passed within the towne and came againe to anchor under the guard of a fort called Puntall [*Puntales*], and with him in front St Mathew, St Thomas [*and*] St Andrew,¹³ some huge gallions and very powrefull. Within them roade too great Ragusines [*ships of Ragusa (Dubrovnik)*], within them the Admirall and Viceadmirall of Terra Nova [*New Mexico*] and the great frigots, and in the flanke of the front 18 gallies, behind these toward Port [*Puerto*] Reale 44 great ships. Hear withall you must understand that the 18 gallies abid first under the fortes of the towne charged all in front with their prowes towardes us who, with the ordinance of the towne and their owne batterie, hoped in so smooth a watter to have stayed us a while from attempting the gallions. As soone as I came to the west fort of the towne the same fort called the Phillip saluted me with all her peeces, which, because they should perceive I wondered not at, nor could be stayed with the noys of gunnes, I only answered everie dischardge with the blur [*sic*] of a trumpett and not otherwise. As I passed on all the gallies made all readie to salute me and gave me all their cannon in good order, hoping, if they could have stumbled the leading ship, it might have made some alteration among the rest. But as to the fortes of the citie so to everie gallie I retorned the blur of a trumpett and no more, never looking aside to these esteemed dreadfull beastes [sic], but bare with the proud Phillip, resolved to revendge the death of The Revendge,[14] or to second it with mine owne. The shipes that folowed bestowed good store of [cannon] bales among them, but I was resolved that the scorne I used towardes them did infinitely discourage them, for soone after they betooke them to their oares and lay on the right wing of the fower Apostles aforesayd. When I came nere the gallions, it being uppon the ebbe, my pylot cryed out that if I stayed not till the fludd [tide] I should be on [sic] ground and that I could not come to beare [= board] the Phillip before the fludd, which was at hand. Whereuppon I lett fall a small anchor and all the rest, finding shallow water, did the like.

Now begunne the most thundring volies of shott that ever I think were heard, the gallies and gallions and the fort beating alltogether uppon The Wastpight. The Lord Thomas took the right hand, with The Marie Rose, but a head [of] her the Marshall [Sir Francis Vere] in The Rainebowe, with The Lyon on the left hand. But, Arthure, thie flesh and blood, single [*HM102 adds*: in the head of all and against whome all the furious battery was bent, after two howers fight I was so beaten] and so often shott betwixt wind and water, and my men torne with uncessant volies of shott powred in as thick as hayle, and being promised two great flyboates to board withall, if I saw cause, because to have boarded with Her Majesties shipes had bene but certeinely to have lost them, I went back in a shallop to my Lord Generall, beseeching him to commaund those hulkes [= *store ships*] and flyboates appointed to come on, that with them I might finish the work.

But feare found so manie delayes [*HM102 has* impediments] as I could not see how to draw anie of the knaves forward, and therefore resolved with Her Majesties servantes to hazzard her ship, for there was little difference in the choice betweene sinking and burning. Of the one I was sure by the riding, as I did of the other by boarding. My Lord Generall of Essex, although it were determined before that the greater shipes should stay, yet his hart was so great that he could indure it no longer but towards x of the clock shouldred in through and came up as neare me as winde and the tide would permit him, and The Foresight after joynde herself on the left hand. The Marshall, who thought it some disgrace to himself that I kept the point [= *lead*] single all the forenoone while I went in my boate to call up the flyboates, slipt a head my ship and took the leadinge. My Lord Thomas, impatient therof, let slip his anchor and headed the Marshall againe. But being resolved to keepe the honour of the day, I let go all and hoist up topsaile and foresaile and gott ahead againe, riding next the enemie at a more distance and more single [*HM102 has*: sayle] and guarded the Marshall wholie, lying my self overth[w]art the channell that none after cowlde ever come by. I then called to my Lord Generall of Essex that I would aboard. He answered that he would not faile to second me upon his honor. My Lord Thomas did the like. I then layd an anchor [*HM102*: by The Phillipe] to warp to her for the winde so scanted [= *dropped*] that I could not lead it with a saile. Now beganne The Phillip to fainte as I approched, and with her The St Mathew and St Andrew and St Thomas ranne themselves a ground, some [*of the crew*] saving themselves with boates, others leaping into the sea, the rest crying *miserecordia*. The noyce and outcrie was marvailous and the spectakle lamentable. The Saint Phillip and Saint Thomas set themselves on fire, a most fearfull and piteous sight to see so huge a flame, so manie drowned, others burning in their shreds [= *shrouds, i.e. rigging*],[15] others half burnt and half drowned, with manie wounded scambling up through the mudde. But before the other 2 gallies [= *galleons*], The Mathew and Andrew, could ridde [= *evacuate*] the better sort, that they [*the ships*] might burne also, I recovered them [*the crews*] with boates and, sparing the lives of the greater part, saved the shipes. The gallions of Lisbone and the three frigotes of warre, being behind the Apostles, also fired themselves, the gallies with oars and shallow water saved themselves, but never so beaten and torne. It was not manie minutes after but the armes of Spain stood in the misentop of The Wastspight, to the great comfort [*sic*] of the soldiers and citizens of Calze.

To conclude, I received manie imbracementes and thankes of the Generall, who hath promised me to doe me right. If it now seeme gratious in her eyes to whom I have given my life I shall count my self blessed, and if God give me a second occasion it shall appeare that it is but borowed breath which I will willingly yeld up at her advantage.

This finished I minded the Earle to desend [= *disembark*] the souldiers and that now the time promised good successe, who, thirsting to finish the rest, used all diligence. But it pleased God to arest me from attending them for the present for I received a greevous blow in my legg, larded with manie splinters which I daylie pull out. Yet I scrambled ashore and my Lord Generall of Essex, att the first landing having driven back a troope of Spanish horse, manie were dismounted. My Lord Admirall, seeing me brought after upon mens shoulders, sent me a horse, which [= *while*] the vangard of the armie, led by the Earle, suddenly and with a fury caried the first port [= *gate*],¹⁶ the soldiers climing up the walls with great resolution. In fowre howres all was taken but the Castle, which afterward also was scaled. All mercy was used,¹⁷ 4000 ladies, gentlewomen and merchantes wives sent out in all their glorious apparell, with their jewells about them, without any tuch[ed], with the greatest honour and respect that ever was used by any nation or in anie warre, to shew that we all serve the greatest ladie of the earth [*Queen Elizabeth*], of most powre and of greatest pitie [= *compassion*].

What I have wrote is to your self.¹⁸ What others shall deliver [= *report*] of me I know not. The best wilbe that ther was 16000 eye witnesses, but they may be cunning in their prayses. That God hath favoured us for her sake whom we serve the glorie and thankes be to him, the honor and profitt to the Queene, prayse and fame to our nation. For ourselves if we could have done more it had bine but duty, yet mixt and made strong with much love.

From my house in Calze 1596 June 21 Eliz. 38¹⁹

1. The argument for identifying the recipient (named as 'Arthur' in paragraph 5) as Arthur Gorges (Lefranc, loc. cit., p. 337), seems compelling, Arthur Throckmorton and Arthur Savage both being with the fleet and Arthur Radford, the only other possibility among Ralegh's circle, of insufficient standing at home to convey the underlying message to those whom Ralegh was so patently anxious to impress. Arthur Gorges (1557–1625) was a younger son of the Somerset branch (Wraxall) of a long-established West Country family. He was a poet as well as a courtier, man-of-affairs and an MP, but his failure to achieve wealth or high office made him something of a rebel. His mother was a Budockside of Devon, making him Ralegh's first cousin on his, Ralegh's, mother's side: R. Gorges, *The Story of a Family*, Boston, 1944 and Hasler II, p. 206.
2. The text printed here is based on Folger V, with significant variations in HM102 noted. Neither clerk, nor perhaps the writer of an intermediate version since lost, was familiar with maritime terminology, transcribing 'aground' as 'on ground'. There are signs in Folger V of corrections in another hand.
3. Ralegh's spelling: see below, Letter 102. The more usual contemporary English spelling was 'Cales'.
4. 'Jan[*uary*]' in the transcript, a scribal error.
5. There is much in this letter which the writer included in his *Relation of Cadiz Action*, first printed in 1700 and reprinted in Cayley 1806, I, pp. 290–301, *Works* 1829, VIII, pp. 667–74, Edwards II, pp. 146–56 and elsewhere.
6. The English fleet arrived off Cadiz soon after sunrise on 20 June, except for Ralegh and his squadron which had been sent 'to tack about the coast' in search of Spanish ships: R.B. Wernham, *Return of the Armadas*, Oxford, 1994, p. 96. This is the best and most detailed modern account of the Sack of Cadiz, but it contains no references to this letter.
7. The Queen had insisted that her ships be returned intact: *HMC Salisbury* VI, p. 239.
8. HM102 has 'evening's work', implying the probable time involved rather than, as in Folger V, the need for daylight, which makes better sense.

9. Apparently regarded as an un-English gesture: cf. Thomas Nash in *The Unfortunate Traveller* (1594), 'It is growen to a common proverbe, Ile give him the Neapolitan shrug, when one intends to play the villaine, and make no boast of it'.
10. Newly built and said to have been a costly failure: M. Oppenheim, *History of the Administration of the Royal Navy*, 1896, p. 130. Ralegh regularly called her the *Wastspight*, i.e. the vessel which exhausted, or wasted, the spite of the enemy.
11. Both transcripts read '*Imparella*' which must be the copyists' error. The *Nonpareil* was one of the Queen's ships.
12. The great Spanish galleon was one of those involved in the defeat of the *Revenge* in 1591.
13. Popularly known as the 'Apostles': see below.
14. The ship in which Sir Richard Grenville had perished at the Azores in 1591.
15. HM102 has 'shreads'.
16. HM102 has 'fort', an obvious error.
17. This is confirmed by Spanish sources (Wernham, op. cit., p. 104) but when it came to plunder the story was rather different (ibid., p. 105), except, apparently for Ralegh, who claimed to have come off rather badly (below, Letter 102), but in so doing he may have had ulterior motives.
18. And hopefully, clearly, for the Queen, though it is odd that Ralegh should not have targeted someone at Court. He delayed writing to Cecil until 7 July (below, Letter 102) by which time his tone had changed somewhat.
19. The date seems correct from his omission both of the failure to take the Spanish merchant fleet and the knighting of the 63 gentlemen, but he may, for his own purposes, have preferred to withhold the bad news and anything which added nothing to his own glorification. The first to leave for home with official reports was Sir Antony Ashley on 9 July (Letter 102). Was Ralegh hoping to steal a march on the rest of the Generals? Ashley did not arrive at Court until the 31st, by which time news of a great victory had already reached London. Only later did it emerge what opportunities had been missed.

---

## 102. To Sir Robert Cecil
### from aboard ship off Cadiz,
### 7 July [1596]

BL, Cotton, Vespasian C XIII, f. 290. In Ralegh's hand. Left-hand margin damaged. Edwards II, pp. 134–5.

# THE SACK OF CADIZ

[*Headed, hand unidentified*]   To Sir Robert Cecill

Sir: This bearer, Sir Antony Ashley,[1] that hath seen all, can better report all then any letter or discource. The xxi of June wee beheld the cytty of Calize, the fleet of the Kinge [*of Spain*] and that of Nova Hispania, all which we mastered the same day. Of every mans desart, both for councell and performance, lett [*i*]t be delivered with what device soever, yet I doubt not [*b*]utt all shall have right.

[*I*] was not secound to any in the fight agaynst the gallions and gallis [*w*]herin I was hurt and could not be first att the taking of the town as att the rest. Ther hath bynn good agrement between the generalls, the victory was caried with great honor and mercye. Ther hath bynn mich [*booty*] gotten by the land cummanders, althought [*I*] do thinke litle posest by the generalls themsealvs.² The King of Spayne never so mich dishonored, neather hath [*h*]ee ever receaved so great loss.

The Earle [*Essex*] hath behaved [= *conducted*] hymesealfe, I protest unto yow by the living God, both valiently and advisedly in the highest degree, without pride with [*sic*]³ crueltye, and hath gotten great honor [*and*] mich love of all.

For particulers your honor shall receve by others which I had rather should so be written then by mee.

I hope Her most excelent Majestye will take my labors and indevors in good part. Other ritches then the hope therof I have none: only I have receved a blow which now, I thanck God, is well amended. Only a little ey sore will remayne. If my life had ended withall I had then payde sume part of my great deabts which I owe her, butt it is butt borrowed and I shall paye it, I hope, to Her Majesties advantage if occasion be offred.

Sir I humble beseich yow to excuse mee that I write thus breifly for the present, and that yow will vouchsawfe also to excuse me to my lord your father [*Burghley*], and I will remayne evermore to be cummanded by yow as your sarvent.
   W Ralegh

[*I*] beseich yow to cummend me to my cussen
[*Hen*]ry Broke,⁴ and to my cussen [*Sir John*] Stanhope.⁵
 To the westward of Calize⁶ sume x leaugs, the 7 of July.

---

1. Clerk to the Privy Council and Secretary to the expedition's Council of War, he was one of those knighted by Essex on the field: BL, Sloane 1303, p. 6.
2. Ralegh and Sir Francis Vere quarrelled violently over the spoils in the town, Vere arguing that the seamen had the enemy's West Indian fleet at their mercy, had they cared to take them, before they were set on fire by the Spaniards themselves. The Quarter-Master General is reported to have claimed that his orders from the Generals were not 'to quarter any seamen under the degree of Sir Walter Ralegh, who ... [he thought] nevertheless had not much, although he deserved very much in this, that he fought so bravely with the Spanish fleet': W. Dillingham (ed.), *Commentaries of Sir Francis Vere*, 1657, p. 44 and W. Birch, *Memoirs of Queen Elizabeth I*, 1754, II, p. 97. But cf. R.B. Wernham, *Return of the Armadas*, p. 119, note 15 for a rather different story.
3. Cf. Edwards who has 'without crueltye', which must be what Ralegh meant to write.

4. Edwards read this as '[blank], my brother', but in spite of damage at the left-hand margin it is still possible to read this as the first mention in Ralegh's letters of what was to be the ill-starred friendship between him and the eldest son of William Lord Cobham, Cecil's brother-in-law: see below, Letters 104, 110, 114, 121, etc.
5. Master of Posts and Treasurer of the Chamber: Hasler III, p. 439.
6. See above, Letter 101, note 3.

---

## 103. To [Sir Robert Cecil][1] from Plymouth, 6 August [1596][2]

BL, Cotton, Otho E IX, f. 365 v. In Ralegh's hand. Top badly injured by fire. The words enclosed in square brackets, except where noted, have been supplied from Edwards's transcription which was made when parts of the manuscript must have been more legible than they are now.

Edwards II, pp. 137–8.

# RETURN FROM CADIZ

*[no address or endorsement]*

... burnt]. Wee had not m[eans to ...]le and men being both wast[ed in the ...] ther is a very dangerus infectio[n[3] ...] and sicke[4] as with great dificultye w[as ...] to the port. I have my sealf labored [...] person. I thanke God shee[5] is now in the p[ort ...] and with us my Lord Thomas in The Honor[6] [...] both which came alitle before by reason [of ...] leakes whereof my Lord Thomas was in gre[at peril]. The rest of the fleet wilbe here tomorrow [in my opi]nion if the winde stand, for the secound of [August] I left them well and [on] the six[th] I[7] arived and they ca[me] above a dusen or twentye leaugs a stern.[8]

This gentleman, Sir Arthure Savage,[9] is dispatcht by the generalls.[10] I know not the effect [= *tenor*] of his message butt, under pardun, I thinke it good for Her Majestye [if] hee be agayne returned with order for the army, w[hich] may for the most be returned into their counties from hence, which, the sooner it shalbe dun, the less charge Her Majestye shalbe att here with continewance of her sea charge.[11] Sir, may it pleas yow to beleve mee this bearer [*Savage*] hathe deserved with the first and had the poynt [= *took the lead*][12] att the entrance of Calize, butt hee came with others in the reregard of profitt and good fortune[13] and I assure your honor by the love I beare yow that yow shall not favor any man more honest and valient. Hee can yeild a good accompt of what soever hath past.

For my particuler I beseich yow if it may be that I may be pardoned for [*not*] cumminge about by sea, for besids the great and dangerus infection I am not well in health my sealf.[14] My Lord Admirall[15] will cum with the fleet and my Lord Thomas likewise. Sir I hope Her Devin Majestye is well: the report whereof hath incountred us with infinit joy.

[*left-hand margin*]  From the port of Plymouth, cuming in this 6th of August.

    Your honors ever to honor and serve yow,
      W Ralegh

1. It is difficult to imagine to whom else this can have been written.
2. The year of the Cadiz expedition.
3. Confined largely to the seamen, the soldiers being apparently in remarkably good shape: Monson, II, p. 357.
4. Edwards reads this as 'siche'.
5. The *Warspite*.
6. Presumably the name by which the *Merhonour* was known in the fleet. The identity of her consort is not known.
7. With Thomas Lord Howard.
8. The Lord Admiral and most of the rest of the fleet reached Plymouth on 7 August, Sir George Carew on the *Mary Rose*, with the Dutchmen, on the 8th, and finally Essex on the *Due Repulse*: Wernham, *Return of the Armadas*, p. 113.
9. A captain in Essex's company.
10. Ralegh seems to be disassociating himself from the rest of the councillors-at-war, but he may have been referring, for some reason best known to him, to the military commanders.
11. Ralegh knew only too well how to play on the Queen's anxieties. In fact, on 9 August, the Privy Council agreed that the 2,200 Low Country soldiers should be sent home by sea after their ships and persons had been searched, presumably for booty, and that most of the rest of the soldiers should go at once to Ireland and the seamen be sent home: *APC* XXVI, pp. 102–5.
12. He was reported as having been the first 'gentleman of quality' to leap down the wall.
13. Too late to fill his pockets.
14. Ralegh had been slightly wounded (see above, Letter 102) and in any case was never a good sailor. His passage down the Channel had not been at all comfortable: see above, Letters 96 and 98.
15. Charles Lord Howard was nearly 20 years Ralegh's senior.

---

## 104. To Sir Robert Cecil, 24 January 1597

Hatfield, CP37/97/2, *HMC Salisbury* VII, p. 35. In Ralegh's hand.
Edwards II, pp. 161–3.

# THE LATE LADY CECIL

[*addressed*] To the right honorable Sir Robert Cecyll knight, Principall Secritray to Her Majestye, etc.
[*endorsed*] 24 January 1596   Sir Walter Raleigh to my master
[*in the hand of the second earl of Salisbury*]   Sir Walter Ra[*legh's*] letter to my father touching the deathe of my mother[1]

Sir: Because I know not how yow dispose of your sealf I forebeare to visit yow, preferringe your plesinge before myne own desire. I had rather be with yow now then att any other tyme if I could therby ether take of[*f*] frome yow the burden of your sorrows or lay the greatest part therof on myne owne hart. In the mean tyme I would butt minde yow of this, that yow should not overshaddo your wisedume with passion butt looke aright into things as the[*y*] are.

Ther is no man sorry for death it sealf butt only for the tyme of death, every on knowinge that it is a bonnd never forfeted to God. If then wee know the same to be certayne and inevitable wee ought withall to take the tyme of his arivall in as good part as the knowledge, and not to lament att the instant of every seeminge adversety, which wee ar asured have bynn on ther way towards us from the begin[*in*]ge. It apartayneth to every man of a wize and worthy spirritt to draw together into sufferance the unknowne future to the known present, lookinge no less with the eyes of the minde then thos of the boddy, theon beholdinge a farr of[*f*] and the other att hand, that thos things of this worlde in which wee live be not strange unto us when the[*y*] approch, as to febleness, which is moved with noveltes, butt that like trew men participating immortalletye and know[*ing*] our destines to be of God, wee do then make our estates and wishes, our fortunes and desires, all on[*e*].

It is trew that yow have lost a good and vertuus wife, and my sealf an honorable frinde and kynswoman,[2] butt ther was a tyme when shee was unknowne to yow, for whom yow then lamented not. Shee is now no more yours nor of your acquayntance butt immortall and not needinge or knowing your love or sorrow. Therfore yow shall butt greve for that which now is as then it was when not yours, only bettered by the difference in this, that shee hath past the weresume jurney of this darke worlde and hath possession of her inheritance.

Shee hath left beind her the frute of her love,[3] for whos sakes yow ought to care for your sealf that yow leve them not without a gwyde, and not by greevinge to repine att his will that gave them yow or by sorrowing to dry up your own tymes [sic] that ought to establishe them.

   Sir, beleve it that sorrows ar dangerus cumpanions, converting badd into yevill and yevill in[to] worss, and do no other service then multeply harms. They ar the treasures of weak harts and of the foolishe. The minde that entertayneth them is as the yearth and dust wheron sorrows and adversetes of the world do as the beasts of the feild, tread, trample and defile. The minde of man is that part of God which is in us, which by how mich it is subject to passion, by so mich it is farther from hyme that gave it us. Sorrows draw not the dead to life butt the livinge to death, and if I weare my sealfe to advize my sealf in the like I would never forgett my patience till I saw all and the worst of yevills, and so greve for all at once, least [= lest], lamenting for sume on, a nother might yet remayne in the poure [= power] of destiney of greater discumfort.

[left-hand margin]   Your[s] ever beyound the pour of words to utter,
     W Ralegh

1. Elizabeth, daughter of William Brooke, 10th Lord Cobham, and sister of Ralegh's current friend, Henry Brooke: *DNB*.
2. Blood relationships were important to Ralegh, however distant, which this certainly was, being through a commmon ancestor five generations back.
3. With two children already, Lady Cecil died during a third pregnancy. Sir Robert never remarried.

---

## 105. To John Rashleigh of Fowey, 14 April 1597

Cornwall Record Office, RS/1/901. Written by a clerk, with signature in Ralegh's hand.

Sir Rennell Rodd, *Sir Walter Ralegh*, 1905, p. 154, spelling modernized; A.L. Rowse, *The Spectator*, 5 May 1939, pp. 76–8.

### THE DEFENCE OF FOWEY

[addressed]   To my lovinge frinde John Rashleigh of the towne of Foye, esquyer[1]

Whereas you have at your owne greate charge made a place of defence in your house at Foye[2] and furnished the same both with ordinance and munytion for the better repulsinge of the enimye uppon anie attempte by them to be made by sea againste the saide towne, which place hath bene seene and very well allowed of by my deputie lieuetennantes. I have therefore thought it requisite for Her Majestes service to require you that you contynewe your care therein and not to suffer the same to be impayred or disfurnished. And for the better effectinge thereof I do hereby assigne and authoryse you, your servantes and famylies, togither with such twelve of your tennantes dwellinge in the said twone [sic] or nere aboutes, as your self shall make choyse of, to be alwaies attendante to the saide place of defence. And for that intente I hereby do discharge you and them from all watchinge, wardinge, trayninge, musteringe and other marsiall services whatsoever. And that it shalbe lawfull for you to furnishe, arm, veiwe and trayne the persons above saide at all tymes and to imploy them in this service from tyme to tyme as occasion shalbe offered, as to your discretion shall seeme convenient.

In which doinge this writinge shalbe your sufficient warrant. Yeoven under my hande and seale the xiiijth of Aprill 1597.
      W Ralegh

1. (1554–1624), son and heir of John Rashleigh senior, a wealthy merchant of Fowey and Member of Parliament for the borough in 1589 and 1597: Hasler III, p. 277.
2. Part of their house survives, incorporated in the Ship Inn in Lostwithiel Street near the quayside. Rashleigh's services were later commended by Thomas Southwell, one of the captains bound for Ireland (*HMC Salisbury* VIII, p. 449), but Richard Carew of Antony gave the credit for the erecting of the defences at Fowey to William Treffry, another substantial resident of Fowey whose house was located above that of the Rashleighs: *Richard Carew's Survey of Cornwall*, ed. F.E. Halliday, 1953, p. 209.

## 106. TO LORD BURGHLEY AND CHARLES LORD HOWARD FROM CHELSEA, 24 APRIL 1597

Hatfield, CP50/46, *HMC Salisbury* VII, pp. 173–4. In Ralegh's hand.

## THE DISCOVERING OF THE SPANISH FLEET

[addressed] To the right honorable my singuler good lorde the Lorde Tresurer and the Lord Admirall of Ingland

[endorsed] 24 April 1597 Sir Walter Raleigh to the Lord Treas[urer], Lord Admirall The *Darling* to be victuald and sent to the seas

Wheras I receved from your lordshipps a letter for the settinge to the seas a smale barke caled The Darling[1] for the discovering of the Spanishe fleett, supposed to be imployed [= *bound*] for Ingland, Irland or Britayne [*Brittany*], and that it pleased your lordships to promis such sumes of mony as the vitles, wages and other charges should amount unto, I have caused accordingly the sayd barke to be putt in order and to be vitled, praying your lordships according to this estimate (if it like your lordships) that the sume of 120*li* be delivered to this bearer, which I will presently sent [*send*] down to the captayne and cumpany[2] who fourthwith shall depart to follow such ins[*truc*]tions as ar geven by your lordships and my lords [*of the Council*].

Thus humble taking my leve I rest reddy to do your lordships all honor and service.

W Ralegh

From Chelsey[3] this xxiiij of Aprill

1. Probably Ralegh's own ship of that name, in which Lawrence Keymis had recently been on a second reconnoitering voyage to Guiana: Caley 1806 II, p. 321.
2. Almost certainly not Keymis.
3. Written over something illegible.

---

## 107. TO SIR ROBERT CECIL FROM WEYMOUTH, 6 JULY 1597

PRO, SP12/264/10, *CSPD 1595–7*, p. 451, Plate 6. In Ralegh's hand. Edwards II, pp. 169–70.

## SUPPLIES FOR THE FLEET

[*addressed*] To the right honorabell Sir Robert Cecyll knight, Principall Secritory to Her Majestye

[*endorsed*] 6 Julii 1597    Sir Walter Raleigh to my master    From Waymouth

In this hast and confusion of bussneses, amonge so many wantes and so great hast,[1] I hope yow will pardon mee if I write litell, and that confusedly. Wee have all written for supply.[2] I beseich yow to further it, or to

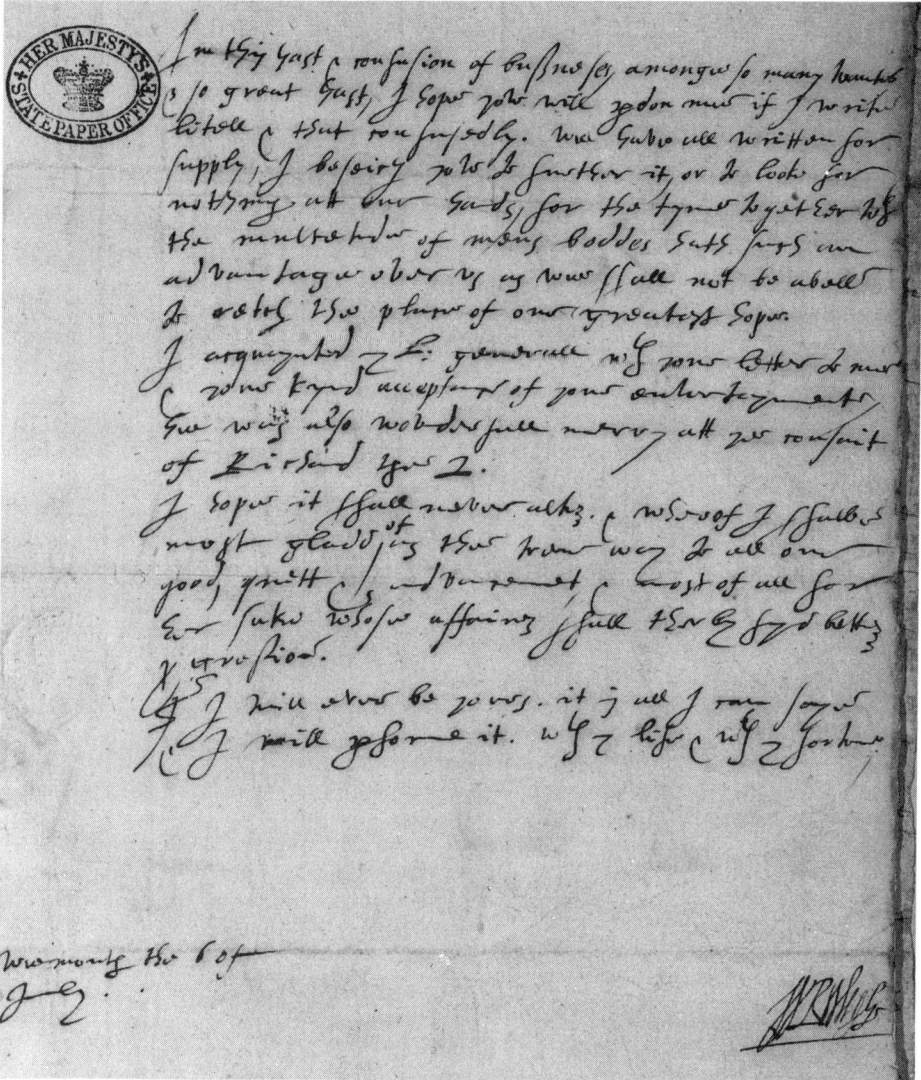

Plate 6. Letter 107: Sir Walter Ralegh to Sir Robert Cecil, 6 July 1597.
(PRO, SP12/264/10)

looke for nothing att our hands, for the tyme together with the multetude of mens boddes hath such an advantage over us as wee shall not be abell to retch [= *reach*] the place of our greatest hope.³

I acqueynted my Lord Generall [*Essex*] with your letter to me and your kynd acceptance of your entertaynment.⁴ Hee was also wonderfull merry att the consait of Richard the 2.⁵

I hope it⁶ shall never alter, and wherof I shalbe most gladd of, as the trew way to all our good, quiett and advancement, and most of all for her sake whose affaires shall therby fynd better progresion.

Sir, I will ever be yours. It is all I can saye and I will performe it with my life and with my fortune.
    W Ralegh

Wiemouth the 6 of July

---

1. In fact, the English and Dutch expedition, the so-called 'Islands Voyage' of 1597, to destroy the Spanish fleet (as the only hope of avoiding further 'descents' on the Queen's dominions) had been planned several months earlier, but as always there had never been an absolutely firm commitment on the Queen's part: R.B. Wernham, *Return of the Armadas*, pp. 143–58.
2. Most recently the leaders of the expedition meeting at Portland on this very day: *HMC Salisbury* VII, p. 291.
3. Presumably, at this stage, this was Ferrol where the Spanish home fleet lay at anchor. On 8 July the Queen promised further supplies provided that her 'lunatic goodness' did not encourage overmanning: *CSPD 1595–7*, p. 453.
4. Probably a reference to the frequent meetings of Essex, Howard and Robert Cecil at Ralegh's house which had been commented on by observers: Wernham, op. cit., pp. 153–4, citing particularly Collins 1746, II, pp. 17, 42, 44, 49 and 55.
5. An interesting anticipation of the political analogy between Elizabeth and Richard II's dependence on favourites of which the rebellious Essex faction was later to make such dangerous use. There is no reason to suspect Ralegh of disloyalty at a time when he had so recently re-established himself at Court.
6. Presumably the recent amity between Essex and Cecil with which Ralegh was credited: Collins 1746, II, p. 24.

---

## 108. To Sir Robert Cecil from Plymouth, 18 July 1597

PRO, SP12/264/32, *CSPD 1595–7*, pp. 483–4. In Ralegh's hand.
Edwards II, pp. 171–4.

## DEFEAT BY THE ELEMENTS

[*addressed*]  To the right honorabell Sir Robert Cecyll knight, Principall Secritory to Her Majestye
   Hast post hast, hast for life   For Her Majesties most especial affairs
   Delivered att Plymouth the 18 of July, att 6 of clocke in the yevening
            W Ralegh
[*endorsed*]   xvii$^{mo}$ Julii 1597   Sir Walter Raleigh to my master from Plymmoth

Although the news of our disseverance and storme beaten fleet be most unpleasinge and discumfortabell, as unto us that have first felt and indured the sorrow and danger as unto Her Majestye, to whom wee had hoped to have presented sume better relation [= *report*], yet the extremet[i]es beinge such as the[y] are I thought my sealf bound to advertize the same.

We[1] departed Plymouth on Sundaye night beinge the 10th of this moneath and held cumpany till Munday night, beinge the 11th, when by reason of fowle weather with thunder and mich winde and rayne, and for abating sayle for The Mathew and The Andrew, I lost sight of my Lorde Generall [*Essex*]. On Twesday morninge my sealf, The Bonaventer, The Mathew and Andrew were together and steered for the North Cape [*Finisterre*], not doubtinge butt to have crost the [*enemy*] fleet within six howres, butt att the instant the winde changed to the south and blew vehemently so as wee putt our sealvs under out [*our*] fore corses[2] and stood to the west in to the sea. Butt on Twesday night I perceved The Mathew to labor very vehemently and that shee culd not indure that manner of standinge of[f] and so putt her sealf a try[3] with her mayne course, which I did also the better to hold her and The Andrew with mee, beinge both of myne own squadron. Notwithstandinge in the morninge I had lost sight of them both and of divers other flibotes nire mee over night.

The storme onn Wensday grew more forsibell and the seas grew very exceeding lofty that my sealf and The Bonaventer had labor enough to beat it up [= *sail across the wind*]. Butt the night following, the Thusday, Freday and Saterday, the storme so increased, the shipps being waighty, the ordenance great and the billoes so raysed and inraged as wee could carry out no saile which, to our judgment, would not have bynn rent of[f] the yeards by the winde, and yet our shipp[s] roled so vehemently and so disjoynted them sealves as wee weare driven ether to force it agayne with our corses or to sinke. In my shipp it hath shaken all her beams, knees [= *right-angled timbers*] and stanchens [= *supports for guard-rails*] well ny asunder, in so mich as on Saterday night last wee made accompt to have yeilded our sealvs up to God, for wee had no way to worke, ether by triinge, hullinge or drivinge,[4] that promised better hope, our men beinge wasted with labor and watchinge and our shipp so open every wher, all her bulk head rent and her verye cookrome [= *galley*] of brike shaken down into powder.

The Saterday morning I spoke with your lordships servant, Cap[tain] Watson, who came from the North Cape,[5] my sealf being, as hee told mee, the windermost man of our fleet, so as it seemed that my Lord Generall was ether more to the westward or more asterne, for Captain Watsonn had not then mett with any butt my sealff. The same day also I spake with another small man of war that came directly from the Cape and hee had not seen any butt my sealf. I therfore, fynding the extremety of the weather such, and perceving that my Lord Generall was asterne mee, bare up with a litle peece of my forsaile to seeke hyme, butt could not crosse any onn that could geve me knowledge of hym, only I know in reason hee cannot butt be forced ether with [= *towards*] Ingland or Irland, and my greatest feare notwithstanding is that hee willbe hymesealf in sume extremetye before hee yeilde to putt backe, although it can be butt too dayes sayling lost and I know that the flibotes which transport the army ar skattered into diver[s] places.[6] Sume of them I found here att Plymouth[7] with great sickness amonge their cumpanyes and the flibots brused, the sailes rent and ther other furneture wasted.

That which most greeveth mee and which I protest before the majesty of God I do constantly beleve, is that ether my Lord Generall hyme sealf will wrestell with the seas to his [uttermost *crossed out*] perrill or, constraynd to cum bake, be found utterly hartbroken, although it be not in the poure [= *power*] of man to fight agaynst ellements.

I here that ther ar between thirtye and fourtye saile putt [*in*]to Falmouth, to which place I have sent overland to know of what sort, butt my Lord [*Essex*] hyme sealf is not among them.[8]

I know not what cource to take here with thos which importune mee to supply them, sume with masts, sume with sayles, sume having wett all their bredd and others that have a great many sicke soldiers which will shortly infect all the rest.

I understand that the [*Spanish*] fleet is strong in Farroll.

What shalbe cum of us I cannot judge, when wee shall cum together, or how wee shall repaire the wracke of this storme, the tyme of the yeare being so advansed. Yow my good lord can judg how wee shalbe abell to beat it up with thes waighty shipps. I dare not advize: it weare to great a presumption, the persons and natures of the affaires being as the[y] are.

God send it a blessed e[n]d. I beseich your honors to direct mee with all speed, and herewithall I humble take my leve from Plymouth this Mondaye yeveni[n]g the 18 of July.

    Your honors to serve you,
        W Ralegh

[*left-hand margin*] Here ar none of Her Majesties shipes butt The Wastpight and The Bonaventer. The Lord send us good newse of The Mathew and Andrew.⁹ I hope to here of them ether in Falmouth or in Torr Baye. The wind doth remayne forcibell att the writing hereof and like rather to increas then slaken.

1. Three squadrons led by Essex, Lord Thomas Howard and Ralegh, containing in all sixteen of the Queen's ships. There were also ten Dutch vessels and some 48 flyboats carrying the soldiers. Ralegh's squadron consisted of his flagship, the *Warspite* (648 tons), the *Bonaventure* (600 tons) and the two former (and slower) Spanish ships captured at Cadiz in 1595, the *St Andrew* (900 tons) and the *St Matthew* (1,000 tons), under the command, respectively, of Sir George Carew, Ralegh's cousin, and Marcellus Throckmorton, Lady Ralegh's uncle. The *St Matthew* had struck a rock coming into Plymouth and was stuck for three hours, but came off without apparent damage: Edwards II, p. 422.
2. Sails set on the foremast.
3. Reducing sail so as to stay in the hollow of the waves.
4. Hulling and driving are moving without the use of rudder or sail and dragging the anchor.
5. In May the Privy Council had sent a Captain George Watson in the *Francis* of Weymouth to report on Spanish preparations at Ferrol and Corunna: *CSPD 1595–7*, pp. 443 and 486. Cf. the mission of the *Darling*, above, Letter 106. Watson was on his way back to the Court so news of the storm probably reached there before Ralegh's letter.
6. Some were driven onto the coasts of France, Wales and even Ireland: Arthur Gorges in Purchas XX, p. 43.
7. Where he had arrived this same day that the letter was written: Collins, II, p. 57.
8. Essex just made it into Falmouth in the leaking *Merhonour* on Tuesday 19 July: see below, Letter 109 and Wernham, op. cit., p. 163. On Saturday 23 July he wrote to Cecil complaining that he had replied to a letter from Ralegh (of 18/19 July) on 20/21 but 'yet we hear not a word': *CSPD 1595–7*, p. 470.
9. See below, Letter 109. Howard fared better than the rest but did not return to Plymouth until 31 July.

## 109. To Sir Robert Cecil from Plymouth, 20 July 1597

PRO, SP12/264/40, *CSPD 1595–7*, p. 466. In Ralegh's hand.
Edwards II, pp. 174–5.

## THE REST OF THE FLEET

[*addressed*]  To the right honorabell Sir Robert Cecyll knight, Principall Secritory to Her Highnes

[*endorsed*]  20 Julii 1597  Sir Walter Raleigh to my master from Plymmoth  The arryvall of 7 of Her Majestes shippes there

Sir: This Wensday morninge my Lorde Generall [*Essex*] is expected here at Plymouth, beinge on Twesdaye night putt into Falmouth in great extremetye and imminent perrill of sinkinge in the sea, which I knew would betyde hyme err hee would yeild to ether seas or winds.[1] The Mathew and Andrew and The Mary Rose (wherin the Marshall [*Sir Francis Vere*] is) ar also arived, The Dreadnought is in Falmouth with The Merehonor, [*and*] the Admirall of Hollande [*Jan van Duivenvoord*] with sume 3 or 4 of his squadron ar also cum in. Most of thes shipps have [spent their main masts *crossed out*] crackt theire masts and ar mervelus leake, especially my Lorde Generalls own shipp. I thinke by this Wensday night all the rest wilbe on the coast. The most of the long botes ar lost and all the barges.

I have herewithall sent your honor a very trew report of the state of the [*Spanish*] army att Farroll.[2] What your honors will resolve I cannot forthinke. In the meane tyme, Sir, I beseich yow to worke from Her Majestye sume cumfort to my Lord Generall who I know is dismayd by thes mischances yeven to death, although ther could not be more dun by any man uppon the yearth, God havinge turned the heavens with that fury agaynst us, a matter beyound the poure or valure or witt of man to resiste, and such accidents as the warr draweth with it sealf.

This mich I thought my sealf bound to lett your honor understand of, beinge among thes misseres herein cumforted that my Lord Generall hymesealf hath escaped such a perrill and those other too shipps, The Mathew and Andrew, saved, which I most vehemently feared.

Plymouth this xxth of July.[3]

    Your honors to do yow service,
      W Ralegh

The shipps alreddy arrived ar:

| | |
|---|---|
| The Merehonor | The St Andrew |
| The Wastspight | The Mary Rose |
| The Bonaventure | The Dreadnought |
| The St Mathew | The Admirall of Holland |

with sume 25 saile of other sortes

1. The *Merhonour* had been leaking before she left Plymouth and the Queen herself had begged Essex not to trust 'the crazed vessell' (*CSPD 1595–7*, p. 453). The English fleet had left Plymouth on 10 July bound for the Spanish port of Ferrol. Within a week it had been forced by violent storms to return either to Plymouth or, in the case of Essex, to Falmouth. For full details see R.B.Wernham, *Return of the Armadas*, Oxford 1994, pp. 143–69.
2. Missing. Based, no doubt, on what Captain Watson had told him during their brief encounter. See above, Letter 108.
3. Ralegh's letter reached London on 22 July and, according to Lord Admiral Howard, the news that Essex was safe brought tears to the Queen's eyes: *HMC Salisbury*, VII, p. 306. His own apparently less hazardous experience must cast some doubt on the seamanship of the two soldiers, Essex and Ralegh: Wernham, op. cit., pp. 163–4. Howard's ships' captains, who included Sir William Monson and Sir John Gilbert, were, by and large, men of more experience than those who served in the other two squadrons. Ralegh, as this letter shows, was in despair, his spirits and his stomach for the enterprise only being revived by the arrival of Essex, who rode overland 'all night post over the rugged mountains of Cornwall': Wernham, op. cit., pp. 164–5.

---

## 110. TO SIR ROBERT CECIL FROM PLYMOUTH, 26 JULY 1597

PRO, SP12/264/55, *CSPD 1595–7*, p. 472. In Ralegh's hand.
Edwards II, p. 176; G. Hadow, 1917, rep. 1978, p. 34, with facsimile.

### GUESTS ON THE *WARSPITE*

[*addressed*] To the right honorabell Sir Robert Cecyll knight, Principall Secritory to Her Highnes

[*endorsed*] 26 July 1597 Sir Walter Raleighe to my master from Plymmoth

Sir: I humble thanke yow for your letters. I can add nothinge of substance to the generall letter.[1] I only send thes to remember my love and service.

My Lord Generall is my guest in The Wast Spite, [*with*] the earle of Ruttland,[2] Sir Thomas Germyne [*Jermyn*], Allexander Racklife [*Ratcliff*] and Sir R[obert] Mansfelde [*Mansell*].[3] I should have taken it unkyndly if my lorde had taken up any other lodging till The Lion[4] cum, and now Her Majestye may be sure his lordship shall sleape sumewhat the sounder, though hee farr the worss by being with me for I am ame an excellent watchman att sea.[5]

Wee only attend the winde, havinge repayred as mich as wee can our bruses,[6] butt we shall not be in any great corage for winter weather and longe nights in thes shipps.[7]

I trust wee shall performe whatsoever and more [that *crossed out*] can be dun with like strenght and means. Sir, I pray love us in your element and wee will love and honor yow in ours and every wher, and remayne to be cummanded by yow for evermore.

W Ralegh

Sir, I pray vouchsauf to remember mee in all affection to my Lorde Cobhame.[8] Plymouth the 26 of July

1. Essex's lengthy report to the Privy Council of a meeting in Plymouth of his Council of War, signed by each of them and probably carried by the same messenger, announcing their intention of setting forth to rejoin Lord Thomas Howard's squadron and seeking out the enemy: PRO, SP12/264/60, *CSPD 1595–7*, pp. 477–8.
2. Roger Manners, 5th Earl, one of the considerable number of gentlemen volunteers who had come on this expedition.
3. Captain of the *Merhonour*. See above, Letter 44, note 6.
4. The *Golden Lion*, sent by the Queen to replace the stricken *Merhonour*: *CSPD 1595–7*, pp. 468, 470.
5. Cf. Letter 119 in which Ralegh confirms his inability to sleep at sea.
6. Essex reported (above, note 1) that all the ships except the *Merhonour* had been 'repayred in reasonable good sort', which, considering the time taken, reflects great credit on Plymouth's shipwrights and moorings. In fact the fleet did not sail again until 17 August.
7. It remains unlikely that the Queen's ships were maintained in as good condition as in Hawkins's day at the Navy Board: J.A. Williamson, *Hawkins of Plymouth*, 1969, pp. 244ff.
8. See above, Letter 102, note 4. He had succeeded his father as the 11th Lord Cobham on the latter's death in March 1597: *DNB*. The family's estates lay largely in the Medway valley in north Kent, with a mansion at Cobham and a London house in Blackfriars. William had been Lord Lieutenant of Kent, Constable of Dover Castle, Warden of the Cinque Ports, Lord Chamberlain and a member of the Privy Council. Henry was appointed to his father's local offices but not to those at Court: *DNB* and Peter Clark, *English Provincial Society from the Reformation to the Revolution*, Hassocks 1977, *passim* and especially p. 261.

---

## 111. To [the Privy Council from Plymouth, end of July 1597][1]

BL, Cotton Otho EIX, f. 377, no date. Upper edges much damaged by fire.[2] In Ralegh's hand.

Edwards II, pp. 191–3.

### AN ALTERNATIVE PLAN

[*no address or endorsement survives*]

[... *how*] this fleet and army of Her [*Majestye* ... *beinge*] now with the latest to lande att[3] [... *many*] dangers and dificultes in the enterprize of Farro[*ll*[4] ... *this*] course,[5] if it shall like Her Majestye and your lordship[s].

[*There have*] past to the Indies this yeare, in March, Aprill and Maye, four [*score ships with purpose*] to returne treasor and marchandize. [*In*] the last yeare, 1596, by reason of the sackage of Calize and burn[*ing of the fleet*], ther was made no returne,⁶ so as this yeare the treasor which sho[*uld have come*] with the last, and what soever is gathered since, is to be transported. [*Now*] because ther is no suspition of any attempt to be made in the Indie[*s this year, and also*] that the Spanishe king would be in effect utterly broken if this duble ret[*urn*] weare surprised, wee do thinke it a matter very feasibell⁷ with the on[*e*] hal[*f of*] Her Majestye[*s*] fleet now att Plymouth and with a third part of the army to [*perform*] the same.

Out of the 16 sayle of shipps of Her Majesties to take eyght and with the vitell of th[*e others to*] furnishet hc rest for on moneath or six weekes to that which now remayneth in [*them*]. The vitell provided here for the supply will make too moneaths vitell more, [*and with*] the remaynder of that which shalbe saved out of the flibotes wee shalbe able to [*furnish*] the fleet by us desired for six moneaths, in which tyme, or less, wee shalbe abell, by [*your lordships*] favor, to go and returne, and sufficient pourfull to master and possess all the kings shipps in the Indies.

The occasion never served so fitly for hee is no way warned, for whensoever this enterprize shalbe undertaken of purpose, and that ther be any suspect therof, the Spanishe kinge will use so many preventions as the labor and charge on our syde will ever more be lost and made frustrate.

The Spanishe fleet now att Farroll is not in any estate to cum out, and by that tyme in which wee shalbe reddy to depart it wilbe no tyme of the yeare to make invasions or incursions by sea. Wee shall only be wantinge in the dead of winter and be abell to returne in the spring sufficient tymely to awnswere any attempt from Spayne. In kepinge the seas uppon the first pretence of Farroll and the Ilands wee shall spend three moneathes wherin wee shalbe shaken and weather beaten, with small hope of profitt, and to possess all his Indien fleet will require butt too moneathes more and the navigation of less perrill and the strenght which wee desire to carry shalbe butt too shipps more then that which was alloted to Sir F[*rancis*] Drake and Sir John Hawkings.⁸

Her Majesties charge is alreddy past, which wee all desire to convert to Her Majesties greate[*r*] profitt, to which purpose wee fynde this enterprize to offer it sealf, which wee asure [*our*]sealves [*sh*]all returne the greatest profitt to Her Majestye and the greatest loss to her enemi[*e*]s then⁹ ever any attempt did in Her Majestyes tyme. [...]¹⁰

1. On 1 August, while awaiting a wind at Plymouth (Letter 110), Ralegh and Essex paid a flying visit to the Court to put to the Privy Council this proposal by Ralegh: Collins 1746, II, p. 59.
2. The words in square brackets have been supplied very largely from Edwards in whose day the manuscript was presumably slightly more legible than it has since become, although he admitted deducing some words from 'the sheer necessity of the context'.
3. Edwards follows this with 'the Islands' but here he was confusing the context.
4. The approach to Ferrol is by a long, winding passage, the hazards of which will have been only too obvious to both Ralegh and Essex.
5. Arthur Gorges stated that Essex never meant to attempt it and took it on board only to calm the Queen's fear of invasion: Purchas, XX, p. 70.
6. From a winter cruise to the West Indies. Ralegh was oddly mistaken: the Indies fleet came home in September 1596: *CSPD 1595–6*, p. 431 and Monson, I, p. 54, note 42.
7. Essex, if not the whole Council of War, seems to have supported what would appear to have been Ralegh's idea.
8. For their voyage of 1595–6 which had ended so tragically.
9. The rest of the sentence is written in the left-hand margin.
10. There is no means of knowing how much more there was, if any, on another sheet, nor whose signatures were appended. The idea received a cool reception in London: Wernham, *Return of the Armadas*, pp. 166–7.

---

## 112. To Sir Robert Cecil from Terceira, 8 September 1597

Hatfield, CP55/21, *HMC Salisbury*, VII, pp. 379–80. In Ralegh's hand.
Edwards II, pp. 177–9.

## NEWS FROM THE ISLANDS

[*addressed*]   To the right honorabell Sir Robert Cecylle knight, Principall Secritory to Her Majestye
       Hast post hast, hast for life   For Her Majesties especiall affaires, delivered att Tercera the 8th of September   W Ralegh

[*endorsed by or for Cecil*]   9 [*sic*] of [October *crossed out*] 7bris   Sir Walter Ralegh to me from the Tercera

[*and by his secretary*]   8 September 97   Sir Walter Ralegh to my master from neere the Tercera

[*by postmasters*]   Rec[*eive*]d by the Mayor of Lyme Regis from the sea the 2 of October at 12 of the clock of the day at noone
       Att Crockerne iii of the clocke afternone the therd October

Sir: I thought my sealf bound by this bearer[1] to lett your honors know the fortuns wee have passed since our departinge Inglande, which was 18 [*sic*] August, att which tyme, havinge the winde [att *crossed out*] very bare att northwest and afterward more westerly, wee weare forst into the Baye of

Biskey² and had great payne in torninge out, in which forsibell weather The St Andrew spent her mayn topmast³ and, as I hard by a barke of the fleet, that [sic] The Mathew had spent her maynemast and was left in the Bay. I hope yow have hard [news] of her, or els God cumfort them.⁴

About the 26 wee recovered the Cape Prior with a very prest sayle and uppon the very doublinge [= *rounding*] I also lost my mayne yeard, broken in to yeven peeces in the midle, which I was forst to lay on over the other and so make it shorter, and have past with it to the hight of the Rocke.⁵ My Lord Generall, after hee had cum unto mee and seen my mishape, stood in with the North Cape and in the yeveninge sent unto mee to stand in also, butt as I was forst to drive before the winde, and not able to ly by a winde without a mayne sayle, the sea beinge also miche growne, I passed on towards the Rocke, being the second rendevous agreed on, and sent word to my lord that I would attend hyme ther. Ther stayd with mee of Her Majesties shipps The Dreadnought only, who never leaft mee in that first and greater mischance, for, tarriinge att the Rocke 3 dayes for my Lord Generall, I receved letters from hyme by a pinnes to follow hyme to the Islands, in which course my mayne mast also fayled. I had with me my cussen Sir W[*illiam*] Broke in The Dreadnought, 20 voluntary barks of the west countrey that came out with mee and 3 flibotes of soldiers of the Low Countres, [*Randall*] Brett, [*Fulk*] Conway and [*John*] Sydney.⁶ Sydnes flibote foundred butt I saved hyme and all the soldiers. I had also that mett mee since 3 of the vitlers of Lundun, The Georg, The Gamaliell and The Gift.⁷

I have notwithstanding followed my lords order to cum to the Ilands and I am now this 8 of [Aug *crossed out*] September in sight of Tercera, havinge chosen rather to perishe then to relinquishe the enterprize, and, the Lord doth know, in a torne shipp. Butt Her Majestye shall fynd that I valew not life,⁸ although I hope Her Majestye would not that I should perishe in vayne. I hope after too dayes to fynd my Lord Generall and the fleet, with whom I thinke all the rest of Her Majesties shipps ar (The Mathew with poore Georg Carew excepted).⁹ It is a carfull and perelus tyme of the yeare for thes wayghty ships. The Lord of Heaven send us all well to returne and send us the good hape to do Her Majestie acceptabell service, to performe which wee have alreddy suffered miche. And for my particuler I have never dared to rest since my wracks and God douth j[*ud*]ge that I never for thes 10 daies came so mich as into bedd or cabbin.¹⁰

In hast I kiss yor hands and will honor yow ever.

Tercera the 8 of September.

        W Ralegh

1. An English merchant whom Ralegh met in Terceira: Arthur Gorges in Purchas, XX, p. 65.
2. Apparently on Essex's orders and against the better judgement of the master of the *Warspite*: ibid., p. 50.
3. She caught up with the rest near Cape Ortegal: *HMC Salisbury* VII, pp. 368–9.
4. See below, note 9.
5. Cape de Roca north of Lisbon.
6. These were soldiers in charge of English companies withdrawn from the Low Countries: *APC* XXVIII, pp. 143–4.
7. A story that Ralegh persuaded a number of ships to follow him rather than the rest of the fleet was dismissed by Arthur Gorges as 'a monstrous untruth, raised out of malice': Purchas, op. cit., pp. 59, 61. Any return to Ferrol was now out of the question, but it was a false report, said to have been picked up by Ralegh from a Southampton ship, that the Spanish fleet had left Ferrol to meet the West Indian fleet, which led Essex to head for the Azores: Wernham, *Return of the Armadas*, p. 172. In fact the Spaniards did creep out on 9 September, only to meet contrary winds: ibid., p. 173.
8. From here written in the left hand margin.
9. Carew refused to leave his ship, taking her first to La Rochelle and thence to England where he begged the *Adventure* from the Queen, reaching the Azores not long after Essex had left: Purchas, op. cit., pp. 50–51, 55–6 and *HMC Salisbury*, VII. pp. 371–2, 384.
10. For the sequel see Wernham, op. cit., pp. 173–90 and below, Letter 113.

---

## 113. To the Earl of Essex, with Lords Thomas Howard and Charles Mountjoy, from Plymouth, 29 October 1597

Hatfield, CP56/61, *HMC Salisbury*, VII, p. 450. In Ralegh's hand, enclosed with Letter 114. Edwards II, pp. 180–2.

## SOUTH WEST DEFENCES

[addressed]   To the right honorable our singuler good lorde the Earle of Essex, Lorde Generall of Her Majesties force and fleet

Delivered att Plymouth att 12 a clock att night the xxix of October

Hast post hast   Hast for life with [all] speed possibell

For Her Majesties most important aff[a]ires from the Leuetenant of Cornewale

        W Ralegh

[endorsed]   1597 29 October   Lord Thomas Howarde, Lord Mountjoy, Sir Walter Raleighe to my Lord of Essex   Capten Summers arryved Capten King [?*Ridgway*] mett nere Falmouthe and fought withall by some of the Spanishe fleet [*by the postmasters*] at As[h]bourton at 8 of the clocke in the morninge At Exeter at 1 in the after nowne At Honyton at halfe an hower after iii of the [*clock in the*] after n[*oon*] Recevyd Crockerne at vi of the clocke after none xxx October At Sherbor[*n*]e paste x of the clocke at nig[*ht*]

Our very good lorde: Wee have this Saterday night receved the cumfortabell newse of George Summers[1] arivall, whos letter wee have here withall sent your lordshipp.[2] Wee do only now want The Andrew, for other small shipps wee hope they will as well profitt by the winde or otherwize to save them sealves as the rest have dunn. Thes beinge all well returned, Her Majesties kyngdoms defended, the enemy dishonored and made a great looser and the warr made uppon our enimis charge, wee hope, together with the considerations of our great travells [= *labours*] and cares, Her Majesty will receve our services in gratius part.[3]

Wee have not hard of any certeyne particuler of the Spanishe fleet since your lordshipps departure[4] other then that sume of ours in returning do discover 10, 12 or more in a cumpany of them as they ar broken.[5] Only I, W[*alter*] Ralegh, receved an advertisment this yevening that the fleet should be nire the coast of Cornwale and by thos very words, not otherwize fortefied by any particuler nor by what means they who wrat the newse receved it.

Notwithstandinge wee have resolved that I the Viceadmirall [*Howard*] will go of[*f*] to the seas with thos few shipps which may be made reddy and that I the Leutenant Generall [*Lord Mountjoy*] will attend this port and the country adjoyning, and I the Leutenant of Cornwale [*Ralegh*] use all mea[*n*]s possibell to defend that countye.[6]

Herewithall wee humble recumend our affections and services to your lordshipps [*sic*] and rest reddy to be cummanded by your lordshipp.

[*postscript*] Captayne Rugway[7] in cumminge by the Lizarde was mett by on[*e*] of the Spanishe fleet nire Falmouth, too of his men kilde and eyght hurt.

        T Howard    C Mountjoye    W Ralegh

[*Ply*]mouth the xxix of October

---

1. George Somers of Lyme Regis, an experienced ship's captain. He wrote to Essex on 29 October saying that he had just arrived at Dartmouth, his crew very sick: *HMC Salisbury* VII, pp. 453–4.
2. Missing.

3. A somewhat battered English fleet had crawled into Plymouth from 26 October, not knowing that the Spanish fleet had left Ferrol on the 9th, the very day Essex had departed from the Azores: Wernham, *Return of the Armadas*, pp. 183–7.
4. Essex had left immediately for London, leaving Ralegh to mobilize the West Country against the expected invasion: *HMC Salisbury*, VII, pp. 445–8, *CSPD 1595–7*, p. 522; Collins 1846, II, pp. 72, 74.
5. These turned out to be friendly: *HMC Salisbury*, VII, pp. 461–2 and 481.
6. Arthur Gorges says that Ralegh had gone ashore at St Ives to quieten the panic in west Cornwall (Purchas XX, p. 125) but did he know of the sailing of the Spanish fleet?
7. Not identified: inexplicably called King in the endorsement.

---

## 114. To Sir Robert Cecil from Plymouth, 30 October 1597

Hatfield, CP56/69 and 81, *HMC Salisbury* VII, pp. 455–6, as two letters. In Ralegh's hand. Edwards II, pp. 182–9.

### NEWS OF THE SPANISH FLEET

[*addressed*]   To the right honorabell Sir Robert Cecyll knight, Principall Secritory to Her Majesty
[*in another hand*]   Plymouth at 12 of the clocke one Sunday nyght
[*endorsed*]   30 October   Sir Walter Raleigh to my master
[*by postmasters*]   R[*eceive*]d Asbourton at vi of the clocke in the morninge   Exeter at 11 of the cloke before nowne   Receved at Hunyton att haff a nower after one   Recevyd the pakett Crockerne at iiij of the cloke after none xxxi October   R[*eceive*]d at Andever at one of the cloke in the afternowne

Sir: Wee have written a joynt letter to my Lord Generall of an advertisment [= *report*] brought by on[e] Bowden of Plymouth[1] who fought with on[e] of the flibots of warr of the Spanishe fleet in 42 degrees and 30 leaugs of[*f*] the Cape [*Finisterre*]. The particuларetes I send yow here inclosed, though not in that forme as in the Lord Generalls letter, for, this being the first examination, we did afterward marshall it.[2] Other newses ther ar none, butt that this day ther came another small barke in, of Sparke of Plymouth,[3] that also mett Georg Carew[4] and sayth hee had repaired his maynmast, so as I hope hee may better shift, both with the weather and the enemy.[5]

      Leving all idle protestations I am your servant,
        W Ralegh

I humble beseich yow to excuse mee to my Lord Admirall and that this coppy may serve his lordshipp also, and to my cussen [*Sir John*] Stanhope and to my Lorde Cobhame,[6] for wee ar here made madd with intricate affaires[7] and want of means.

Plymouth the 30 of October att night.

This captayne [?*Bowden*] reported unto us of his own voluntary that the earle [*Essex*] our generall hath as mich fame and reputation in Spayne and Italy as ever and more then any of our nation had, and that for an enemy hee is the most honored man in Europe. My Lord Thomas Howard was present, my Lord Monjoye, my Lord Marshall [*Vere*] and mysealf, and therfore he shall not take it for flattery on my part. My Lord Monjoy prayeth me to recumend his affection and service unto your honor.

[*new page*]

[*endorsed*]   1597 October   Advises concerning the Spanishe fleet sent by Sir Walter Raleighe

The [*Spanish*] fleet was devided into 4 squadrons, the first that of the Adelantado [*Admiral Don Martin de Padilla*] who had green pe[n]dants [*flags*], the second of Diego Brochero who had yellow pendants, the thirde of Britendona [*Bertendona*] who had redd and the 4th of Cebures [*Zubiaur*] who had white. Ther was a 5th squadron of Marco Arambull [*Arambure*] who was to cume with 30 sayle more and 5000 men for supply. The masters of the campe weare Dun [*sic*] John de Lova, Dun Farnando Brocheroe and Orosa who was expected out of Britayne [*Brittany*].[8]

Sume of the Spanierds examined[9] say ther came out together butt 110, butt the alferes [= *ensign*] of the Spanish captayne avoweth that they weare 160.[10] They say that they departed the Groyne [*Corunna*] St Lucas daye, as they thinck the 10 of October.[11]

They do farther confess severally examined that this fleet came all within 10 [?*20*] leaugs of the Lisard joyntly and entire, and ther meet [*sic*] the storme att east which severed them, after which this ship taken by Bowden never saw butt on[e] of his consortts, which was sume 30 leags from the coast of Spayne.

The Spanish cap[*tain*] is caled John Viveres, a Biscaien. He levied the cumpany hyme sealf in his countrey and he avoweth that ther weare 40 gallions of the kings, of which he knew the names butt of thes: The St Pole in which the Adelantado went, The St Peter, admirante, The St Lucas was cast away coming out of Farrall, The St Francis and The St Johne, 15 great

Biscaien shipps, 60 great esterlings [*Germans*], 10 or 12 flibotes, besids freich [*sic* = ?*freighters*] and carvells.

Ther was also expected 17 sayle of shipps out of the Streyts [*of Gibraltar*], which fleet another bark of Plymoth of Sparke,[12] which arived also this present, saw att the South Cape [*St Vincent*]. Hee sayth that ther weare of infantry betwen 10 and 12000, of horss 500 and 5000 foot are expected with Marco Arambull, a Biscayne.

They all confess that they came six dayes on with good wind and then [*were*] taken with the storme. The[*y*] brought also feld artillery, with store of moyles [= *mules*] and oxen. The generall of the artillery was Dun Pedro de Guavera. Being axed [*asked*] what Inglishe weare in the fleet they say divers, butt the[*y*] knew name of none butt Richard Burley.[13]

Of Irishe ther was on[*e*] cumpany entire.

Being asked what provision of boats to lande soldiers, they say 20 made of purpose capabell of 100 men apeece, besides thos of the shipps. Being demanded what vitell they answere that the fleet had butt 6 weeks for it was determined that assone as the men weare ashore the fleet should returne. They do avow all [*to*]gether that the place of discent should be Falmouth.

This Inglishman, Bowden,[14] passing by the Lisard the 28 of this moneth of October say [*saw*] 12 sayle nire the head land butt could not make them [*out*], and the Spanish prisoners say that they think them not [*to*] be of their fleet because they had no pedants, which wee thinke them sealvs took in because they wear so few.[15] This Bowden also reporteth that he [*saw*] t[*w*]o very great shipps o[*f*]f Silley [*Scilly*] as hee came and, as we gather both by the circumstances and by the confession of the prisoners, that this poore man fought more resolutely and having butt 28 men and boyes took this flibote by an entry [= *boarding*] [*of one*] who had 40 soldiers besids saylers and yet slew not on[*e*] butt at the entrance, of whos good service and the better to incorag others wee humble pray your lordships to have consideration.[16]

1. Not identified: it was a very common Devon surname. Bowden not only fought with the Spanish flyboat but apparently brought her and her crew back to Plymouth.
2. If this was the letter sent to Essex the previous day (Letter 113) it was indeed 'marshalled' to the extent of being totally uninformative. There is no mention of Bowden! Was this deliberate? Did Ralegh and his fellow commanders want to be sure of impressing Cecil and marginalizing Essex?
3. John Sparke, a Plymouth merchant, had been Mayor in 1583 and 1591: R.N. Worth, *Calendar of Plymouth Municipal Records*, 1893, pp. 18 and 21. This informant was probably his son or even his grandson: Vivian, *Devon*, 1895, p. 586.

4. Sir George Carew had encountered him on 1 October and learned that eight days earlier he had been chased by 18 Spanish warships.
5. Carew was limping back to Portsmouth in the *Adventure*: Wernham, *Return of the Armadas*, pp. 189–90. He reached the Downs on 3 November: Purchas, XX, p. 56 and *HMC Salisbury*, VII, p. 465.
6. Letters 102, note 4, and 110, note 8.
7. See above, Letter 113.
8. For the above names, and those of other, presumably junior, officers, see C. Ferdandez Duro, *Armada Española*, 1897, III, pp. 161, 166.
9. Presumably those aboard the ship captured by Bowden.
10. 136 ships and 24 caravels: Duro, op. cit., p. 166.
11. St Lukes's Day is 16 October.
12. See above, note 3.
13. Formerly of Melcombe Regis in Dorset, Burley had lived since 1580 in San Sebastian as a merchant's factor. He had been captain of one of the four Spanish ships which landed the men who burned Penzance in 1595. He was later arrested in Spain on suspicion of being an English spy: H.J. Loomie, *The Spanish Elizabethans*, 1965, pp. 66–8.
14. See above, note 1.
15. The Spaniards were right: they turned out to be 'English, Scotch or Flemings': *HMC Salisbury*, VII, p. 461.
16. Their lordships would no doubt argue that the ship he had captured was reward enough.

---

## 115. To Lord Burghley from Durham House, 16 January 1598

Hatfield, CP48/101, *HMC Salisbury* VIII, p. 18. In Ralegh's hand.
Edwards II, p. 197.

### DEPUTY LIEUTENANTS OF CORNWALL

[*addressed*] To the right honorabell my singuler good lorde the Lord Treasorer of Inglande
[*endorsed*] Sir Walter Rayligh 1597

My very good lorde: Wheras it hath bynn thought fitt that Sir Nicholas Parker[1] should be made a deputy leuetenante in Cornwale, I do for my sealf exceedingly well allow of the gentelman and do farther humble pray your lordshipp that Master Barnarde Grenvile,[2] late sherife of Cornwale and soonn and heire to Sir Richard Grenvile, may be also admitted, because in all the north parts of Cornwale ther are none of the deputes that have any dwellinge.[3] The gentelman is very sufficiente and the rest shall receve great ease therby and Her Majesties service the better performed.[4]

Thus with remembrance of my humbell dewty I rest to be cummanded by your lordshipp as your sarvante,
          W Ralegh

From Derum Howse this 16 of January.

1. Parker had served with distinction as a captain of horse in the Low Countries and had been on the Islands Voyage in 1597: Purchas, XX, p. 77.
2. Grenville (1567–1636) resided at Stowe in the north Cornish parish of Kilkhampton. He married the niece and heiress of Sir William Bevill (see above, Letter 29 and below, note 4): Hasler II, p. 215.
3. This was a prime consideration with Burghley in the appointment of deputy lieutenants.
4. The Council agreed to the appointments on 18 January (*APC* XXVIII, p. 244) and both were listed as deputies on 13 August 1599, together with Sir William Bevill of Killigarth (in Talland) and Master Richard Carew of Antony: *CSPD 1598–1601*, p. 291.

---

## 116. TO SIR WILLIAM MORE[1] AND OTHERS FROM THE COURT, 20 MAY 1598

Surrey Record Office, Guildford, LM/2013/28, formerly at Loseley Park, Guildford, *HMC 7th Report*, pt i, Appendix (W. More Molyneux), p. 657, abstract only, otherwise not hitherto printed. Written by clerk, with subscription and signature in Ralegh's hand.

### FOR ROBERT SHARPE

[*endorsed, in later hand*]  Sir Walter Ralegh to Sir William More, Lawrence Stoughton, William Wright and John Denham[2]

After my very hartie commendations: Whereas I understand that Robert Sharpe,[3] one of Her Highnes servauntes of my band,[4] hath been unjustlie and wrongfullie molested in suites of law and otherwise by one Edward Owen,[5] who deviseth and practiseth meanes to troble and vex him contentiouslie, without anie just cause, as is known to all or some of you, forasmuch as he ought not to commence or prosecute suite against him without leave first obteined from me, and for that I maie not permitt that anie of the number should be wronged, but protected by me in their honest and lawfull actions, I praie you to call Robert Sharp and Owen before you, and such wittnesses and proofes as either of them can produce, and uppon knowledg of the truth of the complaint to certefie me the causes of the suggested molestations and the qualitie of Owen and his accusations and what your opinion is thereof, that I maie take such order therin as maie seeme fytt.

So I commyt you to God, from the Court at Greenewich the 20th of Maie 1598.

>Your assured lovinge fri[n]de,
>W Ralegh

1. See above, Letter 21, note 2.
2. Magistrates of the county of Surrey.
3. The Queen's goldsmith, who supplied gold and silver 'for spangles for the coats of the [Queen's] guards, [etc.]': CSPD 1598–1601, p. 244.
4. Ralegh was Captain of the Queen's Guard.
5. On 13 June 1597, an Edward Owen had been pardoned for causing bodily harm to one Piers Holland for which he had been sentenced in the Court of Star Chamber: CSPD 1595–97, p. 439. On 26 May, Sharpe himself carried to More a letter to the same effect as Ralegh's from the Lord Chamberlain, in which was added the name of 'one Skeers' to that of Owen: HMC 7th Report, p. 657.

---

## 117. To [Sir Thomas Norris][1] from the Court, 15 June 1598

Chatsworth, Derbyshire, Devonshire Papers, Lismore Papers, 1/29. In the hand of a clerk, including a copy of Ralegh's signature, which suggests that it may be a near-contemporary transcript. Now very badly decayed. Some missing or illegible words have been supplied from Grosart.

Grosart, *Lismore Papers*, Series II, v, 1887, p. 14, from the original then at Lismore Castle, co. Waterford.

## THE WARDENSHIP OF YOUGHAL COLLEGE

*[no address or endorsement]*

My very good lord: Whereas Nathaniel Baxter[2] hath my co[nsente] to resigne the wardenship of Youghall,[3] de[siring] to reside here upon h[is parson]ige in England,[4] I hav[e nom]ynated Master Godfery Hering,[5] a Master of Artes and ev[ery w]aie very sufficient to be the [war]den there, as appeareth by lettres written from Sir Robert Cecyll, Her Majestes Principall [Sec]retar[y, in the] course usual there for [?the] presentation thereunto. And therefore do praie your lordship that you will admitt and allow of him in the office and place of ward[en] accordinglie.

And so [com]mitt you to God from the courte at Greenwych [*this 15° of June 1598*].
>   Your very loving fr[ende],
>       W Ralegh

1. Lord President of Munster 1597–9, whose duty it was, on behalf of the Queen, to admit the warden to his temporalities.
2. Warden of Youghal College since 1592, formerly tutor in Greek to Sir Philip Sidney.
3. A Desmond foundation (1464), very richly endowed, the right of the presentation to whose wardenship had come to Ralegh with the estates of the attainted earl. In 1588 Baxter's predecessor had leased the college's property to Sir Thomas Norris for 60 years: S. Hayman, *Ancient Religious Foundations at Youghal*, 1855.
4. In June 1596, Baxter was alleged to have refused to perform covenants entered into with Ralegh: *APC* XII, p. 265. In 1597 he was ordered to resign and did so but only in 1598. He was to be the author of *Oranie* (1606). Clearly Ralegh wanted him out.
5. Not identified, but seems not to have been appointed. On 15 May 1598 [*sic*], John Chardin, Bishop of Down and Connor, became warden, to be followed later the same year by Dr Meredith Hanmer: Hayman, op. cit. In 1602, Norris having died, Warden Hanmer granted the lease to William Jones of Youghal in trust for Ralegh, from whom possession passed in 1602–4 to Richard Boyle. For Ralegh's residence in Youghal, not in the Warden's house but probably in one of the college's properties, see C.H. Orpen, 'Ralegh's House at Youghal', *Proc. Royal Society of Antiquaries of Ireland*, XXXIII, pt iv, 1903, pp. 345–52.

---

## 118. TO SIR ROBERT CECIL, 26 OCTOBER 1598

PRO, SP12/268/93, *CSPD 1598–1601*, pp. 112–13. In Ralegh's hand.
Edwards II, pp. 198–9 and Pope Hennessy 1883, p. 174.

### IRISH REBELS

[*addressed*]  To the right honorabell Sir Robert Cecyll knight, Principall Secritory to Her Majestye
[*endorsed*]   1598  26 October   Sir Walter Raleigh to my master

Sir: It cann be no disgrace if itt weare knowne that the killinge of a rebell weare practised, for yow see that the lives of anoyncted princes ar dayly sought and wee have alwayes in Irlande geve head mony for the killinge of rebells, who ar evermore proclaymed att a price: so was the Earle of Desmond and so have all rebells bynn practised ageyest.[1] Notwithstanding I have written this inclosed[2] to Stafford[3] who only recummended that knave[4] to me uppon his creditt. Butt for your sealf yow ar not to be touched in the matter,⁵ and for mee I am more sorry for being deceved then for being declared in the practize.

        Your honors to do yow service
          W Ralegh

Hee hath nothing under my hand butt a passport

1. What exactly had prompted this letter is not clear, but at the beginning of August 1598, at a time of serious rebellion in Munster, Cecil apparently wrote to Sir Geoffrey Fenton, the Secretary of State for Ireland, instructing him to arrange for the assassination of the Earl of Tyrone. Fenton replied urging that Cecil communicate with the utmost secrecy: *CSPI 1598–9*, p. 221.
2. Missing.
3. Probably Captain Francis Stafford who had served in Ireland since 1585, received a disability pension in 1598 and was well known to Cecil: *HMC Salisbury* VIII, p. 286 and IX, p. 272. A Captain Stafford had been a member of the commission appointed in 1597 (with Ralegh, George Carew and others) to advise on the best way to conduct the war in Ireland.
4. Not identified.
5. Ralegh was well aware that although Cecil, who had recently been appointed Chief Secretary, had no scruples about disposing of rebels by assassination, he took care to show a pair of clean hands himself.

---

## 119. To [Sir Robert Cecil]¹ from the Channel, 25 August [1599]²

Hatfield, CP27/101–2, *HMC Salisbury* XIII, Addenda, p. 514. In Ralegh's hand.
Edwards II, pp. 96–9, dated 1594.

### HAZARDS ON LAND AND SEA

[*endorsed*] Sir Walter Rawleigh

Sir: I beseich yow to geve me leve to trobell yow a littel with my particuler because it concerns all the poore estate I have.³ The preists of Sallisburye have signed and sealed the fee farme⁴ more to benefite on FittJamis,⁵ who hath geven them a good fine, then any way to satisfye or releve mee. They have stoode upon scrupell of consciences [?*not*] to yeild any thinge to Her Majestye, butt without her letters, without her cummandments, they have past [= *transferred*] 50 *li* land to a nother and in such sort as myne must be voyde unless that 50 *li* land pass also, for the[y] have geven myne uppon condission that the other shall pass withall or elce both to be voyde. This bravely they dare to tye the Queen to do what they injoyne or elce they refuse to do what she cummands. Now this wilbe the culler [= *deceit*] of this insolency that unless FittJames have his fee farme the church shalbe in danger to lose 50*li* rent, butt that is meerely falce for if by any trick in law FittJames may pretende [= *presume*] to defraud the church of that rent, yet it was never ment to be so and therfore the [*court of*] Chancery will inforce hyme by a decree att the first motion, and if that should be doubted I will undertake to assure that rent my sealf.[6]

This FittJames is a smooth knave as any liveth, and a falce, and he offers mee 200*li* for my goodwill. Butt first I gave the Queen a jewell worth 250*li* to make [= *persuade*] the byshope; I must geve 60*li* loned to the church for ever of increase [*in the rent*], which will cost mee 1200*li* more [*at 5 per cent*]; the charges will cume to 150*li* more which is demanded, and when all this is spent I am not on farthinge the better butt the assurance of my estate only, which I purchace att a most terribell rate.[7] And I am sure if I weare a Turke I could not be worse dealt withall then I am by them [*the clergy*] who have dun nothinge for Her Majesties sake butt rackt mee yeven a sunder, and notwithstanding have past to a nother 50*li* land better then all Sherburne[8] for their own profitt and to satisfye their frinde [*Fitzjames*]. And if it had not bynn for his sake they would never have past myne, and so it apeereth for the[y] pass myne butt on condission that his shall pass withall or elce both to be voyde.[9] Sir, if yow pleas butt a littell to consider both of the charg they putte mee to, how ernestly Her Majesty hath dealt for mee, how hardly they use me, how undewtifully they dare to condistion [= *bargain*] with the Queen, how, agaynst all presedent that ever was, they pass 50*li* land [*out*] of their own handes which never any church did uncummanded by the prince, I hope yow may favor mee so mich uppon thes advantages as ether to compell them to graunt myn alone or elce that FittJames may ease mee in my charge in a more liberall kynde, which of the too I desire rather. For if by sute or by sume frinde in the Privy Chamber hee shall obtayne his passage from the Queen, then shall I lose that which he offreth mee [*i.e. £200*] and have it caried more to my disgrace, and therfore if I could draw hyme to healp toward my charge I had rather it should pass by mee then by another. On the other syde I hope by this advantage of the byshope and chapter that I may be freed for [?*from*] this increas of rent during myne own life, [*or*] att least during the byshops, who I hope will easely be perswaded to spare mee for his tyme. Butt I desire that this graunt may be inroled [= *in a court of record*] to the Queen before any speach be made att all and then, when it is in [t]her, perchance Master

Aturney [*Coke*] will finde a waye to frustrat that condistion as sure as they think they have made it. Sir, if yow think wee may cum bake in tyme, after it is inrold to the Queen I could wish it rested there, unless my wife be satisfied [= *compensated*] by FittJ[*am*]es to her likinge.¹⁰

Sir, we ar here att the [*North*] Forelande,¹¹ and purpose to run over for the French coast as soon as wee cann, butt I feare that wee shall have a wanton peece of work with thes shipps att this tyme of the yeare, and if wee tarry longe putt them so out of order, if not in danger, as the[*y*] will hardly be reddy for the next yeare when we have more use of them.¹² My Lord Admirall knowes that if they [*sic*] winde blow att south, sowth-west or south-south-west and blow strong, as it will do now every day, that wee must then needs ride att ancor in the Downs, and if wee be driven to shift roades [= *anchorage*] in the dark night here amonge the sands how perrelous it may prove.¹³ Butt we leve it to your wisdumes. Sure I am att this tyme of the yeare wee can do no services unless the enemy cum for the Thames mouthe, and if hee dare enter it with his shipps [hee is worthy of *crossed out*] hee shall do more then wee dare do butt with that feare, deliberation and tyme as no enemy can do the like, nor ever pass up while the world stands, unless hee cume in the beast [*best*] of summer and have gall[*i*]es to sound [*measure*] the channell, which now hee cannot have for this yeare.¹⁴

For our instructions I beseich yow the[*y*] may be certayne, for elce great advantage may be taken of us, I mean for goinge westwarde, wherof I now begin to be afearde, finding the unwildenes of thes huge shipps, in which I shall never sleap [*at*] night if I be here till Chrismass.

   Yours ever to do yow services,
   W Ralegh

25 August

---

1. In all probability.
2. Ralegh was at this time in the Channel on the *Ark Royal* as vice-admiral of a fleet under the command of Lord Thomas Howard: R.B. Wernham, *Return of the Armadas*, 1994, pp. 263–71. See also below, note 4.
3. An exaggeration (see below, note 6) indicating a degree of hysteria, perhaps induced by sea-sickness.
4. = freehold subject to a perpetual fixed rent. This was not a reference to the lease of the Sherborne estate in 1592 (see above, Letter 60, note 9) but to the grant to the Queen by the Bishop, confirmed by the dean and chapter of Salisbury, dated 20 August 1599, which, like the lease, was transferred to Ralegh by the Queen's letters patent dated 11 September of the same year: B.S. Wildman, *Short History of Sherborne*, 1911, p. 149. Ralegh had discovered that the rent now payable to the Bishop was £260, an increase of nearly £60, in spite of the

fact that the estate was marginally reduced in size: see below, note 6. Sir Edward Coke, the Attorney-General, on 29 August 1599 expressed outrage almost as great as Ralegh's at the way in which the Bishop of Salisbury had dictated the terms of the grant to the Queen: *HMC Salisbury* IX, pp. 333–4. Both seem to have forgotten that 99 years had become forever.
5. John Fitzjames of Leweston near Sherborne, a connection of the Somerset family: F. Brown, 'Fitzjames of Leweston', *Somerset Arch. Soc. Proc.*, XXIV, 1878, pp. 32–42.
6. What had happened was that the two former episcopal manors of Longburton and Holnest near Sherborne, which were included in the Bishop's grant to the Queen, were now excluded from Ralegh's grant and conveyed to his neighbour, Fitzjames, also subject to a rent charge, in his case £60 (not £50 as stated by Ralegh). In fact he had a longer interest than Ralegh, having acquired the remainder of a 99-year, rent-free, lease of these made to the Duke of Somerset in 1548 and, either by error or influence, although this was irrelevant by 1599, excluded from a decree in Chancery restoring the rest of the Salisbury estate to the Bishop shortly after. Hence, in his lease from the Queen in 1592, Ralegh had acquired only a reversionary, and virtually valueless, financial interest in the two manors, an interest which he himself had sold to Fitzjames in April 1594: Wildman, op. cit. pp. 138–9. It would seem, on the evidence, that Ralegh had few grounds for complaint.
7. There is no evidence of any purchase price being asked for or paid.
8. In the *Valor Ecclesiasticus* of 1536 (ed. J. Caley and J. Hunter, 1810–34, vol. II, pp. 70–71) the Bishop's Sherborne estate had been valued at nearly £400 net of outgoings. See also below, Letter 177.
9. i.e. Fitzjames.
10. Ralegh's outburst availed him nothing. In fact within a very short time he was on good terms with Fitzjames.
11. Howard had already rounded this but although Ralegh refers to the Downs and of moving westwards, he would appear to have been still sheltering in the Thames estuary: Wernham, op. cit., pp. 269–70.
12. Against another Spanish Armada?
13. Ralegh lost his mainmast on 26 August: Wernham, op. cit., pp. 269–70.
14. Galleys had been known in northern waters much later in the year: *HMC Foljambe*, pp. 98–100. Reports of so many galleys being assembled led the Queen and her ministers to suspect the enemy of intending a landing in the Thames estuary. It was all a false alarm, but it had called forth men and ships, and especially land forces, such as had not been seen since 1588.

---

## 120. To Sir Thomas Fane with Thomas Lord Howard from the Downs, 27 August, 1599

East Sussex Record Office, Rye 47/57/2, *HMC* 13th Report, Appendix IV, p. 119, *in extenso*, a contemporary copy, with imitation signatures.

## SPANISH INVASION ALERT

[*addressed*] To my very loving freind Sir Thomas Fane, Lieutenant of Dover Castle   For Her Majestes most espetiall services   Hast post, etc.
[*left-hand margin*]   Copia vera

Master Fane: Wee have receyved lettres from my lordes of the Councell which were sent unto them from the Governor of Brest[1] to lett their honors know that seaven gallies belonginge to the Spa[nish] fleet were putt into the harborough [*of Le Conquet*] and that 200 sayle of shipps were sene a sea boord standing for our channell.[2] There came also a pincke[3] from the Governor of Callice [*Calais*] this present Monday which wrat [= *wrote*] unto us confyrming the same intelligence. Wee doe therefor pray you, and hartylie requyer you, as you tender Her Majestes services, to cause a couple of small barques of Dover to stand over into the sea as farr to the westward as they can, to give us notices yf they see any fleet commyng this way, that wee may have some tyme to be lose from our anchors, and that you will wryte to the port of Rye to doe the lyke.

And satysfacion for the charge shall be made here by the Threasorer of Her Majesties Navie,[4] Rere-Admyrall of the Fleet. And wee doe further pray you to cause the Mayor of Dover to send about hither to the Downes 50 tonnes of ballast, etc., but these must be presently [= *immediately*] dispatcht.

    Your loving freindes,
        T Howard    W Raleigh [*sic*]

This 27 of August 1599

---

1. René de Rieux, sieur de Sourdéac, an adherent of the French king, Henry IV, was anxious for English assistance in keeping out the Spanish forces who had occupied the nearby Crozon peninsula.
2. It had been on the receipt of this news in July that an English fleet had been hastily mobilized: *CSPD 1598–1601*, *passim* and above, Letter 119. Another message from the Governor of Brest had reached Dartmouth on 23 August warning that an attempted invasion might be expected any day: ibid., p. 307. The '200 sayle', however, turned out to be a Dutch fleet returning from the Canaries.
3. A 'pink' = a small, fast vessel with a narrow stern.
4. Sir Fulk Greville (1554–1628), appointed in September 1598: Hasler II, p. 220.

---

## 121. To Sir Robert Cecil [from Sherborne], 2 February [1600][1]

Hatfield, CP173/36, *HMC Salisbury* VII, p. 55, dated ?1596–7. In Ralegh's hand.
Edwards II, p. 224, dated ?1600/1601.

## NAVAL INTELLIGENCE

[*addressed*]   To the right honorabell Sir Robert Cecyll knight, Principall Secritorye, etc.   Hast haste post haste   W Ralegh
[*endorsed*]   Sir W Ralegh

Sir: If my newse be stale it cost mee butt the labor to write it. A townsmans sonn of Sherburne hath bynn in Spayne in a French bottume [= *ship*] and is now returned. He departed Lysborne [*Lisbon*] the 15 of January, which is late [= *recently*], and reporteth for certeyne that the fleet of treasor is returned,[2] all butt onn great shipp which is doubted of. They had by common fame 17 millions.

Hee spake with divers soldiers at Cascales [*Cascais near Lisbon*] wher ther ar assembled 2000 [*men*] reddy to be imbarked in 30 sayle of shipps. Thos soldiers knew no other butt that they were bo[u]nd for Flanders. It may be for Irland or for sume other purpose.

They take up our small men of warr very fast, not only with the good saylinge Dunkirk[er]s, butt cussen [= *deceive*] them with Frenche bottumes which the Inglishe suspect not. This that I write yow, yow may assure your sealf to be trew.

        Yours as your sarvante,
        W Ralegh

I never receved on worde from my Lord Cobhame,[3] neather of his sute nor of his cumminge[4] or other matter this 3 weekes. Yow have many letters of myne: I pray returne sume awnswere.
    Candelmas Day

---

1. See note 2.
2. Similar news reached London from Liège on 7 April 1600: *CSPD 1598–1601*, p. 419. This time it was substantially correct, the Spanish vessels carrying the American silver arriving towards the end of February, although the main fleet did not return until May: Wernham, *Return of the Armadas*, p. 319.
3. See above, Letter 110, note 8. In July 1600 Ralegh and Cobham went together to Dunkirk: Collins 1746, II, p. 206.
4. Cobham was endeavouring to acquire from the Queen a lease of Otford Park: Collins II, *passim*, and Clark, *English Provincial Society*, p. 262. In September 1600 he and Cecil were Ralegh's guests at Sherborne: Collins II, p. 214.

## 122. TO SIR ROBERT CECIL, [FEBRUARY 1600]¹

Hatfield, CP19/66, *HMC Salisbury* IV, p. 78, dated 1590. In Ralegh's hand.
Edwards II, p. 199, dated 1590.²

### THE ARMY IN IRELAND

[*addressed*]  To the right honorabell Sir Robert Cecyll knight, Principall Secritory to Her Majestye

[*endorsed*]  1599  Sir Walter Raleigh to my master

Sir: I beseich yow to signefye Her Majesties pleasure to my Lord Deputye of Irlande,³ because his lordship is reddy to depart, concerning this gentelman⁴ on whom Her Majestye hath bestowed Poores [*Power's*]⁵ companye.

    Your honors to do yow services,
        W Ralegh

1. See below, note 3.
2. Edwards misread the endorsement, but noted that Cecil was not then Principal Secretary.
3. Charles Blount, Lord Mountjoy, who landed at the Head of Howth in Dublin Bay on 26 February 1600: C. Falls, *Mountjoy: Elizabethan General*, 1955, p. 119.
4. Not identified.
5. Probably Sir Henry Power who, on Essex's departure, had been put in command of all the English forces in Ireland (*CCM 1589–1600*, p. 327) and who in March 1600, having been replaced by Mountjoy, was offered Sir Warham St Leger's company in Leix: APC XXX, pp. 171, 179. But it may have been one of the many other Powers, e.g. 'a brother to Captain Poor' who is referred to in April 1599 as the Earl of Essex's servant (*HMC Salisbury* IX, p. 137), or the Captain William Power who in September 1599 commanded a company of 150 foot (Fynes Moryson II, p. 254).

---

## 123. TO SIR ROBERT CECIL [FROM DURHAM HOUSE, FEBRUARY/MARCH 1600]¹

Hatfield, CP90/150, *HMC Salisbury* X, pp. 439–40. In Ralegh's hand.
BL, Addit. 4106, f. 59, a transcript of the original made for Birch.
Murdin, 1759, pp. 811–12; Edwards II, pp. 222–3, dated February–August 1600.

### MY LORD OF ESSEX

[*addressed*]  To the right honorabell Sir Roberte Cecyll knight, Principall Secritory to Her Majestye

[*endorsed*]  Sir Walter Ralegh 1601

Sir: I am not wize enough to geve yow advise, butt, if yow take it for a good councell to relent towards this tirant yow will repent it when it shalbe to late. His mallice is fixt and will not evaporate by any [of] your mild courses [of action] for he will ascribe the alteration to Her Majesties pusillanimitye and not to your good nature, knowing that yow worke butt uppon her humer and not out of any love towards hyme. The less yow make hyme the less he shalbe able to harme yow and yours, and if Her Majesties favor faile hyme he will agayne decline to a comon parson. For after revenges feare them not, for your own father [Lord Burghley] that was esteemed to be the contriver of Norfolks[2] ruin, yet his soon followeth your fathers soonn and loveth hyme. Humors of men succeed [= are inherited] not, butt grow by occasions and accidents of tyme and poure [power]. Summersett made no revendge on the Duke of Northumberlands[3] heares [heirs]; Northumberland that now is thincks not of Hattons[4] issew; Kelloway lives that murderd the brother of Horsey[5] and Horsey lett hyme go by all his life tyme. I could name yow a thousand of thes and therfore after feares ar butt profesies, or rather conjectures, from causes remote.[6] Looke to the present and yow do wisely. His soonn shalbe the youngest earle of Ingland butt on[7] and if his father be now keipt down Will Cecill[8] shalbe abell to keip as many men att his heeles as hee, and more to[o]. Hee may also mache [= marry] in abetter howse then his, and so that feare is not worth the fearinge. Butt if the father continew he wilbe able to break the branches and pull up the tree, root and all. Lose not your advantage: if yow do I rede [= predict] your destiney.

    Yours to the end,
        W R

[left-hand margin]    Lett the Queen hold Bothwell[9] while she hath hyme. He will ever be the canker of her estate and sauftye. Princes ar lost by securetye and preserved by prevention. I have [fore]seen the last of her [the Queen's] good dayes and all ou[r]s after his libertye.

---

1. No exact date can be established and Ralegh did not even mention the 'tyrant' by name, but there can be little doubt that it was the Earl of Essex he was inveighing against (see below, note 7). Essex had been put under arrest on 1 October 1599, but Ralegh was clearly writing at a time when the Queen and her ministers were weakening in their resolve to punish him. In February 1600 there were rumours to that effect concerning Cecil, and in March Queen Elizabeth's former favourite was freed from custody and allowed, under some restraint, to return to his own house: *DNB*, sub Devereux, Robert, 2nd Earl of Essex. By March 15 Ralegh himself had been given the cold shoulder at Court and was hardly likely to be addressing Cecil with such self-confidence: *HMC De L'Isle and Dudley* II, pp. 97, 98.

2. Thomas Howard, 4th Duke of Norfolk, executed for treason in 1572, whose second son, also Thomas, had been restored in blood in 1584 and in 1597 summoned to Parliament as Lord Howard of Walden.
3. Edward Seymour, eldest son of the Protector.
4. Henry Percy, 9th Earl of Northumberland, whose father had committed suicide in 1585, caused, it was commonly believed, by the machinations of Sir Christopher Hatton.
5. Two of Ralegh's West Country neighbours whose exact identity has not been established: see John Roberts, 'Kelloway lives', *Devon and Cornwall Notes and Queries*, XXXVII, 1995, pp. 271–3.
6. Cecil may have confided his dynastic fears to Ralegh, but it is far more likely that Ralegh was intent on arousing them.
7. The Earl's son and heir had been born in January 1591, confirmation, if such be needed, that Ralegh was targeting the Earl of Essex.
8. Cecil's son, a sure route to his father's heart.
9. The 4th Earl, husband of Mary Queen of Scots.

---

## 124. To Sir Robert Cecil from Durham House, 15 March 1600

Hatfield, CP68/103, *HMC Salisbury* X, p. 71. Written by a clerk, with subscription and signature in Ralegh's hand.

Edwards II, p. 201.

## RECOMMENDATION OF A HISTORY

[*addressed*]  To the right honorable Sir Robert Cecyll knight, Her Majesties Principall Secretary

[*endorsed*]  15 March 1599   Sir Walter Raleigh to my master

Sir: I have perused this translated storie of the Conquest of Portugall and the warrs of Africa[1] and have corrected somethings therein. For the rest I see nothing in the booke but what may well passe.[2] If your honnor please to give allowance therof, which I humblie desire in favor of the translator.[3] And so do take my leave from Dirrham House the xvth of March 1599.

    Your honors to do yow services,
      W Ralegh

1. Jeronimo Conestaggio, *The Historie of the Uniting of the Kingdom of Portugall to the Crowne of Castile containing the last warres of the Portugals against the Moores of Africke, the end of the house of Portugall and change of that government*, London 1600. First published in Genoa in 1585, it was written from a Catholic point of view, for example depicting the Duke of Alva as a hero. The English version was dedicated to the Earl of Southampton.

2. Since 1599 there had been a return to stringency in licensing, the printing of 'Englishe historyes' having to be 'allowed by some of Her Majesties Privie Counsell'. Ralegh, then, was acting as a friend rather than as an official referee.
3. Edward Blount (fl. 1588–1632), who was a translator as well as a stationer, but he attributed the translation to 'a respected friend'.

---

## 125. To Sir Robert Cecil [from Sherborne], 27 March 1600

Hatfield, CP78/7, *HMC Salisbury* X, p. 84. Written by Ralegh in a particularly poor hand, the address more than usually brief.

Edwards II, pp. 202–3.

### YOUNG CECIL AT SHERBORNE

[*addressed*]   To the right honorabell Master Secretarye
[*endorsed*]   27 March 1600   Sir Walter Ralegh to my master

Sir: Because I know that yow can receve no pleasinger newse from hence then to here of your beloved creture[1] I thought good to lett yow know of his good health, and wheras I wrat in my last[2] that he was a littell trobled with a looseness I thank God he is no[w] freed therof and I assure yow better in health and strenght then ever I knew hyme. His stomake that was heretofore weake is altogether amended and douth now eat well and digest perfetly. I hope this eare [= *air*] will agree exceedingly with hyme. He is also better keipt to his booke then any wher elce.[3]

This is all I can say from this poore place and that I am ever your poorest and trewest frind and sarvent,
        W Ralegh

This 27 of March

---

1. William, Sir Robert Cecil's motherless eldest son, aged ten. He went to Sherborne about 22 March and stayed there until the autumn: Collins 1746, II, p. 181, *HMC Salisbury* X, p. 459.
2. Missing.
3. Robert Cecil was later to despair of his son's scholarship, declaring that he had come down from Cambridge not knowing six words of Latin: A. Cecil, *Life of Robert Cecil*, 1915, pp. 367–9.

## 126. To Lord Cobham [from Sherborne], 6 April [1600][1]

PRO, SP12/279/60, *CSPD 1601–3*, p. 27, dated ?1601. In Ralegh's hand.
Edwards II, pp. 203–4.

### THE GOVERNORSHIP OF JERSEY

[*addressed, by a clerk*] To the right honorable my very good lord the Lord Cobham
[*no endorsement*]

I cann write your lordshipp nothing from hence butt that wee live. I have written to Master Secritory [*Cecil*] that I would be gladd that Her Majestye weare butt proved [= *decided*] for Pawletts matter,[2] though I hope not after it, or ought elce.[3] Butt if ther be neather honor nor profitt I must begynn to keip sheep by tyme.[4]

In speaking with my cussen Brett,[5] a very honest gentelman, he cumplayned to me what abuse was offred your lordship aboute your wood sales by [= *near*] Charde.[6] It is certayne that the land will not be lett for half the valew hereafter when ther is left no tree upon it to build or mend a tenement, and it semes they have sold the very hedgro[w]s. Wheruppon I desired my cussen Brett to enquire more particulerly of the matter and this day hee sent me this inclosed letter.[7] I thought good to lett your lordship know of it for thes hireling officers will undo us all.[8]

God hold your lordship in the minde to cum to the Bathe.[9] If your lordshipp receve awnswere that Bakers[10] howse is taken up it is butt for me and your lordship may half [*have*] the onn half notwithstanding.

I am wher I can do your lordship no services. I will not therfore pester yow with idell words in which I cann butt profess what I would more willingly execute.

   Till when and ever your lordships absolutely to cummande,
    W Ralegh

I beseich your lordship to remember me to my Lorde Thomas [*Howard of Walden*].

6 of Aprill att night.

1. See note 2.
2. Sir Anthony Paulet, Governor of Jersey, was known to be dying early in 1600 and did so late in July: *CSPD 1598–1601*, pp. 442, 457.
3. Ralegh had already failed in his hopes of becoming a Privy Councillor and of being Vice-Chamberlain: Collins 1746, II, pp. 156, 179.

4. Cf. Letter 5, 'I would disdayn it as miche as to keap sheepe.' It was noted on 19 April 1600 that 'Sir Walter Rawley is gon into the cowntrey, unsatisfied.': ibid., p. 188. He did in fact get the governorship of Jersey: for his patent (dated 26 August 1600) see Rymer's *Foedera*, XVI, p. 398 and Cayley 1806, II, pp. 382–6.
5. Alexander Brett of White Stanton, Sheriff of Somerset 1599–1600: see below, Letter 165, note 16.
6. The Brookes, Lord Cobham's family, had come from Somerset and owned land at Chard. Between Chard and White Stanton lay many fine oak woods: Collinson, *Somerset*, 1791, III, pp. 303–4. Cf. Edwards who personalizes the word 'Charde'.
7. Not preserved.
8. See below, Letters 141, 144, etc.
9. See below, Letter 128.
10. Dr Baker, one of the physicians who provided accommodation for their patients, among them, in 1595, the Earl of Pembroke: A.L. Rowse, *Ralegh and the Throckmortons*, p. 194. Cf. Edwards who read the name as 'Bate'.

---

## 127. TO SIR ROBERT CECIL FROM SHERBORNE LODGE, 21 APRIL 1600

Hatfield, CP78/83, *HMC Salisbury* X, p. 120. Written by a clerk but subscribed and signed by Ralegh.

Edwards II, pp. 204–5.

## HENRY CAREW, RECUSANT

[*addressed*] To the right honorable Sir Robert Cecyll knight, Her Majesties Principall Secretary

[*endorsed*] 1600 xxith April Sir Walter Raleighe to my master In favour of Master Henry Carye [*sic*]

It may please your honor: I am much importuned by my cosen, Master Henry Carew,¹ to desire your favour towards his distressed sonne,² that his enlargement out of prison maie be procured by good bands [= *bonds*], sufficient suretie or by anie other meanes that were possible. The gentleman offreth 1000*li* caution [= *guarantee*] or a greater sume if it maie be accepted, to have his sonne out upon anie conditions that shalbe required, and his earnest solicitation importuneth me to move yow to direct what course you shall thinke fytt in your honorable wisedome.³

And so do humblie take my leave, from Sherborn Lodg the 21th of Aprill 1600.

   Your honors to do yow service,
    W Ralegh

1. Of Hamworthy near Poole, Dorset, who himself appears on a list of recusants in October 1598 and again in May 1600: Hutchins, *Dorset 1731*, III, p. 359 and *APC* XXIX, p. 203 and XXX, p. 311. Hutchins says he was of a younger branch of the Carews of Antony in Cornwall, and if so this was enough for Ralegh to call him 'cousin'.
2. Also Henry, he was educated at the English college at Eu in Normandy, whence he went to Madrid in the service of a member of the King of Spain's Council. Against his father's advice he returned to England early in 1599, was arrested at Weymouth and accused before Lord Bindon and other Dorset magistrates of having spoken in favour of Spain against the Queen: *CSPD 1598–1601*, p. 186 and *HMC Salisbury* IX, p. 155 and X, p 308.
3. Bindon continued to hound both father and son, and in 1602 was cautioned by Cecil for ignoring the Queen's wish to show clemency. Lord Chief Justice Popham continued to regard the elder Carew as 'a most dangerous man', but Ralegh was said to be confident that if young Henry were liberated he could 'bring him to Church': *HMC Salisbury* XII, pp. 229, 244 and 332.

## 128. To Lord Cobham from Bath, 29 April [1600][1]

PRO, SP14/1/57, *CSPD 1603–10*, p. 5, dated ?1603. In Ralegh's hand. The manuscript is torn at the right-hand corner.

Edwards II, p. 206, dated 1600.

### EXPECTING COBHAM AT BATH

[*addressed*] To the right honorabell my very good lorde the Lorde Cobhame geve thes

My worthy lorde: Here we attend yow and have dunn this senight [= *week*] and [*we*] murne yowr absence, the rather because we feare that your m[ind] is changed. I pray lett us here from yow att least, for if yow cum not we will go hevely home and make butt short tariinge here.[2] My wife will dyspaire ever to see yow in thes parts if your lordship cume not now. We can butt longe for yow and wyshe yow as [?*sharing*] owre lives whersoever [?*you be*].[3]

Your lordships ever most faythfull to honor yow most,
W Ralegh

Bath the 29 of Aprill

1. In 1600, Cobham, preocccupied with several suits at Court and with his impending marriage to Lady Kildare, one of the Queen's maids of honour, put off an intended visit to Bath: Collins 1746, II, pp. 187, 192, 193. On the very day this letter was written he was said to be in too much pain to go to the Court: *HMC Salisbury* X, p. 129.
2. They stayed another two weeks.
3. Edwards inserts 'owne' after 'owre' but this adds nothing to Ralegh's sycophantic phraseology.

### 129. To Sir John Gilbert II, 26 May [1600]¹

PRO, SP9/55/9, an eighteenth-century transcript of an untraced original, with blanks indicating partial illegibility. The words enclosed within asterisks have been supplied by the editors.² An interesting text, not hitherto published. Spelling suggests that the original letter was written by Ralegh.

## A DISPUTED PRIZE

[*addressed*]  For Her Majesties especyall affaires   To my verie loving nephew Sir John Gilbert knight³ at Dartmouth   Hast post hast with speed
[*no endorsement recorded*]

I sent yow worde by my last letters of the clayme which is made to your prize⁴ by the States [*of Holland*], since which tyme I have lerned that their pretences is [*sic*] not so vehement and that they clayme butt a part [? *of the cargo*] and the shipp, which is certenly, if they mistake it not, is [*sic*] belonginge to Heland⁵ and was fraughted for Brasill before the last restraynte and proclimation⁶ and therfore we shall [?*should*] not moche strive for the parts of her.⁷ Bestow no cost on her, nether suffer her impelments [= *gear*] to be conveyed away for yow will pay for all [*that*] is missinge. Take heed that yow deliver no thirds [= *share of the profits*] to your [*ship's*] cumpany *for* that will draw deipe in your *purse* if it be recovered, and if but a *part is* recovered yet that part will eat out your share, and that which the cumpany *have* yow can never recover. W[*het*]her this milder proceedinge of the Duch be tolde mee to make yow more secure I cannot tell, or w[*het*]her it be so in deed. Therfore use your discretion. But howsoever it be, in makinge hast awaye with the goods, though to some loss, cann be no harme. Butt putt *everything* in the Maior's [*of Dartmouth's*] hands *or some other person's* of creditt, for take heed, *for if you leave* them to the cumpany *you* may be only undun. For the rest yow can awnswer no more then yow receve. Look to it therfore. Ther is notorious exclamation [= *clamour*] for the Frenchman, and I think yow will finde it a Frenchman in deed and the fact cummitted since the prize came awaye.⁸ Take heed that yow disavow it, and that yow tuch nothinge that was taken out of her, for if yow do yow ar undon forever. Lett them awnswere it that did it, undo not yoursealf to save others, for no man can helpe yow therin. Yow had a letter to have a commission out of the [*High Court of*]

Admiraltye.⁹ Send me that letter that I may gett out that cummission if I finde it best by councell [= *legal advice*] so to do. Take heed that yow be cleane fingerd about the Frenche and when your shipp cumes do not your sealf so much as know any of them till they cleare themsealvs. I pray beleve mee and follow my councell or elce yow must trust to yoursealf.

I pray send mee word what yow have don *by* Burrell¹⁰ or any elce.

    Your loving unkell,¹¹
        W Ralegh

The 26 of May

I have sent yow the commission yow sent for.

---

1. See notes 4 and 11. Possibly from London.
2. The transcriber does not indicate the number of illegible words, but they seem by the context to be only single ones.
3. Eldest son of Sir Humphrey (ob. 1583) and also nephew and heir of Sir Humphrey's brother Sir John I (ob. 1596). He was about 25 years old in 1600, so Ralegh was some 13 years his senior.
4. Young Gilbert, with various partners, was the leader in capturing many prizes, most of them of doubtful legality, during the last five years of the Queen's reign. Although the text of this letter which has come down to us has no indication of the year, various bits of evidence point to 1600 when, on February 25, John Chamberlain, writing from London, reported that Gilbert had taken a Venetian ship 'to Sir Walter Ralegh's use': Sarah Williams (ed.), *Letters of John Chamberlain*, Camden Society 1861, pp. 68–9. On March 16 of that year, the Privy Council considered 'a complainte by certaine Netherlanders as also by some Englishe merchauntes on behalf of the Venetyans for a sugar prize taken by the shippes of Sir John Gilbert knight and Richard Drake esquier [the latter of Esher in Surrey, brother of the late Sir Bernard Drake of Musbury in Devon]' and referred the matter for speedier conclusion than was likely in the High Court of Admiralty to the Commissioners for Causes of Depredation: *APC* XXX, p. 173. On 24 June, when the Privy Council discussed the matter further (ibid., p. 424), the prize ship was named as the *Mary* of Flushing. Presumably she was taken after she had been to Venice for a cargo of sugar, reported by Chamberlain (Williams, loc. cit.) to be worth £9–10,000. For the activities of English men-of-war in the Mediterranean at this time see also K.R. Andrews, 'Sir Robert Cecil and Mediterranean Plunder', *English Historical Review*, 87, 1972, passim.
5. Either a mistake by the transcriber for 'Holland' or a misreading of 'Zealand'.
6. Probably refers to the Queen's proclamation of 8 February 1699 forbidding the seizure of ships and goods belonging to nations with which England was not at war: P.L. Hughes and J.F. Larkin (eds), *Tudor Royal Proclamations* III, p. 197.
7. Confirms Ralegh's personal involvement in the enterprise. On 2 March the ship employed by Gilbert was said to be 'a bark of Sir Walter Raleighs': *HMC Portland* II, p. 21.
8. This must be another prize ship which had not yet reached Dartmouth.
9. Presumably refers to Gilbert's commission of reprisal, i.e. his licence to seize enemy shipping.
10. Not identified.
11. Further proof, if such be needed, that this letter is of an earlier rather than of a later date by which time relations between Ralegh and Gilbert had deteriorated: see below, Letters 153 and

157. On 22 September 1600, Gilbert was ordered to accompany one of the Queen's 'messengers' to London to appear before the Judge of the Admiralty and the rest of the Commissioners for Depredations or to give his word, with sureties, that he would appear within 10 days of receiving a warrant: *APC* XXX, p. 660.

---

130. TO THOMAS REYNELL, CHRISTOPHER AND ROBERT HAMLYN AND TO JOHN SWETE, FROM SHERBORNE, 1 SEPTEMBER 1600

New York Public Library, Arents Collection 5682, bound into a copy of John Prince's *Worthies of Devon* with a note, quite erroneous, that it was written to a Thomas Prince. Written by a clerk and signed by Ralegh.

Sotheby's *Catalogue*, 14 December 1906, Lot 451, *in extenso*, but not otherwise hitherto published.

## VENLAKE TIN MINE

[*addressed*]   To my loving frends Thomas Reynell esquier,[1] and to Chr[istopher] and Robert Hamlyn[2] or to anie of them   And likewise to Master John Sweete,[3] to whom the lettere is first to be delivered

Whereas I wrate before that each partie pretending or clayming tytle to the tynworke called Venlake[4] should have true copies (taken out of the originals) of all the depositions and interrogatories whereupon anie had been examined, taken or ministred by vertue of any commission, wherby their councell might be instructed, as was desired by both parties. Now I understand that you refuse to deliver the copies as I required but wold give them such as you copie out of other papers contrary to my directions. Therefore I do now againe require you to deliver to Master Sweete the Steward the true and perfect copies of all the depositions and interrogatories which are in anie of your custodies concerning this title, that the poore men[5] may not be driven to such often and great charges and troble, and that they maie acquaint their councell therewith to be ready at my coming down into the cuntrie[6] where I shortlie purpose to heare the cause and order the state of the title my selfe. And if you refuse at this direction to deliver the depositions and interrogatories examined before the Steward to agree with the originals, to theis persons or some of them, I will without faile give order to deliver them and award them the possession of the tynwork.

So fare you well. From Sherborn the first of September 1600.

  Your loving frend,
    W Ralegh

1. Later Sir Thomas, of East Ogwell, near Newton Abbot in south Devon.
2. Not identified. A fairly common name in Devon.
3. Not identified; presumably a clerk, possibly with some legal expertise.
4. Not identified; probably in south Devon, but see below, note 6. 'Venn' (= Fen) or 'Venny' is a fairly common constituent of Devon place-names and 'lake' also denotes the presence of water.
5. Possibly working tinners in dispute with owners of tinworkings, but could also refer to rival owners. Details of the case have not been found.
6. His ultimate destination was Cornwall (see below, Letter 133) but on the way thither on 27 October he attended a Stannary Parliament for Devon at Crockern Tor on the south-western slopes of Dartmoor: H.P.R. Finberg, 'An unrecorded Stannary Parliament', *DAT* LXXXII, 1950, p. 296. No record of the hearing of particular grievances has survived but a substantial number of legislative measures was approved, including 'An act for the drawing of water unto Tinne-mills' which contained a proviso protecting the interests of Plymouth: ibid., pp. 308–9. See also below, Letter 135, note 5.

---

## 131. TO LORD COBHAM FROM SHERBORNE, 14 OCTOBER [1600][1]

PRO, SP12/260/61, *CPSD 1595–7*, p. 294, dated ?1596. Written by Ralegh, addressed by a clerk.

Edwards II, p. 255, dated ?1602.

### RETURN FROM JERSEY

[*addressed*]   To my honorable good lord the Lord Cobham, Lord Warden of the Cinque Portes

My best lorde: I do only write yow thes to salute yow and to desire to here from yow how your particuler and our generall worlde movethe, and withall that yow will vouchsauf to lett me know how the Queen accepted the Jewell.[2] For the littell common wealth whence I came [*Jersey*] I will leve to trobell your lordship withall till God send us to meet. I am now preparing my miserabell jurney into Cornwale:[3] from thence I will hast towards you, wher and elce wher I will ever remayne your most trew frinde and sarvant,
  W Ralegh

Bess remembers her sealf to your lordship with a challendg that she never hard from yow.

I beseich your lordship to favor this poore man[4] who is worthy estimation.

Sherburne this 14th of October.

1. Ralegh went to Cornwall on or about 6 November: see below, Letter 133.
2. Possibly a present in acknowledgement of his appointment, on 26 August 1600 (Collier (ed.), *Egerton Papers*, p. 314), to the Governorship of Jersey.
3. On Stannary business: see above, Letter 130, note 6, and below, Letters 133 and 135.
4. Probably Paul Ivey, a military engineer: see below, Letter 132. As Warden of the Cinque Ports, Cobham might have need of an expert in coastal fortifications.

---

## 132. To Sir Robert Cecil from Sherborne, 15 October 1600

Hatfield, CP250/14, *HMC Salisbury* X, p. 352. In Ralegh's hand.
Edwards II, pp. 206–9.

### THE DEFENCES OF JERSEY

[*addressed*] To the right honorabell Sir Robert Cecyll knight, Principall Secritorye to Her most excelent Majestye

[*endorsed*] 1600 xvth October  Sir Walter Raleigh to my master  By Master Pawle Ivye[1]

May it pleas your honor to receve knowledge from this bearer, Master Paule Ivey, what wee have determined for the fort Isabella Bellisima in the Ilett,[2] wher wee have left workmen to finishe as mich as this season of the yeare will permitt and the rest to be dun in March following. The charge wherof wilbe exceedinge great, as Master Ivey uppon his conscience can wittness, and the profitt of the Iland so farr under the common valuation as untill your honor see the kings [= *the Crown's*] own liger booke yow will not beleve. But howsoever it succeed I hold my sealf unmeasurable bound to Her Majestye for her gratius respect to mee therein,[3] and I will never thinck of any peny receite till that peece of worke be finished and past the recovery of any enemye, be it butt for the name sake which I have presumed to christen it by beinge before without any denomination att all.

It had byn very happy for me if Paule Ivy had remayned to finishe what he began ther, which I assure your honor by the livinge God is as prayse worthy a worke both for his judgment, invention and industry in savinge charge as ever any man behelde, and I have not seene a devize of that state and pride in any place of Europe. Sir, I do assure yow the poore man hathe an excelent gift in thes works and that which is rarely joined to such knowledge, as mich trewth and honestye as any man can have. Your honor, in my poore judgment, shall do Her Majestye good service to be a mean for his reliefe, for such another will not be had.

For the accompts of the late Governoure [*Paulet*] the[*y*] ar strang to me, for Pawle Ivy did more with 300*li* then he [? *the Governor*] did afterward for 1000*li*,[4] and Pawle Ivy is fittest to be used in the accompts because he can cumpare worke to worke and judge of the rest better then a[*n*]y man can, for besyds the unmeasurabell reckninge made by Sir A[*myas*] Pawlett of Her Majesties monies, they ar not ashamed to aske 500*li* debt of Her Majestye dew to them[5] for Mountorguell.[6] I have vewed it and do not finde that I had any cummission to demolishe it, and to say trew it is a stately fort of great capacetye and both a countenance and cumfort to all that part of the Iland next unto Normandy, which stands in vew therof, so as untill I knew further Her Majesties pleasure I have left att myne owne charge sume men in it. And if a small matter may defend it it weare pitty to cast it down, having cost Her Majestyes father, brother and sister, withe her own charge, 10,000 mark[*s*] the erectinge.[7]

I will leve the rest untill my cumming from Cornwale and then lett yow know the estate of that poore place, the importance of it and how it hath bynn handled. Till then and ever I rest reddy to do yow all honor and service,

        W Ralegh

[S]herburn this 15 of October 1600

---

1. Of Christ's College, Cambridge, author of *The Practise of Fortification* and translator of William de Bellay's *Instructions for the Warrs*, both published in 1589, the year he had begun work on the defences of Jersey. Since then he had also worked at Portsmouth (1595–6), Ostend (1597) and at Pendennis Castle in Cornwall (1598–9): E.T. Nicholle, *Mont Orgueil Castle*, Jersey 1921, p. 61.
2. Elizabeth Castle on the island off St Helier, begun by Edward VI. When Paul Ivey was put in charge in 1594 the Queen promised him £500 towards expenses, which were apparently still owing in 1600 (Nicholle, ibid., p. 62), which is presumably why Ralegh repeatedly referred to him as a 'poor man'.
3. Ralegh was being exceedingly accommodating. By custom, the Governor of Jersey defrayed the cost of defending the island out of the Crown's revenues granted to him in his patent of appointment, but after the death of his predecessor in July 1600 it emerged that various other people had claims on them: *HMC De l'Isle and Dudley*, II, 475–9. See also Nicholle, op. cit., p. 64.

4. Edwards has '£2000', and similarly '20,000 marks' near the end of the letter.
5. See above, note 2.
6. Mont Orgueil or Gorey Castle on the east coast, which had served as the seat of government until 1594 when Paul Ivey had declared it too exposed to artillery attack. Attention then shifted to the new fort off St Helier on the south coast: Nicholle, op. cit., pp. 60–62.
7. It had been inspected by royal commissioners in 1531, 1551 and 1562, and between 1549 and 1567 some £4,000 had been spent on its refurbishment: BL, Lansd. 16, f. 85 and Nicholle, op. cit., pp. 43, 49 and 52. It still survives, more impressive to the eye than its Elizabethan successor.

---

## 133. To Lord Buckhurst and Sir Robert Cecil from Radford,[1] 4 November 1600

Hatfield, CP181/33, *HMC Salisbury* X, pp. 374–5. In Ralegh's hand.
Edwards II, pp. 209–10.

## THE PRICE OF TIN

[*addressed*]   To the right honorabell the Lorde of Buckhurst, Lorde High Treasourer of Inglande, and Sir Robert Cecyll knight, Principall Secritarye

[*endorsed*]   4 November 1600   Sir Walter Ralegh to my Lord Thresurer and to my master, from Radford by Master Connock[2]

May it pleas your honors, accordinge to the order which I had from yow[3] I have proceeded in[*to*] Cornwale and agreed with the tynners for a prize [= *price*] certayne,[4] twenty shillings in the thowsand [*weight*] less than I had cummission to geve them, which they desire by petition to have added and which for myne own poore oppinion I could wish that Her Majestye out of her own liberalletye should bestow on them.[5]

Master Brigame[6] and Master Cunnocke can informe your honors how I have proceeded, who can best judge what my littell creditt here hath dun in this bussness.

Master Cunnocke hyme sealf hath taken great paynes herein and furnisht mee with many good arguments and reasons. Your honors could not have imployed any man as I thincke both for his dillegence and knowledge of more sufficiencye.[7] Master Bulmers[8] offer of 29$li$ held us longe uppon that prize, and hath dun us mich wronge in this bussness, and had we not caled such a jurey as wee did of the principall gentelmen,[9] we had had a longe worke of it.

Ther ar yet many things to be dun, which this gentelman can better informe your honors of then mysealf, which your honors will take care of. For my sealf I have performed your cummandments and have littell elce to do butt to see promis keipt with thes poore men to whom my fayth is engaged,[10] and this bearer can informe your honors trewly wh[eth]er they tynners do not more rely theron then on all the rest of our argumentts. I will shortly attend yow mysealf and in the mean while I humble desire to be continewed in your favors and will remayne ever reddy to do all the honor and service I shall bee abell.

                W Ralegh

From Radford by Plymouth this 4th of November[11]

1. In the parish of Plymstock, east of Plymouth, the residence of Master Christopher Harris, Deputy Warden of the Cornish Stannaries.
2. Richard Connock of Calstock in Cornwall, MP for Bodmin in 1593, appointed Auditor of the Duchy of Cornwall in 1603: Hasler I, p. 640. A William Connock was with Ralegh in Guiana in 1595: Harlow, *Discoverie* 1932, p 36.
3. PRO, SP12/270/123, *CSPD 1598–1601*, p. 202, draft of a letter from the Queen to Ralegh, dated 31 May 1599, informing him of her decision to exercise her right to buy 'as much tin of Cornwall as has usually been exported' at a price more favourable to the tinners than they have been receiving from the dealers (see below, note 4). He is to call together representatives of the four Cornish stannaries and agree with them a minimum price. A *docquet* of the letter follows (ibid.), but at what date such an instruction reached Ralegh is not on record. It seems from Ralegh's letter printed here not to have come from the Queen herself and, after reconsideration, to have suggested a maximum price. Ralegh had been much occupied with the affairs of Jersey but it is unlikely that he would have delayed for very long his 'miserable journey into Cornwall'.
4. The reigning monarch (or his/her assigns) had for centuries possessed the right of pre-emption of tin, i.e. to buy it from the tinners (or their assigns) at his/her own price: G.R. Lewis, *The Stannaries*, Cambridge, Mass., 1908, pp. 142–6. The right had not been personally exercised by the Tudors but Queen Elizabeth had for short periods farmed it out to certain individuals for a consideration.
5. At this juncture Ralegh would appear to have been personally exercising the Crown's right of pre-emption: see below, note 11. In an undated draft letter from the Queen herself to the tinners (*CSPD 1601–3*, p. 507) the figure mentioned was £27 the thousandweight.
6. Thomas Brigham, a later patentee: see below, note 11.
7. See below, note 10.
8. Bevis Bulmer, a wealthy mine-owner. In October 1599 an offer he made to the Queen of £10,000 for a tin patent had been found unacceptable: *CSPD 1598–1601*, pp. 330–31.
9. Most of whom will have been interested parties as owners of land or of actual tinworkings.
10. Ralegh prided himself on his care of tinners of all ranks, and a major talking point at the meeting was a suggestion currently being made by the London Turkey merchants, who were exporters of pewter, of which tin was a major component, that the Queen should impose an extra duty of £6 per thousandweight on the export of raw tin. This would have depressed the price paid to the Cornishmen, and Ralegh and Connock will almost certainly have been agreed in their promise to oppose it at the highest level. On 7 December 1600 there was a meeting in London of all the interested parties, including Ralegh and Connock, but on

29 January the Council instructed customs officers to collect the new duty: *HMC Salisbury* X, p. 411 and *APC* XXXI, pp. 131–2. The Queen's letter to the tinners (above, note 5) may have followed, suggesting that both impositions were to be laid, which will have pleased nobody.

11. Within twelve months Ralegh was to be attacked in the House of Commons by Master Martin (probably Richard, MP for Barnstaple: Hasler I, p. 23 and III, pp. 275–6, and Murdin, p. 747) for his personal enjoyment of a monopoly of the pre-emption of tin. Ralegh defended himself by claiming that when tin had been 17s. and more, the working tinners had earned less than 2s. a week, 'but since my patent whosoever will work, be tin at what price soever, they have 4s a week truly paid.': Simonds D'Ewes, 1682, p. 646. He went on to point out that he was acting by virtue of his office of Lord Warden of the Stannaries, an indication that the 'patent' he referred to was no ordinary grant of monopoly rights such as other men possessed in respect of salt, starch, etc., but his appointment in 1585 as the Queen's deputy. Indeed, no ordinary grant to him is on record. Moreover, if further proof be needed, before the Queen's death, a patent of monopoly for the pre-emption of tin was granted to John Brigham and Humphrey Wemmes (*CSPD 1601–13*, p. 274), which must, in effect, have superseded Ralegh's involvement.

---

## 134. To Sir Robert Cecil from Sherborne, 13 November [1600][1]

Hatfield, CP250/102, *HMC Salisbury* X, p. 382. In Ralegh's hand. Edwards II, p. 256.

## NO NEWS

[*no address or endorsement*]

Sir: Since I wrate unto yow out of Cornwale [*sic*] of the agreement with the tynners [*Letter 133*] I have not hard from yow. I miche desire to know how our labors ar accepted of and how the world fareth. I linger here as longe as I cann to dispach my private affaires, except ther be cause to hasten me up.[2] I will herein be directed by yow and in all things elce disposed att your pleasure. I can write yow from hence no other newse butt that wee ar all, littell and great, in good health and ever yours faythfully to cummande wheresoever,

    W Ralegh

Sherburne the 13 of November

1. See above, Letter 133.
2. To London rather than back to his post in Jersey.

## 135. To Sir Robert Cecil from Sherborne, 15 November 1600

Hatfield, CP250/107, *HMC Salisbury* X, p. 383. Written by a clerk, with subscription and signature in Ralegh's hand.

BL, Add. 6177, p. 69, a later transcript.

Edwards II, pp. 211–12; Vera Gray, 'A leat on Roborough Down', *DAT* 122, 1990, pp. 77–8, from BL.

## WILLIAM CRYMES v. TOWN OF PLYMOUTH

[*addressed*] To the right honorable Sir Robert Cecyll knight, Her Majesties Principall Secretary

[*endorsed*] ·15 November 1600 Sir Walter Ralegh to my master in favour of Master Crymes

Sir: This gent[*leman*], Master Crymes,[1] hath erected certein clash mylls[2] uppon Roburghe Down[3] to work the tyn which upon that place is gott with extreame labour and charge out of the ground. And because the townsmen of Plymouth seeke to procure all the commoditie [= *advantage*] thereaboutes into their own hands they alleage that theis mylls are prejudiciall to them and that the course of their water which runneth through Plymouth is diverted, contrary to a statute.[4] I tooke the paines to view the river [*the leat*] and mylls. I found that in my opinion they [*the Queen*] could not disallow the building or using the same for that there are about 200 [*tin*]workes which must lie unwrought without the use of such clash mylls and the benefytt of that river, and no hindraunce at all to the water course. Otherwise Her Highness can receve no commoditie therebie and the poore tynners wilbe undone. I had an especiall care to satisfie them [*the townsmen of Plymouth*] and the tynners made an acte that those clash mylls shold not be prejudiciall to the towne.[5]

Notwithstanding they have procured *sub penas* out of the Starre Chamber to call the matter in question there, the matter being tryable and determinable in the Stannary Courtes where it now dependeth. But if this be sufferd to proceed in the Starre Chamber it will not be avaylable [= *be to no avail*] to speak of Her Majesties late imposition, or encrease of custome,[6] or to establish good lawes amongst tynners when others who can by a great purse or [*by*] procuring extraordinary meanes deminish to their power Her Majesties duties and the common benefytt of the people. I do humblie therefore desire your honorable favour in theire [*the tinners'*] behalfe, that when the question shall grow for this matter in the Starre Chamber that it maie be either respited untill my comming or dismissed to the place and nature of the proper tryall.[7] And so do humblie take my leave.

From my house at Shyrebourne the 15th of November 1600.
    Your honors to do yow service.
        W Ralegh

1. William Crymes, whose grandfather, a London haberdasher, had bought the former Buckland Abbey manor of Buckland Monachorum in 1546. He owned tin works and was a jurat of the Tavistock stannary: Vivian, *Devon*, p. 258, Joyce Youings, *Devon Monastic Lands*, Devon and Cornwall Record Society, New Series I, 1954, pp. 79–81 and Finberg, op. cit., p. 297.
2. Water-powered mills used for breaking up the tin ore.
3. Moorland north of Plymouth in the parish of Buckland Monachorum, across which Sir Francis Drake had diverted the River Meavy in 1590 to supply Plymouth with water. The city fathers were a formidable body, with whom Ralegh had never been on particularly friendly terms. Their chief ally was Thomas Drake, Sir Francis's brother and heir (*APC* XXXII, pp. 134–5), who, as it happened, had tinworks lower down: Gray, op. cit., p. 77. Cecil was the town's High Steward, a purely honorary post except in a crisis. Letters to him on 3 November accused 'the gentlemen', who claimed to have Ralegh's support, of acting 'only upon malice': *HMC Salisbury* XI, pp. 471–2.
4. Presumably 27 Elizabeth, cap. 20, 1585, an Act 'for Preservation of the Haven of Plymouth', which was concerned with pollution caused by the debris of tin-mining: *Statutes of the Realm*, ed. A. Luders, *et al.* 1810–28, IV, pt i., pp. 728–9.
5. At a Stannary Parliament for Devon called by Ralegh and held at Crockern Tor near Tavistock on 27 October 1600, it had already been agreed that tinners should not draw off water to the detriment of Plymouth: H.P.R. Finberg, op. cit., p. 309.
6. See above, Letter 133, note 10.
7. In 1601 the matter was referred to the Justices of Assize, but without being resolved: *CSPD 1601–3*, p. 97. It was finally settled in 1603 in favour of Crymes: R.N. Worth, *Calendar of Plymouth Municipal Records*, 1893, pp. 279–81. But see also above, Letter 130, note 6.

---

## 136. TO SIR ROBERT CECIL [?FROM LONDON, AFTER 17 JANUARY 1601][1]

Hatfield, CP186/132, *HMC Salisbury* X, p. 466. In Ralegh's hand.
Edwards II, pp. 260–61, first dated late 1602, corrected to early 1601.

## DEPARTURE OF ORSINI

[*addressed*]   To the right honorabell Master Secritarye
[*endorsed*]   Sir Walter Ralegh to my master

Sir: Ther came unto mee a gentelman from Flushing who saw the Duke Dun Virginia Ursini² ther. It is trew that hee was imbarked in a Fleminge [*ship*] att Dover, the winde not servinge for Her Majesties shipp to cum about.³ Now wh[*eth*]er this Zelander did cary hyme thither perforce, or whether hee desired it, hering of the Peace of Savoy,⁴ I know not, for I remember he tolde me that hee would see Holland and Zeland if that peace weare concluded. How he shalbe welcum to the Archduke⁵ I conceve not. I thought good to lett yow know this miche.

        Yours to do yow service,
           W Ralegh

1. See below, notes 2 and 3.
2. Virginio Orsini, Duke of Bracciano, nephew of the Grand Duke of Tuscany. According to a letter he wrote to his wife on 21 January, he had been well-received and lavishly entertained by the Queen: L. Hotson, *The First Night of Twelfth Night*, 1954, pp. 208–16. On 9 January, Ralegh and Cobham escorted him to Hampton Court and he and Ralegh ('Guatterrali') rode together from Gravesend to Chatham on the 13th to view the fleet: ibid., pp. 209, 213.
3. Orsini apparently returned to the Continent in some haste on or about 17 January. Unwilling to wait for the Queen's *Vanguard*, which was to have taken him across the Channel, he took passage from Dover on a Dutch ship which fell in with twenty of its compatriots lying in wait for an expected Spanish fleet: Hotson, p. 215.
4. Between Henry IV of France and the Duke of Savoy, concluded at Lyons on 17 January 1601, which severed Spain's principal land link with the Low Countries, the so-called 'Spanish Road': Wernham, *Return of the Armadas*, pp. 372–3.
5. The Cardinal Archduke Albert of Austria, nephew of Philip II of Spain, Governor of the Netherlands since 1596. Ralegh's intelligence was indeed sound: from Calais, Orsini went straight to Antwerp: *CSP Venetian, 1592–1603*, p. 457; *HMC Salisbury* XI, pp. 2, 12, 21 and 100. Neither his reasons for visiting the English Court nor the Queen's for making him so welcome are entirely explicable.

---

## 137. To Sir Edward Coke from Durham House, [between 20 February and 13 August 1601]¹

Holkham Hall, Norfolk, Holkham Library 746, S. de Ricci, *Handlist of Manuscripts ... at Holkham*, 1932, p. 62; *HMC Various Collections* IV, p. 325, *in extenso*. In Ralegh's hand.

V.T. Harlow, *The Discoverie of Guiana*, 1928, p. xxx, from *HMC*.

### EDWARD BAYNHAM TRAITOR

[*addressed*]   To the right worshipfull Master Aturney Generall
[*endorsed*]   Sir Walter Rawlye, his lettre to Sir Edward Coke
[*possibly in Coke's hand*]   Sir Walter Raleigh

Master Aturney: It would greatly expedite my bussness for Baynam[2] if yow would pleas to write me a few lines to this effect:– that where as I intreated yow to know whether Her Majestye might reape any profitt by Baynams death, or wh[eth]er Baynam weare farther in in any of thes treasons then the common sort of my Lord of Essex servants and followers, yow will awnswere that yow have looked into his estate and have delivered your knowledge. For the land in Essex yow shall order it as it shall pleas yow.[3]

  Your most assured loving frind,
   W Ralegh

Derham Howse this Monday morning.

1. See below, note 2.
2. Sir Edward Baynham, condemned to death on 20 February 1601 for complicity in Essex's rising and pardoned by the Queen on 13 August: *APC* XXXII, p. 153.
3. On 11 August 1601, the Lord Chancellor (Egerton) wrote to Robert Cecil to say that Baynham's pardon was signed, and that Ralegh's conveyance was ready but that it had been 'stayed' as Cecil had directed. Two days later, Sir Edward Coke, Attorney-General, wrote to say that he had done his best to complete the instrument and had Ralegh's promise that what his 'councillor' yielded should be performed: *HMC Salisbury* XI, pp. 332, 341. It was, indeed, rumoured not only that Ralegh had been instrumental in obtaining Baynham's release but that he had been paid for his services (William Camden, *History of ... Princess Elizabeth*, 1706, p. 636). However, there is no evidence that he acquired an estate in Essex.

---

### 138. To Sir John Gilbert II [?from London], 14 July [1601][1]

Philadelphia Free Library, Elkins Americana, 63. In Ralegh's hand, written in great haste. Not hitherto printed from the original.

PRO, SP9/55/12x, an eighteenth-century transcript, with minor errors.

J. Roberts, *DAT*, 100, 1968, p. 211, part only, from PRO.

## MISCELLANY OF NEWS

[*addressed*]  To my loving nephew Sir John Gilbert knight, governour of the fortts nire Plymouth, thes

Your man hath all his dyspaches. I marvaile that yow make no awnswere to my letter about your shipp which Master Secritory offred to vitell.[2] I wrat unto yow to send a man with the Spaniard. Newse here is none, butt that Ostend is hardly beseiged. Vere is in it.³ I thinck shortly to cum into Cornwale. Yow here of our new councelors.⁴ I am left out till the parlement they tell me, butt I take no thought for it.

I pray gett [*the nomination of*] sume burgeses if yow can and desire C[*hristopher*] Harris⁵ to write in my name for as many as he can procure. The parlement will be here in October.⁶

      Yours,

          W Ralegh

14 of July

1. See below, notes 2 and 3.
2. The *Refusal*. See Gilbert's letter to Cecil, of 25 July 1601, saying that she was already half-victualled by her captain and was now at Lisbon, victualled for five months: *CSPD 1601–3*, p. 72.
3. Ostend was under siege by the Archduke of Austria, Sir Francis Vere being in command of the defences: R.B. Wernham, *Return of the Armadas*, p. 374. Ralegh and Cobham had recently been there: ibid., p. 330.
4. On 29 June, the Earls of Worcester and Shrewsbury and the Vice-Chamberlain, Sir John Stanhope, were sworn of the Privy Council: *APC* XXXI, p. 467. That there were to be no further additions until Parliament assembled is confirmed by a letter the same day from Cecil to George Carew, in which he declares very robustly that, if he has his way, Ralegh will never be a member of the Council unless he surrenders his Captaincy of the Guard to Carew: J. Maclean (ed.), *Letters from Sir Robert Cecil to Sir George Carew*, Camden Society, 1964, p. 86.
5. See above, Letter 133, note 1.
6. Ralegh was to sit in this Parliament as senior knight of the shire for Cornwall.

---

## 139. TO SIR ROBERT CECIL FROM SHERBORNE, 13 AUGUST [1601]

Hatfield, CP43/84, *HMC Salisbury* X, p. 273–4. In Ralegh's hand, except for the address. Edwards II, pp. 226–7.

### BY SEA AND LAND

[*addressed*]   For Her Majesties speciall affaires   To the right honorable Sir Robert Cecyll knight, Principall Secretarly [*sic*] to Her Majesty at the Court   From Sherborne the 13th of August at 12 in the night

Post hast, hast post hast, with all spede

[*by Ralegh*]   Hast post hast hast for life   W Ralegh

[*postmasters*]  Sarum paste x in the fore none beinge Thursdaye
  Rec[*eived*] at Andever at 4 of the clocke in the after nonne the same Thur[*sday*]
  Rec[*eived*] at Basinge Stoke a[*t*] 8 of the clocke at nite the same daye
[*endorsed*]  13 August  Sir Walter Ralegh to my master

Sir: I humble thanck yow for your letter which I receved this 13th att night at Sherburne, dated from the Court the 11th, so it was to dayes and too nights cumminge. I my sealf went it in half a day less, and if ther [be *crossed out*] weare any danger it would be no otherwise handled. My Lord Cobhame stayd here butt on night butt went on for Cornwale.[1] I could not by any mean disswade hyme. I canot beleve that thos 80 sayle ar Spanierds if they weare seene so high up as St Mallos,[2] for no winde could force them in so farr that hath blowne. Butt if the[*y*] hover about the mouth of the Channell I am here nirer my charg[3] then att Lundun.

I have sent away your letter post to my Lord Cobhame. I humble thanck yow for Vivien.[4] Wee do wishe yow more cordially here then yow can wish your sealf. Tomorrow I go to Rushmore[5] agayne to take thorrow order. The trees I thinck may be released agayne to the first bwyers for they ar not so nire as I thought, and farr derer then worthe, and will stand yow, all wayes considered, 900*li*.[6] If yow send me your pleasure I will leve them. Rushmore will not be fitt for yow to cum to this yeare: it is so ruined as I canott lodge yow or my sealf therin.

I pray beleve that when all harts ar open and all desires tried [*sic*][7] that I am your poorest and your faythfullest frind to do yow service,
        W Ralegh

Sherburn the 13th of Aug[*u*]st att night when I receved yours.

[*left-hand margin*]  Bess returns yow her best wishes notwithstanding all quarrels.[8]

---

1. On 19 July, the Earl of Northumberland had written to Cobham that he understood that he and Ralegh had gone to Sherborne. However, their departure must have been delayed: *CSPD 1601–3*, p. 71.
2. See a report to Cecil from Weymouth, on 7 August, that his informant had been asked by a Spanish fleet of 50 sail at St Malo for a pilot for Flanders or England. An unlikely story, as Ralegh was quick to recognize: ibid., p. 82. But see below, Letter 140.
3. As Lord Lieutenant of Cornwall.
4. Hannibal Vyvyan, esquire (1554–1610), of Trelowarren in the parish of St Mawgan in Meneage, a Vice-Admiral of Cornwall, Captain of St Mawes Castle and Sheriff of Cornwall in 1601–2, he had lately been appointed Attorney-General of the Duchy of Cornwall: Hasler III, p. 559 and *HMC Salisbury* XI, p. 332.

5. A hunting lodge in the parish of Berwick St John, Wiltshire. Cecil had recently been acquiring property there.
6. Cecil's own steward put the figure at £1,000.
7. Ralegh's memory of the liturgy of Holy Communion was slightly at fault, the last word in the *Book of Common Prayer* being 'known'.
8. Cf. below, Letter 140.

---

## 140. To Lord Cobham from Sherborne, 13 August 1601

PRO, SP12/264/81, *CSPD 1595–7* [sic], p. 481, Plate 7. In Ralegh's hand, except for address, postscript by Lady Ralegh. Not previously printed *in extenso*.

### SAME NEWS

[*addressed*] For Her Majestes speciall affairs
To the right honorable my very good lord the Lord Cobham, Lord Warden of the Cinck Ports, Her Majestes Leiftenant Generall of Kent, att Plymouth [*another hand*] From Shirborne the 13th of August at 12 in the night Post hast, hast post, with spede [*in Ralegh's hand*] Hast post hast for life W Ralegh
[*postmasters*] Crewkern at 10 before noone August 14 Hunytun a [? = *half*] paste fow at after non Ry[*ceived*] after 7 in the night thes

I have sent your lordship Master Secritores letter,[1] by which yow may perceve that 80 sayle of Spanierds ar entred in to our seas as high as St Mallos. Your lordship may see that if yow weare not loose [?*travelling*] yow should be tied above [? *at Court*] for awhile. If yow needs will into Cornwale then make hast or I thinck yow wilbe sent for. I can say no more butt that I am your lordshipps before all that love [*sic*].

      W Ralegh

and if I could disgest [*digest*] this last word of Sur Waltars letta I wold exp[*r*]es my love likewies, but unly this I agree and am on in all with Sur Waltar and most in his love to you. I pray hasten your returne for the elecket [= *election's*][2] sake, that we may see the bathe to gether.

      Your trew poour frind,
         E Ralegh

1. To which Letter 139 was his answer.
2. The forthcoming parliamentary election.

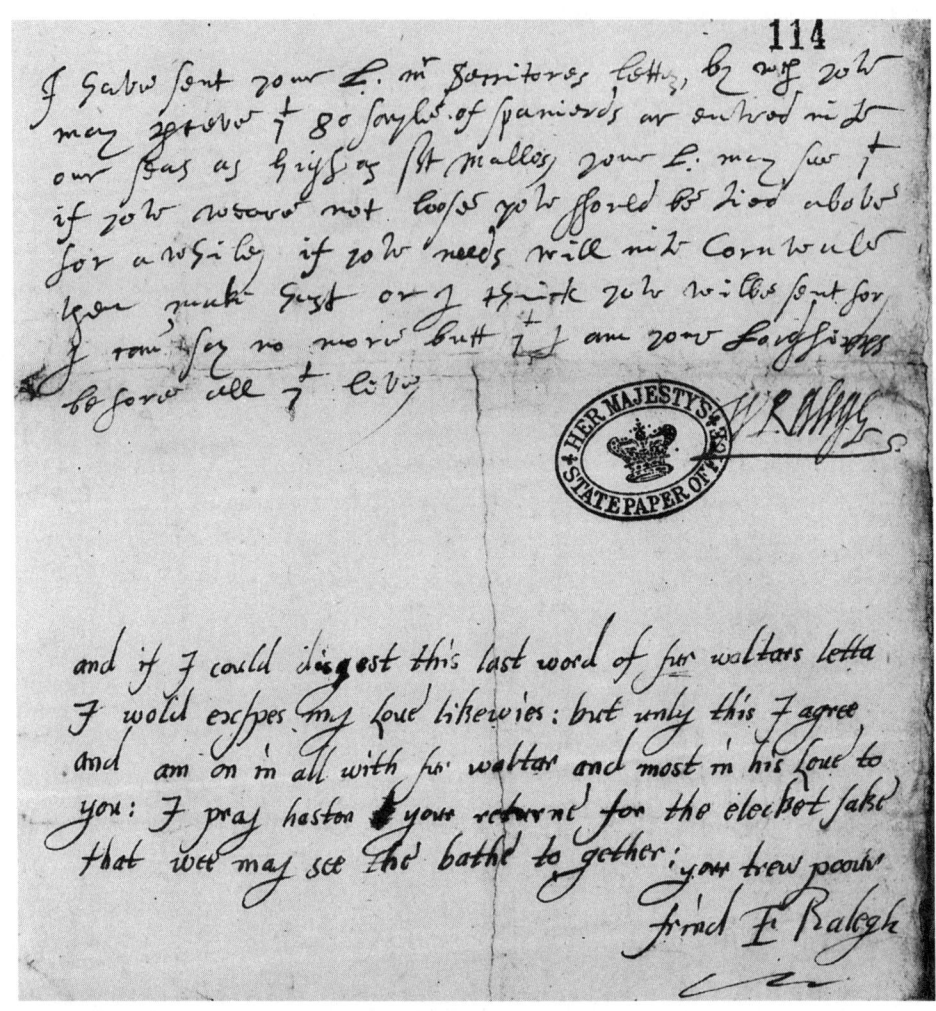

*Plate 7.* Letter 140: Sir Walter Ralegh to Lord Cobham, 13 August 1601, with postscript by Lady Ralegh. (PRO, SP12/264/81)

## 141. TO LORD COBHAM FROM SHERBORNE, [27 AUGUST 1601][1]

PRO, SP12/281/64, *CSPD 1601–3*, p. 87. In Ralegh's hand.

### TROUBLE WITH JOHN MEERE

[*addressed*] To the right honorabell my very good lorde the Lorde Cobhame, Lord Warden of the Cinque Portts and Her Majesties Leuetenant Generall of Kent
[*endorsed*] Wm Ralyee [*sic*]

I have sent your lordship such newse as came to me from above [*see Letter 140*] and your lordships letter to my Lord Treasurer [*Buckhurst*]. Agayne it was brought me by the post att midnight and I opened it in a badd light and half asleep, thincking it had byn to my sealf. I hope your lordship will be here to morrow or a [= *on*] Saterday or elce my wife sayes her oysters wilbe all sp[o]ilt and her partrig stale. If your lordship cannot cum Friday I will wait on yow wher yow ar.

I pray send me word if yow go to Lyme [*Regis*] and Melplashe[2] that I may attend yow, for a Friday I shall dispach my bussness with the Justices [*of the Peace*] here about thos roggs the Meers,[3] wherof the elder hath bynn att Court to cumplayne and brought my Lord Thomas [*Howard of Bindon*][4] to Master Secritory to deale for hyme.[5] The younger [*Meer*] Master Secritory hath now sent for by pursevant, and if it had not bynn so, to have sent informations [= *charges*] agaynst hyme, I had bynn with yowr lordship this morninge.

I feare that my Cornishemen did not repaire to your lordship to do yow service because your passage was so suddyne, but I am sure yow have had an ill jurney. I pray your lordship to send us word wh[*eth*]er yow have taken up the howse att Bath[6] or no, that we may send thither.

Your lordships ever and wholy to cumand,
W Ralegh

Bess remembers her sealf to your lordship and sayes your breach of promis shall make yow fare accordingly.

[*left-hand margin*] The shipp of the South Sea that ar [*sic*] of Hollande is past by, and none of ours stayd her, with a lantern of clean gold in her sterne, and arived att Amsterdame infinit riche. Master [*sic*] Mansfeld hath lien abrod to great purpose.⁷ The Queen is removed to Wards howse on Friday and from thence to Knowlses to Reddinge⁸ wher farther is not yett resolved.

1. See below, note 8.
2. East Melplash in the parish of Netherbury near Beaminster, Dorset, where the Brookes owned a considerable estate: J. Hutchins, *Dorset* II, p. 115.
3. John Meere and his son William. John, with deep roots in local society and some training as a lawyer in London, had been bailiff of the Sherborne estate when it had belonged to the Bishop of Salisbury. In 1592, when the Raleghs took up residence, he was in Newgate Gaol following a conviction for clipping coin. Ralegh secured his release and made him his bailiff, with a house near the Castle: PRO, SP12/242/124. He is mentioned in Ralegh's will of 1597: see Appendix 2. Subsequently they fell out and Meere exhibited a bill in Star Chamber against Ralegh, his half-brother, Adrian Gilbert, who was now in charge of the Dorset estate, and a long list of Ralegh's alleged supporters: J.B., 'Sir Walter Raleigh at Sherborne', *Gentleman's Magazine*, 1853, pt ii, pp. 434–43 and 1854, pt i, pp. 17–23. As was necessary to obtain a hearing in Star Chamber, Ralegh and company were accused of crimes of violence against Meere and his friends. Meere's fury knew no bounds, but whether he had deserved what he claimed to have been his dismissal from Ralegh's service is difficult to determine.
4. The most distinguished of Meere's local supporters.
5. Meere senior was committed to prison by Cecil on 31 July: *HMC Salisbury* XI, p. 403.
6. See above, Letter 126.
7. Sir Robert Mansell (see above, Letter 44), whom Ralegh disparages by failing to give him his right title, was lying off the English coast with the Channel Guard. He could have stopped the Dutch ship and seized any Spanish goods aboard. That the Dutch were allies and lived by their carrying trade would presumably not have inhibited Ralegh.
8. Early in August 1601, the ageing Queen moved to Windsor and on the 28th to the house of her Cofferer, Richard Warde, at Hurst in Berkshire. Until 1 September she was at Reading whence she dined with Sir William Knollys, the Comptroller of her Household, at Caversham Park in Oxfordshire: E.K. Chambers, *Elizabethan Stage*, IV, p. 114. That the Queen moved to Hurst on Friday 28 August 1601, and that Ralegh was expecting Cobham 'tomorrow', i.e. Friday, fixes the date of this letter as Thursday 27 August.

---

## 142. To Sir Robert Cecil from London,¹ 7 September 1601²

Hatfield, CP88/22, *HMC Salisbury* XI, pp. 382–3. In Ralegh's hand except for passages indicated.

Edwards II, pp. 233–4.

### ENTERTAINING MARSHAL BIRON

[*addressed*]   To the right honorabell Sir Robert Cecyll knight, Principall Secritory etc   Haste post hast for life, W Ralegh³

[*bold italic hand*]   For Her Majesties most especiall service

[*another hand*]   London vii^mo Septembr att ix a clock att night
[*endorsed*]   6 [*sic*] September 1601   Sir Walter Raleigh to my master   The entertaynement given to the Duke of Byron[4]
[*by the postmasters*]   And[*over*] xij at night   Harfart Breg [*Hertford Bridge, Staines*] att 6 o clock in the [?*night*]

Sir: I am gladd I came hither for I never saw so great a person so neglected. He hath bynne here now left, not on nobelman nor gentelman to accompany them [*sic*] nor to gwyde them and it is so long er they hard of my Lord of Cumberland[5] as they thought they weare neglected. We have caried them to Westminster to see the monuments,[6] and this Monday we entertayned them att the Bear Garden[7] which they took great pleasure to see. Here hath bynne with them Sir A[*rthur*] Savage and Sir Arthure Gorges, who hath bynne their guids, without whom they had byn left allone. Their horses will not be provided till Wensday morninge. The posts say that they cannot take up horses without cummission from the Lords of the Councell.[8] I sent to and fro and have labored like a moyle [= *mule*] to fashion all things, so as on Wensday night they wilbe att Bagshoot and Thursday att the Vine.[9]

It weare good that A[*rthur*] Gorges and A[*rthur*] Savage weare cummanded to cume with them because they speak French well and ar familliar with them. Crosby Howse[10] this Munday att 6 aclock
    Your honors to do yow service,
      W R

---

1. See below, notes 5 and 10. Cecil was with the Queen at Basing House in Hampshire.
2. Monday was 7 September.
3. Accompanied by a sketch of a gallows.
4. Charles de Gontaut-Biron, Marshal of France, who arrived in London about 5 September with a large retinue, as emissary to the Queen from King Henry IV of France: John Stow, *Annals*, 1613, pp. 795–6. There was some hope, which proved groundless, that France would declare war against Spain: Wernham, *Return of the Armadas*, pp. 376–7.
5. On 28 August, the Privy Council arranged for Biron to be met at Gravesend by the Earl of Cumberland, Lord Zouche, Sir Arthur Savage and others to be taken by water to London, whose Lord Mayor was 'to cause the house of Aldermanne Spencers ... called Crosby Place to be made ready': *APC* XXXII, pp. 190–91.
6. Ralegh had done the same for the ambassador of the Archduke of Austria in 1600: Collins 1746, II, p. 174.
7. In Southwark.
8. Cumberland, who was to conduct the visitors to Basing, wrote to Cecil on 7 September saying that he had been unable to find sufficient horses and adequate accommodation en route: *HMC Salisbury* XI, p. 383–4. The next day the Council authorized him to requisition horses: *APC* XXXII, p. 204.

9. Biron and his party left London on 10 September and were lodged at the Vine, the Hampshire residence of Lord Sandys, where they were visited by the Queen. The English ambassador in Paris, Ralph Winwood, later reported 'some discontents conceaved of the Marshal Biron's entertainment' (E. Sawyer (ed.), *Ralph Winwood: Memorials of affairs of state*, 1725, I, p. 347) and Biron himself reported on his way to London that 'ma bourse me fait beaucoup de bien car on ne nous defraie point en Angleterre', but the Queen reckoned that his entertainment in Hampshire cost her more than that of her own Court: *CSPD 1598–1601*, p. 216.
10. Crosby Place in Bishopsgate, built for a London merchant c.1466, the one-time home of Sir Thomas More, Henry VIII's Lord Chancellor, part of which survives on Chelsea Embankment.

---

143. TO LORD COBHAM FROM BASING, [12 SEPTEMBER 1601][1]

PRO, SP12/281/83, *CSPD 1601–3*, pp. 96–7. In Ralegh's hand.
Edwards II, pp. 234–5.

ADVICE FROM COURT

[*addressed*] To the right honorabell my very good lorde the Lorde Cobhame
[*endorsed, in same hand as Letter 171*] Wm Raylee

I that knew your lordshipps resolution when we parted cannot take on mee to persuade yow. I will only say this mich: it is butt a day and half jurney hither [*from Bath*], the Queen will take it exceeding kyndly and take hersealf more beholding unto yow then yow thincke. They French[2] tarry butt 2 or 3 dayes att most. I will presently returne to the Bath with your lordship agayne. The French weare all black and no kind of bravery [= *adornment*] att all, so as I have only made me a black taffata sute to be in and leve all my other sutes.

This is all I can say, saving I only wish yow a littell to [*for*]beare and make the Queen so mich the more in your debt. It wilbe Thursday er they have a[*u*]dience.[3] It weare too long to tell the Queens discource with me of your lordship and finding [= *learning of*] it I dust [= *dare*] not say that I knew yow weare resolved not to cum but left it to the estate of your boddy. I need not doubt butt that your lordship wilbe leve [*sic*] that I wish yow to hold such a cource as may best fitt your honor and your humor [= *disposition*] together. If yow cum she will take it most kyndly, if yow

cum not it shalbe handled as yow will have it, and herein and all elce I will remayne yours before all the worlde.
   W Ralegh

Basing this Saterday night late.

I am yeven now going all night to Lundun to provide me a playne taffata sute and a playne black saddell and wilbe here agayne Twesday night. And if your French jurney holde it will mich stand yow for them to know what yow are here, for I am resolved that the Queen will most esteeme yow here, and use yow.

1. See note 2.
2. Marshal Biron and his party: see above, Letter 142. The Sheriff of Hampshire met them on 10 September, a Thursday, and took them to the Vine: John Stow, *Annales*, 1613, p. 796.
3. Cf. his own prediction as to the Frenchmen's length of stay.

---

## 144. TO SIR ROBERT CECIL FROM SHERBORNE, 19 SEPTEMBER 1601

Hatfield, CP88/53, *HMC Salisbury* XI, p. 392, listed only. In Ralegh's hand. Edwards II, pp. 235–6.

### THE SPANIARDS IN THE CHANNEL

[*addressed*] To the right honorabell Sir Robert Cecyll knight, Principall Secritory etc.
[*endorsed*] 19 September 1601 Sir Walter Ralegh to my master

Sir: I receved a letter from Jersey dated the 12th of this September by which I was advertised that a barke of St Malos cuminge from Lysbone the first of September reportethe for certayne that the Spanish fleet is still helde ther, together with sume 6 or 7000 soldiers, yeven then reddy to depart, ether for Irland or the Low Countres.[1] Ther weare amonge them of shipps of warr sume 25, the rest weare of all sortts for transportation only. The French man is helde to be an honest man and, as wee beleve in Jersey, will reportt no untrewth. If they be att sea this weather they ar hardly besteede [= *beset*]. The rest I leve to your judgementt.

 I ment to have gone to the Bathe the day after my returne butt I fell sick and so continew, wherby I shall not be abille this yeare to healp my sealf therby.

That rooge Meers² continews his knavery as violently as ever, sent down seven writts out of the Exchequer, one to mee and six more to divers poore men here to vex them only and to shew bravery.³ I must in this matter refer my reputation to your favorabell regard of me, for nothinge ever concerned me more.

I have by this bearer sent yow the gloves⁴ but it is indented [= *stipulated*] that if they serve not your own hands yow must of your grace return them agayne.

>Yours ever to do yow service,
>W Ralegh

Sherburne this 19th of September

1. A Spanish fleet under the command of Juan d'Aquila left Lisbon on 24 August bound for Ireland and apparently unaware that the last six months or so had seen the new Lord Deputy (Mountjoy) and Sir George Carew, President of Munster, achieve remarkable success against the rebels, with whom, no doubt, Aquila planned to make common cause: Wernham, *Return of the Armadas*, p. 377. Half of his troops followed later.
2. See Letters 141, 145 and 156.
3. Vexatious litigation, an indictable offence, was a well-known way of embarassing one's opponents.
4. A present from Lady Ralegh: see Letter 145.

---

## 145. TO SIR ROBERT CECIL FROM SHERBORNE, 25 SEPTEMBER 1601

Hatfield, CP88/62, *HMC Salisbury* XI, p. 395. In Ralegh's hand. Edwards II, pp. 237–9.

### JOHN MEERE

[*addressed*] To the right honorabell Sir Robert Cecyll knight, Principall Secritory, etc.

[*endorsed*] 1601 September 25   Sir Walter Raleigh to my master, concerning Meeres

Sir: It is true that Meere¹ is bounde to the good behavior by Sir George Trencher [*Trenchard*], Sir Raufe Horsey and three or foure other Justices of this shire,² butt the recognisence is not above 40*li*. The rest that ar bound with hyme ar too or thre roggs of the country,³ and wher a councelors cummandment is layde it serveth allwayes for a *supersedeas*, and did it not, yet by me no advantage shalbe taken.⁴

That his wife is a kynswoman to my lady of Essex⁵ it is trew. She was a poor mans wife of this country butt to good for such a knave and, being a broken peece that I thincke few or none would have had, this knave, hopinge therby to have bynn upheld by the earle of Essex, took her. Butt the earle did not make shew to like Meeres nor admitt hyme to his presence. Butt it was thought that secreatly he ment to have used hyme for sume mischief agaynst me and if Essex had prevayled he had bynn used for the counterfeter, for he writes my hand so perfectly as I cannot any way decerne the difference. My wife wrate unto my Lady Walsingame⁶ towching Meeres, for he tooke into his howse a sister of his wives who had sume 200 mark portion which the knave hath cussined her of [= *embezzled*] and turnd her of[f] a begginge. Now that sister, being as dere to my lady [Essex]⁷ as Meers wife, she cannot esteme such a knave who, if he respected her, would not so abuse her sister as he hath, who, being unmaried and begotten with childe in his howse, is now by hyme thus undun, cussned and cast of.

Besyds, I hope that my lady of Essex cannot say butt in matters of more importance it hath pleased yow and your frinds to do her service since her lords death.⁸ Butt howsoever it be, if yow shall not thinck it fitt that he [*Meere*] submitt hym sealf, having used towards me many more cussneges [*sic*] and villanes then ever Daniell⁹ did to my lady of Essex, I shalbe contented with your order therin and dare make my lady of Essex judge in the cause. Meers hath sent down 16 *su*[*b*]*penas* at [*sic*] me and other poor men since he was committed.

[*left-hand margin*]  If the Spanierds be now att sea ther [*they*] ar in great distress.¹⁰ My Lord Cobhame is now with yow. I am sure the Queen must be a godmother and my Lord Admirall [*Charles Howard*] a fitt deputye.¹¹ I beseich yow lett us know what becumes of Ostend and my Lord of Northumberland,¹² to whom I have written of your carefull respect of hyme. And to conclude with Meers, if ther be any nobell man, conceler or gentelman that would be contented to be so provoked by a sarvant and thinck it fitt to disgest so many indignities from a villayne raysed by hymesealf, I wilbe contented to be ordered in this cause by such a one.¹³ Bess sayes that she must envy any fingers whosoever that shall wear her gloves butt your owne.¹⁴

       Yours ever as your sarvant,
           W Ralegh

25 of September

1. See above, Letter 141. Inquiries made of those indicted, along with Ralegh and his half-brother, Adrian Gilbert, in Star Chamber, had resulted in a pretty damning picture of Meere's machinations: J.B. in *Gentleman's Magazine*, 1853–4, loc. cit.
2. He seems to have been released from prison in London: see above, Letter 141, note 3.
3. Named in Meere's bill as Michael Humphrey, Richard Brett, Valentine Hyllard and Stephen Ash. In his answer, Adrian Gilbert added John Meere's son, William, and John Carter.
4. Ralegh himself appears to have entered no defence against Meere's charges in Star Chamber.
5. Lady Essex was Frances, née Walsingham, widow of Sir Philip Sydney, who, as Lady Sydney, had been a guest at Sherborne in February 1600: Collins 1746, II, pp. 168–9. By 1601, Meere had married as his second wife someone called Dorothy, surname unknown. Ralegh's statement, the basic facts of which, if not the innuendo, he is unlikely to have invented, cannot at present be substantiated.
6. Ursula Worsley, née St Barbe, had a daughter and a granddaughter called Dorothy but there is no evidence of either of them being married to John Meere.
7. Sir Francis's widow had died in July 1601, so this must be her daughter, Lady Essex.
8. On 25 February 1601.
9. John Daniel who was brought before Star Chamber for stealing and forging a bundle of letters belonging to the Earl of Essex.
10. See above, Letter 144.
11. Speculations about the Dauphin, born 27 September 1601: *CSPD 1601–3*, p. 107.
12. See above, Letter 138, note 3. Northumberland was in Ostend.
13. In October 1601 Meere wrote from prison apologizing for the words he had used against Ralegh. He was released on 23 October: *HMC Salisbury* XXIII, p. 89. But see also below, Letter 204.
14. See above, Letter 144.

---

## 146. To the Jurats[1] of Jersey from Sherborne, 25 September 1601

Houghton Library, Harvard College, Cambridge, Mass., Locker-Lampson-Warburg-Grimson Album, bMS Eng 870(5a). Written by a clerk and signed by Ralegh.

P. Le Geyt, *Manuscrits sur la Constitution*, Jersey, 1847, IV, p. 324, faulty; Sotheby's *Catalogue*, Manners MSS, 17 June 1870, Lot 1615; P. Ahier, *Governorship of Sir Walter Ralegh in Jersey*, St Helier 1971, pp. 27–8, from Le Geyt.

### DE CARTERET v. PAULET

[*endorsed*] Lettre de Sir Walter Ralegh a la Justice touchant Jean de Carteret et Abra[ham] Poulet

After my verie hartie commendations: Wheras I understand[2] that there is dissention in the Iland between Master John Carterett[3] and Abraham Poulett, his sonne in law, as I am sorrie to heare of it, so I am desirous that there maie be an attonement, the rather because of the ingratitude of the sonne in law to accuse Master Carterett of his unworthines in Justice. And for my parte I protest I never conceaved anie ill of Master Carterett[4] but have found him honest and verie sufficient at the Court and elsewhere in following and dispatching those affaires which he hath undertaken. Therefore I will have have him to continue in his charge and not to desiste by anie mans malicious accusation or to be removed for doing of Justice. And that if his innocencie shall appeare, as it now seemeth to me, that you upon examination and good reguard of his creditt cause satisfaction to be made according to the quallitie of the offence as the lawes and customes of the Iland do permitt, and as in former tymes hath been accustomed.[5] Wherein you must have an especiall care that there maie be no partialitie but justice administered according to the lawes.

And so I committ you to God.

From my house at Shyreborne the 25th of September 1601.

    Your verie loving frend and Governour,

        W Ralegh

1. Members of the Royal Court or governing body of the island.
2. Ralegh's intervention was no doubt triggered by a letter signed by four of the Jurats, mentioning an attack by Abraham Paulet on Carteret at a meeting of the Court on 15 August, and declaring their support for him: copy in Harvard College Library, bMS 870 (5b).
3. Jean de Carteret, Seigneur of the manor of Vinchelez de Haut at St Ouen, a member of the Royal Court of Jersey.
4. Abraham Paulet, son of Sir George and uncle of Sir Anthony Paulet (ob. 1600), Ralegh's predecessor as Governor: see above, Letter 126. The office had almost become hereditary in this Somerset family. Sir George Paulet had been Bailiff to Sir Anthony and, although aged 46, had been appointed Lieutenant by Ralegh in 1600: Ahier, op. cit., p. 13.
5. There was to be further trouble in May 1602 between de Carteret and, on that occasion, Sir George Paulet, and this time Ralegh sent de Carteret to prison until he apologized and made Paulet acccept the apology: Ahier, op. cit., pp. 27–30.

---

## 147. TO SIR ROBERT CECIL FROM WEYMOUTH, 26 SEPTEMBER 1601

PRO, SP12/281/103, *CSPD 1601–3*, p. 105. In Ralegh's hand.
Edwards II, p. 240–41.

## ANOTHER ARMADA

[*addressed*]  For Her Majesties service  To the right honorabell Sir Robert Cecyll knighte, Principall Secritorye etc.  Hast post hast hast for life Sherburne the 26 September att 10 a clock the forenone  W Ralegh [*endorsed*] September 26 1601   Sir Walter Raleigh to my master from Shirbourne [*sic*]

[*postmasters*]   Shaston [*Shaftesbury*] at 3 of the clock in the afternoone
At Sarum [*Salisbury*] at x a cloke at night   R[*eceive*]d at Andever at ix in the morning, being Sound[*ay*]   Hartford Bridge at thre in the after noone

Sir: Ther arived att We[*y*]mouth on Friday the xxvth of this September to Skottishmen, the on called Robert Blanshill, the other Robert Perisonn, merchants of Aburdene. They departed Lysbon the thirde of this present [*month*]. Who affirme on their oathes that they weare stayde att Lysbone and St Uvall [*Setubal, near Lisbon*] eyghteen weekes and that ther departed from Lysbone tenn dayes before their cumminge from thence[1] a fleet of great Spanishe shipps to the number of 36, and with them 3 Irishe shipps, on Irishe byshoppe with many preists and other Irishe men. They all gave out that they intended to land ether att Cork or Lymbrike [*Limerick*].[2] The number of men weare 8000, wherof 6000 soldiers, the other 2000 weare to bringe back the shipps.[3] They weare well furnished with vittell,[4] munition and mony and had also with them many woemen.[5]

It seemeth by this report that a plantation [= *settlement*] is ment. Thes Skottishe seem to be very honest men and this intelligence differeth littell from that I sent yow from Jersey [*Letter 144*], all which I leve to your better judgment and rest your most assured to do yow service.[6]

We[*y*]mouthe this 26 of September,
   W Ralegh

1. Cf. above, Letter 144, note 1. Captain Love met the Spanish fleet on 14 September: Letter 148, note 5, and *CSPI 1601–3*, p. 74.
2. Sir George Carew, Lord President of Munster, thought Cork the most likely but did not rule out Limerick or even Waterford: *Pacata* I, pp. 258–9. Cf. below, Letter 149, note 1.
3. Cf. Captain Morgan's report that not more than 4,000 soldiers were landed, many of them sick: *CSPI 1601–3*, p. 125. In reality there were probably fewer, another report saying that while 6,000 left Spain, 1,000 went back with the ships and 1,000 were put ashore at Baltimore: *Pacata* I, pp. 263, 283, 290, *CSPI 1601–3*, p. 125 and Fynes Moryson II, p. 455.
4. On the contrary, they expected to live off the country: *CSPI 1601–3*, pp. 86, 127. General Aquila wrote home that he was so short of ammunition that he had not landed all his cannon: *Pacata* I, p. 280.
5. John Edey, an escaped galley slave, reported the presence of two or three hundred women and children but explained that many of these were returning Irish refugees: *CSPI 1601–3*, p. 87. See also Letter 150.
6. Mountjoy's letter of 24 September reporting the Spanish landing of the previous day only reached London on 20 October, eliciting a promise of whatever troops he should require: *APC* XXXII, pp. 222 et seq. See also *Pacata* I, p. 288 and H.V. Jones (ed.), 'The Journal of Levinus Munck', *EHR* lxviii, 1953, p. 242.

## 148. TO SIR ROBERT CECIL FROM SHERBORNE, 27 SEPTEMBER 1601

PRO, SP12/281/104, *CSPD 1601–3*, p 105. In Ralegh's hand, clearly in great haste. Edwards II, pp. 241–2, Pope Hennessy, 1883, pp. 196–7.

## FURTHER INTELLIGENCE

[*addressed*]   For Her Majesties speciall affaires   To the right honorabell Robert Cecyll knight, Principall Secritory etc.   Hast post hast hast for life att your uttermost perill[1]   W Ralegh
Sherburne at 4 of the cloke in the afternunn thes
[*endorsed*]   27 September 1601   Sir Walter Raleighe to my master Spanyshe advyses delyvered by certen Scottes merchantes
[*postmasters*]   R[*eceived*] at Shaston [*Shaftesbury*] at 8 at nyght being Sunday   R[*eceived*] at Andever at ix in the morning being Munday

I wrate unto yow the 26 of this present [*Letter 147*] what I receved from certayne Skottishe marchants. It is now manefest that bothe thos advertissments ar trew for thos three pinneses which brought in the great prize at Plymouth of 900 chests of sugar[2] wear chased by the Spanishe fleet seven dayes before their arivall and they arived on Tuesday last, the [?*twenty*] seconde[3] of this moneath, and weare therfore chased of [*sic*] the mouth of the Chanell which was about the 25 of August and so must needs be in Irlande or perished, from whence it seemeth yow cannot here by reason of thes esterly winde.[4]

Thos of Munster had sume warning of ther being on the coast for on Captayne Love[5] or Captain Lone, being on the Irishe coast, forsooke his shippe and went into a bote and tooke horse uppon the shore and gave warnimge to the next adjoining [*place*] about the coast of Dungarven between Yoholl [= *Youghal*] and Waterforde. From thence he took his shipp agayne and arived at Plymoth. Thes pineses tolde [= *counted*] 60 sayle. A Fleming [*vessel*] also cumminge from Lysbone confirmeth the former intellegence and addeth therunto, ether out of conjecture or knowlege or fame, affirming that the soldiers ar 6000, that they have twelve moneaths pay and like vittell before hande, that he sey many with chaynes of golde and that generally the army was very brave [= *splendidly attired*] and well provided of all things, that certayne cannons weare imbarked in four gallions with all other things awnswerabell.[6]

Sir, I beseich [*you*] to acquaynt my Lord Admirall herewith and that yow will vouchsauf to excuse me for not writing to his lordship, knowing that yow ar of on mind and fortune, of on love and one indevor for Her Majesties service.

Sherb[*orne*] the 27 of September,
> Yours ever as your sarvant,
> > W Ralegh

1. Ralegh added a thumbnail drawing of a gallows and a ladder.
2. Two English men-of-war, one of London and one of Fowey, Cornwall, who had captured a San Thomé vessel homeward-bound full of sugar from the Guinea coast, told John Goard, on 14 September, that they had seen the Spanish fleet the day before. He himself had seen it on the 12th and brought the news to Plymouth, whence it was relayed to London by the 21st: *CSPD 1601–3*, p. 100.
3. Either an error in what was clearly a written report or his misreading. The 2 September 1601 was a Wednesday. The pinnaces must have been chased on the 15th, which agrees with John Goad's report.
4. See above, Letter 147, note 6.
5. Owner of the *Plough* of Plymouth, he had reached Ireland on 13 September and reported having seen 45 Spanish ships off Lisbon on 27 August. Sir George Carew relayed this news to Cecil, who received it on 20 September: *Pacata* II, pp. 274–5 and *CSPI 1601–3*, pp. 73–4. Love must have lost no time in returning to Plymouth for Ralegh to have received his news by 27 September, a testimony to the usefulness of small ships to Cecil's intelligence network. See also *CSPD 1601–3*, p. 99.
6. Evidently an exaggeration. Cf. a report that they left Lisbon with a month's victuals and were six weeks at sea: *HMC Salisbury* XI, p. 429. See Letter 151 for what must have been a serious loss of horses.

---

### 149. To Sir Robert Cecil, [*c.*10][1] October 1601

Hatfield, CP89/41, *HMC Salisbury* XI, p. 462, abstract only. In Ralegh's hand.
Edwards II, pp. 244–5; Pope Hennessy 1883, pp. 200–202.

## THE SPANIARDS IN IRELAND

[*addressed*]   To the right honorabell Sir Robert Cecyll knight, Principall Secritorye etc.

[*endorsed*]   October 1601   Sir Walter Raleigh to my master without date

Sir: I am of oppinion that ether Kynsale[2] was not the place purposed [*by the Spaniards*] to be undertaken or elce Florence[3] was the cause thereof, for the port bordereth his country. The towne is of small reseat [= *capacity*], mastered by hills and cumpased with a weake wall. Butt wher as I here that the Deputy [*Mountjoy*] and Presedent [*Carew*] have written that they will make a short work of it,[4] I am not altogether of that minde. And yet I do not thinck that Spayne will supply them in hast, neather will thos Spanierds alreddy ther finde such a party as they hoped, which may be sume cause of their governours hopes. Butt after a few dayes yow shall here more, for if the country stand sounde then the warrs wilbe the easier, butt sure I am if thes Spanierds had cum in the begining of the warrs the kingdome had bynn once lost. Yow shall finde I warrante yow that Tirrone[5] will bestire hyme sealf in the north, and every rebell in his quarter, for this is the last of all hopes.

For Meeres I thinck by this tyme yow finde the strenght of his villanous spirrite, and yet a more notorius cowardly knave never lived. Butt if he do not submitt hyme sealf he will triumph that he hath resisted me and my greatest frinds.[6] All which I leve to your favorabell care and rest most faythfull to do yow service,
    W Ralegh

My wife sayes that yow came hither in an unseasonabell tyme and had no leasure to looke abrode and that every day this place amends and Lundun to her groes worse and worse.

[*left-hand margin*]   I have sent away Her Majesties letters and your honors with all dillegence, not doubting butt the soldiers butt [*sic*] both first apoynted and thes[7] shall be reddy. My deputies [*lieutenants*] have written to me that they will arme the first 50 men. What they will do for thes I know not.

---

1. This letter must post-date the Council's order of 6 October (note 7) for fresh levies from Cornwall, and Mountjoy's confident dispatch of 2 October (note 4) can hardly have arrived in less than a week, but the contents suggest that it preceded Letter 150.
2. On an inlet on the coast, west of Cork.
3. Florence MacCarthy, the rebel, whom Sir George Carew, President of Munster, had sent to the Tower: Wernham, *Return of the Armadas*, p. 368.
4. On 2 October, Mountjoy wrote very cheerfully to Cecil expressing supreme confidence that they could 'beate these Spanish Dons': Fynes Moryson II, p. 461.
5. The rebel Earl of Tyrone who was still at large with a potentially substantial following.
6. See above, Letters 141 and 145.
7. Having ordered, on 29 September, the levy of 50 Cornishmen for service in Ireland, on 6 October the Council doubled its requirements: *APC* XXXII, pp. 225 and 241. The soldiers were to embark at Barnstaple in north Devon on 20 October. But, as usual, most came from London. All together, including 2,000 levied in August, 7,000 were provided: Wernham, *Return of the Armadas*, p. 378. They reached Ireland on or about 14 October: ibid., p. 382.

### 150. To Sir Robert Cecil from Sherborne, 13 and 14 October 1601

Hatfield, CP88/128, *HMC Salisbury* XI, p. 427, abstract only. In Ralegh's hand.
Edwards II, pp. 243–4, Pope Hennessy 1883, pp. 198–9.

## THE SPANIARDS AT KINSALE

[*addressed*]  To the right honorabell Sir Robert Cecyll knight, Principall Secritorye etc.
[*endorsed*]  14 October 1601   Sir Walter Ralegh to my master

Sir: If I cum not to late I would be an humbell suter unto yow for a cumpany in Irland for [this *crossed out*] gentelman, Master Stuckly,[1] who hath served with good reputation both by sea and lande. He was wounded with Sir Richard Grenvile in The Revendge and hath since served longe in Irland and elcewhere. For the rest I will not trobell yow butt will hope for your favor towards hyme and rest your honors to do yow service.
            W Ralegh

Sherburn this 13 of October

This bearer hath brought an Inglishman[2] which came in the Spanish fleet. Hee will tell yow that they imbarked 4000 men but want [= *are missing*] ij great shipps[3] and almost a 1000 of their men. They ar riche in mony. The cummanders have brought their wives and children, which proveth that they mean to abide it and make us a warr ther. They look for great supplies. They have broken down the wall [*to*] mans hight, they have intrenched without the towne, out of which they have bynn beaten twise in a day by Cap[*tain*] Flowre.[4] The Inglish serve with invincibell currage agaynst them, many Spanierds ar alreddy taken. They have too castells uppon the entrance.[5] The Deputy is not yet cum to beseige them butt will shortly.[6] Diego Brochero [*de Araya*] is admirall, Seburo [*Pedro de Cubiaur*] vice-admirall. Brochero is thot dead. They hadd 6 great shipps of 90 toon and one of 1300, all mand for the most with strangers. The most of the shipps ar gonn, the rest tarry yet. I had thought that this bearer had byn Stuckly, which made me write as I did, butt he is still in Irlande and therfore I do not mich desire any thing in his behalf.
            Yours ever to do yow service,
                W R

Sherburn this Wensday night [= *14 October*]

1. Possibly John Stucley (1551–1610), eldest son of Lewis of Affeton in East Worlington, Devon, and one of the gentlemen who had been with Grenville on the Virginia voyage of 1585: D.B. Quinn, *Set Fair for Roanoke*, 1985, p. 67. But if so, he was rather old for a captaincy in Ireland. See below, Letter 223, for John's son and heir, who, as Sir Lewis, was later to betray Ralegh.
2. John Edye: see above, Letter 147, note 5.
3. Seven of the Spanish ships, with the Vice-Admiral (*Cubiaur*), were forced by bad weather into Baltimore, a port west of Kinsale: *CSPI 1601–3*, pp. 125, 128.
4. George Flower, Sergeant-Major of the province of Munster.
5. Rincurren and Castle Park.
6. Mountjoy arrived at Cork on 27 September and camped within five miles of Kinsale on 16 October. Ten days later his army moved within musket-shot and on 30 October opened fire: *CCM 1602–3*, pp. 180–82 and Fynes Moryson II, pp. 1, 10, 15, 92. As Ralegh had prophesied, the Spaniards took some shifting, but Aquila finally surrendered Kinsale and his other occupied territory on 2 January 1602: Wernham, *Return of the Armadas*, p. 386.

---

## 151. To Sir John Gilbert II [from the Court], 31 October [1601][1]

Ransom Center, Pforzheimer 110, Jackson 1940, pp. 856–7, *in extenso*. Worn in several places, even before transcript made. In Ralegh's hand.

PRO, SP9/55/12xi, an eighteenth-century transcript.

Tytler 1833, III, f. 22.

PRIZE GOODS etc.

[*addressed*] To my nephew, Sir John Gilbert, knight, att the Fort att Plymouth   Hast haste

I receved bothe your letters, that wherein yow write of the towns mischance,[2] the other about Brixame [*Brixham, east of Dartmouth*].[3] I will do what I cann in bothe and in all elce that concerns yow, butt yow know this place[4] and the [?*env*]iousness therof. I hope to gett your pu[*rch*]ace 3[5] or 400*li* better cheape then another shoulde.

Yow must remember my wife for purselane [= *porcelain*] and mee with pied [= *multicoloured*] silks for curtens if you meane to bribe mee.[6]

I pray send up the governour of Farname Bucke [= *Pernambuco, South America*] that we may sett a voyage out thither. It may prove a very good voyage. Yow shall have hyme sauf agayne. The commission [*from the Admiralty*] is sent down to try wh[*eth*]er the shipe be prize. I will deale with the Judge [*Sir Julius Caesar*] and do all I can.[7]

Send your ship in to Irland, butt know first how yow shalbe payd and who shall vittell her.⁸ What yow writ about it lett mee see it first. Farewell.

Yours ever,

W Ralegh

This last of October.

1. See notes 4, 6 and 8.
2. Possibly a reference to the disastrous fire which devastated the market town of Tiverton, north of Exeter, in 1598: M. Dunsford, *Historical Memoirs ... of Tiverton*, Exeter 1790, p. 179.
3. See below, Letter 152, note 3.
4. Ralegh was at Court on 11 November 1601: see next letter.
5. See below, Letter 152.
6. Gilbert's privateer, the *Refusal*, had recently taken a Brazilian vessel laden with porcelain and silks: *CSPD 1601–3*, p. 110.
7. Some of the goods aboard were claimed by Flemings and ordered to be seized: *HMC Salisbury* XI, p. 528. Gilbert was suspected of having removed part of the cargo and of allowing it to be 'stolen'.
8. In October 1601 there was a call for shipping to supply the army besieging Kinsale, and on 9 November the *Refusal* departed for Cork, only to be recalled two days later: see below, Letter 152, note 11, *APC* XXXII, p. 322, and *HMC Salisbury* XI, pp. 483, 488, 495.

---

## 152. To Sir John Gilbert II from Court, 11 November [1601]¹

Pierpont Morgan, REIII.EI–I.45, considerably worn and torn. In Ralegh's hand. Not previously printed.

PRO, SP9/55/12xii, an eighteenth-century transcript which supplies some words now missing² but omits some still legible.

### LEASE OF BRIXHAM RECTORY, etc.

[*addressed*] To my lovinge nephew Sir Johne Gilbert knight att Plymouthe

Sir Johne: I receved your letters and we have dun for [= *dealt with*] the parsonage [*of Brixham*]³ butt with the most ado that ever I knew in so small a matter, for Mistris Thynn the mayde,⁴ your old love[r, pro]tested to the Queen that the leas was hers. [The] Queen caused it to be stayde. My Lord Tresorer [*Buckhurst*] mo[ve]d her, butt Greshame with others as nere yow in blud as my sealf had so plotted with Forteskew⁵ as a leas was reddy to be signed uppon the surrender. I [*was*] forst to move Her Majestye and to avow them all to be liers that had tolde her that Greshame had interest, and so shewing the petegre [= *descent*] of the leas from my Aunt Ashley[6] to Sir W. Gorge[7] and so to my brother,[8] and also the necessety which yow stood in, and could not keip howse without it, [*that*] it is past[9] and I take it I saved yow five years purchase. For your leve to cum up, when you ar reddy for it I will procure it.

Now for my sealf and for my wiv[es p]orselayne I here yow have store, and a ce[rta]yne fine saddell, and silk stoc[kin]ges and hangings. Butt yow must not mistake me for I, seing when yow ar furnished yow must sell the rest.[10] I pray be not scripulus [= *scrupulous*] to lett your frinds buy sume of thes things which I have herein named, for ther is nothing of valew butt I will [*not*] pay for. For your shipp, if shee be not gon [? *to Ireland*] yow have order to stay her.[11] If she be gone send for her. Master S[*ecritory*] [*Cecil*] and I and your sealf will sett her out bu[*tt Master*] Secritory will beare half the vente[*r of the*] shipp. And looke [= *see to*] what vittell is wantinge w[*ith*] that which yow have. Take order for it presently and yow shall receve your mony here. Lett me here from yow and I pray stay sume of thes things for your frinds here for their mo[*n*]y.

Thus in hast I leve yow and rest your most assured loving unkell,
    W Ralegh

[*left-hand margin*] My Lord Admirall and Master Secritory have written to Parker[12] to repre[*mand*] hyme. If ther be any Spanishe books[13] save them for my Lord Cobhame and yow must keep us silk stockings for us both.

Court the xi of November.

1. See below, notes 9, 10 and 11.
2. Indicated by roman type enclosed in square brackets.
3. In 1524, while still the property of Totnes priory, the great tithes of Brixham had been leased for 70 years to Sir John Gilbert's grandfather: PRO, SC6 Henry VIII, 597. It was no doubt the expiry of this lease in 1594 which precipitated Sir John Gilbert's claim. In 1597, as heir to his uncle, Sir John the elder (Ralegh's half-brother), Gilbert had sought Sir Robert Cecil's support against Elizabeth, his widowed aunt, and her second husband, Henry, son of Sir John Thynne of Longleat: *HMC Salisbury*, VII, pp. 357, 456.
4. Catherine, daughter of Sir John Thynne by his second wife, Dorothy (née Wroughton). One of the Queen's maids of honour, she was known as 'Gresham', her second name, after her father's first wife, a daughter of Sir Richard Gresham. She was connected with Gilbert through her mother's second marriage to Carew Ralegh, and also through her sister-in-law, Henry Thynne's wife (see note 3).
5. Sir John Fortescue, Chancellor of the Exchequer and responsible for Crown leases.
6. Kate, née Champernon, elder sister of Ralegh's mother and Sir John Gilbert's great-aunt. It is not clear what she had to do with the disputed lease but Ralegh's story presumably had some foundation. Coincidentally, Kate's nephew, Charles Champernon (Ralegh's cousin, son of his mother's brother Arthur), married Ellen, daughter of Sir John Fortescue (see note 5).

7. Probably Sir William Gorges, Ralegh's uncle and Gilbert's great-uncle by marriage, having as his fourth wife Winifred, daughter and sole heir of Roger Butshed and Frances, née Champernon: Vivian, *Devon*, pp. 162, 114.
8. Sir John Gilbert the elder.
9. Gilbert purchased the rectory on 20 November 1601 (PRO, LR6/8/roll 9), apparently, if Ralegh is to be believed, at a preferential price. Paying a rent fixed 70 years before at £13 6s. 8d. and assuming they had not sublet it on the same terms, the Gilberts had already done very well.
10. All the goods mentioned were from the Brazil prize: see above, Letter 151. It is difficult to make sense of this sentence, and the eighteenth-century transcript does not help.
11. See above, Letter 151. In fact, Gilbert's ship was sent to the coast of Spain: *HMC Salisbury* XI, p. 528.
12. Captain William Parker, Mayor of Plymouth 1601–2, with whom Gilbert was frequently at odds, especially over the impressment of mariners: *HMC Salisbury* XI, pp. 481–2, 489–90, 492–3, 503.
13. Gilbert had written several times to Cecil for instructions about the books taken from the Jesuit priests aboard the Brazilian, which were described as 'very scandalous and not fit to be suffered': ibid. p. 480.

---

## 153. TO SIR JOHN GILBERT II [FROM LONDON, LATE NOVEMBER 1601][1]

Ransom Center, Pfortzheimer 111, Jackson 1940, p. 857. In Ralegh's hand.
PRO, SP9/55/12xiii, an eighteenth-century transcript, with gaps.
Tytler 1833, II, f. 20.

### PRIZE GOODS etc.

[*addressed*] To my loving nephew Sir John Gilbert knight, Governor of the Fortt att Plymouth   Haste post haste

I receved your letter and opened Baggs[2] who writes that hee hath 2 partes vitlinge with yow. I send yow back his letter, bothe because yours shalbe the first as also because yow shall know the man. Keip it to your sealf and lett Nicholas[3] see it burnt. It is in vayne for mee to writ for tenthes:[4] they ar all to hungry. I pray send me by Nicholas on of the wisest Spanierds[5] that I may know all particulers. Yow shall have hyme agayne. I care not to make gayne of [= *ransome*] hyme, butt lett it be the best. And if yow have a coopell of fine littell peeces of brass [= *cannon*] betwen minion and faulcon lett me buy them for the castell of Sherburne. Use your fortune wisely in this hard worlde. I here yow spend vaynly and use carowsing. It is tyme to be wize and look to your estate now yow may buy the parsonage,⁶ and therefore harken not to begging companions butt make the best of your fortune.

    Your loving unkell,
        W Ralegh

If the Brasell men have balsem⁷ send me sume, or such tres [sic].

I pray be good to poore Nicholas for his old debt.

Lett no man take any examinations butt your sealf. Send me the Spanierd before any examination be sent up. I go away onn Wensday.

1. Ralegh took part in the great debate on monopolies in Parliament on 20 November, and spoke on several occasions early in December (Hasler III, pp. 275–6); this was clearly written very shortly after Letter 152.
2. James Bagg, a Weymouth man who had made Plymouth a base for his privateering activities. He was Mayor in 1595–6 and 1605–6 and MP in 1601 and 1604 (R.N. Worth, *Calendar of Plymouth Municipal Records*, 1893, pp. 21, 23, 143–4) and also Controller of Customs for the port, which was probably the basis of his unpopularity. His son, also James, was the even more notorious 'Bottomless' Bagg.
3. Ralegh's man, later referred to as Captain Nichols.
4. Due to the Lord Admiral on prize goods: see Andrews 1964, p. 22.
5. From the prize vessel.
6. See above, Letters 151, 152.
7. Balsam, for healing wounds.

---

## 154. TO THE BAILIFF AND JUSTICES OF JERSEY FROM THE COURT, 15 DECEMBER 1601

Found at Vinchelez de Bas manor, St Ouens, Jersey and now in the possession of Major Richard Hyne, photocopy held by the Société Jersiaise, St Helier, Jersey. Written by a clerk with what appears to be a copy of Ralegh's signature.

P. Ahier, *Bulletin of the Société Jersiaise*, XVII, 1960, pp. 345–6 and his *Governorship of Sir Walter Ralegh in Jersey 1600–1603*, St Helier, 1971, pp. 196–7, with errors and omissions.

## DUMARESQ v. CARTERET

[*addressed*]    To my verie loving frendes the Bailiffe¹ and Justices of Jersey

After my verie harty commendations: Whereas the lords of Her Majesties Privie Counsel have referred unto me the ending of controversies betwixt Master John de Carteret and John Dumaresq² at my comming to Jersey, which I purpose to determine at my next arrival, and that Dumaresq, as I understand, hath, without my privitie, contrary to their lordships directions, obteined under hand some commandment[3] that the said John de Carteret and Philip de Carteret, his sonne, with Master Phillip Jorneaux, a man verie aged and unhable to travell and to passe the seas, shall appeare here to answere Dumaresq[s] allegations, forasmuch as Philip de Carteret is now here and likewise an attorney of Dumaresq who have authoritie and power (or els may have) to answere the causes here which can be better decided in Jersey where the particularities and circumstances are better understood and knowne. I pray you to give order for their staye in Jersey untill their [lordships *deleted*] shalbe otherwise informed of the truth of the information or untill my repaire to that island.[4]

And soe I commit you to God.

From the Court at Whitehall the 13th of December 1601.

    Your verie loving frende,
        W Ralegh

In respect that John Dumaresq is here and Phillip de Carteret both, I thincke it fitte that the other justices be spared and not troubled and charged with their repaire in these dangerous times both for storms and Dunkerks.[5]

---

1. George Paulet, son of Sir Anthony, the late Governor.
2. For John de Carteret see above, Letter 146, note 3. John Dumaresq (1548–1606) was seigneur of the manor of Samaurez. His son Daniel is said to have been Ralegh's ward and to have served as his page: Ahier, *Governorship*, p. 100. For his marriage to Ralegh's illegitimate daughter see below, Letter 165.
3. On 16 November 1601, the Privy Council, in response to a petition by Dumaresq, had ordered the disputants to come to England: *APC XXXII*, pp. 369–70.
4. Ralegh was next in Jersey from 3 July to 10 August 1602, by which time Amice de Carteret was Bailiff.
5. French privateers: see above, Letter 121.

---

## 155. To Sir Robert Cecil [?from Sherborne, ?late 1601][1]

Hatfield, CP186/131, *HMC Salsibury* XI, p. 582. In Ralegh's hand, in great haste.
Edwards II, p. 246, dating it c.20 July 1601, from Jersey, but see below, note 3.

## THOMAS FREAKE

[*addressed*] To the right honorabell Sir Robert Cecyll knight, Principall Secritorye, etc.

[*endorsed*] Sir Walter Raleigh to my master without date

Sir: I have now receved of Master Thomas Freake[2] the full sume of foure hundred pounde accordinge to your former letter, which I hope will sett all free. By the next I will send a particuler [= *more details*], easier to be understoode. Master Freake had not so mich mony of his owne att the present but hath taken it up of his frinds. He was exceeding willinge to do yow service therin and wilby in any thinge that yow shall pleas to use hyme, for which I pray yow to returne hyme thancks, for it is a hard matter in this country[3] to make provision of mony. By the next I hope yow shall here that the shipp is gonn that now stayes butt for the winde.[4]

And so having no other matter of importance I rest yours to do yow service.

    W Ralegh

I will returne the last letter by the next packett.

1. See below, notes 3 and 4.
2. Thomas Freke of Iwerne Courtney, near Blandford, Dorset (1565–1633), JP and MP for the county in 1604, was also a land speculator and money lender: Hasler II, p. 158. In December 1601, Ralegh leased Sherborne Barton etc. from a John Freke esquire, also of Iwerne Courtney, and Richard Swayne of London for £6 14s. 11d.: J. Fowler, *Medieval Sherborne*, 1951, p. 397, note 1. The financial settlement was possibly connected with Cecil's property-dealing at Cranborne: see above, Letter 139, note 5.
3. This is unlikely to refer to Jersey as suggested by Edwards.
4. Probably Sir John Gilbert's *Refusal*: see above, Letter 152.

---

## 156. To the Western Assize Judges from the Court, 3 March [1602][1]

Centre for Kentish Studies, Maidstone, U269/1 O0101, a near-contemporary transcript of the missing original, formerly at Knole Park, Surrey, EN.M.1044; *HMC* 4th Report, Appendix (Earl de la Warr) pp. 304–5, summary of part only, suggesting a date of 1604, a year when Ralegh was in the Tower, and in full in *HMC Sackville* I, pp. 46–7, suggesting 1601/2.

## JOHN MEERE AGAIN

[*Headed*]   Sir Walter Raleighes lettre to the Justices of Assise
[*endorsed, in same hand*]   Concerninge John Meere

My verie good lords: Although I knowe it needles to desire justice at your lordshipps hands, who will afford it to the poorest creature, yet I praye your lordshipps to be informed of the vexation of diverse my poore tenaunts and some of my servaunts used by one John Meere,[2] sometime my servaunte, a man not unknowne to your lordshipps for your lordships committed him when my Lord Cheefe Baron Manwood was your lordshipps fellowe and senior judge.[3] Hee was afterwards condempned for clyppinge of goulde and soe before and since in question for forgery and other suche misdemeanors, so many as I will not truble your lordships with the repetition. Your lordships may perceive by this enclosed the greate number of suites which hee is plaintiff in. Hee vexeth soe many poore men that have not anye meanes to wage lawe but ar driven to sell theire poore implements to defend them selves, and the more to undoe these poore creatures hee sues them both in the Star Chamber, Exchecquer and at the Assises for one matter, pledinge a privilidge in the Exchecquer because he oweth the Queene money for a fine sett on him in Starchamber for knavery, which fine hee never yet paid, and therefore I hope your lordshipps will not allowe such a privilidge to such a person.

   I confesse that I thincke that God hath worthily plagued mee for entertayninge suche a wretch, whome I tooke eaten with lyce out of prison because it was tolde me that he had all the aunciert records of Sherborne, his father having been the Bushops officer. And if your lordshipps did knowe what I have done for him, how vylely hee hath used me, with what disdaine and proude words provoked me, your lordships I feare would rather condempne me of basenes then commend my patience, but hee is soe cunninge in counterfeitinge my hand that he will shewe my discharges for all actions that I can bringe against him, for I protest before the everlyving God that I found him my selfe (comminge on him on the sudden) counterfeitinge my hand above a hundred times upon an oyled paper.[4] I therefore most hartely praye your lordshipps to take some order that the poore people bee not thus vexed by him to theire undoinge, for either he sueth or terrifieth all those poore inhabitants that will not joyne with him in his divilish practises, counterfeitinges and perjuries. By this inclosed your lordshipps shall see what actions hee hath a foote and this bearer I beseech

your lordships to heare in this busines, and I will ever remayne redie to be commaunded by your lordshipps.
   Walter Raleighe [sic]

Court, 3 of Marche

[enclosure, in the same hand]
     Touchinge John Meere

Betwene 1580 and 1584 he was often bound to the good behavior and twice committed to the comon gaile, first by the consent of all the Justices of Peace at a Quarter Sessions in Dorset, and the second time by the commandment of both the Justices of Assises of the same countye for dyverse mysdeemeanors. Hee was also comitted to the Fleete out of Starchamber about Mich[ael]mas 1584 and there fined at 100 marckes which he never yet paid.

 About the same time Master Justice Periam[5] committed him at the Assizes at Dorchester, with boultes of iron upon his legges, when the Lord Cheefe Baron Manwood sate on the bench as senior judge and was maister to the saide Meere at the same time.[6]

 After that about 34 Eliz[abeth] R[eg]ine [1591–2] he was condempned at Newegate for clypping of gould, for which the Quene gave him a pardon at the request of the kinge of Portugall[7] who used D[octor] Lopas[8] as his instrum[en]t therein by the mediation of one Rawlinges, Meeres his brother in lawe,[9] they both being interpreters to the same kinge and both of them after hanged at Tiborne for theire severall villanyes. Hee hath beene indicted for a common barretor [= *troublemaker*] and twice sett in the stockes in Sherborne in Dorsetsheere whereas [sic] hee was borne and once at Poyntington in com[itatu] Somerset. He was afterwardes commmitted to the Kinges Bench by the Lord Cheefe Justice Popham. Hee was likewise committed to the Gatehouse by the Lord Admirall and Master Secretary Cecill.[10] Hee hath been often questioned for counterfeiting other mens handes. In Mich[aelm]as terme 43 and 44 Eliz[abeth] [1601][11] he had these actions following on suite, videlicet:

| In all these actions he was pl[aintif]f: | In the Exchecquer | 12 |
|---|---|---|
| | In the Chancery | 03 |
| | In the Kinges Bench | 06 |
| | In the Common Pleas | 5 |
| | In the Starchamber one against 42 severall persons upon which | |

|  |  |
|---|---|
| | hee was comitted and fined for his unjust vexation.     1 |
| In these actions he was def[*endan*]t | In the Chancery     2 |
| | In the Star Chamber     1 |
| | In the Comon Pleas     6 |

1. See below, note 11.
2. See above, Letters 141 and 145.
3. Sir Roger Manwood, Lord Chief Baron of the Exchequer 1578–98: *DNB*.
4. A method of copying signatures much used by clerks when transcribing manuscripts for legitimate purposes.
5. Sir William Periam (1534–1604), an Exonian by birth, was a former Justice of the Common Pleas and, since 1593, Chief Baron of the Exchequer: Hasler II, p. 209.
6. Presumably when Meere was a law student.
7. The Portuguese pretender, Don Antonio Perez, living in exile in England.
8. Roderigo Lopez, a Portuguese Jew (thought to have been the model for Shakespeare's Shylock), formerly the Queen's physician, convicted in 1594, perhaps unjustly, of plotting to poison her and subsequently hanged: *DNB*.
9. Meere's first wife was a Magdalen Rawlinges, but there is no corroboration of this story.
10. Cecil was knighted in 1591.
11. This confirms the date as 1602.

---

## 157. TO SIR JOHN GILBERT II, [LATE APRIL 1602][1]

New York Public Library, Arents Collection 5851, torn, decayed and badly defaced by galls. In Ralegh's hand. Words in roman type enclosed in square brackets have been supplied from the two transcripts, asterisks denoting readings dependent on BL, Addit. 4231.

PRO, SP9/12/55, no 14, an eighteenth-century transcript, with gaps; BL, Addit. 4231, ff. 85v.–86, a more complete transcript, but with errors, made for Thomas Birch *c*.1750.

Edwards II, pp. 193–7, from BL, dated ?1597.

## FAMILY RIFT

[*addressed*]    [To my nephew Sir John Gilbert, knighte]

…….. met I had reason …… [*dis]covered your not trusting …… towards mee bothe in [?which][2] ….. [witness] then himsealf whom … [*importun]ed and vexed in your causes and my … knowe … [care of yow] it is enough that he[3] knowe to … [*that I s]corn otherwize to plead it now but I knew the contents of your letter[4] by arguments used by hym cumparing thos with myne own letter. I also found that somewhat was written that I might not see because he refused to shew me yours.

For the adventure it sealf[5] ther was never any other thinge demanded by me then a third of my Lord A[\*dmirals] forth part. Be the summs more or less, all was and is [?over][6] that third of a forth: ether I will have it or [?hee] shall have it. And when yow were concluded before with a forth part, what was it to yow how the rest had bynn deveded, unless as it seemed it was amiss that I had it. For your feare of my threatnings it was not doubted that yow feard them. Neather did I threaten any thinge but the recovery of that part which I will still have without your healpe, and it is trew I labored foolishly to putt by my cussen Cole and others[7] of whom I could have had as good a part as most of the best adventurers if I had not respected your profitt more then I finde can be in your ungratfull nature to deserve.

Now to the rest, wher yow say yow followed the worst of my fortunes in despight of envy, I pray forgett nott your sealf nor do not so mich mistake my fortunes but that when they were at worst they were better then the best of your owne, and were abell enough to steed [= *support*] my frinds and despise the rest. And for envy, it were a strang[e] consaite to thinck that a nephew should be envied for goinge to the warrs with his unkell,[8] yow beinge then of no abilletye [= *substance*], your unkell[9] livinge. And for your cummand under Sir Jo[hn] Norrice[10] it is not unknown to me what it was, or if it might have bynn more, in who[\*se] respect it had bynn, for Sir Jo[hn] Norrice hyme sea[lf] ever needed me, I never needed hyme nor hi[s h]ealpe and the private jurney to Guiana[11] had as [\*much] honor as the publick jurny of Britayne and yow [\*was] as private in Britayne as in Guiana and [I] adv[\*ise yow] be just as well in Britayne as ... whersoever, and suche ... was no shame to ... the others for spending your ... is a riddell to me for ... had no fortune to spende att [Cadiz][12] ... and the reputation that yow have, forget not [that yow had] it cheifly with your titell in thos, and from which [be]ginnings hath growne the rest what soever. After yow had of your owne yow went for your sealfe and if I did not adventer to your likinge yow must know that ther was more land then to discend unto yow then to any of myne, and my estate beinge but weak and farr in debt, I could not neglect a sonn and a wife.[13] Your fortunes had yowthe and tyme to make them, myne had neather, and yet be not so forgetfull or say that I adventured nothinge, for if I had 200*li* of Lord Cobhame I adventured 400*li* worth of ordenance which I could have sold for so mich mony, which ordenance have bynn fortunate enough unto yow ever since, though contrary to me, for by reason that no man durst buy the sugors without warrantize I lett them with Sanderson who cussned me of the mony. And therefore your passion herein is greater then your allegation.[14] And because yow repeate thes things I pray forgett not that first I saved your parsonage[15] from Cari [*George Cary*] in my brothers tyme and next from [*John*] Thynn in your tyme, and butt in respect of mee I know how your aunt had dealt with yow well enough. Agayne in your pardon[16] do not beleve (how ill so ever my fortune was) butt that for me and by the healp of my frinds yow were discharged in dispight of a stronge opposition. You may remember withall the fort wher yow are[17] that it was not alone for your sealf that yow had it and that I have yet so many enemies for it, both in Court and coun[trey]. And howsoever you may awnswere the world knowe[th w]ell enough what I have dunn and will judge y[ou] accordingly, both for your father,[18] your unkell and y[ours]ealf, which I ment not to have repeted but to [answ]ere the good nature of your owne ... sealf as ... hyme as yow [are] ... [\*in] what soever valuation ... Master Secritory that he is ... [that yow] have lost mee by shewing the ... therfore desire hyme not withstandinge ... rema[yne] your ho[*nourable*] frinde, yow shall not mesure me by your own good nature for I do not labor any man agaynst yow, I may rather bee ashamed to have any man know your ingratetude. I will not defile the neast, nor yet seeke to feed thos that cann now fly so well without mee. Hurt not your sealf. I shall leve yow to your owne courses and holde this of yours no stranger then the usages of others, beinge more natu[ral] to all men rather to pay wrongs then good turnes.

And for the conclusion to that yow say that I dare not offer this dealing to any other butt your sealf, I awnswere that I dare do as muche as your sealfe and have dared and will ever be found so. And for your fortunes otherwize, feare not that I will labor to lessen them, as I will not hereafter looke after them, and when myne shalbe att worst, yet they shall never need your healpe, whatsoever yours have dun myne.[19]

    Your unkell,
    W Ralegh

1. Before 29 April 1602, when Gilbert wrote to Cecil requesting that Ralegh be forbidden to carry through a proposed deal over the sharing out of the profits of a privateering venture with Richard Cole and Robert Bassett: *HMC Salisbury* XII, p. 131 and below, note 7.
2. BL, Addit. has 'both in the ...'.

3. 'He' here and in the following paragraph must be Cecil who had written to Gilbert calling in question his handling of the prize cargo: see next note and *HMC Salisbury* XII, pp. 118–19.
4. The privateering venture in the Channel in which Cecil, Ralegh and Gilbert had been partners. Gilbert's *Refusal*, of which Cecil owned a fourth part, had returned to Plymouth on 6 April with several prizes including a 400-ton Portuguese ship carrying Venetian goods: *HMC Salisbury* XII, pp. 83, 98–9, 100, etc. Cecil had a two-fold interest, his own investment and the inevitable claims of the Venetians, with whom England was not at war.
5. Ralegh and Howard shared a quarter of the victualling: *HMC Salisbury* XII, p. 119.
6. BL, Addit. has 'is only but'.
7. Richard Cole of Slade in north Devon, grandson of Ralegh's maternal aunt, Elizabeth, née Champernon: Vivian, *Devon*, pp. 162, 214. The others included Sir Robert Bassett of Heanton in north Devon: BL, Lansd. 142, f. 125. See also *HMC Salisbury* XI, pp. 539–40, misdated 1601.
8. In 1596 the young Gilbert took part in the assault of Cadiz, where he was knighted.
9. Sir John Gilbert I, Ralegh's half-brother, whose estate young Gilbert inherited, died in September 1596: Vivian, *Devon*, p. 406.
10. Sir John Norris (c.1547–97) had commanded Elizabeth's armies in Flanders and in Ireland but most recently in Brittany: J.S. Nolan, *Sir John Norreys and the Elizabethan military world*, Exeter, 1997. His aunt, Mary Norris, widow of the Sir George Carew who was drowned in the *Mary Rose* in 1545, had married Sir Arthur Champernon, Gilbert's great-uncle: Vivian, *Devon*, p. 163.
11. Gilbert had been one of Ralegh's officers in 1595: Harlow, *Discoverie*, p. 36.
12. Uncertain: PRO, SP9 has 'Law', BL, Addit. 'Cadis', which makes more sense.
13. The loss of the profit from the *Madre de Dios*, the expenditure on Guiana and on the new house at Sherborne, and losses in Ireland following the Rising in 1598 probably meant that Ralegh was now perpetually short of cash. Ralegh's surviving son, Walter, was born in 1594.
14. Presumably a further reference to the Portuguese prize of 1601 for there had not been time for William Sanderson, Ralegh's London partner, to handle the sale of the 1602 prize cargo. Both included large quantities of sugar.
15. The rectory of Brixham: see above, Letter 152.
16. For killing Sir John Burgh in a duel in 1594: J. Roberts, 'The younger Sir John Gilbert', *DAT* C, 1968, pp. 206–7.
17. Young Gilbert had been made Governor of Plymouth Fort in 1601: *APC* XXXI, pp. 284 and 400.
18. Ralegh owed a great deal to his half-brother, Sir Humphrey.
19. The dispute took some time to settle (*HMC Salisbury* XII, pp. 213, 365), but Gilbert visited Ralegh in the Tower in August 1604: *HMC Salisbury* XVII, p. 600. He died without issue in 1608, his heir being Rawleigh, his eldest surviving brother, Sir Humphrey's sixth son: Vivian, *Devon*, p. 406. For his wife see above, Letter 62, note 1.

## 158. To Sir Robert Cecil [from the Court, late June][1] 1602

Hatfield, CP97/104, *HMC Salisbury* XII, p. 559, listed only. In Ralegh's hand.
Edwards II, pp. 256–7.

## THE POOR TAVERNERS OR POOR RALEGH

[*addressed*]  To the right honorabell Sir Robert Cecyll knight, Principall Secreterye etc.

[*endorsed*]  1602  Sir Walter Ralegh to my master

Sir: I have perswaded all the poore taverners of Inglande that I would not depart the Court untill they were assured to injoy their estates and free them from the promoter.² If I shalbe sent away³ before it bee finished I shall not only be thought a cussener [= *cheat*] but in my absence I know ther wilbe a thowsand famylies att the Court. The matter is nothing to Her Majestye. Shee that hath justefied all her actions, words and intents to all the yearth will not finde me out to make example of the contrary. The Queen may take advantage of the acts of her awncestors but neather prince nor private man denieth hyme sealf. Her Majestye used this grace to Sir Henry Ley⁴ for 400*li* lands, and that not of Her Majesties gift.

It gre[v]es mee to finde with what difficulty and torment to my sealf I obtayne the smalest favor. Her Majestye knowes that I am reddy to spend all I have, and my life, for her in a day, and that I have but the keping of that I have, for all I have I will sell for her in an howre and spend it in her service. Lett the Queen then break their harts that ar none of hers: ther is littell gayne in losinge her own. Thes things should not torment mee if I were as other[s] ar, but it is trew, *ubi dolor, ibi amor, exue amorem, exueris dolorem*. Wheras it pleaseth Her Majesty to promis to do it hereafter (although it may be certeyne that *miser est qui ex futuris pendet*), yet I protest before God for my sealf I never care to have it otherwize, butt I cannot live nor shew my face out of my doores without it, nor dare ride thorrow the townes wher they taverners dwell. I beseich yow to offre it: I hope Her Majestye will not refuse it or thinck it agayne to send mee away hartbroken and disgraced.

      Yours to do yow service,
      W Ralegh

---

1. See note 3.
2. Probably to do with a parliamentary bill for the reformation of abuses in taverns which Ralegh had spoken against early in December 1601: Hasler II, p. 275.
3. Ralegh left for Jersey early in July 1602: *CSPD 1601–3*, p. 220. See below, Letter 159.
4. Probably Sir Henry Lee (c.1532–1611) of Quarendon, Bucks, a former Queen's Champion and, since 1580, Master of the Ordnance: *DNB* and Hasler II, p. 449. In 1580 he had received a rare favour, a loan from the Queen: E.K. Chambers, *Sir Henry Lee*, Oxford, 1936.

### 159. To Sir Robert Cecil (and Lord Cobham) from Jersey, 20 July 1602

Hatfield, CP94/56, *HMC Salisbury* XII, p. 239, listed only. In Ralegh's hand, with address by a clerk.
Edwards II, pp. 247–8.

## EXILE IN JERSEY

[*addressed*] For Her Majesties especyall affaires. To the right honorable Sir Robert Cecill knight, Her Majesties Principall Secretary   Hast post hast with speed   Jersey the 21th of July   [*in Ralegh's hand*] W Ralegh
[*endorsed*] July 20   Sir Walter Raleigh to my master   From Jersey
[*postmasters' endorsements*]   Sherborn at 4 in the morninge the 22 of July
   At Shaston [*Shaftesbury*] at ix in the morning
Receved a pacet from Chastone at 4 of the cloke in the afternone the 23de of Julye by a fote man
Receved at Andover at ix at night being Fridaye the 23th of July
Basingstocke att 4 in the morninge ... [*badly torn*] the 24 of Juleye

Sir: Yow will I hope geve me leve to salute my Lord Cobhame and yow both in a letter. I cann send no newse from hence. I here not from any part of the world as yet. I cannot send away a bark for Spayne, the winde blowing continewaly att west and north west. From France I have hard nothing butt that a bark of Granvile [*Granville in Normandy*] told me that the master was offred a hundred crowns to be pilot for this place by Spinola,[1] butt he concluded with a sute for the transporting of sea cole [= *fuel*], to which I suppose his filed [= *false*] tale tended.[2] I feare the cumming of many Norman gentelemen[3] but I cannot prevent it. I shalbe mich pesterd with them.

I besech yow bestow a line or too on me that leve [*live*] in desolation, and if yow find no cause to staye me here I would willingly returne. The newses here of [*the Duc d'*] Epernons flight from Court, the Cunstabells [*Montmorency's*] disgrading and such other Rochell advertisments I beleve not: yow best know what hath past.[4]

I shall ever rest to do yow both service with all I have, and my life to boote.
                    W Ralegh

Bess will convey me your letters if yow send any.

Jersey the 20 of July. I arived here the 3th so I have walked here this 17 dayes in the wilderness.

Cap[*tain Thomas*] Button is gonn with The Vanguard, Captain [*Jeremy*] Turner⁵ is here, and the three Flemings at Garnsey [*Guernsey*].

1. Frederico Spinola, a Genoese employed by the King of Spain to destroy enemy shipping in the Channel. In 1602 he had eight galleys there: see above, Letter 120, note 2 and below, Letter 162, note 2.
2. Possibly Huguenot refugees: Ahier, op. cit., p. 128.
3. Left-hand margin: '? ... loaded'.
4. Cecil was, in fact, already well-informed.
5. Captain of the *Antelope*. Both ships were part of the Queen's Channel squadron which, with the co-operation of the Dutch, was seeking Spinola: Monson II, pp. 169–70 and *HMC Salisbury* XII, pp. 242, 267.

---

## 160. To Lord Cobham from Weymouth, 12 August [1602][1]

PRO, SP12/259/97, *CSPD 1596–7*, p. 266, dated ?1596. In Ralegh's hand, written very carelessly and damaged at the seal and at the lower left-hand margin.

Edwards II, pp. 249–50, correctly dated.

### HOME FROM JERSEY

[*addressed*] To the right honorabell my singuler good lord, the Lord Cobhame, Lord Warden of the Five Portts, etc.
[*endorsed*] Sir W Rawley to Lord Cobham

My worthy lorde: I am now arived, having stayde so long as I had means. I caused The Antelope[2] to be revitled for 14 dayes, which was as mich as that place [*Jersey*] could afforde, and that being spent I durst not tarry to cume home towards winter in a fisher man [*fishing boat*]. I presume ther is no cause to doubt it. The castells ar defensibell enough, the country reasonabell well provided and the Spanierds will ether do sumewhat more prayse worthy or attend a better opportunetye. I am reddy now to obey your cummandme[n]tts. If yow will cum to the Bath [= *the spa*] I will not fayle yow, or what soever elce your lordship will use me in this worlde.

I will now looke for the Lord Henry of Northumberlande[3] who I thinck wilbe here shortly, knowing my returne. And I doubt not butt he will meet us also att the Bathe if your lordship acqueynt hyme with the tyme. It is best if your lordship purpose it to take the end of this monenth att farthest. I here that the Lord Chamberlayn[4] is dead: if it be so I hope that your lordship may be stayde [= *held up*] uppon good cause. If it be so I could more willingly [*go*] eastward [*to Court*] then ever I did in my life. How soever [*it*] be, the[*y*] be butt things of the worlde by which thos that have inioyed them have bynn as littell happy as other poore men. But the good of thes changes wilbe that while men ar of necessety to draw lotts they shall hereby see their chanses and dispose them sealvs accordingly.

I beseich your lordship that I may here from yow. From hence I cann present yow with nothinge butt my fast love and trew affection which [*I*] shall never part from studiing to honor yow till I be in the grave.

[*Wey*]mouth this 12 of Auguste.

· W Ralegh

[*My lord*] Vicount[5] hath so exalted [*John*] Meeres sutes agaynst me in [*m*]y absence as neather Master Sergent Heale[6] nor any elce [*could*] be hard for me to stay [= *delay*] trialls while I was out of [*the*] land in Her Majesties service, a right and curtesy afforded [*to ev*]ery begger. I never busied my sealf with the Vicount [*neit*]her of his extortions or poysoninge of his wife as it [*is he*]re avowed have I [*sic*] spoken.[7] I have forborne hyme in respect of my Lord [*Thom*]as[8] and cheifly because of Master Secritory who, in his love [*to my*] Lord Thomas, hath wisht mee to it, butt I will not [*endu*]re wrong att so pevishe a fooles hands any longer. I will rather loose my life, and I thinck that my lord Puritan Periam[9] douth thinck that the Quean [*shall*] have more use of roggs and villayns then of me, or elce he would not, att Byndons instance, [*have*] yeilded to try actions agaynst me, being out of the lande.[10]

1. In a letter to George Carew on 14 September 1602, Cecil wrote that Ralegh was 'in the West, newly come out of his island': *CCM 1601–3*, p. 326.
2. See Letter 159, note 5.
3. Henry Percy (1564–1632), the 19th Earl, who was a key figure in the current intrigues over the ageing Queen's successor.
4. George Carey, Lord Hunsdon, died on 9 September 1602. Cobham, whose own father had held the office, had long hoped to succeed Hunsdon: Collins 1746, II, p. 179.
5. Thomas Howard, 3rd Lord Bindon, Lord Lieutenant of Dorset since 1601, and no friend of Ralegh.
6. John Hele, sergeant-at-law, was Sheriff of Devon in 1602. He had acted for Ralegh on various occasions but was one of his prosecutors in 1603. He had lent Cobham £4,666: Hasler II, pp. 287–8.
7. Nothing seems to be known of these charges.
8. Lord Howard of Walden (1561–1626), the naval commander, shortly to become Earl of Suffolk: *DNB*.

9. Sir William Periam: see above, Letter 156, note 5. He was, in fact, well known for his Puritan sympathies, but in using the epithet Ralegh may have been implying that he was a stickler for the letter of the law.
10. See above, note 1.

---

## 161. To Sir Robert Cecil from Weymouth, 21 August 1602

Hatfield, CP94/160, *HMC Salisbury* XI, p. 311. In Ralegh's hand.
Edwards II, pp. 251–3; D.B. Quinn (ed.), *New American World*, 1979, III, p. 347.

### THE VIRGINIA PATENT

[*addressed*]   To the right honorabell Sir Robert Cecyll knight, Principall Secritorye, etc.

[*endorsed*]   1602 August 21   Sir Walter Raleigh to my master

Sir: Wheras I wrate unto yow in my last that I was gonn to Weymouth to speake with a pinnes of myne arived from Virginia,[1] I found this bearer Captayne Gilbert[2] ther also who went onn the same voyage. But myne fell 40 leaugs to the west of it and this bearer as mich to the east, so as neather of them spake with the peopell.[3] Butt I do sende bothe the barks away agayne, having saved the charg in sarsephraze [= *sassafras*] woode.[4] Butt this bearer [*Gilbert*] bringinge sume 2200 waight to [*Sout*]hampton, his adventurers have taken away their parts and brought it [? *Gilbert's vessel*] to Lundun. I do therfore humble pray yow to deale withe my Lord Admirall [*Nottingham*] for a letter to make seasure of all that which is cume to Lundun, ether by his lordships octoretye or by the Judge [*of the Admiralty*], because I have a patent[5] that all shipps and goods ar confiscate that shall trade ther without my leve. And wheras sarsephraze was worth 10s, 12s and 20s a pound before Gilbert returned, his cloying [= *flooding*] of the markett will overthrow all myne, and his owne also. Hee is contented to have all stayde, not only for this present butt, being [= *intending*] to go agayne, others will also go and distroy the trade which otherwize would yeild 8 or 10 for on[e] in certenty, and a returne in xx weekes [*wayghts crossed out*]. I desire butt right herein, and my Lord Admirall I hope will not be a hinderance to a matter of trade graunted by the Great Seal of Inglande, his lordship havinge also freedume and an interest in the countrye.[6]

A man of my Lord [*Admiral's*] of Hampton arested a part of Gilberts [*goods*] for the xths [= *tenths*].⁷ I hope my Lord will not take it, belonging not unto hyme, having also hyme sealf poure [= *power*] to trade ther by his interest, and it were pitty to overthrow the enterprize for I shall yet live to see it an Inglishe nation.

Ther was also brought 26 sedar [= *cedar*] trees by Gilbert which on[e] [*Christopher*] Staplyne of Dartmouthe hath. If my Lord [*Admiral*] will vouchsauf to write to C[*hristopher*] Harris⁸ to seaze them we will part them in three parts, to seele⁹ cabinneats and make bords and many other delicate things. I beseich yow vouchsauf to speak to my lord: I know his lordship will do mee right herein. I for hast have not written [*to him*] for if a stey be not made it wilbe spent and sold into many hands. This bearer, Captain Gilbert, who is my Lord Cobhames man, will find out wher it is. Hee came to mee with your post letter. It is he by a good token that had the great diamonde.¹⁰ I beseich yow favor our right and yow shall see what a prety, honorabell and sauf trade wee will make.

   Yours ever to serve yow
    W Ralegh

I hope yow will excuse my cumbersume letters and sutes. It is your destiney to be trobled with your frinds, and so must all men bee, butt what yow thinck unfitt to be dun for mee shall never be a quarrell ether internall or externall. I thank yow evermore for the good, and what cannot be effected farewell hit. If we cannot have what we would, mee thinck it is a great bonde to finde a frinde that will strayne hyme sealf in his frinds cause in whatsoever as this world fareth.

Weymouth this 21 of August

Gilbert went without my leve and therfore all is confiscate and he shall have his part agayne.¹¹

---

1. Letter not extant. Nor is the name of the ship known; but under the command of Samuel Mace, an experienced Weymouth seaman, Ralegh had sent her out from Weymouth in March 1602 in one of several attempts to find his lost colonists of 1587: D.B. Quinn, *England and the discovery of America 1481–1620*, 1974, pp. 405–10.
2. Bartholomew Gilbert (no relation to the Devonshire family), a London goldsmith, Bartholomew Gosnold, probably of Falmouth, and Revd John Brereton, financed by a consortium which included Lord Cobham, had also set out in March 1602, in the *Concord*, apparently unbeknownst to Ralegh, in their case to seek a foothold in North Virginia, the later New England: ibid., pp. 413–16.

3. Mace had made landfall on the Outer Banks of Ralegh's 'Virginia' a considerable way south of Roanoke Island, the colonists' original settlement. He blamed the weather for his failure to find 'the people': ibid., p. 409.
4. The roots were thought to have medicinal uses.
5. For his royal charter of 1584 'for the Discovery and Planting of New Lands in America': see Quinn, *Roanoke 1955*, I, pp. 82–9 and for a suggestion that Ralegh was not in a strong position as his charter concerned 'planting', see D.B. Quinn, 'Thomas Hariot and the Virginia Voyages of 1602', *William and Mary Quarterly*, Series 3, XXVII, 1970, p. 276.
6. The only known reference to Nottingham's investment in the voyages of the 1580s, except that Croatoan Island off the Outer Banks of North Carolina was named Lord Admiral's Island in 1585: Quinn, *Roanoke 1955*, I, p. 283, note 3.
7. His perquisites on privateering booty, which, in Ralegh's eyes, this was not.
8. Deputy Vice-Admiral of Devon.
9. i.e. 'panel' as in 'seeling' and 'Cedar, a sweete wood good for seelings, chests, boxes ... [etc.]': Thomas Harriot, *Report on Virginia 1588*.
10. Thought to have come from the *Madre de Dios* (see above, Letter 54 and *HMC Salisbury* IV, p. 232), it passed through several hands until, in 1597, Sir Anthony Ashley secured it for the Queen with the help of confessions extracted from Bartholomew Gilbert: *HMC Salisbury* VII, pp. 504, 507 and 521, *CSPD 1598–1601*, p. 523.
11. But see below, Letter 165, note 28, for the sequel.

---

## 162. To Sir Robert Cecil from Bath, 15 September 1602

PRO, SP12/285/5, *CSPD 1601–3*, pp. 238–9, Plates 8a and 8b. In Ralegh's hand.
Edwards II, pp. 253–4.

### NAVAL INTELLIGENCE FROM JERSEY

[*addressed*]   For Her Majesties especiall service   To the right honorabell Sir Robert Cecyll knight, Principall Secritorye to Her Majestie, etc.
Hast post hast for life [*drawing of a scaffold: see Plate 8b*]   Bathe the [?15] of September att after nowne
W Ralegh
[*endorsed*]   1602 September xv   Sir Walter Raleigh to my master   With some advertisements from Jersey

Sir: I receved thes inclosed[1] from my leuetenant this present morninge and have dispatched the bearer which came from Jersey unto yow. It seemes to be trew. All that cann be dun is to lay [*in wait*] for them carefully and though the galle[y]s[2] slipp by the shore the flibotts cannot. They speak of galleasses[3] but I understand it not.

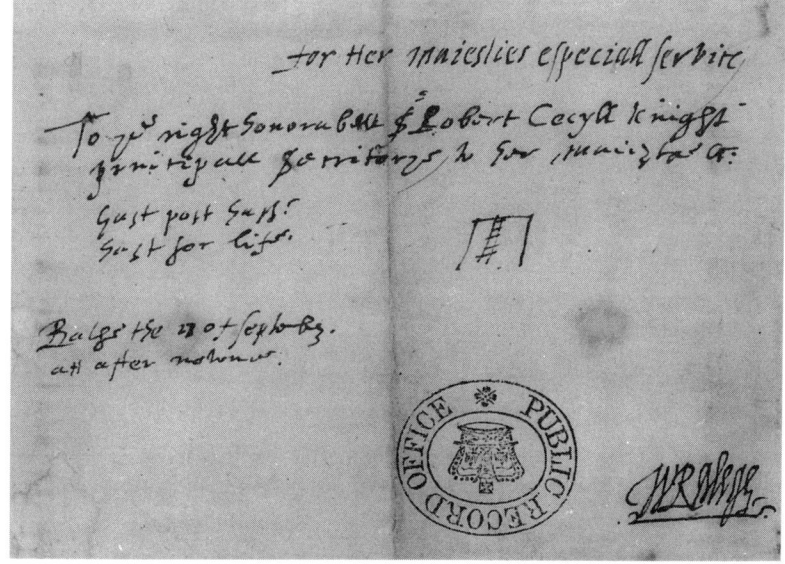

*Plates 8a and 8b.* Letter 162, with flyleaf: Sir Walter Ralegh to Sir Robert Cecil, 15 September 1602. (PRO, SP12/285/5)

I am att this instant in payne and cannot writ mich. I beseich yow be good to this poore man[4] that hath taken payne and cume with speed in his own barck.[5]

    Yours as your sarvent,
        W Ralegh

I beseich yow remember me to my Lord Cobhame.

Bath the xvth.

1. PRO, SP12/285/5/Ii and IV, *CSPD 1601–3*, pp. 238–9. The first, dated 9 September 1602, was from an Englishman, Anthony Bonneville, who wrote from Rennes in Brittany to Sir George Paulet in Jersey about the arrival at Blavet of six galleys and two great flyboats thought to be bound for Flanders with pay for the Spanish army. Bonneville also wrote to Cecil: *CSPD 1601–3*, p. 241. For the sake of security, Paulet sent the news to Ralegh on 13 September in duplicate and wrote again on 18 September confirming it: PRO, SP12//285/5/IIi.
2. Belonging to Frederico Spinola: see above, Letters 120 and 159. When the English complained about the use of Blavet, the French replied that they could not prevent Spinola lying in the bay, but that he would not be made welcome in any French port. On 23 September, Sir Robert Mansell, in command of the English fleet, drove Spinola's ships into the arms of the Dutch who were blockading Sluys and Dunkirk: Monson II, pp. 109, 190–93, *CSPD 1601–3*, pp. 242 and 243.
3. Heavy, low-built ships, powered by both sail and oars.
4. Probably either Phillyp Rockyer or John Cuffe, Paulet's men.
5. Of Spinola's fleet, five were sunk or driven ashore, only Frederico himself reaching Dunkirk: Wernham, *Return of the Armadas*, p. 401. With the English and Dutch fleets now in control of the Channel and the Spanish coast, and with no further need to keep troops in Brittany, English resources could now be concentrated on the subjection of the Irish rebels, an operation in which Ralegh no longer had even an armchair part to play.

---

## 163. To [Sir Robert Cecil, before 25 March 1603][1]

Folger, X.d.459(14), not previously printed. In Ralegh's largely italic hand.

### ON BEHALF OF AN OLD SERVANT OF THE QUEEN

[*no address or endorsement*]

Sir: I sent unto yow in the behalf of an ancient sarvant of Her Majestes to have your hand to signefy [= *endorse*] the contents of his sute. I can asure yow Her Majestye hath graunted the same and willed hyme to send his bill unto her to be sined. But hering that it would not pass without the accustomed sedule he is an earnest suter for the same, which I beseich yow to accomplish in his behalf.

So resting most redy to requit your many cureteses, I take my leve.
>Your most asured frinde,
>>W Ralegh

1. t. Elizabeth I, probably shortly before her death, and if so, almost certainly to her Principal Secretary.

---

### 164. To Sir Thomas Egerton, Sir John Popham and Sir Edward Coke, [on or before 9]¹ June 1603

Huntington, EL 6231. In Ralegh's hand.

J.P. Collier (ed.), *Egerton Papers*, Camden Society, Old Series XII, 1840, pp. 380–81; Edwards II, p. 269, from Collier.

## DURHAM HOUSE

[*addressed*] To the right honorabell my very good lords, the Lorde Keeper of the Great Seale and my Lorde Cheif Justice of Inglande and to my very good frinde His Majesties Aturney Generall
[*endorsed*] Sir Walter Raleghes letter, rec[*eived*] 9 Junii 1603

I receved a warrant from your lordshipps, my Lord Keeper and my Lord Cheife Justice, and signed also by Master Aturney Generall, requiringe mee to deliver the possession of Derum Howse² to the Byshope of Derum³ or to his aturney before the xxiiiith day of June next insewinge,⁴ and that the stabells and garden should be presently [= *shortly*]⁵ putt into his hands. And that I should not remove any seelinge [= *panelling*], glass, iron, etc., without warrant from your lordships or any too of yow. This letter seemeth to mee very strange seinge I have had the possession of the howse almost xx yeare and have bestowed well nire 2000*li* upon the same out of myne own purse. I am of oppinion that if the Kings Majestye had recovered this howse or the like from the meanest gentelman and sarvant hee had in Inglande that His Majestye would have geven six moneaths tyme for the avoydance [= *vacating*] and I do not know butt that the poorest artificer in Londun hath a quarters warni[n]ge geven hyme by his land lord.⁶ I have made my provisions for 40 persons in the springe and I have a fa[m]yley [*household*] of no less number [? *in the howse*]⁷ and the like for allmost xx horse. Now to cast out my my hey and oates into the streats att an howres warni[n]ge and to remove my fa[m]yley and stuff in 14 dayes after is such a seveare expultion as hath not bynn offred to any man before this daye.

But this I would have written to any that had not bynn of yowr lordships place and respect, that the cource taken with mee is bothe contrary to honor, to custome and to civillety, and therfore I pray your lordships to pardon mee till I have acquynted the Kings Majestye with this letter, and then if His Majestye shall thinck it reasonabell I will ob[e]y it. Butt for the cummandment sent mee for the wenscote [= *panelling*] and other things I do not finde that it pleased His Majestye to geve your lordships any suche direction⁸ and if I do any thinge contrary to law the Byshope may take his remedy, and I perceve cannot want good frinds.⁹

And so I humble take my leve and rest your lordships to cummande.

   W Ralegh

1. See endorsement which Collier (op. cit., p. 380) identified as in the hand of Egerton, the Lord Keeper.
2. See Plate 4.
3. Tobias Mathew (Bishop 1595–1606), who entertained the King on the latter's journey south in 1603: J. Nicholls, *Progresses of King James I*, 1828, 1, p. 75. As early as 2 April, the Bishop had arranged to lease Durham House to his own son: Brushfield, *DAT*, 35, 1903, p. 570.
4. Strictly interpreted it means 'immediately', but in the West Country the word was, and still is, used to mean something akin to 'soon'.
5. The three officers of state to whom Ralegh addressed his letter had given judgment in the Bishop's favour on 29 May (*HMC Salisbury* XV, p. 111), and on 31 May the King had signed a warrant ordering Ralegh and Sir Edward Darcy, Ralegh's kinsman and fellow-tenant, to quit the premises at a date to be fixed by Egerton etc., 'with indifferent consideration aswell of the bishops necessary use of the place as also their [Ralegh and Darcy's] convenyency for removing from thence': Huntington Library, EL 6230 and Edwards II, p. 263. See also below, note 9.
6. On 7 June, Bishop Mathew complained of delays by the occupants though they had known since April of his just claim. He had heard that Ralegh was seeking to remain until Michaelmas, which would prevent him carrying out out repairs during the summer: Collier, op. cit., p. 379.
7. Manuscript torn: text as read by Collier.
8. The Bishop claimed that Ralegh was trying 'to gaine tyme to deface the house more then is justifyable by law' but, in fact, as far as the wainscotting and glass were concerned, Ralegh would have been within his rights as neither were regarded as what would now be called 'fixtures'. These were not, in fact, specified in the royal warrant: above, note 5.

9. Although the main part of the house remained with the bishopric of Durham for the time being, the stables and other outbuildings on the Strand frontage, described as 'ruinous', were acquired almost immediately by Ralegh's next-door neighbour, the Earl of Salisbury, doubtless one of the Bishop's 'good friends', to be cleared for the building of his 'New Exchange': T.N. Brushfield, 'Britain's Burse or the New Exchange', *Journal of the British Archaeological Association*, new series, IX, pt i, p. 35.

---

## 165. TO LADY RALEGH [FROM THE TOWER, ON OR SHORTLY BEFORE 27 JULY 1603][1]

All Souls College, Oxford, Codrington Library, 155, ff. 100–102, the only near-contemporary transcript of a lost original, spelling probably to some extent modernized.

J.S. Brewer (ed.), *Bishop Goodman's Court of King James I*, 1839, pp. 93–7; Edwards II, pp. 383–7; Grace Hadow (ed.), *Sir Walter Raleigh: Selections from ... his letters*, 1917, pp. 177–81; A.M.C. Latham, 'Sir Walter Ralegh's farewell letter to his wife', in Percy Simpson (ed.), *Essays and Studies* XXV, 1939, pp. 39–42, all, directly or indirectly, from the All Souls transcript.

## FAREWELL LETTER

[*no address or endorsement but transcript headed*]   Sir Walter Rawleighs letter to his wife after [*sic*] he had hurte himself in the Tower

Receyve from thy unfortunate husband theis his last lynes, theis the last words that ever thow shalt receive from him. That I can live to thinke never to see the[e] and my child[2] more I cannot. I have desired God and disputed with my reason, but nature and compassion hath the victorie. That I can live to thinke howe you are both lefte a spoile to my enimies and that my name shalbe a dishonor to my child I cannot: I cannot indure the memorie thereof. Unfortunate woman, unfortunate child, comfort your selves, trust God and be contented with your poore estate. I woulde have bettered it if I had enjoyed a few [*more*] yeares.[3]

Thowe art a yong woman[4] and forbeare not to marry againe. It is nowe nothing to me: thowe art noe more mine nor I thine.[5] To witnes that thowe didest love me once take care that thowe marry not to please sence but to avoide povertie and so preserve thy child. That thowe didest also love me livinge, witnesse it to others, to my poore daughter[6] to whome I have geven nothinge, for his sake whoe wilbe cruell to himselfe to preserve the[e]. Be charitable to her and teache thy sonne to love her for his fathers sake.

For my selfe I am left [= *deserted*] of all men, [*I*] that have done good to many, all my good turnes forgotten, all my errors revived and expownded to all extremitie of ill. All my services, hazardes and expences for my countrie: plantinges, discoveries, fightes, councells and whatsoever ells, malice hath nowe covered over.⁷ I am nowe made an enimie and traytour by the word of an unworthie man.⁸ He hath proclaimed me to be a partaker of his vaine imag[i]nations,⁹ notwithstanding the whole course of my life hath approved the contrarie, as my death shall approve it. Woe, woe, woe be unto him by whose falsehood we are loste. He hath seperated us asunder, he hath slaine my honor, my fortune, he hath robbed the[e] of thy husband, thy child of his father and me of you both. Oh God thowe doest knowe my wronges, knowe then thowe my wife and child, knowe then thowe¹⁰ my Lord and King that I ever thought them to[o] honest to betraie and too good to conspire againste. But, my wife, forgeve thowe all, as I doe, live humble for thowe hast but a time also. God forgive my Lord Harry¹¹ for he was my heavie enimye, and [*as*] for my Lord Cecill, I thought he woulde never forsake me in extremitie: I woulde not have done it him, God knowes. But doe not thowe knowe [= *admit*] it for he muste be maister [= *guardian*] of thy child¹² and maye have compassion of him.

Be not dismaide that I dyed in dispaire of Gods mercies, strive not to dispute it but assure thy selfe that God hath not lefte me nor Sathan tempted me. Hope and dispaire live not together. I knowe it is forbidden to destroye our selfes but I trust it is forbidden in this sorte, that we destroye not ourselves dispairinge of Gods mercie.¹³ The mercie of God is immesurable, the cogitations of men comprehend it not. In the Lord I have ever trusted and I knowe that my redeemer lyveth.¹⁴ Farr is it from me to be tempted with Sathan: I am onely tempted with sorrowe, whose sharpe teeth devour my harte. O God that art goodnes itselfe¹⁵ thowe must not be but good to me. Oh God that art mercye it selfe thowe canst not be but mercifull to me.

For my [e]state is conveyed to feoffees, to your cosen Brett and others.¹⁶ I have but a bare estate for a shorte life. My plate is at gage [= *as security*] in Lumbard Streete,¹⁷ my debts are many: to Peter Vanlore¹⁸ some 600*li*; to Antrobus as much, but Cumpton¹⁹ is to paye 300*li* of; to Michaell Hext²⁰ 100*li*; to George Carewe²¹ 100*li*; to Nicholas Sanders²² 100*li*; to John Fitz James²³ 100*li*; to Master Waddonn²⁴ 100*li*; to a poore man, one Hawker, for horses, 70*li*; to a poore man called Hunt 20*li*. Take first care of these for Gods sake. To a brewer at Weymouth and a baker for my lord Cecills shippe and myne²⁵ I thincke some 80*li*: John Renolds²⁶ knoweth it. And let that poore man have his true part of my retorne from Virginia,[27] and let the poore mens wages be paid with [*from the sale of*] the goods for the Lords sake.[28]

Oh what will my poore servauntes thinke at their retourne when they heare I am accused to be Spanish, [*I*] whoe sente them, to my great charge, to plant and discover upon his [*the King of Spain's*] territorie.[29] Oh intollerable infamie. Oh God I cannot resiste theis thoughtes. I cannot live to thincke howe I am deryded, to thincke of the expectation of my enimyes, the scornes I shall receive, the crewell words of lawyers, the infamous tauntes and dispightes, to be made a wonder and a spectacle. O death hasten the[*e*] unto me that thowe maiste destroye the memorie of theis and laye me up in darke forgetfullnes. O death destroye my memorie which is my tormentor: my thoughtes and my life cannot dwell in one body.

But doe thowe forget me, poore wife, that thowe maist live to bringe up thy poore child. I recommend unto you my poore brother, A[*drian*] Gilbert. The lease of Sanding [*Sandridge*] is his and none of myne:[30] lett him have it for Gods cause. He knowes what is due to me upon it. And be good to Kemis[31] for he is a perfecte honest man and hath [*suffered*] much wronge for my sake. For the rest I commend me to them and them to God. And the Lord knowes my sorrowe to part from the[*e*] and my poore child, but part I must, by enimyes and injuries, parte with shame and triumph of my detractors. And therefore be contented with this worke of God and forget me in all thinges but thine owne honor and the love of mine. I blesse my poore child. And let him knowe his father was noe traytor. Be bold of my innocencie, for God to whome I offer life and soule knowes it. And whoesoever thowe chuse againe after me, lett him be but thy politique [*= expedient*] husband, but let my sonne be thy beloved for he is parte of me and I live in him, and the difference is but in the nomber and not in the kinde. And the Lord for ever keepe the[*e*] and them and geve the[*e*] comfort in both worlds.

                   [*no signature transcribed*][32]

1. Ralegh was arrested on 15 July and sent to the Tower on or about 20th. The heading of the transcript is in error in dating the letter '*after*' the suicide attempt which occurred on 27 July: *HMC Sackville* II, pp. 136–7. He is quite clearly only *intending* to take his own life, or at least (Latham, op. cit., p. 45) to appear to be about to do so.
2. Walter junior, now aged ten.
3. Since King James's accession in March, Ralegh had lost his main source of regular income, his patent to issue licences to retail wine, which had been suspended with all other monopolies early in May: Stebbing 1899, p. 181.
4. Lady Ralegh was in fact 38.

5. Cf. above, Letter 104 and below, Letter 172.
6. The illegitimate daughter whose mother's name had been revealed by him in his will of 1597: see Appendix 2. See also Letter 31a, printed in Appendix 1. There is some evidence that the daughter married Daniel Dumaresq, Seigneur de Saumarez, of Jersey, Ralegh's ward and page, and that she died of the plague in or near London: A.M.C. Latham, loc. cit., p. 132.
7. Cf. Ralegh's 'Petition to Queen Anne': Latham (ed.), *Poems*, 1951, p. 70.

> All love and all desert of former tymes
> Malice hath covered from my soveraignes eies,
> And largelie laid abroad supposed crimes.

8. Lord Cobham.
9. Cf. below, Letter 169.
10. The transcript reads 'knowe them thowe', but the emendation makes better sense unless 'my wronges' be understood after 'knowe'.
11. Lord Henry Howard (1540–1614), Ralegh's chief detractor with the King, to whom he wrote of Ralegh and Cobham that 'hell did never spew up such a couple': Penry Williams, *Later Tudors*, 1995, pp. 385–6.
12. Cecil had been appointed Master of Wards in May 1601: J. Hurstfield, *The Queen's Wards*, 1958, p. 297. In the event of Ralegh's death he would take over the administration of his heir's estate during his minority.
13. When in the Tower in 1618 Ralegh observed to Sir Thomas Wilson that, 'divers doe hold opinion that a man may doe it [*commit suicide*] and yett not desperatly dispayre of Gods mercy but dy in Gods favor': PRO, SP14/99/101.
14. The Book of Job, chapter 19, verse 25.
15. Cf. below, Letter 172.
16. On 12 April 1603 Ralegh had conveyed the whole of his estate at Sherborne to trustees for the benefit first of himself, then of his son and his heirs and, in the event of his son's death without heirs, of his brother Carew and Carew's three sons. Unlike his conveyance of 1594 (see above, Letter 81), he retained power of revocation: W.B. Wildman, *Short History of Sherborne*, pp. 140–41. Alexander Brett, of White Stanton in Somerset, was married to a cousin of Lady Ralegh. The other trustees were Sir Arthur Throckmorton, Lady Ralegh's brother, and Thomas Harriot, and there were six witnesses, including John Doddridge, Laurence Keymis and John Shelbury. There was no provision for Lady Ralegh, but it was her husband's intention that she should have the wine patent: see below, Letter 172, note 6.
17. See below, Letter 178.
18. The King's jeweller. See below, Letter 213, note 2.
19. Not identified, probably a tradesmen.
20. Michael Hicks, formerly secretary to Lord Burghley. See below, Letter 186.
21. Presumably Sir George, Ralegh's longstanding friend, now Lord President of Munster.
22. Of Ewell in Surrey, MP for Haslemere in 1593, another relative by marriage of Lady Ralegh, rather than his namesake the MP for a Cornish borough in 1601: Hasler III, pp. 344–5.
23. A Dorset neighbour: see above, Letter 119, note 5.
24. Possibly John Waddon, joint owner of the *Spy* of Plymouth, a privateering ship and to be Mayor of Plymouth 1609–10: Andrews 1964, p. 270 and R.N. Worth, *Plymouth Municipal Records*, 1893, p. 147.
25. Cecil, Ralegh and Cobham were currently partners in a privateering venture.
26. A privateer of Weymouth: Andrews 1964, p. 142.
27. Presumably not Reynolds who could hardly be described as 'poor'.
28. Earlier this year Ralegh had sent Bartholomew Gilbert and Thomas Mace in two ships to look for his 'Lost Colonists' in Chesapeake Bay. They had no success and returned home without Gilbert, who had been killed, in September: D.B. Quinn, *Set Fair for Roanoke*, 1985, pp. 335–6.
29. An interesting admission, repeated below in Letter 166.

30. In the parish of Stoke Gabriel. In 1596–7 Adrian Gilbert had conveyed his lease of 'the site and capital messuage of Sandridge together with land called Blindwells' in Devon to Ralegh to hold in trust for his, Gilbert's, benefit. In 1598–9 Ralegh had regranted the property, Gilbert having remained in possession. On Ralegh's attainder the property was seized by the Crown on suspicion of it belonging to him. As late as 1609 the ownership was still in dispute, Ralegh being accused of conspiring to claim ownership and in his turn laying charges against his half-brother: *CSPD 1603–10*, p. 554 and *HMC Salisbury* XXI, p. 153.
31. Captain Laurence Keymis, Ralegh's devoted lieutenant, especially in Guiana. He was imprisoned and subjected to endless questioning concerning his master's affairs. Nothing seems to be known of his background.
32. The authenticity of this text has been called into question, notably by Stebbing (1899, pp. 197–8), but the discovery that Ralegh did indeed father an illegitimate daughter (see above, note 6) now serves as its chief accreditation. The personal details also ring true. The only remaining doubt is whether it was ever read by Lady Ralegh.

## 166. To the Earls of Nottingham, Suffolk and Devonshire and Lord Cecil [from the Tower, shortly after 13 August 1603][1]

BL, Harley 39, f. 369, a contemporary transcript.

Six others, very similar, including Inner Temple London, Petyt 538.51, f. 44, *HMC 11th Report*, p. 288 which has some corrupt readings not in BL, Harley 39; Bodleian, Rawlinson B 151, f. 1021 v., incomplete, Tanner 299, f. 30, by Archbishop Sancroft; BL, Addit. f. 13, as Harley 39; Folger, G.b.9, f. 180 v., *c*.1620, as BL, Harley 39.

*Remains* 1702, 1726, p. 187, as Petyt; Birch, 1751, II, p. 379, as *Remains*; Cayley, 1806, I, p. 367, as Birch; *Works* 1829, VIII, p. 644, as Birch; Edwards II, p. 271, spelling modernized, from *Works*.

### REFUTING HIS ACCUSERS

[*transcript headed*] The coppie of a lettere written by Sir Walter Ralegh to the erles of Nottinham [*sic*], Suffolk and Devonshir[2] and to the Lord Cicille declaring his inosencie in the two points wherwith he was chargede as in point of treason on the xiiith of August anno 1603

[*addressed*] To the right honorable my very good lordes the earles of Nottinham Suffolke and Devonshire, and to the Lord Cecill

I do not knowe whether your lordshippes have seene my answeres to all those matteres which my Lord Henry Howarde, my Lord [*Edward*] Wotton and Sir Edward Cooke examyned me of on Saterdaye the 13th of this presente, which makes me bould to write unto your lordshippes at this time. The two principall accusationes beinge thes, the firste that money was offered me with a pretence to maintaine the amety[3] but the intent was to have assisted His Majesties suprise,[4] or to have done somme other like mischeife. The other that I was privie to my Lord Cobhames Spanish jurney.[5] For the firste I beseech your lordshippes to way it seriously before ther be any further procedinge, for to leave me to the cruelly [= *cruelty*] of the lawe of England and to that *summum jus* before bothe your understandings and consciences be thoroughly informed wer but carlessly to distroy the father and fatherlesse. And you may be assured that ther is noe glory nor any reward that can recompence the shedinge of innocent bloude. And wheras it seemeth to appeare that this money was offered to others longe after it was offered to me, and upon some other conditiones then it was unto me, for my selfe I avowe upon my alleageaunce that I nevere either knewe or suspected either the man or the new intention.[6] To me it was but once propounded and in three weekes aftere I never heard more of it, neither did I beleve it that he had any commissyone to offer it, as the everlastinge God doth witnes. For yf that word amytie had bene used to me coullorably [= *deceptively*] I must have bene also made acqu[a]inted with the trew end for which it should have bene given, which it seemeth was for the surprise, but of any such horrible and fearfull purpose, yf ever I had so much as a suspition I refuse your lordshipes favors and the Kinges mercye.

I knowe that your lordshipes have omitted nothinge to find out the truth herof, but as you have not erred like ill surgeones to laye on plasters too narrowe for so greate woundes, so I truste that you will not imetate unlernede phisitiones to give medescines more cruell then the desease it selfe.

For the jurney into Spaine I knowe that I was accused to be privey therunto, but I knowe that your lordshipes have a reputatione of conscience as well as of industry. By what meanes that revengefull accusatyone was stirred you, my Lord Cecill, knowe right well that it was my lettre about Rensis,[7] and your lordshipes all knowe whether it be maintayned or whether, out of truth and out of a Christyan consyderatyon, it be revoked.[8] I knowe that to have spoken it once is enough for the lawe yf wee lived under a crewell prince, but I knowe that the Kinge is too mercifull to have or suffere his subjects to be ruined by any quirke or uncristian advantage, unlese he be resolvede or can perswade his religeous hearte of the equitie. I knowe that the King thinkes with all good princes *satius est peccare in alteram partem*.[9] God doth knowe, and I can give accompte of it, that I have spente 40000*li* of myne owne againste that King and natyon, that I never reserved so much of all my fortunes as to purchas 40*li* [*per annum of*] lande, that I have bene a violente[10] furtherer of all enterprises againste him. I have served againste them [sic] in person, and howe my Lord Admirall and my Lord of Suffolke can witnes. I discovered my selfe the richest partes of all his Indies, I have planted in his territoryes, I offered His Majestie at my unkell Carews[11] to carry 2000 men to invad him, without the Kinges charge. Alase, to what end should wee live in the world yf all our indevores, if so many tostymonyes, shalbe blowne of[f] with one blaste of breath or be perverted by on[e] manes worde. And in this tyme when wee have a generous prince from whome to purchas honor and good oppinion I had no other hope but by undertakynge upon that cruell and insolent nation.

Thinke therfore I moste humbly beseech you one [sic] my greate afflictyon with compasyon, who have loste my estate and the Kings favore upon one manes worde, and as you would that God should deale with you, deale with me. You all knowe that the lawe of Englande hath neede of a mercifull prince, and yf you put me to shame you take from me all hope ever to recover His Majesties leaste grace againe. I beseech you be resolved of those thinges of which I am accused and distinguish me from otheres as you have trewe honore and as you would your selves be used in the like. Forget all pertyculer mislikes. *Multos clementia honestavit ultio nullum.* Your lordshipes knowe that I am gultelesse of the surprise intended. Your lordshipes knowe, or may knowe, that I nevere accepted of the money, and that it was nott offerede to me for any ill. And of the Spanishe jurney I truste your consciences are resolved. Keepe not then I beseich you these my awnsweres and humble desires from my soveraine lord, *qui est rex pius et miserecors et non leo coronatus.* This humbly beseechinge your lordshipes to have a mercifull regarde of me, I reste your lordshipes humble and misserable supplyante.

           Wal[ter] Raulegh [sic]

1. This was the day on which Ralegh was examined by Henry Lord Howard, Henry Lord Wotton and Sir Edward Coke, the Attorney General.
2. All were old comrades in arms and might have been regarded by Ralegh as his friends, or those most likely to support him.
3. Peace with Spain. Ralegh had confessed to having been offered money for the furthering of the peace but claimed that he gave no undertaking.
4. The Bye Plot to seize the King.
5. It was alleged that he planned to return via Jersey where he was to meet Ralegh.
6. Cobham's alleged suggestion to the Count of Aremberg, the Spanish agent, that if more cash were forthcoming there were ways other than peace.
7. Matthew de la Renzi, a merchant of Antwerp, not 'Keymish' as in some of the transcripts and in the *Remains* and Edwards. Renzi was often used by by Cobham to relay messages.

8. On 4 August, Cecil wrote to the English ambassador in France that Cobham 'seemeth now to clear Sir Walter in most things and to take all the berthen to himself': Cayley 1806, 1, p. 366.
9. The scribe of Harley 39 either wrote or copied bad Latin, i.e. '*satis est perrare in altram parteme*', which has been replaced here by the sound Latin provided by Archbishop Sancroft in BL, Tanner 299, and by Edwards.
10. Some of the transcripts add the words 'persecutor and'.
11. Ralegh's last formal interview with the King had been at the house of Lady Ralegh's uncle, Sir Nicholas Carew, at Beddington, Surrey, in June: J. Nicholls (ed.), *Progresses of King James I*, I, p. 164.

---

## 167. To Lord Cecil [from the Tower, before 10 November 1603][1]

Hatfield, CP102/67(2), *HMC Salisbury* XV, p. 285, dated 'after Nov. 17'. In Ralegh's neatest hand.

Edwards II, pp. 278–80.

## AN APPEAL FOR MERCY

[*addressed*]  To the right honorabell the Lord Cecyll, etc.
[*endorsed*]  Sir W Ralegh

Sir: To speake of former tymes it were needles. Your lordshipe knowes what I have byn towards your sealf and how long I have loved yow and have byn favored by yow, but chang of tymes and myne own errors have worren out thos remembrances (I feare) and if ough[t] did remayn, yet in the state wherin I stand ther can be no frindshipe. Cumpassion ther may be for it is never seperat from honor and vertu. If the poure [= *power*] of law be not greater then the poure of trewth I may justly beseich yow to releve me in this my affliction. If it be, then your lordship shall have cause (as a just man) to bewayle my undeserved miserabell estate. I cannot dispaire but that sume warmth remayneth in cynders[2] to move yow to the first. To the secound I may assure my sealf that even God hym sealf and your lordships love to justice will parswade yow.

Your lordship knowes my accusor and have ever known my affection to that nation [*Spain*] for which I am accused. A hevy burden of God to be in danger of perishinge for a prince which I have so long hated and to suffer thes miseres under a prince whom I have so long loved. Sir, what mallice may do agaynst me I know not. My cause hath byn handled by strong enemyse. But if ever I so mich as suspected this practize layd to my charge, leve me to death if the same by any equety shalbe proved agaynst me. And *equitas* is sayd to be *juris ligitimi emendatio et justitiae directio*.

Your lordship is now a counceler to a mercifull and just kinge (if ever we had any). Yow have ever dealt in matter of justice as knowing no mans face, yet vouchsauf now so to use the poure which God and the King hath geven yow as to defend me from undeserved crewelty. *Potentia non est nisi ad bonum.* The law ought not to overrule piety but piety the law. The law doth warrant all actions before men, but God hath sayde *Innocentem non interficies.* Your lordship hath known in your tyme one in this place condemned and in this place he perished,[3] who, at the houre of his death, receved the sacriment that he was innocent. How therfore I shalbe judged I knowe not. How I have deserved to be judged I know, and I desire nothinge but *secundum meritum meum.* If I should say unto the King that my love so long born hyme might hope for sume grace it would perchance be taken for presumption because he is a king, and my soveraygne.[4] But as the King is a trew gentelman, and a just man besyds his beinge a kinge, so he oweth unto me such a mercifull respect as the resolution most willingly to have hasarded my life and fortune for hyme agaynst all men may deserve.

For your sealf (my Lord Cecill), and for me sumtyme your trew frind and now a miserabell forsaken man, I know that affections ar nether taught nor perswaded, but if ought remayn of good, of love or of cumpassion towards me, your lordship will now shew it when I am now most unworthy of your love and most unabell to deserve it. For even then is love, trew honor and trew vertu expressed. And what I shall leve to pay of so great a debt God will performe to your lordship and to yours.

    Your lordships wreched poor frinde and sarvant,
        W Ralegh

Your lordship will finde that I have bynn strangly practiced agaynst and that others have their lives promised to accuse me.[5] I can say no more but beseich yow to use charety. *Charitas est quaedam participatio spiritus sancti.*

---

1. Ralegh left the Tower ('this place') for Winchester on 10 November 1603.
2. Cf. 'First Draft of a Petition to Queen Anne', Latham (ed.), *Poems*, 1951, p. 68.
        For did in Cinders any heate remayne
        Of those cleare fyres of Love and friendlines
        I could not call for right and call in vaine.
3. Not identified.
4. Cf. below, Letter 168.
5. Presumably a reference to Cobham: see below, Letter 171, note 5.

### 168. To King James [from the Tower, before 10 November 1603][1]

Hatfield, CP102/67/1, *HMC Salisbury* XV, p. 285, dated '1603 after 17 November'. In Ralegh's most formal set hand, the Latin quotations being in italic. Enclosed with Letter 167.

Innumerable contemporary and later transcripts with minor variants. Many times printed, first in *Cabala* 1654, p. 85; Edwards II, p. 280.

## AN APPEAL TO KING JAMES

[no address]
[endorsed]   Sir W R

Most dread soverayne: It is on part of the office of a just and worthy prince to here the cumplaynts of his vassalls, especially of such as ar in gretest missery. I know that among many other presumtions gathered agaynst me Your Majesty hath bynn parswaded that I was one of them who were gretly discontented and therfore the more likely to be disloyall. But the great God so releive[d] me and myne in both worlds as I was the contrary and, as I tooke no greter cumfort then to behold Your Majesty and allways lerninge sume good and betteringe my knowledg by Your Majesties discource, I do therfore most humble beseich my soverayne lord not to beleve any of thos in my particuler who, under pretence of offences to kings do easely work their particuler revenges. I trust that no man (under the culler of making examples) shall parswade Your Majesty to leve the word mercifull out of your stile, for it will no less profite Your Majesty and becume your gretnes then the word invincibell.

It is trew that the lawes of Ingland ar no less jelous of the king then Caesar was of Pompeia his wife, for, notwithstanding that she was clered of the accusation for Claudius, yet for beinge suspected he condemned her. For mysealf I protest before the everliving God, and I speak it to my master and my soverayne, that I never invented [= *instigated*] treason, consented to treason or parformed treason agaynst hyme.[2] And yet I know that I shall fall *in manus eorum a quibus non possum exsurgere* unless by Your Majesties great cumpassion I be sustayned. Our law therfore, most mercifull prince, knowing her owne cruelty and that she is wount to cumpound treasons out of presumtions and circumstances, doth geve this charetabell advice to the king her superior: *Non solum enim sapiens debit esse rex sed et misericors, ut cum sapientia misericorditer sit justus cum tutius sit reddere rationem misericordiae quam juditii.*

I do therfore on the knees of my hart beseich Your Majesty to take councell from your own sweet and mercifull disposition, and to remember that I have loved Your Majesty now twenty yeares,³ for which Your Majesty hath yet geven me no reward, and it is fitter that I should be indebted to my soverayne lord then the king to his poore vassall. Save me therfore most merciful prince, that I may owe Your Majesty my life it sealf, then which ther cannot be a greter debt. Lend it me att lest, my soverayne lord, that I may pay it agayne for your service when Your Majesty shall pleas. If the law distroy me Your Majesty shall put me out of your poure [= *power*] and I shall have then none to feare, none to reverence, but the Kinge of Kings.

Your Majesties most humble and penitent vassall,
WR

1. Ralegh enclosed this with Letter 167 to Cecil, presumably to increase its chances of reaching the King. Whether it did so is not known, but its survival among Cecil's papers is suspicious.
2. Cf. below, Letter 170.
3. The timespan seems to have no particular significance.

---

## 169. To Lord Cobham from Bagshot, [c.11/12 November 1603]¹

Huntington, HM102, f. 14, a contemporary transcript of a lost original.

P. Lefranc, 'Ralegh in 1596 and 1603: Three unprinted letters in the Huntington Library', *Huntington Library Quarterly*, XXIX, 1966, pp. 344–5, *in extenso*.

### REQUESTING EXCULPATION

[*no address or endorsement included*]

I doe not knowe whether your lordship or myself shalbe first araynd. I thinke I shall be the first.² I beseche your lordship as you would have God showld comforte you so deale with me in this matter. You knowe in your soule that you never acquainted me with your Spanish imaginations,³ and that you had really satysfyed me of Cobliffe.⁴ I never suspected you afterwards. You knowe that you offered me the monie *bona fide* for the peace. I trust in God that you never spake those words of the Kynge, and if you be clere of it your peers will never condeme you for your Spanishe intent, seinge as you have chainged your thoughts and discovered it [= *made it known]* to the Kynge first. Your brother[5] is no lawefull wittnes against you, havinge sought to injure you as he hath heretofore. Good my lord, according to the truth wright accordingly and that effectually. And directe it to my Lord Cheefe Justice [*Popham*] and the rest of the Commission.

From Bayshall [*Bagshot, Surrey*] and so I hope God will blesse you for it in doinge me right.[6]

   Your poore and unfortunate frend
    W R

1. Ralegh left the Tower, under escort, on Thursday 10 November and arrived at Winchester on the Saturday.
2. In the event, Ralegh was dealt with first, on 17 November.
3. See above, Letter 166.
4. Anthony Copley, a young Catholic gentleman and professional soldier who was among the others arrested.
5. George Brooke, a fellow-prisoner.
6. At his trial Ralegh stated that he had written to Cobham in similar terms from the Tower, i.e. before 10 November, but that the reply 'was not to [*his*] contenting'. To his second letter, presumably the above, he said that he had received from Cobham 'a very good letter' which, with the first, he had returned, 'lest the Lieutenant of the Tower [*Sir George Harvey, a kinsman*] might be blamed if itt were discovered [*that*] letters passed ...': BL, Harley 39, f. 321. Neither the originals nor transcripts of these have survived, but there is extant a contemporary transcript of a third letter from Cobham, even more to Ralegh's advantage: Lefranc, p. 345. This letter must have been written by Cobham at Winchester, where he arrived three days ahead of Ralegh, on or about 19 November.

---

## 170. TO KING JAMES I [FROM WINCHESTER, SHORTLY AFTER 17 NOVEMBER 1603][1]

Hatfield, CP102/111, *HMC Salisbury* XVI, p. 9, dated, from Edwards, 21 January 1604. In Ralegh's best hand. There also survives (Somerset Record Office, DD/M1 Box 18, FLIV 82, pt i, *HMC 7th Report*, pp. 591–2) an unsigned draft of this letter, in Ralegh's less neat hand, from the papers of Sir George Harvey, Lieutenant of the Tower in 1603, significant differences in which are inserted below, indicated by the letter *D*.

Many transcripts, e.g. BL, Addit. 34631, f. 63, 44848, f. 166v. and Huntington, EL. 102, f. 13.[2]

*Remains* 1702 and 1726, p. 191, faulty; Birch 1751, II, p. 382, from *Remains*; Cayley 1806, I, p. 31, from Birch/*Remains*; *Works* 1829, p. 646, more accurate; Edwards II, p. 296, from Hatfield;[3] and elsewhere.

### BEGGING HIS LIFE

[*addressed*] To the Kinges most excelent Majesty my Soverayne Lorde
[*endorsed*] S W Ralegh

The life which I had, most mighty prince, the law hath taken from mee and I am now but the same earth and dust [*D: and dust missing*] out of which I was made. If my offence had proportion with [*D: could be cumpared to*] your Majesties mercy I might dyspayre, or if my deserving had quantety with your Majesties unmeasurabell goodnes I might hope.[4] But [*D: it is*] your great [*D: great omitted*] Majesty, and not I, must judg of both. Name, bludd, gentillety or estate I have none [*D: not*], no not so mich as a being, no not so mich as *vita plantae*. I have only a penetent sowle in a body of iron which moveth [*D: fast inserted*] towards the loadstone [= *magnet*] of death and cannot be witheld from towchinge it unles [*D: except*] your Majesties mercy turne the poynct [*D: that poynt*] towards it [*D: mee*] which repelleth. Lost I am for heringe a vayne man,[5] for heringe only, but never belevinge or [*D: nor*] acceptinge, and [*D: and missing*] so littell accompt I made of that speach of his (which was [*D: thos speaches (which now were*] now my condemnation), as the livinge God doth trewly wittnis, that I never remembred any such thinge till it was att my triall objected agaynst mee.[6] So did he repay my care, who cared to make hyme good, which I see no care of man can effect [*D: which most cared for hyme and loved hyme then when all men else abandond hyme*]. But God for my offences to hyme hath layd this hevy burden on mee, misserabell and unfortunate wrech [*D: that I am*]. [*D: But*] For not lovinge yow, my Soverayne, God hath not layde this sorrow on mee, for the same [*D: the same omitted*] God knowes, with whom I may not [*D: now*] dissembell that I have trewly [*D: first*] honored your Majesty by fame and trewly [*D: afterward*] loved and admired your Majesty [*D: yow*] by knowledge, so as wh[*eth*]er I live or dy [*D: dy or live*] your Majesties trew and humbell [*D: lovinge*] sarvant I will live or [*D: and*] dy. If I now write what doth not now becum mee [*D: becums me not*], most mighty kinge [*D: marcifull prince*] vouchsaufe to ascribe it to the councell of a dead hart and to a minde which sorrow hath broken. But the more my misery is the more is your Majesties mercy if yow pleas to behold it, and the less I can deserve, the more liberall your Majesties gift. God only herein [*D: herein missing*] your Majesty shall imitate [*D: herein*], both in geving frely and by gevinge to such a one from whom ther can be no retribution savinge [*D: but*] only a desire to pay agayne a lent life and to repay it with [*D: and ... with omitted and which inserted*] the same great love which the same great goodness shall pleas to lend it. This beinge the first letter which [*D: that*] ever your Majesty receved[7] from a dead man, I humble submyt [*D: leve*] my sealf to the will of my supreme lorde and shall willingly and patiently suffer what his great and generus hart shall determyne [*D:* to your Majesties will, being reddy patiently to suffer whatsoever it shall pleas your Majesty to lay on mee].

>by that humbell vassell which yet breatheth by your Majesties permission and meere mercy,
>[*D:* your most humblest vassall]
>
>W R[8]

1. The date on which Chief Justice Popham pronounced Ralegh guilty of high treason: Cayley 1806, II, p. 31.
2. Collation of the original with these transcripts shows that they derive neither from the final version nor from the draft drawn upon below but from a second draft which does not appear to survive, since they incorporate readings sometimes from the one and sometimes from the other. Presumably it was this second draft, and not the copy sent to the King, which was made available for circulation.
3. Edwards attributes his text to Hatfield, CP102/111, but dates it 21 January 1604 from an endorsement by Sir Julius Caesar on BL, Lansd. 157, f. 155, a contemporary transcript, although admitting in a footnote to some doubts.
4. This elaborately balanced sentence was frequently misread in the transcripts.
5. i.e. listening to Cobham's offer of Spanish money.
6. It was during his examination in the Tower on 13 August that Ralegh confessed to having heard Cobham speak of 'his Spanish imaginations': see above Letter 166, note 1.
7. He must have had doubts as to whether his letter would be read by the King. In fact, according to Cecil, writing to Ralegh's keeper on 4 December, the King had read 'every woord' of it: *HMC Salisbury* XV, p. 305.
8. Subscription and initials in a minute hand at the foot of the sheet.

---

## 171. To the Earls of Suffolk and Devonshire, Lord Cecil, Henry Lord Howard and Henry Lord Wotton [from Winchester, 27/28 November 1603][1]

Hatfield, CP102/25, *HMC Salisbury* XV, p. 285, dated after 17 November. In Ralegh's minutest hand, in some haste.

Edwards II, pp. 274–7, dated October, but corrected, vol I, p. 439, to November.

### REFUTING NEW CHARGES

[*addressed*] To the right honorabell my singuler good lords the Earles of Suffolke and Devon, the Lorde Cecyll, the Lorde Henry Howard and the Lorde Wutton

[*endorsed, by or for Cecil*] Sir Walter Ralegh

It was so late er your lordships came² as I could not, in good manners, beseich yow of longer tyme. It was your pleasures to tell me of a new accusation, of the landing of Spanyerds att Milford Haven.³ I beseich yow for the love of God, and as your lordships will looke ether for mercy or justice att Gods hands, to consider and wey the likelode hereof, and trewly and charitable to thinck butt of this one circumstance. First I was accused to have perswaded the Lord Cobhame to have gon into Spayn and to have brought mee 600,000 crowns to Jersey. I was strongly suspected that the mony offred mee for the peace was for the surprize,⁴ or for sume other ill intent. The first accusation for which I was committed, indyted and arrayned your lordships do know to be falce,⁵ and yet it was by your lordships most constantly beleved, and my Lord Cheif Justice [*Popham*] avowed that it could not be otherwize because the Lord Cobhame accused hyme sealf also therin. Then, my lords, if I had perished therfore [= *on that account*] yow all finde that I had perished innocent and that the presumption of the mony was also inferred agaynst mee and would have strenghtned [*sic*] my condemnation: and yet neather trew. And for a third, the letter delivered by Rensey⁶ in my presence, being unknown to be the Count Arramberke⁷ by mee, was yet a third presumption ageynst mee.

But now for this other. I do beseich yow for his sake that shedd his blud for us to thinck of this one argument. Your lordships see that from the beginninge that the Lord Cobhame hath had a crewell desire to distroy me, hoping therby to extenuate [= *lessen*] his owne offences. How he hath bynn therto perswaded I have seene: hyme sealf sent me the letters. And if this matter of Milford [*Haven*] had bynn trew what needed the Lord Cobham [*to*] have invented a treason agaynst me which was not trew. Secondly it had bynn easier to have remembred that which was then that which was not. And thirdly in this accusation he might have indangered me and spared hyme sealf. And this was also as great a treason as the other, and this, if it had been trew, he might have justefied and bynn confident therin. Thes considered, good my lords, judg as yow would be judged, and remember his letter which he ment no creature should see but my sealf.⁸

A man can have butt one sowle and one faythe, and therfore if your lordships will every day recave new inventions agaynst mee then it is vayne for mee to contend. Your lordships also saw that the night before my arrynment [*17 November*] he spake not a word of this when he then studied [= *applied himself*] all he could to distroy me. It was not therfore without cause that the most wize and mercifull God gave thes cummandments towchinge the sheding of bludd, and his lawes ar the trew lawes to christien men and christien kings. God sayde in the 35 [*chapter*] of Numbers: *Non poterit testis unus testari contra aliquem ut moriatur.* God renewed his cummandment in 17 and 19 of Detrinomy [*sic*]: *Ex sermone duorum aut trium testium morte afficitur is qui moritur, nec morte afficitur ex sermone testis unius*, and agayne, *ne surgite testis unicus in quenquam pro ulla iniquitate aut pro ullo peccato ex omnibus peccatis quibus quis peccat.* The same also is confirmed by Christ in Mathew and in John,⁹ and as St Augustine sayes, *Non divina humanis, sed humana divinis sunt judicanda.* And, good my lords, beleve: *Nemo postest melius aut aliud fundamentum ponere quam posuit Dominus.*¹⁰

But the law is past agaynst me, the mercy of my Soverayne is all that remayneth for my comfort, and I know that this law of God wilbe an argument of remorce to my Soverayne Lorde, how soever mens lawes take place. And I desire your lordships for the mercy of God not to doubt to move so mercifull a prince to cumpassion, and that the extremety of all extremeties be not layd on mee. Lett the offence be estemed as your lordships shall pleas in charety to beleve it and valew it. Yet it is butt the first offence and my service to my country and my love so many yeares to my supreme lord I trust may move so great and good a kinge who was never estemed cruell, and I trust will nevir prove so to be. And if I may not begg a pardon, or a life, yet lett me begg a tyme att the kings mercifull hands. Lett me have one yeare to geve to God in a prison and to serve hyme. I trust his pitifull nature will have cumpassion on my sowle, and it is my sowle that beggeth a time of the kinge. Ther is no prejudice [= *injury*] cum to the kinge nor never could any prejudice have cum by that supposed horid intent which the Lord of Heaven knowes I never imagined [= *conceived*]. And if the kinge my mercifull lord pleas to withdrawe all his grace from me, it must be the last breath that I shall draw in the worlde that I dy his trew vassall and that [*I*] have and do love his very person.

Although I must confess that I am most worthy of this hevy affliction for the neglect of my dewty in giving eare to sume things and in taking on me to harken to the offer of mony, but his [= *the king's*] mercy I trust is greater and the Lord that hathe made hyme a lord of many nations will incline his royall hart to pitty.¹¹ And I beseich your lordships, as every yow tendred the sorrowes of a penetent hart, that yow will present thes unto His Majesties knowledg and afford me your favors for grace and cumpassion.

        Your lordships most humble,
        W Ralegh

1. See note 2.
2. On Sunday 27 November, Cecil and the rest of the commissioners visited the prisoners in Winchester Castle: H.V. Jones, 'The Journal of Levinus Munck', *EHR* LXVIII, 1953, p. 248.
3. On 22 November, Cobham, facing conviction as a traitor, had come up with new information that earlier that year, showing 'great discontentment', Ralegh had asked him to arrange with Count Aremberg the sending of an army to land at Milford Haven: PRO, SP14/4/91. Cobham was to repeat this at his trial on 25 November: Cayley 1806, II, p. 14.
4. The so-called Bye Plot.
5. Cobham had retracted his accusations in a letter to Ralegh (see above, Letter 169, note 6) which the latter had produced at his trial.
6. La Renzi (see above, Letter 166, note 7), who had given evidence that he had delivered a letter from Aremberg to Cobham when he was in conference with Ralegh at Durham House.
7. For Count Aremberg see above, Letter 166, note 6.
8. See above, note 5.
9. Matthew 18.16 and John 8:17.
10. Corinthians 3:11.
11. Last two words omitted by Edwards.

---

## 172. To Lady Ralegh [from Winchester, 4–8 December 1603][1]

BL, Sloane 3520, ff. 14v.–17, a transcript of the lost original made for Sir Robert Cotton (1571–1631), one of many, lacking Ralegh's usual spelling.

*Remains* 1702, etc.; *Works* 1751, p. 383; Edwards II, pp. 294–7, from PRO, SP14/96/71, collated with BL, Sloane 3520 and Hatfield, CP102/19; Hadow, op. cit., 1917, pp. 181–4.[2]

### A FAREWELL IN EXPECTATION OF DEATH

[*headed*] The Coppy of a Letter written by Sir Walter Raleigh to his wife the night before he expected to be putt to death att Winchester in 1603

You shall nowe receive (my deare wife) my last words in these my last lynes. My love I send you, that you may keepe itt when I am dead, and my counsell, that you may remember itt when I am no more. I would not by my will present you with sorrowes (dear Besse). Lett them goe into the grave with mee and bee buried in the dust. And seeing itt is not the will of God that I shall see you any more in this life, beare itt patiently and with an heart like thy selfe.

First I send you all the thankes which my heart can conceive or my words can express for your many travailes [= *labours*] and care taken for mee, which, though they have not taken effect as you wished, yett my debt to you is not the lesse, but pay itt I never shall in this world.

Secondly, I beseech you, for the love you bare mee liveing, doe not hide your selfe many dayes after my death but by your travailes seeke to help your miserable fortunes and the right of your poore child. Thy mourninge cannot availe mee: I am but dust.

Thirdly you shall understand that my land was conveyed *bona fide* to my childe. The writeings weere drawne att Midsomner twelve monthes.[3] My honest cosen Brett can testifie soe much, and Dalberrie[4] too can remember somewhat therein. And I trust that my blood will quench the malice that have thus cruelly murthered mee, and that they will not seeke alsoe to kill thee and thine with extreame povertie. To what freind to direct thee I knowe not,[5] for all mine have left mee in the true tyme of triall. And I plainely perceive that my death was determyned from the first day.

Most sorrie I am (God knowes) that being thus surprised with death I can leave you in noe better estate. God is my wittnesse I meant you [*to have*] all my office [= *grant*] of wynes,[6] or all that I could have purchased by selling itt, halfe my stuffe and all my jewells, but some on't for the boy. But God hath prevented all my resolutions and even that great God that ruleth all in all. But if you can live free from want, care for noe more: the rest is but vanitie.

Love God and beginn betymes to repose yourselfe on him, and therein shall you finde true and lasting riches, and endlesse comfort. For the rest, when you have travailled and wearied all your thoughts over all sorts of worldly cogitations, you shall but sitt downe by sorrowe in the end. Teache your sonne alsoe to love and feare God whilst hee is yett younge, that the feare of God may growe upp with him, and the same God will bee a husband to you and a father to him, a husband and a father which cannot bee taken from you.

Baylie[7] oweth mee 200*li* and Adrian Gilbert 600*li*. In Jersey I have alsoe much monye oweinge mee besides.[8] The arrerages of the wynes[9] will pay my debts. And howsoever you doe, for my soules sake, pay all poore men.[10] When I am gone no doubt you shall bee sought by many, for the world thinks that I was very rich. But take heed of the pretences of men, and theire affections, for they last not, but in honest and worthie men, and noe greater misery can befall you in this life then to become a prey and afterwards to bee despised. I speake not this (God knowes) to disswade you from marriage, for it will bee best for you, both in respect of the world and of God.

As for mee, I am noe more yours, nor you mine. Death hath cutt us a sunder and God hath devided mee from the worlde and you from mee.

Remember your poore child for his fathers sake, who chose you and loved you in his happiest tymes.

Gett those letters (if it bee possible) which I writt to the lords [*Letter 171*] wherein I sued for my life. God is my wittnesse, itt was for you and yours I desired life. But itt is true that I disdaine my selfe for begging itt. For knowe it (deare wife) that your sonne is the sonne of a true man, and one who, in his owne respect, dispiseth death, and all his mishapen and ouglye shapes.[11]

I cannot write much. God hee knowes how hardly I steale this tyme while others sleepe, and itt is aloe high tyme that I should separate my thoughts from the world. Begg my dead body which liveinge was denyed thee[12] and either laye itt att Shirbourne (if the land continue) or in Excester church by my father and mother.[13] I can say noe more, tyme and death call mee away.

The everlasting, powerfull, infinite and omnipotent God, that Almightie God whoe is goodnesse itt selfe, the true life and true light, keepe thee and thine. Have mercy on mee and teach mee to forgive my persecutors and accusers, and send us to meete in his glorious kingdome.

My deare wife farewell. Blesse my poore boye. Pray for mee and lett my good God hold you both in his armes. Written with the dyeing hand of sometyme thy husband but now (alasse) overthrowne.
    Wa Raleigh[14]
        Yours that was but nowe not my own
        W R

1. None of the manuscript or printed versions give the day of the month. On Sunday 4 December, the Bishop of Winchester reported that he had found in Ralegh 'a lingering expectation of life': *HMC Salisbury* XV, p. 306. On 6 December, Ralegh witnessed the beheading of George Brooke, Cobham's brother. His own reprieve came on 9 December: Stebbing 1899, pp. 236–9.
2. There are two versions of this letter, both of them contemporary transcripts, of which this is the longer and almost certainly, apart from the spelling, what Ralegh actually wrote when he was expecting to die. The second, of which PRO, SP14/96/71 is one of many copies, was almost certainly also composed by him at a later date, and was no doubt intended for public circulation. It omits most of the more immediate practical instructions and reads more like a work of art than a personal message and an unburdening of the writer's misery. It was this which was printed in 1644, with the misleading date: see Introduction, p. xxx. All editions of the *Remains* before 1702, beginning with the *Sceptick* (1651), contain the shorter version.
3. See above, Letter 165, note 16. He is thinking of the first draft rather than the final engrossment.
4. Robert Dolberry, an employee at Sherborne.

5. Lady Ralegh had written an almost hysterical letter to Cecil. She was to write again, in more measured terms, later in December: Edwards II, pp. 406–9.
6. Withdrawn in May 1603.
7. Possibly the sea-captain who was to desert Ralegh on the second Guiana voyage: see below, Letter 217, note 6.
8. In 1605 the King granted John Spilman, the London jeweller, all goods, chattels and money owing to Ralegh in Jersey, in payment of a debt, but it took Sir John Peyton, Ralegh's successor as Governor, until 1609 to collect what was due: *CSPD 1580–1625 Addenda*, pp. 515–16.
9. These were to be claimed by his successor, the Earl of Nottingham, although they had accrued while Ralegh held the patent.
10. Peter Van Lore remarked of Ralegh that he was 'the best payer of debts that ever he knew': A.L. Rowse, *Ralegh and the Throckmortons*, 1962, p. 247.
11. Possibly a reference to his sentence of death by hanging, drawing and quartering rather than by the beheading normally allowed to gentlemen. On 29 November he had probably seen the hanging of the two priests, Watson and Clarke: Stebbing 1899, p. 236.
12. There had been a ban on her visits to the Tower and there is no evidence that Lady Ralegh went to Winchester.
13. Walter senior and Kathleen, his wife, had died in 1581 and 1594, in the parish of St Mary Major, Exeter: T.N. Brushfield, *DAT* xxviii, 272–312. This is the sole reference in the letters to his parents.
14. An unlikely spelling.

---

## 173. To the Lords Commissioners for the Trial [from Winchester, 9 December 1603][1]

Hatfield, CP102/110, *HMC Salisbury* XV, p. 321, dated 10–15 December. In Ralegh's hand. Edwards II, p. 282, dated 10 December.

## PLEA FOR MERCY

[*addressed*]   To the right honorabell my singuler good lords of His Majesties most honorabell Privey Councell, commissioners for the trial of the late treasons
[*endorsed, by or for Cecil*]   Sir W Ralegh

We have this day beheld a worke of so great mercy[2] and for so great offences as the like hath byne seildome, if ever, known, not after the manner of men, or of kings, *sed coelestis judicis, eternique regis more*. And although my sealf have not yet byn brought so nire the very brinck of the grave,[3] yet I trust that so great a cumpassion will extend it sealf towards me also, every way being as hopeless as the rest, and who shall as trewly pay that most great debt of borrowed life as any that ever hath or ever shalbe therto bound. Only the memory of myne own unworthinis made mee to dispayre of so great grace, who otherwize beheld piety in the face, the voyce, the writinge and life of my soverayne. I did fear that it would be sayde that I, beinge now poore, would live but a discontented life, but the lord of heaven doth know that, if it shall pleas my most good and gratious lord the King to geve me that poore life, that [sic] I shall as faythfully and thanckfully serve hyme, eating but bread and drinkinge water, as whosoever that hath receved even the greatest honor or the greatest profyte. For a greater gift none can geve, none receve, then life.

What the Lord Cobhame hath confest,[4] and how mich it differeth from the receved oppinion, I leve to their reports who know it. I will not in charety condeme his [good] fayth because he was nirer death, though not nirer the expectation, then I was, but will only for this tyme accuse his memory or mistakinge.[5] Good my lords, do me this grace to beleve, and vouchsaufe to say it for mee to my Soverayne Lorde, that the loss of my estate [= *income*] (which I have deservedly lost) cannot make mee less faythfull or less lovinge his [*the King's*] estat and parson. For as I have to this day loved both his estate and parson, so have I in my prayers besought God to inclyne his mercifull hart towards me [sic].[6] I will leve your lordships farthur trobell, remembringe this gratefull oppinion: *non hostiliter saeviit qui omnia cum possit, fortunas abstulit, spem vitaque reliquit.*

Your lordships most humbell to cummande.

W Ralegh[7]

1. See note 2.
2. Cobham, Grey and Markham, Ralegh's fellow-prisoners, were reprieved by the King, then at Wilton, on Friday 9 December: Stebbing 1899, p. 239.
3. Each of the others had been led to the place of execution, watched by Ralegh, before being informed of his reprieve. Ralegh's execution was scheduled to take place on 12 December, but his death warrant had not yet been signed by the King: Cayley 1806, II, p. 21, quoting Carlton.
4. It can be assumed that Ralegh knew that at the scaffold, earlier in the day, Cobham had declared that 'what he had said of him was true': ibid.
5. Cobham's memory had led him more than once to retract his charges.
6. Did he intend to write 'him', i.e. the King?
7. This letter was sent to their lordships on 10 December from Winchester Castle by the Sheriff, Sir Benjamin Tichbourne, together with letters to the King from the other three prisoners: *HMC Salisbury* XV, pp. 319–20.

174. TO LORD CECIL [FROM WINCHESTER, ON OR SHORTLY AFTER 10 DECEMBER 1603][1]

Hatfield, CP102/112, *HMC Salisbury* XV, p. 345, dated 10–15 December. In Ralegh's hand. Edwards II, p. 288, dated December 1603.

## THANKS FOR GOOD OFFICES

[*addressed*]  To the right honorabell the Lorde Cecyll, Principall Secritorye, etc.
[*no contemporary endorsement*]

My Lorde Cecyll: To geve yow thancks, to promis gratefullnis, to returne words, is all I can do, but that your lordship will esteeme them I cannot promis my sealf, no not so miche as hope it. To use defences for the errors of former tymes I cannot, for I have fayled both in frindshipe and in judgment. Therfore this is all that I can now say for my sealf. Vouchsaufe to esteeme me as a man raysed from the dead, though not in body yet in mind, for neather fortune, which sumetyme guyded me, or rather vanety (for with the other I was never in love), shall agayne turne myne eyes from yow toward her while I have beinge. Nor the world, with all the cares or intisements belonging unto it, shall ever way down (though it be of the greatest wayght to mortall men) the memory alone of your lordships trew respects had of me, respects tried by the touch, tried by the fier, trew wittnises in trew tymes and then only when only avaylabell. And although I must first attribute unto God, who inclined, and secoundly, and essentially after God, to my deere soverayne who had goodnes apt to be inclyned, goodness and mercy without cumparison and exampell, yet I must never forgett what I find was in your lordships desire, what in your will, what in your words, and works, so farr as coulde becume yow as a counceler, and farr beyound all dew to me, as an offendor. Thes I have fixed to my hart inseperabelly; from thes neather tyme nor perswation, or ought elce wonnt to chang affections, or to wast them, shall beat from mee, or make old in mee, who will acknowledg your lordship with a love without maske or cover, and follow yow to the end.
 W Ralegh

Sir: all the rest have written to His Majesty since ther rec[e]aving of his grace. I hope I may presume to do the like.[2]

1. See above, Letter 173, note 2.
2. Cecil did not reply until 20 December and then only indirectly when he asked the Lieutenant of the Tower to tell Ralegh, in effect, that he wished him well: Edwards II, p. 486. He also encouraged Ralegh to write to the King and to thank him as his sole deliverer. Presumably he was unaware of Ralegh's letter to the King (below, Letter 175) doing just that.

---

### 175. To the King [from Winchester, 11–15 December 1603][1]

Hatfield, CP102/109, *HMC Salisbury* XV, pp. 321–2, dated 10–15 December. In Ralegh's very best set hand, almost pure italic.

Edwards II, p. 289, dated December, from Winchester.

#### THANKS FOR HIS REPRIEVE

[*addressed*]   To the Kings most excellent Majestye, my Soverayne Lorde
[*endorsed by or for Cecil*]   Sir W Ralegh to the King

Most mighty and most mercifull Kinge: Seing it hath pleased Your Majestye to breathe into dead yearth [= *the prospect of death*] a new life, I amonge others do presume to offer my humblest thancks, thancks and acknowledgments, which, God knowes, cann neather in words be exprest or presented. For wheras Your Majestye hath reason[2] to reckon mee among thos who have foolishly imagined [= *plotted*] meischeif, who have wickedly intended the greatest ill towards the greatest goodnes, and yet have pleased to spare the blowe which both exampell hath taught and law hath warranted Your Majestye to strike. Alas, what waight have words, or vowes, or protestations, or wherwith cann so unworthy a creture make payment of so uncountabell a debt. To promis my fydellety: I know that I am bound by God both to promis and performe it though I had never receyved any such great grace as this. To vow my service: in what sort soever I know it to be the dewty of every vassall towards his soverayne. To say that I will hassard my life for Your Majestye: I have done it for my frind, for my country, ey, even sumetyme for vayne glory. And if I should directly yeilde it up for Your Majestye, what thancks can be deserved therby, seinge I shall but offer that which is none of myne and in which I have neather right nor property. What therfore to promis, or what to pay, I know not. God only, who doth wittnis my thoughts, what they have byne and ar, must speake for mee. It is true that I have allreddy suffred diversly but deservedly: I have bynn beaten with sorrow, *sed mea culpa*, for it was myne own error that opened the passage to that passion. I have bynn beaten by fortune, but it was myne own unthankfullnis, who would not know when shee had dealt liberally with mee. And I have bynn beaten by God hymesealf but with a souft hand, in respect of my greatest offences to hym. Only my Soverayne Lorde, who might justly have beaten mee, and justly have distroyde mee, have vouchsaufed to spare mee, and hath pleased to geve mee every dropp of bludd in my body, to hold mee back from shame, and to stopp his ears from the voyce of publick law and private hatred. For thes works of mercy, of manly gentelnes, of kingly magnanimity, what deeds to be performde by mee cann hope itsealf flatter mee withall. No, in place of deeds would to God I could but in my very thoughts attribute what I ought [= *owe*], what is dew. Here is all of cumfort which remayneth, that as Your Majestye hath imitateth God the celestiall kinge in gevinge,[3] that Your Majestye wilbe pleased to do the like in receyvinge. Other retribution [= *recompence*] then acknowledgment and love God looketh not for, nether can Your Majestye have other of mee, *sed miserationum tuarum nunquam obliviscar*, but remayn Your Majesties,

> most humblest and most bound and indebted vassall,
> W Ralegh

1. It is impossible to be more precise. It seems unlikely that Ralegh wrote this letter in time for it to be sent on 10 December with his letter to Cecil, whose advice he sought on the very propriety of writing a letter of thanks to the King, or that he waited until he received Cecil's reply: above, Letter 174, note 2. Indeed, it is clear from Letter 179, note 5, that he wrote before 16 December when, along with the rest of the prisoners, he was escorted back to the Tower: Stebbing 1899, p. 241.
2. Note that Ralegh falls short of saying that the King was right to regard him as a traitor.
3. Cf. Letter 170, 'God only herein Your Majestye shall imitate ... in geving frely.'

---

## 176. To Lord Cecil [from the Tower, late December 1603–early January 1604][1]

Hatfield, CP102/22, *HMC Salisbury* XV, p. 259. In Ralegh's hand. Edwards II, pp. 291–3, dated December 1603.

### HARD TIMES

[*addressed*] To the right honorabell my singuler good lord the Lord Cecyll, Principall Secritory, etc.

[*endorsed*] Sir Walter Ralegh to my lord

*Plate 9.* Sir Walter Ralegh's quarters (marked T) in the Tower of London, with adjacent garden, from the *Plan of the Tower of London*, 1597, by William Hayward and J. Gascoyne. Much enlarged. (Courtesy of the Society of Antiquaries of London)

If thes letters cume out of tyme [= *too late*] to your lordshipe I beseich yow to lay them asyde and to pardon mee. It pleased the Kinge to promis my wife her goods and chatells.² I have willed her to sew for them. She thincks it to littell purpose untill she have a bill drawn for them: that she cannot have without a warrrant to Master Aturney [*Sir Edward Coke*] or Solliciter [*Lord Ellesmere*].

My debts are trebell to my goods: the everliving God doth know it to be trew. And ther fore the Kings Majesty shall ease hyme sealf both of charg and trobell by refusing to meddell with ether. I speak it not to geve a reason for the Kings charety, for it hath respect but to it sealf and to God, but to deliver trewly my miserabell estat. And thos small debts which ar owing to me I cannot recover untill it pleas the Kinge to enable me or sume body for mee.³

My lands ar tied uppon my child and my brother.⁴ If I plead that conveyance I cannot use the poure [= *power*] of revocation in the conveiance who have lost all poure. Then can I never satisfy my creditors, and besyds I shall live a ward to my child and to my brother. If I take my land from the Kinge I may then dispose of sume part of it to free me from clamor. That the conveyance was made att Midsomer was twelvemoneth Dodrige⁵ can witnis, and if he have law or honesty it is good.⁶

Yet I do humble desire that, as I hold my life, so I may that littell land that I have of the Kings gift, that nothing may be myne but what his mercy hath gaven me. The trew valew of my land I have delivered this bearer, all but xii*li* a yeare in Devon.⁷ I protest upon my alleage[n]ce that this is the trew state of it to my knowledge, and God doth know that it will not gave me and myne bread and cloath. I pay here 4*li* a week for my diet. I must pay it if the Kinge geve me my poore estate agayne. And, my Lord Cecill, the lord in heaven doth witnis that I and my wife and child must proportion our sealvs such a famely as we must all live att 4*li* a week for all our dietts, or elce we must all go naked, for it takes too parts [= *thirds*] of all the rent I have in the world. If by your goodnis thes things might cum to sume question or end I shalbe most bound unto yow.

My tenants refuse to pay my wife her rent. I hold divers leases uppon forfeture in that manner of myne own tenants.⁸ Alas, all goes to ruin of that littell which remayneth. My woods ar cutt down, my grounds [= *home farm*] wast, my stock which made up my rent sold, and except sume end [= *solution*] be had by your good favor to the Kinge I perishe every waye.

This I leve to your tyme and charetabell care, and rest your lordships miserabell poore frind, ever to be cummanded by yow,
    W Ralegh

of 3000*li* a yeare ther remayns but 300*li*, and upon that 3000*li* debt.

1. It is impossible to be more precise but an early rather than a later date is more likely, for the matter was urgent. After Christmas Day, Ralegh was moved for a while to the Fleet prison.
2. As early as 16 October 1603, Cecil had informed a suitor for Sherborne that Lady Ralegh had reason to hope that the King, presumably in the event of her husband being found guilty, would give her Ralegh's movable goods, all of which, Cecil surmised, would barely pay his debts: *HMC Salisbury* XV, p. 259.
3. On 14 February 1604, Ralegh's goods and chattels were granted by the Crown to John Shelbury (see below, Letter 179) and Robert Smith, to be used towards the payment of his debts and the maintenance of Lady Ralegh and her child: *CSPD 1603–10*, p. 36 and T. Rymer, *Foedera* xvi, p. 569. They were still busy on his behalf in 1611: see below, Letter 204, note 3.
4. See above, Letter 165, note 16. This is the conveyance which was later discovered to have been incorrectly drafted: see below, Letter 185.
5. John (later Sir John) Doddridge (1555–1620), Solicitor-General from October 1604. He hailed from Barnstaple in north Devon.
6. Note Ralegh's slight misgivings about Doddridge's competence.
7. Not identified. Hawkerland in Colaton Raleigh had already been sold: Letter 13, note 7. He also had land in Cornwall: see Appendix 2.
8. A reference to his own cash flow. For some of his leases, see J. Fowler, *Medieval Sherborne*, p. 385.

---

## 177. To the Lords Buckhurst and Cecil and Sir George Hume [from the Tower, soon after 14 February 1604][1]

Hatfield, CP109/15, *HMC Salisbury* XVI, p. 260. In Ralegh's hand.
Edwards II, pp. 307–11.

## THE SHERBORNE ESTATE

[*addressed*] To the right honorabell my singuler good lords the Lord Treasorer of Ingland [*Buckhurst*], the Lord Cecyll and the Lord Humes [*sic*], Chancelor of His Majesties Exchequer

[*endorsed*]  1604   Sir Walter Raleigh to the lords   A particular of Shirborne

If ther be any more rents then thes to my knowledg but [= *except*] the herbage [= *grass etc.*] of the parke which was never in mee but purchased in my childs name tenn year since, and a lease of Pinford grounds in Master

Heriot[2] for 58 years, then I refuse all grace of and from His Majesty, except I may miscast a matter of foure or five pound in the whole or leve out sume five or six akers of ground in summ quillet [= *small piece*]. But this is the substance of all uppon my alleagence and therfore if it pleas your honors to make further inquiry I submit my sealf unto it, and I beseich your lordships that a copy hereof may be delivered to the commissioners.[3]

All that greevs mee herein is that so infamus and detested a wrech as Meere[4] is made a commissioner, as hee hath vaunted [= *boasted*] and sent me worde, and who dares not otherwise shew his face, having so many executions [= *convictions*] agaynst hyme, and hath not forty shiling worth of ground in the world but of my gift, and who now rooteth up my copp[i]s woods and promiseth to pay all his creditors with the part promised hyme out of Sherburn, spreding it abrod that sume one of your honors hath imployed hyme withe a purpose to procure this, the remaynder of all which I had in the world of [= *from*] His Majesty, and to turne my poore wife, child and famely a begging. But I trust that God hath not geven so cruell a hart to any worthy man whom the spoyle of me and myne cannot inrich, but that all your lordships will in charety stand my good lords herein, having lost allreddy 3000*li* a yeare.

        And I shall remayne your humbell sarvant,
            W Ralegh

[*enclosure, abstract only*]

| | |
|---|---|
| Manor of Sherburne with hundred, liberties, park, farm and other 'demayne grounds', rent of assize[5] yearly | £150 16s 4d |
| Village of Casteltoun in which the old castle[6] stands, rent of assize | £3 12s |
| 'Secound street or village' in Sherburn towne called Newland, rent of assize | £3 13s 4d |
| Village of Caundell Byshope 3 miles from Sherburn, part of Sherburn, rent of assize | £21 11s 2d |
| Village outside park wall, part of Sherburn, old rent of assize | £7 13s 10d |
| Farm of Whitfeildes, old rent | £13 8s |
| Manor of Yetminster, old rent of assize,[7] 'but this manner is a kind of fee simpell to the tenants and the lord hath but a small fine att every death or alienation' | £12 5s 11d |
| Total old rent | £207 8s[8] |

| | |
|---|---|
| Sherburn is worth net 'by improvement ... if it do not decay' | £250 |
| Certain demesne land in Whitfield let for the yearly rent of | £60 |
| Other land at Caudell Byshope and Down 'redeemed out of the tenants' hands', worth yearly | £40 |
| Pasture rented from tenant called Swetnam, profit net of rent | £12 |
| Other land around Sherburn worth yearly about | £30–£40 |
| Total | £400 |
| Rent charge from Sir Robert Miller for Upcern 'in consideration of the feefarm of them which I procured hyme' | £22 10s 3d |
| Half of demesne of Pinford manor, old rent yearly | £5 |
| Half of the manor of Prumsly [= *Primsley*], old rent yearly | £7 2s 7d |
| Mill in Sherburn and 20 acres of land purchased from Queen Elizabeth, let to Arthure Swayn for 3 lives at old rent of | £6 4s 10d |
| Close behind the Castle, 5 acres, and 2 or 3 others, let for | £6 5s |
| Total rents | £22 10s 3d |
| Total old rent of these parcels | £18 7s d |
| Rack rent of the closes | £6 5s |
| Sum total | £629 8s 4d 'or nire therabout' |
| Outgoings: To the Bishop 'for ever' | £260 |
| To Edmonnd Lane for 25 or 30 years | £30 |
| Fees to 'officers and others' | £44 13s |

'besyds payments to the King for the household' etc, 'butt wheras in this deduction of fees the Bayly is to have 8*li* a yeare and the Receiver summ 7*li* a year, I do not pay the Baylife [*John Meere*] because he is myne enemy and hath abused me, and the Receiver,[9] being my sarvant, douth not exact it of me. Butt yet all thes be dew and have ever bynn payd.'

| | |
|---|---|
| Total deductions | £334 14s |
| Clear | £295 |

'Now the reason why by the office [= *inquiry*] ther is found but fourscore pound to the Kings Majesty is because the farm valued att 240*li* or 250*li* being in lease and the assignment not found, ther is but the old rent found for the King. As also because it hath pleased His Majesty to geve too of my sarvants all my goods, leases and chattells.¹⁰ And then if the rackt rent of the farm which is 240*li* or 250*li* be deducted ther remayneth according to the office about fourscore and odd pounds.'

1. Probably very soon after the assignment of Ralegh's goods: see below, note 10.
2. Thomas Harriot, the 'mathematical practitioner' employed by Ralegh: see above, Letter 87, note 8.
3. Little seems to be know about the identity of the commissioners but they were probably local men, friends of Meere rather than of Ralegh.
4. See above, Letter 141, note 3.
5. Old fixed rents.
6. The medieval castle of the bishops of Salisbury in which the Raleghs had lived pending the building of their new 'Lodge'.
7. Ralegh had augmented the Queen's grant of 1599 with a number of small purchases: J. Fowler, *Medieval Sherborne*, p. 397. He bought Pinford and Primsley in 1602 from Richard Arnold, husband of Sir John Horsey's sister and heiress: Hutchins, *Dorset*, IV, pp. 297–8.
8. Actually £213 0s. 8d.
9. John Foster or Robert Dolberry.
10. John Shelbury and Robert Smith: see above, Letter 176, note 3.

---

## 178. To the Privy Council [from the Tower, after 14 February 1604]¹

Hatfield, CP102/23, *HMC Salisbury* XVI, p. 454–5. Right-hand edge damaged. In Ralegh's hand.
Edwards II, pp. 298–300, dated ?1603–4.

### FINANCIAL STRAITS

[*addressed*]   To the right honorabell my very good lords the Lords and others of His Majesties most honorabell Privey Councell
[*endorsed*]   Sir Walter Ralegh to the Lords

My dewty most humble remembred: Wheras it pleased your lordshipp[*s to*] write your letters for the stay of the sale of such poore stufe as [*re*]mayneth in my howse att Sherburne, I understande that notwithstan[*ding*] your lordships letters that [*sic*] the cummissioners do go on for the finding of [*my*] lands, and because my conveyance of thos lands² is here in Lon[*don*] in the custody of my sarvant John Wood,³ vitler for the province o[*f*] Munster, and that he is now att the Bathes [= *Bath*] so as I cannot gett [*the*] writings out of his hands, I do most humble beseich your lordships to be pleased to write your letters to Master Sergent Phillips[4] and the rest to putt of[f] the execution of their cummission for sume eyght or ten dayes. And although I had rather be altogether bound unto the Kings Majesty for thos lands then to hold them by any other strenght of law, yet that it may apere that the conveyance by me made was drawn in our late Queens tyme,[5] as Master Dodreg [*John Doddridge*] can witnis, who drew it, and that I had never any ill intent therin, I do beseich your lordships that the same may be perused by the cummissioners before they proceed to finde [= *determine*] the lands by jury, on way or other.

The whole receat of thos lands, with the parke and a stock of 400*li* in sheep in the sayd parke, is but on thowsand marke [= £666 *13*s. 4d.], out of which I pay unto the byshops of Sallisbury for ever t[*wo*] hundred and sixty pound a yeare, and in fees and pensions wherwith the land is charged, and towards the provision of the kings howse, to maymed soldiers and to the poore above fifty pound a yeare more. So the clere valew is not four hundred pound with a stock. My charges in this place for diet only is 208*li* a yeare, and if His Majesty do allow the rest of this sume [to make it 300*li* *interlined*] unto me for all other necessaries ther remayneth not above on hundred mark [= £66 *13*s. 4d.] a yeare for my poore wife and childe and their sarvants, which, God knowes, will not geve them bread and cloathe.

My debts ar above 3000*li*; all my goods that I have left in the world I protest before the majesty of God ar not worth on thowsand marke. All my rich hangins I sold my Lord Admirall [*Nottingham*] for 500*li*; I had but on riche bedd which I solde the Lord Cobhame for 300*li*; all my plate which was very fayre[6] is now lost or eaten out with interest att on Chenes[7] in Lumbord Street; that which I have alreddy lost by Jersey, the wine office, the Stannery,[8] Gillingam and Portland[9] is at least 3000*li* a yeare, so as I trust His Majesty wilbe mercifull unto me for the rest which, after[10] the payment of my debts, wilbe but a miserabell estat, God knowes.

Herein I humble beseich your lordships favors that I may not be left to utter beggory and that your lordships wilbe pleased in the mean while to write your letters for the stay of this cummission. And I shall ever rest your lordships most humble
        W Ralegh

1. After the grant of his goods at Sherborne: see above, Letter 176, note 3.
2. The grant to trustees of 1603: see above, Letter 165, note 16.
3. He is named as 'Captain Wood' by Van Loon in 1600: PRO, Chancery Proceedings, C2, James I, R1/55.
4. Edward Phelips of Dorset and the Middle Temple: see below, Letter 204.

5. i.e. before his indictment as a traitor and the need to protect his estates from confiscation by process of attainder.
6. Cf. Ralegh's will of 1597, Appendix 2.
7. Master Henry Cheyney, goldsmith: PRO, C2, James I, R1/55.
8. See below, Letters 179–80.
9. The Rangership of Gillingham Forest, Dorset, which Ralegh had shared with his brother Carew since 1593 (Hutchins, (*Dorset* III, p. 624) and the Lieutenancy of Portland Castle (BL, Lansd. 52, p. 6).
10. The rest is written in the left-hand margin.

---

### 179. To Lord Cecil [from the Tower, 16/17] June 1604[1]

Hatfield, CP109/10, *HMC Salisbury* XVI, p. 260. In Ralegh's hand.
Edwards II, p. 294, dated December/January 1603/4.

## WARDENSHIP OF THE STANNARIES

[*addressed*]   To the right honorabel my singuler good lord and Lord Cecyll
[*endorsed*]   1604   Sir Walter Raleigh to my lord

May it pleas your lordship: Ther came a sarvant unto me of the Earle of Penbrooks for the seal of the Duchy of Cornwale,[2] having a letter of your lordships to Master Leuetenant [*of the Tower*] for his access unto mee. I beseich yowr lordship to excuse mee in that I did not deliver the seale unto his man, for I received it from Her Majesty upon the death of the Earle of Bedford,[3] and I thinck when your lordship gave up the Duchy [*of Lancaster*] yow delivered the seales by warrant from her.[4] I had thought to have taken this good occasion to have written to His Majesty which I never did since my returne from Winchester,[5] although all others have don. If your lordship do not thinck it unfitting me I would willingly do it, but if your lordship thinck it not best for mee I will forbeare it and then write unto your lordship and send yow the seale to deliver [*to*] the King. I do not desire to offend the earl but I hope he will thinck it reasonabell that I deliver it by order as I receved it and not uppon a message by his man.

I humble beseich your lordship, by Shelbury[6] or sume[*one*] elce to vouchsaufe your favorabell advice, whose I shall every remayne to the end of my life to do yow service.

    W Ralegh

1. See note 2.
2. William Herbert, 3rd Earl of Pembroke, had received the stewardship of the Duchy of Cornwall and the Wardenship of the Stannaries on 18 January 1604: *HMC Salisbury* XV, p. 68 and *CSPD 1603–10*, p. 68. On 16 June 1604, Cecil gave permission for Pembroke's manservant to 'speak with' Ralegh: *HMC Salisbury* XVII, p. 601.
3. In 1585.
4. Cecil had been Chancellor of the Duchy of Lancaster from 1597 until May 1599.
5. Proof that Letter 175 was written before Ralegh left Winchester.
6. John Shelbury (1557–c.1641) was the son of a London grocer who studied at Oxford and afterwards at Lincoln's Inn. He was MP for West Looe in Cornwall in 1593, probably due to his service to Ralegh. From 1596, with Robert Smith, he administered Ralegh's wine licences, continuing to do so even after they were taken into the King's hands on Ralegh's attainder. He seems to have had easy access to Ralegh in the Tower: Hasler III, pp. 372–3 and *HMC Salisbury* XV, pp. 305, 307; XVI, pp. 192–3; XVII, pp. 601 and 444. See also above, Letter 176 and below, Letters 186–8.

---

## 180. To Lord Cecil [from the Tower, shortly after 16 June]¹ 1604

Hatfield, CP109/12, *HMC Salsibury* XVI, p. 260. In Ralegh's hand.
Edwards II, p. 295.

### THE DUCHY SEAL

[*addressed*] To the right honorabell my singuler good lord the Lord Cecyll
[*endorsed*] 1604 Sir Walter Raleigh to my lord

I have sent your lordshipe herewith the Duchy seale and have written to the Kings Majesty that I have besought your lordship to deliver the same unto His Majesties hands, to whom only it appartayneth to dispose therof. I humble beseich your lordship also to deliver for me this enclosed [*Letter 181*] wherin I have humble prayed His Majesty to continew and perfait his mercies begun. Good my lord, remember your poore awntient and trew frind, that I perish not here, whose health weres awaye and whose short tymes run fast on in misery only. Those which plotted to surprize and assaile the person of the Kinge, thos that ar papists, ar att liberty.² Do not forgett me, nor doubt me, for as God liveth I shall never forgett your trew honor and remorce of me,
        but will rem[a]yne as yow thought to serve yow,
        W R

1. See above, Letter 179, note 2. Before 20 August when Cecil became Lord Cranborne.
2. Of those convicted of plotting to 'surprise' the King, the so-called Bye Plot, only the two priests and George Brooke had died on the scaffold.

---

## 181. To King James [from the Tower, shortly after 16 June 1604][1]

PRO, SP14/8/123, *CSPD 1603–10*, p. 138, a near-contemporary transcript of a missing original. There is a second, almost identical, transcript (ibid., 124) which supplies the address and signature. Previously printed only in abstract.

### THE DUCHY SEAL AND A PLEA FOR LIBERTY

[*addressed*]   To the Kings most excellent Majesty, my soverain lord

May it please Your most excellent Majesty: I was of late sent unto for the seale of the Dutchy of Cornwale which, together with the office of Warden and Chancelor, I received at the hands of my late soverain. This seale appertayneth not to me to dispose but to Your Majesty only, and therefore I have intreated my Lord Cecyll [*Letter 180*] to present the same.

For my sealf I have interest in nothing but in Your Majesties mercy only. God, who knows what faith I do [*bear*], and have ever born, to Your Majesty, move your emperiall heart to parfayt your graces begun. I be here restrayned until the poures [= *powers*] both of my body and mind shall be so enfeebled as I cannot hope to do Your Majesty some acceptable and extraordinary service, whereby I may trewly approve [= *prove*] my faith and intentions to my soverayn lord, God douth know that then it had bin happiest for mee to have died long since. For the everliving God doth bear me record that it is to no other cheif end that I desire to live a day. I most humbly beseich Your Majesty, even for the love of our Lord Jesus, to thinck that I can never forgett the mercies of the King who hath vouchsaufed to lift mee out of the grave, being then friendless, lost and forsaken of all men. Pardon me, most renowned King, but to say this mich, that if it pleas Your Majesty to have compassion of mee while I have yet lymes and eyes, that Your Majesty shall never have cause to accuse or repent [= *regret*] Your Majesties mercies towards mee, beseiching the lord of all

poure and justice to strike me with the greatest miseries of body and sowle when I shall not remayne a most faithfull and humble and gratfull vassall.
      WRaleige [sic]

1. Original enclosed with Letter 180.

---

### 182. To Lord Cecil from the Tower, [between 25 March and 3 August][1] 1604

Hatfield, CP109/17, *HMC Salisbury* XVI, p. 261, dated before 20 August. In Ralegh's neatest hand.

Edwards II, pp. 300–303.

#### FAVOURS PAST AND FUTURE

[*addressed*]    To the right honorabell my singuler good lord the Lord Cecyll etc.

[*endorsed*]    1604   Sir Walter Raleigh to my lord from the Tower

My lord: If all christien and lawfull pour [= *power*] directs it sealf equaly by the counsell of reason and of charity, theon teaching us humayn pollecy, the other celestiall, your lordship, whose mind hath bynn ever moderat, doth witnes that yow have received this grace from God, and light from virtu to know that cumpassion hath ever bynn repayd with cumpassion, and cruelty with cruelty, and if ever this rule have fayled in the life of man (which is rare) it hath bynn performed everlastingly elcwher. I do therfore humble pray your lordship that yow will looke into that justice which is never seperate from mercy, by which and in which, whosoever useth it, hee douth both pleas and imitate God. And therin, first but to consider thes too: what my offences have bynn to my soverayn and what my errors were towards my frinds, and then, laying both in the balance, together with my losses and afflixions, to consider and way the fault with the payn and the counterperjures and person by whom I have perished.[2]

    To be equall herein is the office of a just magistrat. To respect the trewth and not the law is celestiall polecy, by which wee must all hope to be judged, and shalbe judged as wee judge and be dealt withall, as wee deal with others in this life, if wee beleve God hym sealf. To be cunpassionat and moderating is an effect of piety, for which God was never debtor to any man. And if God have moved others to preserve me from the worst of evells, I may trust that the thoughts of my sowle have found grace with hym, in which hee never beheld any desire of mans ruin or destruction, mallic or revendg. Lastly, to undertake the cause of any man in misery is ether out of trew honor and generosety, which geveth freely, and out of no other respect then sealf vertu, or out of love, which beholds the ill a farr of and the good at hand.

Now your lordship hath used the first and second to all, and for affection, if nothing be left, it hath cast all his leves of late and withereth in the spring, which I cannot beleve. Seeing in my darck and dead winter it made that most trew and adventurus proof of it sealf, which I could not hope for and can never repay, for thos lines writen in a nother hand of which I knew the phraze ar also writen on my hart, and which my sowle can never leve to repeat while it liveth in my body. And if any cunning toong [= *tongue*] of man, or if an angell tell your lordship the contrary, do not beleve hym. Neither shall I ever distinguish that demonstration of my lives care, which the effect sealed,[3] while I have being or know ther is a God which hath ever hated that ingratetud to the ministers of his goodness.

A seconnd effect of your lordships great favor was the preservation of my moveabells which the ravenous sherifs were in hand [= *preparing*] to have seised, and att my gates to have rifled, if your lordships letters had not then cum to have countermanded it, which it also pleased yow soon after to procure mee.[4]

The last [*favour*] is now humble desired of mee and myne, which is the obtayning of that poore estate which remayns, that the life which your lordship hath stayd at the graves brinck may have wherwith to releve it, and that my poore childe may be your poore creature forever, as I am. Which being doon, I protest before the living God I shall take my loss for a gayne, nothing being lost that could have bettered any of myne but the lease of the wines which was desperat [= *at great risk*] before my trobells.

And for conclusion I beseich your lordship from my hart, which shall ever devise how to honor yow, that yow will resolve, and do me right therin to beleve, that my thoughts and my love can never be seperat from yow, and that I may be of sume use unto yow if yow pleas to finishe the worck for me which yow have begun, which I shall imprint in the harts of all myne, and remayne forever so tied unto your lordship as, if ther be any life and body yours which yow may accompt of to expose to what yow pleas, it is my sealf,

      Your lordships trew poore frind and trew sarvant,
        W Ralegh

1. Endorsement indicates a date after 25 March, and it was on 3 August 1604 that the Crown placed the estate in the hands of trustees for the benefit of Lady Ralegh and her son: see below, Letter 183, note 3. Another son, Carew, was born later that year, or early in 1605: see below, Letter 184, note 1.
2. Presumably a veiled reference to Cobham.
3. Cf. (Letter 183) 'your lordship who hath first saved my life and estate ...'. Ralegh continues to credit Cecil with his partial reprieve, or at least to pretend to do so, although Cecil had replied to Ralegh's letter from Winchester (Letter 174) indicating that thanks were due only to the King (ibid., note 2).
4. On 14 February 1604: see above, Letter 176, note 3.

---

## 183. TO LORD CECIL FROM THE TOWER, [BEFORE 3 AUGUST][1] 1604

Hatfield, CP109/16, *HMC Salisbury* XVI, p. 260. In Ralegh's hand.
Edwards II, pp. 303–5.

## ONE STEP AT A TIME

[*addressed*]   To the right honorabell my singuler good lord the Lord Cecyll
[*endorsed*]   1604   Sir Walter Raleigh to my lord from the Tower

My wife told me that shee spake with your lordshipe yesterday about my poore estate and hers, and that it pleased your lordship to tell her that yow would be pleased to deale for the assurance of my land unto sume feoffees of trust to the use of her and my childe, but that for my pardon it could not yet be dunn. Whatsoever your lordship shall do herein it is of your great goodness and beyonnd my poure [= *power*] to deserve, and if my pardon may not be had then I most humble beseich yow that the land may bee so obtayned in the mean while, which to the end of my life I shall acknowledg. But wheras it pleased your lordship to add that yow would be contented that sume body elce should hereafter procure mee a pardon, I do rather desire to attend your lordships leasure therin then to ingage my sealf to any man living for so great a benefyte, but to your lordship who hath first saved my life and estate and keipt mee and myne from utter ruin. For it cannot bee but a great debt from mee to any man and a challendg of my service and love to hyme forever that shall procure it. And good my lord, lett mee bee your trew and only creature without any other dependency. I may yet do your lordship sume kind of service, ether by word, deed or writinge, all which God douth know I will imploy to do your lordship honor forever.

If I had a pardon I may notwithstanding be restraynd or confined. If I may not be here about Londun (which God cast my sowle into hell if I desire but to do your lordship sume kind of service) I shalbe most contented to be confined within the hundred of Sherburn, or if I cannot be allowed so mich I shalbe contented to live in Holland wher I shall perchance get sume imployment uppon the Indies. Or elce if I be apoyncted to any bishope, or other gentelman or nobel man, or that your lordship would lett me keip but a parke of yours which I will buy from sume one that hath it, your lordship shalbe sure that I will never break the order which yow shall pleas to undertake for me. And if I bee any wher nire yow, yow shall find that in sume kind or other I shall do your lordship service.

For God douth know that if I cannot go to the Bathe this fall I am undun for my health [for ever *crossed out*] and shalbe dead or disabled forever. Good my lord, make an[2] end one way or other, that I may witness to the world the great debt I owe yow, and your lordship shall find it from God and with men in sume proportion to your lordships advantage, to whom I will remayne your [*sic*] the most thanckfullest man that ever received good from your lordship or ever shall.[3]

        W Ralegh

1. See note 3.
2. From here to the end is written in the left-hand margin.
3. On 3 August 1604, the Castle, manor, etc. of Sherborne etc., were granted by letters patent to Sir Alexander Brett and George Hull in trust for Lady Ralegh and her son for a term of 60 years 'should Sir Walter so long live': *CSPD 1603–10*, p. 138. Brett was Lady Ralegh's cousin (see above, Letter 165, note 16) and Hull, who came from Exeter and moved into Dorset, was the second husband of Ralegh's sister Margaret: Vivian, *Devon*, pp. 492, 637 and 639.

---

## 184. To Lord Cranborne [from the Tower, late] 1604[1]

Hatfield, CP109/13, *HMC Salisbury* XVI, p. 291. In Ralegh's hand.
Edwards II, pp. 314–15.

### LOSS OF FRIENDSHIP

[*addressed*] To the right honorabell my singuler good lord the Lord Cecyll, Viscount Cranborn, etc.

[endorsed]   1604   Sir Walter Raleigh

Since the tyme that my wife was last with your lordshipe² I have withered in body and mind, by whom [*Lady Ralegh*] I perceived a sad chang in your lordships favor towards me, on which all my hopes have ever lived and made me live. Not for the discumfort of liberty only but in that it pleased your lordship to thinck that I had dealt ungratfully with yow since my trobels, which, as there is a God, I never did, nor could so mich as thinck to do.

For the tymes past, whatsoever your lordship hath conceived, I cannot thinck my sealf to have bynn ether an enemy or such a viper,³ but that this great downfall of myne, this shame, loss and sorrow, may seme to your lordships hart and sowle a sufficient punishment and revendg. And if ther be nothing of so many years love and familiarety to lay on the other scale, O my God, how have my thoughts betrayd me in your lordships nature, compassion and piety. For to dy in perpetuall prison I did not thinck that your lordship could have wished to your strongest and most mallicious enemyes. I know that law and condemnation ar formal arguments to men of iron harts, but God that must judg us all, and extend infinit compassion towards all, or elce we must all perish in the never ending sorrows to cum, that God, when the sorrowfull night of death shall cum uppon us, will remember the cries and grones of the miserabell whom we have suffred to perish and not releived.

I have presumed att this tyme to remember your lordship of my miserabell estate [= *condition*], dayly in danger of death by the palsey,⁴ nightly of suffocation by wasted and obstructed lungs, and now the plaug [*plague*]⁵ being cum att the next dore unto me, only the narrow passage of the way between, my poore child⁶ having lien this 14 dayes next to a wooman with a running plaug sore and but a paper wall betwen, and whose childe is also this Thursday dead of the plauge.

So as now my wife and child and others in whom I had cumfort have abandoned me,⁷ and in what fearfull estate the Lord knowes. My most humble desire is to be removed elsewher, even to what place which Gods goodness and charitey shall move your lordships hart, that I be not left alone and remedeless, as well for this visitation as for other as lamentabell deseases which possess me.

That I shall not ever acknowledg your lordships great and cumfortabell favours, God make yow to know the contrary, the same God that knowes that I was never farther from my Lord Cecyll but that I would have sett

my life betwen hyme and harme. God geve me cumfort as it is trew, and as I shall evermore be found gratfull in the highest degree and remayne your lordships poore disconsolate
        W Ralegh

1. After 20 August 1604, when Cecil became Lord Cranborne, but before the birth of Carew, who was baptized on 15 February 1605.
2. Lady Ralegh saw Cecil in July and was promised that Sherborne would be placed in trust, which was done on 30 July: see Letter 183, note 3.
3. At Ralegh's trial the Attorney-General told Ralegh that 'there never lived a viler viper upon the face of the earth than thou': Cayley 1806, II, p. 425.
4. Some form of paralysis. Dr Poe, one of the Royal physicians, had permission to visit Ralegh on 20 September: *HMC Salisbury* XVII, p. 600.
5. London was never entirely free of plague but it was not particularly virulent in late 1604: Paul Slack, *The Impact of Plague in Tudor and early Stuart England*, 1985, p. 146.
6. Walter junior, aged about ten.
7. Although the whole family appears to have been normally resident in the Tower at this time (see below, Letter 209, note 3), Lady Ralegh acquired a house on Tower Hill, near All Hallows Barking.

---

## 185. To Lord Cranborne [from the Tower, winter 1604–5][1]

Hatfield, CP102/24, *HMC Salisbury* XVI, p. 455. In Ralegh's hand.
Edwards II, pp. 311–13.

### DEEP DEPRESSION

[*addressed*]  To the right honorabell my singuler good lorde the Lord Cecil, Vicount Cranborne etc.
[*endorsed*]  Sir W Ralegh

That life which cann be of no use to others and is now also weery of mee, at parting putts mee in mind of thos whom nature and charetie commands me not to neglect—a wife and a childe and a wife with childe whom, God knowes, have nothing elce to inherit then my shame and ther own misery. How to healp it or to whom to cumplayn I know not, whose fortune is over darck for the reason of the world to peirce. And I, who cann nether pay old debts nor deserve new trust, cannot be so partiall to my sealf but to know that to press your lordshipp (who have alreddy cast back unto me all I have) were ether foolishness or impudency. And while I know that the best of men are but the spoyles of tyme and certayne images wherwith childishe fort[u]ne useth to play, kiss them to day and break them tomorrow, and therfore cann lament in my sealf but a common destiney. Yet the pitifull estate of thos who are altogether healpless, and who dayly wound my sowle with the memory of their miseries, force mee in dispight of all resolvedness both to bewayle them and labor for them. Not that I wish them (God knowes) the least proportion of plenty, having forgotten (that happines) [sic] which found to mich, to littell. But my thoughts are now guyded by thos affections which povertie hath begotten, who contemplate it to bee a sufficient felicitie for them but to be able to eat of their own bread.

Now, if it shall please your lordship to pardon the necessetie of my presumtion, I most humble beseich yow to receve the opinions of my Lord Cheif Justice [*Sir John Popham*] and Master Aturney [*Sir Edward Coke*] for the conveyance.[2] Master Dodrige knowes that it had [= *would have*] bynn sealed almost too yeere err the Queen died if the feoffees[3] had not bynn so farr asunder, and God doth witness with me that att that tyme when it was dun Sir A[*lexander*] Brett was the sole cause in respect of my quarells with Gorge and Preston.[4] If they shall judg fraud herein God judg them with more grace then they have judged of it and mee.[5]

Howsoever it be, it seemed to me that His Majestye (by your lordshipp moved to compassion) promised to leve me what was left, and that the more it appeared in valew that His Majestie would the [*more*] willingly graunt it. This mich I had cause to hope for, the rather because your lordship tolde me at Winchester that yow were sorry that I had resigned Jersey,[6] words which, God knowes, peirced my hart to the center, as witnesing a feeling of his adversetie whom yow had once loved. That, and other things of the greatest debts layd onn me, makes me still presume that your lordships hart (which God for goodness hath blest), being ether moved with the past, or by the compassion of my present, would yet vouchsauf to save this quarter which remayneth from the ravens of this tyme which feed onn all things. For as it is, so are my tenants made afeard, as I protest before God ether I must spoyle all and receve 20*s* for 20*li* or elce want altogether, and in the mean tyme cann neither pay debts, releve my sealf or assure bread to my children.

For myne owne tyme, good my lord consider that it cannot be calde a life but only misery drawn out and spoone [= *spun*] into a long thride without all hope of other end then death shall provide for mee, who, without the healp of kings or frinds, will deliver mee out of prison.

If your lordship shalbe pleased to do any thing herein I shall but offer myself for recumpence who am but as a broken reed. But [I] shall hope that God shall pay your lordship all my debts. If your lordship forsake mee herein all I can do is to lett them know that I cannot healp them, that they may try for themsealvs, while by my life they have yet a possession of their birthright.

For the rest lett the pollecy of the world be it what it will, as ther is a God I know my sealf bound unto your lordshipp, and which I would pay agayne if I could with a gratetud never surmounted.

    W R

1. As above, Letter 184, note 1.
2. Of the Sherborne estate to trustees in April 1603: see above, Letter 165, note 16. The conveyance was first drafted in January, the indenture dated 20 February 1603 and signed and sealed on 13 April following: Wildman, *Short History*, pp. 140–41. This is the first positive intimation in Ralegh's surviving letters that the conveyance was flawed, but see above, Letter 176. Who actually first drew attention to the possibility is not clear, but Ralegh himself may have had his reasons for wanting it declared null and void: see Introduction, pp. xlvii–xlviii.
3. Alexander Brett, Thomas Harriot and Sir Arthur Throckmorton.
4. Either Sir Arthur Gorges (see above, Letter 101) or, more likely, Sir Ferdinando Gorges, Governor of Plymouth Fort 1595–1601 and 1604–29, and Sir Amyas Preston, a native of Somerset, knighted by Essex at Cadiz. Both had been involved in the Earl of Essex's rising in 1601.
5. See above, Letter 178, where Ralegh denies any 'ill intent'.
6. He surely had no option but to forfeit the post following his conviction.

---

## 186. To Sir Michael Hicks from the Tower, 10 November 1604

Longleat, Wiltshire, Portland Papers I, f. 202, *HMC BATH* II, p. 54, almost a full transcript. In Ralegh's hand.

## ON BEHALF OF JOHN SHELBURY

[*addressed*] To my loving frind Sir Michell Hext knight
[*endorsed*] 10 November 1604 Sir W Raleighe

Sir Mihell Hext: I pray spare John Shelbury[1] for a little tyme, for I protest before God wee have no means in the world to discharg it[2] as yet. Hee stands bound for mee for 1500*li* and if hee bee arested for my part hee must ly in prison for all, and, God is my witness that, if hee be restrayned that [*sic*] hee cannot recover the wine arrearages,[3] [*and*] thes debts will never be payd. It cannot profite yow any way to molest hym, but it may bee his undowing and I may therby lose all thos debts of the wine office[4] and then never abell to pay myne own. If I live I shall find sume what to make yow recumpence.

        Your assured loving frind,
            W Ralegh

1. See above, Letter 179, note 6.
2. For Ralegh's debts, including £100 to Hicks, see above, Letter 165 and below, Letter 190.
3. On 21 February 1604, Ralegh's wine licensees had been instructed by the Privy Council, following the grant of all his goods and debts to Shelbury and Smith (above, Letter 176, note 3), to go to Ralegh's steward 'at his house over against Durham Place ... as they were wont to do' and pay their arrears: *HMC 4th Report* (Lord Bagot), 331.i. On 28 April, Shelbury was formally appointed to administer the revenue from the wine licences: *CSPD 1603–10*, p. 102.
4. Ralegh was still confident, as he had been a year before (Letter 172, note 9), that the arrears would be at his disposal, but see below, Letter 187. As yet the patent had not been assigned to anyone else.

---

## 187. To Lord Cranborne [from the Tower, late December][1] 1604

Hatfield, CP105/50, *HMC Salisbury* XVI, p. 453. In Ralegh's hand.
Edwards II, p. 316.

### THE WINE ARREARS

[addressed] To the right honorabell my singuler good lord the Vicount Cranborn, etc.
[endorsed] 1604 Sir Walter Raleigh to my lord

I might feare that this my importunety might offend your lordshipp if I did not withall hope that the proportion of your lordships favor sett by for me cannot by any weakness of this nature be recalde or cast back into that heape out of which your lordships justice taketh out to releive all men.

   Thos seasons which honor and good fortune accumpany seeme but short and steale from us un[a]wares, but their tymes whose days runn out in misery only appeare exceeding longe and draw sloely to their end. Sorrow rydes the Ass, prosperitie the Eagell.

   That which makes me adventure to beseich your lordship herein is the nireness of the term,[2] att which tyme the kinges councell in law wilbe more busied and much deerer, the bussness intricate³ and therfore dangerus in a careless hand, for my sealf being unpardoned I must wholy trust other mens consciences wherin, howsoever the fathers deale, God knowes how the soonns may.⁴

Besides, I have keipt my steward [*John Shelbury*]⁵ here ever since your lordships first cumfort geven mee, a man whom I can better intreat then know how to reward, his owne estate requiring his presence more then it doth my love, as it hath pleased God to order it. All which I leve to your lordships goodness to valew, for whom charitie only must finde out frinds.

        Your lordships ever to serve yow,
        W Ralegh

1. Between 8 December 1604 (see note 4) and 11 January 1605 (see note 2).
2. The Hilary term began on 11 January.
3. Collection of arrears of payment for wine licences was complicated by the mismanagement of Ralegh's agents.
4. On 8 December 1604, the King appointed the Lord Admiral, the elderly Earl of Nottingham, and his son, Lord Charles Howard of Effingham, to administer the granting of wine licences: PRO, SP14/10/56. A fortnight later, the Howards leased the 'business' to a syndicate comprising Sir John Fearne, Sir Arthur Ingram and James Cullimore: R.H. Tawney, *Business and Politics under James I*, Cambridge 1958, pp. 118–19. In March 1605 the number of partners was increased to eight. They continued to maintain headquarters 'near Charing Cross'.
5. See above, Letter 179, note 6.

---

## 188. TO LEVINUS MUNCK [FROM THE TOWER, c.APRIL 1605]¹

Hatfield, CP102/21, *HMC Salisbury* XVI, p. 454. Right-hand margin torn. In Ralegh's hand.

Edwards II, pp. 305–6.

### RECOVERY OF A DEBT

[*addressed*]  To my loving frinde Master Levinus, or in his absence to Master Bruerton,² secritores to my Lord of Cranborn
[*endorsed*]  1605  Sir Walter Raley

Master Levinus: If necessitie were not impudent, or if povertie could heal it sealf, I would not take this boldness to trobell my lorde, who hath alred[y] putt many debts uppon hyme that is abell to repay nothing, and every day less then other, forsaken of frinds and of health and of all but God.

I solde of late to peeces of ordenance to one Master Aleblaster,³ a merchant whome yow know. Hee that made the bargayne between us was one Thom[as] Scott,⁴ a broker, one that I have dunn mich for in my tyme and one that since I came back from Winchester [*on 16 December 1603*] offred to sell his howse for [?*to*] me⁵ if I wanted, with protestations to shamless to be dissembled [= *disguised*]. But, having gotten my mony into his hands which Master Aleblaster sent mee, and five pounds waight of tobacco promised, hath sold the tobacco and retayneth my mony, finding me now fitt for all men to tread onn. Hee hath goods in a shipp of Master Aleblasters which Master Aleblaster advised me to attach [= *arrest*], but he hath cunningly shippt them in other mens names so as I have lost that charge. Arrest hyme I cannot nor sew hyme because the law knowes me but for dead.

My humble sute is to have pursevant [= *royal messenger*] and my lords letter to take hyme. He means to go away for Speyne in Master Aleblasters shipp, so as if the pursevant find hyme not this Sunday hee will imbarck on Munday, onless it would pleas my lorde to write a commandment to the master of Master Aleblasters shipp called The Prudence of London to command the master not to take hyme abord here or elcewher till hee have payd me the mony.

If yow thinck it not offencive, good Master Levinus, procure it. If yow do I must have patience till God geve end to my miseres or to me.

    Your poore frinde assur[ed],
    W Ralegh

1. Before 4 May 1605, when Cecil became Earl of Salisbury, and the endorsement places it after 25 March.
2. See A.G.R. Smith, 'The Secretariat of the Cecils', *EHR*, LXXXIII, 1968, especially pp. 481–2.
3. In 1605, when he gave advice on a diet for the lion cubs in the Tower, Aleblaster was described as 'a merchant of good understanding that has frequented Barbary': *HMC Salisbury* XVII, p. 375.
4. Not identified, but clearly a man of parts.
5. Possibly near the Tower, for Lady Ralegh's use.

---

## 189. To the Earl of Salisbury from the Tower, [shortly before 16 July]¹ 1605

Hatfield, CP109/9, *HMC Salisbury* XVII, p. 624. In Ralegh's hand.
Edwards II, pp. 317–19.

## THE SHERBORNE ESTATE

[*addressed*] To the right honorable my singuler good lorde the Lord Vicount Cranborn, Earle of Sallisbury, etc.
[*endorsed*]  1605  Sir Walter Ralegh to my lord

Your lordshipp being now reddy to depart hence[2] (and being otherwise imboldned by your lordships cumfortabell promises) makes me adventure once agayne to beseich your [*lordship*][3] to remember my long sute.[4] I do not press your lordship as doubtinge your lordships favor therin. My life had sauftie without your words and therfore no cause for me to doubt my land with it.

But it is true, *dant animum ad loquendum libere ultimae miseriae*, and being in such estate [= *condition*] brought, I lay before your lordship the trew cause of my importunetie. Theon is (which I speake in the presence and feare of God) that I am every second or third night in danger ether of suddayne death, or of the loss of my lymes and sense, being sumetyme two howres without feeling or motion of my hand and whole arm.[5] I complayn not of it: I know it vayne for ther is none that hath compassion therof. Theother [*is*] that I shalbe made more then weary of my life by her [*Lady Ralegh's*] criing and bewayling, who will return [*from Dorset*] in post [= *haste*] when shee heares of your lordships departure and nothing don. She hath alreddy brought her eldest sonn in one hand and her sutting [= *sucking*] child in another, criing out of her and their destruction, charging me with unnaturall negligence and that, having provided for myne own life, I am without sense and compassion of theirs.[6]

Thes torments, added to my desolate life, receiving nothing but torments and outcries wher I should look for sume cumfort, together with the consideration of my cruell destiney, my dayes and tymes worn out in sorrow and imprisonment, is sufficient ether utterly to distract me or to make mee curse the tyme that ever I was born into the world and had a being, did I not hope that God wilbe pleased to accept thes misires of myne in this world for thos eternall sorrowes which my neglect of hyme and offences agaynst hyme have deserved.[7] I beseich your lordship, even as yow must one day begg cumfort from God and cry unto hyme for his aboundant mercie, that yow wilbe pleased to spare the tyme and to finish and effect in sume sort your harts intents toward me. If I could ether healp, or blame [= *censure*] their cries and impatience, I would for my sealf leve all to God and your lordship, but if your lordship spare one thought towards this estate of myne I cannot but hope for sume happie end, which I leve to your lordships goodness to resolve of.

  And rest your most miserable creture, to do yow service,
    W Ralegh

1. See below, note 2.
2. The King's progress, on which his Principal Secretary would be in attendance, began on 16 July 1605: E.K. Chambers, *Elizabethan Stage*, Oxford 1923, IV, p. 120.
3. Word omitted. Edwards has 'yow' but Ralegh definitely writes 'your'.
4. Regarding the Sherborne estate: see above, Letter 185.
5. In March 1606, Peter Turner, doctor of physic, reported as follows:
   > Sir Water Raleghs complayning is ... [that] all his left syde is extreme cold, out of sens and motion or num. His fingers on the same syde beginning to be contracted. And his tong taken in sum parte, in so mych that he speketh wekely and it is to be fered he may utterly lese the use of it.
   
   Turner advised that Ralegh be moved to warmer quarters, if only to 'a litle roome which he hath bilt in the garden adjoyning to his stilhows [= *laboratory*]': PRO, SP14/19/112. See Plate 9. Again, it must be remembered that Ralegh was an accomplished actor.
6. In fact, Lady Ralegh was already assured of residence at Sherborne for her husband's lifetime: see above, Letter 183, note 3.
7. Traditional popular orthodoxy, although the Elizabethan Church discouraged belief in purgatory, i.e. atonement for earthly sins, emphasizing instead the benefits of good works.

---

## 190. To the Earl of Salisbury [from the Tower, before November][1] 1605

Hatfield, CP109/11, *HMC Salisbury* XVII, p. 624. In Ralegh's hand.
Edwards II, pp. 319–21.

### ASSURANCE OF SHERBORNE

[*addressed*] To the right honorable my singuler good lord the Lord Vicount Cranborn, Earle of Sallisburie, etc.
[*endorsed*] 1605 Sir Walter Ralegh to my lord

As all my cumforts and sorrowes are in your lordships poure, so it pleaseth your lordship often to mixe them, though with a gentell hand. My wife tolde mee that your lordship had pleased to move His Majestie for Sherburne, and that His Majestie was graciously disposed toward the releif of her and her poore children.[2] My thanckfullness I know your lordship cannot valew: thos bonds of debts are only layd up wher payment may be hoped for, but all dew from me I must leve to the world to pay your lordship, withe a great part of the honor it hath to geve, and to God to allow for, satisfied in your great accompt towards hyme the compassion yow shew towards others. All men have one entrance into life, and a like going out. In the dust we live by glorie, in the heavens by mercie: *prudentia humana mortalis, misericordia aeterna.*

Ther is nothing more trew then that the greatest prosperitie hath the greatest envie, and though wise men do not therfore neglect the blessings of God in this world, yet they carefully distinguish her two natures, the one biting att prosperitie it sealf, att what prise soever vertue hath bought it, the other att that poure accumpaned with serveritie, especially agaynst thos whom it hath sumetyme loved and are afterward become miserabell. *Ea prosperitas maxime invidiosa est, in qua est asperitas, praecipue in amicos afflictos ac miseros ac in nostram potestatem redactos*: for the plentie of happines is never decreased by imparting cumfort to others wher God hath geven sufficient for both. How your lordship may thinck that I acknowledg your lordships liberalitie towards my sealf I can no otherwise gess then by the continewance of your favor. To geve your lordship farther assurance of my desire to honor your lordship with all the poures of my sowle I find no other argument then trewth in my sealf, and uttered by thes emptie voyces which your lordships charitie pleaseth to accept.

For the sute it sealf with which I have so often trobled your lordship, as I must take most thanckfully whatsoever your lordship shall vouchsauf to procure mee, so, if the land be tied with a remaynder a third of the valew is therby lost. Besids that, neither can I have means to pay my debts (owing to Master [*Peter*] Vanlor and Sir J[*ohn*] Spilman[3] 1300*li*, and, as God liveth, as mich more elcewher, and the debts [= *arrears*] of the wines allreddy assigned).[4] Agayne, the church of Sallisburie which hath no great estate might therby loose 260*li* a yeere which I pay,[5] for the King can be no mans tenant nor hold land of any vassall.

I did desire it free[*hold*], the rather in hope to bargayn with your lordship for it, for ther is no seat within the cumpass of your titells[6] so fitt for your lordship as that, and I will make it appere [= *demonstrate*] that your lordship may save 10,000*li* in respect of building, imparking and setling elcewher.

It was once intayled uppon my brothers children but I might have revoked it agayn and ment it [= *to do so*].[7] I beseich your lordship do me that grace as I may be therin no less free then heretofore, and if your lordship do not find reason in my offer towards your sealf (my debts being payd), I protest before God I will then tie it as your lordship shall advise me or command mee.

And howsoever I shall remayne your lordships faithfull sarvant to the end,
    W Ralegh

1. Surely predates the Gunpowder Plot: see below, Letter 191.
2. There are undated instructions at Hatfield (*HMC Salisbury* XVII, pp. 624–5) from King James to Salisbury which read:
   Wheras we understand that by rigour of law the reversion of Sir Walter Raleigh's land may come unto our hands, yet seeing his conveyance was made in the Queen our sisters time, as also because we have given himself those lands for his own life, our pleasure is that you cause a grant to be drawn wherin all our title and interest may be passed over unto his wife and children, that we be no more troubled with their pitiful cries and complaints for that business.
   That these royal instructions, which seem on the face of it intended as a genuine act of mercy, were not followed by Salisbury may be due to Ralegh's insistence later in this letter that he wanted nothing less than freehold for himself.
3. For Van Lore see above, Letter 165, note 18. Sir John Spilman, a jeweller and money-lender, had Salisbury's permission to visit Ralegh on 10 August 1605: *HMC Salisbury* XVII, p. 600.
4. To Shelbury, etc.: see above, Letters 172, 186 and 187.
5. See above, Letter 119, note 4.
6. Salisbury needed a country 'seat' but he was unlikely to be interested in Sherborne which was too far from London. In 1607 he was to exchange with the King Theobalds in Hertfordshire for Hatfield: *CSPD 1603–10*, p. 358.
7. See Letter 165, note 16. He seems to have forgotten his own earlier doubt as to whether, being a convicted traitor, he had the power to exercise the right of revocation.

---

## 191. To the Privy Council [from the Tower], 9 November 1605[1]

Hatfield, CP107/108, *HMC Salisbury* XVII, p. 480. In Ralegh's hand.
Edwards II, pp. 387–8, from BL, Addit. 6178, f. 469, an early transcript of the original.

### GUNPOWDER, TREASON AND PLOT

[*no address*]
[*endorsed, by or for Salisbury*]    1605 9 November    Sir Walter Raleigh

I have not had any other affaire with Captain Whitlock[2] then familier and ordinarie discource, neither do I know any other cause of his cumming unto me then to visite me, having not mich wherwith to busie hymsealf. I have sumetyme spoken to hym to finde the Earle of Northumberlands disposition towards me, from whom I never received other then a drie and frindless awnswere.³ From the Earle I neither [sent nor *crossed out*] received letter nor sent hym any, ether by Whitlock or any man elce since my trobells.

With the French imbasator⁴ I have no affaires. His wife came hither once with the Ladie of Effingam⁵ and, the pale [= *partition*] being then down,⁶ she saluted me and desired me to geve her a little balsemum of Guiana. Whitlock being then in her cumpany I sent it by hym to her.

    W Ralegh

I sent your lordships in the beginnings of my trobells a letter from Sir John Bodley concerning Rensay⁷ and others and the same was my utter ruin. I did it to do the Kings service. If I now knew any thinge or could devise how this horribell and fearful practize might be discovered, [then *crossed out*] if it were with the loss of myne own life, as God liveth, I would geve the one to perform the other. I beseich you lordships to call to minde my many sorrowes and the causes and to remember my services and love to my countrie, and I beseich yow in charitie and for the love of God not to make me more odious then ever the earth brought forth any—by suspecting me to be knowing this unexampled and more then develishe invention.

    Your humble servant,
    W R

1. The date on the dorse is confirmed by a list of 'letters come about this treason' compiled by Salisbury's secretary, Levinus Munck, which, for 9 November, includes an item entered on that day in 1605 as 'Sir Walter Ralegh, his declaration concerning Whitlock': *CSPD 1603–10*, p. 256.
2. Captain Edmund Whitelock, formerly an associate of the Earl of Essex and latterly a pensioner of the Earl of Northumberland, who was to be convicted of complicity in the Gunpowder Plot.
3. Before the Queen's death, Northumberland had commended Ralegh to the future King James as one who while 'insolent [and] extreamly heated' he knows there to be in him 'excellent good parts of natur': J. Bruce (ed.), *Correspondence of James VI*, Camden Society 78, 1861, p. 67. He adds the interesting reflection that while Ralegh likes to be regarded as one able 'to sway all men's fancies', when the time comes he will never do James 'muche good nor hearme'.
4. Christopher de Harlay, Count of Beaumont, from 1602.
5. Anne, née St John, wife of William, Lord Howard of Effingham, the Lord Admiral's son.
6. This was the 'slender pale' between the Lieutenant of the Tower's lodgings and the garden where Ralegh walked (see Plate 9). On 19 August 1605, the new Lieutenant, Sir William Waad, had sought Salisbury's permission to have it replaced by a brick wall to preserve his own privacy: *HMC Salisbury* XVII, p. 378. Ralegh's remark suggests that this had been authorized and quickly done.
7. The letter which provoked Cobham's first accusation in 1603. For a short time in July 1603, Ralegh was under house arrest in the custody of Sir Thomas Bodley in Fulham: G. Wheeler (ed.), *Letters of Sir Thomas Bodley*, 1927, pp. 92–3. For Matthew de Renzi, see above, Letter 166, note 7.

## 192. To the Earl of Salisbury [from the Tower, c.July]¹ 1607

Hatfield, CP124/121, *HMC Salisbury* XIX, pp. 454–5. In Ralegh's larger set hand.
Edwards II, pp. 389–91, dated ?1608/9, from BL, Addit. 6178, f. 827, a transcript; Harlow, *Last Voyage*, 1932, pp. 100–102, from Edwards.

## PROPOSAL FOR A SECOND VOYAGE TO GUIANA

[*addressed*] To the right honorable my singuler good lord the Earle of Salsburye etc. geve these
[*endorsed*] 1607 Sir Walter Ralegh to my lord

I have hard· that Sir Amias Preston² informed your lordshipe of certain menerall [= *mineral*] stones brought from Guiana of which your lordshipe had sume doubt, for so yow had att my first returne. Secondly that your lordshipe thought it but an invention of myne to procure unto my self my former libertie, suspitions which might rightly fall into the cogitation of a wise man.

Now, what soever difference your lordshipe shall make between your own inriching and my misery, of which as yet I cannot by any means feare the worst, for the first I protest before the majestie of God that one of those minerals here, and never before, tried was not only found and gathered on the land of Guiana by my self but therof ther may be had an aboundance sufficient to please every appetite, the mountayn being nire the rivers side and of easy cariage thither. Secondly, I take the same God to wittnes that I never esteemed this minerall att any price, both in respect of the quantetie and of the similitude it had with other merquesite [= *marcasite*]³ formerly found, and had not a refiner cum unto me to try another mettall, to whom I presented this stone by chance and without hope, I protest before the everliving⁴ God that it never had cum into question all my life, for it had byne many tymes in my hand heretofore [*only*] to cast [it *crossed out*] away.

The refiner that made the assay is a man very skilfull but poore and it is trew that I promised hym twentie pound if he could find gold or silver in the oare. Now if he have delt justly, or in hope of the mony falcely, it may easely be examined, and yet that which most perswades me is that he offers to go in person and is content to be hanged ther if he aprove not his assay to be good. And for the more surtie I have reserved a little quantitie of each to make a second triall.

I beseich your lordshipe then to consider what I offer and I beseich yow to way it in the ballance of your wisedome and pietie, which I cannot suspect but that the same doth yet hang in your hand by sume one thride [= *thread*] or string of your lordships great and auntient love towards mee. And because it may be objected that when I have a shipp [*or*] two or three that I may turn my course sume other way, although I trust that your lordshipe will not for your self judg that in my old years I would becum a runnegate and live from my wife, children and frinds in a strang countrie, yet that others may not say that ther was not care enough and caution had, I am content both to go and cumm as a private man, that both the charg of the shipp be geven to a nother, which I desire might be the bearer hereof,[5] and that he have order that if I do but perswade [= *argue*] a contrary course to cast mee into the sea. Your lordshipe may also appoynt the master and all other officers, only if God geve us leve to arive in sauftie that upon the land they may be derected by mee or by any joynt commissioners if your lordshipe shall so please.

The charg of the jurney will amont to 5000*li*, of which if the Queens Majestie[6] (to whom I am bound for her compassion) and your lordshipe will beare two parts, I and my frinds will beare a therd, or if Her Majestie and your lordshipe will not adventure I will finde means to beare all and present Her Majestie and your lordshipe with the one half, so [= *provided*] wee may be assured to injoy the rest. The charg wilbe the greater in this respect, because wee would ride at ancor 3 or 4 moneths in the river and, cariing with us six paire of great bellowes and brick in ballast, wee would melt down the minerall into ingats as fast as wee gather it, for to bring all in oare would be more notorious [= *conspicuous*].

My tymes are not long in the world and I shall not be able hereafter (if now) to performe such a jurney. Your lordshipe may have gold good cheap and may joyne other of your honorable frinds in the matter if yow please, for ther is enough. Your lordshipe may releive mee and my distroyed estate and bynde me more then ever to live and dye your sarvant.

The jurney may go on under the culler [= *pretence*] of Virginia[7] for Neuport[8] will [go *crossed out*] shortly return. Wee will break no peace, invade none of the Spanish towns. Wee will only trade with the Indiens and see none of that nation [= *Spain*] except they assayle us. If your lordship will send my Lord Carew[9] or any elce I will satisfye them in all particulers.

   And rest your lordships evermore to serve yow,
    W R

1. See note 8.
2. See above, Letter 185, note 4.
3. Base metal with some gold and silver content.
4. Edwards, p. 390, followed by Harlow, has 'everlasting'.
5. Probably either Lawrence Keymis (see Letter 206) or Viscount Haddington (see Letter 193).
6. Queen Anne, wife of James I.
7. Ralegh had put it about that he was bound for Virginia at the time of his first voyage to Guiana in 1595: V.T. Harlow (ed.), *Discoverie of Guiana by Sir Walter Raleigh*, 1928, p. 13. See also Harlow, *Last Voyage*, p. 146.
8. Captain Christopher Newport who had been sent out in January 1607 in command of a fleet bound for Virginia. He sailed for home on 15 June and reached Plymouth on 29 July (Purchas XVIII, p. 463), which, assuming that Ralegh knew his sailing plans, indicates a date for this letter not later than mid-July.
9. Ralegh's cousin and friend, who had been in the service of the Queen since giving up the Presidency of Munster and, since June 1605, had been Baron Carew of Clopton.

## 193. To Viscount Haddington [from the Tower, c.July 1607]¹

Hatfield, CP103/49, *HMC Salisbury* XXI, pp. 282–3, dated ?1610. In Ralegh's hand.

BL, Addit. 6177, f. 241, an eighteenth-century transcript, dated 1603.

Edwards II, pp. 392–4, from BL but dated 1610; Harlow, *Last Voyage*, 1932, pp. 102–3, from Edwards but dated 1609.

## GUIANA PROPOSAL

[*addressed*] To the right honorable my very good lord the Vicount Haddington²
[*endorsed*] 1603 [*sic*] Sir Walter Raleigh to my lorde

I gave commission to sume of [*my*] frinds to move your lordshipe in a matter of great importance, if the attayning of honor and ritches may be so accompted. To troble your lordshipe with the particulers I will forbeare till such tyme as I may know whe[*the*]r any good thing offred by me may be accepted. For if in my late soverayns tyme, in whose favor I had sume little interest, I could not obtayne leve to adventure myne own life and myne own estate to inrich her, because myne own honor, fame and benefite had in all likelehode byne adjoyned, what may I hope for now, being altogether frindles in the world, except His Majestie, who, according to the trust geven hym by God, do vouchsauf to remember that ther is no prise nor ransume for innocent blood, and that to suffer those to perrish that are his (what soever a Middlesex jurie³ hath sayd to the contrary) hath no distinction to satisfie that great God by whom kings raygne and whom for ther mercie and trewth he hath preserved.

But, my lord, leving the succes to Gods providence, it is a jurney of honor and ritches that I offer yow, an enterprise fesible and certayne. And thought [= *though*] it may be sayd that miserie feareth no chang and that my pretences and intents are diverse, yet I beseich your lordshipe to beleive that I am more in love with death then with falcesode and that what soever tyme, or fortune, or I know not what elce, hath taken from me, yet neither of them nor any poure [= *power*] elce under heaven shall teach me or force me to be a knave. A base and an unworthy remedie it were agaynst imprisonment to forsweare God, to betray the Kings mercie and to cast away my frinds, to undertake a jurney full of haszards and ille fair [= *fare*],⁴ to return agayne a perjured, falce and foolish knave. No, my lord, when myne enemies have done ther worst and distroyed me amd mine, yet the former (which is in myne owne minds poure) shall never be my destiney.

Yet because I desire no trust and that wise men may have warrant for their jelosies I am content, your lordship liking it, to follow your self in this enterprise as a private man. If your lordship cannot obtayne the expence of such a tyme⁵ I am content to be committed to others, and setting down the course and project in writing, if att any tyme I perswade the contrarie, lett them cast me into the sea.⁶

Secondly, when God shall permitt us to arive, if I bringe them not to a mountayn nire a navigable river covered with gold and silver oare, lett the commanders have commission to cutt of my head their.

If this bee not sufficient I will presume to nominate unto His Majestie such commanders as His Majestie will like of, who wilbe bound bodie for bodie to returne me agayne, alive or dead, and if I have mistaken my self and may be yet of more prise [= *price*] His Majestie shall have fortithowsand pound⁷ bond to boot.

Lastly, I pray your lordshipe not to marvaile why I have desired to ingage yow in this enterprise and desire that your self may be the commander, for I know that you are valient and without falcesode, qualleties rarely found in one man in this age. I know that yow are deere to the King and I hope withall that by your means we shall injoy the frutes of our travells and such parts [= *shares*] as we adventure for and deserve.

    With which hope I rest your lordships to do yow service,
      W Ralegh

1. See note 2 which indicates a date not earlier than June 1606, and the similarity to Letter 192 points to its being about the same time. Harlow's choice of 1609 was based on a report of that year by the Spanish ambassador, that Ralegh 'has left [i.e. lost] his fortune so that the King may give it to a Scotchman' and that he now expects to be released and to go to Guiana (*Last Voyage*, p. 113), but the fortune was Sherborne and the Scotsman was Sir Robert Carr.
2. John Ramsay (c.1580–1626), a Scotsman and royal favourite, created Viscount Haddington in June 1606.
3. On 21 September, Ralegh had been indicted at Staines in the county of Middlesex and jurors summoned for his trial, although in the event the hearing was held in Winchester: Stebbing 1899, p. 207.
4. Edwards, followed by Harlow, has 'soe farr', but *HMC*, as here, is undoubtedly correct. Ralegh often complained of ship's victuals.
5. i.e. cannot spare the time.
6. Note in this and the following paragraphs the similarities to Letter 192.
7. It is difficult to imagine where Ralegh could have raised such a sum which is twice what Sherborne was worth.

---

194. TO HENRY PRINCE OF WALES [FROM THE TOWER, c.NOVEMBER 1607][1]

Bradford (Yorks.) District Archives, Hopkinson 19, ff. 87v.–88v., a seventeenth-century transcript, probably the nearest of the seven surviving to the lost original, *HMC*, 3rd Report, p. 293, list only. The Bradford text is the only one to retain Ralegh's superscription and signature, but it is readable only with the greatest difficulty owing to ink penetration from the reverse side.

BL, Cotton, Otho E.vi, f. 208, badly burnt; National Maritime Museum, Greenwich, Lec/6, faulty; *HMC* 6th Report (Leconfield), p. 304; Duke of Bedford's MSS, Woburn 261, f. 438; Dr Williams's Library, Jones B 60, p. 23; Bodleian, English History d. 138, f. 2, *HMC* 4th Report (Mostyn), p. 353.

Sir Walter [Ralegh], *Judicious and Select Essays*, 1650, pp. 8–15, not in letter form; *Sceptick*, 1651, pp. 126–33, spelling modernized; *Maxims* 1656; *Remains*, 1657 etc., p. 189; Birch, *Works* 1751, II, p. 359, as *Remains* 1702; Cayley 1806, II, p. 400, as Birch; *Works* 1829, VIII, p. 657; Edwards II, p. 330, all, directly or indirectly, from *Sceptick*.

## ADVICE TO A PRINCE ON BUILDING A SHIP

[*headed*]   Sir Walter Raleighe unto Prince Henry touching the modell of a ship

[*addressed*]   To his highnesse the most excellent Prince of Wales, etc.

Most excellent Prince: If the ship Your Highnesse intends to build[2] be bigger than The Victorie then her beames which are layd overthwarte from side to side will not serve againe, and many other of her timbers and other stuffe will not serve, wherfore if she be a size lesse the timber of the old ship will serve well to the building of a new.

If she be bigger she wilbe of lesse use, go very deepe to water and of mightie chardge [= *burden*], our channells decayeing every year,³ lesse nimble, less mannable [= *manageable*] and seldom to be used. *Grande [Navio], grande satica* saith the Spaniard.

A ship of sixe hundreth tunes will carry as good ordinance as a ship of twelve hundreth tunnes and where the greater hath double her ordinance the lesse will turne her broad side twice before the great ship can wind [= *turn about*] once, and soe noe advantage in that overplus of guns. The lesser will go over cleare where the greater shall stick and perishe. The lesser will come and goe, leave or take and is yare [= *quick*],⁴ whereas the greater is slow, unmanable and ever full of incumbers.

In a well conditioned ship these things are chiefly required: that she be strong built, swifte in sayle, stout-sided; that her ports be soe laid as that she may carry out her guns all weathers; that she hull and trye⁵ well, that she staye well when boarding or turneing on a wind is required.⁶

To make her stronge consisteth in the care and truth of the workemenn; to make her swifte is to give her a large run or way forward, and so afterwarde, done by art and just proportion and that, in layeing out of her bowes before and quarters behind, the shipwright be sure that she neither sinke nor hange into the water but lie clear and above itt, wherein shipwrights do often faile and then is the speed in sayleing utterly spoiled.

That she be stout-sided, the same is provided by a long beareing [= *flat*] floare⁷ and by shareing [= *shearing*] of from above waters to the lower edge of the ports, which done, then will she carry out her ordinance all weathers.

To make her to hull and to trie well, which is called a good sea-ship, there are two thinges principally to bee regarded, the one that she have a good draughte of water, the other that she be not over-chardged. And this is seldome done in the Kinges shipps and therefore we are forced to lye or trye⁸ in them with our main course and mizen, which, with a deep keel and standing streak [= *strake*],⁹ she would perform.

The extreame length of a ship makes her unapt to staye, especially if she be floatye [= *buoyant*] and want sharpenesse of way forward.¹⁰ And itt is most true that such overlong shipps are fitter for the Narrowe Seas [*the English Channel and southern North Sea*] in summer then for the Ocean or long voyages. And therefore an hundreth foote by the keele and thirtye five foote broad is a goode proportion for a great ship.

It is to be noted that all shipps sharpe before, not having a long floar, will fall roughe into the sea from a billowe and take in water over head and eares. And the same qualitie have all narrow-quartered ships to sinke after the tayle. The high chardgeing of ships is that that bringes many ill qualities: it makes them extreme leeward, makes them sinke deep into the seas, makes them labour sore in foul weather and oftymes oversett. Safety is more to be respected then showes or niceness for ease: in sea-journeys both cannot well stand together and therefore the most necessarye is to be chosen.

Two decks and and [sic] halfe is enoughe and no building at all above that but a lowe masters cabbin. Our maisters and mariners will saye that the ships will bear more well enough, and true itt is if none but ordinarye mariners served in them. But menn of better sort, unused to such a life, cannot so well endure the rolling and tumbling from side to side where the seas are never soe litle grown which comes by high chardgeing. Besides those high cabbin-workes aloft are very dangerous in fight to tear menn with their splinters.[11]

Above all other thinges have care that the great gunnes be foure foote cleare above water when all ladeing is in, or els those best peeces are idle at sea. For if the ports lie lower and be open it is dangerous, and by that default was a goodly ship and many gallant gentlemen lost in the days of Kinge Henry the Eight before the Ile of Wight in a ship called by the name of Mary-Rose.[12]

So Sir, humbly submetteing this and all other my labours unto your highnesse princely pleasur and now humbly takes leave, remaineing

Your highesse most humble vassall,
Walter Raleighe [sic][13]

1. See note 2. The date preferred here is very soon after Pett had displayed his model in November 1607 in an effort to persuade the prince to build an entirely new and bigger ship, and well before the storm of criticism which Ralegh would surely have mentioned. But cf. C.H. Firth, 'Sir Walter Raleigh's "History of the World"' in *Essays Historical and Literary*, Oxford 1938, p. 39 and E.C. Wilson, *Prince Henry and English Literature*, 1946, who place it later. In any case, as allowed by both Firth and Wilson, the laying of the keel in September 1608 made the main thrust of Ralegh's advice superfluous.
2. In 1606, King James had given the twelve-year-old Prince Henry an old ship, the *Victory*, and instructed his master shipwright, Phineas Pett, to rebuild her. In November 1607 Pett produced a model of a new and bigger ship, 'fairly garnished with carving and painting and placed in a frame, arched, covered and curtained with crimson taffety'. The keel frame was in place by 13 August 1608 and the keel laid on 20 October: W.G. Perrin (ed.), *Autobiography of Phineas Pett*, Navy Records Society, 51, 1918, pp. 31–2, 36–7. There is much in this letter which echoes passages in Ralegh's other naval discourses, especially his 'Discourse on the Invention of Ships' published in *Judicious and Select Essays*, 1650.
3. This was especially the case, as Ralegh well knew, of West Country river navigation: 'I my selfe remember when Falmouth in Cornwall had three foote more of water at the entrance

then now it hath, and Plymouth little lesse' in Dr Williams's Library, Jones B60, f. 233 and his speech in Parliament in 1601 on the Dover harbour tax: H. Townshend (ed.), *Historical Collections*, 1680, p. 299. See also M. Duffy *et al.* (eds), *New Maritime History of Devon*, vol. I, 1992, p. 100.
4. The sort of attacking tactics referred to in N.A.M. Rodger, 'The development of Broadside Gunnery, 1450–1650', *MM* LXXXII, 1996, pp. 301–24.
5. See above, Letter 108, note 4.
6. Numbered 1–6.
7. i.e. with the maximum beam, and thus able to carry the heavy armament of which he later expresses his disapproval. Dr Nicholas Rodger comments, in a letter to the editor, that this contradicts the English shipbuilding tradition 'but corresponds to one of the most significant ways in which the *Prince Royal* broke with that tradition'.
8. See Letter 108, note 3.
9. = garboard, the first line of planks laid on a ship's bottom.
10. = 'bluff-bowed, so having much buoyancy forward and rising easily to the waves, but by the same token losing way rapidly when luffing up into the head sea to go about': Dr Rodger, as above, note 7, who goes on to comment that in the next paragraph Ralegh 'notes the opposite disadvantage of a fine entry, giving a wet ship which pitches deeply'. He finds the letter 'most interesting read in the context of Pett's [*probable*] borrowing of a Danish design, and Prince Henry's intention to build a new and radically different ship ...' and in the way Ralegh's comments largely 'echo the standard criticism of hull form of the *Prince Royal* as she eventually turned out'. I am most grateful to Dr Rodger for his expert assistance but in no way hold him responsible for my interpretation of his remarks.
11. Ralegh, no doubt, still had painful memories of his own injury at Cadiz: see above, Letters 101 and 102.
12. Among them Sir George Carew, his father's 'cousin', and the late Sir Richard Grenville's father, Roger. Note that Ralegh was quite clear as to the cause of the disaster of 1545, as now well established: N.A.M. Rodger, *The Safeguard of the Sea*, 1997, p. 183.
13. When built, the *Prince Royal* was of vast dimensions, 1,147 tons, keel 115 feet, breadth 43 feet, depth 18 feet and carrying 55 guns. By 1609 (Prince Henry died in 1612) there was much criticism on account of the ship's cost, unconventional design, and allegedly poor timber: Perrin, op. cit., pp. lxxii, lxxix and 217.

---

## 195. To [?Sir Henry Hobart from the Tower, mid-1608][1]

Longleat, Wilts, Portland Papers I, f. 201, *HMC Bath* II, pp. 54–5, *in extenso* dated 1604–8. In Ralegh's set hand.

## THE SHERBORNE ESTATE

*[no address and endorsement crossed out]*

Sir: Least yow might charg me with breach of promis I desire by these to excuse my self, seeing the resolution required from me uppon an offer made me in your name was the next day by the same partie disavowed to proceed from any other but himself. I was also presently uppon your departure sommoned by process to awnswere the law. So was my wife, my childe and divers other of my frindes, and therby the dispute of the former proposition att an end.²

Since then I understand by Master Felwall [*sic*]³ that if I make yow no offer between this and Saterday next that it will not be your pleasure hereafter to herken to any composition. What the law will determine in this controversy⁴ your self shall better judg if it please yow but once to heere my councell⁵ with your owne. For it is trew that I have no propertie at all in the land [*at Sherborne*] in question, for His Majesties mercifull graunts both of the land and leases are to the use of my wife and for the present releife of my children, and not to me.⁶ They have also divers other leases in their owne names in which I have no other interest but as a father during the infancie of my childe and as a husband during my wives life. And therfore as ther is left in me no other powre then my perswasion only, who am but a dead husband to theone and a dead father to the other (your sute in law agaynst us having made them know mich of their owne strenght) it will not now be easy for me to order them concerning their whole livelehode and estates, who [*himself*], being destined to endless misery in this life, can never more harme them by my mislike nor healp them by my indevor.⁷ For otherwise to perswade them to their own expulsion and beggery and to leve them no habitation uppon the face of the earth, theon having no husband, the other no father, were [= *would be*] agaynst the law of nature and the honor of man kinde.⁸

But Sir, if it may please yow to be a mean for the recovery of His Majesties grace,⁹ that I may dye but with the marke of his mercie, I will disavow the one for my wife and the other for my childe if they do not willingly give yow satisfaction.¹⁰ And if His Majestie have bine informed that those offences layde to my charg were not only not subscribed by my accuser but were denied uppon the holie sacramentes att the instant when he expected death,¹¹ it shall not be hard for yow to draw some few dropps of commiseration from him who is the worlds great fountayne of all goodnes.

These things I leve to your honorable consideration, hoping that yow will rather chang the cries and sorrowes of my wife and children into their prayers for yow then that yow will ether increase them or continew them.¹²

    I rest att your service,
    W Ralegh

1. Undated and lacking an addressee, this letter cannot be dated with any certainty, but it cannot be earlier than 1604–5 when his son Carew was born, for Ralegh twice refers to his 'children'. It was almost certainly written in 1608 while Ralegh's case over the Sherborne estate was being contested in the Court of Exchequer, necessitating the attendance of Lady Ralegh and her elder son. In 1608, Sir Henry Hobart (who had succeeded Sir John Popham as Attorney-General in 1607) called on Ralegh to defend the legality of the conveyance to trustees of 1603 (see above, Letter 165, note 16): S.R. Gardiner, *History of England*, 1905, II, p. 45. The recipient of this letter was clearly someone with access to the King but it was addressed in a somewhat stiffer tone than Ralegh's usual style when writing to Salisbury. The letter's survival at Longleat offers no obvious clue.
2. Edwards (vol. I, p. 473) states that it had already been proposed to Ralegh early in 1608 that he should sell Sherborne to the King, citing a letter (200) which he dates 29 January 1608 but which the present editors date 1609.
3. Bevis Thelwall, a member of the royal household and Carr's agent: see below, Letter 196, note 4.
4. About the legality of the 1603 conveyance.
5. Ralegh had been allocated Sergeant Harris jun., Sergeant Nicholls and Master Brocke: Hutchins, *Dorset* IV, p. 217.
6. See above, Letter 183, note 3.
7. See above, Letter 176, where Ralegh envisages being a ward of his children if the 1603 conveyance *be found good*.
8. Helps confirm date by indicating that they were still in occupation.
9. i.e. good will, an indication that Ralegh was determined to exact a price.
10. Was his anxiety for a pardon now taking precedence over his concern for his family? See below, Letter 196, note 5.
11. Probably a harking back to the trial of 1603 and the part played by Cobham. Cf. above, Letter 173, when with mock courtesy he referred to Cobham's '[*bad*] memory or mistakinge'.
12. The invalidity of the deed was proclaimed on 27 October 1608: Wildman, *Short History*, p. 143.

---

## 196. To [?Lord Salisbury from the Tower, ?1608][1]

*Collection of Letters made by Sir Tobie Mathew*, 1660, pp. 66–7, edited by John Donne the younger, spelling standardized.

Edwards II, pp. lxvi–lxvii, doubting authenticity.[2]

## THE SHERBORNE ESTATE

[*headed*] Sir Walter Rawley to a great lord whom he entreates to give him just assistance in his business

May it please your lordship: I humbly beseech your lordship to give me leave, and pardon too (if I need it), for the answering of [*to answer*] those things which you were lately pleased to object [= *impute*] against me and that you will charitably also consider both of my demands and of the reasons which embolden me to make them. Those answers go here, in a paper which is inclosed,[3] apart, and my letter shall say but thus much, that the gentleman who is so greatly in favour [*Robert Carr*][4] hath many faire fortunes before him, and we nothing to look for but misery, and that he is better able to give us above the worth of the land than we [*are*] in condition to abate any part therof.[5] And therefore we humbly beseech your lordship that your compassion and care of honour may be the judge between his prosperous navigation and our shipwrack, and that your charity for us, and your desire of satisfaction for him, may equall the ballance between us.

I hope so heartily to find all just favour at your hands as I will venture upon this to assure you that I will do all my uttermost to make my wife and my son forget their misery in themselves and to be ever mindfull of their duty towards your lordship, to whom I hope they will be, as I am sure my self have been and am, a most faitfull humble servant, etc.

[*no signature printed*]

1. There can be little doubt, both on the grounds of content and of style, that the recipient of this letter was Salisbury, now Lord Treasurer. Ralegh could not expect help from anyone else, and, indeed, Salisbury was virtually a forlorn hope. In date it almost certainly follows Letter 195 and precedes Letter 197, the reference to Ralegh's wife and family indicating that it preceded the court verdict in October 1608.
2. There are no grounds for doubting the letter's authenticity or for connecting it with Lady Ralegh's own estate at Mitcham in 1618: cf. Oldys in *Works* 1829, I, p. 471.
3. Missing.
4. See below, Letter 197, note 2, and the King's letter to Salisbury late in 1608 (*HMC Salisbury* XX, p. 269) welcoming the Earl of Northampton's suggestion that 'yon manor of Sherburne' be given to Carr.
5. i.e. Ralegh was prepared to entertain the idea of a sale, which may indicate that he already knew the verdict of the Court of Exchequer (see above, Letter 195, note 10) which may have made him less mindful of his wife and son's welfare. He was still staking all on his own release from the Tower.

---

## 197. TO SIR ROBERT CARR FROM THE TOWER, 2 JANUARY 1609

Inner Temple Library, Petyt 538.36, f. 80v. (identical with BL, Harl. 6908), a contemporary copy, one of more than a dozen to survive, including BL, Add. 4106, which is clearly faulty (identical with Huntington HM 267), BL, Add. 34761 (identical with BL, Sloane 3520), BL, Harl. 787, (identical with Pierpont Morgan Library, Cecil-Stanford Towneley MS, p. 214), Longleat, Portland Papers II, f. 20b, in the hand of Michael Hicks, and many others.

Eight or more slightly varying versions have been printed, including *Cabala*, 1654, Supplement, p. 86; *Works* 1829, VIII, p. 650, from *Cabala*; J.P. Collier, *Catalogue of the library of Bridgewater House*, 1837, pp. 348–9 (now Huntington EL 6232), a good text but with a facsimile of a signature which he claims, quite obviously erroneously, to be Ralegh's and Edwards II, 326–8, from BL, Add. 4106.[1]

## LOSS OF SHERBORNE

[*addressed*] To the honourable knight, Sir Robert Carr,[2] at the Court
[*endorsed*][3] December 1608 [*sic*] Coppie of Sir Walter Raleigh's letter to Sir Robert Carr

Sir: After many[4] great losses and many yeares sorrowes, of both which I have cause to feare that I was mistaken in their endes, it is come to my knowledg that your self (whom I know not but by an honourable fame) have been perswaded to give me and myne our last fatall blowe, by obtayning from His Majestie the inheritance of my children and nephewes,[5] lost in the law for want of a word.[6] This done there remaynes nothing with me but the name of life, dispoiled of all ells but the title[7] and sorrow thereof. His Majestie, whom I never offended (for I ever helld it unnaturall and unmanlie to hate goodnes) staied me at the graves brinke, not (as I hope) that His Majestie thought me worthy of many deaths and to beholld all myne cast out of the world with myself, but as a king who, judging the poore in truth, hath receaved a promise from God that his throne shalbe established forever.[8]

And for your self Sir, seeing your faire day is but now in the dawne and myne drawen to the evening,[9] your [*own*][10] vertue and the Kings grace assuring you of many good fortunes and much honor, I beseech you not to begin your first buildings upon the ruines of the innocent, and that their and my sorrowes may not attend your first plantation. I have byn ever bound to your nation aswell for many other graces as for their true report of my triall to the Kings Majestie,[11] against whom had I byn found malignant the hearing of my cause would not have changed enemies into friends, malice into compassion and the myndes of the greatest number present into the consideration[12] of my estate. It is not the nature of fowle treason to begett such faire passions. Neither could it agree with the duty and love of faithfull subjects (especially of your nation) to bewaile his overthrowe that had conspired against their most liberall and naturall lord. I therfore trust Sir, that you will not be the first that shall kill us [*outright*][13] [*cut*][14] down the tree with fruites and undergoe the curse of them that enter into the fields of the fatherless[15] which (if it please you to know the truth) are farr lesse fruitfull in valew then in fame, but that soe worthie a gentleman as yourself will rather binde us to your service, being six gentlemen not base in birth and alliance which have interest therin.[16]

And my self with my uttermost thankfullnes will ever remayne ready to obey your commaund.

From the Tower, January 2 1608 [*1609*][17]

W.R.

1. Detailed comparison of the Petyt transcript with all other versions suggests that it is nearest to what Ralegh actually wrote to Carr. The variations, except those noted below, are of little substance. In 1837 J.P. Collier published a version of this letter almost identical to the Petyt text which he claimed to have copied from the original then in the Egerton library at Manchester House, but his facsimile of Ralegh's signature, in large italic capitals, has no counterpart: *Catalogue of English Literature ... at Bridgewater House*, 1837, pp. 247–8.
2. Carr (c.1587–1645) was a penniless Scotsman from Roxburghshire who had come south with King James in 1603 and, by 1607, was the King's favourite courtier.
3. From Portland Papers II.
4. As in Collier, loc. cit., but Portland Papers II has 'some'.
5. See above, Letters 165, note 16.
6. See above, Letters 172, 176 and 185.
7. BL, Add. 4106 has 'tithe' which makes no sense.
8. Proverbs 29:14: 'the king that faithfully judgeth the poor, his throne shall be established for ever'.
9. Cf. in the Preface to the *History of the World*, 'the day of tempestuous life, drawn on to the very evening ere I began': *Works* 1829, II, i, p. i.
10. Not in the Petyt text, but in several others, including Collier.
11. See Hicks to the Earl of Shrewsbury, 6 December 1603, 'divers gentlemen, and others, of the Scottish nation were exceedingly moved towards hym in favour': J. Nichols, *Progresses of King James I*, 1828, I, p. 296.
12. Other copies, including BL, Add. 4106, have 'the' or 'a commiseration', which makes little sense. Cf. his use of the word in the sense of coming to an unbiased conclusion in Letter 166 where he speaks of Cobham 'out of truth and out of a chrystyan consideration' revoking his first accusation.
13. Petyt 538 reads 'right out', some other copies 'root out', but both have been rejected in favour of Collier's 'outright'.
14. Petyt 538 reads 'roote', other copies 'cut', including Collier, which is probably what Ralegh wrote.
15. Proverbs 23:10: 'Enter not into the fields of the fatherless, for their redeemer is mighty; he shall plead their cause with thee.'
16. A reference to the conveyance of 1603 (Letter 165, note 16) whereby, failing his own two sons, on Ralegh's death his estate was to go to his brother, Sir Carew, of Downton, Wilts, and then to Carew's three sons, Gilbert, George and Walter. Ralegh had not yet acccepted the Exchequer decree of the previous October: above, Letter 195, note 12.
17. A week after this letter was written the Sherborne estate was granted to Carr: Wildman, *Short History*, p. 143. In 1611, Carr became Viscount Rochester and in 1613 Earl of Somerset, only to fall into disfavour himself, though not before surrendering Sherborne to the King in February 1610 for £20,000. It was then passed to Prince Henry who, it is suggested, intended giving it back to his friend Ralegh. When he died in 1612 it was resold, for £25,000, back to Rochester, on whose attainder in 1616 it passed to Sir John Digby whose descendants still own it: Wildman, op. cit., pp. 145–6.

## 198. To John Shelbury, 3 January 1609[1]

PRO, SP14/43/7, *CSPD 1603–10*, p. 484, Plate 10. Almost certainly a forgery.[2]
Edwards II, p. 326; John Shirley, *Huntington Library Quarterly* 13, 1949, p. 69.

### LEASE FOR JOHN MEERE

[*no address or endorsement*]

John Shelbury:[3] I preye give John Meere a promis under your hand to make him a good and perfet lease of all Bishops Down[4] so soon as it shalbe known to whom the land doth belong which I will that you performe unto him freely and without all question or cavill, and this shalbe your sufficient warrant. Written the 3 of January 1608 [*sic*][5]
        W Ralegh

1. See note 5.
2. Edwards (II, pp. 325–6) was inclined to the view that this note was forged by John Meere and finds some support in Ralegh's own convictions: see above, Letter 156. It is unlikely that Meere could at this time have persuaded Ralegh to agree to a lease, but cf. J.W. Shirley, loc. cit. If it is a forgery, it is a very convincing one, the hand being virtually indistinguishable from Ralegh's larger, set hand: see Plate 10.
3. Ralegh's right-hand man: see above, Letter 179.
4. See above, Letter 177.
5. The letter, even if a forgery, should possibly have been dated 1608 but it has been dated 1609 on the assumption that the usual practice was followed of converting years on legal documents before 31 March to the following year.

---

## 199. To the Earl of Salisbury [from the Tower, c.29 July 1609][1]

Hatfield, CP120/36, *HMC Salisbury* XX, p. 34, dated 29 January 1608. In Ralegh's hand.
Edwards II, pp. 323–5, also dated 1608.

### SHERBORNE

[*addressed*] To the right honorable my singuler good lord the Earle of Salsburie, Lord Treasorer of Inglande, etc.
[*endorsed by or for Salisbury*] Sir Walter Raleigh

Doubting that something may be sayde unto your lordshipe of my proceeding towching Sherburne I humble pray your lordshipe to judge of me herein by the same goodnes and charitie which hath hitherto directed all

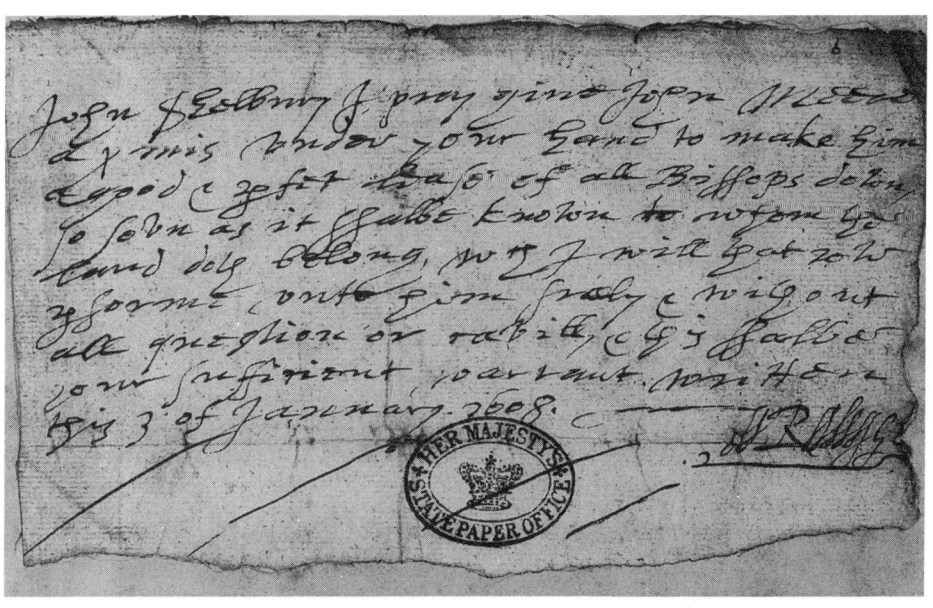

*Plate 10.* Letter 198: Sir Walter Ralegh to John Shelbury, 3 January 1609. Probably a forgery. Much reduced. (PRO, SP14/43/7)

your actions, for that the graunt required of me and others² is indeed fearfull unto us I cannot deny because wee therin pass unto His Majestie those things which are out of our powre to performe and wherby those that joyne with mee do not only inthrale [= *entangle*] their own estates but my wife and sonn therby forfeat their anuetie.³ For if those that never had fee simple [= *freehold*] graunt a fee simple, if wee covenant to graunt all the lands free and unstated, if wee also binde ourselves to deliver all writings, all evidences, courtroles etc. which we never had, wee do presently [= *immediately*] fayle and fall under I know not how many inconveniences, dangers and trobles, and from which the proviso offred doth no way deliver us.⁴

I protest before the majestie of God that I deale cleerly in this busenes and that as I have alreddy delivered many things for the good of the lord that shalbe,⁵ so I will make it appeere that I will reserve nothing in my knowledg that may assure those lands to the propriator [that shalbe *crossed out*]. Only this mich I humble desire (that as I would be glad never to heere the place named henceforth) so in parting from it I might also part from all future troble and vexation concerninge it, and that for those bonds and covenants entred into for the injoying of estates and anueties by me and mine I may be, with them which have dealt for mee,⁶ freely and cleerly discharged. I mean for such and no other as do appeere just and are found by the last survey.⁷

And if it shall please your lordshipe to be advised by mee heerein, I thinck it farr better that such a graunt be devised for us to signe so indifferent [= *fair*] and equall as that the same shall not hold any dispute in parlement then that the parties which joyne with mee therein shall seeke to be releived in that great court, and so their desires retarded which [*who*] would be glad of a free passage and expedition.

For the rest, if Master Thelwal⁸ have told your lordshipe that hee found unwillingnes in me to bee at any charge for the [*letters*] patents,⁹ it is trew that I prayd him that all might come free unto us, but my meaning was for the future. For this charge is not great, and in lew therof I am content (because it cannot be otherwise) to yeild so mich longer time to the farmers of custome¹⁰ as the interest would amount to 40*li*. For as ther is demanded above tenn pound for the tallies,¹¹ so do the[y *crossed out*] officers tell us that the fees going out of the 400*li* wilbe att the least 20*li* yeerly, which if wee had had a lease of land would have bine saved, and to which I would have held my sealf, had I not feared your lordships construction that I sought delay and a prolongation of the busenes.¹²

But in all these I submit my sealf to your lordships charitie and rest your humble sarvant,

        W Ralegh

1. Both the month and the year in *HMC Salisbury* and Edwards must be in error, for Salisbury did not become Lord Treasurer until 4 May 1608. Mid-1609 better fits the contents of the letter: see below, note 2.
2. In fact, the first stage in the trustees' conveyance of the Sherborne estate to the King was dated 24 July 1609: Wildman, *Short History*, p. 144. It took the form of articles of agreement between Salisbury, Henry Howard, Earl of Northampton, Sir Julius Caesar and Carr on the one part and George Lord Carew, Ralegh, George Hull, Thomas Harriot, John Shelbury, Robert Smythe and Laurence Keymis on the other. The King was to pay Ralegh's nominee 6 years' purchase based on a new valuation of the estate plus a sum not exceeding £2,000 to be raised by way of fines for new tenancies. Lady Ralegh and Walter junior were to have an annuity, for as long as either should live, of £400.
3. Presumably a reference to the provision Ralegh claimed he had made in 1598: see above, Letters 60, note 9, and 81, note 8.
4. Ralegh seems still not to have accepted the Exchequer ruling of October 1608: above, Letter 195, note 12. Was he, perhaps, having a last shot at confusing the situation in order to delay Carr's taking possession? In fact, he did not actually formally revoke his conveyance to trustees of 1603 until 14 June 1614: Wildman, op. cit., p. 145.
5. The legal transfer to the King was not completed until 9 February 1610: Wildman, op. cit., p. 145.
6. His trustees: see above, note 2.
7. The second survey was made in July 1609: Wildman, p. 146. For the earlier survey of 1603/4 see above, Letter 177. On 23 September 1609, Keymis told Salisbury that the second survey was defective:

    'Shortness of time, and perhaps the commissioners' desire to leave your lordship occasion to deal extraordinarily well with Sir Walter Ralegh and his [*family*] caused them not to take so precise instructions as was requisite': PRO, SP14/48/50, *CSPD 1603–10*, p. 544.
8. Carr's agent: see above, Letter 195, note 3.
9. Presumably for the conveyance to Carr.
10. Presumably the source of payment of the annuity to Lady Ralegh and her son.
11. Form of receipt.
12. See above, note 4. The annuity was finally granted on 15 January 1610: *CSPD 1603–10*, p. 581.

---

## 200. To [the Earl of Salisbury[1] from the Tower], December 1609

    Woburn Abbey, Beds., 3rd Earl/Somerset ALN 30/11/5, Plate 11. In Ralegh's hand. Torn at right-hand edge. Not hitherto published.

## TERMS OF DISPOSAL OF SHERBORNE

[*no address*]

[*endorsed*]   The acknowedgment of Syr Walter Ralegh and others touching their good usage for their interest in Sherborne, etc. December 1609

May it please your lordship: I understand by Master Thelwall[2] that it is your lordships pleasure to allow us 2000*li* for the fines[3] which might be made in the manner of Sherburn and the rest, and not only to performe the six yeeres purchace promised for the rents and profitts of those lands but withall to make addition of 300*li* over [*and*] above the valew found by the survey.[4] And that it is also [*His*] Majesties most gratious pleasure to bestow on my w[*ife and son*] and to the longest liver of them an annuitie of 4[oo*li with*] assurance for the same to their liking,[5] all which yo[*ur lordships*] most honorable dealing and His Majesties great goodnes [*and*] charitie wee shall now and forever acknowledg and by our utmost service strive to deserve, and shalbe att all times reddy and willing to make what farther assurance wee shalbe able, as well of our present estate as of the gran [*sic*] lease, and all other leases, and yeild to any confirmation by parlament or otherwise which shalbe offred us or required att our hands.

Reddy to do your lordship all faythfull service,

[*in another hand*]

Wytnesses of the signinge by Sir Walter Ralegh    [*signed*] W Ralegh
and Dame Elizabeth                                             E Raleg[*h*]
    [*signed*] Jo. Shelberye    Lau. Kemys[6]
Wittnesses of the signinge by Walter Ralegh        Waltherus Ralegh
the sonn [*Master*] Gilbert Hathorne, Bacheler                filius[7]
of Divinitie and fellow of Corpus Christi
College in Oxford[8]

1. It is difficult to think to whom else this 'letter' can have been sent. Carr was not ennobled until 1611 and did not become Earl of Somerset until 1613.
2. Carr's agent: see above, Letter 195, note 2.
3. See Letter 199, note 2. The number '2' has been superimposed on another, possibly an '8', an anticipation, perhaps, of the settlement finally achieved in February 1610: see below, note 5.
4. See above, Letter 199, note 7.
5. A final settlement was made in the Court of Chancery on 9 February 1610 whereby £8,000 and an annuity of £400 was to be paid to Thomas Harriot, John Shelbury and Lawrence Keymis, as trustees, the annuity being payable for the lives of Lady Ralegh and Walter junior: J. Fowler, *Medieval Sherborne*, p. 397. According to Stebbing (1899, pp. 262–3) part of the £8,000 was put out on loan by Ralegh (presumably by his trustees) to the dowager Duchess of Bedford, which is presumably how this letter became part of the Bedford archives.
6. Named as trustees in the settlement of 1610: see above, note 5.
7. Young Walter was a student at Corpus Christi from 1607–10: J. Foster, *Alumni Oxonienses*, p. 1230. Now in his early teens he was said by his tutor to be given to 'strange company and violent exercises': Anthony Wood, *Athenae Oxonienses*, ed. P. Bliss, 1813–20, III, p. 158.
8. Gilbert Hawthorne, a Somerset man, had been vicar of Dymock, Brecon, since 1608 (Foster, op. cit., p. 679), and his name appears on a list of persons to whom the Lieutenant of the Tower was licensed, in 1605, to allow access to Ralegh: *HMC Salisbury* XVII, p. 444.

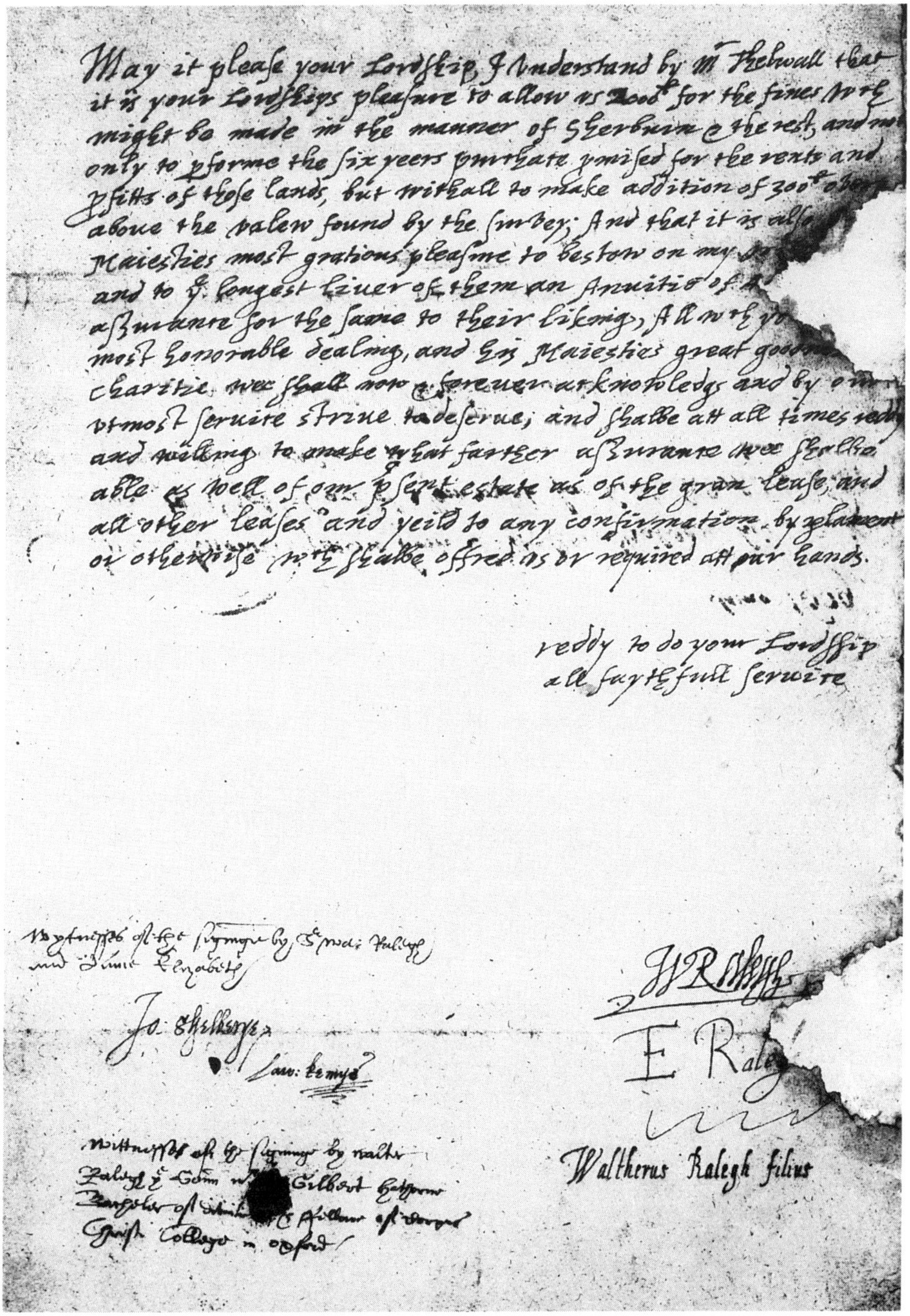

May it please your Lordship, I vnderstand by Mr Thelwall that it is your Lordships pleasure to allow vs 2000ᵗ for the fines wᶜʰ might be made in the manner of Sherborne & the rest, and not only to pforme the six yeers purchase pmised for the rents and pfitts of those lands, but withall to make addition of 300ᵗ aboue the valew found by the survey; And that it is also his Maiesties most gratious pleasure to bestow on my [...] and to y longest liuer of them an Annuitie of [...] assurance for the same to their likeing, All wᶜʰ yo[...] most honorable dealing, and his Maiesties great goo[...] charitie, wee shall now & foreuer acknowledge and by o[...] vtmost seruice striue to deserue; and shalbe att all times [...] and willing to make what farther assurance wee sh[...] able as well of our psent estate as of the graunt lease, and all other leases and yeild to any confirmation by pliament or otherwise wᶜʰ shalbe offred vs or required att our hands.

reddy to do your Lordship all faytefull seruice

W. Ralegh

E Rale[gh]

Waltherus Ralegh filius

*Plate 11.* Letter 200: Sir Walter Ralegh and others to [the earl of Salisbury], December 1609. (Woburn Abbey, 3rd Earl/Somerset ALN 30/11/5) (Courtesy of the Marquess of Bedford and the Trustees of the Bedford Estate)

## 201. To Queen Anne [from the Tower, ?late 1609/early 1610][1]

BL, Harl. 39, f. 359, a contemporary transcript of a lost original. BL, Harl. 6908, f. 89; National Library of Wales, Aberystwyth, Porkington 29, p. 33; Inner Temple, Petyt 538.36, f. 81; Longleat, Misc. MSS, p. 284; Yale University, Newhaven, Osborn 212/3, p. 1a; Folger, G.b.9, f. 179v., all very similar to BL, Harley 39, f. 359.

Edwards II, pp. 333–4, from BL, Harley 39, f. 359, dated ?1610; Harlow, *Last Voyage*, p. 106, from Edwards.

### PROPOSING A VOYAGE TO VIRGINIA

[*headed*]  The letter written by Sir Walter Raleghe to Queen Anne the [*blank*] of [*blank*] anno 16[*blank*]

The same blessinge which God doth contynewe towarde Your Majestie will (I hope) put Your Majestie in minde of your charritie towards otheres. I longe since presumed to offer Your Majestie my service in Virginia[2] with a shorte repeti[t]ion of the comoditie, honor and safetye which the Kings Majestie might reape by that plantation yf it were followed to effecte. I doe still hombly beseech Your Majestie that I may rather die in servinge the Kinge and my countrey then to perrish here. I did also presume hertofore to set doune my answeres to all objectyones [= *provisos*] that could be made, to wit, that yf I wente not by a day sett that I would forfete my life and estate, that I wold leave my wife and two sonnes pleadges for my faith, and that my wife shall yeald herselfe to death yf I performe not my duty to the Kinge.[3] And yf this suffice not that it may be towld the masteres and marrineres that transporte me that yf I offer [= *declare my intention*] to saile elsewhere that they may caste me into the sea.[4]

But were ther nothinge ells, let Your Majestie, I beseech you, be resolved that it shall never be said of me that the Queen of England gave her worde for this man, that the Queen took him out of the hands of death [*and*] that he, like a villaine and perjured slave, hath betrayde so worthy a princes and hath brokene his faithe. Noe, Maddam, as God lyveth ther is no bound, noe not the lose of 20 sonnes, cane tye me so faste as the memory of your goodnes, and ther is neither death nor life that can allewere [*allure*] me or feare me from the performance of my duty to soe worthie and charritable a lady.[5]

This I knowe Your Majestie may effecte for me, and the sooner yf you please, to engage your worde for me to the earle of Salesbury. And yf Your Majestie thinke me worthie of life, or that I have any bloud of a gentlman in me, I beseech you vouchesafe it, and Your Majestie shall never repente you or receave lose [*loss*] by your goodness towards me, from whose reverence and service no power (but that of God by death) shall ever seperat [me *in Harl. 6908*] but that I will ever rest,

    Your most humble vassall,
        W Raleghe

1. Immediately following the settlement of the Sherborne problem seems the most likely date. Ralegh had lost his own chartered rights in 'Virginia' on his attainder in 1603. The Virginia Company had been founded in 1606 but progress was slow until after the grant of its new charter in 1609. In July of that year the Spanish ambassador reported that Ralegh, who was considered in England 'a very great personage', had written a paper on the subject: Quinn 1962, p. 235. It has been suggested (Stebbing 1899, p. 288) that as Ralegh's main interest was now in Guiana, the date of this letter is more likely to have been 1611, but he is unlikely to have risked hoodwinking the Queen. However, see below, note 4 and also above, Letter 192, in which he had suggested to Salisbury that his proposed expedition to Guiana might set forth under the pretence of going to Virginia.
2. The eastern seaboard of North America.
3. Such a drastic declaration has not been traced.
4. Cf. his pledge made in 1607 regarding Guiana, above, Letter 192.
5. Two of Ralegh's closest friends and relatives, Lord Carew of Clopton, and Sir Arthur Gorges, were members of the Queen's household.

## 202. TO WALTER RALEGH JUNIOR [FROM THE TOWER, ?c.1610][1]

BL, Addit. 22587, ff. 16v.–17, a contemporary copy. Inner Temple, Petyt 538.18, f. 215, ditto, but with the second person singular transposed into the third person. Both extant copies, which are otherwise virtually identical, seem to break off very abruptly, lacking subscription or signature, suggesting that the text was incomplete.[2]

A.M.C. Latham, 'Sir Walter Ralegh's *Instructions to his Son*', in Herbert Davis and Helen Gardner (eds), *Elizabethan and Jacobean Studies presented to F.P. Wilson*, Oxford 1959, pp. 207–8, *in extenso*.

## PATERNAL ADVICE

[*headed*] Sir Walter Rawleigh to his sonn

I would have thee my sonne awaken thyself to industrye and rowse upp thy spiritts for the world. Greate possessions would make thee lazie: I would have thee to be the sonne of thyne owne fortunes aswell as my sonne. I have ever aymed at a competencye and God hath fitted mee thereafter. Nevertheles I deny not that I have affected promotion, but it hath beene with a mynd, as God knoweth, to honor him and to doe good in the common wealth. And the same holy and just ambition I bequeath to thee my deare and wellbeloved sonne.

I feele noe more perturbation within mee to depart this world then I have donne in my best health to arise from table when I have well dyned and thence to retyre to a pleasant walke. I have had my parte in this world and nowe must give place to fresh gamesters. Farewell. All is vanity and wearynes, yet such a wearynes and vanitye that wee shall ever complayne of it and love it for all that. And in all vanityes oure owne imaginations are most yrkesome, and of all imagynations that the most foolish when, being by God and nature sized out [= *ranked*] to be a vessel of smalle content, wee yett stryve to hold either as much of understandinge or fortune as larger vessells, and therein strive against Gods ordinance and providence.

But see wee rather that wee make that measure that is ours full and that the falt is not in us though we bee but pinte whereas others are pottle. Oure heades swymme and our harts beate within us as if wee were att sea. It is [not *in Petyt 538*] enough that oure owne thoughts perplexe us but wee ever and anon are shipwrackt and seasick. Wee are toyled and hazarded with tempests and stormes that arise abroad. Oure good or ill depends not simply in oure owne counsells and resolutions but more often upon adventures that lye not in oure management. Publicke affaires are rockes, private conversations are whirlepooles and quickesandes. Itt is alike perilous to doe well and to doe ill. Opinion befoggs us and faire and smooth calemenes [calemes *in Petyt 538*, = *calumnies*] befool us.

Nevertheles, my sonne, take harte and courage to thee. Thy adventure lyes in this troublesome barque. Strive if thou canst to make good thy station in the upper decke. Those that live under hatches are ordained to be drudges and slaves. Endeavoure rather to be parte of the tymber of the howse then lath or mudwall, but be beame tymber not threshould stuffe. Farewell. God only is sure and true evermore to those that are true to him. Noe gospell truer then this in proofe.

    [*no signature*][3]

---

1. Clearly written in advancing years but not at a time of acute depression. Between 1608 and 1614 Ralegh was intellectually active, writing not only his *History of the World* but a variety of political pamphlets. In 1610, though still in the Tower, he had settled his affairs and was again planning new but modest ventures overseas. Also, he had the example of his fellow-prisoner, the Earl of Northumberland, whose *Advice to his Son* (ed. G.B. Harrison, 1930) was completed in 1609. More to the point, in June 1610 young Walter, aged 16, completed his BA at Oxford: see above, Letter 200, note 7.

2. The letter was probably intended as an introduction to the *Instructions to his Sonne*, published by Benjamin Fisher of Aldersgate in 1632 as Ralegh's, and reprinted in *Maxims* 1650, etc., *Remains* 1657, etc., and *Works* 1751 and 1829, a much longer and probably authentic Ralegh composition, not in the form of a letter.
3. Whether Ralegh ever actually sent his son a copy is not known.

---

### 203. To Sir Robert Cotton[1] [from the Tower, ?c.1610][2]

BL, Cotton Julius C III, f. 311, damaged by fire, missing words supplied from Edwards II, pp. 322–3, dated 'probably between 1605 and 1612', who obtained them from an early, unidentified copy. In Ralegh's hand.

## SEEKING A LOAN OF BOOKS

[*no address or endorsement*]

Sigeberts Cronikells[3]
Vincents Speculum Histor[*iale*]
Gervasius Tilesberius
Phillip Bergomus
Natalis Talipes
Aniandus Zirexens
Caius Londinius

Joh[*annes*] Major de Gestis Scotorum,
Lessabius of Herault
Alex[*ander*] Evesham
Brute Booke
Cronikell of Teuxberry
Peter de Icham

Sir Robert Cotton: If yow have any of thes old books or any manuscrips wherein I [*cann reade any*] of our Britton [*sic*] antiquites, if yow pleas to lend them mee [*for a little while I will*] safly restore them and thinck my sealf miche [*behoulding unto yow, or if yow have any old French his*]tory wherin our nation is mentioned, or any [*else in what language soe*]ver.

    Your poore frind,
        W Ralegh[4]

---

1. The well-known antiquary and collector of books and manuscripts (1571–1631), who had a London residence by the river in Westminster. He had been knighted by James I in 1603: *DNB*.
2. The first part of Ralegh's *History of the World* was first published in 1611, and it was his intention to follow this with a second part, which was already 'hewn out' (*Works* 1829, VII, p. 901), dealing with his own country. It was never completed.
3. For an attempt, clearly only partly successful, to identify this and the following books and manuscripts, see Edwards II, pp. 322–3.

4. An undated catalogue, not earlier than 1606, of Ralegh's library in the Tower includes copies of two of the items listed: Walter Oakeshott, 'Sir Walter Ralegh's Library', *Library*, 5th ser., 23 (1968), pp. 286–7.

---

## 204. To Sir Edward Phelips [from the Tower] 19 June [1611][1]

Somerset Record Office, DD/PH/219/23, formerly at Montacute House, *HMC 3rd Report*, p. 282, mistakenly dated 29 June. Not hitherto published *in extenso*. In Ralegh's large set hand.

## THE SANDERSON SUITS

[*addressed*]  To my honorable frinde Sir Edward Phillips[2] knight, Master of the Rolls
[*no endorsements*]

Sir: Having herd that the commission sent into Devon is returned,[3] I beseich yow to give us some end of the unchristian sute which Sanderson[4] hath agaynst me.[5] Before the commission was sent it was proved by Mr Heriots[6] oath that my release to Sanderson was but conditionale, yea, his owne borrowing of it [*the release*] for certayne dayes to shew his creditors, and his restoring of it to Heriot agayne, did sufficiently prove it. For the bond of myne for a braslett of seed perrell [= *bracelet of seed pearls*], I trust, Sir, that yow will not thinck it reasonable that I pay that bond before he deliver up bonds of myne for twenty or thirtye thowsand pound which, as I am told, he hath gotten assigned over to him self. I was ever contented to allow him that bond uppon his accompt, though it be 200*li* for 20*li*, but if he be ten thowsand pound in my debt I trust that yow will not charge me to pay him who hath little or no meanes to pay mee. For a paper which he sheweth of myne, noated in the margent [= *margin*] by my self, I beseich yow, Sir, to understand it aright, which is that I never signed to any thing therin but to myne owne margent to the end to give allowance to pass in his acccompt such somes agaynst which I did not accept. For he told me that he had no warrant for them and that therfore my auditor [*Harriot*] would not allow them, which perswaded mee to the signing of that paper in the margent, not that I ever acknowleged any of those summs payd by him otherwise than with my mony.

And, Sir, wheras he made but a slight matter of the careck[7] accompt, I will shew it yow if yow please that he received of the carrek goods six and thirty thowsand pound, which, with the two and forty thowsand which he chargeth him self withall, amounteth to seventy eyght thowsand pound.

Lastly, Sir, this pernitious miscreant hath vaunted to one of the custome howse to whom he is indebted, that he was promised a judgment of 500*li* agaynst mee in the Roles before the matter was herd, and he that will dare to abuse a man of yowr vertue and reputation in the world will easely scandale a man in adversitie and frindles.

But for my self, as [= *although*] it was never in my power to do yow[8] service, so [= *nevertheless*] have I ever loved and honored yow and will rest reddy to be commanded by yow.[9]

June the 19 [*sic*]

   W Ralegh

1. Somerset man and builder of Montacute House, Sir Edward Phelips (c. 1560–1614) was Speaker of the House of Commons from 1604 until 1611: Hasler III, p. 386. He became Master of the Rolls in January 1611 and as such presided over the hearing of both actions.
2. William Sanderson (see below, note 4) brought his countersuit (see below, note 5) in May 1611.
3. This was in connection with Sanderson's suit, but previous to this, in February 1611, the trustees of Ralegh's chattels, John Shelbury and Robert Smith (see above, Letter 176, note 3) had commenced an action in the High Court of Chancery, against William Sanderson (below, note 4), charging him with non-payment of £60,000 raised by him to pay for Ralegh's Guiana voyage of 1595. For details see J.W. Shirley, 'Sir Walter Ralegh's Guiana finances', *HLQ* XIII, i, 1949, pp. 55–69 and the same author's *Thomas Harriot: a biography*, Oxford 1983, pp. 218–22.
4. William Sanderson, a London merchant (?1548–1638), who had married Ralegh's sister's daughter. He had helped to finance a number of Ralegh's voyages, including those to Virginia: Ruth A. McIntyre, 'William Sanderson: Elizabethan Financier of Discovery', *WMQ* 3rd ser., XIII, 1956, pp. 184–201.
5. In May 1611, Sanderson had countercharged Ralegh, Shelbury, Smith and Thomas Harriot (see below, note 6) in the Court of Star Chamber with withholding a release of liability and with forgery of certain documents: PRO, St Ch 8/260/4.
6. Harriot (see above, Letter 177, note 2) was still in Ralegh's service in 1611, although increasingly devoting himself to the Earl of Northumberland, Ralegh's friend and fellow-prisoner: Shirley, *Harriot*, pp. 223–4.
7. The *Madre de Dios* captured by Ralegh's ships in 1592: see above, Letters 54 and 56. Sanderson had been named, as Ralegh's representative, to assist the commissioners for the sale of the prize goods: *HMC Salisbury* IV, p. 239.
8. From here the remainder is written horizontally in the left-hand margin.
9. The judgments of neither court are on record. If one might hazard a guess on the basis of the surviving evidence it would be that neither party obtained satisfaction and that this was an equitable outcome, there being little to choose between them for vexatious litigation. The letter to Phelips adds very little to the evidence except Ralegh's admission that he would have expected some favours if he had had any claim on the judge. In fact it has been suggested that in 1593 Ralegh had helped procure Phelips the Cornish parliamentary borough of Penryn: Hasler III, p. 386.

205. TO THE EARL OF SALISBURY [FROM THE TOWER, 1611][1]

In private hands, formerly deposited in Fitzwilliam Museum, Cambridge, Bradfer-Lawrence 61, f. 138, a contemporary transcript headed in Ralegh's own hand: see Introduction, pp. xxvii–xxviii.

Longleat, Wilts, Portland Misc., f. 377, *HMC 3rd Report*, Bath, p. 185, similar to the above but lacking heading and in poor condition; BL, Addit. 73087, ff. 26–9, also similar and including copy of signature.

C. Deedes, *Notes and Queries*, 8th Ser., 1893, IV, pp. 21–2, from BL, Addit. 73087 then in his possession; Harlow, *Last Voyage*, 1932, p. 109, from Deedes.

## GOLD IN GUIANA

[*headed*]  Coppie of my letter to the Treasorer Secyll 1607[2]

The offer which I made for Guiana some foure yeares since[3] I was of late perswaded by some honorable freindes of mine[4] once more to present unto your lordshipp, which I was the more willing to presume when I considered with what difficultie such somes are raysed in England[5] as may serve His Majesties occasions and answere the great liberalitie and goodnes of his heart.

Uppon my first offer [*in 1607*] it was required that a shipp[6] might be first sent thither for the triall of the riches of the place, upon the returne of which (the truth appearing) your lordshipp promised to be a meane[7] for[8] my libertie and my lande. But your lordshipp may be pleased to remember upon what difference that resolution was broken off,[9] and that if the same tryall be againe required that the bargaine is now twentie thousand pounde[10] worse for me then the former, my land being now disposed.

Notwithstanding which, I will never hinder so great a service for any respect of my selfe if the charge of the triall by sending may be borne. Neither would I desire so much could I be assured that the gentleman[11] sent might live to arrive there, and not dye in his passage, either by sicknesse, by shipwracke or by the sworde, by which both the enterprise would be for ever lost and all in effect that remaines to relieve my wife and children cast awaye.

Now the inconveniences of sending for a triall I have allredie sett downe, and though I cannot doubt but that your lordshipp hath redd that paper, yet to the end your lordshipp might the better consider of them, I have herein under written them on[c]e againe.

As first because it is now sixteene yeares since Kemish and my selfe sawe the place, the countrie being desolate and overgrowne, I resolve that it will be enough for us both to finde the same peece of grounde againe, in which difficultie, and in a matter of soe great importance, two guides are better then one.

Secondly, if Kemish dye or perish by shipwracke in the waye thitherward, or before he finde the mine, the charge of the voiage is not only lost but the enterprise it selfe, for I dare not trust mine owne memorie and mine owne markes for the finding it.

Thirdly, if this yeare be spent in the triall it will be two years and more ere His Majestie can reape any profite from thence, wheras if both he and I be imployed all may be done in nine moneths.

Fourt[h]ly, if the mine be once opened and discovered those Spaniards which dwell upon the same river and which, since my being there, have tormented above an hundred of the naturall [= *native*] people to deathe to finde the place, will worke it out to the last pound weight ere any second companie can be sent.

For if the mine laye deepe in the ground, or in any rock or harde sparr, it were not easely taken up but by time and by inhabiting the place. But seeing that the gold oare is founde but at the roote of the grasse, in a broade and flatt state,[12] the neighboring Spaniards will easely worke it out in a short time, so as [= *before*] Kemish can returne and a new fleete be prepared here, and can arrive there, ten moneths will be spent and when it shall arrive the next year what can we otherwise looke for but to be laught at by our enemies for having discovered for them, at our charge, a mine of golde which, themselves having inhabited upon the same river twentie year,[13] neither by tormenting others nor by their owne travaile could ever finde.

Lastly, wheras this treasure may be had upon the first opening of the mine without breach of peace, because the Spaniards hath neither knowledge nor possession of the place where it is, it cannot be gotten by a second voiage without publique force. It may now be brought away by twoe shipps, the next yeare hardly with twentie, and better it were (so farre as my weake judgment can discerne) that the Spaniards should give cause of quarrell to us then we to them.

Now that which may be objected is the importance of my libertie. Certainly, if it be thought better for His Majestie to loose so great riches then that I be employed in his service I know noe reason why such a one as I am should be suffred to live. If it be thought that being at libertie I would runne hence to some other prince or state: if I did, yet I doe not heare of any wonders that have been wrought to this daye by any runnegat of ours, and sure I am that the one halfe of that which I enjoye in England by His

Majesties grace would buye any unnaturall knaves heade that is beyond the seas, wheresoever he think himself most sure. And for ought I heare, those that have the best entertainement elsewhere would most willingly returne into their owne countries upon exceeding easy conditions.

For the rest, for me to purchase a yeares libertie, or perchaunce lesse, by perjurie and infamie, for me to leave my wife and children to be spurned at as the wife and children of a faithlesse and ungratefull traitor, I trust that your lordshippe will never beleeve it of me.

For other worthie men who (howsoever your lordshipp stand indifferent) may diswade His Majestie in all they can from this enterprise, and passe it over with the same slight contempt which some of King Henrie the seavenths councelers did the offer of Columbus,[14] I should greatly feare (if the case were mine) that when His Majestie should understand that the Spaniards have found this place, who endangered all the states of Europa by the like, that he may justly laye it to my charge that this treasure might have beene his for the haszard of a reede, for the adventuring of an olde and sorrow-worne man whom death would shortly have delivered *invito domino*, and who, if he had done well, it had beene for the King; if ill, the shame, infamie and losse had beene his owne, his enemies had had a greater advantage over him then ever and only his owne freinds who were content to adventure themselves and their fortunes with him he had betrayed.

Thus much I say His Majestie may say in the future, whither justly or noe, your lordshipp can better judge then I can. For mine owne parte God doth witnesse it with me that I finde litle cause of hope to outlive another winter. Happie, therfore, should I thinck my selfe if I might repaye that life to the King which he hath lent me with some good interest and not leave it to death who will shortly sease it, either at a base price or for nothing.

But to Gods providence I must leave it and rest your lordshipps humble servant,[15]

Walter Raleigh [sic][16]

---

1. Ralegh's heading is misleading: this is a renewal of a proposal of that year written 'sixteen yeares since Kemish and my selfe sawe the place [*1595*]', i.e. 1611. Meanwhile, there had been two other English voyages to Guiana, that led by Robert Harcourt in 1609 and that of Sir Thomas Roe's in 1610 in which Ralegh had invested £600. Roe wrote to Salisbury on 28 February 1611 displaying a sober confidence in the area's mineral resources and the weakness of its defences: Harlow, *Last Voyage*, pp. 104–6. In 1607, Ralegh's lands had not yet been 'disposed'.
2. *Sic*: see above, note 1. This is almost certainly the transcript mentioned below, Letter 210.
3. See above, Letter 192.
4. George Carew, Lord Clopton, was one: see below, Letter 210.

5. A shrewd thrust considering James's difficulties with his first Parliament which he dissolved in December 1610 after a quarrel over supplies: Cf. 'grunting subjects', below, Letter 208.
6. Longleat copy has 'small barke'.
7. ibid. has 'undertook'.
8. ibid. has 'the restitution of' inserted.
9. Probably a reference to the Exchequer case of 1608 concerning the Sherborne estate: see above, Letter 195.
10. The price the King paid Carr for relinquishing Sherborne in 1611–12.
11. Addit. 73087 has a marginal note naming Captain Harcourt (see below, Letter 220, note 9) but Ralegh is much more likely to have been referring to Keymis, who, it had been suggested, might be sent to Guiana.
12. Ralegh described no such mine in 1596. The gold he saw near the Caroni river was in quartz and specimens were detached with difficulty: Harlow, *Discoverie*, 1932, pp. 43–4 and 55. In his letter to Salisbury in 1607 (Letter 192) he recommended the mine he was proposing to open upon the evidence of a stone which he implied he had himself casually picked up.
13. San Thomé was founded in 1595 but the Spaniards were on the Orinoco before that.
14. Cf. below, Letter 212. Ralegh's choice was significant: he saw himself following in the wake of Columbus rather than of Cabot.
15. Longleat has 'to do you service'.
16. From BL, Add. 73087.

## 206. To [the Earl of Salisbury] and the Privy Council from the Tower, [before July][1] 1611

In private hands, Bradfer-Lawrence 61, f. 135 v., a contemporary transcript (see heading to Letter 205).

BL, Harley 39, f. 350, another, very similar but addressed throughout to more than one lord.

Edwards II, pp. 337–9, from Harley 39, with errors and a substantial portion omitted; Harlow, *Last Voyage*, 1932, pp. 112–13, from Edwards.

## NEW PROPOSALS

[*headed, in Ralegh's hand*]   1611   An agrement betweene me and the Lords [*sic*] for the jurney of Guiana in the yeer above[2]

[*no address or signature*]

Your lordshipp [*sic*] as I remember did offer to be at the charge to transport Kemish into Guiana with such a proportion of men in two shipps as should be able to defend him against the Spaniards inhabyting upon Orenoke,[3] if they offred [= *attempted*] to assaile him. Not that it is ment to offend the Spaniards there or to beginne any quarrell with them except themselves shall beginne the warre.

To know what numbers of men shall be sufficient may it please your lordshipp to informe your selfe by Captain Moore,[4] a servant of Sir John Watts,[5] who came from Orenoke this last spring and was oftentimes ashore at St Thome where the Spaniards inhabite.

Which numbers made knowne to your lordshipp and to the captaines which you shall please to imploye with Kemish, those captaines shalbe able to judge with what force they will undertake to secure Kemishes passage to the mine, which is not above five miles from the navigable river, takinge the nearest waye.

Now your lordshipp doth require of me that if Kemish live to arrive, and shalbe garded to the place,[6] and shall then faile to bring into England halfe a tunn, or as much more as he shalbe able to take up, of that slate golde oare wherof I gave a sample to my Lord Knevit,[7] that then all the charge of the journie shalbe laide upon me, and by me to be satisfied, wherto I willingly yeilde.[8] And though it be a matter of exceeding difficultie for any man to finde the same acre of ground againe in a countrie desolate and overgrowne which he hath seene but once, and that sixteen yeares since, which were harde enough to doe upon Salusberie Plaine, yet that your lordshipp may be satisfied of the truth I am content to adventure all I have (but my reputation) upon Kemish memorie, hoping that it may be acceptable to the Kings Majestie and to your lordshipps [sic] so to doe, considering that if Kemish misse of his marckes my poore estate is utterly overthrowne and my wife and children as utterly beggerd.

Now that there is noe hope after this triall made to fetch any more riches from thence, I have allreadie given your lordshipp my reasons in my former letter [Letter 205] and am readie upon a mapp of the countrie to make demonstration therof if it shall please your lordshipp to give me leave, but to the Kings Majesties wisdome and your lordshipps I submitt my selfe.

That which your lordshipp doth promise me is that halfe a tunn of the former oare being brought home that then I shall have my libertie and in the meane while my free pardon under the great seale, to be left in Her [sic][9] Majestie[s] hand till the end of the journie.

[no signature transcribed]

---

1. In July 1611, Ralegh attracted the censure of the Lords of the Privy Council (below, Letter 207, note 3), so much so that he is unlikely, after that, to have addressed them so optimistically with what he assumed would be an acceptable agreement.
2. Ralegh seems unsure whether he is addressing one lord (who could only be Salisbury) or the

whole of the Privy Council, some of whose members would have been very unsympathetic. The entire heading is optimistic and raises the possibility that both transcripts were no more than drafts.
3. The territory either side of the River Orinoco.
4. John Moore, master of the *Archangel*, had twice been in Trinidad and up the Orinoco in 1610, buying tobacco for Sir John Watts and his partners, returning to London early in 1611: Joyce Lorimer, 'The English Contraband Tobacco Trade', in K.R. Andrews *et al.* (eds), *The Westward Enterprise*, Liverpool, 1978, pp. 133–5. Harley 39 could be read as 'Moure' which Edwards, followed by Harlow, loc. cit., reads as 'Moate'.
5. For Sir John Watts see above, Letter 37, note 3.
6. 'and ... place' omitted by Edwards, followed by Harlow. Ralegh made no secret of the likelihood of a brush with Spanish settlers.
7. Thomas Lord Knyvet of Escrick in Yorkshire, Warden of the Mint and a member both of Queen Anne's Council and the Privy Council, but best known as the discoverer of the Gunpowder Plot: *DNB*.
8. 'consent' in Harley 39.
9. Both manuscripts clearly read 'Her', i.e. the Queen. Edwards and Harlow read 'His'.

---

## 207. To Queen Anne [from the Tower, after 11 July 1611][1]

PRO, SP14/67/126, *CSPD 1611–18*, p. 105, undated, Plate 12. In Ralegh's best italic hand. Edwards II, pp. 334–5; Harlow, *Last Voyage*, 1932, p. 107, from Edwards.

## REGRETTING REJECTION

[*addressed*]   To the Queens most excellent Majestie
[*endorsed*]   Sir Walter Ralegh to the Queene

I did lately presume to send unto Your Majestie the copie of a letter written to my Lord Treasurer towching Guiana.[2] That ther is nothing done therin I could not but wounder with the world, did not the mallice of the world exceede the wisedome thereof. In mine owne respect the ever living God doth witness that I never sought such an imployment, for all the gold in the earth could not invite me to travell after miserie and death, both which I had bine likeler [*sic*] to have overtaken in that voyage than to have returned from it. But the desire that ledd me was the approving of my fayth to His Majestie, and to have done him such a service as hath seildome bine performed for any king.

But, most excelent Princes, although His Majestie do not so mich love him self for the present as to accept of that riches which God hath offred

I did lately presume to send unto your Maiestie the coppie of a letter written to my Lord Treasorer towching Guiana, that ther is nothing done therin I could not but wounder with the world, did not the mattere of the world exceede the wisedome therof. In mine owne respect the euerliuing God doth witnes that I neuer sought such an imployment, for all the gold in the earth could not inuite me to trauell after miserie and death, both which I had bine likeler to haue overtaken in that voyage, than to haue returned from it. But the desire that ledd me, was the approuving of my fayth to his Maiestie, and to haue done him such a seruice as hath seildome bine performed for any king. But most excellent Princes although his Maiestie do not so mich loue him self for the present as to accept of that riches which God hath offred him, therby to take all presumption from his enemies, arising from the want of treasor, by which (after God) all states are defended: yet it may be that his Maiestie will consider more deiply therof hereafter, if not to late, and that the dissolution of his humble vassall do not preceede his Maiesties resolution therin; for my extreeme shortnes of breath doth grow so fast on me, with the dispaire of obtayning so mich grace to walke with my keeper up the hill within the tower; as it makes me resolue that God hath otherwise disposed of that busenes and of me; who after eyght yeers imprisonment am as strayght-ly lokt up as I was the first day, and the punishment dew to othermens extreame negligence layd altogether uppon my patience & obedience. In which respect (most worthy Princes) it were a sute farr more fitting the hardnes of my destinie, (who every day suffer and am subiect every day to suffer for othermens offences) rather to desire to dye once for all, and therby to giue end to the miseries of this life, than to striue agaynst the ordinance of God; who is a trew iudg of my innocencee towards the king, and doth know me.

for your Maiesties most

humble and most

bound. vassall

W Ralegh

*Plate 12. Letter 207: Sir Walter Ralegh to Queen Anne, after 11 July 1611. (PRO, SP 14/67/126)*

him, therby to take all presumption from his enemies arising from the want of treasor, by which (after God) all states are defended, yet it may be that His Majestie will consider more deiply therof hereafter, if not to late, and that the dissolution of his humble vassall do not preceede His Majesties resolution therin.

For my extreeme shortnes of breath doth grow so fast on me, with the dispaire of obtayning so mich grace to walke with my keeper up the hill within the Tower, as it makes me resolve that God hath otherwise disposed of that busenes [?*Guiana*] and of me who, after eyght yeers imprissonment, am as straygtly lockt up[3] as I was the first day and the punishment dew to other mens extreame negligence[4] layd altogetheer uppon my patience and obedience. In which respect (most worthy Princes) it were a sute farr more fitting the hardnes of my destinie (who every day suffer and am subject every day to suffer for other mens offences) rather to desire to dye, once for all, and therby to give end to the miseries of this life, than to strive against the ordinance of God, who is a trew judge of my innocencie towards the King, and doth know me,

for Your Majesties most humble and most bound vassall,

W Ralegh

1. 'after eight years imprissonment' = 1603–11, and his being 'strayghtly lockt up' indicates late summer: see below, note 3.
2. Letter 205. See below, Letters 208 and 210 for further references to the letter to Salisbury.
3. In July 1611, Ralegh was charged with some offence, the nature of which can only be surmised. He was apparently examined by some members of the Privy Council, including the Earl of Salisbury and the decidedly hostile Earl of Northampton (Henry Howard), and in Letter 209 Ralegh speaks of 'sharp words' from the former and of 'three monethes close imprissonment'. On 12 July, Northampton told Viscount Rochester (Carr) that after visiting the Earl of Northumberland in the Tower about charges related to the Gunpowder Plot (of 1605) brought by his servant, they had 'a bout with Sir Walter Ralegh and found him as bold, proud and passionate as ever. The lawless liberty of the Tower, so long cockered [= *nourished*] and fostered with hopes exorbitant, hath bred suitable desires and affections. And yet your lordship may assure His Majesty that by this publication he hath won little ground.': PRO, SP14/61/26, *CSPD 1611–18*, p. 58. The 'publication' may have been his 'Discourse upon the marriages with the house of Savoy' proposed early in April 1611 for Prince Henry and his sister, which Ralegh circulated in manuscript: see Edwards II, pp. lix–lxi. Both the Earls favoured a Catholic alliance and, it as been suggested, were suspicious of Ralegh's growing influence on the heir apparent: S.R. Gardiner, *History of England*, 1853–4, II, p. 137. Whatever his offence he was punished with a stricter regime which, together with the stalemate over Guiana, induced a mood of almost suicidal despair. Or was he playing on a woman's sympathy?
4. Assuming the above suggestion to be correct, Ralegh may have been referring to a 'leak' by someone in the Prince's entourage of what was intended as a private document.

## 208. To King James [from the Tower, after July 1611][1]

In private hands, Bradfer-Lawrence 61, f. 136 (see heading to Letter 205).

BL, Addit. 73087, ff. 24v.–26, another early transcript with minor variants.

C. Deedes, *Notes and Queries*, 8th ser., III, 1893, p. 481, from BL, Addit. 73087, then in his possession; Harlow, *Last Voyage*, pp. 108–9, from Deedes.

## MORE REGRETS FOR GUIANA

[*headed, by Ralegh*]   A coppie of my letter to His Majestie anno 1607[2] [*sic*] concer[n]ing Guiana

I hope that your most excellent Majestie will pardon this presumption of mine. I have besought the Queene[3] that out of her wounted charitie towards me shee would be pleased to offer unto your Majestie theise few lines, for wheras I have beene toulde[4] that it pleased your Majestie to reade over a letter of mine [*Letter 205*] written to my Lorde Treasurer [*Salisbury*] for a voiage to Guiana, I most humbly beseech your Majestie to beleive that I never had other respect to my selfe in that project then to make it apparent that I ever have beene and ever will remaine your Majesties faithfull servant. That ever I sought my libertie therby for the love of libertie, or that I had any trick therin, as it pleaseth some men to terme it, the living God doth witnes the contrarye, for to him that hath not beene bredd a slavish marriner the imprisonment of a longe navigation is farre more greivous than the Tower of London, into which as I was never cast for any knavery or villanie, so will I never seeke to be delivered therby. But maye it please your most excellent Majestie, it is true that I did lament the refusall made because your Majestie hath thereby refused a most easie waye of being inriched, both in despight of your malitious enemies abroade and of your grunting subjects at home.[5]

And wheras it hath beene inforced against me that it had bin a great levitie [= *lack of judgement*] of state to have trusted a man in my estate, it had beene indeede well said if I had desired the trust of any great some of monie, of any great armie or any great fleete, or of any thing else wherby your Majestie might have received prejudice [= *injury*]. But where nothng had beene put in haszarde with me but myne owne shame and infamie, where I was to be trusted in nothing but to make my selfe a ridiculous lier and a begger and to leave that marke upon my children and posteritie, I should have thought it (under pardon) when [= *while*] I lived in the worlde, a great levitie of state to have refused such an adventure, seeing [*that*] whatsoever profite had beene made, the same had beene your Majesties and there was nothing else wherof your Majestie had been in danger but of the ill bestowing of your mercie. For, alas, what am I in respect of that which hath beene offerd, to make which good why was I not rather inforst than forbidden. If it had beene but a promise of mine, why was it not tryed, seing the promise was so great and I soe litle. Or why should so notable a service for your Majestie be ballanced with the libertie of one man, whose fortune when it was at greatest never overshadowed any thing but itselfe. But seing it is in the providence of God that (your Majestie refusinge it) some other king or kingdome shalbe inriched therby, for it cannot lye hidden longe, yet I most humbly beseech your Majestie to doe me that grace as to beleive that I who have spent my sorrowfull times of imprisonment in the studie of your Majesties service and safetie,[6] of which I hope one daye to make good proofe, would in the rest nevre have prooved false, nor never have beene founde ungratefull to such a king as tooke me out of the handes of death when noe man elce that had power in the worlde had compassion of me.

[*in same hand as heading*] Your M[*ajesties*] humble vassall,
      W R

1. Despite Ralegh's heading (see note 2), this letter clearly dates from after the setback of his Guiana plans in July 1611.
2. As in Letter 205, this date refers to his earlier proposals. It is closely linked with Letter 207 which certainly belongs to 1611. This, too, is almost certainly the transcript mentioned by Ralegh below, Letter 210.
3. No covering letter to the Queen survives.
4. Had he heard that Letter 207, in which he expressed surprise at the lack of response to his proposals, had been regarded by the Queen as a reflection on her effectiveness?
5. See above, Letter 205, note 5.
6. A reference to his considerable literary output, published and unpublished.

---

## 209. To Sir Walter Cope [from the Tower], 5 October [1611][1]

Pierpont Morgan, New York, REIII.EI–l.46. In Ralegh's hand.

J.P. Collier, *Archaeologia* XXXV, 1853, pp. 219–20, from the original then in private hands, with some faulty readings and dated 1610; Edwards II, pp. 328–9, from Collier but (I, p. 503) correcting date to 1611; V. Klinkenborg, W. Cahoon and C. Ryskeep (eds), *British Literary Manuscripts*, series I, New York 1981, plate 19, facsimile.

## FOR LADY RALEGH TO LIVE IN THE TOWER AGAIN

[addressed]   To my very worthy frind Sir Walter Cope knight[2]
[endorsed]   Sir Walter Rawleigh

Sir Walter Cope: Yow are of my old acquayntance and were my familier frind for many yeeres, in which time I hope yow cannot say that ever I used any unkind office towards yow. But our fortunes are now changed and it may be in your power greatly to bynde me unto yow, if the bynding of a man in my estate be worth any thing.

My desire unto yow is that you wilbe pleased to move my Lord Treasorer [Salisbury] in my behalf, that by his grace my wife might agayne be made a prisoner with me, as she hath bine for six yeeres last past,[3] shee being now devided from me and therby to my great impoverishing I am driven to keip to howses. A miserable sute[4] it is and yet great to me who, in this wretched estate, can hope for no other thing than peacible sorrow.

It is now, and I call the lord of all power to wittnes, that I ever have bine and am resolved that it was never in the worthy hart of Sir Robert Cecyll[5] (whatsoever a counceler of state and a Lord Treasorer of Ingland must do) to suffer me to fall, mich less to perrish. For what soever termes it hath pleased his lordship to use towards mee which might utterly dispaire any bodie elce, yet I know that he spake them as a counceler, sitting in councell and in company of such as would not other wise have bine satisfied. But, as God liveth, I would have bought his presence[6] att a farr deerer rate than those sharp words and these three monethes close imprisonment, for it is in his lordships face and countenance that I behold all that remaynes to me of comfort, and all the hope I have and from which I shall never be beaten till I see the last of evills and the dispayre which hath no healp. The blessings of God cannot make him cruell that was never so, nor prosperitie teach any man of so great worth to delight in the endles adversitie of an enemie, mich less of him who in his very sowle and nature can never be such a one towards him.

Sir, the matter is of no great importance (though a cruell destinie hath made it so to me) to desire that my wife may live with me in this unsavery place. If by your mediation I may obtayne it I will acknowledg it in the highest degree of thanckfullnes and rest reddy in trew fayth to be commanded by yow.

October the 5
    W Ralegh

1. Almost certainly 1611, the year when he fell foul of the Privy Council: see above, Letter 207, note 3.
2. Chamberlain of the Exchequer since 1609. Presumably the friendship claimed by Ralegh went back to his years at Court in the 1590s.
3. The appointment of a new Governor of the Tower in 1607 had led to tighter regulations, including an order in the King's name that Lady Ralegh 'resort to her house on Tower Hill or elswhere with her women and sonnes': Stebbing 1899, p. 252.
4. Collier, followed by Edwards, reads this as 'fate'.
5. A wistful harkening back to Elizabethan days.
6. Possibly a reference to Salisbury's visit to the Tower in the previous July: see above, Letter 207, note 3. Salisbury's regime was about to come to an end: he died on 24 May 1612: *DNB*.

---

### 210. TO SIR RALPH WINWOOD [FROM THE TOWER], JULY 1615

In private hands, Bradfer-Lawrence 61, ff. 137–137v. (see heading to Letter 205), a contemporary transcript headed in Ralegh's own hand.

BL, Harl. 39, f. 351v.–52, an inferior contemporary copy, known to Edwards (I, p. 508) but omitted from vol. II.

Harlow, *Last Voyage*, 1932, pp. 114–16, from Harley 39.

## MORE PROPOSALS FOR GUIANA

[*headed*] Coppie of my letter to Master Secritorie Winwood[1] in Julie 1615

Honorable Sir: Having beene of late visited by two gentlemen of my olde acquaintance and your devoted servants,[2] we fell into the discourse of an enterprise which I had heretofore propounded to the late Treasurer Secill,[3] which, although at sundrye times he seemed willing to imbrace, yet allwayes upon the conclusion he had his *ariere bouticque* [= *back room, i.e. entrenched position*] into which he withdrew himselfe. Notwithstanding, when he had pawsed[4] a yeare or two and founde that by his subtilitie (in which the greatest part of his wisdome consisted) he coulde not raise those buildings for His Majestie of which he had conceived the idea, he dealt with the Lorde Carew my kinsman to perswade me to renew my former offers, making shew of a great desire to have some what done therin, wherto, although [= *in spite of*] the scornes with which (after the change of our fortunes) he had oftner then honestly paid my many yeares affection towards him, yet, for the reasons remembred in this inclosed letter of mine written unto him [*Letter 205*], by my Lorde Carews perswasions, I was moved to obey him. With which letter to the Treasurer I have also made bolde to send your honor a transcript of a letter written unto His Majestie [*Letter 208*] about the same time, to satisfie His Majestie in those things which I knew the Treasurer would object, for the Treasurer knew that I had besought the Queene [*Letter 207*] to [*show*] His Majestie the coppie of my letter written to himselfe [*Salisbury*] which he never ment to have imparted unto His Majestie but to have spoken of my offers in generall tearmes and slightly enough.

Now Sir, it is true that although my times are soe farre gone, as I am unfitt and, as I feare me, unable to undergoe soe great a travaile, yet seing the same death which strikes us downe in the worthiest actions doth not spare to strangle us in taking our unprofitable ease, I should thinck myselfe exceeding happie to incounter him in the waye of His Majesties service.

I heare of many inventions to inrich His Majestie, at least to supply his present occasions,[5] but some of them are litle ones, some require too longe a time and other are rather devised to inrich those that shalbe imployed in them than to inable the King. This of mine, in which I have noe other end nor desire then to paye His Majestie some parte of the debt I owe him (having beene more bounde to his goodnes before my troubles, in my troubles and since my troubles then any freindlesse man hath ever beene) shall cost His Majestie nothing. I will give noe cause of offence to any Christian prince. I will take none[6] with me not only not suspect but such as His Majestie shall acknowledg for his faithfull servants. And lastly, whatsoever I shall returne of riches His Majestie may be pleased to make election of his own proportion.[7]

This last offer of mine I doe now leave to your honors judgment whether or noe (perusing what hath past by the inclosed) it may please you to favoure it.[8] If it goe on and succeed well, His Majestie shall have reason to acknowledg it towards you as the meane of a service, and perchance the greatest that hath beene done and if it shall please God that I perish in it yet His Majestie shall loose but a man allreadie lost, who will ever remaine your humble servant,

W R

1. Sir Ralph Winwood (c.1563–1617), Principal Secretary since 1614. His diplomatic service in France, the Low Countries and Germany had bred in him no love for Spain.
2. Not identified, but see below, Letter 211, note 4.
3. See Letters 192 and 205. Salisbury had died on 24 May 1612.
4. Harley 39, followed by Harlow, has 'passed'.
5. This was the great age of industrial and commercial projects, each of whose promotors promised a handsome commission to the Crown: see Joan Thirsk, *Economic Policy and Projects*, Oxford 1978.

6. Harley 39, followed by Harlow, has 'now'. It also omits a number of words of minor significance.
7. Implying some contribution from the King, contrary to Ralegh's undertaking in his third paragraph.
8. Exactly what part Winwood was to play in securing Ralegh's release is not on record, but see below, Letter 218. The Venetian ambassador reported to his master that Winwood actually urged Ralegh to attack the Spaniards: *CSP Venetian 1617–19*, p. 339.

211. TO SIR RALPH WINWOOD FROM THE TOWER, [EARLY 1616][1]

Bradford (Yorks.) District Archives, Hopkinson 19, f. 81, a seventeenth-century transcript, unique in including subscription and a date and spelling probably nearer the original than the many other transcripts. Legible in spite of ink penetration from reverse.[2]

Bodleian, Eng. Hist.d.138, f. 6, *HMC 4th Report*, p. 353 (Mostyn), Dr Williams's Library, Jones B 60, p. 243, and Northamptonshire Record Office F.H. 3641/4, p.[D], the two last in the same hand.

*Sceptick*, 1651, pp. 69–74, as Jones B 60; *Maxims*, 1656; *Remains* 1657, pp. 158–61, etc., as *Sceptick*; Birch, 1751, II, pp. 362–3; Cayley, 1806, II, pp. 58–60; *Works* 1829, VIII, pp. 629–30, from Birch; Edwards II, pp. 339–41, from *Maxims* and *Remains* 1657, dated 1615–16; Harlow, *Last Voyage*, 1932, p. 113, from Bodleian, dated 'probably 1615'.

## ANOTHER PLEA FOR A GUIANA VOYAGE

[*headed*] Sir Walter Raleighe to Master Secretarye Winwood before his journey to Guiana

[*addressed*] To the honorable Rafe Winwood knight, Secretarye of State to His Sacred Majestie

Honorable Sir:[3] I was lately perswaded by two gentlemen, my antient freinds,[4] to acquainte your honor with some offers of mine made heretofore for a journey to Guiana, who were of opinion that it wold be better understoode now[5] then when itt was first propounded, which advice haveing surmounted my dispaire, I have presumed to send unto your honor the copyes of those letters which I then wrote, both to His Majestye [*Letter 205*] and to the Treasorer Cecille [*Letter 208*], wherin aswell the reasons that first moved me are remembred as the objections by him made are briefely answered: that I knowe of the riches of that place not by heresaye but what myne eyes have seene. I have said itt often but it was then to noe end because those that had the greatest trust were resolved not to beleeve me, not because they doubted the truth but because they doubted my disposition towards themselves. Where (if God had blessed me in the enterprise) I had recovered His Majesties favour and good opinion, other cause then this or other opinion they never had any. Our late worthy Prince of Wales[6] was extreame curious in searching out the nature of my offences, the Queenes Majestie[7] hath informed herselfe from the beginning, the Kinge of Denmarke[8] at both tymes of his being here was thoroughly satisfied of my innocencie: they wold never have otherwise moved His Majestie upon my behalfe. The wife, the brother[-*in-law*] and the sonne of a king doe not use to sue for menn suspect, but Sir, since they all have done itt out of their charitie and but with reference to me alone, your honor (whose respect hath onely relation to His Majesties service), strengthened by the example of these princes, may with the more hardnesse doe the like, being princes to whome His Majesties good estate is noe lesse deare, and all menn that shall oppugne [= *question*] itt noe lesse hatefull then to the kinge himselfe.

It is true, Sir, that His Majestie hath sometimes answered that his [*privy*] councell knewe me better then he did, meaneing some twoe or three of them, and indeed it was my infelicitye, for had His Majestie knowne me I had never bene here where now I am, or had I knowne His Majestie they had never beene so longe there where now they are. His Majestie not knoweinge of me hath beene my ruine and His Majesties misknowing of them hath been the ruine of a goodly part of his estate,[9] but they are all of them nowe, some liveing and some dyeing, come to His Majesties knowledge.[10] But, Sir, howe litle soever His Majestie knewe me and howe much soever he beleeved them, yet have I bene bound to His Majestie both for my life and all that remaines, of which, but for His Majestie, my life nor aught els had remained. In this respect, Sir, I am bound to yeild up the same life, and all I have, for His Majesties service: to dye for the King and not by the Kinge is all the ambition I have in the world.

So, Sir, most humbly takes leave, recommending yow to youre more serious affaires, remaineing,

        Your honors much bounden
           Walter Raleighe

From the Tower, the [*blank*] 1617 [*sic*]

---

1. The date at the foot of the text must be a slip of the pen on the part of the transcriber for Ralegh was conditionally released from the Tower on 19 March 1616 and, although kept under close surveillance thereafter, was not back in the Tower until after his return from Guiana in 1618. It was clearly written not long after Letter 210 which also mentions the visit by Ralegh's two 'antient frends'.

2. I am indebted to Miss Letitia Lawson of the West Yorkshire Archive Service for her assistance and to Mrs Audrey Erskine for demonstrating that it is possible to read this text: JY.
3. By 1702 this had become 'Honoured Sir' in the printed texts.
4. Still unidentified: see above, Letter 210. One may have been Sir William St John (see Letter 214), who in 1614 suggested to Ralegh that he set down on paper details of the project (E. Strathmann, 'Ralegh plans his last voyage', *MM* 50, 1964, p. 268), and the other the man most likely to accompany him, Lawrence Keymis.
5. Possibly a reference to the King's dire need for money, but more likely to be connected with the death of Salisbury in 1612.
6. See above, Letter 194.
7. See above, Letters 201 and 207.
8. Christian IV of Denmark, brother of the Queen, visited England in 1606 and 1614, on the second occasion trying, unsuccessfully, to secure Ralegh's release to do him some naval service: Stebbing 1899, pp. 293–4.
9. Cf. Ralegh's attack in *The Prerogative of Parliaments*, not published until 1628, but written in the summer of 1615 (Lefranc 1968, chapter VIII, *passim*), on the King's advisers as 'men ambitious and greedy without proportion', who 'ruined his estate': *Works* 1829, VIII, pp. 178, 219.
10. With the deaths of Salisbury (1612) and Northampton (1614) and the disgrace of Rochester (Robert Carr) early in 1616, most of Ralegh's implacable obstacles in high places were now removed.

---

## 212. To Sir George Villiers [from the Tower], 17 March [1616][1]

Longleat, Wilts, Portland Papers II, f. 9, *HMC Bath* II, p. 64, abstract only, a seventeenth-century transcript.

Oldys 1736, p. 162, 'from the original in the library of James West Esq.'; *Works* 1829, I, p. 468; Cayley 1806, II, p. 56 and Edwards II, p. 341, both from Oldys.

### THANKS FOR RELEASE FROM THE TOWER

[*headed*]   From the original   To Sir George Villiers[2]

Sir: You have by your mediation put me againe into the world. I can but acknowledge it, for to [re]pay any part of your favour by any service of myne as yet it is not in my power. If it [*the Guiana voyage*] succeed well a great part of the honour shalbe yours, and if I doe not also make it profitable unto you I shall shew my self exceeding ungratefull. In the maine while, and till God discover the success, I beseech you to reckon me among the number of your faithfull servants, though the least able.
      W Ralegh[3]

March the 17

1. Ralegh was released from the Tower on 19 March 1616: *APC 1615–16*, p. 456.
2. (1592–1628), the King's new favourite, the later Marquess of Buckingham, who was at this time, with Secretary Winwood, in the anti-Spanish lobby.
3. The transcriber was at pains to imitate Ralegh's signature, including the spelling.

---

## 213. To Master Peter Van Lore, 1 July 1616[1]

Folger, Addit. 991, the subscription and signature (see note 5) supplied from Oldys. In Ralegh's hand.

Oldys 1736, pp. cxciii–cxciv, spelling modernized, transcribed from the original, then in the possession of Browne Willis of Whaddon Hall, Bucks; *Works* 1829, I, pp. 472–3; Edwards II, pp. 342–3 and Harlow, *Last Voyage*, p. 116, both from Oldys.

### DUTCH SUPPORT FOR GUIANA

[*addressed*] To Master Peter Vanlore[2]

[*endorsed*] This letter was showne unto Mathias Penewart at the tyme of his examination on the part and behalf of Sir Peter Van Lore knight, defendant, against Dame Elizabeth Rowleigh, complainant[3]     12 daie Junii 1623
        Martin Basill.[4]

[This is the letter which I desire you to write to your brother[-*in-law*] in Amsterdam, and for any assurance [= *guarantee*] you shall give I will again put you in sureties to save you harmless [= *free of legal liability*].
        W Ralegh][5]

Brother Tibotes:[6] There is a marchant in Amsterdam[7] that for the love he beares to my honourable frinde Sir W[*alter*] Ralegh is content to discover some what of importance unto him in Guiana,[8] to which country Sir W[*alter*] Ralegh is now preparing to go, but he [*the merchant*] doth require assurance from Sir W[*alter*] Ralegh that he him self may be assured to injoy such part of the commoditie discovered as he shall agree uppon with Sir Walter Ralegh bi his [*the merchant's*] deputie, Master Henry Hovenar.[9] I do therfore pray yow to speake with the partie which Master Hovenour [*sic*] will bring unto yow, and to know what assurance he will require which, to pleasure Sir Walter, I shalbe willing to give: that is to say, to give him assurance that uppon Sir Walters returne into Ingland (the charges being deducted) the discoverer shall receive from Sir Walter such part of the sayd [*sic*] marchandise as Sir Walter and he shall agree on, although their needs no such assurance to be given because His Majestie doth assure all Sir Walters partners by the great seal of Ingland[10] that they shall freely and quietly injoy all their parts and shares of what goods, marchandise or treasure soever shall be returned.[11] Out of which great seal of Ingland the discoverer shall have an assignment for so much as belongs unto him, to be delivered here in London to whom soever he shall appoynt to receive it.

1. Oldys does not include a date in his transcript but notes that the letter 'is dated July 1 1616'.
2. The well-known London goldsmith and jeweller, born in Utrecht but now a naturalized subject of the Crown. He was to be knighted in 1621. Ralegh did a lot of business with and through him: see above, Letter 165, note 18.
3. In June 1622, Lady Ralegh, Sir Walter's widow, alleged in the Court of Chancery that in 1605 Van Lore had deducted £600 from the proceeds of the sale of a jewel belonging to her in settlement of an allegedly unpaid debt: PRO, C2 James I, R1/55, R11/56.
4. Not identified.
5. From Oldys, who makes it plain that Ralegh's request was written below the draft letter to the Dutch merchant, the missing lines having presumably been torn off for the autograph. The order has been reversed here for clarity.
6. No doubt Adrian Thibaut of Amsterdam, who was the brother of Van Lore's wife, Jacomina, a daughter of Henry Thibaut of London, merchant-stranger.
7. Not identified. The unknown merchant cannot have been Adrian Thibaut.
8. The 'discoverer' seems to have been a sleeping partner, but his particular interest (perhaps precious stones) is not disclosed. Neither is Ralegh explicit about the particular contribution he is hoping for, but it was probably cash or some form of credit, not, as has been suggested, information about the mine. Ralegh was certainly hoping for some Dutch ships and also for a company of English soldiers to be recruited from those currently serving the Prince of Orange: Harlow, *Last Voyage*, pp. 144 and 164 and *CPSD 1611–18*, p. 412.
9. Not identified.
10. Ralegh was hoping for the authority of the Great Seal, which would have been tantamount to a pardon, but on 26 August 1616 his commission was granted under the Privy Seal: Harlow, *Last Voyage* 1932, p. 341, *CSPD 1611–18*, pp. 387–8 and Rymer's *Foedera*, XVI, 789.
11. The repayment was clearly to be in goods.

---

### 214. TO SIR WILLIAM ST JOHN FROM LEE, ESSEX, 19 MARCH [1617][1]

National Library of Wales, Aberystwyth, Bute L 3/5. In Ralegh's hand.

David Iffans, 'A Sir Walter Ralegh letter', *National Library of Wales Journal*, vol. XXII, 1981–2, p. 349.

## SUPPLIES FOR THE VOYAGE TO GUIANA

[*no address or endorsement*]

Sir William St Johns [*sic*]:[2] Besyds the monie dew to Tite the anker smith[3] ther is fifty pound that this bearer, Wi[*llia*]m Ston[*e*],[4] hath given bond for to a linnen draper for shirtts for the companie. I pray yow to speake with

Master Herbert the pencioner[5] that he will satisfy [*pay*] that fifty pound out of my cussen Herberts[6] monie and in the meane while free this poore man who hath bine arested[7] for it.

    Your loving frinde,
      W Ralegh

From Lee,[8] reddy to sett sayle, this 19th of March

1. The year Ralegh sailed to Guiana.
2. Sir William St John of Highlight, Glamorgan, a naval captain who, it has been suggested, had worked with Villiers (see above, Letter 212) to secure Ralegh's release.
3. Lewis Tite (or Tayte) who supplied ironwork for Ralegh's newly built ship the *Destiny*.
4. Not identified.
5. Arnold Herbert, a Gentleman Pensioner of the King, who was knighted in July 1617.
6. William Herbert, whose remote relationship with Ralegh seems to have rested on a connection with the Throckmortons. For his quarter share in the *Destiny* see below, Letter 225. That this was William Herbert of Glamorgan (ob. 1628) is suggested by the survival of this letter among manuscripts relating to the Herberts of Cogan Pill: *ex infer*. National Library of Wales. Both St John and Herbert were to betray Ralegh on his return.
7. Presumably meaning that Stone's goods had been seized. Why the linen-draper should have been arrested is not clear.
8. A small port on the Thames estuary. Ralegh's main fleet was currently assembled at the Isle of Wight but the *Thunder*, commanded by Sir Warham St Leger, was still at Lee, whither Ralegh had presumably made a quick dash to get her away: Harlow, *Last Voyage*, p. 318, from Ralegh's *Apology* which he reads as 'at lee'. Ralegh then moved to Plymouth where he faced further delays. He set sail from there on 12 June 1617: Stebbing 1899, p. 313.

---

## 215. TO MONSIEUR DE BISSEAUX FROM PLYMOUTH, 14 MAY [1617][1]

Archivo General de Simancas, Valladolid, Legajo de Estado 2598 no. 65. Written by a clerk, signed and possibly dated, by Ralegh. Punctuation and capital letters and the absence of apostrophes and accents are, in this instance, printed exactly as in the original manuscript, to which is appended a rough translation into English.

S.R. Gardiner, 'The case against Sir Walter Ralegh', *Fortnightly Review*, VII, May 1867, p. 611, with several textual errors; Edwards II, pp. 346–7 and Harlow, *Last Voyage*, 1932, pp. 127–8, both from Gardiner.

### SEEKING A COMMISSION FROM THE KING OF FRANCE

[*addressed*]   A Monsieur Monsieur de Bisseaux,[2] cons[*eill*]er du Roy en ses conseils destat et prive

Monsieur

   estant Sur le point de faire Voile³ Jay entendu le heureux changement des afaires de France⁴ qui me donne beaucoup d'esperance et de courage, Masurant que le party éspagnol' ne sera par⁵ si apres si puissant, et qui ma occasionne renvoyer par devers vous [m]on fidelle amy le Cappitaine Faige⁶ avec Ample Commission de conduire certains Navires promis et autes⁷ qui desireront avoyr part a ma fortune, et luy ay asigne le temps et les places⁸ ou il me doibt trevaer⁹ aux Indes, et Cepandant Jetravailleray aux Mines, que si Je ne¹⁰ les treuve suffisantes et telles que Je desire, Il vous dira la resolution que iay prinse, la luy ayant [con]fiee Il y a long temps,¹¹ Laquelle jespere me reusiya au contentement de ceux qui me font lhonneur de Maymer,¹² Cest pourquoy Je vous prie de donner au present Gentilhomme¹³ la mesme croyance que autrefoys, et lasister pour obtenir le brevet qui mest promis¹⁴ [par] celuy quil ma aporte et lequel Je retiens par devers Moy, toutefoys remettant le tout a votre prudence de Voyr si le temps le permet, ce que atendant Je vous coniure de croyre que vous pouves et pourres ajamais [sic] disposer de moy comme de vostre treshumble et affectionne serviteur,
      W Ralegh

de Plemouht ce14' May 1616 [sic]¹⁵

[*Translation*] Being on the point of setting sail³ I have heard of the happy turn of events in France⁴ which give me much hope and strength, being assured that the Spanish faction will not be henceforth as powerful and which prompts me to send to you my faithful friend Captain Faige⁶ with full authority to command certain promised ships, and others who will want to share in my fortune, and I have indicated to him times and the places⁸ where he has to meet me in the Indies. And meanwhile I shall work the mines, and if I do not¹⁰ find them satisfactory and of the quality I want, he will tell you what decisions I have taken as I have revealed to him a long time ago,¹¹ which I hope I shall be successful in, to the pleasure of those who do me the honour of being my friends.¹² For this reason I ask you to give this gentleman¹³ the same credence as before and to assist him to obtain the commission I have been promised¹⁴ like the one he brought me and which I have in front of me, however leaving all to your wisdom to see if time permit. Awaiting which I beg you to believe that you can and will be able always to use me as your very humble and loving servant.
      W Ralegh

From Plymouth this 14 of May 1616¹⁵

1. The year Ralegh departed for Guiana.
2. Samuel Spifame, seigneur de Bisseaux, French ambassador to England 1611–12.
3. Ralegh spent the whole of May 1617 in Plymouth.
4. A reference to the murder of Concini, the French Queen Mother's favourite, on 14 April 1617.
5. Gardiner, followed by Edwards and Harlow, reads this as 'pas'.
6. Captain Charles Faige, a native of La Rochelle, whom Ralegh trusted.
7. Gardiner, etc. have 'autres'.
8. A reference to a map of Guiana showing the route Ralegh expected to follow which he had entrusted to Faige and to another of his French friends, Antoine Belle of Dieppe. It survives, with this letter, in the archives of Simancas: see below, note 14.
9. Gardiner, etc. read as 'trouver'.
10. Gardiner, etc. omit the crucial 'ne' which indicates that in his negotiations with the French Ralegh was being uncharacteristically realistic. His relaxed air suggests that he did not feel threatened by the French.
11. The only alternative was an attack on the Spanish plate-fleet or on the coastal towns, and indeed Ralegh confessed as much to his men in order to keep their spirits up. In the event the desertion of Whitney and Woolaston (see below, Letter 218, note 11) left him too weak to take any such aggressive action.
12. Gardiner read this as 'armer' but there is quite clearly a 'y' superimposed on the 'r'.
13. Faige or possibly his accomplice, Antoine Belle of Dieppe.
14. Presumably the commission Ralegh hoped for from the French King. All that he had so far obtained was a commission from Admiral Montmorency dated 20 April 1617. This gave him leave to trade and use arms in self-defence in South America, and also what he really wanted, permission, on his return, to enter any French port from which, if necessary, to negotiate with King James. He was thus able truthfully to claim at his trial that he had never received any favours from the King of France: Harlow, *Last Voyage*, pp. 126–7. The original 'brevet' remained with Antoine Belle who later sought absolution in Rome for aiding 'Huguenots' and was told to take the incriminating document, presumably supported by this letter and the map, to Spain, where a Spanish translation of Montmorency's commission (Simancas E 2597/104) was identified some years ago by Pierre Lefranc.
15. A mistake for 1617. It is unlikely that Ralegh wrote the last two words. I am grateful to my colleague, Professor Keith Cameron, for his invaluable help with the translation. In his opinion Ralegh's written French is good, 'some of the deviations' being explicable 'by regional differences in pronunciation', a reminder that Ralegh had learned his French while soldiering with the Huguenots.

## 216. TO SIR RICHARD BOYLE FROM ROSTELLAN, CO. CORK, 28 JUNE 1617

Chatsworth, Derbyshire, Devonshire Papers, Lismore Papers VIII/70, previously at Lismore Castle. In Ralegh's larger hand. There is damage to the right-hand margin and a horizontal tear, probably worse now than when Grosart saw it, though some words which he misread are still legible and he overlooked, in his conjectural readings, what space was available. Words no longer readable are prefaced by 'G' when supplied from Grosart.

A.B. Grosart, *Lismore Papers*, Series 2, 1887, II, p. 85.

## STORMBOUND IN CORK HARBOUR

[*addressed*]   To the right honorable Sir Richard Boyle knight, Barron of Youghell[1]

[*endorsed by Boyle*]   29 Junii 1617[2]   From Sir Walter Raleigh

My very good lord: After as many crosse[*s on land*] and sea as ever man was subject unt[*o, I am*] by extremitie of weather driven into [*the harbour*] of Corcke. I was first forst into Ply[*mouth and*] from the French coast into Falmout[*h. Meeting*] with a violent storme on Midsom[*er Eve*] and Midsomer Day (my smaler shipp[*s unable to*] beare it out),[3] I putt into this port[4] [G: *with eight*] sayle, not heering yet any newse of [*my flyboat*][5] in which I had bestowed a great par[*t of my*] provisions. This hard beginninge [G: *nevertheless*], God I trust will bless us with a [G: *good wind*]. If I had had horses I would hav[*e waited on your lordship myself ere t*]his, but now hav[*ing met with*] my old [*serva*]nt Manus Macsh[G: *uhy*,[6] *if your*] lordshipp will do mee the favor [*to oblige*] mee with a few hackenes I [*shall make*] bold with Master Thomas Fitts Ger[*ald*[7] *to go*] to Cloyne on Twesday morning [*with three*] or four gentlemen and a coople of [G: *hawks*]. This much I make bold with [*your lordship*]. If God bless me with good succes [*my under*]takings being certayne and well y[*et, I will*] then acknowledge your lordships favor [*or I will*] perish (for ther is no middle course [*but perish*] or prosper).[8] I will then intreat my [G: *messenger*] to give your lordship thancks for m[*e and*] ever remayne your lordships to be c[*ommanded*].

    [G: *W Ralegh*]

From Rostillon this Sunday morning.

## 216a. To Sir Richard Boyle [from Rostellan, ?early/mid August 1617]

Chatsworth, as above, VIII, 70, a fragment only. In Ralegh's hand, signature missing.

Grosart, op. cit., p. 86, dating it 17 June 1617, at which time Ralegh was still in Falmouth.

## THANKS AND COMPLIMENTS

[*addressed*]   To the right honorable Sir Richard Boyle, knight, Barron of [*Yougal*]

[*endorsed by Boyle*]   [*Sir Walter R*]alighes letter I cut off and sent to [*R*]edmond Fitz John by hi[*s o*]wn messenger incontinently.

... I have written to my honorable frends how much I am indebted to your lordshipp[9] and withall what services yow have don the state in strenghning this part of the kingdome, with all elce that becometh a frinde to performe.

[*no signature*]

[*postscript*]  ... idle foole poore I have quitted him.
 ... received the young gentlemen.

1. Richard Boyle (1566–1643), clerk to the Council of Munster and soon to be Earl of Cork. In 1602 he had bought Ralegh's Irish estates: D. Townshend, *Life and Letters of the Great Earl of Cork*, 1904, pp. 31–2, 38. Ralegh was still grateful to Boyle for his paying him the cash outstanding after his attainder in 1603, and for the gift of 32 gallons of 'choice aqua-vite' before he left England: Grosart, op. cit., p. 145.
2. The day Boyle received the letter, a Monday.
3. They had hit a storm eight leagues west of the Scillies and lost one ship (captain John Chidley) sunk and the *Supply*, a pinnace (captain Samuel King), driven into Bristol: Harlow, *Last Voyage*, p. 319.
4. Rostellan, on Cork harbour, 2.5 miles SW of Cloyne (and not Kinsale as stated by Grosart, followed by Harlow and others), where his ships lay from 25 June to 19 August: Harlow, *Last Voyage*, pp. 232 and 320. They carried over three hundred mariners and no less than ninety gentlemen, a company of soldiers and numerous servants and labourers, probably not far short of one thousand men: ibid., pp. 51–2.
5. The *Supply*.
6. Manus Macshihy of Kylnetora, who had acted as Ralegh's attorney in the sale of Youghall, etc., to Boyle: Townsend op. cit., p. 38.
7. Thomas Fitzgerald, son of Ralegh's old ally, John FitzEdmund Fitzgerald (above, Letter 5, note 6), who held Rostellan by a grant of 1608: C. Smith, *Cork*, 1890, p. 85.
8. Adversity had not destroyed the gambling instinct of the owner of the *Destiny*.
9. Before Ralegh left Ireland Boyle lent him considerable sums of money and, besides affording invaluable supplies to his captains, gave him 'six barres of Spanish yron and a hogshead of salmon': Grosart, op. cit., pp. 158–60. In his 'Apologie', which he composed on his return to England (Harlow, *Last Voyage*, p. 320), Ralegh wrote,
   That we staied longe in Ireland it is true; but they muste accuse the clowdes and not me for our stay there, for we lost not a day of a good wynde and there was not any captaine in the fleet but had creditt, or might have had, for a great deal more of the victualls then we spent there. ...

---

## 217. TO LADY RALEGH FROM CAYENNE, 14 NOVEMBER 1617

Bradford District Archives, Hopkinson 19, f. 82, a seventeenth-century transcript, unique in certain respects but suffers from ink penetration.

BL, Harl. 39, f. 371 is the next best. Derby Record Office, General 67/6, *HMC* 9th Report (Pole-Gell), p. 386 and Folger Library, G.b.9, ff. 183–4 are very similar, but University Library Cambridge Ec.5.23 and Bodleian, Ashmole 830, f. 104, which lacks the final paragraph, show signs of editing. Dr Williams's Library, Jones B60, pp. 247–9 is corrupt.

Sceptick 1651, p. 75, from Jones B60; *Maxims* 1656; *Remains*, 1656, etc., and Birch 1751, II, p. 363, from *Sceptick*; Cayley 1806, II, p. 63, as Birch and 'Harleian and other collections'; *Works* 1829, VIII, p. 631, from Ashmole 830, amended.

Edwards II, p. 347, as *Remains* 1656–7 with a few variations suggesting that he had seen other copies; Harlow, *Last Voyage*, p. 158, as Edwards.

## NEWS FROM GUIANA

[*heading*]   Sir Walter Ralieghe [*sic*] to his ladie from Guiana
[*addressed*]   For my dearest wife, the Ladye Raleighe[1]

Deare[2] heart: I can yette write unto yow but with a weake hand for I have suffered the moste vyolent calenture[3] for fifteene dayes that ever man did and lived. But God, that gave me a stronge heart in all my adverseties, hath also now strengthened itt in the hell fire of heate.

Wee have had [?*the*] moste greevous sicknesses in our ship [*The Destiny*] of which fortye two have died and ther are yette many sicke. But havinge recovered [= *reached*] the land of Guiana this twelfthe of November I hope wee shall recover them. Wee are yett two hundreth menn and the reste of my fleet are reasonable stronge, stronge enoughe I hope to performe what wee have undertaken—if the diligent care at London to make our strength knowne to the Spanishe kinge by his ambassador have not taughtt the Spaniardes to fortefie all the entrances againste us.[4] Howesoever wee must make the adventure, and yf we perishe itt shalbe noe honor for England nor gaine for His Majestie to loose amonge many other an hundreth gent[*lemen*] as valiante as England hath in itt.[5]

Of Captaine [*John*] Bailyes base runninge from me at the Canaries see a letter of Master [*Lawrence*] Kemishes to Master Scory,[6] and of the unnaturall weather, stormes, raine and windes, he hath be [= *by*] the same letter given a towch of the waye itt hathe ever beene sailed in forteene dayes now hardly performed in fortye dayes.[7] God, I hope, will give us comforth in that which is to come. In the passage to the Canaries I stayed at Gomerah where I tooke water in peace because the Country durste not denie itt me.[8] I received there [from the Countes][9] of an English race a present of orenges, lemmons, quinces[10] and pomegranets, without which I shold not have lived. Those I preserved in fresh sands and I have of them yet to my great refreshinge.

Your sonne [*Walter jun.*] had never soe good helth, havinge no distemper in all the heate under the line [= *south of the Equator*]. All my servants have escaped [= *survived*] but Crab and my cooke, yet all have had the sicknesse. Crofts and March and the rest are all well. Remember my service to my lord Carew and to Master Secretarye Winwood. I write not to them for I can write of naught but miseries as yet. Of menn of [the better] sort wee have lost our Serjant Major, Captaine [John] Pigot, and his leiftenante; Captain Edward Hastings,[11] who wold have died at home, for both his liver, spleene and brains were rotten; my sonnes leuftenant, [Thomas] Payton, and my cousin;[12] Master Hughes; Master Mordant; Master Gardiner; Master [John] Hayward; Captaine Jennings; the marchant Kemishe of London[13] and the master chirurgeon [Newball];[14] the master refiner [John Fowler of London];[15] Master [Richard] Moore, the Governor of the Beimudas;[16] our provoste marshall, William Steed, Leiftenant Vesier, but [sic] to mine inestymable greife [Christopher] Hamond and [John] Talbot.[17] By the nexte I trust you shall heare better of us. In Gods hands wee are, in him wee trust. This bearer Captain [Peter] Alley for his infirmitie of his head I have sent backe, an honeste, valliante man.[18] He can deliver you all that is passed. Commend me to my worthy freinds at Lothburye [London],[19] Sir John Leigh[20] and Master B[owyer],[21] whose nephew Knevet is well, and to my cosen Blundell,[22] and my most devoted and humble service to Her Majestie.

To tell yow that I myghte be here kinge of the I[ndyans][23] nowe were a vanitye, but my name hath still lyved amonge them.[24] Here they feede me with freshe water and all that the country yeildes, and all offer to obey me.

Commend me to poore Carew, [my sonne. Soe God blesse yow.][25]

From Calliana in Guiana the 14th of November 1617

    Yours,

        Walter Raleighe [sic]

---

1. From BL, Harl. 39.
2. Unique to the Bradford transcript and more like Ralegh's usual form of address to his wife than the 'Sweet heart' of all the other transcripts.
3. A tropical disease conducive to delirium suffered by sailors. In his 'Journal' Ralegh attributed it to getting out of bed in a hot sweat when a sudden storm had made it necessary to haul down the *Destiny*'s sails: R.H. Schombergk (ed.), *The Discoverie ... of Guiana ...*, Hakluyt Society, Series I, iii, 1848, p. 197.
4. In March 1617, Ralegh had been instructed to set down full details of his plan which were made known to the Spanish ambassador and promptly relayed by him to Madrid: Stebbing 1899, p. 305. See also Letters 218 and 219. The Spaniards had not, in fact, fortified the approaches although the delays suffered by Ralegh on his outward voyage had given them plenty of time to do so.
5. The young gentlemen who accompanied Ralegh, including his ships' captains, will have been soldiers rather than seamen and navigators. See above, Letter 216, note 4. Including the ships' captains, this round figure was no great exaggeration.

6. Harlow, op. cit., pp. 53–4 and 160–61 (from a transcript in Cambridge U.L. Ec. 5. 23). For Skory see Letter 219, note 6. Bailey had deserted at Lanzerote, reporting on his return to England that Ralegh had turned pirate, a charge he later retracted.
7. This transcript has the number of days reversed, but the sense demands that the order followed in all other transcripts be preferred. See below, Letter 218, which gives an account of these circumstances.
8. Cf. Keymes who reports that they had to use force to obtain water, something Ralegh would have had more sense than to admit: Harlow, *Last Voyage*, pp. 55 and 160. See also ibid., p. 146.
9. From BL, Harl. 39. The Governor's wife was apparently an Englishwoman.
10. BL, Ashmole 830 has 'limes', which is what Ralegh almost certainly wrote.
11. Younger brother of the Earl of Huntington, he had been captain of the *Encounter* and rear-admiral of the fleet.
12. Customer of Plymouth, his wife was Lord Carew's niece and hence Ralegh's distant 'cousin': Vivian, *Devon*, p. 290.
13. He was the 'cape merchant' in charge of the ship's cargo.
14. On the *Destiny*, ibid., p. 151.
15. Grosart, *Lismore Papers*, ser. 1, I. p. 163.
16. First holder of the post (from 1612), he had come home in 1615: Purchas XXIX.
17. A longstanding servant of Ralegh's who had lived with him in the Tower: Harlow, *Last Voyage*, p. 151.
18. Suffering from vertigo, he was sent home with a friendly Captain Janson of Flushing, arriving early in February 1618 with this letter: *CSPD 1611–18*, pp. 520–21.
19. In the city of London. Lady Ralegh was living in Broad Street in the same ward.
20. A former adventurer in Guiana.
21. From BL, Harl. 39. Not identified.
22. Not identified.
23. From BL, Harl. 39.
24. And still does: information from a recent English missionary.
25. This, together with the signature, is unique to the Bradford transcript.

---

## 218. To Sir Ralph Winwood from St Christophers, 21 March 1618

Somerset Record Office, DD/M1, 18/82, *HMC* 7th Report, App. (Sir John Mildmay), p. 592, a contemporary copy, one of over a score (of varying reliability) to have survived and very close to PRO, SP14/96/70 which was almost certainly made for Sir Thomas Wilson, Keeper of the Archives, but it is badly torn.

*Skeptick* 1651, pp. 81 and 109; *Maxims* 1656; *Remains* 1657, etc.; Birch, *Works*, 1751, II, pp. 365 and 374, from *Remains* 1702; Cayley 1806, II, p. 69, from Birch; *Works* 1829, VIII, p. 632, from *Remains* etc; Edwards II, pp. 350–58, from PRO, SP46/70 and Hatfield, CP242/f.12; C. Pérez Bustamente, *El Conde de Gondomar*, Santiago, 1928, p. 74, and A. Ballasteros y Beretta, *Correspondencia Oficial de Diego Sarmiento*, Madrid, 1936, p. 274, both from a contemporary Spanish translation; Harlow, *Last Voyage*, p. 238, from Edwards and others.

## FAILURE OF THE MINE

[*heading*]¹ To the right honorable Sir Ralphe Winwood knight, one of His Majesties Principall Secretaires and one of his most honorable Privy Counsell

[*endorsed*] Coppie of a letter from Sir W. Raleghe to Sir Ralph Winwood, at Whitehall 14 May 1618²

Sir: [*As*] I have not hitherto given you anie accompt of our proceedings and passage towards the Indies soe I have no other subject to write of since our raivall then of the greatest and sharpest misfortunes that have ever befalne anie man. For whereas for the first all those that navigate betweene Cape Verde and America doe passe it in 15 or 20 daies at most, we found the windes so contrarie (which is alsoe contrary to nature) and so manie violent stormes and raynes as wee spent six weekes in that passage,³ by reason whereof and that in so greate heate wee wanted water (for at the Isle Bravo off Cape de Verde wee lost our cables and anchors and our water caske, beeinge driven from the Island with a huricano⁴ and were all like to have perished). Greate sicknes fell amongst us and carried away great numbers of our ablest men, both for sea and land.

The 17th of November 1617 wee had sight of the coast of Guiana and soone after came to anchor in five degrees of the river Caliana. Heere we staide till the 4th of December, landed our sicke men, sett up the barges and shallops which wee brought out of England in quarters, washed our shipps and tooke in freshe water, beeinge fedd and assisted by the Indians of my old acquayntance with a greate deale of love and respect. My selfe haveinge ben in the hands of death without hope some six weekes, and not yet able to move otherwise then I was carried in a chayre, gave order to five small shipps to sayle into [*the river*] Orenoke, haveinge Captayne Keynis for their conductor towards the Myne, and in these five shipps five companies of fifties under the comaund of Captayne [*Charles*] Parker and Captayne [*Roger*] North, brothers to the Lord Mountegle and the Lord North, valiant gentlemen and of infinite patience for the labour, hunger and heate which they have endured. My sonne had the third company, Captayne Thornix [*Thomas Thornehurst*] of Kent the fourth, Captayne [*John*] Chudlie [*of Ashton, Devon*]⁵ by his leiuetenant [*Pridiaux, also of Devon*] the fift. But as my Serjeant Major, Captayne Pigott of the Low Countries, dyed in the former miserable passage, so my leiuetenant, Sir Warham St Leger [*of Kent*], lay sicke without hope of life and the charge [*was*] conferred upon my nephewe George Raleghe [*son of Sir Carew*], who had allso served longe with singuler commendations in the Low Countries, but by reason of my absence and Sir Warhams was not so well obayed as the enterprize required. As they passed up the river the Span[i]ards begann the warr and shott at us, both with theire ordnance and musketts, whereuppon the companies were forced to charge them and soone after beate them out of theire towne, in the assalt whereof my sonne, haveinge more desyre of honour then of saftie, was slayne, and with whom (to saie the truth) all respect of the world hath taken end in me. And although the five captaynes had as weake companies as ever followed anie valiant leaders, yet were there amongst them some 20 or 30 verie adventurous gentlemen and of singuler courage, as of my sonnes companie Master Knevet, Master Hammon,[6] Master Langworth and John Plesington, his officers; Sir John Hamden, Master Simon Leake (corporall of the feild), Master Hamons elder brother, Master Nicholls of Buckingham, Master Roberts of Kent, Master Perin, Master Tresham, Master Mullineaux, Master Winter and his brother, Master Way, Master Miles Herbert, Master William Harbert,[7] Master Bradshawe, Captain Hall and others. Sir, I sett downe the names of these gent[lemen] to th'end that if His Majestie shall have cause to use theire service yt maie please you to take notice of them for very sufficient men.

The other five shipps staide a[t] Trinidado, haveinge no other port capeable of them neere Guiana. The second shippe was comanded by my Vice Admirall, Captayne [John] Pennington, of whom to doe him right I must confesse is one of the most sufficient gent[lemen] for the sea that England hath; the third by Sir Warham St Leger, an exceedinge valiant and worthy gentleman; the fourth by Sir John Fearne, the fift by Captayne Chudley of Devon. With these five shipps I daylie attended that armada of Spayne which, had they sett uppon us, our force devided, th'one halfe in Orinoke, [1]50 myles from us, wee had not onlie bene torne in peeces but all those in the river had allso perished, beeinge of no defence at all for a sea fight, for wee had resolved to have burnt by theire sides, and to have dyed there, had the armada arived. But belike they stay for us at Margarita, by which they knowe wee must passe towards the Indies.

For it pleased His Majestie to vallewe us at so little as to commaund me uppon my alleageance to sett downe under my hand the country and the very river by which I was to enter it, to sett downe the number of men and the burthen of my shipps, with what ordnance every shipp caried, which beeinge made knowe to the Spanishe ambassador, and by him in post to the Kinge of Spayne, a dispatch was made by him and his letters sent from

Madrill [*Madrid*] before my departure out of the Thames, for his first letter, sent by a barque of advise was dated the 19th of March 1617 at Madrill, which letter I have here inclosed[8] [*and*] sent your honour. The rest I reserve, not knowinge whether this may be intercepted or not. The second, of the King, dated the 17th of May, sent allso by a carvill to Diego de Pallomeque, Governor of Guiana, El Dorado and Trinidado,[9] the third by the Bushoppe of Puerto Rico and delivered to Palomeque the 15th of July at Trinidado, and the fourth was sent from the farmur and secretarie of the Customes in the Indies at the same tyme. By that of the Kinges hand sent by the Bishopp there was allso a commission for the speedie levyinge of 3000[10] men and 10 peices of ordnaunce to be sent from Puerto Ricco for the defence of Guiana, 150 from Neuvo Reyno de Granado under the commaund of Captayne Anthonio Musica, and the other 150 [*sic*] from Puerto Ricco to be conducted by Captayne Francisco Zanchio. Now Sir, if [?*as*] all that have traded [*with*] the Indies since His Majesties tyme knowe it, that [*sic*] the Spaniards have flead alive those poore men that they have taken beeing but merchants men, what death and torment shall we expect if they conquer us. Certaynly they have hitherto fayled grossly, beeinge sett out unto them as wee were, both for numbers, tyme and place.

Lastly, to make an apologie for not workinge the myne, although I knowe not (His Majesty excepted) whom I am to satisfie as much as myself, haveinge lost my sonne and my estate in the enterprize, yet it is true that the Spaniard[*s*] tooke more care to defend the passages leadinge unto it then they did theire towne, which haveinge the Kinges instructions they might easilie doe, the country beeinge *aspera et fragosa* [= *rough and overgrown*]. But it is true that when Kemis found the river lowe and that he could not aproach the bancks in most places neere the myne by a myle, and where he found a discent, a volley of musketts came from the woods uppon the bancks and slewe two of our rowers, hurt six others and shott a valiant gent[*leman*], Captayne Thornix, in the head, of which wound he hath languished to this day, he (to wit, Kemis), following his owne advice that it was in vayne to discover the myne (for he gave me this for excuse at his returne), that the companies of English which were in the towne of St Thomas [*San Thomé*] were hardly able to defend it against the dayly and nightly alarams and assalts of the Spaniards, that the passage to the myne was of thick and impassable woods, that beeinge discovered they had no men to worke it, did not discover it at all. For it is true that the Spaniards, haveing two gold mynes neere the towne, th'one possessed by Pietro Roderigo de Perama, the second myne by Herman Fruntino, the third, of silver, by Francisco Fashardo, complayne for want of negroes to worke them. For as the Indians cannot be constrayned by a lawe of Charles the fift [*1542*], so the Spaniard[s] will not, neither can they indure the labour of these mynes, whatsoever that braggadoccio the Spanishe ambassador saies. I shall prove it under the proprietaries hands, by the custome bookes and by the Kinges quinto, of which I recovered a[n] ingote or two. And I shall make it appeare to any prince or state that will undertake it how easie these mynes and five or six more may be possest, and the most of them in those places which never yet have bin attempted by any enemye, nor any passage unto them ever discovered by the English, Dutch or French.

But at Kemis returne from Orenoke, when I rejected his counsayle and his course, and told him that he had undone me and wounded my creditt with the Kinge past recoverye, he slewe himselfe. For I told him, seeinge my sonne was lost I cared not if he had lost a hundred more in opening of the myne, so my credditt had bin saved. For I protest before God had not Captayne Whitney[11] (whom I gave more countenance to then to all the captaynes of my fleete) runn from mee at the Granadoes and carried another shippe with him of Captayne Wollastons, I would have left my body at St Thomas by my sonnes, or have brought with me out of that and other mynes so much gold ore as should have satisfied the Kinge that I had propounded no vayne thinge.

What shall become of mee now I knowe not. I am unpardoned in England and my poore estate consumed, and whether any other prince will give me bread I knowe not. I desyre your honour to hold me in your good opinion, and to remember my service to my lords of Arundell and Pembroke,[12] to take some pittie on my poore wife, to whom I dare not write for renewinge of her sorrrowe for her sonne, and beseeching you to give a coppie of these to my Lord Carewe, for to a broken mynde, a weake body and weake eyes it is a torment to write manie letters. I have found many thinges of importance for discoveringe the state and weaknes of the Indies which, if I live, I shall hereafter impart to your honour, to whom I shall ever remayne,

      A faithfull servant,
        W Raleghe

[*postscript*] Sir, since the death of Kemis yt is confessed by the Sergeant Major [*George Ralegh*] and others of his inward freinds that he told them when he was at the rivers mouth comeinge thence that he could have brought them to the myne within two howers march from the rivers side, but because my sonne was slayne, myselfe unpardoned, and not like to live, he had no reason to open the myne for the Spaniard, or for the Kinge [*of England*]. They answeard that the Kinge (though I were not pardoned) had graunted me a pattent under the greate seal [sic]. He replyed that the graunt to me was to a man that was *non ens* in lawe and therfore of no force. This discourse he had which I knewe not of till after his death. But when I was resolved to write to your honour he prayde me to joyne with him in excuseinge his not goeinge to the myne. I answered him I would not doe it, but if himselfe could satisfie the Kinge and the state that he had reason not to open it, I should be gladd of it, but for my part I must avowe it that he knewe it and that with little losse he might have done it. Other excuses I would not frame. He told me he would waite on me presentlie and give me better satisfaction, but I was no sooner come from him into my cabbon but I heard a pistoll goe off over my head and, sending up to knowe who shott it, word was brought that Kemis had shott it out of the cabbon windowe to clense it. His boy, goeinge into his cabbon, found him lyinge uppon his bedd with much blouud by him and, lookinge on his face, sawe he was dead. The pistoll beeinge but little did but cracke his ribbe but he, turninge him over, found a longe knife in his body, all but the handle.

Sir, I have sent into England by my cosen Harbert, a very valiant and honest gentleman, divers other unworthy persons, good for nothing either by land or sea and, though it was at theire owne suite, I knowe they will wronge me in all they can. I beseech your honour that these scumme of men may not be believed of me who have taken more paynes and suffred more then the meanest rascall in the shippe. These beeinge gone I shalbe able, if I live, to keepe the sea till the end of August with some four reasonablie good shipps.

Sir, whensoever God shall permitt me to arrive in any parte of Europe I will not fayle to let your honour knowe what we have done. Till then and ever,

        Your honours servant,
          W Raleghe

[From St Christophers, one of the Ilandes
of the Antillias, the 21th of March 1617][13]

1. Not in Mildmay copy, only in BL, Addit. 40838, f. 32v. and one other.
2. Winwood had died, very suddenly, on 27 October 1617.
3. See above, Letter 217.
4. In his 'Journal' (Schomburgk, op. cit., p. 187) Ralegh wrote that he was 'so wete as the water ran in att my neck and out att my knees as if it had bine powred on me with pailes'.

5. For John Chudleigh see below, Letter 220, note 15.
6. For Knevet and Hammon see above, Letter 217.
7. He had a quarter share in the *Destiny* (see below, Letter 225) but he later turned king's evidence.
8. Not extant.
9. Don Diego Palomeque de Acuna, a relative of Gondomar, had been appointed in 1615: Harlow, *Last Voyage*, pp. 132-3.
10. Several other copies, followed by Edwards and Harlow, have '300 soldiers', which is probably what Ralegh wrote.
11. Possibly distantly related to Lady Ralegh through her uncle, Sir Francis Carew. See also Letter 219. After deserting Ralegh, he and Woolaston went after prizes, ravaged Newfoundland, and took their cargo of dried fish to the Mediterranean: R. Whitbourne, *Discourse of Newfoundland*, 1622, and Harlow, *Last Voyage*, p. 85.
12. Ralegh's sureties: see Harlow, ibid., p. 309.
13. From PRO, SP14/96/70.

---

## 219. TO LADY RALEGH FROM ST CHRISTOPHERS, 22 MARCH 1618

BL, Addit. 34631, ff. 47-8, a seventeenth-century transcript, the best of over a dozen copies, the rest very similar.

*Sceptick* 1651, p. 98, as BL and followed by Birch 1751, II, pp. 370-71, Cayley 1806, II, p. 78 and *Works* 1829, VIII, p. 638; Edwards II, p. 359, from BL, Sloane 3520 and Harley 4781 and Harlow, *Last Voyage* 1932, pp. 243-4, from BL, Addit. 34631, with minor errors.

## DEATH OF YOUNG WALTER

[*Heading*] The copie of a lettre written by Sir W[alter] Ralegh to his wife from the Isle of St Christophers touching the ill successe of his last voyage to Guiana, bearing date the 22th of March 1617
[*No address or endorsement copied*]

I was loath to write because I know not how to comfort you. And God knowes I never knew what sorrow meant till now. All that I can say to you is that you must obey the will and providence of God and remember that the Queenes Majestie bare the losse of Pr[ince] Henry with a magnanimous heart and the Lady Harrington of her onely sonne.[1] Comfort your heart (deare Bess): I shall sorrow for us both and I shall sorrowe the lesse because I have not long to sorrowe, because not long to live.

I referr you to Master Secret[ary] Wynwoods lettre [*218*] who will give you a coppie of it if you send for it. Therin you shall know what hath past, which I have written by that lettre, for my braines are broken[2] and tis a torment to mee to write, espetially of miserie. I have desired Master Secretary to give my Lord Carew a coppy of his lettre.

I have clensed my shipp of sick men and sent them home and hope that God will send us somewhat ere we returne. Commend mee to all at Loathbury.[3] You shall heare from mee, if I live, from New-found-land[4] where I meane to cleane my shipp and to revictuall, for I have Tabacco[5] enough to pay for it.

The Lord blesse you and comfort you, that you may beare patientlie the death of your most valient sonne.

    Your
        W Ralegh

March the 22th from the Isle of St Christophers

[*postscript*] I protest before the Majestie of God that, as Sir Fr[*ancis*] Drake and Sir John Hawkins died heart-broken when they failed of their enterprize, I could willinglie doe the like did I not contend ag[*ains*]t sorrow to comfort and releive you. If I live to returne resolve yourself that it is the care for you that hath strengthened my heart.

It is true that [*Lawrence*] Keymish might have gone directlie to the myne and meant it [*sic*], but after my sonnes death hee made them beleive that hee knew not the way and excused himself upon the want of water in the river, and, counterfeiting many impedimentes, left it unfound. When hee came back I told him that hee had undone mee and that my credit was lost for ever. Hee answered that when my sonne was lost and that [*sic*] he left mee soe weake as he resolved [= *expected*] not to finde me alive, hee had noe reason to enritch a company who, after my sonnes death made no account of him. Hee further tolld mee that the English sent up into Guyana could hardly defend the Spanishe towne of St Thome which they had taken, and therefore for them to passe through the thick woodes it was impossible, and more impossible to have victualls brought them into the mountaine. And it is true that the Governor, Diego Palomeque, and fower other captaines being slaine (of which my sonne Watt slew one), [*John*] Plessington (Watts serjeant) and John of Morocos (one of his men) slew each two, I say five of them slaine in the entrance of the towne, the rest went off in a whole bodie and tooke more care to defend the passages to their mynes (of which they had three within a league of the towne, besides myne, which was about five miles off) then they did of the citie itself. Yet Kemish at the first was resolved to goe to the myne, but when hee came to the bankes side to land hee had two of his men slaine outright from the banke, six others hurt and Captaine Thornex [*Thornhurst*] shott in the heade, of which wound and the accidentes thereof hee hath pined away these twelve weekes.

Now, when Keymish came back and gave mee the former reasons which moved him not to open the myne, the one, the death of my sonne, a second, the weaknesse of the English and their impossibilitie to worke it and to be victualled, a third, that it was follie to discover it for the Spaniard, and, the last, both my weaknesses and my being unpardoned and that [*sic*] I rejected all these argumentes and tolld him I must leave him to himself to answere it to the King and the State, hee shutt himself into his cabbine and shott himself with a pockett pistoll which brake one of his ribbs. And, finding that it had not prevailed, hee thrust a long knife under his short ribbs up to the handle and died.

Thus much I have written unto Master Secretary, to whose lettres I referr you. But because I thinke my friendes will rather hearken after you then any other to knowe the trueth, I did, after the sealinge, breake open your lettre againe to let you know in briefe the state of that businesse, which I pray impart to my Lord of Northumberland and Sil[*vanus*] Skory[6] and to Sir John Leigh.[7] For the rest, there was never poore man soe exposed to the slaughter as I was, for, being commanded upon my allegiance to sett downe, not onely the countrey but the very river by which I was to enter it, to name my shipps, nomber my men and my artillery, this was sent by the Spanish ambassador to his master the King. The King wrote his lettres to all partes of the Indies, and espetially to the governor, Palomeque, of Guiana, Eldorado and Trinidado, of which the first lettre bare date the 19th of March at Madrid when I had not yet left the Thames, which lettre I have sent Master Secretary. I have also two other lettres of the King [*of Spain'*]s which I reserve and one of the Counsell. The King also sent a commission to levie 300 soldiers out of his garrisons of Nuevo Reigno de Granado et [*sic*] Puarto Rico with tenn peeces of brasse ordnance to entertaine [= *to engage*] us. Hee also prepared an armado by sea to sett upon us. It were too long to tell you how wee were preserved. My braines are broken and I cannot write much. I live yet and I have told you why. Whitney, for whom I sold my plate at Plymouth and to whom I gave more credit and countenance then to all the captaines of my fleet, ranne from mee at the Granados and Wolleston with him, soe as I am now but five shipps and one of those I have sent home, my flyboate and in her a rabble of idle rascalls which I know will not spare to wound mee, but I care not.

I am sure there is never a base slave in the fleet hath taken the paines and care that I have done, hath slept so little and travailed [= *worked*] so much. My friendes will not beleive them and for the rest I care not. God in Heaven blesse you and strengthen your heart.
    Your
        W Ralegh

1. John, son of Lord Harrington (ob. 1613), who died in 1614: *DNB*.
2. A common Elizabethan expression: cf. Shakespeare, *2 Henry IV*, IV, v. 69, 'Have broken ... their brains with care'.
3. See above, Letter 217, note 19.
4. Ralegh told Sir Warham St Leger of his intention to re-fit in Newfoundland, after which he would lie off the Azores and hope eventually to find asylum in France or elsewhere. In the event he did not land: Harlow, *Last Voyage*, p. 236.
5. From San Thomé.
6. Son of John Skory, a former bishop of Hereford, who in 1617 had advised Ralegh to stay at home and assert his moral superiority rather than attempt feats of valour: BL, Cotton Titus C7, f. 94.
7. See above, Letter 217, note 20.

---

## 220. TO LORD CAREW FROM PLYMOUTH, [c.11][1] JUNE 1618

Archivo General des Indias, Seville, a Spanish translation of the original, which is missing, sent by the Spanish ambassador to King Philip of Spain, printed here from Hume's translation with minor rephrasing using the printed Spanish texts.[2]

M.A.S. Hume, *Sir Walter Ralegh*, 1897, pp. 383–91, a translation into modern English; C. Perez Bustamente, *El Conde de Gondomar*, Santiago, 1928, pp. 85 and 113, the complete Spanish text; Harlow, *Last Voyage* 1932, pp. 247–9, from Hume but lacking second part; A. Ballesteros y Beretta, *Correspondencia Oficial de D.Diego Sarmiento de Acuna*, Madrid, 1943, I, pp. 282–7.

## RETURN HOME TO FACE CHARGES

[*headed*] Walter Ralegh to Baron Carew, Master of the Ordnance, of the Privy Council of the King of England, written at Plymouth 1 [*sic*] June 1618

Sir: I am sure your lordship has received a copy of my letter [218] sent with Captain North to Secretary Winwood, of whose death I heard with great sorrow in Ireland.[3] From that letter your lordship will have learned the reasons given by [*Lawrence*] Keymes for not discovering the mine, which could have been done, notwithstanding his obstinacy, by using a cacique [= *chief*] of the country, an old acquaintance of mine, if the companies had remained up the river two days longer, for the cacique himself offered pledges to do it.

Moreover the [*Spanish*] Governor's servant [*Christoval Guayacunda*], who is now with me, could have led them to two gold mines not two leagues from the town [*San Thomé*] as well as to a silver mine not three arquebus [= *light handgun*] shots distant, and I will demonstrate the truth of this when my health allows me to go to London. As for the rest, if Whitney and Wollaston had not deserted me at the Granadas[4] and the rest had not abandoned me at Nevis[5] as if they had some great enterprize in hand, I would have returned from Newfoundland to Guiana and either died there or fulfilled my undertaking.

When they deserted me I resolved to steer for Newfoundland to take in water and clean the ship [*The Destiny*], which had been agreed six days before they left me, but when I was approaching land I was informed that a hundred of my men had determined to go ashore and join the English settlers, or to do so when the ship was hauled up on the beach for cleaning. Their intention was to board the best ship of the English fleet at night and with it to plunder all the friends of England and the Portuguese in the ports, knowing that I should not be able to get my ship ready to follow them in less than ten or twelve days and that I had no men to navigate it. I thereupon called all the [*ships*] company together and told them that I had no wish to accuse any of them but as I had been told by some of the men themselves of the violence they intended to commit I had decided to return without taking in water or other provisions rather than enter the Newfoundland ports to the great prejudice of my countrymen, of men of other nations and of the fishermen there. And I therefore ordered the master [*Robert Burwick*] to set sail for England.

In consequence the conspirators revealed themselves, resisting and shouting that they would rather die than return to England. They were certainly a majority, some of them the best men I had, some of them being gentlemen. All the arquebusses and swords were in the magazine with the armour for cleaning and the mutineers had taken possession, refusing me entrance. Finding myself in this peril I gave way to the mutiny for a time, during the night setting my course again for Newfoundland and treating with two or three of the leaders to abandon their side, which, with great difficulty, they agreed to do, on condition that I would promise on oath not to return to England until they had obtained pardon for past piracies.[6] At last we agreed to go to Ireland and they chose Killibeg in the north, a miserable place frequented by desperate corsairs [= *pirates*]. If I had not agreed they would have killed me and those who stood by me, or else I should have killed them, in which case, as the mutineers were the ablest of my men, I should have been unable to bring the ship into port. It is true that when they calmed down for a while they told me that if I returned home poor I should be despised, to which I answered that even if I were a beggar I did not want to return a robber or do anything base, nor would I abuse the commission and confidence of the King and that before doing that I would choose not only poverty but death itself.

  I am well aware that, with my ship, than which there is no better in the world, I could have enriched myself by £100,000 in the space of three months and could have collected a company which would have impeded the traffic of the whole of Europe. But those who have told the King that I feigned the mine and decided to turn corsair are mistaken in their malice, for after failing in the business of the mine through the fault of another and having spent my estate and lost both it and my son, and being without pardon for myself or security for my life, I have held it all as nought and offer myself to His Majesty to do with me as he will, without making any terms. As for the mutineers, the majority have fled to Ireland and some of them I have persuaded to surrender themselves to His Majesty's mercy.

  Since my arrival in Ireland I have been not a little alarmed to be told that I have fallen into the grave displeasure of His Majesty for having taken a town in Guiana [*San Thomé*] which was in the possession of the Spaniards.[7] When they heard this my men were so afraid of being hanged that they were on the point of forcing me to sail away again. With regard to the taking of the town, although I gave no authority for it to be done, it was nevertheless impossible to avoid because when the English were landed at night to secure Keymes's passage the Spaniards attacked them with the intention of destroying them, killing several and wounding many. Our companies thereupon fired at them and, pursuing them, found themselves inside the town before they knew it. It was at the entrance to the town that my son was killed, and when the men saw him dead they were so enraged that if the King of Spain himself had been there in person they would have shown him little respect. With regard to the burning of houses overlooking the Plaza [= *Square*] they were obliged to do it because the people had made loop-holes in the walls and kept up so hot a fire that in a quarter of an hour they would have killed them all.[8]

  And, my lord, that Guiana be Spanish territory can never be acknowledged for I myself took possession of it for the Queen of England by virtue of a cession by all the native chiefs of the country. That His Majesty knows this to be true is proved by the grant by him under the great seal of England to [Robert] Harcourt.⁹ Henry IV [of France], who also considered it a country not justly in the possession of any Christian prince, gave it to [Reneé Maree, Sieur de] Montbariot, and Xavarhere, his lieutenant, held it until, for lack support, he was captured and taken prisoner to Lisbon. Your lordship has a copy of the patent that Count Maurice and the States [General] gave to some Flemings who held part of the country for ten years until, by negligence, they were surprised and defeated by the Spaniards who are now again beginning to settle there. It will thus be seen that His Majesty has a better right and title than anyone.

I heard in Ireland that my enemies have declared that it was my intention to turn corsair and flee, but at the manifest peril of my life I have brought myself and my ship to England. I have suffered as many miseries as it was possible for me to suffer, which I could not have endured if God had not given me strength. If His Majesty wishes that I should suffer even more let God's will and His Majesty's be done, for even death itself shall not make me turn thief or vagabond, nor will I ever abuse the noble courtesy of the several gentlemen who gave sureties for me.¹⁰

    Your poor kinsman,
    W Ralegh

I beg your lordship will excuse me to my lords [of the Privy Council] for not writing to them. Want of sleep for fear of being surprised in my cabin at night has almost deprived me of my sight and some return of the palsy¹¹ which I had in the Tower has so weakened my hand that I cannot hold the pen.

Plymouth 1st June 1618

Sir: Since my arrival here I have been handed a copy of the statement given to your lordships against me.¹² They are bound to plead their own case: the truth is that all of them except [Sir] Warham St Leger wanted to turn thieves if they had a chance, but they were obliged to return. I myself was in manifest peril because I wished to return.

They say I lingered at Plymouth [on the outward journey]: they knew I would not have stayed there a day but for [awaiting] Pennington, St Leger, Bailey, Whitney and Wollaston.¹³ I entered Falmouth by reason of head winds and put into Ireland because of a heavy gale in which Chidley's pinnace and all her men were lost, and one of my boats driven into

Bristol. Of the provisions I obtained in Ireland they all had their share although they had credit there for their needs. The only things I got in the Canaries were a basket of oranges and three loaves of sugar sent to me by the countess of Gomera.¹⁴ Chidley was in no want of provisions for he brought a supply for eight months from his home in England,¹⁵ and [*on the return voyage*] the rest took great quantities from Ireland where, not knowing what vile accusations they had made against me, I used my influence with the Lord President [*of Munster, Sir Oliver St John*] that he should not send them as prisoners to England as he would otherwise have done. With regard to the sacking of San Thomé I have told you the truth in the other [*sic*] letters. In all they have said there is not one word of truth.

As for their last accusation that I was intending to abandon my country and bring them into trouble, if I had been so minded I could certainly have carried it out with their full consent, but I risked my life to oppose it. The fact of my having come here freely and unconditionally and cast myself on His Majesty's mercy is sufficient proof of my intention. If I had left here to live elsewhere because I had no pardon, why did I return. I only give your lordship a brief answer to the accusations. I hope to live to answer them to their [*lordships*] faces and to prove them [*the mutineers*] all cowards, liars and, in spirit, thieves.

I wrote this after having sealed the other letters and I pray you give a copy of them to my poor wife who, with the loss of her son and these rumours, I fear will go mad. I forgot to answer the third accusation in which they accuse me of having sacked the town before seeking the mine. I have already told your lordship the manner in which the men entered the town at night before they knew where they were and that they burned the part near the Plaza to save their lives, which probably they would not otherwise have done because thereby everything of value in those houses was burnt. But with regard to the rash assertion that the entering of the town and the burning of the houses was contrary to all my promises and undertakings, I shall be content to suffer death if [*it can be proved that*] I had any part or knowledge whatever of the burning or sacking. I knew nothing about it. It took place through the circumstances stated and I could not have protested against something which I had not anticipated. At the end of the accusation they say that it was done without their consent, and it is true that it was never proposed. But their desire to appear ignorant of the enterprize, whatever it was, is impudent for I never did anything without consultation. [*Captain John*] Pennington had a company there under his lieutenant and Chidley had one which he undertook to command himself but apparently did not dare to do. St Leger also had his company there. So it appears that they participated in the enterprize and were not ignorant of it, whatever it may have been.¹⁶

1. It is impossible to be precise about the date of this letter except that a Spanish translation was sent to Spain from London on 24 June: Ballesteros, op. cit., I, pp. 268–73. The *Destiny* arrived at Plymouth shortly before 14 June (*CSP Venetian 1617–19*, pp. 235, 241 and Ballesteros, p. 269) and Ralegh may have begun to write what was to be an unusually long letter while still at sea, having learned in Ireland of his likely reception in England. The copyist's date of 1 June is clearly a mistake, perhaps for 11 June, but certainly not for 21 June, the date favoured by Hume (op. cit., p. 388) and those who followed, right down to Harlow, *Last Voyage*, p. 86. Ralegh does not refer particularly to the royal proclamation which was dated 9 June (see below, note /) nor to the order to Sir Lewis Stucley, Vice-Admiral of Devon, to place him under arrest which was dated 12 June (T.N. Brushfield, *DAT* XXXVII, 1905, p. 28), the news of which, on or about the 14th, would have made him at least temporarily incapable of mounting such a reasoned defence. The aborted attempt to escape across the Channel occurred on or about 20 July.
2. While the text, having been translated twice, cannot do more than approximate to what Ralegh actually wrote, it does, on the whole, ring true, not only to form but also to his later, more official 'Apologies'.
3. The *Destiny* had reached Kinsale late in May.
4. Most of the manuscript evidence relating to Ralegh's second voyage to Guiana will be found in Harlow, *Last Voyage*, 1932, *passim*, except for the postscript to this letter which has hitherto been published in English only in Hume, loc. cit.
5. One of the Leeward Islands. It was here, on 21 March, that Ralegh's remaining captains learned of Keymis's suicide and deserted the *Destiny*, first contemplating piracy and then deciding to go home and make their tale good, which they did in a letter written on their behalf to the Privy Council: Harlow, op. cit., pp. 232–7.
6. There is some evidence that Ralegh was actually locked in his cabin during the Atlantic crossing.
7. It was not until 9 June, shortly before Ralegh reached Plymouth, that the King published a proclamation declaring his 'utter mislike and detestation of the ... insolences and excesses' committed by Ralegh's men at San Thomé and soliciting further reports (J.F. Larkin and P.L. Hughes (eds), *Stuart Royal Proclamations*, Oxford 1973, pp. 391–3), but news of Gondomar's growing success with the King must have been widely reported some time before.
8. This is confirmed by a Spanish source: Harlow, p. 168. The fires consumed a great quantity of tobacco.
9. In February 1609 Robert Harcourt received a royal commmission to explore part of Guiana; on 14 August he took formal possession of the Oyapok in the King's name and on 28 August was granted proprietory rights by letters patent: C.A. Harris (ed.), *A Relation of a voyage to Guiana*, Hakluyt Society LX, 1926, pp. 7, 10, 13.
10. See above, Letter 218, note 12.
11. The manuscript has 'perlesia'. Ralegh several times (e.g. Letters 224 and 225) complained of a swelling on his side but this paralysis in his hand, if that is what it was, sounds more like a minor stroke.
12. See note 5 above. Captain Edward Giles sent a copy to Lady Ralegh from Plymouth on 24 May: Trinity College, Cambridge, R.5.12, f. 170.
13. See Ralegh's 'Apologie', Harlow, *Last Voyage*, p. 318.
14. See above, Letter 217, where he tells his wife a slightly different story.

15. John Chudleigh's father, also John, a somewhat foolhardy adventurer, had died in the Straits of Magellan in 1589: Hasler I, p. 608.
16. It is not clear whether these three remained loyal to Ralegh, but Pennington, Sir John Ferne, and Samuel King were in command of three of Ralegh's ships which had reached Kinsale in Ireland by 24 March: *CCM 1603–24*, p. 123.

## 221. To King James [from Plymouth],[1] 16 June 1618

Centre for Kentish Studies, Maidstone, U269/1 Oo147, formerly one of the Sackville Papers at Knole Park, Surrey. Not hitherto published except from transcripts. Written by a clerk, addressed and signed, in a very shaky hand, by Ralegh.

Over 20 early transcripts, only one of them dated, including PRO, SP14/99/69i and 70, *CSPD 1611–18*, p. 576, two copies made in late September 1618 by one of the clerks of Sir Thomas Wilson, Ralegh's keeper in the Tower, and Bodleian, Eng. hist. d.138, dated 24 September 1618.

*Sceptick* 1651, p. 113; *Maxims* 1656; *Remains* 1657 etc.; John Prince, *Worthies of Devon*, 1701, 1810 edn, p. 676; Edwards II p. 368, from PRO; Bustamente, *El Conde de Gondomar*, 1928, pp. 99–100, from copy in Spanish at Simancas; Harlow, *Last Voyage* 1932, p. 277, from Bodleian; Ballasteros, *Correspondencio*, 1943, II, pp. 66–8, as Bustamente.

### AN ANSWER TO GONDOMAR'S COMPLAINTS

[*addressed*]   To the Kings most excellent Majestie
[*no contemporary endorsements*]

May it please your moste Excellent Majestie: If in my journey outwards bound I had [*some*] of my men murdered at the Ilands[2] and yet spared [= *declined*] to take revenge; if I did discharge some Spanish barkes taken, without any spoyle;[3] if I forbare all parts of the Spanish Indies wherein I might have taken twentie of their townes on the sea coste, and did only follow my enterprise which I undertooke upon Guiana, where (without any directions from me) a Spanish village [*San Thomé*] was burnt which was newly sett up within three miles of the mine; by your Majesties favour, I finde no reason why the Spanish embassador should complayne of me.

If it were lawfull for the Spaniards to murder twentie seven Englishmen,[4] tying them back to back and then cutting their throats, when they had traded with them a whole moneth, and came to them without so much as one sword amongst them all, and that it may not be lawfull for your Majesties subjects, being charged first by them, to repell force by force, wee may then justly say: O miserable English. If Parker and Moutam tooke

Campeche and other places in the Honduras, seated in the hart of the Spanish Indies,[5] burnt townes and killd the Spaniards and had nothing sayd unto them at their returne; and that my selfe forbare to looke into the Indies because I would not offend, I may justly say: O miserable Sir Walter Ralegh. If I have spent my poore estate, lost my sonne, suffered by sicknesse and otherwise a world of miseries; if I have resisted with the manifeste hazard of my life the roberies and spoyles which my companies would have made;[6] if, when I was poore, I could have made my selfe rich; if when I had gotten my libertie (which all men, and nature itselfe, do so much prise) I voluntarily lost it; if when I was master of my life I have rendred it agayne; if I might elsewhere have solde my shipp and goods,[7] and have putt five or six thousand pound in my purse, I have brought hir [the *Destiny*] into England;[8] I beseech your Majestie to beleeve that all this I have done because it should not be sayd to your Majestie that your Majestie had given libertie and trust to a man whose end was but the recoverie of his libertie and who had betrayed your Majesties trust.

My mutineers tolde mee that if I returned for England I should be undone, but I believed more in your Majesties goodnesse then in their arguments. Sure I am that I am the first that, being free and able to inrich myselfe, that [*sic*] hath embraced povertie and perill, and as sure I am that my example shall make me the last. But your Majesties wisdome and goodnesse I have made my judges, who have ever beene, and shall ever remayne, your Majesties

      Moste humble vasall,
      W Ralegh

16th Junii[9]

1. He was at Plymouth until the end of July. See also below, note 8, and Introduction, p. liii.
2. At Lanzarote and the Canary Islands on his outward voyage when he called in for water: Harlow, *Last Voyage*, p. 233.
3. On leaving Gomera on the outward voyage he returned two small Spanish ships: ibid.
4. During the fight for San Thomé: see above, Letter 218 and below, Letter 222.
5. William Parker, a privateer of Plymouth, was frequently in the West Indies. For his exploits in 1594 and 1595 see K.R. Andrews (ed.), *English Privateering Voyages 1588–95*, Hakluyt Society, Series 2, CXI, 1959, pp. 308–25. Moutam, whose name is quite clear, with slight variations, in the transcripts, has not been positively identified, but Parker's regular 'consort' was one Jeremias Raymond of Cherbourg.
6. Especially in Newfoundland: see above, Letter 220.
7. The goods were in the form of tobacco: see below, Letter 225.
8. His first port of call on his return to Europe had been Kinsale: Harlow, *Last Voyage*, p. 86.
9. I am grateful to Mr Carter of the Centre for Kentish Studies for kindly checking the text of this letter for me, the present owner being unwilling for it to be photographed.

## 222. To [Lord Carew,[1] late July/early August 1618][2]

Bodleian, Carte 77, ff. 41–2, a contemporary transcript.

Over twenty transcripts identified, including BL, Cotton, Vitellius C, XVII, ff. 439–40, badly damaged by fire.

Sir Walter Rawleigh, *Judicious and Select Essays*, 1650, p. 58; Birch 1751, II, p. 275; Cayley 1806, II, p. 117, amended; Edwards II, p. 375, from BL, Cotton, assuming it to be the original letter; Harlow, *Last Voyage*, 1932, p. 250, from Edwards.

## A SHORT DEFENCE

[*no address*]

[*endorsed*] The coppie of Sir Walter Raleigh his appologie [*sic*] to the Kinge [*sic*] at his returne from Guiana in July 1618

Because I knowe not whether I shall live to come before the lords [*of the Privy Council*] I have, for His Majestes satisfaction, sett downe as much as I can say, either for my owne defence or against my self as thinges are now construed.

It is true that though I acquainted His Majestie with my intent to land in Guiana, yet I never made it knowne to His Majestie that the Spaniards have any footing there,[3] neither had I authoritie by any patent to remove the Spaniards from thence. And theirfore His Majestie had noe interest in the attempt of [= *attack on*] St Thome by any fore knowledge in His Majestie.

But, knowing His Majestes title to the countrey to be the best and most Christian because the naturall [= *native*] lordes did most willingly acknowledge Queen Elizabeth to be their soveraigne, who by me promised to defend them from the Spanishe crueltye, I made noe doubt but I might enter the land by force, seeing the Spaniards had noe other title but force (the Popes donation excepted),[4] considering also that they gott a possession there divers yeares since my possession taken for the Crowne of England [*in 1595*]. For were not Guiana His Majesties, than [= *then*] might I aswell have bene questioned for a theife for taking the gold out of the King of Spaines mynes, as the Spaniards doe nowe call me a peacebreaker, for from any territorie confest to be the King of Spaines it is noe more lawfull to take gold than lawfull for the Spaniard to take tynne out of Cornewall. Nowe, were this possession of theirs a sufficient barre to His Majestes right, the Kinges of Spaine may aswell call themselves Dukes of Brittaine [= *Brittany*] because they held Bluets[5] and fortified there, and Kinges of Ireland because they possessed Smerike[6] and fortified there, and soe in other places. That His Majestie was well resolved of his right there I make no kinde of doubt because the Englishe both under Master Charles Leigh and Master Harcourt[7] had leave to plant and inhabit the countrey.

That Oronoque[8] it selfe [*would have*] had long ere this 5000 Englishe in it I assure my selfe, had not my imployment at Cales [= *Cadiz*] the next yeare after my returne from Guiana, and after that our jorney to the Islands, hindred me for those two yeares, after which Tyrones Rebellion made Her Majestie unwilling that any great number of shippes should be taken out of England till that rebellion were ended. And lastly, Her Majestes death and my long imprisonment gave tyme to the Spaniards to sett up a towne of sticks covered with leaves of trees upon the bankes of Oronoque which they call St Thome. But they have neither reconciled nor conquered any of the casiques or naturall lords of the countrey, which casiques are still in armes against them,[9] as by the Governors letteres to the Kinge of Spaine it may appeare. That by landing in Guiana there can be any breach of peace I think it, under favour [= *if I may say so*] impossible, for to breake peace where there is noe peace, it cannot be.

That the Spaniardes give us noe peace there it doth appeare by the Kinges letteres to the Governor that they should put to death all those Spaniard[s and] Indians that trade *con les Anglos inimicos*, with Englishe enemyes. Yea, those very Spaniards which wee encountred at St Thome did of late yeares murder 36 of Master Hales men of London and myne[10] who landed without weapon upon the Spaniard faith to trade with them. Master Thorne also, of Tower Streete in London,[11] besides many other Englishe, was in like sorte murdred in Oronoque the yeare before my deliverie out of the Tower.

Nowe, if this kinde of trade be peaceable there is than [*sic*] a peaceable trade in the Indies betweene us and the Spaniard, but if this be cruell warre and hatred and noe peace than [*sic*] there is n[o]e peace broken by our attempts.

Againe, howe does it stand with the greatnes of the Kinge of Spaine, first to call us enemyes when he did hope to cutt us in pieces, and than, having failed, to call us peacebreakers, for to be an enemye and a peacebreaker in one and the same action is impossible, but the Kinge of Spaine in his letter to the Governor of Guiana, dated at Madrill [*Madrid*] the 9th of March before we lefte the Thames calls us *Engleses inimicos*, English enemies. If itt had pleased the Kinge of Spaine to have written to His Majestie in 17[12] monethes tyme (for wee were soe long in preparing) and have made [= *let*] His Majestie knowe that our landing in Guiana would drawe after it [*a charge of*] a breach of peace, I presume to thinke that His Majestie would have stayed our enterprise for the present. This he [*the King of Spain*] might have done with lesse charge than to leavie 300 [*sic*] soldiers[13] and transport 10 pieces of ordinance from Porto Rico, which soldiers added to the garrison of St Thome, had they arrived before our coming, had [= *would have*] overthrowne our raw companies and there would have followed noe complaint.

For the maine point of landing neere St Thome, it is true that wee were of opinion that we must have driven the Spaniards out of theire towne before we could passe the thicke woodes upon the mountaine of the myne,[14] which I confesse I did first resolve, but better bethinking my self I referred the takinge of the towne to the goodnes of the myne, which, if they [*were*] found to be soe rich as it might perswade [= *argue*] the leaving of a garrison there, to drive the Spaniards thence, but to have it burnt was never my intent, neither could they give me any reason why they did it.[15]

Upon the[*ir*] returne I examined the Sergeant Major [*George Ralegh*] and [*Laurence*] Kemishe why they followed not my directions for the tryall of the myne before the taking of the towne and they answerd me that although they durst hardly goe to the myne leaving a garrison of Spaniards betweene them and their boates, yet they finde [*sic*: ?*followed*] their latter directions and did land betwcene the towne and the myne, and that the Spaniards, without any manner of parley, sett upon them unawares and charged them, calling [*them*] *Perros Engleses* [= *English dogs*],[16] and by skirmishing with them drew them on [*to*] the very entrance of the towne before they knewe where they were, soe as if any peace had bene in those partes the Spaniards first broke the peace and made the first slaughter, for as the Englishe could not but land to seeke the myne, being come thither to that end, soe being first reviled and charged by the Spaniards, they could doe no lesse than repell force by force.

Lastly, it is a matter of noe small consequence to acknowledge we have offended the King of Spaine by landing in Guiana. For first it weakens His Majesties title to the country or quitts it. Secondly there is noe king that hath ever given the least way to any other king or state in the traffique of the lives and goods of his subjects (to wit as in our case) that it shalbe lawfull for the Spaniards to murder us, either by force or treason and not lawfull for us to defend our selves and pay them with their owne coyne, for this proves superioritie and inferioritie which no absolute monarch ever yealded unto or ever will. Thirdly it shewes the English beares [*sic*] greater respect to the Spaniards and are more doubtfull of their forces than either the French or Dutch are who invade all partes of the Indies without being questioned at their returne. Yea at my nowe being at Plymouth a French gentleman called Flory went thence with 4 seale [= *sail*] and 300 land men [= *soldiers*] with commission to land, to burne and to sacke all places in the Indies that he could maister, and yet the French kinge married a daughter of Spain.[17]

This is all I can say other than that I have spent my poore estate, lost my sonne and my health and endured as many sortes of miseries as ever man did in hope to doe His Majestie service, and have not to my understanding committed any hostile acte other than entrance upon a territorie belonging to the Crowne of England, where the Englishe were first sett upon and slaine by the usurping Spaniardes. I invaded noe other partes of the Indies pretended [= *claimed*] by the Spaniards. I returned into England with the manifest perill of my life, with a purpose not to hold my life with any other acte than His Majesties grace, and from which noe man nor any perill could disswade me. To that grace and goodnes and kingelines I referre my selfe, which, if it shall finde that I have not yet suffred inough, it may please adde more affliction to the remaynder of a wretched life.

[*no signature transcribed*]

1. That the letter was intended for Lord Carew rests entirely on a statement of the editor of *Judicious and Select Essays*, 1650. It is, to say the least, likely that Ralegh would want to be sure that his one remaining friend in high places knew the gist of his defence and could pass it on to such of his fellow-members of the Privy Council as were inclined to listen.
2. See endorsement. None of the many copies carries an exact date but the original letter was almost certainly written before, or, more likely, shortly after Ralegh composed what became known as his *Apology* to King James (which it largely summarizes) at Salisbury, while under escort from Plymouth to London in late July 1618. He reached London early in August. For the text of the *Apology* see Harlow, *Last Voyage*, pp. 316–34.
3. He had certainly been frank about this in 1611: see above, Letter 205 (to Salisbury) and Letter 206 (to the Privy Council).
4. The bull of Pope Alexader VI of 1493 conferring the Indies, *inter alia*, on the King of Spain.
5. Blavet, the modern St Louis, a Spanish naval base in France.
6. The Spaniards landed at and fortified Smerwick on the south-west coast of Ireland in 1580.
7. For Leigh and Harcourt see above, Letters 217, note 20 and 220, note 9.
8. The land in Guiana either side of the Orinoco river.
9. Confirmed by Spanish records: see Harlow, *Last Voyage*, pp. 169, 178, 191, 227–8.
10. Cf. Letter 221 where Ralegh himself wrote 27, but it is possible to read it as 37.
11. Not identified.
12. Was this a reference to the period between his release from the Tower (19 March 1616) and his departure from Cork harbour on 19 August 1617?
13. On 19 August 1618, a Spanish contingent of 33, instead of the 50 called for, arrived in San Thomé from Santa Fé and Tunja: Harlow, *Last Voyage*, pp. 132–3 and 182–3.
14. Ralegh regularly refers to *one* mountain and *one* mine but seventeenth-century scribes are unreliable on final e and s, and too much cannot be read into their usage, especially in the case of transcripts.

15. It seems to have been a deliberate but pointless act.
16. BL, Harley 1576 reads *diegos Ingleses*.
17. Louis XIII married Anne of Austria in 1615.

---

## 223. To the Marquess of Buckingham from the Tower,[1] 12 August 1618

Bodleian, Tanner 74, f. 126. In Ralegh's hand.

*Cabala* 1654, pp. 308–9, edited; Oldys 1736, pp. CCxxi–ii, part only; Birch, 1751, II, pp. 387–9, from *Cabala*; *Works*, 1829, VIII, pp. 651–2, from Birch; Edwards II, pp. 373–4, from *Works*.

## A CRY FOR HELP

[*addressed*]   To the right honorable my singuler good lord the Marquise of Buckingame[2]

[*endorsed, at a later date*]   Sir Walter Raleigh to the Duke [*sic*]

If I presume to much I humble beseich your lordshipe to pardon me, especially in presuminge to write to so great and worthy a parson who hath byne tolde that I have don him wronge.[3] I herd it but of late, but most happy had I byne if I might have disproved that villanye agaynst me when ther had byne no suspicion that the desire to save my life had presented my excuse. But, my worthy lord, it is not to excuse my self that I now write. I cannot, for I have now offended my Soveraigne Lord, for all past [*sic*] even all the world, and my very enemies have lamented my loss, whom now, if His Majesties mercie alone do not lament, I am lost. Howsoever, that which doth comfort my sowle in this offence is that even in the offence it self I had no other intent than His Majesties service, and to make His Majestie know that my late enterprise was grounded upon a trewth, and which, with one shipp spedely sett out I ment to have assured or have died, being resolved as it is well knowne to have don it from Plymouth had I not byne restrayned.[4] Hereby I hoped not only to recover His Majesties gracious oppinion but to have destroyed all those mallignant reports which had byne spread of me. That this is trew that gentleman whom I so much trusted, my keiper,[5] and to whom I opened my hart, cannot but testifye, and wherin, if I cannot be beleeved living, my death shall wittness, yea, that gentleman cannot but avow it that when wee came back towards London I desired to save no other treasor than the exact discriptions of those places in the Indies.⁶

That I ment to go hence as a discontented man, God, I trust, and myne owne actions will disswade His Majestie, whom neither the loss of my estate, thirteene yeers imprissonment and the denial of my pardon could beat from his service. No,⁷ the oppinion of being accounted a foole, or rather distract[ed], by retur[n]ing as I did, ballanced with my love to His Majesties parson and estate, had no place att all in my hart. It was that last severe letter from my lords [*of the Privy Council*]⁸ for the speedy bringinge of me up, and the impatience of dishonor, that first putt me in feare of my life or [*of*] injoying it in perpetuall imprisonment, never to recover my reputation lost, which strengthened me in my late, and to late lamented, resolution. If His Majesties mercie do not abounde, if His Majestie do not pitty my age and scorne to take the extremest and uttermost advantage of my errors, if His Majestie, in his great charitie, do not make a difference betweene offences proceeding from a life havinge naturall impulsion without all ill intent, and those of an ill hart, and [*if*] that your lordshipp, remarkable in the world for the noblenes of your disposition, do not vouchsafe to become my intercessor, whereby your lordshipp shall bynde a hundred gentlemen of my kyndred to honour your memorie, [*then*] bynde me for all the time of that life which your lordshipp shall begg for me to pray to God that yow may ever prosper and ever bynde me to remaine your most humble sarvant,
    W Ralegh

From the Tower this 12 of August


1. Ralegh returned to the Tower on 10 August.
2. George Villiers (above, Letter 212) had become Marquess of Buckingham on 1 January 1618. His dukedom did not follow until 1623. He was currently promoting a Spanish alliance and was no longer, if he had ever been, a friend of Ralegh.
3. By twice attempting to flee the realm, Buckingham having supported his release on good behaviour, in 1616.
4. He had actually embarked and set sail for France, almost certainly with the full knowledge of his 'keeper', Sir Lewis Stucley (see note 5), but changed his mind and returned to Plymouth. For confirmation of his story that he hoped, with French help, to return to Guiana see Harlow, *Last Voyage*, p. 276.
5. Sir Lewis Stucley of Affeton in north Devon, Vice-Admiral of Devon, who kept Ralegh on a somewhat loose rein in Plymouth and on the journey to London in late July.
6. The inventory of his possessions, taken on his admission to the Tower, included 'one plott [*map*] of Guiana and Nova Regnia and another of the river of Orinoque'. He was also made to

hand over 'three sea cards [*charts*]' of the West Indies which he said he would not have parted with for £300: PRO, SP14/98/79, 103/67, *CSPD 1611–18*, pp. 565 and 589.
7. All previous editors have printed this as 'Nor' or 'And', but it is quite clearly 'No'. Ralegh is anxious to give the impression, with considerable justification, that he had not only returned to England but had aborted his two attempts to escape overseas of his own free will.
8. On 23 July, Stucley was ordered to bring Ralegh from Plymouth to London: *APC 1617–19*, p. 220. This marked the real beginning of his being in custody.

---

## 224. TO LADY RALEGH FROM THE TOWER, 18 SEPTEMBER 1618

PRO, SP14/99/9, *CSPD 1611–18*, p. 573, possibly an extract from a longer letter, copied for Sir Thomas Wilson,[1] with a note in his hand.

Edwards II, p. 370; Harlow, *Last Voyage*, p. 263.

## WEAK AND IN PAIN

[*headed*] 18 of September 1618[2]   Sir Walter Rawley to his lady by Ed[*ward*] Wilsons [*sic*]

I am sycke and weak. This honest gent[*leman*], Master Ed[*ward*] Wilson, is my keeper and takes much payne with me. My swolne syde[3] keeps me in perpetual paine and unrest. God comfort us.[4]

    Yours,

        W R

[*by Sir Thomas*]   Memorandum that I asked Master Secretarys co[*u*]nsell if I myght send Edward with the box of spiritts and cordialls.[5] He told me ther was noe danger to send to her [*Lady Ralegh*] but to observe what came from her. Yett I kept the boxe till I had talked with the apothecare.[6]

1. Sir Thomas Wilson, who was Keeper of State Papers, was put in charge of Ralegh on 10 September and he appointed Edward, possibly a relative, to act, in effect, as the prisoner's personal servant and, no doubt hopefully, his confidant: *CSPD 1611–18*, pp. 568 and 570.
2. On 15 September, Sir Thomas informed Sir Robert Naunton, the Principal Secretary, that Ralegh had asked that Edward be sent to see Lady Ralegh 'to see howe shee doeth'. He added 'I know him to be faythfull and Sir W. R. affects him already, and therby something may be found out': PRO, SP14/99/12.
3. On 12 September, Wilson reported that Ralegh was 'syck of a rupture' but the patient himself blamed his trouble on the King's Physician having applied fomentations 'too strong and too hot': Harlow, *Last Voyage*, p. 263.
4. On the same sheet is a copy of Lady Ralegh's reply that ''tis meerly sorrow and greaf that with wynd hath gathered into your syde': Edwards II, p. 370.

5. During his earlier incarceration Ralegh had occupied himself with chemical distillations and his laboratory had apparently been left comparatively undisturbed during his absence. They no doubt added both to the aura and to the suspicion with which he was regarded.
6. When Wilson asked some doctors to identify the spirits they replied that 'noe man in the world knowes what they are unless he had seen the extraction of them': PRO, SP14/99/48.

---

## 225. To Lady Ralegh from the Tower, 4 October 1618[1]

PRO, SP14/103/22 and 21 [sic], CSPD 1611–18, p. 583, a copy made for Sir Thomas Wilson.[2]

Edwards II, pp. 372 and 498.

## GUIANA RECKONING

[no address]
[headed]  Coppy of Sir W Raleghs lettere to his lady in answer of hers[3] touchinge his shipp called The Desteny[4]
[endorsed by Wilson as heading]

Yow have a note what the shipp cost, in which every perticuler is sett downe and it is signed by Master [*William*] Harbert.[5] The lyke note he hath of myne and signed by me. I gave yow myne att Plymouth with other writtings of Peningtons and Ferns.[6] As I remember the shipp and her furniture, to witt her cabells, ancors, sayles, ordnance, bulletts, powder, joyners worke, carving, paynting and all ells, doth amount unto 7000*li* or neare it, as yow may perceive by the inventory under my hand and Master Harberts hand.

And as I do remember Master Harbert hath disburssed towards his fourth part 11 hundred pounds. Yow say that hee demands [= *claims*] twelve and it may be true. Yow have also an inventory of all that is now remaining and belonging to the shipp. Yow have also a writing from C[*aptain John*] Pennington of the forth part of his shipp which I pray deliver to Sir Char[*les*] Snell,[7] to whome it belongs. Yow have also a writting from Sir John Ferne[8] to discharge me for 1700*li* which I was some way entangled for him, with whome I adventured of Master Harberts mony 200*li*. There is a paper booke which Samuel King[9] kept of all particulers of the shipp and to whome the mony was paide.

My sonn whome I have lost hath also signed that note, inventory and agreement betweene me and Master Harbert.[10]

    Your desolate husband,

        W R[11]

[*postscript*] When the shipp shalbe praysed Master Harbert is to have a fourth part wanting [= *less*] a thride, for he adventured 11 hundred [*pounds*] and the fourth part came to seventeene hundred or therabouts. And so, after that rate he is to have a 4th part as the shipp is praysed, deducted a third.

Ther is in the bottome of the sedar cheist [= *chest*] some paper bookes [*writings*] of myne. I pray make them up alltogether and send them me. The title of one of them is The Art of War by Sea.[12] The rest are notes belonging unto it.

Ther is amongst the litle glasses the powder of steele [= *iron*] and pumex [= *pumice*] for to stay the flux [= *dysentry*]. If you can finde it now, [*send it*], for I have a greevous loosenes and feare that it will turne to the bloddy flux.

Send some more bitony.[13]

[*added by Wilson*] My la[dy] Rawley hath noe other wrytings but only articles of agreement what parts of the goods or treasur gotten in the viag [*the adventurers*] shold have for furnishing or setting out the shypps, viz: Pennington 24*li* 6*s* of every hundred [*pounds*], Sir John Ferne 12*li* 6*s* [*and*] Sir Warham Sellenger 10*li* 6*d* on every hundred. They are ingrossed on parchment and signed and sealed by Sir Walter Rawley. She saith that all other things that are mentioned in this lettere wer delivered to Sir G[eorge] Calvert[14] and the chiests are with Alderman C[ockay]ne.[15]

1. See below, note 11.
2. See above, Letter 224, note 1.
3. Lady Ralegh's letter, which has not survived, reached Ralegh via Naunton, the Principal Secretary, who asked Wilson to give him details of Ralegh's reply for relay to the Privy Council: PRO, SP14/103/18–20.
4. Begun in April 1616 and launched on 16 December, the *Destiny*, 621 tons, had been built by Phineas Pett, the King's shipwright, at Woolwich and had cost Ralegh £2,500: W.G. Perrin (ed.), *Diary of Phineas Pett*, NRS, 1918, pp. 115–16. See also above, Letter 214.
5. See above, Letter 214, note 6.
6. See below, notes 7 and 8.
7. Of Kington St Michael in Wiltshire. According to Aubrey, Snell was one of the friends of Ralegh's youth, who sold land in order to build a ship for the voyage to Guiana: Clark (ed.), *Brief Lives*, 1898, II, pp. 183–4. She was the *Jason*, captained by John Pennington (see above, Letter 218), and, having served as Ralegh's 'vice-admiral', she was arrested in Ireland on orders from the King and handed over to the Spaniards as compensation for the burning

of San Thomé: *CSPI 1615–25*, p. 209. John Pennington, although he had not been at San Thomé, was jailed: ibid., p. 562.
8. Sir John Ferne was a hardened privateer who had himself sailed with a French commission: see above, Letter 218. His *Flying Hart* was also arrested in Ireland but he had friends in high places: Harlow, *Last Voyage*, pp. 203, 274 and 279.
9. Captain of Ralegh's flyboat, the *Supply*. He had twice commissioned ships to carry Ralegh to France. He was later to place on record his version of how Ralegh was 'betrayed', the text of which was printed two hundred years later (*Works*, 1829, I, p. 513), although the original manuscript cannot now be traced.
10. Ralegh's own *Destiny* was also confiscated by the King but Lady Ralegh was compensated to the tune of £2,250. William Herbert was awarded £750 which was withdrawn to pay for tobacco taken or destroyed at San Thomé: *CSPD 1619–21*, p. 428 and *APC 1619–21*, pp. 177–8. Meanwhile, Phineas Pett failed to recover what he reckoned was owed to him: Perrin, op. cit., p. 218.
11. Presumably to save time, Wilson sent Naunton Ralegh's original letter, which has not survived, for he asked to have it back so that he could take it to Lady Ralegh and 'gett those wrytings he saith she hath concerning the ship': PRO, SP14/103/18–20. Having taken this, copy Wilson may well have left the original with Lady Ralegh, who probably destroyed it, though it was hardly incriminating.
12. This was seen by Wilson who, on 2 November 1618, advised its seizure, but only fragments have survived: PRO, SP14/103/67, BL, Cotton Titus B, VIII, f. 21 and Dr Williams's Library, Jones B60. See P. Lefranc, *Sir Walter Ralegh Écrivain*, pp. 596–601.
13. *Stachys betonica*, recommended by the herbalist John Gerrard for rupture: see above, Letter 224, note 3.
14. Sir George Calvert, one of Robert Cecil's secretaries who became Clerk to the Privy Council in 1609 and, after the death of Winwood, Assistant Secretary of State. One of the many English Catholics interested, as investors, in colonial projects, he had served in Ireland and been an 'undertaker' there: D.B. Quinn, *England and the Discovery of America*, 1974, pp. 393–4.
15. Sir William Cockayne, a London merchant/financier, best known for his ambitious attempt in 1614 to manipulate the English cloth industry.

---

## 226. TO KING JAMES FROM THE TOWER, 4 OCTOBER 1618[1]

Archivo General de Indias, Simancas, E 2597, f. 96, being a translation into contemporary Spanish of a now missing original or contemporary transcript. What is printed below is a new translation from the Spanish text.[2]

J.A. St John, *Life of Sir Walter Ralegh*, 1868, II, pp. 331–3, translated, somewhat freely, from Simancas E 2597; Harlow, *Last Voyage*, pp. 280–81, from St John.

## NEGOTIATIONS WITH FRANCE

[*no address or heading survives*]

Sir: Having by Your Majesty's express command been many times questioned, both as concerning the commission from France to put to sea and the hopes of aid which the French had promised me, I have always feared to tell the truth of this business lest I should cause pain and trouble to those who promised me many good things and afterwards wished for my liberation. But seeing that Your Majesty would very much like to know the truth and would command me most strictly that I should put it all in writing for you, now, to keep Your Majesty no longer in suspense and doubt of the truth, and seeing myself bound in conscience to give satisfaction to my king and natural sovereign and to none other (hoping that, inasmuch as I have always desired to give him satisfaction in this, so he will have compassion on my hard and cruel state and on my old age), I will speak the truth to Your Majesty.[3]

I received a commission from the Duke de [*Montmorency*], Admiral of France, to put to sea. This was given to me by a Frenchman named Faggio [= *Faige*] who told me that the French ambassador, Monsieur des Marets [= *Le Clerc*] would favour me with his letters to the Duke de [*Montmorency*] for this purpose.[4]

And as for the other point on which Your Majesty desires greatly to know the truth, I will declare it. It is true that a French gentleman called [*Monsieur de la Chesnee*][5] came three times to see me, the first in [*Brentford*] and the other two in my house in London,[6] where, on each of these three times he assured me on behalf of the French 'agent' that he would give me every assistance and favour to escape to France, would find me a vessel for this purpose and would furnish me with very favourable letters so that certain French gentlemen should cause me to be very well received by the Most Christian King [= *Louis XIII*], and to be honourably employed by him so that I should have every favourable occasion to be most contented and satisfied. And the third time the agent himself came in person to me to confirm all these things, and, to tell Your Majesty the truth, seeing that my enemies had great power to harm me in this kingdom, I resolved to make the effort to save myself by whatever means. And for this I pray Your Majesty with all humility to pardon me, begging you to have compassion on me, for that, if it pleases Your Majesty to grant me life, even in prison, I will disclose matters of great service to the state, whence much wealth and advantage will result,[7] while my death can but give satisfaction to all who seek it with such violent haste, contrary to the natural disposition of Your Majesty, who has always been inclined towards goodness and clemency.

And these alone are all the hopes I have in this world, which will cause me to pray to God to give Your Majesty as much happiness as I desire for myself, being, Sir, Your Majesty's most humble and unhappy subject and vassal,

        W Ralegh

From the Tower of London, 5 October 1618

1. The date on the Spanish translation. St John, followed by Harlow, seems to have assumed that the Spanish translator would have replaced Ralegh's old style date but there is no precedent for this: cf. above, Letters 220 and 221. Harlow (op. cit. p. 277) confused this with Letter 221, but this was before the discovery of the original Letter 221 dated 16 June. On 4 October, Wilson wrote to say that he despaired of getting anything more out of the prisoner and asked to be released: Harlow, op. cit. p. 284. This was possibly Ralegh's cue for bypassing him.
2. The editors are indebted to various friends and colleagues, including Dr Richard Hitchcock of the University of Exeter, for help with the translation. Inevitably, having been translated twice, the present English text will only be an approximation of what Ralegh actually wrote.
3. For Ralegh's two previous letters to the King which were forwarded in late September by Sir Thomas Wilson (see above, Letters 224 and 225), which seem not to have survived in any form: see Harlow, *Last Voyage*, pp. 272–6. The three letters provide ample corroboration of Ralegh's frequent assertion that his dealings with the French were known to King James.
4. See above, Letter 215.
5. David de Novion, Sieur de la Chesnaye, a member of the French ambassador's staff: *APC 1617–19*, p. 261.
6. He lived in Lady Ralegh's house in Broad Street in the city of London from his arrival in the capital in late July until he was committed to the Tower on 7 August: see above, Letter 217, note 19 and *CSPD 1611–18*, p. 565.
7. At this point he was probably thinking in particular of his knowledge of the New World and of the Spanish presence there, but see also below, Letter 227, note 1. Certainly as late as 21 October some of those around the Court thought his chances of survival to be good: PRO, SP14/ 103/14, *CSPD 1612–18*, p. 586.

---

## 227. TO KING JAMES FROM THE TOWER, [?BETWEEN 24 AND 28 OCTOBER 1618][1]

Dr Williams's Library, Jones B 60, f. 229, a seventeenth-century transcript of part of a lost original, hitherto unpublished.

## SOMETHING TO SAY

[*headed*] Fragmentes of Sir Walter Raleighes

For weere it not out of a singuler devotion to doe Your Majestie service I take it (under [= *with*] Your Majesties gracious pardon) for a libertie *mal entendu* [= *unintended*] to be removed out of this steddy tower into a rowling shipp,[2] to change the dyett of soft bread and fresh meat for hard biskett and salt beife, to drinke unsavory water in steed of wyne and beare and to disorder an aged, worne and weake bodie with watching, travell and [the] distempered heat of the Indies, besides a world of other harmes and hazardes. For the rest (most renowned soveraigne) I most humbly beseech Your Majestie to conceive that I never had any hidden or any dishonest intention in this point.

There have bene in all ages some that have risen againe after a civill death. Yea, wee have of them now liveing which take them selves to be honest men and so beleive of them. Why they may not write while they lyve in Nature I knowe not, if by writing they may serve their countrie and be profitable to others.³ They are dead in charitie that thinke the contrary and to be numbred amongst those *qui gloriantur in malitia* of whome I have spoken before.

/To⁴

1. The note of desperation points to a date very late in his last incarceration. It was on 24 October 1618 that Ralegh knew that he was to be executed and on the 28th that he was removed from the Tower: Stebbing, 1899, pp. 364–5. Although suffering physically at this time, his mind was still clear. See also below, note 3.
2. Presumably referring to his release to go on his second voyage to Guiana, during which he had suffered particular hardship: see above, Letter 217.
3. Was this more than a vain hope that he could gain at least a temporary reprieve by persuading the King that he had important matters to report? As late as 21 October, contemporary observers believed that he could still save himself by revealing incriminating evidence against the Earls of Suffolk and Salisbury: PRO, SP14/103/45, *CSPD 1611–18*, p. 586.
4. Suggesting continuation on next page, but what follows on pp. 230 *et seq.* is clearly from Ralegh's other writings.

---

## 228.  To [?Queen Anne from the Tower, ?late October 1618]¹

[John Donne (ed.)], *Collection of letters made by Sir Tobie Mathews [sic]*, 1660, pp. 65–6. Edwards II, pp. lxvii–lxviii, doubting letter's authenticity.²

## DECLARATION OF LOYALTY

[heading]  Sir Walter Rauleigh to King James, which seemes rather to acknowledge favours than to desire them

May it please Your Majesty:³ My sad destiny hath been such that I could never present Your Majesty but with a prospect upon my complaints and miseries, in stead of doing you services which might have been acceptable to you. I have not spared my labour, my poor estate and the howerly hazard of my life, but God have otherwise disposed of all, and now end the dayes of my hope. I must nevertheless, in this little time which I am to live, acknowledge and admire your goodnesse and in all my thoughts, and even with my last breath, confesse that you have beheld my affliction with compassion. And I am yet in nothing so miserable as in that I could never meet [= *face*] an occasion wherin to be torn in pieces for [= *driven mad to perform*] Your Majesties service.

    I, who am still your, etc.

        [*no signature*]

1. The date of this letter is entirely conjectural. It seems to refer to failure in services attempted, i.e. after his return from the second voyage to Guiana, and his anticipation of death suggests late October, although if it was a 'last letter' one would have expected to find other copies. Ralegh's reference to his 'affliction' links it with Letter 222 (July/August), but he is clearly no longer acting a pretence. All things considered, a date late in October 1618 seems the most likely.
2. That it was not a forgery is indicated by the relaxed tone, one which Ralegh himself was quite capable of assuming when he knew his situation was hopeless. A forger would have introduced more bravura or more despair.
3. In spite of its heading, which could well have been an editorial assumption, was it perhaps addressed to Queen Anne, who had certainly been Ralegh's friend? This might explain his failure to mention the loss of his son, which he usually included with the loss of his health and his estate, a tactful omission in view of the death of Prince Henry. Its elegance, which must have been its main appeal to its collector, makes it an appropriate piece of Ralegh's epistolary prose with which to end this collection.

# APPENDIX 1

### 31a. To Master [James] Gold from the Court, 10 October [1589][1]

Present location unknown. From J.P. Collier, 'Some letters and documents of the time of Elizabeth I', privately printed, 1869, pp. 52–1.[2] The spelling suggests, as might be expected, that it was in Ralegh's hand.

## AN INDISCRETION IN IRELAND

[*endorsed*]   Sir Walter Rawley, xiv [*sic*] October

Master Gould [*sic*]:[3] I have it from my cussen Sir George Carewe[4] that you have harknd to a malicious knave, on Nebucodonozer Jewell,[5] who sayth that I have bin to forward with your daughter. He [*is*] one of my undertakers, a phello[6] that oweth me mich, and this he sayth, I kno not for what reson, but it is fales[7] and I pray you to suppress it as mich as you are able, for your sake and for your daughters, a gentle-wo[*man*] I swear before the [ever- *crossed out*] living God whom I have ever held in trew honor and respect.

If you desier a leass of Castle [*illegible*] in my seignory[8] as [*I*] have hard yow wold, I will have the papers drawn for you this Michaelmas. I have written to my Lord Deputy[9] for your sute against Donogh McCormac[10] and the othe[r]s and will put an end to ther cavellations [= *quibbling*].[11] I cum not into Irland for my nireness to Her Majestie[12] makes me mich busnes hire. I pray you look not for me.

   Your frinde as I shal finde yow,
      From the Court[13] this xth day of October
         W Ralegh

Cummend me to the gentlewoman your daughter

1. Ralegh was in Ireland in the summer of 1589, probably from early August, the Court gossip being that he had been 'chased ... from the Court' by the Earl of Essex: see Letter 33. He was at Lismore with Sir George Carew (see below, note 4) in late September (*CCM 1589–1600*, pp. 11–13) and still there on 1 October when, witnessed by Carew, he granted to his 'servant', Robert Maple gentleman, the stewardship of his castle, manor, lands and liberties of Lismore: Chatsworth, Devonshire Collection, Lismore Papers, I, 6a. He returned to London a few days later accompanied by his friend, the poet, Edmund Spenser (W. Maley, *Spenser Chronology*, 1994, pp. 52–3) and probably also by Carew. The date of the endorsement of the letter to Judge Gold cannot have been that of its receipt and is presumably that of its arrival at one of the posts.

2. The immediate source of the text, and most of the annotation, is a transcript made by Agnes Latham in the early 1980s, found among her papers after her death. In spite of exhaustive searches no copy of the pamphlet, which she describes as 'rare', has been found by the present editor and until one is discovered the authenticity of this letter must remain in doubt. The name of J.P. Collier, the notorious Victorian forger of literary manuscripts, must also arouse suspicion, but that Ralegh's mistress was a Miss 'Goold' (or 'Gold'), and that her daughter by Ralegh was in Ireland, were not known until the discovery of Ralegh's will in 1971 (see below, note 7), which Collier cannot have seen, virtually rules out the possibility of a forgery by Collier. According to Agnes Latham, Collier states that he had the original from 'a gentleman'.

3. James Gold of Cork, Attorney-General of Munster, was shortly to be appointed second Justice of the province: *CSPI 1588–92*, p. 255. He had been one of those commissioned by the Crown to survey the lands confiscated from the Earl of Desmond and other rebels for distribution among the English undertakers: *CSPI 1586–9, passim*. Ralegh no doubt knew him well and had probably stayed in his house in Cork.

4. Sir George Carew (see above, Letters 32 and 33), had been a soldier in Ireland since 1574 and Master of the Ordnance there since February 1588: Hasler I, p. 539–40. His cousinage with Ralegh was on his mother's side: Vivian, *Devon*, p. 162.

5. In her original transcript Agnes Latham first wrote and crossed out 'W[*illia*]m Maryes', and omitted this in her fair copy. Jewel's name is on a list dated 12 May 1589 of Ralegh's copyhold tenants in Co. Waterford: *CSPI 1588–92*, p. 170. The surname was very common in Elizabethan Devon.

6. Cf. above, Letter 45.

7. Cf. Ralegh's Will made in 1597 (Appendix 2) in which he makes provision for his 'reputed daughter begotten on the bodye of Alice Goold now in Ireland'.

8. Ralegh had been granted a seigniory of 42,000 acres in 1587: Quinn, 1962, p. 13.

9. Sir William Fitzwilliam had succeeded Sir John Perrott as Lord Deputy in 1588: Bagwell III, p. 167.

10. Donagh MacCormack was in possession of certain land which had been leased to Master Justice Gold by Cahir MacDonagh, father of Donagh MacCahir, the lawful heir: *CCM 1589–1600*, p. 26.

11. Cf. above, Letter 33.

12. Cf. above, Letter 33, for Ralegh's use of the same striking phrase at about the same time.

13. Ralegh's usual London address for correspondence from 1583 to 1592. For a subsequent reference by Ralegh to his daughter, see above, Letter 165.

# APPENDIX 2

## Sir Walter Ralegh's Will, 8–10 July 1597[1]

Sherborne Castle, Dorset. Parchment, 79 cm × 60 cm.

In the hand of a clerk, with signature in Ralegh's hand, the following signing as witnesses: Adrian Gilbert,[2] William Strode,[3] Christopher Harris[4] and John Meere.[5]

Not hitherto printed in full, but there are extracts in A.M.C. Latham, 'Sir Walter Ralegh's Will', *Review of English Studies*, New Series XII, 86, May 1971, pp. 129–36 and short passages in J.W. Shirley, *Thomas Harriot*, Oxford 1993, pp. 235–8.

IN THE NAME of God the father, the sonne and holye ghoste, three persons and one God, the eighth daye of Julye *anno domini* 1597.

I, Walter Raleghe, of Colliton Raleghe in the countye of Devon,[6] knighte, Captaine of Her Majesties Garde and Lord Warden of the Stanneryes in the countyes of Devon and Cornewall, acknowledging that all fleshe ys grasse and that the daye of our birthe ys the firste steppe to death, though the hower be uncertaine when the spiritt shall retorne to the Lord that gave it, doe ordeyne, declare, and make this my laste will and testament in manner and effecte followinge:

FIRST I humblye restore my sole to that moste blessed and indivisible Trinitye, one God most gloryous, almightye and eternall, on whome by mercye and grace I firmelye relye, by faithe, for the remissyon of my sinnes, and diligentlye attende [= *await*], by grace everlastinge, unspeakable and most comfortable heavenlye blisse. As for my bodye, I will it be bestowed with all due rightes apperteyninge to the same, by the discretion of my executors or my deere frindes my overseers of this my last will.[7]

AND as concerninge all my signioryes, honours, castells, mannors, landes, tenementes and heredytamentes within the realme of Ireland,[8] my will is that my brother [*sic*] Adryan Gilberte shall have yssuinge out of the same one yearlye rent [*charge*] of one hundred poundes of currant Englishe moneye during the tearme of the naturall liffe of the said Adryan Gilberte, payable at the feaste of St Michell Tharkangell and Thannunciation of our Blessed Ladye, St Mary the Virgin, yearelye, by even and equall portions duringe the said tearme. And which said signioryes ... [*etc.*] I will and bequeath to Walter Ralegh esquire,[9] my son and heire apparant, and to his heirs, for ever, PROVIDED ... [*that Adrian receive his annuity*]. And my will ys that all my said signiories, ... [*etc.*] within the said realme of Ireland and all other my landes, tenementes and heradytamentes of inherytance[10] within the realme of England, of what nature soever they be of [sic], shalbe to the heires males of my bodye lawfully begotten, and for defaulte of such yssue ... to Dame Elizabeth, my now wiffe, for tearme of her liffe, and after her deccase to the right heires of me the said Sir Walter Raleghe.

AND as touchinge my tearme or tearmes for yeares in that Castell, lordshippes, mannors, landes, libertyes and hundreds of Sherborne, Newland, Casteltowne, Wotton, Whitefeild, Yetminster and Candell Bishoppe in the countye of Dorset or Somerset, and all other landes, tenementes, rentes, profittes and hereditamentes within the hundredes of Sherborne and Yetminster or anie of them, late parcell of the possessions of the bishiprike of Sarum, or of anie other person or persons whatsoever,[11] I will and bequeathe the occupation and profitt thereof [sic] to the said Dame Elizabeth, my wiffe, untill my said sonne, Walter Ralegh (or, yf he dye, to anie other my heire of my bodye, male or female, to whome the same, by this my last will and testament, shalbe bequeathed) shalbe marryed or accomplishe the full age of one and twentye yeares, if the said Elizabeth shall soe longe lyve.

AND my will is that at the tyme of my said sonnes or heires marryage aforesaid, or at such time as my said sonne or anie my heire aforesaid shall accomplyshe the age of one and twentye yeares aforesaid or at the tyme of the death of the said Elizabeth, or at either of the said tymes first happeninge, that then my said tearme or tearmes of yeares of the said Castle ... [etc.] shalbe and remaine to my said sonne, Walter Raleghe, for, by and duringe all the said severall tearmes then to come or unexpired of and in the same.

Item: As touchinge my lease, tearme and intereste for yeares to me granted by our soveraigne Ladye the Queenes Majestie that nowe ys, by Her Highnes letters patentes under the Greate Seale of England, of full power, libertye, interest and aucthoritye concerninge the grauntinge and erectinge, geevinge or makinge, of licences for the utteringe, retaile or [whole]sayle, of wynes, and keepinge of tavernes throughout Her Majesties realme of England and domynions of Wales,[12] with all my rentes, revenewes, yearlye sommes, profittes, and comodityes for, or in respect [of], or anie wise touchinge or concerninge, the same licences and makinge and grauntinge of licences as aforesaid, I declare my will and testament to be, and I geeve, legate, and bequeathe my said tearme of yeares in and concerninge the same licences and makinge of licences and all my rentes, revenues, yearely soomes and paymentes, and all counterpartes of licences, bondes, obligations and other escriptes and assurances to me or to my use made concerninge the same in anie degree, to my said sonne Walter Raleghe. But neverthelesse to thintentes, meaninges, uses, purposes, and effectes followinge: that ys to saye to thende, use, and intent, and my will ys, that my said wiffe shall yearelye and yeare by yeare have and receave in, uppon, and by the rentes or yearelye paymentes reserved or granted for and in respecte of the said licences, the yearelye soome of fyve hundred poundes, at the feastes of St Michaell Tharkangell and of Thannunciation of Our Lady St Marye, by even portions at the handes of my overseers untill my said sonne shalbe marryed or shall or maye by computation of tyme come to thage of xxi yeares, yf he shall soe longe lyve. And after my said sonne shalbe, or might be, by computation of tyme, of full age, that then my said wiffe shall have and receave the said yearelye soome or payment at the feastes aforesaid duringe my tearme therein, yf shee shall soe longe lyve, by the handes and deliverye of my said sonne, in, by and out of the said yearlye rentes, soomes and anuall paymentes reserved, graunted, or agreed uppon, for, touchinge, or in respect of the said licences, allwais willinge, ordeyninge, and my full mynde ys, that my said overseers shall have the orderinge, usance, and goverment of my said tearme, right, and interest for the grauntinge of licences as is aforesaid for thuse and benifitt of my said sonne. And for the payment and discharge of the said yearelye soome of fyve hundred poundes to my said wiffe uppon accompt to my said sonne to be made untill my said sonne be married or be of full age, and noe longer.

And I geeve, dispose, and bequeathe all that cheefe messuage or tenement and all such messuages, tenementes, landes, and hereditamentes as I have or ought or shall or maye have in possession, reversion, or remainder, with there rightes, members, and appertenances, in Haselberye Plucknet in the countye of Somerset,[13] unto the said Elizabethe my wiffe duringe all my tearme and intereste therein, yf shee shall soe longe lyve, provided allwais that shee shall not falle [= *fell*], cutt downe, waste, nor distroye the tymber, woodes nor coppices standinge or growinge uppon the same fearme or tenementes or anie of them, all which said woodes and coppices I geeve and devise to my said sonne or his assignes. And yf my wiffe shall happen to dye before thend and expiration of the said tearme, then I geeve and dispose the same lease, ... [*etc.*] in Haselberye Plucknett aforesaid, in the same lease, estate, or tearme mentioned, unto my said sonne Walter Raleghe and his assignes.

ITEM, I will, devise, and bequeathe to my said sonne the lease of Spilmane, Her Majesties Juillers, house neere Durham House, London,[14] and all the estate, tearme of yeares, and demaunde [= *issues*] therewith, to reedeeme twoe greate flagons of silver gilte wayinge six and twentye poundes, eight ounces, or there aboutes. Allsoe twoe great silver pottes, guilte, of the same suite [= *pattern*], wayinge twentye poundes, ten ounces or thereaboutes and one silver bason and one ewer wayinge xxvii$^{en}$ poundes or thereaboutes, the which I allsoe geve to my said sonne Walter Raleghe. I geeve allsoe to my said sonne Walter one bed steede of mother [*of*] perele and one chyna [= *Chinese*] bed of silke ymbrodered with silke and china gould, with the bedsted guilte, and furniture thereto belonginge, and eight peeces of my richest hanginges havinge my armes on them. AND moreover I geve and bequeath to my said sonne Walter Raleghe one suite of porcelane [= *porcelain*] sett in silver and gylt, that ys to saye, two basons and eweres with twoe flaggons and twoe boles sutable [= *to match*], willinge and appointinge hereby that yf my said sonne shall happen to dye without heire of his bodye before he be of full age, that then my right honorable good frinde Sir Roberte Cecill[15] shall have the said whole suite of porcelane soe bequeathed to my sonne.

AND further I geve to my said sonne the moyetye of all my plate, bedinge, householdstuffe, furniture of house, jewels, my wyves [= *wife's*] perls excepted, and the other moyetye I doe give and bequeathe, togeather with my wives perles aforesaid, unto the said Elizabeth, my nowe wiffe, provided allwais, and my meaninge ys, that yf my said sonne shall happen to dye before he be married or of full age, and have noe heire of his bodye, that then the said Elizabeth my wiffe shall have all the residue of my said plate, beddinge, household stuffe, furniture of house and jewels.

ITEM, the Statutes [*Staple*] of my lord of Huntington[16] and of Sir John Throkemorton deceased,[17] and one obligation of fyve hundred poundes of the nowe Earle of Derbye,[18] I will that the benifitt thereof shalbe ymployed by my overseers of this my last will and testament to the payment of my debtes, and the remaine [*sic*] thereof to be devided betweene the said Elizabeth my wiffe and the said Walter Ralegh my sonne, prayinge my said overseers that they will take and have a specyall care that such soomes of moneye as shall yearelye and from tyme to tyme be receaved by them maye be converted to a reasonable profitt and benifitt for the use and behouffe [= *benefit*] of the said Walter Raleghe my soone untill he shalbe marryed or accomplishe the age of xxi yeares.

ITEM: I will, ordeyne, and appointe that soe soone as my debtes are paid and dulye discharged, without fraude or delayed practise, which I specyallye will and earnestlye require be not attempted nor used in anie sorte, that then Thomas Harryott of London, gent[*leman*],[19] shall yearlye at the feastes of St Michaell Tharkangell and of Thanunciation of Our Ladye the Virgin, duringe my said tearme graunted for or in respecte of the makeinge of licences for the sale or retayle of wynes and keepinge of tavernes aforesaid, yf the said Thomas Herryott [*sic*] shall soe longe lyve, have, and receave out of said rentes, revenues, and paymentes touchinge the said licences, one anuitye or yearelye soome of one hundred poundes, by the handes of such persone and persons as by this my last will shall or ought to have the rule, estate, and goverment of the said tearme concerninge the said licences accordinge to the purporte and trewe meaninge hereof. Moreover I geeve to the said Thomas Harryott all my bookes and the furniture in his owne chamber and in my bedchamber in Durham House, togeather with all such blacke suites of apparell as I have in the same house.

ITEM: I will and ordeyne that all those my three partes in the shippe called The Robucke,[20] with her ancores, tackle and furniture, and all my artylerye and greate ordinance therein, shalbe sold by my said overseers, and of the moneye and profittes there uppon risinge I will that my reputed daughter begotten on the bodye of Alice Goold, now in Ireland,[21] shall have the soome of fyve hundreth markes [£333 6s. 8d.]; that Thomas Harryott shall have twoe hundred poundes; allsoe Lawrence Kemishe[22] one hundred poundes. And I will that the residue of the moneye and profittes of the said shippe, with furniture [= *gear*] and ordynance, shalbe ymployed, converted, and bestowed by my said overseers towardes and for the payment of my debtes.

ITEM: I geeve to Sir Arthur Throkemorton my beste horse and my best saddle with the furniture; to Sir George Carewe[23] my next best horse and saddle, and to Alexander Brett my longe blacke velvett cloake now in my wardrobe at Durham House. And I geeve to my lovinge kinsman Arthur Gorges my best rapyer and dagger, and I clearelye and freelye acquite, release, and discharge him of and for all debtes and soomes of moneye to me by him due in anie sorte.[24]

PROVIDED and my further will ys, concerninge all my leases, ... [*etc.*] within the hundreds of Sherborne and Yetminster aforesaid, ... [*that in the event of his son Walter dying unmarried or a minor, remainder to go to Sir Walter's eldest male heir, then to his heirs female and then to his wife, Elizabeth*] and after her deathe to such person or persons as I, the said Sir Walter Ralegh, shall nomynate or appointe in writinge subscribed with my signe or hand writinge.²⁵

PROVIDED allsoe and my will ys that soe longe as I, the said Sir Walter Ralegh, or my soone Walter Raleghe, have anie yssue of either of our bodyes, the said Elizabethe my wiffe shall not make anie grauntes by copie of courte role, by her selfe or anie of her officers, of anie of the premisses laste bequeathed, nor shall disparke my parke of Sherborne or plough upp anie parte of the same parke, or comitt anie wilfull waste, spoyle or distruction in the said Castell or in other the premisses or newe erected buildinges in the said parke, gardens, orchardes, walkes, fishe pondes, conduit pipes of lead, tymber, trees, newe planted trees or hedges in the same parke, nor shall take anie woodes or under woodes out of the severall groundes inclosed called by the name of Honycombe woodes, Thornye Leaze, Whitefeild woodes or Candell woodes,²⁶ parcell of the premisses.

PROVIDED allsoe and my will ys wheresoever I have bequeathed by this my will to my said sonne Walter Raleghe anie legacye or legacyes of anie goodes and chattells, jewels, plate, bedinge and household stuffe (the leases ... [*etc.*] in the hundredes of Sherborne and Yeatminster aforesaid onlye excepted), ... [*further details regarding residuary legatees*].

ITEM, I geeve to my servant John Meere of Casteltowne aforesaid one annuall or yearelye rent of twentye poundes of currant English moneye, to be paid him yearelye out of and from my mannors, landes and tenementes in Sherborne aforesaid, at the fower most usuall feastes and tearmes of the yeare, by even and equall portions, duringe all my tearme that I have yet to come amonge other thinges of and in my mannors of Sherborne aforesaid, yf the said John Meere soe long shall lyve, charginge and requiringe him hereby that he doe contynue like faithfull and diligent servant to my said wiffe and sonne as he hath byn to me, and with all [*sic*] by all diligent care to be aiding unto my said wiffe and sonne for the better effectinge of this my last will and testament, accordinge to my true meaninge.²⁷

All the reste of my goodes, shippinge, ordynance, debtes, and chattells whatsoever they be, not alreadye geven and bequeathed, I doe geeve and bequeath to the said Walter Ralegh my sonne when he shalbe marryed or accomplish the age of xxi yeares, ... [*with remainder to any other of Sir Walter's heirs and then to*] Elizabeth my wiffe.

AND I doe ordeyne and make the said Walter Ralegh my sonne the executor of this my last will and testament, ... [*and in default, Sir Walter's next heirs and then his wife, Elizabeth*]. AND I doe further ordayne and make my trustye and faithfull frindes Arthur Throkemorton of Pawlersburye in the countye of Northampton knight,²⁸ George Carewe of London, knight, Alexander Brett of Whitechurche in the county of Dorset, esquire²⁹ and Thomas Harryott of London, gent[*leman*], aforesaid, the overseers of this my last will and testament. AND my will and desire ys that they will take the admynistration of all my goodes uppon them duringe the mynorytye of my said sonne Walter Raleghe and duringe the mynorytye of anie other that shalbe myne executor within age untill such executor shall marrye or accomplishe the age of one and twentye yeares. FURTHER I doe earnestlye requeste and praye my said overseers by the bandes of amytye that they will with all care and regard faithfullye and truelye admynister my goodes according to the trust reposed in them and according to my true meaning expressed in this my last will and testament.

AND I do utterlye revoke ... [*all former wills*].³⁰

IN WITNES whereof I have to this my present will and testament subscribed my name and affixed my seale the daye and yeare firste above written.

Sealed and signed and published by the above named Sir Walter Ralegh as his last will and testament the tenth day of July 1597, in the presens of [*signed*] Adryan Gylbarte, William Strode, Chr[*istopher*] Harris, Jo[*hn*] Meere
        W Ralegh

[*later endorsement*]   Sir Walter Raleyghe will made the yeare 1597

1. Having returned, comparatively speaking, to royal favour, early in July 1597 Ralegh was preparing, as second-in-command to the Earl of Essex, to take a large English (and Dutch) fleet to attack the Spanish fleet at Ferrol. The will was signed on the very day they made their first departure from Plymouth. The progress of the London flotilla down the Channel had been slow and as recently as 6 July Ralegh had been at Weymouth in Dorset, desperately awaiting supplies (above, Letter 107). He seems, however, to have used the time to attend to his own affairs, foregathering, with a clerk and his four witnesses, either at Sherborne Castle, where John Meere, his steward, a professional lawyer, will have been on hand, or, more likely, after riding overland, accompanied by Meere and Adrian Gilbert, his half-brother, at Radford, Christopher Harris's house near Plymouth. William Strode lived nearby. No doubt Ralegh had already arranged some time in advance for the will to be drafted and its detailed provisions settled, but the fair copy which has so miraculously survived gives every impression of having been engrossed ready for signing within its two covering dates. Within six years its contents were irrelevant and it totally disappeared, to be discovered over three hundred years later, in a packet of old deeds, in the estate office at Sherborne.
2. Ralegh's half-brother who for some years in the 1590s lived at Sherborne and supervised Ralegh's improvements to the park and gardens: Latham, op. cit., p. 135.
3. Of Newnham in the parish of Plympton St Mary, currently MP for Devon. See above, Letter 84.
4. Of Radford in the parish of Plymstock, recently appointed by Ralegh as his deputy Vice-Admiral of Devon: Hasler, p. 259.
5. Of Castleton, near Sherborne, formerly steward to the Bishop of Salisbury, whom Ralegh had re-engaged on grounds of his experience and local knowledge, in spite of his conviction for forgery. See also below, note 27.
6. Cf. Ralegh's use of the same address in his wine licences (above, Plate 2).
7. Cf. above, Letter 72.
8. In 1587 Ralegh had become the proprietor of some forty thousand acres, largely in Munster.
9. Walter junior, Ralegh's only surviving son, born in 1594.
10. At this time Ralegh owned practically no freehold land in England but he had considerable leaseholdings, which at this time included the estate at Sherborne (see above, Letters 13, note 7, and 60, note 9).
11. ibid.
12. See above, Letter 12.

13. The parish of Haselbury Plucknett lies some 10 miles south west of Sherborne, but nevertheless in the county of Somerset. Note that Ralegh also held his farm there by leasehold.
14. Since the early 1580s Ralegh had occupied part of Durham House in the Strand in London, but only at the Queen's pleasure: see above, Letter 60, note 9.
15. For Ralegh's penchant for fine china see above, Letters 50, 151, 152. His avowals of his private devotion to Robert Cecil are a feature of his letters at this time, the support of one who had recently been appointed Principal Secretary of State, being, of course, essential if Ralegh was to retain the Queen's newly-revived confidence. But, if indeed Cecil was ever privy to Ralegh's testamentary intentions, he could hardly have been flattered by the distinctly residuary nature of this token of friendship.
16. In February 1572, Sir Nicholas Throckmorton had left the sum of £500 for a dowry for his only daughter, Elizabeth, the later Lady Ralegh, then aged six, which her mother had subsequently lent to the impecunious nineteenth Earl of Huntington (ob. 1595): P. Lefranc, 'La Date du Mariage de Sir Walter Ralegh', *Etudes Anglaises*, 1956, pp. 197–8. The debt now stood at £1,000.
17. Lady Ralegh's uncle, a Catholic lawyer who had prospered during the reign of Queen Mary, had been disgraced and died in debt in 1597: A.L. Rowse, *Ralegh and the Throckmortons*, 1962, *passim* and pp. 73–4. The nature and extent of his debt to the Raleghs has not been identified.
18. William Stanley, Earl of Derby, 1561–1642, who had succeeded to the title in 1594.
19. Thomas Harriot, the mathematician, who had for some years been a member of Ralegh's household, usually residing at Durham House in London but occasionally joining the family at Sherborne.
20. Built by Ralegh himself, it had already seen considerable service.
21. See Appendix 1.
22. Lawrence Keymis, soldier and navigator, who had recently been employed by Ralegh on his first Guiana voyage.
23. Ralegh's distant cousin, his best, and arguably his only, friend in high places.
24. Another West Country relation on his mother's side, in whom Ralegh placed considerable trust (above, Letter 101), shortly taking him as Captain on his flagship, the *Warspite* (Purchas XX, p. 34).
25. No such provision survives.
26. Ralegh was very proud of his landscaping at Sherborne.
27. Very soon after this, relations between Ralegh and his Steward became very strained (see above, Letters 141 and 149) and indeed there are indications here that already Ralegh did not entirely trust his agent.
28. Lady Ralegh's brother.
29. Brett's wife was a cousin of the Throckmortons of Coughton in Warwickshire.
30. There is no evidence of a previous will, or indeed of any later revisions between 1597 and 1603 when his attainder deprived him of freedom to dispose of his estate.

# APPENDIX 3

## AGNES M.C. LATHAM
## BIBLIOGRAPHY

'Sir Walter Ralegh's *Cynthia*', *Review of English Studies*, 4, 1928, pp. 1–6.
Ed., *The Poems of Sir Walter Ralegh*, London and Boston, 1929, revised edition London and Cambridge, Mass., 1951.
'Ralegh's Letters', *Times Literary Supplement*, 4 February 1938, p. 74.
'Sir Walter Ralegh's farewell letter to his wife in 1603: a question of authenticity', *Essays and Studies*, 25, 1939, pp. 39–58.
'Satire on literary themes and modes in Nashe's *Unfortunate Traveller*', *English Studies*, New Series 1, 1948, pp. 85–100.
'Sir Walter Ralegh's Gold-mine: new light on the last Guiana voyage', *Essays and Studies*, New Series 4, 1951, pp. 94–111.
'A Birth-date for Ralegh', *Etudes Anglaises*, 3, 1956, pp. 243–5.
'Sir Walter Ralegh's *Instructions to his Son*', *Elizabethan and Jacobean Studies: Presented to Frank Percy Wilson*, Oxford, 1959, pp. 199–218.
Ed., *The Poems of Sir Walter Ralegh*, new edition London and Cambridge, Mass., 1962.
'Shakespeare, poet and dramatist', *Filoloski Pregled* I–II, 1964, pp. 85–90.
*Sir Walter Ralegh*, *Writers and their Work*, for the British Council and the National Book League, London and New York, 1964.
Ed., *Sir Walter Raleigh: Selected Prose and Poetry*, London, Oxford, and New York, 1965.
'Sir Walter Ralegh', in *Shakespeare's Contemporaries: Playwrights, Poets*, for the British Council and the National Book League, London and Tokyo, 1968.
'Sir Walter Ralegh's Will', *Review of English Studies*, New Series XXII, 86, 1971, pp. 129–36.
'Raleigh, Sir Walter', *Encyclopaedia Britannica*, 15th edition, vol. 9, 1974, pp. 913–14.
Ed., *As You Like It*, Arden edition of The Works of William Shakespeare, London and New York, 1975, New Delhi, 1976.
'Sir Walter Ralegh (c.1554–1618)', in *British Writers*, edited under the auspices of the British Council, 8 vols, New York, 1979, 1, pp. 145–59.

# INDEX

Arabic numbers refer to the Letters. The numbering sequence is shown in the List of the Letters, starting on p. vii, which also indicates the page reference for each letter.

Roman numbers refer to pages of the Introduction. App., followed by italic page numbers, refers to the Appendices.

The names of recipients of letters are printed in bold type.

Aberdeen (Aburdene), 147
Admiralty,
   High Court of, 22, 93, 129
   Judge of, see Caesar, Sir Julius
Albert, Cardinal Archduke, 136
Aleblaster, Thomas, merchant, 188
Alley, Captain Peter, 217
Alresford (Alsford), Hampshire, letter from, 81
Amsterdam, 141, 213
Andover (Andever), Hampshire, 114, 139, 142, 147, 148, 159
**Anne of Denmark, Queen of James I,** xl, xlvi, liii, 192, 208, 211, 217, 219
   letters to, 201, 207, 228
Antrobus, —, 165
Antwerp, 44
Aremberg (Arambull, Arambure, Arramberke, Arumbur), Count Marco of, 114, 166
Argyll (Argile), Earl of, see Campbell
armourers, 51
Arscot, Tristram, of Tetcott, 29
Arundel (Arundell, Arundle),
   Sir John, of Laherne, 69
   Sir John, of Trerice, 29
   Master, 66
   Thomas, 18th Earl of, see Howard
Ashburton (Asbourton), Devon, 113, 114
Ashley,
   Sir Anthony, 102
   Kate, 152

Askeaton (Asketon) Castle, Ireland, 4
**Assize Judges, Western,** letter to, 156
Aubrey, John, 13
Azores, the islands of the, 50, 112

Bagg, James senior, 153
Bagshot (Bagshoot), Surrey, 142, 169
Bailey (Bailye, Baylie),
   —, 172, 217
   Captain John, 217, 220
Baker, Dr, of Bath, his house, 126
bakers, 51
balsam (balsemum), 153
   of Guiana, 191
Bantry, Ireland, 4
Barbary, North Africa, captives in, 17
Barking Creek (Barking Shelf), 96
Barnes (Barnishe),
   Captain Arthur, 2
   Sir George, of London, 52
Barnstaple, north Devon, mayor of, 26
Barry (Barre) Court Castle, 3, 4
Barry (Barrey),
   David (Davey) Fitzjames, later Lord, 2–4, 68; his lands, 2; his mother, 3, 4
   James FitzRichard, Viscount Barrymore, 2
Basill, Martin, 213
Basingstoke (Basing), Hampshire, 139, 143, 159

Bath, Somerset,
  letters from, 128, 162
  the spa, lv, 60, 126, 140, 141, 143, 144, 160, 178, 183
Bath, William, 4th Earl of, see Bourchier
Baynham (Baynam), Sir Edward, 17
Bayonne (France), ship of, 49
Baxter (Baxster),
  —, 12, 15
  Nathaniel, 117
Bear Garden, London, 142
Bear Haven, Ireland, 4
Bel Isle, France, 75
Belle, Antoine, of Dieppe, 215
Berkeley (Barckeley, Bartle, Bartley), Captain Edward, 4
Berry Pomeroy, Devon, 9
Bertendona (Britendona), 114
Bevill,
  Peter, 64
  Sir William, of Talland, 29, 40
Billingsley, Henry, of London, 52
Bisse, James, see Wells, Subdean and Chapter
Blackwall (Blake Wale, Bralkwale), London, 93, 96
Blackwater River, Munster, xxxix, 5
Bland, John, 53
Blanshill, Robert, Scotsman, 147
Blarney Castle, Ireland, 2
Blavet (Blewett), France, 75
**Blount, Charles, Lord Mountjoy, Earl of Devonshire,** 113, 121, 149, 150
  letters to, 166, 171
Blount, Sir Michael, 51
Bodley, Sir John, 191
Bonetti, Signor Rocco, 21
books, liv, 203, App. 2, *p. 384*
  Spanish, 152
Bordeaux (Burdeus), France, 60
Borough (Burres, Burroes, Burrough), William, 93, 96
Bothwell, 4th Earl of, 123
Bourchier (Bowcer, Bowser),
  Sir George, 4
  John, 3rd Earl of Bath, 4, 88
  William, 4th Earl of Bath, xxxvii, xlix, 36
Bowden, —, of Plymouth, 114
**Boyle, Sir Richard,** later 2nd Earl of Cork,
  letters to, xxxvii, xl, 216
Boyse, Sir Richard, 10
Bradshawe, Master, 218

Brazil, 129
Brest, port of, France, 75
  Governor of, 120
Brett, Sir Alexander, 126, 165, 172, 183, 185, App. 2, *pp. 384, 385, 387*
brewers, 51, 165
bribery, 77, 78, 119
Bridgwater, Somerset, 88
Brigham (Brigame), Thomas, 133
Bristol,
  merchants of, 49
  port of, 37
Brittany (Britaigne, Britayne, Brittaine, Bryton), 22, 48, 79, 88, 106
  campaign in, 60, 157
  coast of, 50, 75
  Spaniards in, 114
Brixham, near Dartmouth, Devon, 151
  rectory, 152, 153, 157
Brochero (Brocheroe) de Araya,
  Diego, 114, 150
  Farnando, 114
Brooke (Broke), family, 126
Brooke, George, 169
Brooke, Henry, 11th Lord Cobham, xxxvi, 102, 104, 110, 114, 121, 145, 152, 157, 159, 165, 170, 171, 173, 178, 182
  letters to, xxvii, 126, 128, 131, 140, 141, 143, 160, 169
  his marriage, 128
  his servant, see Gilbert, Bartholomew
  his Spanish journey, 166, 169, 171
Brooke, Sir William, 112
Brooke, William, 10th Lord Cobham, 104, 110
  Elizabeth (Cecil), his daughter, death of, 104
Broughton (Brouton), Hugh, 92
Browne,
  Maurice, 6
  Richard, 28, 31
Bruerton, Master, 188
Buckhurst, Thomas Lord, see Sackville
Buckingham, 1st Duke of, see Villiers
Bulmer, Bevis, 133
Burgess (Burges), Peter, 57
Burgh, Sir John, 41, 50
Burgh, Thomas Lord, 60
Burghley, William Lord, see Cecil
Burke, Ulick, 47
Burley, Richard, 114
Burrell, —, 129
Burwick, Robert, 220

Butler, Thomas, 10th Earl of Ormonde, xxxviii, 2–4
  his kindred, 3
Button, Captain Thomas, 159
Bye Plot (the Surprise), 166, 171, 180

Cadiz (Calize, Calze), Spain, 93
  letters from, 101, 102
  sack of, xxxvi, 101–103, 111, 157
Caesar, Sir Julius, 22, 49, 55, 99, 151, 161
Calais (Callice), Governor of, 120
Callice (Callis), John, 10
Calvert, Sir George, 225
Cambridge, University of, xliii, 12, 15, 16
Campbell, Archibald, 7th Earl of Argyll, 60
Canary Islands, xxxvi, 61, 63, 217
canvas, 51
**Carew (Carye), Sir George,** (from 1605) Lord Carew of Totnes, xxvii, xxxix, 32, 46, 48, 51, 108, 112, 114, 149, 165, 192, 210, 217–19, App. 1, *p. 379*, App. 2, *p. 384*
  letters to, xxxvii, 33, 220, 222
Carew, Henry senior, 127
  Sir Nicholas, 166
  Sir Peter, 32
  Richard, of Antony, 29, 36
Carey,
  George, 2nd Lord Hunsdon, Lord Chamberlain, death of, 160
  Henry, 1st Lord Hunsdon, 13, 14
Carigtohill, Co. Cork, 3
**Carr, Sir Robert,** xlviii, 196
  letter to, xxvi, xxxvii, 197
Cary (Cari), George, of Cockington, 26, 30, 39, 157
Cascaes (Cascales), Portugal, 121
Cashel, archbishop of, *see* Magrath, Miles
Castletown, Dorset, App. 2, *pp. 382, 385*
Catholic League, ships of, 49
Caundle (Candle) Bishop, Dorset, 177, App. 2, *p. 382*
Cayenne (Calliana), letter from, 217
**Cecil, Sir Robert,** (from 1603) **Lord,** (1604) **Viscount Cranborne,** (1605) **Earl of Salisbury,** xxvi, xxxv, xxxix, xliii, xlvii, xlviii, 52–54, 58, 60, 117, 141, 152, 156, 157, 160, 165, 181, 201, 209
  letters to, xxxvii, xlv, xlvi, 36, 41, 45–47, 62–69, 74, 76, 79–87, 89, 91–100, 102–104, 107–10, 112, 114, 118, 119, 121–27, 132–36, 139, 142, 144, 145, 147–50, 155, 158, 159, 161–63, 166, 167, 171, 174, 176, 177, 179, 180, 182–85, 187, 189, 190, 192, 196, 199, 200, 205, 206
  his late wife, lvi, 104
  his ship, 165
  his son William, 125
**Cecil, William, Lord Burghley,** 12, 15, 25, 64, 71, 76, 78, 85, 92, 102, 123
  letters to, xxxvii, xlii, 8, 16, 26, 31, 37, 44, 49, 51–56, 61, 73, 105, 115
Champernon (Champernowne),
  Sir Arthur, 9
  Elizabeth, his daughter, 9
  Sir Philip, 14
Chancery, High Court of, 156
Chard (Charde), Somerset, Brooke estate at, 126
Chatham, Kent, 41, 52
Chelsea, London, 106
Cheyney (Chene), Henry, goldsmith, 178
Chudleigh (Chydle), Captain John, 22, 218, 220
cider, xli, 22, 38, 39, 42
Clifford, George, 3rd Earl of Cumberland, 30, 52, 82, 142
  his ships, 53, 54, 56
cloth,
  silk, 151, 152
  woollen, 51
Cloyne, Co. Cork, 216
Clyst Honiton, Devon, 9
Cobham, Lord, *see* Brooke
cochineal, 37
Cockayne, Alderman Sir William, 225
coining of money, 67
**Coke (Cooke), Sir Edward,** Attorney-General, 119, 166, 176, 185
  letters to, 137, 164
Colaton (Colliton, Colyton) Raleigh (Raleghe), Devon, 9, 13, App. 2, *p. 381*
Cole, Richard, 157
Collier, J.P., lawyer and forger, App. 1, *p. 380*
Columbus, Christopher, 205
Common Pleas, Court of, 11, 17, 156
Commons, House of, 58; *see also* Ralegh, Sir Walter, positions of influence
Compton (Cumpton), —, 165
Condon (Conndon),
  David, 73
  Patrick, 2, 3, 61, 73, 74
Conestaggio, Jeronimo, *History of ... Kingdom of Portugal*, 1600, recommended by Ralegh, 124

Connock (Cunnocke), Richard, 133
Conolothe Wood, Ireland, 4
coopers, 51
Cope, Sir Walter, 209
Copley (Cobliffe), Anthony, 169
Cork, city of, xxxix, 3, 147
    letters from, 1–4
Cornelius (*alias* Moone), John, 69
Cornwall (Cornwale), county of, 88
    deputy lieutenants of, 64, 115, 149
    Duchy of, Seal of, 179–81
    impressment of seamen in, 40
    manpower in, 79
    militia in, 29, 36, 88, 89, 105, 141, 149
Corsini (Corsina), Filippo, 55
Corunna (the Groyne), 114
**Cotton, Sir Robert,** xxvi, xxxvii
    letter to, 203
Council, Privy, *see* Privy Council
Courtenay (Courtney),
    Peter, 64
    Sir William, 9, 26
Crewkerne (Crockerne), Somerset, 112–114, 140
Crosby Place (House), London, 142
Crosse, Captain Robert, 54
Crozon, Finistere (Old Croydun), France, 75
Crymes, William, 1, 135
Cumberland, Earl of, *see* Clifford

**Dale, Dr Valentine,** letter to, 11
Dallison (dalyson), 'my man', 19
Dantzig, ships of, 27
Dart, River, 9, 53, 55
    estuary, 30
Dartmouth, Devon, port of, xlvi, 37, 39, 50, 52–54, 62, 75, 79, 88, 129, 161
    letters from, 53
    mayor of, 129
    seamen in, 40
Davis,
    Captain John, navigator, 55, 67
    Nevil, 44
De Acuna,
    Diego Palomeque, 218, 219
    Diego Sarmiento, Count of Gondomar, liii, 218, 219, 221
De Bisseaux, *see* Spifame
De Carteret,
    Jean (John), 146, 154
    Philip, 154

De Guavera, Don Pedro, 114
De Lova, Don John, 114
De Padilla, Don Martin, Admiral of Spain, 114
De Perama, Pietro Roderigo, 218
Delves, George, 32
Denham, John, 116
Denmark, King of, 211
Dennis,
    Sir Robert, 26
    Sir Thomas, 30
Denny, Edward, 1
Denshire, —, 71
Derby, Earl of, *see* Stanley
Desmond, Earl of, *see* FitzGerald
**Devereux, Robert, 2nd Earl of Essex,** xxxv, xxxvi, 82, 83, 96, 101, 102, 107–110, 112, 114, 123
    letter to, xxxvii, 113
    his reputation in Europe, 114
    his supporters, 137
    his wife, 145
Devon, county of,
    deputy-lieutenants of, 10, 26
    Earl of, *see* Blount
    impressment of seamen in, 40
    **Justices of the Peace of,** letter to, 57
    knights of, in Parliament, 22
    manpower in, 79, 88, 89
    militia in, 26
    parish constables of, 57
    Quarter Sessions of, 57
    Ralegh's land in, 176
    sheriffs of, 9, 160
    subsidy in, 24, 36
    vice-admirals of, 10
    *see also* tin
Dieppe, France, ship of, 49
Dingle peninsula, Ireland, 4
Dobb, William, 71
Doddridge, Sir John, xlviii, 165, 176, 178, 185
Dolberry, Robert, 172, 177
Dorchester, Dorset,
    Assizes at, 156
    letter from, 68
Dorset, county of,
    havens in, 89
    magistrates of, 145, 156
    sheriffs of, 9, 182
Dover, Kent, 98, 136
    Castle, 120
    Lieutenant of, 98
    Mayor of, 98

# INDEX

Dowdall, Captain John, later Sir, 4, 45
Drake,
   Bernard, 11, 22
   Sir Francis, 23, 27, 30, 53, 84, 85, 89, 111, 219
   Thomas, 1, 135
Dublin, Ireland, seat of English government, 1–3
   Castle, 2
Dudley, Robert, 86
**Dudley, Robert, 14th Earl of Leicester,** 12
   letters to, xxxviii, xlii, 5, 20, 23
Duhallow (Dowhalla), Ireland, 4
Duivenwoorde, Admiral Jan van, 109
**Duke, Richard,** letter to, 12
Dumaresq,
   Daniel, 154, 165, 172
   John, 154
Dungarvan, Ireland, 148
   Castle, 1
Dunkirk (Dunkerks), France, seamen of, 121, 154
Dunster, Somerset, 88
Durham, bishop of, 164
Durham (Derum) House, London, liv, 60, 89, 164, App. 2, *pp. 383, 384*
   letters from, 36, 37, 44, 45, 47, 48, 55, 56, 61, 80, 115, 123, 124, 137
   Ralegh's household there, lv, 164
Dyer, Elinor (Ellner), 72

East Melplash, Dorset, 141
Edgcombe, Peter, 26
**Egerton, Thomas,** later Sir and Lord Ellesmere, Lord Chancellor, 176
   letters to, 7, 28, 71, 164
**Elizabeth I, Queen of England,** xxxv, xxxvii, 3, 6–8, 20, 25, 28, 30, 32, 36, 38, 39, 41, 47, 48, 51–57, 62, 68, 88, 96, 97, 99, 102, 107, 110, 113, 119, 123, 126, 132, 141, 143, 145, 152, 156, 158, 163, 179, 193
   her cash, 51, 52, 56, 111
   her customs, 52
   her debts, 78
   her ships, 44, 50, 51, 56, 75, 90, 101, 103, 108, 111, 159
   letter to, 58
   tin-mine dispute in Devon, 135
Elizabeth Castle (Fort Isabella Bellisima), Jersey, 132
Epernon, Duke d', 159
Essex, Earl of, *see* Devereux

Evelegh (Eveleigh),
   George, 24
   John, 24
Exchequer,
   Barons of the, 18, 19
   Court of, 24, 31, 156
Exe, River, 9
Exeter,
   citizens of, xlix
   city of, 11, 26, 53, 113, 114, 172
   Dean and Chapter of, 99
   deputy-lieutenants of, 26
Exmouth, port of, 39

Faige, Captain Charles, 215
Fal, River, 88
falcon, 63
Falmouth, Cornwall, 113, 114
   port of, 37, 39, 40, 43, 56, 108, 109, 216
**Fane, Sir Thomas,** letter to, 120
Fanshaw, Thomas, 31
Fashardo, Francisco, 218
Fearne (Fern), Sir John, 218, 225
Fenton, Geoffrey, later Sir, 4, 109, 118
Ferrol (Farroll), Spain, 108, 111, 114
Finisterre, Cape, 44, 108
fish, 42, 49
   from Newfoundland, xli, 38
   as prize cargo, 64
FitzGerald,
   Gerald, 16th Earl of Desmond, 1–3, 118; his wife, 4
   James FitzMaurice, 2
   John FitzEdmund, of Cloyne, 2
   John FitzEdmund, Seneschal of Imokilly, xxxviii, 2
   Thomas, 216
Fitzherbert (Fitzharbert, Fizharbert),
   Nicholas, 62
   Thomas, priest, 62
FitzJames (FittJamis),
   —, 91
   John, 119, 165
**Fitzwilliam, Sir William,** xxxix, 33, 34, 45, 47, 61, 63, App. 1, *p. 380*
   letter to, 32
Flanders, 121
Florence, ship of, 55
Floyer (Fleor, Floire, Flowre),
   Captain George, 150
   Captain John, 39, 49

forgery, 156
Fortescue (Forteskew),
  Hugh, 26
  Sir John, 64, 152
Fowey, Cornwall, defence of, 105
Fowler, John, metal refiner, 217
Freake, Thomas, 155
Frobisher (Furbresher), Sir Martin, 41, 43, 54
fruit, 217
Fruntino, Herman, 218

Gamage,
  Barbara, 14
  Catherine, 14
  Robert, 14
Gascoigne, George, *The Steel Glasse*, 5
Geraldines (Garantines), 3
Gibraltar, straits of, 114
Gifford, George, 97
Gilbert (Gilberd, Gylbarte),
  Adrian, xxxv, 87, 165, 172, App. 2, *p. 381*
  Ann, née Aucher, widow of Sir Humphrey, 30
  Captain Bartholomew, 161
  Elizabeth, née Chudleigh, 38, 43
**Gilbert, Sir Humphrey,** xxxv, xxxvii, 3, 6, 10, 157
  his portrait, 6
  letter to, xxix, xxxvii, 6
**Gilbert, Sir John I,** xxxv, xlix, 10, 26, 53, 62, 75, 84, 109, 152, 157
  letters to, xxix, xxxvii, 22, 27, 30, 38–40, 42, 43
  his residences, 42
**Gilbert, Sir John II,**
  his ship, 138, 151, 152, 155
  letters to, xxix, xxxvii, xli, 129, 138, 151–53, 157
Gillingham Forest, Dorset, 63
ginger, 37
Glanville (Glanvyle), Sir John, 57, 64
Gold (Gould), Alice, daughter of James, App. 1, *p. 380*, App. 2, *p. 384*; her daughter by Ralegh, App. 2, *p. 384*
**Gold, Judge James,** xxxix; letter to, App. 1, *p. 379*
gold, lii, 87, 89, 192, 193, 205, 207, 218
  chains of, 148
  clipping of, 156
  slate, 206
Gondomar, Count of, *see* De Acuna

Goodwin (Gooden) Sands, 98
Gorges,
  **Arthur,** later Sir, 7, 25, 47, 112, 113, 142, App. 2, *p. 384*; letter to, 101
  Sir Edward, 25
  Sir Ferdinando, 185
  Nicholas, 20
  Tristram, 53
  Sir William, 152
Goring, George, 92
Grante, Patrick, 94
Granville, Normandy, 159
Gravesend, London, 93, 96
Greenwich Palace, 8, 116, 117
Grenville (Granvile, Grenvill, Greynvyll),
  Bernard, 115
  Sir Richard, xxxvii, xlix, 26, 29, 150; son of, 115
**Grey, Arthur, 11th Lord Grey of Wilton,** Lord Deputy of Ireland, 2, 3, 5
  letter to, xxxviii, 4
Guiana, South America, li–liii
  map of, lii, 206
  mines in, liii, 215, 218–20
  natives of, li, 220
  operations in, 218, 220, 222
  Ralegh's expeditions to: in 1595, xxxvi, 80–87, 89, 97, 157; in 1617–18, proposals for, 192, 193, 201, 205, 206, 210, 211; rejection of, 207, 208; preparations for, 212–15; route to, 216; return from, 220, 221; mutiny at sea, 220
  San Thomé, liii, 206; siege of, liii, 219, 220, 222
Gunpowder Plot (1605), 191
guns, ships', 194, App. 2, *p. 384*

Hall, Master, 218
Hamden, Sir John, 218
Hamlyn, Christopher and Robert, 130
Hamond (Hammon), Christopher, 217, 218
Hancock, Edward, Ralegh's Secretary, 62, 89
Harcourt, Robert, 220, 222
Harlay, Christopher de, Count of Beaumont, French ambassador, 191
  his wife, 191
Harrington, Lady, 219
Harriot (Harryott, Heriott), Thomas, xxxvii, 87, 177, 185, 204, App. 2, *pp. 384, 385*
Harris, Christopher, of Radford, 53, 133, 138, 161, App. 2, *p. 381*

Hartley Row, Hampshire, letter from, 53
Harwich, Essex, 54
Haselbury Plucknet, Somerset, App. 2, *p. 383*
Hastings,
    Captain Edward, 217
    Henry, Earl of Huntington, App. 2, *p. 384*
Hatton, Sir Christopher, 7, 8, 46
Hawker, —, 165
Hawkins (Hawkings),
    Sir John, Comptroller of the Navy, 48, 50, 51, 56, 85, 86, 90, 111, 219
    William, of Plymouth, 3
hawks, 216
Hawthorne (Hathorne), priest, his signature, 200
Hayes, East Budleigh, 12
Hayward, John, 217
Heaton, Thomas, 80, 81
Hele, John, sergeant-at-law, 160
Heneage, Sir Thomas, Vice-Chamberlain, 17, 32
Henry VIII, xlvii, 194
**Henry, Prince of Wales,** letter to, xlii, 194, 211, 219
Herbert (Harbert),
    Arnold, 214
    William, 3rd Earl of Pembroke, 179, 218
    William, of Glamorgan, 214, 218, 225
Hering, Godfrey, 117
Hertford (Harfart, Hartford), Bridge, Middlesex, 142, 147
**Hickes (Hext), Sir Michael,** 50, 165
    letters to, xxxvii, 77, 78, 186
Hide, Arthur, 73, 74
hides, 37, 50
Hilliard, William, 99
**Hobart, Sir Henry,** letter to, 195
Holland, States of, 129
Honiton (Hunyton), Devon, 113, 114, 140
Hooker, John, of Exeter, xxxviii, 2
Hoorne (Horne), Holland, 96
horses (hackneys), 29, 165, App. 2, *p. 384*
    at Durham House, 164
Horsey,
    Sir Edward, 31
    Sir Ralph, 69, 72, 145
**Hovendon, Dr Roger,** letter to, 25
**Howard, Charles, Lord Howard of Effingham, Earl of Nottingham, Lord High Admiral,** xl, 30, 38, 41, 63, 64, 76, 79, 86, 101, 114, 119, 145, 148, 152, 156, 161, 178
    letters to, xxxviii, 48–50, 53, 55, 75, 90, 106, 166
    his ships, 41, 52
    his tenths, 161
    his wife, 191
**Howard, Henry, Earl of Northampton,** 8, 165, 166
    letters to, 171
Howard, Thomas, 4th Duke of Norfolk, 123
Howard, Thomas, 18th Earl of Arundel, 218
Howard, Thomas, Lord, 56, 101, 103, 110, 113, 160
**Howard, Thomas, Lord Howard of Walden, Earl of Suffolk,** 123, 126
    letters to, 166, 171
Howard, Thomas, Viscount Howard of Bindon, 127, 141, 160
**Howland, Dr Richard,** letter to, 12
Hull, George, of Exeter, 183
**Hume (Humes), Sir George,** letter to, 177
Hunsdon, Baron, *see* Carey
Hunt, —, 165
Huntington, Henry, Earl of, App. 2, *p. 384*

Imokilly, Co. Cork, Seneschal of, *see* FitzGerald
impressment of seamen, 40
Indians, 217, 218
Indies, West, voyages to, 23
Ireland,
    Army in, 122
    bishop of, 147
    Council of, 32, 61
    invasion of, 121, 147
    Scots in, 60
    Spaniards in, 58, 106, 144, 148, 149
    *see also* Ralegh, Sir Walter
Islands,
    Atlantic, 36
    Voyage, xxxvi, 36, 111, 112
Ivey, Paul, military engineer, lv, 131, 132

**James I, King of England,** xxxvi, xli, 164, 166, 167, 169, 171, 174, 176–78, 185, 190, 193, 195, 197, 201, 205–207, 210, 218, 219
    letters to, xxvi, xxvii, xxxi, xxxvii, liii, 168, 170, 175, 179, 181, 208, 221, 226, 227
    his ships, 194
Jennings, Captain, 217
Jermyn (Germyne), Sir Thomas, 110
Jersey, Channel Islands, 144, 162
    defences of, 132
    Governorship of, 116
    **Jurats (Justices) of,** letters to, 146, 154; letters from, 159

Jesuits, *see* Cornelius, John
Jewell, Nebucadnezer (Nebucodnozer), App. 1, p. *379*
jewels, 50, 53, 119, 161, 172
Jones, [Nicholas, of Weymouth], 17
Jorneaux, Phillip, 154
Jukes, Edward, 20

Kelly,
   John, of Tavistock, 62
   Richard, of Dartmouth, 62
Keymer, John, 12, 14
Keymis (Kemish, Keymys),
   —, merchant, of London, 217
   Lawrence, lii, 165, App. 2, p. *384*; death of, 219; his signature, 200; voyages to Guiana: (1596), 106, 205; (1617–18), lii, liii, 192, 206, 217–20, 222
Kilkenny (Kilkeny), Ireland, 4
Killibeg, Co. Donegal, 220
Killigrew (Killegrewe), William, 41, 47, 53
King, Samuel, 225
King's Bench, Court of, 156
Kinsale (Kynsale), Co. Cork, xxxix, liii, 149, 150
Kintyre (Cantirr), 60
Knevett (Knevit),
   Lord, 206
   Master —, 218
   Randell, 31
   Thomas, 8
Knoyle, Edward, 72

Lancaster, Duchy of, 179
Langford (Lanxford), Richard, 57
Langherne, William, 7
Langworth, Master, 218
Leake, Simon, 218
Lee (Leigh),
   Master Charles, 222
   Sir Henry, 158
   Sir John, 217, 219
Leicester, Earl of, *see* Dudley
Leigh (Lee), Essex, 96
   letter from, 214
**Lewis, Dr David**, letter to, 10
Lieutenants, deputy Lords, 149
Limerick (Limbricke),
   county of, 4
   port of, 147

Lisbon (Lysbon, Lysborne), Portugal, 121, 147, 148
Lismore (Lesmore), Co. Waterford, 5
   Castle, 33
   and Waterford, bishop of, 45, 92
Lizard, the, Cornwall, Spaniards off, 114
London (Lundun), 52, 90, 161, 217
   Blackfriars in, 21
   Corporation of, 56
   Gilds of, 56
   goldsmiths of, 53
   Lombard (Lumbard, Lumbord) Street, 165, 178
   Lord Mayor of, 17, 52
   Mile End in, 59
   Ralegh departs from, 1
   Tower of, letters from, 49–51, 165–68, 176–86, 188–97, 199–205, 207–11; Lieutenant of, 179
Lopez (Lopas), Roderigo, 156
**Lore, Peter Van,** 87, 165, 190
   letter to, 213
Love (Lone), Captain, 148
Low Countries, *see* Netherlands
Lower, Thomas, of Lewannick, 29
Lowman,
   John, 9
   Philip, 9
Luscombe, —, 40
Lyme Regis, Dorset, 86, 141
   Mayor of, 112

MacCarthy (Cartey, Macartey, Mac Cartye),
   Charles, xxxix, 76, 77, 83, 94
   Sir Cormac MacTeighe, 2
   Donnell More, 2
   Florence (Finnin), 2, 4, 68, 149
   Teig MacDermot, *see* Onorsi
Macshuhy, Magnus, 216
MacTeige, Callough, 2
Madrid, 218
Magrath, Miles, archbishop of Cashel, 92
Makerell, —, ship's master, 75
Manners, Roger, 5th Earl of Rutland, 8, 110
Mansell (Mansfelde, Mansfield, Maunsfeld), Sir Robert, 44, 110, 141
Manwood, Sir Roger, Lord Chief Baron of the Exchequer, 156
marcasite (merquesite), 192
Margarita, 218

mariners, xli, 37, 96
  impressment of, 40, 42
  restraint of, 27
  shirts for, 214
  wages of, xli, 41, 48, 52, 54
Martin (Marten), Sir Richard, of London, 53
Meere (Meer, Meeres),
  John junior, xlvii, 156
  John senior, 141, 144, 145, 149, 160, 177, 198, App. 2, *p. 385*; his brother-in-law, 156
  William, 72, 141
Middleburg (Middleborough), in Zealand, merchants of, 44
Middleton, Thomas, of London, 55
Milburn, —, 67
**Mildmay, Sir Walter,** letter to, 24
Mile End, London, 94, 95
Miller, Sir Robert, 177
militia, *see* Cornwall, Devon
Minehead (Minniett), Somerset, 88
minerals, 192, 206
Mohun, Sir William, 26
Moile, Henry, 2
Monson, Sir William, 109
Mont Orgueil (Mountorguell) or Gorey Castle, Jersey, lv, 132
Montmorency, Constable of France, 159
Moore, Captain, 206
More,
  Donnell Macarthy, Earl of Clancare, 2
  Richard, 217
  **Sir William,** letters to, 21, 116
Morgan, Sir William, 1
Mountjoy, Charles Blount, Lord, *see* Blount
Mounts Bay, Cornwall, 88
Mullineaux, Master, 218
**Munck, Levinus,** letter to, 188
Munster, Ireland, province of, 178
Musica, Captain Anthony, 218
Muskerry, Ireland, lordship of, 94

Naunton, Sir Robert, 224
Navy Board, Treasurer of, 120
Netherlands, 23
  Governor of, *see* Dudley
Newfoundland, 10, 22, 48, 219, 220
  fleet, 79
  *see also* fish
Newhaven (Le Havre), France, ship of, 49
Newland, Dorset, App. 2, *p. 382*

Newport, Captain Christopher, 192
Nicholas (Nichols), Captain, Ralegh's servant, 154
Nichols, Master, 218
**Norgate, Robert,** letters to, 15, 16
Norris (Norrice),
  Sir John, 60, 157
  **Sir Thomas,** letter to, 117
North,
  Sir John, 21
  Captain Roger, 218, 220
Northfleet, Kent, 96
Northumberland, Earl of, *see* Percy
Nottingham, Earl of, *see* Howard

O'Donnell, Hugh, 60
Okehampton, borough of, 57
Okenif, —, 4
Okham, Richard, 31
O'Neill,
  Hugh, 3rd Earl of Tyrone, 60, 86, 149
  Shane, 47
Onorsi (a Nursey), Teig, 34
oranges, 220
ordnance, ships', 153, 157, 225, App. 2, *p. 384*
Orinoco (Orenoke), Guiana, 206
  river, 218
Ormonde, Earl of, *see* Butler
Oroso, 114
Orsini (Ursini), Virginio, Duke of Bracciano, 136
Ostend, siege of (1601), 138, 145
O'Sullivan, Philip, 2, 4
Otterton (Otertowne), Devon, manor of, 13
Owen,
  Edward, 116
  John, of London, 17
Oxford,
  Earl of, *see* Vere
  University, All Souls College, lands of, 7, 25

Padstow (Padstowe), Cornwall, 88
Panama, 90
papists, 180
Parker,
  Captain Charles, 218
  Sir Nicholas, 115
  Captain William, 152, 221
Parliament, *see* Ralegh, Sir Walter, positions of influence

Paulet (Poulet),
　Abraham, 146
　Sir Anthony, 126, 132
　George, 154
Payton (Payden), 53
　Thomas, 217
pearls, lii, 53, 54, 87
　seed, 204
Pelham, Lord Justice, 2
Pembroke, Earl of, *see* Herbert
Penewart, Mathias, 213
Pennington, John, 218, 220, 225
Pepler, —, 87
pepper, 50, 55
Percy, Henry, 19th Earl of Northumberland, 145, 160, 191, 219; *see also* Harriot, Thomas
Perez, Don Antonio, pretender to the throne of Portugal, 156
Perin, Master, 218
Pernambuco (Farname Bucke), 151
Perranporth (St Piran), Cornwall, 88
Perriam, Sir William, Chief Baron of the Exchequer, 156, 160
Perrison, Robert, Scotsman, 147
**Phelips (Phillips), Sir Edward**, Master of the Rolls, 178
　letter to, 204
Pigot, Captain John, 217, 218
pikes, Spanish, 42
Pinford, Dorset, manor of, 177
'pioneers', 20, 29, 79
plague, 40
　in London, 184
　in Sherborne, 80
plate, silver and gold, 165, 178, 219
Plessington, John, 218, 219
Plymouth, Devon, xl, li, 22, 38, 39, 49, 50, 53–55, 88, 90, 98, 103, 148, 216, 219, 223, 225
　corporation of, 1, 84, 135
　Fort, governor of, *see* Gilbert, Sir John II
　letters from, liii, 99, 100, 108–11, 113, 114, 215, 219–21
　mayor of, *see* Parker, William
　tin-mine dispute, 135
Pointington (Poyntington), Somerset, 156
Pomeroy estate, 9
poor people, 45, 57, 72, 156, 165, 172
　wages of, 165
Pope,
　Robert, 96
　William, 93, 96

**Popham, Sir John,** Lord Chief Justice, 31, 127, 156, 169, 171, 185
　letters to, 164
porcelain (purselane), 50, 151, 152
Port Reale, Cadiz, 101
Portland, Dorset, 42
　Castle, *see* Ralegh, Sir Walter, positions of influence
　stone, lv, 70
Portsmouth, 52, 54
postmarks, 89, 112–14, 139, 140, 142, 147, 148, 159
Powderham, Devon, 9
Power, Sir Henry, 122
Powell, Morgan, 17
Preston, Sir Amyas, 185, 192
Prideaux (Prideux), Edmund, 13
Primsley (Prumsly), Dorset, manor of, 177
privateering, 37, 52, 53, 64, 129, 148, 151
　profits of, 55, 56, 129, 153, 157; *see also* Ralegh, Sir Walter
**Privy Council, Her/His Majesty's,** 1, 17, 30, 52, 55, 57, 61, 63, 64, 71, 73, 74, 88, 89, 94, 106, 111, 120, 142, 154, 178, 211, 223
　letters to, 29, 173, 178, 191, 206
　membership of, 138
Privy Seal, 41
prize goods, 151–53
　Lord Admiral's tenths of, 153
proclamations, 40, 50
Puerto Rico, Bishop of, 218
Puntales (Puntall), Fort, Cadiz, 101
Pyne, Henry, 63
Pytt, Master, 70

Queenborough, 97

Radford, near Plymouth, letter from, 133
Ralegh, Carew, Sir Walter's second surviving son, 182, 189, 217
**Ralegh, Elizabeth, Lady,** xxxv, lii, 40, 80, 81, 119, 128, 131, 139, 141, 145, 149, 151, 152, 157, 159, 172, 176, 178, 182–85, 189, 190, 192, 195, 196, 209, 218, 220, App. 2, *pp. 381–387 passim*
　handwriting of, lvii
　letters to, xxii, xxvi, xxxvii, xlv, liii, 165, 172, 217, 219, 224, 225
　postscript by, 140
　her son (Walter), xlviii, 196, 197, 200
　her two sons, xlviii, lv, lvi, 201, 206

Ralegh family, xxxv
**Walter junior,** Sir Walter's eldest surviving son, 80, 81, 157, 165, 172, 176–78, 182–85, 189, 195, 217, 218, 225, App. 2, *pp. 381–387 passim*; death of, liii, lvi, 218, 219; letter to, 202
Walter senior, Sir Walter's father, xlvi, xlix, 13
Ralegh, George, Captain, 218, 222
Ralegh, Sir Walter,
  brief biography, xxxiv–xxxvii
  his birthplace, xxiv, 13
  his burial, 172, App. 2, *p. 381*
  his cloth patent, 18, 52
  his clothes, 143, 152, App. 2, *p. 384*
  and Cobham, Lord, xlv, 128, 139, 140, 143, 145, 159, 160, 162, 165–67, 169–71, 173, 182
  and Cornish tin, 133, 134; and Devon tin, 135; and the pre-emption of, 1
  his daughter, xxii, xxxix, 165, App. 2, *p. 384*
  and the Earl of Essex, xlv, 102, 109, 110, 114, 123
  entertaining at Sherborne, lv, 125, 139, 141, 149
  his expeditions to Guiana, *see* Guiana
  his expeditions to Virginia, *see* Virginia
  his expeditions to the West Indies, xxxvi, 40, 49, 81
  his finances, xli, li, lvi, 95, 119, 157, 165, 166, 172, 173, 176, 178, 185, 188, 190, 204, 209, App. 2, *p. 384*
  his friends, 58–60, 77, 80, 119, 172, 209, 215, 219
  his handwriting, lvii–lviii; his clerks, lviii–lix; the carriers of his letters, lix
  his health, xl, xli, 47, 48, 60, 85, 101–103, 110, 144, 162, 180, 181, 183, 184, 189, 207, 210, 217–19, 220, 224, 225
  in Ireland, xxxviii, xl, 220; as a soldier, 1–5, 45; as an 'undertaker', xxxv, xxxviii, xxxix, 33, 45, 61, 63, 73, 74
  his attitudes to Ireland, xxxvi, xxxix, 47, 60, 68, 75, 89
  and the Church in Ireland, xxxix, 92
  his Irish lands, 45, 47, 92, App. 2, *p. 381*
  his Irish tenants, 45, 92
  and King James, xlvii, xlviii, li, liii, 173, 223; *see also* Anne of Denmark
  his marriage, xxxv, xlvi, xlvii, lv, lvi, 41, 45, 47, 48

  as a naval commander, xl, xlii, 44, 79, 101, 102, 108, 110, 112, 119
  and overseas intelligence, xxxix, xlii, xlix, 75, 79, 86, 90, 114, 120, 121, 136, 138, 139, 144, 147, 148, 150, 159, 160, 162
  his pardon, xlvi, lii, 206, 220, 223
  his parents, 172
  his political ambitions, 126
  his positions of influence: as Captain of the Guard, xliii, xliv, 22, 29, 33, 46; as Governor of Jersey, lv, 126, 131, 132, 146, 154, 159, 160, 162, 172, 178, 185; as Lieutenant of Portland Castle, 178; as Lord Lieutenant of Cornwall, xlvii, xlix, 88, 113, 139; as Member of Parliament, xlvii, l, 58, 60, 138; as Ranger of Gillingham Forest, 178; as Steward/Chancellor of the Duchy of Cornwall and Lord Warden of the Stannaries, xli, xlix–li, 20, 22, 26, 44, 57, 66, 71, 130, 131, 133, 178–81; as Vice-Admiral of Devon and Cornwall, xli, xlix, 22
  as privateer, xli, 22, 37, 48, 49, 51, 55, 56, 129, 157
  his property, 7, 9, 22, 157, 165, 166, 172, 182, 183, 196; ancient records of, 156, 199; in North America, xxxv; his residence, xlvi; in Sherborne, xxvi, xxxvi, xlvi–xlviii, 46, 60, 72, 81, 176, 177, 183, 185, 189, 190, 195, 199, 200, App. 2, *p. 382*
  and Queen Elizabeth, xlii, xlvi, xlix, lii, 33, 46, 51, 52, 58, 60, 75, 90, 131, 158
  his relations, xxxv, xliv, xlix, 11, 14, 25, 32, 33, 75, 84, 92, 97, 101, 102, 104, 112, 114, 126, 127, 129, 152, 157, 170, 183, 214, 217
  his religion, liv, 104, 189, App. 2, *p. 381*
  his servants, *see* Dallison; Dolberry; Hancock; Langherne; Luscombe; MacCarthy, Charles; Macshuhy; Meere, John junior; Nicholas; Smith, Richard and Robert; Wood
  shipbuilding, his knowledge of, xlii, 194
  his ships, 22, 30, 41, 53, 54, 56, 82, 83, 161
  spelling of his name, lviii, 9, 11, 22, Plate 2
  his views on foreign policy, 48, 60, 87, 167
  his wife, *see* Ralegh, Elizabeth
  his will (1597), xxxiii, xxxvii, xlvi, xlvii, App. 2, *pp. 381–387*
  his wine licences, xliii, xlvi, 12, 15, 16, 28, 30, 158, 172, 182, App. 2, *p. 382*; arrears in payment for, 172, 186, 190

**Ramsay, John, Viscount Haddington** (1606), letter to, 193
Randoll, John, of Weymouth, 100
ransoms, 17
**Rashleigh, John, of Fowey,** letter to, xxxviii, 105
Ratcliff, Alexander, 110
Ratcliff (Ratcleife), London, 93
Rawlinges, —, see Meere, John junior
Raymond (Rimonde), George, of Chichester, 64
Reagh, MacCarthy, 2
rebels
  in England, 145
  in Ireland, 2, 3
recusants, 69
refiner of metals, 217
Renzi (Rensay, Rensis), Matthew de la, 166, 171, 191
Requests, Court of, 11
Reskemer, John, of Helston, 29
Reynell, Thomas, 130
Reynolds, John, 165
Richmond, Surrey, Palace of, 6
Ridgway, Captain, 113
Rigges, Lieutenant Gregory, 3
Roberts, Master, 218
Roborough Downe, in parish of Buckland Monachorum, Devon, tin mills on, 135
Roche,
  Maurice (Morrice), 2
  Lord, 2
Rochelle, La, France, news from, 159
Rostellan (Rostillon), Co. Cork, letter from, 216
Rowe, Barrey, 4
Rowleigh, Dame Elizabeth, 213
Rushmore, Wiltshire, 139
Russell,
  Francis, 2nd Earl of Bedford, death of, xlvii, 179
  John, 1st Earl, xlvii
Rutland, Earl of, see Manners

**Sackville, Thomas Lord,** Lord Treasurer, letters to, 55, 133, 152, 177
St Christophers (St Kitts), Island of, letters from, liii, 218, 219
St Ives (St Tees), Cornwall, 88
**St John (John's),**
  **Sir Oliver,** 220
  **Sir William,** letter to, 214

St Leger,
  family, 5
  Sir Warham, 2, 5, 218, 220, 225
St Malo (Mallos), 44, 139, 140
St Vincent, Cape, 114
Salcombe (Saltcombe), Devon, 88
Salisbury,
  bishop of, xlvii, 60, 119, 177, 178, 190, App. 2, p. 382
  Plain, 206
  town of, 139, 147
Saltash, Cornwall, 53
Salter, —, 38, 39
Sanders, Nicholas, 165
Sanderson, William, 157, 204
Sandridge (Sanding, Sandrige), Devon, 9
sassafras wood, 161
Savage, Sir Arthur, 103, 142
Savoy, Peace of, January 1601, 136
Scilly Isles, 56
  enemy ships off, 114
Scotland, Spanish faction in, 58
Scotney, Kent, manor of, 7
Scotsmen, 10
  in Ireland, 60
Scott, Thomas, 188
sea coal, 159
Setubal (St Uvall), Portugal, 147
Seymour,
  Edward, Duke of Somerset, 9
  **Master Edward,** letter to, 9
Shaftesbury (Chastone, Shaston), Dorset, 147, 148, 159
Sharpe, Robert, 116
**Shelbury, John,** 176, 177, 179, 186, 187
  signature of, 200
  letter to, forged, 198
Sherborne, Dorset, 9, 113, 156, 159, 172
  almshouses at, 72
  Castle, 60, App. 2, p. 382; park at, App. 2, p. 385; cannon for, 153; letters from, 60, 62, 65–67, 70–72
  letters from, 69, 73–79, 82–90, 121, 126, 127, 130–32, 134, 135, 139–141, 144–46, 148, 150
  Lodge, lv, 60, 70; household there, lv; letter from, 127; goods at, 178, 182
  pictorial map of, lv, note 23, Plate 5
  plague in, 80
  young man of, 121
  see also Ralegh, Sir Walter, property

sheriffs, 182
shipping,
  of Dunkirk, 121
  Dutch, 141
  English, 48, 75, 96, 98, 101, 218; of London, 101; of the west country, 112
  Flemish, 136, 148
  French, 48, 64, 86, 159
  German, 114
  Irish, 147
  Portuguese, 101
  Ragusan, 101
  restraint of, 27, 39, 81
  Spanish, 44, 50, 75, 79, 89, 101, 106, 108, 111, 113, 114, 120, 139, 140, 144, 145, 147, 148, 150, 218, 219
  voluntary, 112
ships,
  *Adrian*, 43
  *Antelope*, 159, 160
  *Ark Royal*, 101
  *Bark Ralegh*, 6
  *Bonaventure (Boaventer)*, 108, 109
  *Dainty*, 53, 54, 56
  *Darling*, 106
  *Destiny*, liii, 217, 220, 221, 225
  *Disdain*, 41
  *Dragon*, 53
  *Dreadnought*, 109, 112
  *Due Repulse*, 101
  *Foresight*, 41, 53, 54, 101
  *Gamaliell*, 112
  *Garland*, 41, 44, 50
  *George*, 96, 112
  *Gift*, 112
  *Great Susan*, 48
  *Harry and John*, 37
  *Jacob*, 96
  *John*, 37
  *Joshua (Jusua)*, 96
  *Lion (Golden Lion, Lyon)*, 101, 110
  *Lion's Whelp*, 41, 44, 52
  *Madre de Dios (Deus)*, xli, 50–56, 204
  *Margaret and John*, 30, 44
  *Mary Rose (Marirose)*, 101, 109, 194
  *Merhonour (Honour)*, 101, 103, 109, 110
  *Nonpareil (Nonparella)*, 101
  *Prudence*, 188
  *Rainbow (Rainebowe)*, 101
  *Refusal*, 138, 151, 152, 155
  *Revenge (Revendge)*, 101, 150

*Roebuck (Robuck, Row Bucke, Rowbuck)*, 30, 44, 54, 56, App. 2, *p. 384*
*San Andrew (Andrew, St Andrew)*, 101, 108, 109, 112, 113
*San Francis (St Francis)*, 114
*San John (St John)*, 114
*San Lucas (St Lucas)*, 114
*San Mathew (Mathew, St Mathew)*, 101, 108, 109, 112
*San Peter (St Peter)*, 114
*San Phelippe (St Phillip)*, 101
*San Pole (St Pole)*, 114
*San Thomas (St Thomas)*, 101
*Susan Bonaventure*, 44
*Uggara Salvania*, 55
*Vanguard*, 159
*Victory*, 194
*Warspite (Wast Spite, Wastpight)*, 101, 103, 109
ships',
  carpenters, 51
  companies, 41, 52
  gear, 225
**Shrewsbury, Countess of, (Bess of Hardwick),** letter to, xxxviii, 59
Sidney,
  Sir Henry, 5
  Sir Philip, 3, 14
  Robert, 14
silver,
  coins, 37
  ore, 192, 193
Simcotes (Symcottes), 17
Simpson, Egis, 81
Skory, Silvanus, 219
Slapton, Devon, 88
Sleeman (Sleman), Anthony, 57
Smith (Smythe),
  George, of Exeter, 38
  Gilbert, of Exeter, 62
  Richard, 40
  Robert, 176, 177
  widow, 81, 82, 95
smiths, 51
Snell, Sir Charles, 225
soldiers,
  Irish, 114
  of the Low Countries, 112
  sea, 75, 101, 103, 108, 147
  Spanish, 147
Somers, Captain George, later Sir, 113

Somerset, county of, 4
  militia, 88, 89
**Sotherton (Sowtherton), John,** letters to, 18, 19
South West, the,
  economy of, 60
  land defences of, 88
Southampton, port of, 161
Southcott, Thomas, 43
Southwell, Francis, 8
Spain, 20
  army of, 109
  coast of, 56
  king of, xxvii, 50, 56, 102, 111, 166, 217–19;
    hostility of, 58, 79, 88; supporting Irish rebels, 86; territory of, 165
  merchants of, 50
  naval preparations in, 36, 75
  ships of, attacks on, 22; *see also* shipping
Spaniards in Ireland, 58, 60, 149, 150
Spanish Armada, 30
Sparke, John, of Plymouth, 114
**Spifame, Samuel, Seigneur de Bisseaux,** letter to, 215
Spilman, Sir John, 81, 190
Spinola, Frederico, 159, 162
Sprente (Sprinte), Gregory, 13
Spring, Captain Edward, 78
Stafford,
  Captain Francis, 118
  Lady Jane, 25
Stanhope, Sir John, 102, 114
Stanley, William, Earl of Derby, App. 2, *p. 384*
Stannaries, the, charter and customs of, 57
Staplyne, Christopher, 161
Star Chamber, Court of, 71, 135, 156
Statutes Staple, App. 2, *p. 384*
Steed, William, 217
Stepney (Stupey), Clement, 7
Stevens, —, 71
Stocker, John, 9
Stockman, William, 57
Stoke Gabriel, Devon, 9
stones, precious, 53, 54, 87
Stoughton (Stauton),
  Lawrence, 116
  Thomas, 91
Stourton, Lady, 69
Stradling,
  **Sir Edward,** letter to, 14
  Sir Thomas, 14

Strode, William, 84
Stukeley (Stuckly),
  John, 150
  Sir Lewis, Vice-Admiral of Devon, 223
succession to the throne, 58
sugar, 37, 148, 157, 220
Swete, John, 130

Talbot, John, 217
Tanner, Captain Roger, 2
Taswell (Tawswell), William, 35
taverners, 158; *see also* Ralegh, Sir Walter, wine licences
Tawstock, north Devon, 4
Terceira (Tercera), Azores, letter from, 112
Thelwall (Felwall), Bevis, 195, 199
Thibaut, Adrian, of Amsterdam, 213
Thornehurst (Thornix), Captain Thomas, 218, 219
Throckmorton,
  Sir Arthur, 53, 58, 94, 185, App. 2, *p. 384*
  Sir John, App. 2, *p. 384*
Thynne,
  Captain Henry, 65
  Sir John, of Longleat, 6, 157; his daughter, Catherine (Gresham), 152
timber,
  cedar, 161
  in Dorset, 176, App. 2, *p. 385*
  Irish, xxxix, 61, 63
  in Somerset, 126
  in Wiltshire, 139
tin,
  mills, 135
  mines (works), 66, 130
  miners, tinners, xlix–l, 20; of Cornwall, 133, 134; of Devon, 57, 130, 135; privileges of, 57, 71
  price of, 133
Tite, —, anchor smith, 214
tobacco, 188, 219
Torbay (Torr Baye), Devon, 39, 42, 88, 108
Tower of London, *see* London
Towse (Touse), William, 7
trade, 26; *see also* timber, Irish
Trelawney, Jonathan, of Menheniot, 29
Trenchard (Trencher), Sir George, 69
Tresham, Master, 218
Trinidado, 218
Truro (Trewro), Cornwall, 88
Tucker (Toiker), —, 11

# INDEX

Turner, Captain Jeremy, 159
Tyrconnell, 60
Tyrone, Earl of, *see* O'Neill
Tywardreth (Trewardreth), Cornwall, 88

Ulster (Ustell), 60
undertakers, App. 1, *p. 379*
Uphill on Severn, Somerset, 49

Venlake tin mine, Devon, 130
Vere,
    Edward de, Earl of Oxford, 8
    Sir Francis, 101, 102, 109, 114, 138
Vesier, Lieutenant, 217
victualers, 51, 178
victuals,
    army, 4, 29
    ships', 22, 38, 39, 42, 48, 51, 90, 107, 111, 138, 153, 160
**Villiers, Sir George, 1st Duke of Buckingham,** xliv, liii
    letters to, 212, 223
Vine, the, Hampshire, 142
vintners, xliii, 12, 15
Virginia, voyages to, xl, 20, 161
    patent for, 161
    profits from, 165
    pretended voyages, 192, 201
Viveres, Captain John, 114
Vyvyan (Vivien), Hannibal, 139

Waddon (Waddonn), John, 165
Wallop, Sir Henry, 2
**Walsingham, Sir Francis,** 20
    letters to, 2, 3, 34
    his wife, 145
Wards, Court of, xlviii, 64
wardship, 64
Waterford, Ireland, 4, 148
Watson, Captain George, 108
Watts,
    George, 90
    John, later Sir, 37, 206
Way, Master, 218
weather, 42, 49, 93, 96, 101, 108, 112, 119, 216, 218
**Wells, Subdean and Chapter,** letter to, 35
Wentworth, Peter, 58
Weymouth (Weemouth), Dorset, xlii, 90, 107, 147, 161

    bailiff of, 100
    brewer of, 165
    letters from, 64, 91, 147, 160
Whiddon, Captain Jacob, 22
Whitelock, Captain Edmund, 191
Whitestone, Devon, 9
Whitford, Thomas, 71
Whitgift, Archbishop John, 92
Whitney, Captain, 218–20
Wight, Isle of, 1, 52, 194
Wilcox, Peter, 31
Wilkes, Thomas, 81
Wilkinson (Wilkenson), Captain Edward, 60
Willoughby, Lord Peregrine, 21
Wilson,
    Master Edward, 224
    Hugh, 11
    Sir Thomas, 224
Winchester, Hampshire, letters from, 170–75
Windsor, letter from, 23
wine, 22
    casks, 30; *see also* timber
    from Spanish ships, 30
    licences, *see* Ralegh, Sir Walter
Wingfield (Winckefeld), Richard, 45
Winter, Master, and brother, 218
**Winwood, Sir Ralph,** 217
    death of, 220
    letters to, xxvi, lii, liii, 210, 211, 218–20
Wolridge (Wollridge, Wulredge), John, 64
Wood, John, 178
Woolaston, Captain, 218–20
woollen cloth,
    aulnage of, 19
    in Yorkshire, 19
Wootton, Lord Edward, 166, 171
Wrey, John, of Sourton, 29
Wright, William, 116

Yarde,
    Edward, 9
    Francis, 9
    George, 9
Yetminster, Dorset, 117, App. 2, *p. 382*
Youghal (Yoholl), Co. Cork, 3, 4, 45, 148
    College, Wardenship of, 117

Zachio, Captain Francisco, 218
Zubiaur (Cebures, Seburo), Pedro de, 114, 150

94